New Zealand Wines

2020

Michael Cooper's Buyer's Guide

upstart press

A catalogue record for this book is available from the National Library of New Zealand

ISBN 978-1-988516-87-5

An Upstart Press Book
Published in 2019 by Upstart Press Ltd
Level 6, BDO Tower, 19–21 Como St, Takapuna
Auckland, New Zealand

Designed by www.cvdgraphics.nz
Printed by Opus Group Pty Ltd

Front cover photograph: Winter vineyard in Kumeu, Auckland — iStock

Reviews of the latest editions

'For anybody who is interested in New Zealand wine, it doesn't come any better. A great book – it always is.' – Leighton Smith

'Michael has a lovely, laid-back tasting notes style that doesn't scream at you. A very reliable taster.' – Caro's Wine Merchants

'So when Cooper says a wine is great – and great value – you sit up and listen.' – Josie Steenhart, *Stuff*

'[Michael Cooper is] New Zealand's leading consumer advocate in wine.' – Allan Scott, *Marlborough Man*

'The softcover book that first made its presence felt in 1992 has become somewhat of a bible for wine lovers here at home and, more recently via his website, overseas.' – Tessa Nicholson, *New Zealand Winegrower*

'. . . the Gandalf of New Zealand wine critics, Michael Cooper . . .' – Yvonne Lorkin, Canvas, *New Zealand Herald*

'Michael is deeply entrenched in the landscape of New Zealand wine. . . . We consider his extensive knowledge and long experience vital as a benchmark tool when reflecting on our wines.' – Dry River

'It comes out just before Christmas and makes an ideal stocking-filler for almost all wine drinkers who are interested in New Zealand wine.' – *Raymond Chan Wine Reviews*

Michael Cooper is New Zealand's most acclaimed wine writer, with 44 books and several major literary awards to his credit, including the Montana Medal for the supreme work of non-fiction at the 2003 Montana New Zealand Book Awards for the first edition of his magnum opus, *Wine Atlas of New Zealand*. In the 2004 New Year Honours, Michael was appointed an Officer of the New Zealand Order of Merit for services to wine writing.

Author of the country's biggest-selling wine book, the annual *New Zealand Wines: Michael Cooper's Buyer's Guide*, now in its 28th edition, he was awarded the Sir George Fistonich Medal in recognition of services to New Zealand wine in 2009. The award is made each year at the country's largest wine competition, the New Zealand International Wine Show, to a 'living legend' of New Zealand wine. The weekly wine columnist for the *New Zealand Listener*, he has also been the New Zealand editor of Australia's *Winestate* magazine for many years, and he writes regular wine features for *North & South* magazine.

In 1977 he obtained a Master of Arts degree from the University of Auckland with a thesis entitled 'The Wine Lobby: Pressure Group Politics and the New Zealand Wine Industry'. He was marketing manager for Babich Wines from 1980 to 1990, and since 1991 has been a full-time wine writer.

Cooper's other major works include *100 Must-Try New Zealand Wines* (2011); the much-extended second edition of *Wine Atlas of New Zealand* (2008); *Classic Wines of New Zealand* (second edition 2005); *The Wines and Vineyards of New Zealand* (published in five editions from 1984 to 1996); and *Pocket Guide to Wines of New Zealand* (second edition 2000). He is the New Zealand consultant for Hugh Johnson's annual, best-selling *Pocket Wine Book* and the acclaimed *World Atlas of Wine*.

Michael's comprehensive, frequently updated website, *MichaelCooper.co.nz*, was launched in 2011.

Contents

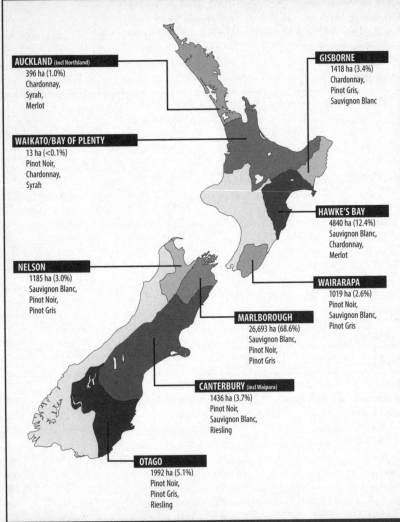

The Winemaking Regions of New Zealand

Area in producing vines 2019 (percentage of national producing vineyard area)

AUCKLAND (incl Northland)
396 ha (1.0%)
Chardonnay,
Syrah,
Merlot

WAIKATO/BAY OF PLENTY
13 ha (<0.1%)
Pinot Noir,
Chardonnay,
Syrah

NELSON
1185 ha (3.0%)
Sauvignon Blanc,
Pinot Noir,
Pinot Gris

GISBORNE
1418 ha (3.4%)
Chardonnay,
Pinot Gris,
Sauvignon Blanc

HAWKE'S BAY
4840 ha (12.4%)
Sauvignon Blanc,
Chardonnay,
Merlot

WAIRARAPA
1019 ha (2.6%)
Pinot Noir,
Sauvignon Blanc,
Pinot Gris

MARLBOROUGH
26,693 ha (68.6%)
Sauvignon Blanc,
Pinot Noir,
Pinot Gris

CANTERBURY (incl Waipara)
1436 ha (3.7%)
Pinot Noir,
Sauvignon Blanc,
Riesling

OTAGO
1992 ha (5.1%)
Pinot Noir,
Pinot Gris,
Riesling

These figures (rounded to the closest percentages) are from New Zealand Winegrowers' *Vineyard Register Report 2017–2020*. During the period 2017 to 2020, the total area of producing vines was predicted to expand from 36,943 to 38,886 hectares – a rise of just over 5 per cent.

Preface

First, the good news. Our wine quality has never been better, reflecting steady increases in vine maturity and winemaker experience, plus intense competition in the marketplace. And over the next year or two, the 2019 vintage should yield wines that are well worth celebrating.

The 2019 harvest was lighter than expected, yielding a smaller crop than even 2014, despite a recent steady expansion in the area of bearing vines. However, quality expectations are high. During one of the country's hottest, driest, mid to late summers on record, moisture levels in the soils plummeted. The vines responded by reducing shoot and leaf growth, focusing their energy on ripening their fruit.

In early March, when the harvest got into full swing, the weather was still hot and dry, but the second half of March was very wet in Marlborough. April was also a mixed bag, with above-average rainfall in Marlborough and Central Otago, but the dryness persisted in Hawke's Bay, which reported an exceptional vintage.

The country's winegrowers, however, are grappling with huge challenges in the marketplace. Over 40 per cent of the wine we drink in New Zealand is imported. During the past decade, the amount of New Zealand wine consumed by Kiwis has declined by 20 per cent, and the average export price achieved by Marlborough Sauvignon Blanc has fallen markedly.

Chris Yorke, global marketing director at New Zealand Winegrowers from 2004 until earlier this year, rejects the argument that the slump in export prices means growth does not indicate success. 'Prices have come down because the volumes have exploded,' he argues. 'If you compare us to the rest of the world, the two countries that achieve the highest average prices for their wines are France and New Zealand.'

Overseas-owned wineries, which produce over a third of all New Zealand wine, have often been criticised for lowering retail prices abroad, thereby shifting international perceptions of the country's wine quality. However, a recent PwC Strategic Review found that foreign-owned companies pay their grape suppliers more than local wine companies, and they are less inclined than New Zealand-owned wineries to ship their wines in bulk containers, rather than bottles.

A few producers are pushing boundaries on the price front. 'We have the ability to make stellar, world-class wines,' says Nick Aleksich, general manager of Mills Reef, a medium-sized winery on the outskirts of Tauranga. From its shingly Mere Road vineyard, in the Gimblett Gravels of Hawke's Bay, since 1994 Mills Reef has produced a stream of Cabernet Sauvignon, Merlot and Syrah-based reds under its $50 Elspeth label. This year brought its new pair of flagship reds, priced at $350.

After tasting the wines 'blind' (identity hidden) against famous French reds, Mills Reef decided they were of similar quality. 'You've got to stake your reputation at the top,' believes Aleksich, 'and it really does take a certain price to be able to do that. There are a few of us who have been brave and are leading the way . . .'

About 1000 bottles each were made of Mills Reef Arthur Edmund Cabernet/

Merlot and Arthur Edmund Syrah. From the highly acclaimed 2013 vintage, the grapes were hand-picked from the oldest vines, pruned to extremely low yields, and the wines were matured for 20 months in 100 per cent new oak barrels. Ensconced in a boxed collector's set, they are beautifully packaged.

The key challenge now facing Mills Reef is to command such a lofty price, when the wines haven't had the time to build up the global reputation of prestigious French reds. As Aleksich points out: 'You have to start somewhere.'

Which raises the overall question: is New Zealand wine getting cheaper or more expensive? A basket of goods and services that a decade ago cost $100 will now set you back about $117, according to the Reserve Bank's inflation calculator. So have wine prices risen similarly?

To find out, I compared the prices of wines in the 2009 edition of the Buyer's Guide with those in the 2019 edition. Supplied by the producers, these are the wines' suggested 'normal retail' prices.

First, I looked at six mid-priced wines from long-established, mostly family-owned wineries – Babich Sauvignon Blanc, Brookfields Bergman Chardonnay, Hunter's Riesling, Mission Merlot, Saint Clair Pinot Gris and Seifried Gewürztraminer. A decade ago, this collection would have cost you $118. Since then, half of the wines have not altered their prices; the others have each risen or fallen by no more than three dollars; and their total price is identical – $118.

What about brands often stacked in supermarkets? I looked at Brancott Estate Sauvignon Blanc, Church Road Chardonnay, Church Road Merlot/Cabernet Sauvignon, Kim Crawford Sauvignon Blanc, Lindauer Brut, Oyster Bay Sauvignon Blanc, Roaring Meg Pinot Noir, Stoneleigh Sauvignon Blanc and Villa Maria Cellar Selection Chardonnay.

Down by 19 per cent! How can that be? Six years ago, legislation came into force that banned the advertising of discounts over 25 per cent on alcoholic beverages, except inside licensed premises. Until then, wineries commonly 'priced up to price down', thereby creating the scope for discounts that always looked far better on paper than in the glass. Once the advertising of '50 per cent off' discounts was banned, the supposed 'normal retail' prices of many wines dropped dramatically.

How about the country's 'icon' wines? It's bad news – at least for consumers. The average price of such prestigious reds as Church Road Tom, Craggy Range Le Sol, Esk Valley Heipipi The Terraces, Felton Road Block 5 Pinot Noir, Te Mata Coleraine and Trinity Hill Homage Syrah has climbed over the past decade by 40 per cent.

As the world gradually wakes up to the fact that New Zealand makes some truly distinguished wines, you can expect their prices to keep climbing.

— *Michael Cooper*

Vintage Charts 2009–2019

WHITES	Auckland	Gisborne	Hawke's Bay	Wairarapa	Nelson	Marlborough	Canterbury	Otago
2019	7	7	7	6	6	5	6	6
2018	3–4	4	4	4	3–4	4	4	4
2017	3	4	4	3	3	2–5	3–4	5
2016	3	4	4	5	3	4–5	5–6	5
2015	5	5	5	5	4	6	6	4
2014	6	6	5–6	5–6	5–6	5	3–5	5
2013	7	7	7	6	5	6–7	6–7	5–6
2012	3–4	2	3–4	3–4	4	4–5	4–5	4–6
2011	3	3	4	4	4	4	4	3
2010	7	6–7	7	6	7	7	6	6
2009	4	6–7	4	5	6	5	6	3–5

REDS	Auckland	Gisborne	Hawke's Bay	Wairarapa	Nelson	Marlborough	Canterbury	Otago
2019	7	7	7	6	6	7	6	5
2018	3–4	4	4	4	3	3	4	4
2017	2	3	3	3	3	3–5	3–4	5
2016	3	4	4	5	3	5	5–6	5
2015	4	4	5	5	4	5	6	4
2014	5–6	5–6	5–6	5–6	5–6	5	3–5	5
2013	6–7	7	6–7	6	6	6–7	6–7	5–6
2012	3–5	2	3	3–4	4	4–5	4–5	4–6
2011	2	2	3–4	4	3	4	4	3
2010	7	6	6	6	6	6–7	5	5–6
2009	5	6–7	6	5	6	6	6	3–5

7 = Outstanding 6 = Excellent 5 = Above average 4 = Average 3 = Below average 2 = Poor 1 = Bad

2019 Vintage Report

The new season's wines are pouring onto the shelves. After the rain-disrupted 2017 and 2018 harvests, what can we expect from 2019?

The news is good, overall. During the country's third-hottest summer on record, with low rainfall in January and February, soil moisture levels in the vineyards dropped, reducing foliage growth and encouraging the vines to pour their energy into ripening their grapes.

In early March, when most harvesters swung into action, the weather stayed hot and drier than usual in east coast wine regions. April proved a mixed bag, with higher than average rainfall in Marlborough and Central Otago, but the dryness persisted in Hawke's Bay.

Every vintage is a great one, if you believe some winemakers – who are keen to sell their wine – but Hawke's Bay's growers seem especially excited about 2019. 'I've never seen a season with the threesome of Chardonnay, Syrah and the Cabernet family all shining so well in one season,' enthused Warren Gibson, of Trinity Hill. Others in the region have described 2019 as 'the greatest', 'superb' and even 'sublime'.

In Central Otago, a wet spring and warm summer, with temperatures hitting 32.8°C in Cromwell on Christmas Day, was followed by an exceptionally hot March but cool, wet April. One winery noted others 'have been fighting powdery mildew and botrytis, due to the heavier rainfall', but another predicted 'excellent' wine.

In Marlborough – source of about three-quarters of the country's wine – wet, cold weather during the vines' flowering reduced their potential crops. During January and February, the region had high temperatures, plentiful sunshine and just 12 mm of rain, compared to 261 mm in 2018.

After the exceptionally hot, dry summer, the harvest began early, but March rainfall proved the highest since 1984 and April was also wetter than normal. Due to the early water stress, many grapes were picked unripe, according to one viticulturist, who described quality as a 'mixed bag'.

However, several producers reported small crops of extremely promising Pinot Noir. With Sauvignon Blanc, reported Villa Maria, the procession of warm days and nights meant a close watch needed to be kept, to preserve the fruit's fresh, appetising acidity. Saint Clair described its grapes' flavours as 'incredible'.

Auckland (and Northland)

The two northernmost regions, Auckland and Northland, accounted for just 0.5 per cent of the national grape crop. However, it was still a bumper harvest – for Auckland growers, the grape crop was 101 per cent heavier than in 2018, and in Northland, production soared by 183 per cent.

Spring kicked off with a dry but cloudy September, followed by a dry October and warm, wet November. Goldie Estate, on Waiheke Island, described spring as 'warm and windy. . . . Flowering and fruit set took place in early November, between rain events, which led to an abundance of fruit . . .'

Early summer was very wet, with Auckland experiencing above-average temperatures and record December rainfall. January, however, was notably warm and dry, with NIWA stations at Whenuapai (in West Auckland) and Kerikeri (in Northland) recording some of their highest temperatures since 1945. By February, which brought only 30 per cent of normal rainfall, the regions' soils were severely dry.

In autumn, the weather stayed fine: a very warm, dry March was followed by an unusually sunny, drier than average April. The Landing, in the Bay of Islands, reported 'a huge harvest by our standards of just over 58 tonnes, around four times what we brought in the year before. The 2019 vintage was exceptional for us.'

Te Motu, on Waiheke Island, reported on 28 March that '2019 could be one of the greats. . . . The perfect summer conditions allowed ripening to accelerate', yielding 'juicy, sweet and concentrated Malbec'. At Goldie Estate, where the harvest began with Chardonnay on 5 March, 'the grapes were harvested at optimal ripeness, retaining fine natural acidity and delicate aromatics'. In the barrel, the estate's reds displayed both 'concentration' and 'finesse'.

Gisborne

At 16,238 tonnes (25 per cent more than in 2018), Gisborne's growers picked 4.1 per cent of the national harvest. Quite apart from the distinct lift in production, expectations were also high for wines of memorable quality.

After a wet spring and moderate December, January was the region's sunniest and second warmest since records began in 1905. In February, parts of Gisborne experienced above average rainfall, but March was hot – the fourth warmest since 1905. Gisvin, a contract winemaking company, praised the 2019 crop as 'fantastic', attributing the quality to a 'good, long, hot, dry ripening period'.

Indevin, a huge contract winemaker, reported a 'really good' vintage. 'It was quite dry early on and then we had a little bit of moisture, but rainfall was down on the long-term average. We got everything in at optimum ripeness, with a good amount of sugar and flavours, and the aromatics are very good too.'

Annie Millton, of The Millton Vineyard, was also highly enthusiastic in her vintage report. 'Chardonnay has shone again. Our Viognier was absolutely beautiful. The Syrah was superb.'

Hawke's Bay

At 37,173 tonnes, Hawke's Bay's grape crop was 9 per cent down on 2018, accounting for 9.3 per cent of the national harvest. All indicators point to wines of exceptional quality.

Spring got off to a wet start – Hastings recorded its second-wettest September on record. By the end of October, soil moisture levels were below normal, but November brought above-average temperatures and rainfall.

Summer kicked off with near-average temperatures in December. January was extremely warm (3.5°C above average in Hastings) but wetter than usual, based on several days of rain in the middle of the month. Gordon Russell, of Esk Valley, reported in mid-January that although the vines' flowering had gone well, heat and humidity were creating a lot of work, leaf trimming and plucking. In February, however, the weather was warmer and drier than normal.

In autumn, the warmth continued, with March temperatures 1.5°C above average at Napier, and a low total rainfall of 18 mm, compared to the normal 50 mm. In April, temperatures were near average, but the weather stayed drier than usual.

'It was a late season,' says Chris Wilcox, of Ash Ridge, who began picking Chardonnay in early May, a month later than in 2018. 'It was a very, very good vintage – very wet until after Christmas, then completely dry. You could pick whenever you liked and you could let the flavours really come through.' Church Road viticulturist Claire Pinker agreed, stating Chardonnay was being left on the vines 'a lot longer than last year, so . . . the flavours would be given time to develop fully.'

Russell believes 2019 is 'going to be a legend. All varieties are superb.' Hugh Crichton, of Vidal, was especially excited by his Syrah and Cabernet Sauvignon.

Te Awa winemaker Richard Painter pointed to Chardonnay and Cabernet Sauvignon as 'real highlights'. Warren Gibson, of Trinity Hill, was also extremely upbeat, lauding the trio of Chardonnay, Syrah and Cabernets. Julian Grounds, winemaker at Craggy Range, was the most enthusiastic of all, praising the 2019 vintage as 'sublime'.

Wairarapa

At 4390 tonnes, Wairarapa winegrowers harvested 4 per cent less than in 2018, accounting for just 1.1 per cent of the national grape crop.

Spring brought devastating frosts. Te Hera Estate, a 5-hectare vineyard at Te Muna, near Martinborough, lost half of its potential grape crop in October. Martinborough Vineyard got off more lightly, reporting its coldest frost since November 2006 had caused a fruit loss of 5 to 10 per cent. 'Some parts of town got hit fairly hard, whilst other parts were untouched.'

Summer began with near-average temperatures in December, followed by a favourably dry January (the driest on record at Masterton), and a cool February (Martinborough had its third-lowest daily maximum air temperatures since 1986). Escarpment Vineyard viewed the region's summer as 'ideal, with no disease pressure. We started and finished vintage earlier than ever before,' due to 'large canopies driving small crops, so things ripened rapidly and very successfully'.

Escarpment Vineyard reported that temperatures over the growing season were 15 per cent warmer than the long-term average. Pinot Noir was picked in 'fantastic' condition, with 'deep, ripe colours, loads of fruit and soft, ripe tannins'. The winery also praised its Chardonnay as 'classic', with 'very clean, ripe flavours and adequate acidity'; and Pinot Gris showed 'real depth of flavour, edging into Gewürztraminer flavour profiles'.

Nelson

At 12,370 tonnes of grapes (36 per cent more than in 2018), Nelson winemakers harvested 3.1 per cent of the national crop. Nelson Winegrowers, the regional association, reported that 'vintage 2019 has been a great one. . . . There are some awesome wines taking shape in tank and barrel.'

Patrick Stowe, of Rimu Grove, described the growing season as 'one of extremes – an early spring with early flowering, followed by a hot, dry summer, culminated in the earliest harvest ever'.

Following a dry November, soil moisture levels were below average by the start of summer.

December brought warm, sunny weather, and January proved notably sunny, warm and dry. In February, the region recorded just 9 per cent of its usual rainfall, causing extreme soil dryness.

'Drought conditions persisted over January and February,' Stowe reported, 'with water restrictions for those irrigating on the plains. Older vines in the Moutere were surprisingly unaffected by these conditions, with healthy canopies and little vine stress.' However, unirrigated young vines didn't fare as well, 'suffering defoliation and fruit dehydration towards the end of the season'.

In early autumn, Nelson was officially classified on 12 March as suffering a medium-scale drought. After a week of moderate rain in early to mid March, which freshened up the vines, April also proved drier than normal. 'Overall, yields were close to average or better,' says Stowe, 'with great fruit ripeness. . . . The resulting wines exhibit good balance, fruit concentration and varietal expression. There is a quiet optimism among the winemakers for one of the best vintages we've seen in a while!'

Marlborough

Leading into the 2019 harvest, Marlborough's winegrowers were hoping that 2019 was 'not going to be a repeat of the vintages in 2017 and 2018, with the problems that the rain over those two vintages caused,' observed Rob Agnew, a scientist at Plant and Food Research (Marlborough). They got their wish. In January and February 2018, Marlborough had a total rainfall of 261.4 mm, the highest on record. In January and February 2019, the region's rainfall totalled just 11.8 mm.

At 305,467 tonnes, Marlborough's growers handled 76.6 per cent of New Zealand's total grape harvest. Their fourth-largest crop to date was 2.5 per cent lighter than in 2018 (313,038 tonnes), and well below the record 329,571 tonnes harvested in 2014.

Spring began with a dry, sunny September, followed by a warm, sunny and dry October and warm, but cloudy and wet, November. According to Cloudy Bay, wet, cold weather during the vines' flowering reduced crops, especially of Pinot Noir and Chardonnay. Hans Herzog also reported that some of our varieties 'flowered when the weather was not favourable, with rain and cold gluing the tiny flowers together, causing poor fruit set and very little crop'.

In summer, a warm, wet, cloudy December was followed by a sunny, exceptionally warm and dry January. Mean air temperatures at Blenheim were the second-highest since 1932. With rainfall just 8 per cent of the monthly long-term average, by the end of January, *Winepress* reported, 'there was almost no available moisture left in the topsoil'.

February was also notably warm, sunny and dry. Blenheim reported its fourth-highest mean maximum air temperatures since 1932 (2.3°C above average), with just 12 per cent of its normal rainfall.

By late February, according to *Winepress*, there was 'a long list of water rights switched off across the region, some almost continuously since late January. . . . Some vineyards are trucking water from town to try to save their vines.' Wairau River noted in March that 'where water restrictions are biting, increased [grape] sugars are due to "shrivel", rather than ripening. Some vines appear to be shutting down.'

Overall, Marlborough's summer rainfall was 46 per cent of the long-term average (despite the wet December). Summer was also the fourth-equal hottest on record for Blenheim since 1932, with 16 days above 30°C (six more than the previous highest total of 10, recorded in the summer of 1989–90).

In early autumn, the government announced a medium-scale drought classification for the region. However, the weather changed abruptly – by the end of the month, Marlborough had experienced its wettest March since 1984, with total rainfall 237 per cent of the long-term average. April also brought above-average rainfall.

The year 2019 was a notably early harvest. Rob Agnew, of Plant and Food Research, noted that some companies 'harvested some blocks of Pinot Noir for table wine in the last week of February, the earliest start they had ever experienced'. Cloudy Bay, in *Winepress*, reported it started picking Pinot Noir and Chardonnay for sparkling wine on 16 February, 'two weeks before a typical season would kick off'.

In terms of wine quality, hopes are high. One viticulturist noted that 'a lot of very low brix [sugar level] fruit was picked, due to the water stress'. Helen Morrison, Villa Maria senior Marlborough winemaker, observed in *New Zealand Winegrower* that the warm growing season meant 'the wines don't have as much acidity as they normally would have. While we will make some very good Sauvignons, with good palate weight, I am not sure they will have that striking acidity we are used to.'

Brenton O'Riley, a grower/viticulturist of Giesen, made similar comments about Sauvignon Blanc. 'Probably not as much aromatics as the winemakers would like . . . but they have good texture and palate weight.'

Two Rivers on 29 March reported 'an amazing vintage – pristine fruit, small berries and great concentration'. Hans Herzog was equally enthusiastic: 'We could not be happier with the quality.' Saint Clair described its grapes' flavours and concentration as 'incredible'.

'If there is a standout variety from Marlborough this year, it is Pinot Noir,' according to *New Zealand Winegrower*. Yields were down, due to adverse weather during the vines' flowering, but Villa Maria reported the berries had 'thick skins and intense colour and flavour'. James Healy, of Dog Point Vineyard, says Pinot Noir was picked in 'the best condition I have ever seen'.

Canterbury

At 8535 tonnes of grapes (a 24 per cent lighter crop than in 2018), Canterbury – including its dominant sub-region, Waipara, in North Canterbury – produced 2.1 per cent of the country's wine in 2019.

Spring was cool and wet in North Canterbury, with a cool September followed by a wetter than average October. In November, the NIWA station at Waipara West recorded its second-highest rainfall since records began in 1973.

After a wet start to the summer in December, 'at the beginning of the year, somewhere, a switch was turned on,' reported Dunnolly Estate, at Waipara. 'It has been HOT, HOT, HOT, and DRY, DRY, DRY!'

In January, Cheviot, north of Waipara, had its highest mean maximum air temperatures since 1982 (3.7°C above average). Rainfall across North Canterbury was well below normal. February brought similarly warm, dry weather.

Autumn opened with a warm March – Waipara West recorded 32.4°C on 5 March. Further south, in March Christchurch had well above average temperatures. 'The season has been absolutely amazing,' enthused Dunnolly Estate on 21 March, 'giving consistency of ripening and no disease pressures. The best season we have experienced in at least 10 years.'

Otago

At 11,909 tonnes, 2019 was a record crop in Central and North Otago (the Waitaki Valley), exceeding the 2018 vintage by over 3 per cent, but it still accounted for only 3 per cent of the national grape harvest.

The growing season was 'bookended by frosts' and 'not without its challenges,' according to Nick Paulin, chair of the regional association, Central Otago Winegrowers. In spring, a wet September was followed by severe frosts in mid-October, and a cool, extremely wet November.

The frost-fighting peaked on the nights of 12 and 13 October. *New Zealand Winegrower* noted that 'an earlier than usual bud burst had left vines vulnerable'. Some young plants were 'nuked', and shoot damage was also reported at sites usually viewed as frost-free.

In early summer, 'December flowering was patchy and drawn out,' reported *New Zealand Winegrower*. However, the two driest locations in the country were Clyde and Cromwell (where temperatures hit 32.8°C on Christmas Day). A hotter than usual January, with average rainfall, was followed by a significantly cooler February.

In early autumn, 'March surprised by being warmer than February,' observed Grasshopper Rock, at Alexandra, 'bringing the harvest forward by about 10 days to 5 April.' Cromwell recorded its highest mean maximum air temperatures for March since records began in 1949 – 3.7°C above average.

April, however, was colder and wetter than normal. 'Late rains which arrived right before harvest time increased berry size and saved growers from what was looking to be a leaner crop,' according to *New Zealand Winegrower*. Several April frosts meant some grapes had to be harvested for rosé, rather than red wine. Misha's Vineyard, at Bendigo, noted on 18 April that some vineyards 'have been fighting powdery mildew and botrytis, due to the heavier rainfall during the season'.

Predictions about the likely quality of Central Otago wines from 2019 have varied. Misha's Vineyard was 'delighted with the quality (and quantity) of fruit', describing 2019 as 'a great season'. Grant Taylor, of Valli, praised 2019 as 'a stellar year for whites', and Grasshopper Rock expects 'the 2019 grapes will make excellent wine'.

However, *New Zealand Winegrower* noted that 'some vineyards saw the effects of larger berry size in wines which lacked a bit of concentration'. Terra Sancta, at Bannockburn, predicted the 2019 harvest will yield wines somewhere between the concentrated 2017 vintage and the lighter 2018s.

Best Buys of the Year

Best White Wine Buy of the Year

Villa Maria Cellar Selection Marlborough Sauvignon Blanc 2019
★★★★☆, $18 (down to $15)

From one year to the next, this is one of New Zealand's greatest wine bargains. When the 2016 vintage featured as Best White Wine Buy of the Year in the 2017 *Buyer's Guide*, I enthused that 'this classy wine has pretty much everything you could hope for in a Marlborough Sauvignon Blanc, for $20 or less . . . often a lot less'. Now comes the 2019 vintage, offering equally irresistible value.

Ripely scented, it is weighty and sweet-fruited, with deep, vibrant passionfruit/lime flavours, and a crisp, dry, long finish. As usual, it's a great buy, especially on special at under $15, and for downright drinkability, it's hard to beat.

Positioned above the popular, huge-volume, low-priced Private Bin wines and below the rarer, more expensive Reserve and Single Vineyard ranges, Villa Maria's Cellar Selection wines often offer a magical combination of high quality and affordable price. Made in sufficient volumes to be sold nationwide in supermarkets, when on special, they can offer simply unbeatable value.

In Marlborough, January and February 2019 brought high temperatures, abundant sunshine and just 12 mm of rain, compared to 261 mm in 2018. Helen Morrison, Villa Maria's senior Marlborough winemaker, observed early that the warm growing season meant 'the wines don't have as much acidity as they normally would have. While we will make some very good Sauvignons, with good palate weight, I'm not sure they will have that striking acidity we are used to.'

If you are looking for a pungently herbaceous, grassy, zingy Sauvignon Blanc, with leap-out-of-the-glass intensity, the 2019 Cellar Selection will probably not be your first choice. Rather, I enjoy its satisfying fullness of body, rich, ripe flavours and well-rounded finish.

Vineyard blocks from the warmer Wairau Valley were selected for their concentrated tropical-fruit flavours, while the cooler, windier Awatere Valley gave grapes with herbal and green-capsicum characters. Harvested in cool night temperatures, to protect the grapes' aromatics, the juice was cool-fermented in stainless steel tanks, and the wine was matured on its yeast lees 'to build palate weight and texture into the wine, without compromising freshness'.

According to one retailer, the gold label on Villa Maria's Cellar Selection is 'the gold standard in wine value'. Given the 2019 Sauvignon Blanc's 'normal' retail price of $18, frequently discounted to around $15, it's hard to argue.

Best Red Wine Buy of the Year

Alexander Dusty Road Martinborough Pinot Noir 2018
★★★★☆, $27

'I'm very cynical about wine competitions,' Michael Finucane declared in 2003, 'but I'd love to win one, because that's what guides the consumer.' Finucane, co-owner of Alexander Vineyard, is still sceptical about the variation in results from one show to the next, but Alexander's reds have since won a host of accolades. On the same day I spoke to him about giving the Best Red Wine Buy of the Year award to Alexander Dusty Road Martinborough Pinot Noir 2018, he learned that the judges at the New Zealand International Wine Show had also given the wine a gold medal.

Designed for early drinking, but also age-worthy, the Dusty Road Pinot Noir 2018 is an estate-grown, single-vineyard wine, hand-picked and matured for 11 months in French oak barriques (20 per cent new). Bright ruby, with a fragrant, savoury bouquet, it is mouthfilling, with concentrated, ripe, plummy, spicy flavours, showing good complexity, and the structure to mature well. Approachable now, it should be at its best from 2022 onwards.

Alexander's wines stand out not only for their quality but also for their consistently great value. Dusty Road, the second-tier red, is sold at $27, compared to $38 for the top label, Alexander Pinot Noir, which is barrel-selected, with a slightly stronger new oak influence.

Over many vintages, I have rated Dusty Road Pinot Noir with four or four and a half stars, out of five, on a quality level that matches many Pinot Noirs in the $40–$45 category. The 2016 and 2014 vintages of Dusty Road Pinot Noir were also awarded gold medals at the New Zealand International Wine Show.

Finucane, a surveyor, and his partner, Roz Walker, a clinical psychologist, arrived from the UK in 1996. Today, their 5-hectare vineyard is planted principally in Pinot Noir, with pockets of Merlot and Chardonnay. Both are involved in the winery, with Walker in overall charge of the winemaking.

The couple's description of Dusty Road Pinot Noir sums up its quality and style so well, it will surely whet your appetite. 'Made from hand-picked fruit off our home Hinakura Vineyard, the newly released 2018 vintage has a full and densely packed nose of ripe, dark raspberry, cherry and dark berry fruits, with liquorice and spicy notes on a well-structured, elegant palate with plenty of fruit weight. A concentrated, full-bodied Pinot Noir with fine-grained tannins, energy and power with a smooth finish and great mouthfeel, it should be matched with duck, venison, grilled meat and game dishes over the next five to six years. Cellaring will be rewarded with greater complexity and subtle expression.'

Dusty Road has been described by retailer Fine Wine Delivery Co. as 'always a great Pinot Noir that could well be New Zealand's best-kept secret'. Being a tiny operation, Finucane often finds himself serving in the winery's cellar door. 'People often say: "What's wrong with your wine?" They've earlier been somewhere else and seen Pinot Noirs selling at $50 or $75, and then they see Dusty Road at $27. So I invite them to try it, and they say ours is better. Then they buy a bottle or often a case.'

Other shortlisted wines

Whites

Askerne Hawke's Bay Gewürztraminer 2018 ★★★★☆ $23
Askerne Hawke's Bay Viognier 2018 ★★★★☆ $23
Dashwood by Vavasour Marlborough Riesling 2019 ★★★★ $16
Dashwood by Vavasour Marlborough Sauvignon Blanc 2019 ★★★★ $16
Delegat Awatere Valley Sauvignon Blanc 2019 ★★★★☆ $20
Delegat Crownthorpe Terraces Chardonnay 2018 ★★★★ $20
Durvillea Marlborough Pinot Gris 2019 ★★★☆ $15
Esk Valley Hawke's Bay Pinot Gris 2019 ★★★★☆ $20
Greenhough River Garden Nelson Sauvignon Blanc 2019 ★★★★★ $22
Kumeu Village Hand Harvested Chardonnay 2018 ★★★★ $18
Main Divide North Canterbury Gewürztraminer 2018 ★★★★★ $21
Mount Brown Estates North Canterbury Pinot Gris 2018 ★★★★ $16
Mount Riley Marlborough Gewürztraminer 2019 ★★★★ $15
Old Coach Road Nelson Sauvignon Blanc 2019 ★★★☆ $14
Seifried Nelson Gewürztraminer 2019 ★★★★☆ $18
Thornbury Marlborough Sauvignon Blanc 2019 ★★★★ $16
Vidal Reserve Hawke's Bay Chardonnay 2018 ★★★★☆ $20
Vidal Reserve Marlborough Sauvignon Blanc 2019 ★★★★☆ $20
Villa Maria Private Bin East Coast Pinot Gris 2019 ★★★★ $15
Villa Maria Reserve Clifford Bay Awatere Valley Marlborough Sauvignon Blanc 2019 ★★★★★ $25

Reds

Brookfields Back Block Syrah 2018 ★★★★☆ $20
The Crater Rim Waipara Valley Pinot Noir 2016 ★★★★☆ $28
Delegat Gimblett Road Merlot 2018 ★★★★☆ $20
Domaine-Thomson Explorer Central Otago Pinot Noir 2018 ★★★★☆ $29
Mission Hawke's Bay Merlot/Cabernet Sauvignon 2018 ★★★☆ $16
Nor'wester by Greystone North Canterbury Pinot Noir 2017 ★★★★☆ $32

Classic Wines of New Zealand

A bumper crop of 61 new Potential Classics, 20 new Classics and 8 new Super Classics are the features of this year's closely revised list of New Zealand wine classics.

What is a New Zealand wine classic? It is a wine that in quality terms consistently ranks in the very forefront of its class. To qualify for selection, each label must have achieved an outstanding level of quality for at least three vintages; there are no flashes in the pan here.

By identifying New Zealand wine classics, my aim is to transcend the inconsistencies of individual vintages and wine competition results, and highlight consistency of excellence. When introducing the elite category of Super Classics, I restricted entry to wines which have achieved brilliance in at least five vintages (compared to three for Classic status). The Super Classics are all highly prestigious wines, with a proven ability to mature well (even the Sauvignon Blancs, compared to other examples of the variety).

The Potential Classics are the pool from which future Classics will emerge. These are wines of outstanding quality which look likely, if their current standards are maintained or improved, to qualify after another vintage or two for elevation to Classic status. All the additions and elevations on this year's list are identified by an asterisk.

> Some wines on the classics list are not reviewed every year. If a wine is not currently on sale, this generally reflects a lack of favourable weather in recent vintages.

Super Classics

Branded and Other White Wines
Cloudy Bay Te Koko, Dog Point Vineyard Section 94

Chardonnay
Ata Rangi Craighall; Church Road Grand Reserve Hawke's Bay; ***Church Road Tom; Clearview Reserve; Clos de Ste Anne Naboth's Vineyard; Dry River; Fromm Clayvin Vineyard Marlborough; Kumeu River Estate; Kumeu River Hunting Hill; Kumeu River Mate's Vineyard; Neudorf Moutere; Sacred Hill Riflemans; Te Mata Elston; Villa Maria Reserve Barrique Fermented Gisborne; Villa Maria Single Vineyard Keltern

Gewürztraminer
Dry River Lovat Vineyard; Johanneshof Marlborough; Lawson's Dry Hills Marlborough

Pinot Gris
Dry River

Riesling
Carrick Bannockburn; Dry River Craighall Vineyard; Dry River Craighall Vineyard Selection; Felton Road Bannockburn; Pegasus Bay

Sauvignon Blanc
Cloudy Bay; Saint Clair Wairau Reserve; Seresin Marlborough; ***Te Mata Cape Crest

Viognier
***Te Mata Zara

Sweet Whites
Forrest Estate Botrytised Riesling; Framingham Noble Riesling; Villa Maria Reserve Noble Riesling

Bottle-fermented Sparklings
Deutz Marlborough Cuvée Blanc de Blancs; Nautilus Cuvée Marlborough

Branded and Other Red Wines
Craggy Range Le Sol; Esk Valley Heipipi The Terraces; Puriri Hills Harmonie Du Soir; Stonyridge Larose; Te Mata Coleraine

Cabernet Sauvignon-predominant Reds
Church Road Tom Cabernet Sauvignon/ Merlot; Te Mata Awatea Cabernets/ Merlot; Villa Maria Reserve Gimblett Gravels Cabernet Sauvignon/Merlot

Merlot
Esk Valley Winemakers Reserve Merlot-predominant blend; Villa Maria Reserve Hawke's Bay

Pinot Noir
Ata Rangi; ***Burn Cottage Burn Cottage Vineyard; Dry River; ***Felton Road Bannockburn; Felton Road Block 3; Felton Road Block 5; Fromm Clayvin Vineyard Marlborough; Neudorf Moutere; Pegasus Bay; Pegasus Bay Prima Donna; ***Quartz Reef Bendigo Estate Single Ferment; Rippon Tinker's Field Mature Vine; ***Valli Gibbston Vineyard; Villa Maria Reserve Marlborough

Syrah
Esk Valley Winemakers Reserve Gimblett Gravels; Passage Rock Reserve; ***Stonecroft Gimblett Gravels Reserve; Te Mata Estate Bullnose; Trinity Hill Homage Gimblett Gravels Hawke's Bay

Classics

Chardonnay
Babich Irongate; Cloudy Bay; Dog Point Vineyard; Esk Valley Winemakers Reserve; **Felton Road Bannockburn; Felton Road Block 2; Greenhough Hope Vineyard; Greywacke Marlborough; **Mahi Twin Valleys Vineyard; Martinborough Vineyard; **Mission Jewelstone; **Nautilus Marlborough; Pegasus Bay; **Pyramid Valley Vineyards Lion's Tooth Canterbury; Seresin Reserve; Te Whau Vineyard Waiheke Island; Vidal Legacy Hawke's Bay; Villa Maria Reserve Hawke's Bay; Villa Maria Reserve Marlborough

Chenin Blanc
Millton Te Arai Vineyard

Gewürztraminer
**Greystone Waipara Valley; **Lawson's Dry Hills The Pioneer Marlborough; Pegasus Bay; **Spy Valley Envoy Johnson Vineyard Marlborough; Vinoptima Ormond Reserve

Pinot Gris
Greystone Waipara; Neudorf Moutere; Villa Maria Single Vineyard Seddon

Riesling
Carrick Josephine; **Felton Road Dry; Framingham Classic; Misha's Vineyard Limelight; **Misha's Vineyard Lyric; Rippon

Sauvignon Blanc
Auntsfield Single Vineyard Southern Valleys; Brancott Estate Letter Series 'B' Brancott Marlborough; Clos Henri Marlborough; **Dog Point Vineyard Marlborough; **Greywacke Marlborough; Greywacke Wild; Lawson's Dry Hills Marlborough; Pegasus Bay Sauvignon/Sémillon; Staete Landt Annabel Marlborough; Villa Maria Reserve Clifford Bay; Villa Maria Reserve Wairau Valley

Viognier
Clos de Ste Anne Les Arbres

Sweet Whites
Alpha Domus AD Noble Selection; Framingham F Series Riesling Trockenbeerenauslese; Pegasus Bay Encore Noble Riesling

Bottle-fermented Sparklings
Deutz Marlborough Prestige Cuvée; Quartz Reef Méthode Traditionnelle [Vintage]

Rosé
Terra Sancta Bannockburn Central Otago Pinot Noir Rosé

Branded and Other Red Wines
Alpha Domus AD The Aviator; Babich The Patriarch; Craggy Range Aroha; Craggy Range Sophia; Destiny Bay Magna Praemia; Destiny Bay Mystae; **Gillman; **Mission Jewelstone Gimblett Gravels Antoine; Newton/Forrest Cornerstone; Puriri Hills Pope; Sacred Hill Brokenstone; Sacred Hill Helmsman; Te Whau The Point; Trinity Hill The Gimblett

Cabernet Sauvignon-predominant Reds
Babich Irongate Cabernet/Merlot/Franc; Brookfields Reserve Vintage ['Gold Label'] Cabernet/Merlot; Vidal Legacy Gimblett Gravels Cabernet Sauvignon/ Merlot

Pinot Noir
Akarua Central Otago; Bannock Brae Central Otago; Carrick Bannockburn Central Otago; **Doctors Flat Central Otago; Dog Point Vineyard Marlborough; Felton Road Cornish Point Central Otago; Fromm Fromm Vineyard; Gibbston Valley Le Maitre; Gibbston Valley Reserve; Grasshopper Rock Earnscleugh Vineyard; Greenhough Hope Vineyard; Palliser Estate; Pisa Range Estate Black Poplar Block; **Prophet's Rock Home Vineyard Central Otago; Quartz Reef Bendigo Estate Single Vineyard; Rippon 'Rippon' Mature Vine Central Otago; **Two Paddocks Central Otago; Valli Bannockburn Vineyard Central Otago; **Valli Bendigo Vineyard

Central Otago; Villa Maria Single Vineyard Seddon Marlborough; Villa Maria Single Vineyard Southern Clays Marlborough

Syrah

Brookfields Hillside; Church Road Grand Reserve Hawke's Bay; Craggy Range Gimblett Gravels Vineyard; La Collina;

**Mission Jewelstone Hawke's Bay; Sacred Hill Deerstalkers Hawke's Bay; Stonyridge Pilgrim Syrah/Mourvedre/Grenache; Vidal Legacy Hawke's Bay; Villa Maria Reserve Hawke's Bay

Tempranillo

**Hans Herzog Marlborough

Potential Classics

Albariño

*Nautilus Marlborough; *Villa Maria Single Vineyard Braided Gravels Hawke's Bay

Chardonnay

*Alpha Domus AD Hawke's Bay; Auntsfield Cob Cottage Southern Valleys Marlborough; Auntsfield Single Vineyard Southern Valleys Marlborough; Bilancia Hawke's Bay; *Boneline, The, Sharkstone Waipara; Carrick Cairnmuir Terraces EBM; *Collaboration Aurulent Hawke's Bay; Elephant Hill Reserve Hawke's Bay; Greystone Erin's Reserve; Kumeu River Coddington; *Mills Reef Elspeth Gimblett Gravels; *Pegasus Bay Virtuoso; *Pyramid Valley Vineyards Field of Fire; Spy Valley Envoy Marlborough; Trinity Hill Gimblett Gravels [Black Label]; Villa Maria Single Vineyard Ihumatao; Villa Maria Single Vineyard Taylors Pass

Chenin Blanc

*Astrolabe Wrekin Vineyard; Clos de Ste Anne La Bas

Gewürztraminer

Seifried Winemaker's Collection Nelson; Stonecroft Old Vine; Villa Maria Single Vineyard Ihumatao

Pinot Gris

Georges Road Selection; Greywacke Marlborough; *Hans Herzog Marlborough; Misha's Vineyard Dress Circle; Spy Valley Envoy Marlborough

Riesling

Framingham F-Series Old Vine; Greystone Waipara Valley; Greywacke Marlborough; *Pegasus Bay Bel Canto Dry; *Prophet's Rock Central Otago Dry; Saint Clair Pioneer Block 9 Big John

Sauvignon Blanc

*Astrolabe Vineyards Taihoa Vineyard Marlborough; *Babich Winemakers' Reserve Barrel Fermented Marlborough; Church Road Grand Reserve; *Churton Best End Marlborough; Churton Marlborough; Clos Marguerite Marlborough; *Fairbourne Marlborough; *Folium Reserve Marlborough; Hans Herzog Sur Lie; *Lawson's Dry Hills Reserve; *Mahi Marlborough; Spy Valley Envoy Johnson Vineyard; Villa Maria Single Vineyard Taylors Pass Marlborough; *Whitehaven Greg Awatere Vineyard Single Vineyard

Sweet White Wines
*Esk Valley Late Harvest Chenin Blanc; Felton Road Block 1 Riesling; Framingham F Series Riesling Auslese; Framingham Select Riesling; *Mondillo Nina; Pegasus Bay Aria Late Harvest Riesling; *Pegasus Bay Finale Noble Barrique Matured Sauvignon Blanc/Sémillon; *Riverby Estate Marlborough Noble Riesling; *Seifried Winemaker's Collection Sweet Agnes Nelson Riesling

Bottle-fermented Sparklings
Cloudy Bay Pelorus NV; *Daniel Le Brun Blanc de Blancs Méthode Traditionnelle; *Daniel Le Brun Vintage Méthode Traditionnelle; *Hunter's Miru Miru Reserve; *Nautilus Cuvée Marlborough Vintage Rosé

Branded and Other Red Wines
Clearview Enigma; Clearview Old Olive Block; Clearview The Basket Press; Destiny Bay Destinae; *Elephant Hill Hieronymus; Frenchman's Hill Estate Blood Creek 8; Messenger; Obsidian Reserve The Obsidian; *Passage Rock Magnus

Cabernet Franc
*Clearview Reserve Hawke's Bay

Cabernet Sauvignon-predominant Reds
*Awaroa Requiem Waiheke Island Cabernet/Merlot/Malbec; Church Road McDonald Series Cabernet Sauvignon; Mills Reef Elspeth Cabernet/Merlot; Mills Reef Elspeth Cabernet Sauvignon; *Stonecroft Gimblett Gravels Cabernet Sauvignon

Malbec
Stonyridge Luna Negra Waiheke Island Hillside

Merlot
Church Road McDonald Series Hawke's Bay; Elephant Hill Reserve Hawke's Bay Merlot/Malbec; Hans Herzog Spirit of Marlborough Merlot/Cabernet

Montepulciano
Hans Herzog Marlborough

Pinot Noir
*Akarua The Siren Bannockburn; *Akitu A1 Central Otago; *Alexander Martinborough; Amisfield Central Otago; *Amisfield RKV Reserve Central Otago; *Auntsfield Heritage Marlborough; *Auntsfield Single Vineyard Southern Valleys Marlborough; Black Estate Damsteep North Canterbury; *Burn Cottage Valli Vineyard Gibbston; Carrick Excelsior Central Otago; Cloudy Bay Te Wahi Central Otago; *Coal Pit Tiwha Central Otago; Craggy Range Te Muna Road Vineyard Martinborough; Felton Road Calvert Central Otago; *Folding Hill Bendigo Central Otago; *Folium Reserve Marlborough; *Fromm Cuvée 'H' Marlborough; Gibbston Valley China Terrace Bendigo; Gibbston Valley School House Central Otago; Greystone Thomas Brothers; *Greystone Waipara Valley Canterbury; Greywacke Marlborough; Lowburn Ferry Home Block; *Maude Mt Maude Vineyard Wanaka Reserve; Misha's Vineyard The High Note Central Otago; *Mondillo Bella Reserve; Mondillo Central Otago; Mount Edward Central Otago; *Mt Difficulty Bannockburn; Mt Difficulty Single Vineyard Long Gully; Mt Difficulty Single Vineyard Pipeclay Terrace; Nautilus Four Barriques Marlborough; *Nga Waka Martinborough Lease Block;

Peregrine Central Otago; *Rippon Emma's Block; Rockburn Central Otago; Rockburn The Art Central Otago; *Rock Ferry Trig Hill Vineyard; *Spy Valley Envoy Johnson Vineyard Waihopai Valley; Tarras Vineyards The Canyon Single Vineyard; *Te Kairanga John Martin Martinborough; Terra Sancta Jackson's Block; *Terra Sancta Slapjack Block Bannockburn; Two Paddocks Proprietor's Reserve The Fusilier Bannockburn Vineyard; Two Paddocks Proprietor's Reserve The Last Chance Earnscleugh Vineyard; Urlar Select Parcels; *Valli Burn Cottage Central Otago; Villa Maria Single Vineyard Taylors Pass Marlborough; *Whitehaven Greg Southern Valleys Single Vineyard; Wooing Tree Central Otago; Wooing Tree Sandstorm Reserve Single Vineyard

Syrah
Awaroa Melba Peach Waiheke Island; Church Road McDonald Series; *Church Road Tom; Clos de Ste Anne The Crucible; *Elephant Hill Airavata; Elephant Hill Reserve Hawke's Bay; *Fromm Syrah Fromm Vineyard; Man O' War Dreadnought; Mission Huchet; Passage Rock; Trinity Hill Gimblett Gravels Hawke's Bay

Cellar Sense

Most wine in New Zealand is young and consumed on the day it is bought. A few producers, such as Pegasus Bay, Puriri Hills and Hans Herzog, regularly offer bottle-aged vintages for sale, but around the country, barely 1 per cent of the wine we buy is cellared for even a year.

So it's great news that more and more wineries are releasing or rereleasing mature, bottle-aged wines, up to a decade old, including Pinot Noirs, Cabernet Sauvignons, Merlots, Chardonnays, Rieslings – even barrel-fermented Sauvignon Blancs. Age has not wearied most of these beauties, proving the country's finest wines can mature well for a decade or longer.

Sauvignon Blanc, which accounts for over 70 per cent by volume of all New Zealand wine, is not usually seen as a variety that needs time to develop. Only a decade ago, Marlborough winemakers often stated that the region's Sauvignon Blanc 'should be picked, pressed and pissed by Christmas'.

Today, most Sauvignon Blancs develop soundly for a couple of years, but the popularity of New Zealand Pinot Noir has done far more to persuade consumers around the world that this country's wine can mature gracefully – as it must, if New Zealand is to be accepted as a serious wine producer.

'To gain true international recognition, an industry has to be capable of making wines that improve with age – that's the ultimate quality factor,' stresses John Buck, co-founder of Te Mata Estate, acclaimed for its long-lived Hawke's Bay Cabernet/Merlots. 'People need to be able to put wine into their cellars with confidence and know that when they pull them out they will be a damn sight better than when they put them in.'

But do all winemakers share that view? Geoff Kelly, a Wellington-based critic, believes too much emphasis is placed on young wines in New Zealand, partly because many wine judges are winemakers. 'Generalising, winemakers . . . speak most highly of fresh and fruity smells and flavours in wine. How else can they sell their young wines? Consequently, it is quite rare to find New Zealand winemakers who really enjoy old wines or attend tastings of them.'

If you are keen to build up a cellar of distinguished Chardonnays, Rieslings, Pinot Noirs, Syrahs or Cabernet/Merlots, how do you decide what to buy? Confidence comes from 'vertical' tastings, where several vintages of a wine are tasted side by side. Vertical tastings, staged more and more frequently in New Zealand, let you assess the overall quality of a wine, the evolution of its style, the impact of vintage variation and its maturation potential.

To sum up, I suggest drinking most New Zealand Sauvignon Blancs at nine months to two years old. Screwcaps preserve the wines' freshness markedly better than corks did. Most fine-quality Chardonnays are at their best at two to five years old; top Rieslings at three to seven years old.

Middle-tier Pinot Noirs, Merlots and Syrahs typically drink well for five years;

outstanding examples can flourish for much longer. New Zealand's top Cabernet/ Merlot blends from Hawke's Bay and Waiheke Island are still the safest bet for long-term cellaring over decades.

Cellaring Guidelines

Grape variety	Best age to open
White	
Sauvignon Blanc	
(non-wooded)	6–24 months
(wooded)	1–3 years
Arneis	1–3 years
Albariño	1–4 years
Gewürztraminer	1–4 years
Grüner Veltliner	1–4 years
Viognier	1–4 years
Pinot Gris	1–4 years
Sémillon	1–4 years
Chenin Blanc	2–5 years
Chardonnay	2–5 years
Riesling	2–7+ years
Red	
Pinotage	1–3 years
Malbec	1–5 years
Cabernet Franc	2–5 years
Montepulciano	2–5 years
Merlot	2–5+ years
Pinot Noir	2–5+ years
Syrah	2–5+ years
Tempranillo	2–5+ years
Cabernet Sauvignon	3–7+ years
Cabernet/Merlot	3–7+ years
Other	
Sweet whites	2–5 years
Bottle-fermented sparklings	
(vintage-dated)	3–5+ years

How to Use this Book

It is essential to read this brief section to understand how the book works. Feel free to skip any of the other preliminary pages, but not these.

The majority of wines have been listed in the book according to their principal grape variety, as shown on the front label. Villa Maria Private Bin Marlborough Sauvignon Blanc, for instance, can be located simply by turning to the Sauvignon Blanc section. Wines with front labels that do not refer clearly to a grape variety or blend of grapes, such as Dog Point Vineyard Section 94, can be found in the Branded and Other Wines sections for white and red wines.

Most entries are firstly identified by their producer's name. Wines not usually called by their producer's name, such as Kim Crawford Marlborough Sauvignon Blanc (from Constellation New Zealand), or Rocky Point Central Otago Pinot Noir (from Prophet's Rock), are listed under their most common name.

The star ratings for quality reflect my own opinions, formed where possible by tasting a wine over several vintages, and often a particular vintage several times. *The star ratings are therefore a guide to each wine's overall standard in recent vintages*, rather than simply the quality of the latest release. However, to enhance the usefulness of the book, in the body of the text I have also given a *quality rating for the latest vintage of each wine*; sometimes for more than one vintage. (Since 2010 wineries have been able to buy stickers to attach to their bottles, based on these ratings.)

I hope the star ratings give interesting food for thought and succeed in introducing you to a galaxy of little-known but worthwhile wines. It pays to remember, however, that wine-tasting is a business fraught with subjectivity. You should always treat the views expressed in these pages for what they are – one person's opinion. The quality ratings are:

★★★★★	Outstanding quality (gold medal standard)
★★★★☆	Excellent quality, verging on outstanding
★★★★	Excellent quality (silver medal standard)
★★★☆	Very good quality
★★★	Good quality (bronze medal standard)
★★☆	Average quality
★★	Plain
★	Poor
No star	To be avoided

These quality ratings are based on comparative assessments of New Zealand wines against one another. A five-star Merlot/Cabernet Sauvignon, for instance, is an outstanding-quality red judged by the standards of other Merlot/Cabernet Sauvignon blends made in New Zealand. It is not judged by the standards of overseas reds of a similar style (for instance Bordeaux), because the book is focused solely on New

Zealand wines and their relative merits. (Some familiar New Zealand wine brands in recent years have included varying proportions of overseas wine. To be featured in this book, they must still include at least some New Zealand wine in the blend.)

Where brackets enclose the star rating on the right-hand side of the page, for example (★★★), this indicates the assessment is only tentative, because I have tasted very few vintages of the wine. A dash is used in the relatively few cases where a wine's quality has oscillated over and above normal vintage variations (for example ★–★★★).

Super Classic wines, Classic wines and Potential Classic wines (see page 20) are highlighted in the text by the following symbols:

Super Classic	Classic	Potential Classic

Each wine has also been given a dryness-sweetness, price and value-for-money rating. The precise levels of sweetness indicated by the four ratings are:

DRY	Less than 5 grams/litre of residual sugar
MED/DRY	5–14 grams/litre of residual sugar
MED	15–49 grams/litre of residual sugar
SW	50 and over grams/litre of residual sugar

Less than 5 grams of residual sugar per litre is virtually imperceptible to most palates – the wine tastes fully dry. With between 5 and 14 grams, a wine has a hint of sweetness, although a high level of acidity (as in Rieslings or even Marlborough Sauvignon Blancs, which often have 4 to 6 grams per litre of residual sugar) reduces the perception of sweetness. Where a wine harbours over 15 grams, the sweetness is clearly in evidence.

At above 50 grams per litre, most wines are unabashedly sweet, although high levels of acidity can still disguise the degree of sweetness. Most wines that harbour more than 50 grams per litre of sugar are packaged in half bottles, made to be served with dessert, and can be located in the Sweet White Wines section. However, a growing number of low-alcohol, sweet but not super-sweet, mouth-wateringly crisp Rieslings, not designed as dessert wines and usually packaged in 750-ml bottles, can also be found in the Riesling section.

Prices shown are based on the average price in a supermarket or wine shop (as indicated by the producer), except where most of the wine is sold directly to consumers from the winery, either over the vineyard counter or via mail order or the Internet.

The art of wine buying involves more than discovering top-quality wines. The real challenge – and the greatest satisfaction – lies in identifying wines at varying quality levels that deliver outstanding value for money. The symbols I have used are self-explanatory:

–V	=	Below average value
AV	=	Average value
V+	=	Above average value

The ratings discussed thus far are all my own. Many of the wine producers themselves, however, have also contributed individual vintage ratings of their own top wines over the past decade and the 'When to drink' recommendations. (The symbol **WR** indicates Winemaker's Rating, and the symbol **NM** alongside a vintage means the wine was not made that year.) Only the producers have such detailed knowledge of the relative quality of all their recent vintages (although in some cases, when the information was not forthcoming, I have rated a vintage myself). The key point you must note is that *each producer has rated each vintage of each wine against his or her highest quality aspirations for that particular label, not against any absolute standard.* Thus, a 7 out of 7 score merely indicates that the producer considers that particular vintage to be an outstanding example of that particular wine; not that it is the best-quality wine he or she makes.

The 'When to drink' (**Drink**) recommendations (which I find myself referring to constantly) are largely self-explanatory. The **P** symbol for PEAKED means that a particular vintage is already at, or has passed, its peak; no further benefits are expected from aging.

Here is an example of how the ratings work:

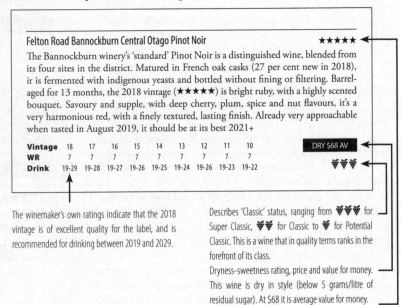

Felton Road Bannockburn Central Otago Pinot Noir ★★★★★

The Bannockburn winery's 'standard' Pinot Noir is a distinguished wine, blended from its four sites in the district. Matured in French oak casks (27 per cent new in 2018), it is fermented with indigenous yeasts and bottled without fining or filtering. Barrel-aged for 13 months, the 2018 vintage (★★★★★) is bright ruby, with a highly scented bouquet. Savoury and supple, with deep cherry, plum, spice and nut flavours, it's a very harmonious red, with a finely textured, lasting finish. Already very approachable when tasted in August 2019, it should be at its best 2021+

Vintage	18	17	16	15	14	13	12	11	10
WR	7	7	7	7	7	7	7	7	7
Drink	19-29	19-28	19-27	19-26	19-25	19-24	19-26	19-23	19-22

DRY $68 AV

The winemaker's own ratings indicate that the 2018 vintage is of excellent quality for the label, and is recommended for drinking between 2019 and 2029.

Describes 'Classic' status, ranging from ❦❦❦ for Super Classic, ❦❦ for Classic to ❦ for Potential Classic. This is a wine that in quality terms ranks in the forefront of its class.

Dryness-sweetness rating, price and value for money. This wine is dry in style (below 5 grams/litre of residual sugar). At $68 it is average value for money.

Quality rating, ranging from ★★★★★ for outstanding to no star (–), to be avoided. This is generally a wine of outstanding quality.

White Wines

Albariño

Coopers Creek's 2011 bottling was the first true example of Albariño from New Zealand or Australia. Called Albariño in Spain and Alvarinho in Portugal, this fashionable variety produces light, crisp wines described by Riversun Nurseries at Gisborne as possessing 'distinctive aromatic, peachy characteristics, similar to Viognier'. With its loose clusters, thick skins and good resistance to rain, Albariño could thrive in this country's wetter regions. New Zealand's 38 hectares of bearing Albariño vines in 2020 are mostly in Gisborne (20 hectares) and Hawke's Bay (7 hectares), but there are also pockets in Marlborough (4 hectares), Nelson (3 hectares) and Auckland (2 hectares). Of all white-wine varieties to emerge in New Zealand over the past decade, Albariño is one of the most exciting.

Astrolabe Vineyards Sleepers Vineyard Marlborough Albariño ★★★★☆

Grown at Kekerengu, the 2018 vintage (★★★★) was hand-picked and fermented and matured for six months in an even split of tanks and old French oak puncheons. Made in a fully dry style, it is lively, crisp and very youthful, with citrusy, spicy flavours, a touch of complexity and good intensity. Best drinking 2021+. Still on sale, the 2016 vintage (★★★★☆) is maturing well. Still bright and youthful in colour, it has strong, citrusy, peachy, spicy flavours, dry and lasting. Drink now or cellar.

Vintage	18	17	16
WR	6	7	7
Drink	21-23	19-22	19-21

 DRY $30 –V

Babich Family Estates Headwaters Organic Marlborough Albariño ★★★★

The vibrant 2017 vintage (★★★★) was estate-grown in the Headwaters Vineyard, near Renwick, in the Wairau Valley, tank-fermented and lees-aged for five months. Medium to full-bodied, it is invitingly scented, with strong, citrusy, slightly appley flavours, woven with mouth-watering acidity, a slightly minerally streak, and a long, dryish (8 grams/litre of residual sugar) finish. Certified organic.

MED/DRY $25 AV

Coopers Creek Select Vineyards Bell-Ringer Gisborne Albariño ★★★★

Still unfolding, the 2018 vintage (★★★★) is a fragrant, full-bodied, punchy wine. Light lemon/green, it is fresh and tightly structured, with youthful, ripe, citrusy, slightly appley and spicy flavours, showing very good vigour and depth, and a crisp, dry, racy finish. Best drinking 2020+.

Vintage	18	17	16	15	14	13	12	11
WR	6	5	6	7	7	7	4	4
Drink	19-20	P	P	P	P	P	P	P

 DRY $22 V+

Forrest Marlborough Albariño ★★★★

The 2018 vintage (★★★★) is already drinking well. Partly (10 per cent) handled in old oak casks, it is fresh and full-bodied, with strong, peachy, spicy, slightly gingery flavours, and a dryish (5 grams/litre of residual sugar), crisp finish.

 MED/DRY $25 AV

Hunting Lodge, The, Marlborough Albariño   ★★★★☆

Albariño, according to The Hunting Lodge, 'offers the best parts of a Riesling and Viognier, but with none of their hang-ups'. The attractive 2018 vintage (★★★★☆) is a single-vineyard wine, grown and hand-picked in the Awatere Valley. It was mostly fermented and lees-aged for four months in tanks, but 10 per cent was handled in seasoned oak barriques. Invitingly scented, it is mouthfilling, fresh and vibrantly fruity, with strong, peachy flavours to the fore, hints of spices, apples and ginger, and a dryish (5.3 grams/litre of residual sugar), appetisingly crisp finish.

 MED/DRY $26 AV

Left Field Gisborne Albariño   ★★★★☆

Offering great value, the 2018 vintage (★★★★☆), handled mostly in stainless steel (tanks and barrels), is a racy, strongly varietal wine. Fresh and full-bodied, it is youthful, with concentrated, peachy, citrusy, slightly spicy flavours, a touch of complexity, and a crisp, dry (2.5 grams/litre of residual sugar), lasting finish. (From Te Awa.)

Vintage	18	DRY $19 V+
WR	6	
Drink	19-23	

Mahurangi River Winery Matakana Albariño   ★★★★

Grown north of Auckland, the 2016 vintage (★★★★) was fermented in a concrete egg. Full-bodied, with good concentration of citrusy, slightly peachy and spicy flavours, showing a touch of complexity, and a dry, harmonious, lingering finish, it's a good, all-purpose wine. (2016 is the last vintage of this label.)

Vintage	15	14	DRY $29 –V
WR	6	7	
Drink	P	P	

Nautilus Marlborough Albariño   ★★★★★

This consistently classy wine is handled without oak. Attractively scented, the 2019 vintage (★★★★★) is fresh and full-bodied, with strong, vibrant, citrusy, peachy, spicy flavours, a slightly salty streak, and a finely balanced, persistent, dry (3 grams/litre of residual sugar) finish. A great all-purpose wine.

DRY $30 AV

Redmetal Vineyards Bridge Pa Triangle Block Five Hawke's Bay Albariño   ★★★★☆

The highly impressive 2018 vintage (★★★★★) is already delicious. Handled without oak, it is a bright, light yellow/green, mouthfilling, sweet-fruited wine. Distinctly peachy, with citrusy notes and a hint of passionfruit, balanced acidity and a dry (3.2 grams/litre of residual sugar), spreading finish, it's a very generous wine, with a real sense of youthful impact. Drink now or cellar.

Vintage	18	DRY $27 AV
WR	6	
Drink	19-24	

Sileni Grand Reserve Advocate Hawke's Bay Albariño   ★★★★☆

The powerful 2018 vintage (★★★★☆) was estate-grown in the Bridge Pa Triangle. Bright, light yellow/green, it is full-bodied, with concentrated, peachy, spicy flavours, and a dry (1.9 grams/litre of residual sugar), crisp, long finish.

DRY $25 V+

Smith & Sheth Cru Heretaunga Albariño   (★★★★★)

Compelling in its youth, the debut 2018 vintage (★★★★★) was grown in the Howell Vineyard, in the Bridge Pa Triangle, Hawke's Bay. A very powerful Albariño, it is weighty and highly fragrant, with fresh, deep, citrusy, peachy flavours that build to a dry, resounding finish. Still youthful, it's full of personality.

DRY $28 V+

Stanley Estates Single Vineyard Awatere Valley Marlborough Albariño   ★★★★

The 2017 vintage (★★★★) was mostly handled in stainless steel tanks (60 per cent), but 40 per cent of the blend was fermented with indigenous yeasts in seasoned oak barrels and oak-aged for 10 months. Fresh and full-bodied, it is vibrantly fruity, with good intensity of citrusy, tangy flavours, dry (2.9 grams/litre of residual sugar) and crisp.

Vintage	17	16
WR	6	5
Drink	19-23	19-22

DRY $23 AV

Terrace Edge North Canterbury Albariño   ★★★★★

A bold expression of Albariño, the 2018 vintage (★★★★☆) is a dryish style, grown at Waipara and fermented with indigenous yeasts in seasoned oak barrels. Richly scented, it is full of youthful vigour, with good intensity of vibrant tropical-fruit flavours, firm acidity, and a long, tightly structured finish. Best drinking 2020+.

MED/DRY $25 V+

Tohu Single Vineyard Whenua Matua Upper Moutere Nelson Albariño   (★★★★)

Drinking well in mid-2019, the 2018 vintage (★★★★) is a characterful wine, bright, light yellow/green, with very good depth of stone-fruit and spice flavours, slightly toasty notes adding complexity, and a crisp, dryish finish.

MED/DRY $28 –V

Torlesse Waipara Albariño   (★★★☆)

Tasted in early 2019, the 2017 vintage (★★★☆) was fermented in old oak barrels and made in a medium-dry (9 grams/litre of residual sugar) style. Bright yellow/pale gold, it is fleshy, with very good depth of ripe tropical-fruit flavours, a subtle oak influence and balanced acidity. It's drinking well now.

MED/DRY $25 –V

Villa Maria Cellar Selection Gisborne Albariño   ★★★★☆

Bargain-priced, the 2018 vintage (★★★★☆) was partly hand-picked and mostly tank-fermented, with some use of indigenous yeasts and old oak puncheons. Light lemon/green, it is mouthfilling and vibrantly fruity, with deep, citrusy, peachy, slightly spicy flavours and a dry finish. A strongly varietal wine with good intensity and vigour, it should be at its best 2020+.

Vintage	18	17
WR	6	7
Drink	19-22	19-20

 DRY $19 V+

Villa Maria Single Vineyard Braided Gravels Hawke's Bay Albariño   ★★★★★

Full of youthful impact, the 2018 vintage (★★★★★) is a highly scented wine, mouthfilling and punchy, with citrusy, peachy, slightly spicy flavours, showing a distinct touch of complexity, appetising acidity, and excellent vigour and intensity. Made in a dry style, it's well worth cellaring.

Vintage	18
WR	7
Drink	19-22

 DRY $32 AV

Waimea Nelson Albariño   ★★★☆

Showing clear-cut varietal character, the 2017 vintage (★★★★) is a punchy, medium-bodied wine, with firm acid spine, a slightly salty streak and strong, peachy, citrusy, spicy flavours. Drink now or cellar.

DRY $20 AV

Wairau River Marlborough Albariño   ★★★★

This punchy wine is estate-grown in The Angler Vineyard, on the north side of the Wairau Valley. The 2017 vintage (★★★★☆) is freshly scented and mouthfilling, with good intensity of lively, citrusy, slightly appley flavours, racy acidity, and a crisp, dry (2.5 grams/litre of residual sugar), lingering finish.

Vintage	17	16	15
WR	6	6	6
Drink	19-20	P	P

DRY $30 –V

Arneis

Still fairly rare here, with 20 hectares of bearing vines in 2020, Arneis (pronounced 'Are-nay-iss') is a traditional grape of Piedmont, in north-west Italy, where it yields soft, early-maturing wines with slightly herbaceous aromas and almond flavours. The word 'Arneis' means 'little rascal', which reflects its tricky character in the vineyard; a vigorous variety, it needs careful tending. First planted in New Zealand in 1998 at the Clevedon Hills vineyard in South Auckland, its potential has been explored by numerous producers, but after peaking at 40 hectares in 2016, plantings are now declining. Coopers Creek released the country's first varietal Arneis from the 2006 vintage. Most of the remaining vines in 2020 are clustered in Gisborne (10 hectares) and Hawke's Bay (9 hectares).

Coopers Creek SV Gisborne Arneis The Little Rascal ★★★★☆

The well-priced 2017 vintage (★★★★☆) is a fleshy, weighty wine, with strong, vibrant, peachy, slightly spicy flavours. Scented, with excellent intensity and harmony, it's an ideal, all-purpose, dryish wine, offering delicious drinking from now onwards.

MED/DRY $22 V+

Hans Herzog Marlborough Arneis ★★★★

Certified organic, the 2017 vintage (★★★☆) is an unoaked wine, fleshy and dry. Pale straw, it is full-bodied and fleshy, although not highly aromatic, with peachy, slightly spicy flavours, showing very good depth, a touch of complexity, and a rounded finish.

DRY $39 –V

Branded and Other White Wines

Dog Point Vineyard Section 94, Craggy Range Les Beaux Cailloux – in this section you'll find all the white wines that don't feature varietal names. Lower-priced branded white wines can give winemakers an outlet for grapes like Chenin Blanc, Sémillon and Riesling that otherwise can be hard to sell. They can also be an outlet for coarser, less delicate juice ('pressings'). Some of the branded whites are quaffers, but others are highly distinguished.

Aurum Central Otago Amber Wine ★★★★★

Looking for something completely different, made by ancient techniques? The orange/amber-hued 2016 vintage (★★★★☆) is a single-vineyard Pinot Gris, estate-grown and hand-harvested at Lowburn. Made with prolonged skin maceration and indigenous yeast fermentation, it was bottled unfined and unfiltered. Full-bodied, it is a tightly structured wine, with generous flavours of peaches, strawberries, spices and apricot, showing excellent complexity, and a firm, dry finish. Definitely a 'food wine', rather than for casual sipping, it's certified organic.

DRY $45 AV

Bellbird Spring Aeris (★★★★★)

The distinctive, non-vintage wine (★★★★★) on sale in 2019 reminded me of Spanish amontillado sherry. Grown at Waipara, in North Canterbury, it is described by winemaker Guy Porter as 'an old nutty dry white wine aged in old oak barrels under a veil of yeast'. Made from Pinot Gris, it is unfortified, but has an alcoholic strength of 17.5 per cent, 'achieved through evaporation in cask'. Gold/amber, it has concentrated, sherry-like aromas and flavours, weighty, rich and complex, and a long, dryish, yeasty, nutty finish. Worth discovering.

MED/DRY $48 (500ML) AV

Bellbird Spring Home Block White ★★★★

The 2015 vintage (★★★☆) is a field blend of four aromatic grape varieties – Pinot Gris, Riesling, Muscat and Gewürztraminer – hand-picked at Waipara and fermented and lees-aged for five months in old oak barrels. Pale yellow, it is medium-bodied, with peachy, slightly spicy flavours, gentle sweetness, fresh acidity, a touch of complexity, and a smooth finish. Ready.

MED $32 –V

Bellbird Spring Sous Voile ★★★★★

The non-vintage wine (★★★★★) released in late 2017 is unique for New Zealand, but echoes wines from Jura, France, and amontillado sherry. Made in a deliberately 'oxidative' style from Waipara Pinot Gris, it was fermented dry and matured for about three years in old oak barriques under a layer of flor yeast ('sous voile' means 'under veil'). Light yellow, it's an unfortified wine (although 15.5 per cent alcohol), with a yeasty, complex bouquet. Peachy, yeasty and dry, it's lively and slightly sherry-like, with impressive complexity. A distinctive wine, it's well worth trying.

DRY $42 (500ML) AV

Brennan Gibbston Central Otago Orange (★★★★★)

A memorable mouthful, the 2017 vintage (★★★★★) is a blend of Pinot Gris (73 per cent), Muscat (15 per cent) and Riesling (12 per cent), made 'following ancient winemaking traditions', including fermentation on skins for two months in old French oak barriques. Probably at its peak now, it is highly aromatic and full-bodied, with an orange/slight amber hue, deep, peachy, spicy flavours, showing excellent complexity, gentle tannins and loads of interest.

DRY $50 AV

Brennan Gibbston Central Otago Trio   ★★★★

Drinking well in its youth, the 2018 vintage (★★★★☆) is a blend of three aromatic varieties – Gewürztraminer (45 per cent), Riesling (45 per cent) and Muscat (10 per cent). Bright, light lemon/green, with a perfumed, gently spicy bouquet, it is full-bodied and vibrantly fruity, with a splash of sweetness and excellent depth of stone-fruit and spice flavours, finely balanced and lingering. Best drinking mid-2020+.

 MED/DRY $33 –V

Carrick Central Otago Electric No 1   (★★★★☆)

Named after a dredge, the 2017 vintage (★★★★☆) was estate-grown at Bannockburn and matured for eight months in seasoned oak barrels. A field blend of 'all white varieties grown at Carrick', especially Pinot Gris (40 per cent of the blend), it was designed to be a 'dry wine, textural rather than varietal'. Bright, light lemon/green, it is mouthfilling and vibrantly fruity, with strong, citrusy fruit flavours to the fore, fresh acidity, a subtle seasoning of oak adding complexity, and obvious potential. Best drinking 2020+. Certified organic.

 DRY $36 –V

Cloudy Bay Te Koko   ★★★★★

Te Koko o Kupe ('The Oyster Dredge of Kupe') is the original name for Cloudy Bay; it is also the name of the Marlborough winery's intriguing oak-aged Sauvignon Blanc. Highly refined, the 2016 vintage (★★★★★) was grown in the Wairau Valley, fermented in French oak barrels (only 8 per cent new, to ensure a subtle oak influence), and matured in wood on its yeast lees for 11 months. Bright, light lemon/green, it has a fragrant, fresh, complex bouquet. Full-bodied and youthful, it is tightly structured, with intense, vigorous tropical-fruit flavours to the fore, a herbal undercurrent, balanced acidity and a finely textured, long finish. A complex, age-worthy wine, it should be at its best 2021+.

Vintage	16	15	14	13	12	11	10
WR	7	7	7	7	6	7	7
Drink	19-26	19-25	19-20	19-20	P	P	P

 DRY $60 AV

Craggy Range Les Beaux Cailloux   ★★★★★

After the impressive 2009–2011 vintages, this prestigious Gimblett Gravels, Hawke's Bay Chardonnay was discontinued, due to the removal of virus-infected vines, but it resumed production in 2016. Les Beaux Cailloux means 'the beautiful pebbles'. The 2011 vintage sold at $63, but the price has surged to $150 for the 2017 vintage (★★★★★). Still very youthful, it is weighty and tightly structured, with a lovely sense of delicacy and harmony. Matured for 10 months in French oak barriques (38 per cent new), it is full-bodied, very savoury and complex, with grapefruit-like flavours, enriched with biscuity oak, and a well-rounded finish. Best drinking 2022+.

 DRY $150 –V

Dog Point Vineyard Section 94   ★★★★★

This ranks among the country's greatest oak-aged Sauvignon Blancs. Looking for 'texture, rather than rich aromatics', Dog Point fermented and lees-aged the 2016 vintage (★★★★★) for 18 months in seasoned French oak casks. Hand-harvested in the Dog Point Vineyard (for which 'Section 94' was the original survey title), at the confluence of the Brancott and Omaka valleys, and fermented with indigenous yeasts, it is a powerful, tightly structured wine, full of potential. Bright, light lemon/green, it has highly concentrated, citrusy, gently herbaceous flavours, showing excellent vigour and complexity, balanced acidity, and a fully dry, lasting finish. (The very classy 2013 vintage (★★★★★), held back to acquire bottle-age, is also on sale in late 2019. Proving the ageability of well-crafted Marlborough Sauvignon Blanc, it is still very vigorous, with light colour, a real sense of youthful drive, and lovely depth and harmony.)

Vintage	16	15	14	13	12	11	10
WR	7	7	7	7	5	7	7
Drink	19-28	19-24	19-23	19-22	P	19-21	P

DRY $40 AV

Eaton Marlborough Fortissimo   (★★★★★)

Well worth cellaring, the powerful, debut 2017 vintage (★★★★★) is a distinctive, rare Sauvignon Blanc – only 648 bottles were produced. Grown at two sites, it was hand-picked, given extended skin contact, fermented with indigenous yeasts in a new French oak puncheon, oak-aged for 11 months, and bottled unfined and unfiltered. Bright, light yellow/green, with a fragrant, complex bouquet, it is mouthfilling, fresh and youthful, in a vigorous, ripely herbaceous style with intense flavours, oak complexity, crisp acidity and a tight, dry finish. Best drinking 2020+.

DRY $48 AV

Hans Herzog Marlborough Mistral   ★★★★★

The 2015 vintage (★★★★☆) is a blend of traditional Rhône Valley grape varieties – Viognier (mostly), Marsanne and Roussanne. Hand-picked, fermented with indigenous yeasts and matured for 20 months in French oak puncheons, it is a golden, powerful, fleshy wine, with stone-fruit and toasty oak flavours, showing good richness and complexity. Peak drinking now to 2020.

Vintage	13	12
WR	7	7
Drink	19-23	19-22

DRY $53 AV

Hunting Lodge, The, White Mischief   ★★★★

The 2018 vintage (★★★★) is a secret blend of several varieties, hand-picked in various regions. Fermented and lees-aged in a mix of tanks and seasoned French oak barriques, it is bright, light yellow/green, with a peachy, gently spicy bouquet. A full-bodied wine, it has strong flavours of stone-fruits, spices and ginger (I see Pinot Gris as probably a key part of the varietal recipe), fresh acidity, a finely balanced, dryish finish (5.1 grams/litre of residual sugar), and loads of drink-young appeal. Drink now to 2020.

MED/DRY $30 –V

Lawson's Dry Hills Marlborough Ranu   (★★★★☆)

For the distinctive 2017 vintage (★★★★☆), Pinot Gris, Riesling and Gewürztraminer were co-fermented (Ranu means 'to mix') with indigenous yeasts in old oak barrels. Fragrant, citrusy and spicy, it's a mouthfilling, concentrated wine, finely textured, with a sliver of sweetness (5.8 grams/litre of residual sugar), fresh acidity and impressive complexity and harmony. Well worth cellaring.

MED/DRY $28 AV

Man O'War Gravestone ★★★★☆

Maturing very gracefully, the 2016 vintage (★★★★★) is a blend of Sauvignon Blanc (65 per cent) and Sémillon (35 per cent), estate-grown at the eastern end of Waiheke Island. Hand-picked and barrel-fermented with indigenous yeasts, it is light lemon/green, with a slightly smoky, toasty bouquet. Full-bodied, it is vibrantly fruity, with concentrated, ripe tropical-fruit flavours, developing excellent complexity, a minerally streak, and a crisp, dry, lingering finish.

DRY $29 AV

Millton Gisborne Les Trois Enfants (★★★★☆)

Full of personality, the light gold 2017 vintage (★★★★☆) is a blend of Gewürztraminer, Riesling and Muscat, co-fermented in tanks and large oak barrels. Weighty, with a spicy, vaguely honeyed bouquet, it is a strongly Gewürztraminer-influenced style, with concentrated, peachy, spicy, slightly honeyed flavours and a firm, dryish (7.4 grams/litre of residual sugar) finish. Certified organic.

MED/DRY $24 V+

Providore Luminaire Central Otago Blanc de Noir (★★★★)

Very pale pink, the distinctive 2018 vintage (★★★★) was made from Pinot Noir grapes, removed immediately from their skins. Veering towards rosé, it's a gentle, mouthfilling wine with good weight, peach, strawberry and spice flavours, a vague suggestion of sweetness and a smooth finish.

MED/DRY $25 AV

Pyramid Valley North Canterbury Orange (★★★★☆)

The 2018 vintage (★★★★☆) was hand-harvested in the Porter Vineyard, at Waipara, tank-fermented, lees-aged for six months in seasoned French oak demi-muids, and bottled unfined and unfiltered. The label makes no mention of grape varieties, but given its copper-coloured skins, Pinot Gris would be a good guess. Full-bodied, it's a complex wine, with gentle tannins, strong strawberry, watermelon and peach flavours, and hints of spices, apricots and oranges. A very harmonious wine with good personality, it's already drinking well.

DRY $35 –V

Sileni Estate Selection Hawke's Bay Alba ★★★★

The 2016 vintage (★★★★) is an unusual blend of Pinot Gris, Sauvignon Blanc, Albariño, Muscat and Chardonnay, barrel-aged for five months. Weighty, fleshy and dry (2.9 grams/litre of residual sugar), it's an aromatic wine, with peach, pear and spice flavours, showing excellent complexity and depth.

Vintage	16	15
WR	6	7
Drink	19-25	19-25

DRY $33 –V

Tantalus Waiheke Island Cachette Reserve   (★★★★★)

Delicious in its youth, the refined, weighty 2017 vintage (★★★★★) is a Chardonnay, estate-grown at Onetangi and barrel-aged for 10 months. Light lemon/green, with a fragrant, biscuity bouquet, it is mouthfilling and well-rounded, with concentrated, ripe, citrusy, peachy flavours, finely integrated oak and excellent complexity, structure and harmony. Best drinking 2020+.

DRY $70 AV

Te Kano Central Otago Blanc de Noir   (★★★★)

A 'dry white from Pinot Noir', the 2017 vintage (★★★★) is a single-vineyard wine, grown at Bannockburn. Skilfully crafted, it is highly fragrant, with mouthfilling body and generous, ripe, peachy, slightly spicy flavours, dry (2.5 grams/litre of residual sugar) and smooth.

DRY $27 –V

Vergence White by Pegasus Bay   (★★★★★)

Offering good value, the 2016 vintage (★★★★★), released in early 2019, was made from 'ultra-ripe' Sémillon, matured in old barrels for the extended period of 30 months, then blended with Chardonnay, Muscat and Gewürztraminer, to add 'aromatics and balance'. Estate-grown at Waipara, in North Canterbury, it is pale straw, with a fragrant, complex bouquet. Weighty and fleshy, it has concentrated stone-fruit flavours, hints of herbs and spices, impressive mouthfeel and complexity, fresh acidity and a lasting finish. A distinctive wine, it's well worth discovering.

DRY $27 V+

Wooing Tree Blondie   ★★★☆

This 'blanc de noir' – a white (or rather faintly pink) Central Otago wine – is estate-grown at Cromwell. It is made from hand-picked Pinot Noir grapes; the juice is held briefly in contact with the skins and then fermented in tanks. Offering very easy drinking, the 2018 vintage (★★★☆) is fresh and smooth, in a dryish style (4.7 grams/litre of residual sugar), with vibrant, peachy, spicy flavours, showing very good delicacy and depth.

DRY $28 –V

Breidecker

A nondescript crossing of Müller-Thurgau and the white hybrid Seibel 7053, Breidecker is rarely seen in New Zealand. There were 32 hectares of bearing vines recorded in 2003, but less than 1 hectare in 2020 (0.4 hectares in Central Otago). Its early-ripening ability is an advantage in cooler regions, but Breidecker typically yields light, fresh quaffing wines, best drunk young.

Black Ridge Central Otago Breidecker (★★★★★)

Still on sale, the 2016 vintage (★★★★★) is the best Breidecker I've tasted – and there were quite a few in New Zealand about 30 years ago. Weighty, fleshy, soft and gently aromatic, it has generous, vibrant, citrusy, peachy flavours, a slightly spicy, earthy streak, a splash of sweetness (16 grams/litre of residual sugar) and finely balanced acidity. Drink now.

MED $22 V+

Chardonnay

Do you drink Chardonnay? Sauvignon Blanc is our biggest-selling white-wine variety by far, and Pinot Gris is riding high, but neither of these popular grapes produces New Zealand's greatest dry whites. Chardonnay wears that crown. It's less fashionable than 20 or 30 years ago, but Chardonnay is our most prestigious white-wine variety. No other dry whites can command such lofty prices; many New Zealand Chardonnays are on the shelves at $50 or more. And although it has lost ground to Sauvignon Blanc and Pinot Gris, Chardonnay is still a big seller. Winegrowers are currently reporting a surge in sales, suggesting that Chardonnay is coming back into fashion. However, New Zealand Chardonnay has yet to make the huge international impact of our Sauvignon Blanc. Our top Chardonnays are classy, but so are those from a host of other countries in the Old and New Worlds. In 2018, Chardonnay accounted for 1.9 per cent by volume of New Zealand's wine exports (far behind Sauvignon Blanc, with 86 per cent). There's an enormous range to choose from. Most wineries – especially in the North Island and upper South Island – make at least one Chardonnay; many produce several and the big wineries produce dozens. The hallmark of New Zealand Chardonnays is their delicious varietal intensity – the leading labels show notably concentrated aromas and flavours, threaded with fresh, appetising acidity.

The price of New Zealand Chardonnay ranges from under $10 to over $100. The quality differences are equally wide, although not always in relation to their prices. Lower-priced wines are typically fermented in stainless steel tanks and bottled young with little or no oak influence; these wines rely on fresh, lemony, uncluttered fruit flavours for their appeal. Chardonnays labelled as 'unoaked' were briefly popular a few years ago, as winemakers with an eye on overseas markets worked hard to showcase New Zealand's fresh, vibrant fruit characters. But without oak flavours to add richness and complexity, Chardonnay handled entirely in stainless steel tanks can be plain – even boring. The key to the style is to use well-ripened, intensely flavoured grapes.

Mid-price wines may be fermented in tanks and matured in oak casks, which adds to their complexity and richness, or fermented and/or matured in a mix of tanks and barrels (or handled entirely in tanks, with oak chips or staves suspended in the wine). The top labels are fully fermented and matured in oak barrels (normally French barriques, with varying proportions of new casks); there may also be extended aging on (and regular stirring of) yeast lees and varying proportions of a secondary, softening malolactic fermentation. The best of these display the arresting subtlety and depth of flavour for which Chardonnay is so highly prized.

Chardonnay plantings have been far outstripped in recent years by Sauvignon Blanc, as wine producers respond to overseas demand, and in 2020 it will constitute 8.4 per cent of the national bearing vineyard. The variety is spread throughout the wine regions, particularly Marlborough (where 34 per cent of the vines are concentrated), Hawke's Bay (32 per cent) and Gisborne (20 per cent). Gisborne is renowned for its softly mouthfilling, ripe, peachy Chardonnays, which offer very seductive drinking in their youth; Hawke's Bay yields sturdy wines with rich grapefruit and stone-fruit flavours, power and longevity; and Marlborough's Chardonnays are slightly leaner in a cool-climate, appetisingly crisp style.

Chardonnay has often been dubbed 'the red-wine drinker's white wine'. Chardonnays are usually (although not always, especially cheap models) fully dry, as are all reds with any aspirations to quality. Chardonnay's typically mouthfilling body and multi-faceted flavours are another obvious red-wine parallel.

Broaching a top New Zealand Chardonnay at less than two years old can be unrewarding – the finest of the 2016s will offer excellent drinking during 2020. If you must drink Chardonnay when it is only a year old, it makes sense to buy one of the cheaper, less complex wines specifically designed to be enjoyable in their youth.

144 Islands Northland Chardonnay   (★★★★☆)

Grown at Mangawhai Heads, the 2017 vintage (★★★★☆) is an elegant, single-vineyard wine with lots of youthful drive. Hand-picked, it was fermented and matured for 11 months in French oak casks (25 per cent new). Fresh and full-bodied, with an oaky, buttery fragrance, it has generous, peachy, slightly toasty flavours, showing good complexity, balanced acidity and a long, tightly structured finish. Best drinking 2021+.

DRY $35 –V

747 Estate Gisborne Chardonnay   (★★★☆)

Labelled as a 'Chablis style', the 2017 vintage (★★★☆) is from Denis Irwin, ex-Matawhero. Medium-bodied, it is a fruity, flavoursome, finely balanced wine, only moderately complex, but drinking well in 2019.

DRY $24 AV

Aitken's Folly Riverbank Road Wanaka Central Otago Chardonnay   ★★★★

Retasted in May 2019, the distinctive 2016 vintage (★★★★☆) is based solely on Chardonnay clone 548. Estate-grown at Wanaka, it was fermented and matured for a year in French oak casks (30 per cent new). Bright, light yellow, it has strong, citrusy aromas and flavours, showing very good complexity, and a crisp, long finish. Best drinking now to 2020.

DRY $28 AV

Alchemy Hawke's Bay Chardonnay   ★★★★☆

Offering very good value, the 2016 vintage (★★★★☆) is a single-vineyard wine, hand-harvested at Puketapu, in the Dartmoor Valley, and fermented and matured in French oak barrels (35 per cent new). Fragrant, rich and lively, it is a weighty, finely textured wine, with strong, ripe stone-fruit flavours, well seasoned with toasty oak, balanced acidity and good complexity. Delicious now, it should be at its best 2020+.

DRY $29 V+

Alexander Martinborough Chardonnay   ★★★★☆

Labelled as a 'Chablis style', the 2018 vintage (★★★★☆) is a single-vineyard wine, hand-picked and fermented and matured in two-year-old French oak casks. The bouquet is fragrant and complex; the palate is full-bodied and dry, with strong, youthful, citrusy, peachy flavours, balanced acidity and very good complexity. A stylish wine with obvious potential, it's well worth cellaring to 2021+.

DRY $29 V+

Allan Scott [Black Label] Marlborough Chardonnay   (★★★★)

Made in an extroverted style, the 2018 vintage (★★★★) is a pale gold wine, hand-picked in the Wairau Valley and fermented and matured for eight months in French oak puncheons. Full-bodied, it has strong, ripe stone-fruit flavours, seasoned with toasty oak, excellent complexity and a creamy-smooth finish.

DRY $26 AV

Allan Scott Eli Marlborough Chardonnay

(★★★★☆)

The debut 2016 vintage (★★★★☆) is rare – just one barrel was produced. Fermented with indigenous yeasts and given 'lots' of lees-stirring, it's a weighty, harmonious wine, concentrated and finely textured, with deep, citrusy, peachy flavours, biscuity and well-rounded.

 DRY $100 –V

Allan Scott Generations Marlborough Chardonnay

★★★★

The 2016 vintage (★★★★☆) is a powerful style, estate-grown in the Wallops Vineyard, in the Wairau Valley, and fermented and matured for 12 months in French oak puncheons (80 per cent new). Given a full, softening malolactic fermentation, it is weighty, rich and lively, with substantial body, concentrated grapefruit and peach flavours, and toasty, buttery notes adding an upfront appeal. Drink now to 2021.

 DRY $31 –V

Allan Scott Marlborough Chardonnay

★★★☆

Priced right, the fresh, vibrantly fruity 2018 vintage (★★★☆) was fermented in French oak puncheons and wood-aged for eight months. Light lemon/green, with a citrusy bouquet, it has lively grapefruit and peach flavours, slightly biscuity notes adding complexity, balanced acidity and good depth.

 DRY $18 V+

Alpha Domus AD Hawke's Bay Chardonnay

★★★★★

The powerful, savoury 2016 vintage (★★★★★) was estate-grown in the Bridge Pa Triangle and fermented and matured for a year in French oak casks. A classic regional style, it is ripely fragrant and full-bodied, with generous, citrusy, peachy flavours, seasoned with biscuity oak, excellent complexity, and a tightly structured, long finish. Full of youthful potential, it should be at its best 2020+.

 DRY $38 AV

Alpha Domus The Skybolt Hawke's Bay Chardonnay

★★★★

The 2016 vintage (★★★★) is a single-vineyard wine, estate-grown in the Bridge Pa Triangle and fermented and matured for 11 months in French oak barriques. Mouthfilling, it has generous, ripe stone-fruit flavours, a gentle seasoning of biscuity oak adding complexity, and a slightly creamy texture. Ready.

DRY $26 AV

Anchorage Family Estate Nelson Chardonnay

★★☆

Made in a 'lightly oaked' style, the 2018 vintage (★★☆) is pale straw, with peachy, creamy, buttery notes, a vague hint of honey and firm acid spine. Drink young.

 DRY $18 –V

Archangel Central Otago Chardonnay   ★★★★

The 2017 vintage (★★★★) was fermented and matured for nine months in French oak casks (42 per cent new). Light lemon/green, with a creamy bouquet, it is mouthfilling and smooth, with citrusy, biscuity, mealy flavours, showing considerable complexity, and good mouthfeel and harmony. Enjoyable young, it's also well worth cellaring.

DRY $35 –V

Aronui Nelson Chardonnay   ★★★★

Drinking well now, but also worth cellaring, the 2016 vintage (★★★★) was hand-picked and barrel-fermented. Bright, light lemon/green, it is mouthfilling, with vibrant, citrusy, peachy flavours, showing very good depth, and slightly biscuity and buttery notes adding complexity. (From Kono, also owner of the Tohu brand.)

DRY $22 V+

Ash Ridge Estate Hawke's Bay Chardonnay   ★★★☆

The 2017 vintage (★★★☆) was estate-grown in the Bridge Pa Triangle and mostly barrel-fermented. It's a fragrant, medium to full-bodied wine, with peachy fruit flavours to the fore, a hint of butterscotch, considerable complexity and lots of drink-young appeal.

DRY $20 AV

Ash Ridge Premium Bridge Pa Triangle Hawke's Bay Chardonnay   ★★★★

Crafted in a 'bold' style, the 2017 vintage (★★★★) was made using 'high impact' French oak barrels and 'lots' of malolactic fermentation. Bright, light lemon/green, it is rich and rounded, with balanced acidity and strong, peachy, toasty, buttery flavours.

DRY $32 –V

Ash Ridge Reserve Hawke's Bay Chardonnay   ★★★★☆

Estate-grown in the Bridge Pa Triangle, the 2017 vintage (★★★★☆) was fermented and matured in French oak casks (40 per cent new). Designed for cellaring, it is bright, light lemon/green, with a fragrant, complex, slightly smoky bouquet. An elegant, medium to full-bodied, tightly structured wine, it has generous, peachy, citrusy, slightly nutty flavours, fresh acidity and a long, savoury finish. Best drinking mid-2020+.

DRY $42 –V

Ashwell Martinborough Chardonnay   ★★★★

The 2017 vintage (★★★★), grown on the Martinborough Terrace, was barrique-fermented. Light lemon/green, it is lemon-scented, with vibrant grapefruit-evoking flavours, finely integrated oak and a crisp, dry finish. An elegant, youthful wine, it should break into full stride 2020+.

Vintage	17	16
WR	5	5
Drink	19-25	19-24

DRY $28 AV

Askerne Hawke's Bay Chardonnay ★★★★

Offering good value, the 2018 vintage (★★★★) was estate-grown and fermented and matured in predominantly French oak barrels (28 per cent new). Bright, light yellow/green, it is a full-bodied, generous, creamy-textured wine, with strong, ripe stone-fruit flavours, showing considerable complexity, and a harmonious, well-rounded finish.

 DRY $23 V+

Askerne Reserve Hawke's Bay Chardonnay ★★★★☆

The powerful young 2018 vintage (★★★★☆) was fermented and matured in French oak barrels (35 per cent new). Bright, light yellow/green, it is mouthfilling and sweet-fruited, with strong, ripe stone-fruit flavours, seasoned with toasty oak, excellent complexity and a rich, smooth finish. Best drinking 2021+.

 DRY $32 AV

Astrolabe Marlborough Chardonnay ★★★★

The 2018 vintage (★★★★) was hand-picked at two sites, in the lower Wairau Valley and the Southern Valleys, and fermented and matured for 10 months in French oak barriques and puncheons. Fragrant and mouthfilling, it has excellent depth of ripe, peachy, slightly toasty flavours, showing good complexity, gentle acidity and a creamy-smooth finish. It's already drinking well.

Vintage	18
WR	6
Drink	20-26

DRY $30 –V

Ata Rangi Craighall Martinborough Chardonnay ★★★★★

This memorable wine has richness, complexity and downright drinkability. From a company-owned block of low-yielding Mendoza-clone vines in the Craighall Vineyard, planted in 1983, it is hand-picked, whole-bunch pressed and fermented with indigenous yeasts in French oak barriques (around 25 per cent new). The 2017 vintage (★★★★★) is bright, light lemon/green, with a fragrant, slightly creamy bouquet. A refined, subtle wine, it is full-bodied, with fresh, youthful, peachy, citrusy, slightly biscuity flavours, showing excellent delicacy and depth, finely integrated oak, balanced acidity and a long finish. Best drinking 2021+.

Vintage	17	16	15	14	13	12	11	10
WR	7	7	7	7	7	6	7	7
Drink	19-25	19-24	19-23	19-22	19-21	P	P	P

DRY $55 AV

🍇🍇🍇

Ataahua Waipara Chardonnay ★★★★

Still youthful, the 2017 vintage (★★★★) was fermented and matured for a year in seasoned oak barrels. Full-bodied, with a creamy, buttery fragrance, it has peachy, slightly spicy and biscuity flavours, showing considerable complexity, and a rounded finish. Best drinking mid-2020+.

Vintage	18	17
WR	6	7
Drink	19-25	19-27

 DRY $29 AV

Auntsfield Cob Cottage Southern Valleys Marlborough Chardonnay   ★★★★★

This single 'block' – rather than just single 'vineyard' – wine is estate-grown on the south side of the Wairau Valley. The outstanding 2016 vintage (★★★★★), matured for 11 months in French oak casks (20 per cent new), is a weighty wine, slightly creamy-textured, with deep, youthful citrus and stone-fruit flavours, and very finely integrated, biscuity oak. Combining power and elegance, it is highly concentrated, vibrant and 'complete'.

Vintage	16	
WR	7	
Drink	19-28	

Auntsfield Single Vineyard Southern Valleys Marlborough Chardonnay   ★★★★★

This consistently rewarding wine is estate-grown on the south side of the Wairau Valley, hand-harvested and fermented and matured in French oak barrels (18 per cent new in 2017). The elegant, youthful 2017 vintage (★★★★☆) is fragrant, fresh and full-bodied, with vibrant, citrusy, peachy, slightly biscuity flavours, fresh acidity, very good intensity and a fully dry, tightly structured finish. Best drinking mid-2021+.

Aurum Organic Central Otago Chardonnay   ★★★★

The 2017 vintage (★★★☆) was estate-grown, fermented and matured for 15 months in French oak barrels (25 per cent new), and bottled unfined and unfiltered. Bright, light lemon/green, with fresh, lemony scents, it is lively, crisp and citrusy, with a restrained oak influence and obvious potential; open 2020+. Certified organic.

Awatere River Marlborough Chardonnay   ★★★★

The youthful 2017 vintage (★★★★) was fermented and matured in French oak barriques. Light yellow/pale gold, with a strong, lemony fragrance, it is mouthfilling and slightly creamy, with citrusy, toasty flavours, fresh acidity and good complexity. Best drinking 2021+.

Babich Black Label Hawke's Bay Chardonnay   ★★★★

The Black Label range is aimed primarily at the restaurant trade. Finely balanced for current consumption, but also worth cellaring, the 2018 vintage (★★★★) is a fragrant, vibrantly fruity wine with generous, ripe stone-fruit flavours to the fore, a subtle seasoning of oak adding complexity, slightly buttery notes and a well-rounded finish.

DRY $23 V+

Babich Family Estates Headwaters Organic Marlborough Chardonnay ★★★★☆

Estate-grown near Renwick, in the Wairau Valley, the classy 2017 vintage (★★★★☆) is great value. Fermented and matured for eight months in French oak barriques, it is fragrant and vibrantly fruity, with strong, citrusy, peachy flavours, fresh acidity, slightly buttery and nutty notes, and excellent depth, vigour, complexity and harmony. Best drinking 2020+.

 DRY $25 V+

Babich Hawke's Bay Chardonnay ★★★☆

Drinking well in its youth, the 2018 vintage (★★★☆) is an unoaked style, fresh, full-bodied and vibrantly fruity, with ripe stone-fruit flavours to the fore, good mouthfeel and texture, and a rounded finish.

 DRY $20 AV

Babich Irongate Chardonnay ★★★★★

Babich's flagship Chardonnay. A stylish wine, Irongate was traditionally markedly leaner and tighter than other top Hawke's Bay Chardonnays, while performing well in the cellar, but the latest releases have more drink-young appeal. It is based on hand-picked fruit from the shingly Irongate Vineyard in Gimblett Road, fully barrel-fermented (about 20 per cent new), and lees-matured for up to 10 months. Fragrant and finely textured, the 2018 vintage (★★★★★) is a weighty wine, with deep peach and grapefruit flavours, mealy notes adding complexity and a seamless, lingering finish. Fresh, youthful and finely poised, it's already enjoyable, but likely to be at its best 2022+.

Vintage	17	16	15	14	13	12	11
WR	6	7	7	6	7	4	6
Drink	19-27	19-27	19-26	19-25	19-25	P	19-20

 DRY $40 AV

Bilancia Hawke's Bay Chardonnay ★★★★★

The 2015 vintage (★★★★☆) was estate-grown, hand-picked and fermented with indigenous yeasts in French oak puncheons (30 per cent new). Light lemon/green, with a fragrant, smoky ('struck match') bouquet, it is full-bodied, with excellent depth of vigorous grapefruit-like flavours, integrated oak, and a dry, lingering finish.

Vintage	15	14	13
WR	6	6	7
Drink	19-22	19-20	P

 DRY $34 AV

Black Barn Barrel Fermented Hawke's Bay Chardonnay ★★★★☆

Estate-grown in the Havelock North hills, hand-picked and barrel-fermented, this is typically a classy wine, in a classic regional style. The youthful 2018 vintage (★★★★★) was fermented and matured for 11 months in French oak casks (20 per cent new). Bright, light lemon/green, it has a fragrant bouquet of stone-fruit and toasty oak. Weighty and savoury, it has ripe, peachy, slightly spicy flavours, generous and complex, and a finely balanced, long finish. Best drinking 2021+.

DRY $39 –V

Black Cottage Reserve Marlborough Chardonnay   ★★★☆

Priced right, the 2017 vintage (★★★☆) was hand-picked in the Wairau Valley (mostly) and the Southern Valleys. Bright, light lemon/green, it is drinking well now, with fresh, vibrant, grapefruit-like flavours, savoury notes adding complexity, and a creamy-smooth finish.

DRY $20 AV

Black Estate Home Vineyard North Canterbury Chardonnay   ★★★★☆

The 2017 vintage (★★★★☆) is from the Home Vineyard at Omihi, Waipara, where the oldest vines were planted in 1994. Hand-picked and fermented with indigenous yeasts in French oak barrels, it was bottled unfined and unfiltered. Light yellow, it is a tightly structured wine, medium to full-bodied, with excellent intensity of peachy, slightly toasty flavours, a slightly minerally streak, appetising acidity and plenty of personality. Best drinking 2020+. Certified organic.

DRY $45 –V

Blackenbrook Nelson Chardonnay   ★★★★

Estate-grown, the 2018 vintage (★★★★) was hand-picked and partly barrel-fermented, then matured for a year in American (60 per cent) and French (40 per cent) oak casks. A bold style, it is fresh and full-bodied, with peachy, citrusy flavours, seasoned with biscuit oak, good complexity and a slightly creamy texture. Best drinking mid-2020+.

Vintage	18
WR	6
Drink	20-24

DRY $25 AV

Boneline, The, Barebone Waipara Chardonnay   ★★★★☆

Drinking well now, the 2017 vintage (★★★★) was matured for an extended time (15 months) on its yeast lees, with some use of old oak barrels. Bright, light lemon/green, it is full-bodied, with generous, vibrant grapefruit and peach flavours to the fore, and a dry, well-rounded, slightly creamy finish.

DRY $30 AV

Boneline, The, Sharkstone Waipara Chardonnay   ★★★★★

An emerging classic from North Canterbury. Already delicious, the striking 2018 vintage (★★★★★) was estate-grown, hand-picked from mature vines and fermented with indigenous yeasts in French oak barrels. Bright, light lemon/green, it is fragrant, tightly structured and intense, with searching, grapefruit-like flavours, gentle biscuit and buttery notes adding complexity, and a long, seamless finish. A notably elegant, distinctly cool-climate style, it's a very 'complete' wine, set to unfold gracefully for a decade.

DRY $45 AV

Brancott Estate Identity Wairau Valley Marlborough Chardonnay   (★★★☆)

Drinking well young, the debut 2018 vintage (★★★☆) was grown in the Renwick and Brancott districts, and partly oak-fermented (17 per cent of the blend was fermented in French oak foudres). Mouthfilling, it has good depth of fresh, ripe, peachy flavours, showing a touch of complexity, and a harmonious, slightly creamy-textured finish.

DRY $22 AV

Brancott Estate Letter Series 'O' Marlborough Chardonnay   ★★★★☆

Named after the company's Omaka Vineyard, this typically powerful, high-flavoured wine is hand-picked at sites on the south side of the Wairau Valley, fermented with indigenous yeasts in French oak barriques (about 40 per cent new), and given a full, softening malolactic fermentation. An upfront style, the 2017 vintage (★★★★☆) is bright, light lemon/green, with a fragrant, smoky bouquet, mouthfilling body and strong, ripe, peachy, slightly toasty flavours. Weighty and youthful, it should be at its best 2020+.

DRY $25 V+

Brancott Estate Terroir Series Southern Valleys Marlborough Chardonnay   ★★★★

Offering great value, the 2016 vintage (★★★★) was grown in the Southern Valleys sub-region and fermented and matured in large French oak cuves. Weighty, it has vibrant grapefruit-like flavours, a subtle seasoning of oak, very good complexity and depth, and a slightly mealy, dry, harmonious finish.

DRY $20 V+

Brennan Gibbston Central Otago Chardonnay   ★★★★

Full of youthful drive, the 2018 vintage (★★★★☆) of this tightly structured, estate-grown wine was barrel-fermented and lees-aged. Bright, light yellow/green, it is full-bodied, with ripe stone-fruit and toasty oak flavours, showing impressive complexity and depth, fresh acidity, and a finely balanced, lengthy finish. Best drinking 2021+.

DRY $33 –V

Brick Bay Matakana Chardonnay   ★★★★☆

Well worth cellaring, the 2017 vintage (★★★★) was estate-grown and barrel-fermented. Mouthfilling, fresh and lively, it is youthful, with ripe, citrusy, peachy, nutty flavours, complex and savoury, finely balanced acidity and a lingering finish. Best drinking mid-2020+.

DRY $44 –V

Brightside Organic Chardonnay   ★★★☆

Certified organic, the bargain-priced 2016 vintage (★★★☆) was fully fermented in seasoned oak barrels. Light lemon/green, with a fresh, slightly buttery bouquet, it is mouthfilling, with generous, peachy, lemony flavours, showing some savoury complexity, a creamy texture and a dry, well-rounded finish. (From Kaimira.)

DRY $17 V+

Brightwater Vineyards Lord Rutherford Barrique Nelson Chardonnay ★★★★★

This classy, single-vineyard, estate-grown wine is hand-picked and fermented and matured for up to a year in French oak barriques (25 per cent new in 2016). The 2016 vintage (★★★★★) is a refined, vibrant, tightly structured wine, mouthfilling, with concentrated, citrusy, peachy, slightly toasty flavours, creamy notes, excellent complexity and a lingering finish. Best drinking 2020+.

Vintage	16
WR	7
Drink	19-22

 DRY $40 AV

Brightwater Vineyards Nelson Chardonnay ★★★★

The attractive 2016 vintage (★★★★) was estate-grown, fermented and matured for 10 months in French oak barrels (20 per cent new), and given a full, softening malolactic fermentation. It is fragrant, mouthfilling, fresh and lively, with considerable complexity, balanced acidity and good intensity of lemony, peachy, slightly toasty and buttery flavours.

 DRY $28 AV

Bronte Nelson Chardonnay ★★★☆

From Rimu Grove, the 2016 vintage (★★★☆) was grown at Moutere and French oak-aged. Light lemon/green, with a fragrant, citrusy, peachy bouquet, it is full-bodied and vibrant, with ripe-fruit flavours to the fore, fresh acidity and good depth. Enjoyable young.

Vintage	16	15
WR	6	7
Drink	19-27	19-26

 DRY $24 AV

Brookfields Bergman Chardonnay ★★★★

Named after the Ingrid Bergman roses in the estate garden, this wine is grown alongside the winery at Meeanee, in Hawke's Bay, hand-picked, and fermented and matured on its yeast lees in seasoned French and American oak casks. The 2017 vintage (★★★★) is delicious young. Bright, light yellow/green, it has a fresh, slightly buttery bouquet. Full-bodied, it's an upfront style, with generous, peachy, slightly toasty flavours, fresh acidity and loads of drink-young appeal.

Vintage	17	16	15
WR	7	7	7
Drink	19-20	19-21	19-20

DRY $21 V+

Brookfields Marshall Bank Chardonnay ★★★★★

Brookfields' top Chardonnay is named after proprietor Peter Robertson's grandfather's property in Otago. Grown in a vineyard adjacent to the winery at Meeanee and fermented and matured (with weekly stirring of its yeast lees) in French oak barriques (50 per cent new in 2018), it is a powerful, classy, concentrated Hawke's Bay wine. The refined, generous 2018 vintage (★★★★★) has a fragrant, complex bouquet. Already delicious, it is weighty, with deep stone-fruit flavours, balanced acidity, and impressive richness, complexity and harmony. Best drinking 2021+.

Vintage	18
WR	7
Drink	21-26

 DRY $35 AV

Bushmere Estate Classic Gisborne Chardonnay   ★★★★

The age-worthy 2017 vintage (★★★★) was grown in the Central Valley and French oak-fermented. Bright, light lemon/green, it is still youthful, with fresh, ripe, citrusy, peachy flavours, integrated oak, and a finely poised, rounded finish. Best drinking mid-2020+.

DRY $25 AV

Byrne Northland Puketotara Chardonnay   ★★★★☆

This powerful wine is grown in the Fat Pig Vineyard. The 2016 vintage (★★★★☆) was fermented in French oak barriques (33 per cent new). Fragrant and mouthfilling, it is fresh and creamy-textured, in a concentrated, strongly oak-influenced style, complex and lingering.

DRY $30 AV

Carrick Bannockburn Central Otago Chardonnay   ★★★★☆

Certified organic, the 2017 vintage (★★★★) was hand-picked, barrel-fermented with indigenous yeasts and bottled unfined and unfiltered. Bright, light yellow/green, it is full-bodied, with strong, peachy, toasty, slightly buttery flavours and a crisp, dry finish. A youthful, vigorous wine, it should be at its best 2020+.

Vintage	17	16	15	14	13	12	11
WR	7	6	5	6	7	7	6
Drink	19-24	19-23	19-21	19-21	19-20	P	P

DRY $39 –V

Carrick Cairnmuir Terraces EBM Chardonnay   ★★★★★

From a region producing increasingly fine, often underrated Chardonnays, this is one of the best. EBM means 'extended barrel maturation'. Estate-grown at Bannockburn, the stylish 2016 vintage (★★★★★) was fermented and matured for 18 months in French oak barrels (10 per cent new). Showing obvious potential, it is full-bodied and vibrantly fruity, with strong, citrusy, slightly peachy flavours, gently seasoned with oak, excellent complexity, and a tight, persistent finish. Still youthful, it should break into full stride from 2020 onwards. Certified organic.

Vintage	16	15	14	13	12	11	10
WR	7	5	6	7	7	6	6
Drink	19-26	19-22	19-21	19-20	P	P	P

DRY $47 AV

Catalina Sounds Single Vineyard Sound of White Marlborough Chardonnay   (★★★★☆)

The elegant, youthful 2017 vintage (★★★★☆) was estate-grown and hand-harvested in the Waihopai Valley, and fermented and matured in French oak puncheons. Fragrant, fresh and full-bodied, it is vibrantly fruity, with vigorous grapefruit and peach flavours, biscuity, mealy notes adding complexity, and a long, creamy-textured finish. Best drinking mid-2020+.

DRY $35 –V

Chard Farm Closeburn Central Otago Chardonnay   ★★★☆

The 2016 vintage (★★★★) was fermented and lees-aged in tanks, with no oak handling. Fresh, mouthfilling and creamy-textured, it's a 'fruit-driven' style, with ripe, peachy flavours, showing good concentration, and a smooth, dry finish.

Vintage	16
WR	6
Drink	19-22

DRY $28 –V

Chard Farm Judge & Jury Central Otago Chardonnay   (★★★★☆)

The 2016 vintage (★★★★☆) was designed to showcase its delicious, vibrant fruit characters – 70 per cent of the blend was handled in tanks, but 30 per cent was matured in old and new oak barrels. It has a creamy, slightly citrusy and biscuity bouquet, leading into a mouthfilling, buoyantly fruity wine, with fresh, rich, grapefruit-like flavours, very generous, smooth and harmonious.

Vintage	16
WR	6
Drink	19-23

DRY $39 –V

Church Road Grand Reserve Hawke's Bay Chardonnay   ★★★★★

This very classy wine sits above the McDonald Series (but below Tom) in the Church Road hierarchy. Hand-picked in the Tuki Tuki Valley and fermented with indigenous yeasts in French oak barrels (30 per cent new), the 2017 vintage (★★★★★) combines power and elegance. Tightly structured, with a slightly smoky bouquet, it has concentrated, youthful grapefruit and peach flavours, well-integrated biscuity oak, excellent complexity and a finely poised, lasting finish. Fine value.

DRY $34 V+

Church Road Hawke's Bay Chardonnay   ★★★★

This mouthfilling, rich wine is made by Pernod Ricard NZ at Church Road winery in Hawke's Bay. Described by winemaker Chris Scott as 'unashamedly just a little bit old school', it is typically fleshy and smooth, with ripe stone-fruit flavours, showing good complexity and depth. It is fermented mostly in Hungarian and French oak barrels (about 25 per cent new), given a full, softening malolactic fermentation, and oak-matured for six months. The 2017 vintage (★★★★) is a great buy, as usual. Bright, light lemon/green, with a fragrant, biscuity, complex bouquet, it is mouthfilling, ripe and rounded, with peachy, slightly yeasty and buttery flavours, harmonious and lingering.

Vintage	17	16	15	14	13
WR	5	5	7	7	7
Drink	19-20	P	P	P	P

DRY $19 V+

Church Road McDonald Series Hawke's Bay Chardonnay   ★★★★★

Typically a great buy, with greater richness and complexity than most $25 Chardonnays. Still youthful, the 2017 vintage (★★★★☆) is a refined wine, hand-harvested and fermented with indigenous yeasts in French oak casks. Bright, light yellow/green, it is mouthfilling, with a slightly toasty bouquet, strong, vibrant, peachy flavours, showing good complexity, and fresh acidity keeping things lively. Best drinking 2020+.

Vintage	17	16	15	14	13	12	11
WR	5	5	7	7	7	6	5
Drink	19-21	19-20	19-20	P	P	P	P

Church Road Tom Chardonnay   ★★★★★

Still unfolding, the tightly structured 2016 vintage (★★★★★), released in September 2019, was estate-grown in the Tuki Tuki Vineyard, 4 kilometres from the coast, on a west-facing clay slope cooled by afternoon sea breezes. Hand-picked, it was fermented with indigenous yeasts and matured for 11 months in French oak barriques (43 per cent new). Bright yellow/pale gold, with a fragrant, slightly smoky, toasty bouquet, it is a powerful wine, mouthfilling, with deep, youthful citrus and stone-fruit flavours, barrel-ferment complexity, fresh acidity and a very long finish. Best drinking 2021+.

Vintage	16	15	14	13	12	11	10
WR	7	NM	7	7	NM	NM	7
Drink	19-23	NM	19-21	19-20	NM	NM	P

Clearview Beachhead Hawke's Bay Chardonnay   ★★★★☆

This Hawke's Bay winery has a reputation for powerful Chardonnays, and top vintages of this good-value label are no exception. Estate-grown and hand-harvested on the coast at Te Awanga, the 2017 vintage (★★★★☆) was fermented and matured for nine months in seasoned French oak barrels (one and two years old) and given a full, softening malolactic fermentation. Bright, light lemon/green, with a fragrant, complex bouquet, it is mouthfilling, with loads of vibrant, peachy, slightly toasty flavour, a hint of butterscotch, balanced acidity and a dry, tight finish. Best drinking 2020+.

Vintage	17	16	15	14	13
WR	5	5	7	7	7
Drink	19-22	19-21	19-21	19-20	P

Clearview Endeavour Hawke's Bay Chardonnay ★★★★★

One of New Zealand's highest-priced Chardonnays, this wine is estate-grown at Te Awanga, hand-picked from (Mendoza-clone) vines planted in 1989, fermented with indigenous yeasts and matured for an unusually long period in barrels. It typically makes a very bold statement. The 2015 vintage (★★★★★) was matured for 29 months in all-new French oak barriques. Bright, light yellow/green, it is a highly fragrant, very powerful, weighty, concentrated and complex wine, with notably rich, citrusy, peachy flavours, seasoned with toasty oak, lively acidity, and a real sense of youthful drive and potential. A 'statement' wine, revealing just how flavour-drenched Hawke's Bay Chardonnay can be, it is already delicious, but should break into full stride 2020+.

Vintage	15	14	13
WR	7	NM	7
Drink	19-22	NM	19-20

 DRY $175 –V

Clearview Reserve Hawke's Bay Chardonnay ★★★★★

For his premium Chardonnay label, winemaker Tim Turvey aims for a 'big, grunty, upfront' style – and hits the target with ease. It's typically a hedonist's delight – an arrestingly bold, intense, savoury, mealy, complex wine with layers of flavour. The 2017 vintage (★★★★★) was hand-picked from vines up to 30 years old at Te Awanga, fermented and matured for 11 months in French oak barriques (42 per cent new), and given a full, softening malolactic fermentation. Bright, light lemon/green, it is fragrant and full-bodied, with deep, peachy, toasty flavours, showing notable vigour and complexity, invigorating acidity, excellent harmony and a powerful finish. Coupling a sense of youthful drive with lots of drink-young appeal, it should break into full stride from 2020 onwards.

Vintage	17	16	15	14	13	12	11	10
WR	5	6	7	7	7	6	6	7
Drink	19-27	19-26	19-25	19-25	19-23	19-21	19-20	19-20

 DRY $45 AV

Clos de Ste Anne Chardonnay Naboth's Vineyard ★★★★★

Millton's exceptional Chardonnay is based on ungrafted, unirrigated vines, over 25 years old, in the steep, north-east-facing Naboth's Vineyard in the Poverty Bay foothills. Grown biodynamically and hand-harvested, it is fermented with indigenous yeasts in mostly second-fill French oak barriques, and has usually not been put through malolactic fermentation, 'to leave a pure, crisp mineral flavour'. A powerful wine, it is also notably stylish and complete. The 2015 vintage (★★★★☆) is a good but not great vintage. Bright, light yellow/green, it has a restrained bouquet, leading into a weighty, rich palate with deep grapefruit and peach flavours, showing excellent complexity, fresh acidity, and a well-structured, faintly buttery, long finish. It should be at its best 2020+.

Vintage	15	14	13	12	11	10
WR	6	7	7	NM	NM	7
Drink	19-29	19-29	19-28	NM	NM	19-25

 DRY $75 AV

Cloudy Bay New Zealand Chardonnay ★★★★★

A powerful Marlborough wine with impressively concentrated, savoury, lemony, mealy flavours and a proven ability to mature well over the long haul. The grapes are sourced from numerous company-owned and growers' vineyards at Brancott, Fairhall, Benmorven and in the Central Wairau Valley. The wine is fermented with indigenous yeasts in French oak barriques (15 per cent new in 2017), lees-aged in barrels, and most goes through a softening malolactic fermentation. The 2017 vintage (★★★★★) is typically refined. Bright, light lemon/green, it is fragrant and tightly structured, with good acid spine, citrusy, peachy flavours, a subtle seasoning of oak, and excellent delicacy and depth.

 DRY $41 AV

Vintage	17	16	15	14
WR	7	7	7	7
Drink	19-26	19-25	19-24	19-20

Collaboration Aurulent Hawke's Bay Chardonnay ★★★★★

The refined 2018 vintage (★★★★★) was fermented and matured for 11 months in French oak casks (22 per cent new). Bright, light yellow/green, it has a fresh, smoky fragrance. Mouthfilling, it is vibrantly fruity, with strong, youthful, grapefruit-like flavours, hints of biscuity oak, excellent complexity and a long, slightly creamy finish. Best drinking 2021+.

 DRY $37 AV

Vintage	18	17	16	15	14	13	12	11
WR	6	6	6	7	7	7	6	5
Drink	19-25	19-24	19-23	19-23	19-22	19-21	P	P

Collaboration Impression White Hawke's Bay Chardonnay ★★★★

Already delicious, the 2018 vintage (★★★★☆) was matured for eight months in seasoned French oak barrels and given a full, softening malolactic fermentation. Bright yellow, with a fragrant, slightly buttery bouquet, it is sweet-fruited, well-rounded wine, with generous stone-fruit flavours, gentle, nutty oak characters adding complexity, and loads of drink-young appeal.

DRY $27 AV

Coniglio Hawke's Bay Chardonnay ★★★★☆

Currently on sale, the 2015 vintage (★★★★☆) was estate-grown in the inland, elevated Riverview Vineyard, hand-harvested, fermented with indigenous yeasts and barrel-aged for 18 months. Bright, light lemon/green, it is full-bodied, with concentrated, peachy, toasty flavours, showing very good vigour and complexity, fresh acidity and a long finish. Drink now or cellar.

 DRY $90 –V

Vintage	15
WR	7
Drink	19-25

Coopers Creek Gisborne Chardonnay ★★★☆

A good-value, drink-young style, this is typically a mouthfilling, vibrantly fruity wine with plenty of peachy, citrusy flavour, slightly toasty and creamy-smooth. Partly barrel-fermented, the 2017 vintage (★★★☆) is full-bodied, with very good depth of peachy, slightly toasty flavours, and fresh acidity keeping things lively.

 DRY $18 V+

Coopers Creek Select Vineyards Big + Buttery Gisborne Chardonnay   ★★★★

Crafted deliberately in the 'full-on' style popular in the 1980s, the 2017 vintage (★★★★) was fermented in American oak barrels (30 per cent new) and given a full, softening malolactic fermentation. Bright, light yellow/green, it is fragrant, with fresh, strong, peachy, toasty flavours, showing good complexity, balanced acidity and a slightly creamy texture.

DRY $25 AV

Coopers Creek Select Vineyards Limeworks Hawke's Bay Chardonnay   ★★★★

If you like toasty, creamy, full-flavoured Chardonnays, try this. Grown in the Havelock North hills, the 2018 vintage (★★★★) was fermented and matured for 10 months in American oak casks (30 per cent new), and given a full, softening malolactic fermentation. Fragrant and full-bodied, it has generous stone-fruit flavours, strongly seasoned with toasty oak, and good complexity.

DRY $25 AV

Coopers Creek Select Vineyards Plainsman Hawke's Bay Chardonnay   ★★★★

The subtle, creamy-textured 2018 vintage (★★★★) was fermented and matured for 10 months in barrels, but with no use of new oak. Fresh and full-bodied, it has very good depth of ripe, peachy, slightly yeasty flavours, considerable complexity, balanced acidity and lots of drink-young charm.

DRY $22 V+

Coopers Creek Swamp Reserve Chardonnay   ★★★★☆

Based on the winery's best Hawke's Bay grapes, this seductive Chardonnay has a finely judged balance of rich, citrusy, peachy fruit flavours and toasty oak. Hand-picked in the company's Middle Road Vineyard at Havelock North, it is fermented and matured in French oak barriques (30 per cent new in 2018), and given a full, softening malolactic fermentation. The 2017 vintage (★★★★☆) is full-bodied and youthful, with strong, smoky, 'struck match' aromas, intense, vibrant stone-fruit flavours, showing very good complexity, and a tightly structured finish. The 2018 vintage (★★★★★) is a very classy, harmonious wine. Full-bodied, it has concentrated, peachy, slightly spicy flavours, gentle biscuity and smoky notes adding complexity, and a finely balanced, lasting finish. Best drinking 2022+.

DRY $39 –V

Craft Farm Home Vineyard Hawke's Bay Chardonnay   ★★★★☆

The 2017 vintage (★★★★☆) was estate-grown at Puketapu and barrel-fermented with indigenous yeasts. Bright, light lemon/green, with a fragrant, complex bouquet, it is medium to full-bodied, with rich, ripe stone-fruit flavours to the fore and a tightly structured, long finish. A youthful, very age-worthy wine, it should be at its best mid-2020+.

DRY $35 –V

Craggy Range Gimblett Gravels Vineyard Hawke's Bay Chardonnay ★★★★★

This stylish wine is typically mouthfilling and savoury, with complexity from fermentation and maturation in French oak barriques (19 per cent new in 2018). The 2018 vintage (★★★★★), barrel-aged for 10 months, shows lovely freshness and harmony, with a slightly smoky bouquet. Bright, light lemon/green, it is mouthfilling, vibrant and youthful, with finely balanced acidity, deep stone-fruit flavours, mealy, biscuity notes adding complexity, and a lingering finish. Best drinking 2021+.

Craggy Range Kidnappers Vineyard Hawke's Bay Chardonnay ★★★★

Grown near the coast, at Te Awanga, the pale 2018 vintage (★★★★) was handled for 10 months in French oak puncheons (10 per cent new). Very fresh and vibrant, it is medium to full-bodied, with vigorous, citrusy, peachy flavours, a gentle seasoning of biscuity oak, and a crisp, dry, lingering finish. Best drinking mid-2020+.

Crater Rim, The, Waipara Valley Chardonnay ★★★★☆

The 2016 vintage (★★★★) is an estate-grown wine, hand-picked and fermented and lees-aged for 15 months in French oak barriques (partly new). Bright, light yellow/green, with a fragrant, citrusy bouquet, it is mouthfilling, with good intensity of grapefruit-like flavours, slightly buttery and toasty, and obvious potential; best drinking 2020+.

Crazy by Nature Gisborne Shotberry Chardonnay ★★★☆

From Millton, this is an unoaked style. The attractive 2017 vintage (★★★★) was blended with Viognier (7 per cent) and Marsanne (4 per cent) to 'extend the palate weight' and tank-fermented. Pale straw, it is mouthfilling and sweet-fruited, with ripe, citrusy, peachy flavours, good acid balance, a touch of complexity, and excellent depth and harmony. Certified organic.

DRY $21 AV

Cypress Terraces Hawke's Bay Chardonnay ★★★★☆

From a sloping, 2-hectare site at Roys Hill, the highly attractive 2016 vintage (★★★★☆) was hand-harvested and fermented with indigenous yeasts in French oak casks (25 per cent new). A classic Hawke's Bay style, it is full-bodied and sweet-fruited, with generous, ripe stone-fruit flavours, a subtle seasoning of toasty oak, slightly buttery notes, and excellent complexity and harmony.

Vintage	16
WR	7
Drink	19-21

DRY $32 AV

Dashwood by Vavasour Marlborough Chardonnay ★★★☆

Enjoyable young, the 2018 vintage (★★★☆) offers great value. Bright, light lemon/green, it is fragrant, with good weight and depth of fresh, ripe, peachy flavours, slightly toasty and buttery notes, and a creamy-smooth finish.

De La Terre Reserve Hawke's Bay Chardonnay ★★★★☆

Still on sale, the 2015 vintage (★★★★☆) was hand-picked at Havelock North and fermented in French oak barriques (50 per cent new). A powerful, tight-knit wine, it has rich grapefruit and stone-fruit flavours, slightly buttery and complex, a minerally thread, and excellent cellaring potential.

Vintage	15	14	13
WR	6	7	6
Drink	19-22	19-23	19-22

 DRY $40 –V

Delegat Crownthorpe Terraces Chardonnay ★★★★

From one vintage to the next, this is a great buy. The 2018 vintage (★★★★) was estate-grown at the company's cool, elevated, inland site at Crownthorpe, in Hawke's Bay, and fully fermented and matured for a year in French oak barriques (new and one year old). An elegant, youthful wine, it is full-bodied, with strong, ripe, peachy, citrusy, slightly biscuity flavours, fresh acidity, good complexity and a finely poised, lengthy finish. Best drinking 2021+.

 DRY $20 V+

Delta Hatters Hill Marlborough Chardonnay ★★★★☆

Still youthful, the 2018 vintage (★★★★☆) was grown principally in the Ure Valley, south of the Awatere Valley, and fermented in French oak barriques (just over 50 per cent new). Bright, light lemon/green, it shows obvious potential, with fresh, strong grapefruit-like flavours, gently seasoned with toasty oak, lively acidity, and very good intensity, vigour and complexity. Fine value.

 DRY $27 V+

Delta Marlborough Chardonnay ★★★☆

Already enjoyable, the 2018 vintage (★★★☆) was grown in the lower Wairau Valley and handled in an even split of tanks and oak barrels. Light lemon/green, with a citrusy bouquet, it is fresh, mouthfilling and smooth, with lively grapefruit and peach flavours, showing a touch of complexity, finely balanced acidity and a slightly creamy texture.

 DRY $20 AV

Dog Point Vineyard Marlborough Chardonnay ★★★★★

This classy, single-vineyard wine is grown on the south side of the Wairau Valley, hand-picked, fermented and matured for 18 months in French oak barriques (10 per cent new in 2017), and given a full, softening malolactic fermentation. Still a baby, the 2017 vintage (★★★★★) is bright, light lemon/green, with a fragrant, slightly earthy bouquet. Mouthfilling, it has vibrant, intense, citrusy flavours, woven with fresh acidity, that build well to a tightly structured, lasting finish. Best drinking 2022+. Certified organic.

Vintage	17	16	15	14	13	12	11	10
WR	7	7	7	7	7	5	7	6
Drink	19-29	19-28	19-27	19-26	19-21	P	P	P

 DRY $40 AV

Domain Road Defiance Vineyard Central Otago Chardonnay ★★★★☆

Offering good value, the 2017 vintage (★★★★☆) of this Bannockburn wine was fermented and matured for 10 months in French oak barriques (35 per cent new). Light lemon/green, with a fresh, complex, citrusy, slightly smoky bouquet, it is elegant and youthful, with grapefruit-evoking flavours, showing good complexity, savoury, biscuity notes and a lengthy finish. Best drinking mid-2020+.

Vintage	17	16
WR	6	6
Drink	19-23	19-22

DRY $28 V+

Dry River Martinborough Chardonnay ★★★★★

Elegance, restraint and subtle power are the key qualities of this classic wine. It's not a bold, upfront style, but tight, savoury and seamless, with rich grapefruit and nut flavours that build in the bottle for several years. Based on low-cropping 20 and 30-year-old vines in the Craighall and Dry River Estate vineyards, it is hand-harvested, whole-bunch pressed and fermented in French oak barrels (with a low proportion of new casks). The proportion of the blend that goes through a softening malolactic fermentation does not usually exceed 15 per cent. The 2017 vintage (★★★★☆) was matured for a year in French oak hogsheads (15 per cent new). Light lemon/green, with a complex, biscuity bouquet, it is crisp and tightly structured, with strong, peachy, citrusy flavours, slightly buttery notes and firm acid spine. Open mid-2020+. The 2018 vintage (★★★★★) is very refined. Light lemon/green, it is vibrant, generous and age-worthy, while reflecting a restrained winemaking touch. Weighty, with ripe stone-fruit flavours, mealy and biscuity notes adding complexity, fresh acidity, and notable delicacy and harmony, it's already delicious, but should break into full stride 2021+.

Vintage	17	16	15	14	13	12	11	10
WR	5	7	7	7	7	5	7	7
Drink	19-25	19-25	19-25	19-24	19-23	19-22	19-20	19-20

DRY $60 AV

Dunnolly Estate Reserve Waipara Valley Chardonnay ★★★★

Showing obvious potential, the refined 2017 vintage (★★★★☆) was matured for nine months in French oak barriques (30 per cent new). Fresh and mouthfilling, it has excellent depth and delicacy of grapefruit, peach and pear flavours, with a cool-climate thread and a lingering finish. Best drinking 2020+.

DRY $32 –V

Durvillea by Astrolabe Marlborough Chardonnay ★★★☆

Offering good value, the 2018 vintage (★★★☆) is a regional blend, hand-harvested, barrel-fermented and given a full, softening malolactic fermentation. Bright, light lemon/green, it is fresh and vibrantly fruity, with good depth of ripe-fruit flavours, a touch of complexity and a creamy-smooth finish. Enjoyable young.

Vintage	18
WR	7
Drink	19-22

DRY $18 V+

Elephant Hill Hawke's Bay Chardonnay ★★★★☆

The tightly structured, vigorous 2017 vintage (★★★★☆) was estate-grown at Te Awanga (90 per cent) and in the Bridge Pa Triangle (10 per cent), and fermented and matured for a year in French oak casks (25 per cent new). It has a fragrant, complex bouquet, leading into a full-bodied wine with good intensity of fresh grapefruit and peach flavours, integrated toasty oak, and a crisp, long finish. Best drinking 2021+.

DRY $34 AV

Elephant Hill Reserve Hawke's Bay Chardonnay ★★★★★

The highly impressive 2016 vintage (★★★★★) was estate-grown at Te Awanga (80 per cent) and in the Bridge Pa Triangle (20 per cent), fermented with indigenous yeasts and matured for a year in French oak barrels (26 per cent new). Retasted in July 2019, it is an elegant, youthful wine, well worth cellaring. The bouquet is highly fragrant and complex; the palate is full-bodied and tightly structured, with concentrated grapefruit and peach flavours, smoky, mealy, biscuity notes adding complexity, good acid spine and a rich finish. Best drinking 2021+.

DRY $54 AV

Elephant Hill Salomé Hawke's Bay Chardonnay ★★★★★

The very youthful, tightly structured 2017 vintage (★★★★★) was estate-grown at Te Awanga (principally) and in the Bridge Pa Triangle, and fermented and matured for a year in French oak casks (33 per cent new). Bright, light lemon/green, it has an inviting, complex, fragrant bouquet. Intensely flavoured, it is vibrant, peachy and citrusy, with well-integrated, biscuity oak, good acid spine and a persistent, harmonious finish. Full-bodied, crisp and highly concentrated, with obvious potential, it's well worth cellaring to 2022+.

DRY $75 AV

Esk Valley Hawke's Bay Chardonnay ★★★★

Top vintages can offer irresistible value. The youthful 2018 vintage (★★★★) was predominantly (92 per cent) fermented in French oak barriques (12 per cent new); 8 per cent of the blend was cool-fermented in tanks. Mouthfilling and vibantly fruity, it has generous, ripe stone-fruit flavours to the fore, with slightly spicy and smoky notes adding complexity, and obvious potential; best drinking 2021+.

Vintage	18	17	16	15	14	13
WR	6	5	7	7	6	6
Drink	19-22	19-21	19-20	P	P	P

DRY $20 V+

Esk Valley Winemakers Reserve Hawke's Bay Chardonnay ★★★★★

Often one of the region's most distinguished Chardonnays. The sturdy, rich 2017 vintage (★★★★★) was hand-picked at Bay View and fermented with indigenous yeasts in French oak barriques (35 per cent new). Bright, light lemon/green, it is fragrant, with a hint of gunflint. The flavours are ripe, citrusy and peachy, with excellent vigour, intensity and complexity, and a tightly structured, finely balanced, powerful finish. Already delicious, it should be at its best 2020+.

Vintage	18	17	16	15	14	13
WR	7	7	7	7	7	7
Drink	19-25	19-25	19-23	19-25	19-24	19-23

DRY $32 V+

Falconhead Hawke's Bay Chardonnay ★★★

The good-value 2017 vintage (★★★☆) was fully barrel-fermented and oak-aged for a year. Drinking well now, it is fresh and mouthfilling, with peachy, slightly toasty flavours, showing considerable complexity, balanced acidity and good depth.

Family Company, The, Gisborne Chardonnay (★★★)

The 2018 vintage (★★★) was hand-harvested in the Kawatiri Vineyard at Hexton and fermented in French oak casks (30 per cent new). Light gold, it is mouthfilling, with strong, peachy, slightly toasty flavours, showing considerable development.

Felton Road Bannockburn Central Otago Chardonnay ★★★★★

This classy, distinctive wine is grown at Bannockburn and matured in French oak barriques, with restrained use of new oak. Bright, light lemon/green, the 2018 vintage (★★★★★) was estate-grown in The Elms and Cornish Point vineyards, and barrel-aged for 13 months (10 per cent new). A lovely wine, it has a highly fragrant, complex bouquet. Fresh and full-bodied, it is sweet-fruited, with deep, peachy, citrusy flavours, slightly biscuity notes, finely integrated oak, and a well-rounded finish. Best drinking 2021+.

Vintage	18	17	16	15	14	13	12	11	10
WR	7	7	7	7	7	7	7	6	7
Drink	19-32	19-32	19-30	19-29	19-28	19-24	19-26	19-22	19-22

Felton Road Block 2 Central Otago Chardonnay ★★★★★

This outstanding wine is grown in a 'special part of The Elms Vineyard in front of the winery', which has the oldest vines. The 2018 vintage (★★★★★) was matured for 17 months in seasoned French oak barrels (avoiding the use of new oak), and bottled unfined and unfiltered. Bright, light lemon/green, it has a fragrant, citrusy, complex bouquet. Weighty, it has youthful, vibrant, grapefruit-like flavours, peachy and spicy notes, a subtle seasoning of biscuity oak, finely balanced acidity and obvious potential. Best drinking 2022+.

Vintage	18	17
WR	7	7
Drink	19-34	19-33

Felton Road Block 6 Central Otago Chardonnay ★★★★★

Estate-grown in The Elms Vineyard at Bannockburn, the classy 2018 vintage (★★★★★) was matured for 17 months in seasoned French oak casks (with no use of new wood), and bottled unfined and unfiltered. Full-bodied and fleshy, it is a very age-worthy wine, with concentrated grapefruit and peach flavours, a subtle oak influence, fresh acidity and a finely poised, sustained finish. Best drinking 2022+.

Vintage	18	17
WR	7	7
Drink	19-34	19-33

Forrest John Forrest Collection Wairau Valley Marlborough Chardonnay   ★★★★★

Tasted in August 2018, the 2011 vintage (★★★★★) was seemingly in full stride. Grown at three sites, it is weighty and rounded, with concentrated peach and grapefruit flavours, biscuity notes adding complexity, balanced acidity and a rich, harmonious finish. From a much cooler season, the 2012 vintage (★★★★☆) is slightly more austere, with mouthfilling body, strong, citrusy flavours, showing good complexity, and a crisp, tightly structured finish. Likely to be very long-lived, the impressive 2013 vintage (★★★★★) is fragrant, youthful and finely balanced, with concentrated, peachy, citrusy flavours, slightly toasty, savoury and creamy, and a lasting finish. Best drinking 2020+.

Forrest Marlborough Chardonnay   ★★★★

Currently on sale, the 2014 vintage (★★★★) was fermented and matured in a 60:40 split of barrels and tanks. It has a fragrant, citrusy, slightly toasty bouquet, leading into a full-bodied wine with good intensity of grapefruit-like flavours, gently seasoned with oak, good acid spine, and an emerging, bottle-aged complexity.

Framingham Marlborough Chardonnay   ★★★★

The elegant 2016 vintage (★★★★) was fermented and matured in a 50:50 split of tanks and barrels. Fresh and vibrantly fruity, it has citrusy, peachy flavours, showing very good depth, savoury, biscuity notes adding complexity, and a slightly creamy finish.

Fromm Clayvin Vineyard Marlborough Chardonnay   ★★★★★

Fromm's finest Chardonnay is grown on the southern flanks of the Wairau Valley, where the clay soils, says winemaker Hätsch Kalberer, give 'a less fruity, more minerally and tighter character'. Fermented with indigenous yeasts in French oak barriques, with little or no use of new wood, it is barrel-aged for well over a year. It is a rare wine – only three barrels were produced in 2016 – and top vintages mature well for a decade. The 2016 vintage (★★★★★) is highly refined. Light lemon/green, it is vigorous and youthful, with deep grapefruit and nut flavours, complex and savoury, gentle acidity and a highly fragrant bouquet. A very 'complete' wine with a long finish, it should be at its best 2020+.

Gibbston Valley 95 China Terrace Central Otago Chardonnay   ★★★★★

A wine to ponder over, the classy 2017 vintage (★★★★★) is a single-vineyard Bendigo wine, estate-grown at 320 metres above sea level, and hand-picked solely from highly regarded clone 95 vines. Fermented with indigenous yeasts in French oak barriques and puncheons (22 per cent new), and barrel-aged for 10 months, it has a real sense of youthful drive. Bright, light lemon/green, it is very refined and tightly structured, with deep, citrusy, peachy flavours that build well across the palate, integrated oak, finely balanced acidity, and a lasting finish.

DRY $55 AV

Gibbston Valley China Terrace Bendigo Single Vineyard Chardonnay   ★★★★☆

Here's more evidence that Central Otago has great Chardonnay potential. The 2017 vintage (★★★★★) was estate-grown, at 320 metres above sea level, and fermented and matured for 10 months in French oak barriques and puncheons (25 per cent new). Slightly more extroverted than its '95' stablemate (above), it is full-bodied and savoury, with concentrated, peachy, citrusy, slightly biscuity and buttery flavours, showing excellent complexity, and a rounded finish.

 DRY $42 –V

Giesen The Fuder Series Single Vineyard Clayvin Marlborough Chardonnay   (★★★★★)

Certified organic, the 2015 vintage (★★★★★) was hand-harvested from mature vines in the Clayvin Vineyard and fermented and matured in large (1000 litres capacity) German oak fuders. Pale yellow, with a fragrant, highly complex bouquet, it is a powerful, full-bodied wine, with concentrated citrus and stone-fruit flavours, fresh acidity, a minerally streak, gently nutty notes adding complexity, and a real sense of youthful drive and depth. Best drinking 2021+.

 DRY $50 AV

Goldwater Nelson Chardonnay   (★★★☆)

The 2017 vintage (★★★☆) was grown at Ruby Bay and French oak-aged for 11 months. Pale yellow, it is a fruit-driven style, fresh and mouthfilling, with ripe stone-fruit flavours, showing good vibrancy and depth, and lots of drink-young appeal. (From Foley Family Wines.)

 DRY $25 –V

Greenhough Hope Vineyard Chardonnay   ★★★★★

This consistently impressive wine is estate-grown at Hope, in Nelson, hand-picked, barrel-fermented with indigenous yeasts and matured in French oak barriques. The very elegant, finely poised 2016 vintage (★★★★★) is bright lemon/green, with deep, vibrant, citrusy, peachy flavours, gentle biscuity notes, and a lasting finish. Fragrant, with a long future ahead, it should be at its best 2021+. Certified organic.

Vintage	16	15	14	13	12	11
WR	6	5	7	6	6	6
Drink	19-21	19-20	19-20	P	P	P

DRY $36 AV

Greenhough Nelson Chardonnay   ★★★★

This consistently enjoyable wine is designed to express a 'fresh, taut' style, with background oak providing 'some subtle, savoury complexities'. The youthful, lemon-scented 2017 vintage (★★★★), grown at Hope, in the Morison and Greenhough vineyards, was barrel-fermented (16 per cent new) and French oak-aged for 10 months. Bright, light lemon/green, it is fresh and citrusy, with peachy, biscuity notes adding complexity, a slightly minerally thread, and obvious potential; best drinking 2020+.

Vintage	17	16	15	14	13
WR	7	5	6	6	6
Drink	19-22	19-20	19-20	P	P

 DRY $28 AV

Greyrock Hawke's Bay Chardonnay ★★★

The easy-drinking 2018 vintage (★★☆) is fresh, with lively, citrusy, peachy flavours in an uncomplicated, fruit-driven style, with a smooth (4 grams/litre of residual sugar) finish. (From Sileni.)

 DRY $19 AV

Greyrock Te Koru Hawke's Bay Chardonnay (★★★★)

The elegant, youthful 2018 vintage (★★★★) is a medium-bodied style, with strong, vibrant, peachy, citrusy flavours, a touch of complexity, fresh acidity, and good drive and length. Best drinking mid-2020+.

 DRY $20 V+

Greystone Erin's Reserve Waipara Valley Chardonnay ★★★★★

Greystone views Chardonnay as 'the finest white wine variety'. The outstanding 2015 vintage (★★★★★) is exceptionally rare – just 44 cases were produced. Grown on steep, north-facing limestone slopes, it was hand-harvested, fermented with indigenous yeasts, given a full, softening malolactic fermentation, and matured for 15 months in French oak casks (50 per cent new). It is a highly fragrant, weighty wine (14.5 per cent alcohol), tightly structured, with intense grapefruit and peach flavours that have effortlessly lapped up the new oak. Showing lovely mouthfeel, complexity and length, it's a memorable mouthful.

Vintage	15
WR	7
Drink	19-29

 DRY $95 –V

Greystone Waipara Valley North Canterbury Chardonnay ★★★★★

The richly fragrant, weighty 2017 vintage (★★★★★) was barrel-fermented with indigenous yeasts and given a full, softening malolactic fermentation. Bright yellow/green, it is powerful, deep and complex, with lush, vibrant, peachy, gently toasty flavours, balanced acidity, and a long, very harmonious finish. Best drinking 2021+.

 DRY $39 AV

Greywacke Marlborough Chardonnay ★★★★★

Retasted in mid to late 2019, the youthful 2016 vintage (★★★★☆) was fermented with indigenous yeasts in French oak barriques (20 per cent new), and wood-matured for 18 months. Bright, light lemon/green, it has a smoky bouquet, leading into a mouthfilling, complex wine with concentrated, ripe, peachy, slightly toasty flavours, fresh and tightly structured. Best drinking 2020+. Retasted in mid-2019, the 2015 vintage (★★★★★) is an elegant, generous, complex wine, currently delicious. Bright, light yellow/green, with a smoky fragrance, it is mouthfilling and concentrated, with strong grapefruit and peach flavours, finely integrated oak and a tightly structured, long finish. These wines richly reward cellaring, breaking into full stride at about five years old.

Vintage	16	15	14	13	12	11	10
WR	6	6	6	6	5	6	6
Drink	19-28	19-27	19-26	19-25	P	19-23	19-23

 DRY $42 AV

Grove Mill Wairau Valley Marlborough Chardonnay ★★★★

Bargain-priced, the full-flavoured 2018 vintage (★★★★) was matured for 10 months in French oak casks (20 per cent new). Bright, light yellow/green, with a fragrant, slightly toasty and smoky bouquet, it is mouthfilling, with peachy, toasty flavours, showing good complexity, finely balanced acidity and very good depth. Drink now or cellar.

Vintage	18
WR	6
Drink	19-25

DRY $20 V+

Haha Hawke's Bay Chardonnay ★★★☆

Delicious young and offering great value, the 2018 vintage (★★★★) was barrel-fermented and given a full, softening malolactic fermentation. Very pale straw, it is mouthfilling and sweet-fruited, with strong, peachy, slightly biscuity flavours, gentle acidity and a creamy-smooth finish.

DRY $18 V+

Haha Marlborough Chardonnay ★★★☆

The 2017 vintage (★★★☆) is a partly oak-aged wine, very well balanced for early enjoyment. Fresh and full-bodied, it's a 'fruit-driven' style with youthful vigour, good flavour depth and a well-rounded finish. Bargain-priced.

Vintage	17	16	15	14	13
WR	7	7	7	7	7
Drink	19-21	19-20	P	P	P

DRY $18 V+

Hancock & Sons Bridge Pa Hawke's Bay Chardonnay (★★★★)

The distinctive 2018 vintage (★★★★) from winemaker John Hancock and his son, Willy, was hand-harvested in a single vineyard and principally handled in tanks; a quarter to a third of the blend was fermented in French oak barrels (mostly seasoned). Bright, light lemon/green, it is fragrant, with very good weight and depth of grapefruit and peach-like flavours, a subtle seasoning of nutty oak, and impressive vigour, delicacy and harmony. An elegant, 'fruit-driven' style, still unfolding, it should be at its best 2020+.

Vintage	18
WR	5
Drink	19-23

DRY $25 AV

Hans Herzog Marlborough Chardonnay ★★★★★

At its best, this is a notably powerful wine with layers of peach, grapefruit and nut flavours. The age-worthy 2017 vintage (★★★★★) was estate-grown in the Wairau Valley, hand-picked, fermented with indigenous yeasts in a French oak puncheon, barrel-aged for 22 months, and bottled unfined and unfiltered. A pale gold, sturdy wine, it is very fleshy and harmonious, with concentrated, ripe stone-fruit flavours, finely integrated oak adding complexity, and an enticing fragrance. Best drinking 2021+. Certified organic.

DRY $44 AV

Hihi Classic Gisborne Chardonnay (★★★★)

The 2018 vintage (★★★★) was hand-harvested in the EIT vineyard, fermented in French and Hungarian oak casks (one to three years old), and barrel-aged for 10 months. A fresh, medium to full-bodied style, it is vibrantly fruity, with ripe, citrusy, peachy flavours, showing considerable complexity, and a smooth, slightly creamy finish. Best drinking mid-2020+.

DRY $25 AV

Hopesgrove Single Vineyard Hawke's Bay Chardonnay ★★★★★

Tasted in mid-2019, the rich 2016 vintage (★★★★☆) was estate-grown, hand-harvested and barrel-aged for nine months (30 per cent new). Bright, light lemon/green, it is mouthfilling, with finely balanced acidity and generous, peachy, slightly buttery and toasty flavours, showing good complexity. The 2015 vintage (★★★★★), also tasted in mid-2019, is a classic regional style, maturing very gracefully. Full-bodied, it is rich but elegant, with deep, concentrated, peachy, slightly toasty flavours, showing excellent complexity, and a fragrant, complex bouquet. Delicious drinking now onwards.

Vintage	16	15
WR	6	5
Drink	19-22	19-20

DRY $35 AV

Huntaway Reserve Gisborne Chardonnay ★★★☆

Ready to roll, the easy-drinking 2017 vintage (★★★☆) is weighty, ripe and rounded. It has generous, peachy, slightly toasty flavours, showing a touch of complexity, and a smooth finish. (From Lion.)

DRY $22 AV

Hunter's Marlborough Chardonnay ★★★★

This wine has traditionally placed its accent on vibrant fruit flavours, overlaid with very subtle wood-aging characters. The youthful 2018 vintage (★★★★), grown in the Rapaura, Renwick and Omaka districts, was fermented with indigenous yeasts and lees-aged for 10 months in French oak casks. Bright, light lemon/green, it is full-bodied, with fresh, citrusy, peachy, gently biscuity flavours, showing good complexity, and a lingering finish. Best drinking 2021+.

Vintage	18	17	16	15	14	13	12
WR	6	5	7	7	7	6	6
Drink	19-26	19-25	19-21	19-20	P	P	P

DRY $25 AV

Hunter's Offshoot Marlborough Chardonnay (★★★★☆)

Estate-grown at Rapaura, the youthful 2017 vintage (★★★★☆) was hand-picked from mature vines, fermented with indigenous yeasts in large (900-litre) oak casks (40 per cent new), and barrel-aged for a year. Light lemon/green, it is an elegant, tightly structured wine, with good intensity of vibrant, citrusy flavours, gently seasoned with oak, lively acidity and obvious potential; best drinking 2021+.

DRY $35 –V

Hunting Lodge, The, Hawke's Bay Chardonnay   ★★★★☆

The 2018 vintage (★★★★☆) is a single-vineyard wine, grown at Crownthorpe and fermented and lees-aged for nine months in French oak barriques (40 per cent new). Bright, light lemon/green, with a fragrant, savoury bouquet, it is mouthfilling, vibrantly fruity and tightly structured, with generous, citrusy, peachy flavours, showing impressive complexity and persistence. Best drinking 2021+.

DRY $30 AV

Hunting Lodge, The, Waimauku Home Block Chardonnay   (★★★★★)

From the old site of Matua Valley, in West Auckland, the debut 2017 vintage (★★★★★) was harvested from nine-year-old vines, hand-picked, and fermented and lees-aged for nine months in a single, second-fill French oak barrique. Bright, light yellow/green, with a fragrant, inviting bouquet, it is a very elegant, youthful wine, with highly concentrated grapefruit and peach flavours, well-integrated oak, smoky notes adding complexity, and a very persistent finish. A tightly structured, age-worthy wine, it's well worth cellaring to 2020+.

DRY $55 AV

Jackson Estate Shelter Belt Single Vineyard Marlborough Chardonnay   ★★★★

Retasted in May 2019, the youthful 2016 vintage (★★★★) was estate-grown and hand-picked in the Homestead Vineyard, in the heart of the Wairau Valley, and mostly barrel-fermented (25 per cent new oak); 25 per cent of the blend was handled in tanks. Bright, light lemon/green, it is full-bodied, with fresh, citrusy, peachy, slightly appley flavours, gentle, biscuity notes adding complexity, finely balanced acidity, and a dry, very harmonious finish.

Vintage	16
WR	5
Drink	20-26

DRY $24 V+

Johner Wairarapa Chardonnay   ★★★☆

The 2018 vintage (★★★★) was fermented and lees-matured for a year in French oak casks (20 per cent new). Bright, light yellow/green, it is a mouthfilling, generous, slightly creamy wine with ripe, peachy, slightly toasty and biscuity flavours, showing excellent complexity and depth. Best drinking mid-2020+.

Vintage	18
WR	6
Drink	19-23

DRY $26 –V

Jules Taylor Marlborough Chardonnay   ★★★★

The 2018 vintage (★★★★) was grown at two sites 'that rest below the hills in Marlborough's Southern Valleys'. Partly oak-aged, it is a bright, light lemon/green, mouthfilling, fruit-driven style, with lots of drink-young appeal. It has vibrant, peachy, citrusy flavours to the fore, gently seasoned with biscuity oak, balanced acidity, and a very harmonious, slightly creamy finish. Fine value.

Vintage	18	17	16	15
WR	5	6	6	6
Drink	19-23	19-22	19-21	19-20

DRY $23 V+

Jules Taylor OTQ Limited Release Single Vineyard
Marlborough Chardonnay

★★★★★

The powerful 2018 vintage (★★★★★) was grown in the Meadowbank Vineyard, on the south side of the Wairau Valley, and handled in old and new oak barrels. Bright, light lemon/green, with a fragrant, smoky bouquet, it has strong personality, with mouthfilling body, concentrated, vigorous, slightly toasty flavours, showing excellent complexity, finely balanced acidity and a dry, lasting finish. Still very youthful, it's well worth cellaring to 2021+.

Vintage	18
WR	6
Drink	19-24

DRY $43 AV

Kahurangi Estate Nelson Chardonnay

(★★★★)

Already drinking well, the 2018 vintage (★★★★) has plenty of youthful impact. Bright, light lemon/green, it is a fruit-driven style, with a subtle seasoning of oak and strong, vibrant, peachy flavours, fresh, crisp and lingering.

DRY $25 AV

Kahurangi Mt Arthur Reserve Nelson Chardonnay

(★★★★☆)

Made in a bold, upfront style, the 2018 vintage (★★★★☆) has a fragrant, toasty, creamy bouquet. Mouthfilling, it has strong, peachy, buttery, oaky flavours, showing good complexity, and a creamy-textured, well-rounded finish. Drink now or cellar.

DRY $30 AV

Kaimira Estate Brightwater Chardonnay

★★★★

Certified organic, the 2016 vintage (★★★★) was estate-grown at Brightwater, in Nelson, fermented in French oak barrels (30 per cent new), and oak-aged for nearly a year. It is mouthfilling and fleshy, with generous, ripe, peachy, slightly biscuity flavours, a slightly creamy texture, and good harmony. The youthful 2017 vintage (★★★★) was fermented with indigenous yeasts in French oak casks (20 per cent new). Light lemon/green, it is an elegant, lemon-scented, full-bodied wine, with strong, vibrant grapefruit and peach flavours, a subtle seasoning of oak, fresh acidity and obvious potential; best drinking 2020+.

Vintage	17	16	15
WR	6	6	6
Drink	19-24	19-22	19-20

DRY $25 AV

Kalex Alex Kaufman Waipara Valley Chardonnay

(★★★★)

The powerful 2015 vintage (★★★★) is a single-vineyard, hand-picked wine, fermented and matured in barrels (33 per cent new). Pale gold, it is weighty and fleshy, with strong, peachy, toasty flavours, woven with fresh acidity. Drink now.

DRY $40 –V

Karikari Estate Chardonnay ★★★★

Estate-grown in Northland, the 2015 vintage (★★★★) was hand-picked and fermented and matured in an even split of French and American oak barrels. Bright yellow/pale gold, it is a powerful, weighty wine, with the ripeness and roundness typical of northern whites. A distinctive wine with generous, peachy, toasty flavours, it's probably at its peak.

DRY $45 –V

Karikari Estate Northland Calypso Chardonnay ★★★★

Grown on the Karikari Peninsula, in the Far North, and retasted in early 2019, the attractive 2015 vintage (★★★★) is full of northern warmth, while retaining freshness. Fermented and matured in French oak casks (partly new), it is light yellow/green, with a mature bouquet and a fleshy, ripe, well-rounded palate, showing balanced acidity and generous, peachy flavours.

DRY $27 AV

Kidnapper Cliffs Hawke's Bay Chardonnay ★★★★★

From Te Awa, the classy 2014 vintage (★★★★★) was estate-grown, mostly in the Bridge Pa Triangle, hand-picked, fermented with indigenous yeasts in French oak hogsheads (40 per cent new), and barrel-aged for 10 months. It has a fragrant, complex bouquet, with a distinct whiff of 'struck match'. Mouthfilling, with concentrated peach and grapefruit flavours, a subtle seasoning of oak, and very impressive vibrancy, poise and length, it's an elegant, tightly structured wine, likely to be at its best 2020+.

Vintage	14	13
WR	7	6
Drink	19-21	19-20

DRY $55 AV

Kim Crawford Hawke's Bay Small Parcels Chardonnay (★★★★☆)

Delicious young, the age-worthy 2016 vintage (★★★★☆) was fermented with indigenous yeasts and matured in French oak barriques (36 per cent new). Bright, light lemon/green, it is fragrant and mouthfilling, with rich, ripe stone-fruit flavours, very good complexity and a long, harmonious finish. Fine value.

Vintage	16
WR	6
Drink	19-22

DRY $25 V+

Kim Crawford New Zealand Chardonnay ★★★☆

The easy-drinking 2017 vintage (★★★☆), grown in Marlborough and Hawke's Bay, is 'uncluttered by oak'. Light lemon/green, it is mouthfilling, fleshy and smooth, with good depth of fresh, ripe, peachy, citrusy flavours, balanced acidity, and lots of drink-young appeal. Priced right.

DRY $17 V+

Koha Marlborough Chardonnay   (★★☆)

The easy-drinking 2018 vintage (★★☆) is a 'lightly oaked' style. Light lemon/green, it is fresh, fruity and uncomplicated, with ripe, peachy, slightly appley flavours, showing decent depth, and a smooth finish. (From te Pā.)

DRY $19 –V

Kōparepare Marlborough Chardonnay

Tasted in mid-2019, the 2016 vintage (★★★☆) offers very good value. Made by Whitehaven, it is sold through fishing clubs in support of LegaSea and its commitment to restore inshore fisheries to abundance. Bright, light yellow/green, it is full-bodied, with fresh, generous, peachy flavours, slightly buttery and toasty notes, and a dry, smooth finish. It's drinking well now.

DRY $16 V+

Kumeu River Coddington Chardonnay   ★★★★★

This typically powerful, rich wine is grown in the Coddington Vineyard, between Huapai and Waimauku. The grapes, cultivated on a clay hillside, achieve an advanced level of ripeness (described by Kumeu River as 'flamboyant, unctuous, peachy'). Mouthfilling, complex and slightly nutty, it's typically a lusher, softer wine than its Hunting Hill stablemate (below). The 2018 vintage (★★★★★) was hand-picked, fermented with indigenous yeasts in French oak barriques and wood-matured for 11 months. A weighty, well-rounded wine, bright, light lemon/green, it is mouthfilling and vibrant, with strong, ripe stone-fruit flavours, gently seasoned with oak, finely balanced acidity and a tight finish. Open 2021+.

Vintage	18	17	16	15	14	13	12	11	10
WR	5	6	7	7	7	7	5	5	7
Drink	20-26	19-23	19-22	19-22	19-21	19-20	P	P	P

DRY $55 AV

Kumeu River Estate Chardonnay   ★★★★★

This wine ranks fifth in the company's hierarchy of six Chardonnays, after four single-vineyard labels, but is still outstanding. Grown at Kumeu, in West Auckland, it is powerful, with rich, beautifully interwoven flavours and a seductively creamy texture, but also has good acid spine. The key to its quality lies in the vineyards, says winemaker Michael Brajkovich: 'We manage to get the grapes very ripe.' Grown in several blocks around Kumeu, hand-picked, fermented with indigenous yeasts and lees-aged (with weekly or twice-weekly lees-stirring) in Burgundy oak barriques (typically 25 per cent new), the wine normally undergoes a full, softening malolactic fermentation. Delicious in its youth, the 2018 vintage (★★★★★) is already very expressive. Full-bodied, it has strong, ripe stone-fruit and nut flavours, finely integrated oak, smoky notes adding complexity, and a long, finely balanced finish. Best drinking 2021+.

Vintage	18	17	16	15	14	13	12	11	10
WR	5	6	6	7	7	7	5	5	7
Drink	20-26	19-22	19-21	19-20	19-20	P	P	P	P

DRY $32 V+

Kumeu River Hunting Hill Chardonnay ★★★★★

This outstanding single-vineyard wine – my favourite in the Kumeu River range – is grown on slopes above Mate's Vineyard, directly over the road from the winery at Kumeu (originally planted in 1982, the site was replanted in 2000). A notably elegant wine, in its youth it is generally less lush than its Coddington stablemate (above), but with good acidity and citrusy, complex flavours that build well across the palate. The 2018 vintage (★★★★★) was hand-picked, fermented with indigenous yeasts in French oak barriques and wood-aged for 11 months. Bright, light lemon/green, it is mouthfilling and vibrantly fruity, with a strong sense of youthful drive, depth and potential. Layered and long, it should be at its best 2022+.

Vintage	18	17	16	15	14	13	12	11	10	DRY $70 AV
WR	5	6	7	7	7	7	5	5	7	
Drink	20-26	19-24	19-23	19-22	19-21	19-20	P	P	P	

Kumeu River Mate's Vineyard Kumeu Chardonnay ★★★★★

This extremely classy, single-vineyard wine is Kumeu River's flagship. It is made entirely from the best of the fruit harvested from Mate's Vineyard, planted in 1990 on the site of the original Kumeu River vineyard purchased by Mate Brajkovich in 1944. Similar to Kumeu River Estate Chardonnay, but more opulent and concentrated, it offers the same rich, harmonious flavours, typically with a stronger seasoning of new French oak (about 30 per cent). The 2018 vintage (★★★★★) was hand-picked, barrel-fermented and oak-aged for 11 months. Bright, light yellow/green, it's a weighty, very youthful wine, with concentrated, ripe stone-fruit flavours, slightly smoky notes, excellent mouthfeel and complexity, and a finely textured finish. Best drinking 2022+.

Vintage	18	17	16	15	14	13	12	11	10	DRY $80 AV
WR	5	6	7	7	7	7	5	5	7	
Drink	20-26	19-23	19-23	19-22	19-21	19-20	P	P	P	

Kumeu River Rays Road Chardonnay (★★★★★)

Estate-grown, the debut 2018 vintage (★★★★★) is from an elevated (180 metres above sea level), north-facing site in Hawke's Bay. Hand-picked, fermented with indigenous yeasts in older French oak barrels and wood-aged for 11 months, it's a fresh, crisp, Chablis-like wine, revealing excellent vibrancy and intensity. Bright, light yellow/green, it is full-bodied, with strong, citrusy, slightly appley flavours, gently seasoned with oak. A distinctive, subtle, very harmonious wine, it's already delicious, but also well worth cellaring.

DRY $40 V+

Kumeu Village Hand Harvested Chardonnay ★★★★

Kumeu River's lower-tier, drink-young wine is hand-picked from heavier-bearing Chardonnay clones than the Mendoza commonly used for the top wines, and is typically fermented with indigenous yeasts in tanks and seasoned French oak casks. The 2018 vintage (★★★★), grown in Kumeu and Hawke's Bay, was 80 per cent barrel-fermented. Offering great value, it is full-bodied, with ripe, citrusy, peachy flavours, showing considerable complexity, and excellent mouthfeel and depth. Already enjoyable, it's a drink-now or cellaring proposition.

DRY $18 V+

Lake Chalice The Falcon Marlborough Chardonnay

As a drink-young style, the 2017 vintage (★★★☆) has plenty to offer. Grown mostly in the company's Falcon Vineyard, in the central Wairau Valley, and partly barrel-fermented, it has a buttery bouquet, leading into a full-bodied, vibrantly fruity wine with fresh acidity, toasty, buttery notes adding a touch of complexity and good depth.

DRY $19 V+

Lake Chalice The Raptor Marlborough Chardonnay

Offering terrific value, the 2017 vintage (★★★★☆) is an elegant, single-vineyard wine, grown at Dillons Point and fermented with indigenous yeasts in French oak barriques. Light lemon/green, it is fresh and youthful, with a smoky bouquet, good weight and strong grapefruit-like flavours, showing excellent complexity. Very age-worthy.

DRY $23 V+

Landing, The, Bay of Islands Chardonnay

Estate-grown at a coastal site in the northern Bay of Islands, the 2017 vintage (★★★★☆) was matured for a year in French oak barriques. Already drinking well, it is a weighty, fleshy, rich wine, with concentrated, ripe stone-fruit flavours, seasoned with toasty oak, excellent complexity and harmony, and a long finish.

Vintage	17	16	15	14	13
WR	4	4	5	5	6
Drink	19-21	19-20	19-20	P	P

DRY $40 –V

Last Shepherd, The, Gisborne Chardonnay

The 2017 vintage (★★★★) is mouthfilling, fresh and smooth, with generous, ripe, peachy flavours, slightly buttery notes and considerable complexity. A distinctly regional style, it's drinking well in 2019.

DRY $25 AV

Lawson's Dry Hills Marlborough Chardonnay

★★★★

The 2018 vintage (★★★☆) is a good example of the fresh, very lightly oaked Chardonnay style. Fermented with indigenous yeasts and lees-stirred, mostly in tanks, it was 10 per cent barrel-fermented (in old casks). Vibrantly fruity, it is crisp, dry and lively, with toasty, buttery notes adding a touch of complexity. Best drinking mid-2020+.

Vintage	18	17	16	15	14
WR	6	6	6	6	6
Drink	19-22	19-21	19-21	19-20	P

DRY $20 V+

Lawson's Dry Hills Reserve Marlborough Chardonnay   ★★★★☆

Estate-grown in the Chaytors Road Vineyard, near the coast in the Wairau Valley, the 2018 vintage (★★★★☆) was fermented with indigenous yeasts in French oak barriques (25 per cent new). Already enjoyable, it has a fragrant, smoky bouquet, leading into a mouthfilling, sweet-fruited wine with concentrated, youthful, peachy, citrusy flavours, toasty notes adding complexity, and good cellaring potential. Best drinking 2021+.

Vintage	18	17	16	15	14	13
WR	7	6	7	7	6	6
Drink	19-25	19-25	19-25	19-22	19-20	P

 DRY $28 V+

Le Pont Grand Vin Blanc Chardonnay   ★★★★☆

Grown in Gisborne, the bold 2017 vintage (★★★★☆) was fermented and matured in French and Hungarian oak barrels (20 per cent new). Bright, light lemon/green, it is mouthfilling, with rich, ripe stone-fruit flavours, strongly seasoned with toasty, nutty oak, fresh acidity and a slightly buttery finish. Still unfolding, it should be at its best 2020+. (From Poverty Bay Wine.)

 DRY $36 –V

Left Field Hawke's Bay Chardonnay   ★★★★

Fermented in a 50:50 split of tanks and barrels (with 10 per cent new oak overall), the good-value 2017 vintage (★★★★) is classier than most sub-$20 Chardonnays. Light lemon/green, it is mouthfilling and vibrantly fruity, with good intensity of grapefruit-like flavours, slightly smoky notes adding complexity, restrained oak, fresh acidity and a lingering finish. Far from the 'big, fat and buttery' style, it's an unexpectedly elegant wine. (From Te Awa.)

Vintage	17
WR	5
Drink	19-23

 DRY $18 V+

Leo Nelson Chardonnay   (★★★)

Enjoyable young, the 2017 vintage (★★★) is a light lemon/green, mouthfilling, sweet-fruited wine. It's not complex, but offers plenty of ripe, peachy flavour.

DRY $17 AV

Leveret Estate Hawke's Bay Chardonnay   ★★★★

The elegant, good-value 2017 vintage (★★★★) was fully fermented in French oak barrels (35 per cent new). It has a fragrant, slightly biscuity, smoky bouquet. Fresh and mouthfilling, it has vibrant grapefruit and peach flavours, finely integrated oak adding complexity, and very good depth. Enjoyable now, it should be at its best mid-2020+.

Vintage	17	16
WR	5	6
Drink	19-25	19-21

 DRY $22 V+

Leveret Estate Reserve Hawke's Bay Chardonnay ★★★★

Still on sale, the tightly structured, elegant 2014 vintage (★★★★☆) was estate-grown at cool inland sites and fermented and matured for nine months in French oak casks (35 per cent new). Mouthfilling, it is finely poised, with concentrated grapefruit-like flavours, slightly smoky and toasty notes adding complexity, and a long finish. Best drinking 2020+.

Vintage	14	
WR	6	
Drink	19-24	DRY $26 AV

Linden Estate Esk Valley Hawke's Bay Chardonnay ★★★★

Showing good personality, the 2018 vintage (★★★★) is a sturdy, high-flavoured wine with a slightly biscuity bouquet. Mouthfilling, it has ripe stone-fruit flavours to the fore, considerable complexity and a soft, creamy-textured finish.

DRY $25 AV

Linden Estate Reserve Hawke's Bay Chardonnay ★★★★☆

The classy 2016 vintage (★★★★★) was hand-harvested in the Esk Valley and fermented with indigenous yeasts in French oak barriques. A classic regional style, it is a bright, light yellow, mouthfilling, slightly buttery wine with rich, youthful grapefruit and peach flavours, showing excellent delicacy and complexity, gentle acidity and a long, harmonious finish. Already delicious, it's a top vintage of this label, likely to be at its best 2020+.

Vintage	16	15	
WR	7	6	
Drink	19-21	P	DRY $35 –V

Luna Eclipse Vineyard Martinborough Chardonnay ★★★★

From 'mature' vines on the Martinborough Terrace, the 2017 vintage (★★★★) was fermented and matured for a year in French oak barriques (20 per cent new), and given a full, softening malolactic fermentation. Bright, light yellow/green, it has strong, peachy, slightly toasty flavours, threaded with fresh, lively acidity, and good complexity. Already drinking well, it should be at its best mid-2020+.

DRY $35 –V

LV by Louis Vavasour Marlborough Chardonnay (★★★★☆)

The powerful, bold 2016 vintage (★★★★☆) is mouthfilling and rich, with deep, ripe stone-fruit and toasty oak flavours, and a well-rounded, harmonious finish. Showing very good complexity, it's a drink-now or cellaring proposition. (From Awatere River Wine Co.)

DRY $49 –V

Mahi Alchemy Single Vineyard Marlborough Chardonnay

Well worth cellaring, the youthful 2017 vintage (★★★★☆) was grown at Rapaura, hand-picked, and fermented and matured for 15 months in French oak barriques. Bright, light yellow/green, it has a fragrant, complex bouquet, with lifted 'struck match' aromas. Fresh and lively, it is full-bodied, with strong, youthful peach and grapefruit flavours, gently seasoned with toasty oak, and a persistent finish. An elegant, intense, distinctly smoky wine, it should be at its best 2021+.

DRY $40 –V

Mahi Marlborough Chardonnay   ★★★★☆

The 2017 vintage (★★★★☆) was hand-harvested at four sites in the Wairau Valley, fermented with indigenous yeasts in French oak barrels and wood-aged for 11 months. Full of youthful drive, it has fresh, strong, citrusy, peachy flavours, showing good complexity, a minerally streak, firm acid spine and a long, dry finish. Best drinking 2020+.

Vintage	17	16	15	14	13
WR	6	6	6	6	6
Drink	19-24	19-24	19-21	19-21	P

DRY $29 V+

Mahi Single Vineyard Twin Valleys Marlborough Chardonnay   ★★★★★

Grown and hand-picked in the Twin Valleys Vineyard, at the junction of the Wairau and Waihopai valleys, the 2016 vintage (★★★★☆) was fermented with indigenous yeasts and matured for 15 months in French oak barriques. Bright, light yellow/green, it is tightly structured and youthful, with strong, citrusy, slightly toasty flavours, crisp and long. Showing obvious potential, it should be at its best 2021+.

Vintage	16
WR	6
Drink	19-24

DRY $40 AV

Mahurangi River Winery Field of Grace Chardonnay   ★★★★☆

Still on sale – although production has ceased – this impressive wine was estate-grown at Matakana, in the Field of Grace Block, hand-picked and matured in French oak barriques. The 2015 vintage (★★★★★) has strong personality. Invitingly fragrant, it is full-bodied, with generous, ripe peach and grapefruit flavours, full of northern warmth, oak complexity, and a slightly toasty, long finish. The 2016 vintage (★★★★☆) is a tight, elegant wine, full of promise, with citrusy, peachy flavours, integrated oak, fresh acidity and a finely poised finish.

DRY $34 AV

Main Divide North Canterbury Chardonnay   ★★★★

The 2018 vintage (★★★☆) was fermented and matured for a year in old oak casks. Bright, light yellow/green, it is fresh and moderately complex, with a slightly honeyed bouquet, mouthfilling body, fresh acidity and good flavour depth. Drink now to 2020. (From Pegasus Bay.)

Vintage	18
WR	5
Drink	19-21

DRY $21 V+

Maison Noire Hawke's Bay Chardonnay ★★★★

The flavour-packed 2018 vintage (★★★★) was fermented in French oak barrels (20 per cent new). Enjoyable young, but also well worth cellaring, it has strong flavours of stone-fruit and toasty oak, fresh acidity, and very good vigour, complexity and depth. Best drinking 2021+

DRY $25 AV

Man O' War Valhalla Waiheke Island Chardonnay ★★★★☆

This tightly structured wine is estate-grown at the remote, eastern end of Waiheke Island. Hand-harvested and fermented with indigenous yeasts in French oak casks, the highly refined 2017 vintage (★★★★★) is light lemon/green, with a fragrant, complex, slightly smoky bouquet. Mouthfilling and vibrantly fruity, it is sweet-fruited, with strong stone-fruit flavours, showing excellent delicacy and complexity, finely integrated oak, fresh acidity, and a long, very harmonious finish. It should be long-lived.

DRY $49 –V

Man O' War Waiheke Island Valkyrie Chardonnay (★★★★☆)

The lively 2017 vintage (★★★★☆) has a complex, fragrant bouquet. Full-bodied, it has concentrated, ripe, peachy flavours, slightly toasty and smoky notes, fresh acidity and a long finish. Best drinking 2020+.

DRY $38 –V

Margrain Barrique Fermented Martinborough Chardonnay (★★★★☆)

Offering good value, the 2015 vintage (★★★★☆) was handled for 16 months in French oak barriques of varying age. Bright, light yellow/green, it is fresh and full-bodied, with citrusy, peachy flavours, lively acidity, and biscuity, toasty and nutty notes adding excellent complexity.

DRY $28 V+

Marsden Bay of Islands Black Rocks Chardonnay ★★★★

Grown at Kerikeri, this Northland wine is impressive in favourably dry seasons – sturdy, with concentrated, ripe sweet-fruit flavours, well seasoned with toasty oak, in a typically lush, upfront, creamy-smooth style. The 2018 vintage (★★★☆) was fermented and matured for 11 months in French oak barriques. Light gold, with a very toasty bouquet, it is full-bodied, with strong, peachy, oaky flavours in a strongly wood-influenced style, probably best drunk young.

Vintage	18	17	16	15	14	13
WR	4	5	6	6	6	6
Drink	19-22	19-22	19-23	19-22	P	P

DRY $40 –V

Martinborough Vineyard Home Block Chardonnay ★★★★★

The refined 2018 vintage (★★★★★) was fermented and matured for a year in French oak casks (23 per cent new). Bright, light lemon/green, it is fresh, youthful and weighty, with generous, ripe stone-fruit flavours, finely integrated nutty oak, excellent complexity and a rich, well-rounded finish. Well worth cellaring, it should be at its best 2021+.

Vintage	18	17
WR	7	7
Drink	19-28	19-28

DRY $39 AV

Martinborough Vineyard Te Tera Martinborough Chardonnay   (★★★★☆)

French oak-aged for 10 months, the 2016 vintage (★★★★☆) is worth cellaring. Bright, light lemon/green, it is fresh, full-bodied and sweet-fruited, with generous grapefruit and peach flavours, well-integrated oak adding complexity, slightly smoky notes, and a lingering finish.

Vintage	16
WR	7
Drink	19-23

DRY $30 AV

Matahiwi Estate Holly Hawke's Bay Chardonnay   ★★★★

Made in a rich, upfront style, the 2018 vintage (★★★★) was fermented and matured for 11 months in French oak casks (30 per cent new). Bright, light yellow, with bold, peachy, toasty, slightly buttery flavours and a smooth finish, it's already drinking well, but likely to be at its best 2020+.

Vintage	18
WR	6
Drink	19-24

DRY $30 –V

Matawhero Church House Barrel Fermented Gisborne Chardonnay   ★★★★☆

The bold 2018 vintage (★★★★☆) is a fairly upfront style, but age-worthy too. Bright, light yellow/green, it is mouthfilling and youthful, with generous, ripe stone-fruit and toasty oak flavours, slightly buttery notes and very good complexity. Best drinking mid-2020+. The 2017 vintage (★★★★☆) is a classic regional style – rich and rounded. Fermented in old oak barrels and given a full, softening malolactic fermentation, it is full-bodied and creamy-textured, with generous, ripe stone-fruit flavours, showing good complexity, and a very smooth, harmonious finish.

DRY $30 AV

Matawhero Irwin Gisborne Chardonnay   ★★★★★

Made in a 'full-on' style, the bright, light yellow/green 2017 vintage (★★★★★) was grown in the Tietjen Vineyard and fermented and matured in a 2:1 mix of American and European oak casks (30 per cent new). Weighty and fleshy, it has concentrated stone-fruit flavours, showing excellent ripeness and richness, a strong seasoning of toasty oak, fresh acidity and a lasting finish. A powerful, complex, very age-worthy wine, it's well worth cellaring to 2021 onwards.

DRY $60 AV

Matawhero Single Vineyard Gisborne Chardonnay ★★★☆

The softly seductive 2018 vintage (★★★★) is from a warm growing season. Tank-fermented and given a full malolactic fermentation, it is weighty and sweet-fruited, in a classic regional style with generous, ripe stone-fruit flavours and a fresh, well-rounded finish. Very forward in its appeal, it's already drinking well.

DRY $23 AV

Matt Connell Wines Lowburn Single Vineyard Chardonnay (★★★★☆)

Already delicious, the 2017 vintage (★★★★☆) was hand-picked in Central Otago and fermented in French oak barriques (10 per cent new). Light lemon/green, it is fragrant, mouthfilling and rich, with generous, citrusy, peachy flavours, a hint of butterscotch, savoury, mealy notes adding complexity, and a well-rounded finish.

DRY $38 –V

Maude Mt Maude Vineyard Wanaka Chardonnay Reserve ★★★★☆

This classy Central Otago wine is hand-harvested from estate-grown vines, planted in 1994, and fermented and matured in French oak puncheons (15 per cent new in 2018). The refined 2018 vintage (★★★★★) is already delicious. Bright, light lemon/green, with a fragrant, slightly creamy bouquet, it is mouthfilling, vibrantly fruity and youthful, with deep, peachy, citrusy flavours, finely integrated oak, excellent complexity and a lasting, very harmonious finish.

DRY $38 –V

Maui Hawke's Bay Chardonnay (★★★☆)

Enjoyable young, the 2017 vintage (★★★☆) is a 'fruit-driven' style, tank-fermented, with some oak handling. Bright, light lemon/green, with a fresh, slightly buttery bouquet, it is full-bodied, with grapefruit and peach flavours, showing good depth, and a slightly spicy, smooth finish. Very user-friendly. (From Tiki.)

Vintage	17
WR	7
Drink	19-20

DRY $19 V+

Maui Waipara Chardonnay (★★☆)

The 2017 vintage (★★☆) is a bright yellow/pale gold wine, full-bodied, with peachy, vaguely honeyed flavours, crisp acidity and a rustic streak. Ready.

DRY $18 –V

Milcrest Nelson Reserve Chardonnay ★★★☆

The 2016 vintage (★★★★) is an estate-grown, single-vineyard wine, fermented and matured for 11 months in French (97 per cent) and American (3 per cent) oak barriques. Bright, light yellow/green, it has a fragrant, slightly buttery bouquet. Full-bodied, it has good concentration of peachy, slightly toasty flavours and a well-rounded, harmonious finish.

DRY $44 –V

Mills Reef Bespoke Hawke's Bay Chardonnay ★★★★

A tribute to the 'famous old-school style' of Chardonnay, with 'lashings of toasty oak', this wine is handled in a combination of French and American oak casks, and given a full, softening malolactic fermentation. The 2017 vintage (★★★★) is full-bodied, with ripe, peachy, buttery, toasty flavours, in a generous, well-rounded style, for drinking now to 2020.

DRY $35 –V

Mills Reef Elspeth Gimblett Gravels Hawke's Bay Chardonnay ★★★★★

Mills Reef's flagship Chardonnay is consistently rewarding. The quietly classy 2017 vintage (★★★★★) is a single-vineyard wine, hand-picked and fermented and matured for 10 months in French oak casks (34 per cent new). Refined and youthful, it is full-bodied, with deep, citrusy, peachy flavours, biscuity, savoury notes adding complexity, balanced acidity, and a tightly structured, very finely balanced finish. Best drinking 2021+.

Vintage	16	15	14	13	12	11	10
WR	7	7	7	7	NM	7	7
Drink	19-22	19-21	19-20	P	NM	P	P

DRY $40 AV

Mills Reef Estate Hawke's Bay Chardonnay ★★★

Fragrant and fleshy, the 2018 vintage (★★★☆) is already drinking well. Bright, light yellow/green, it has generous, ripe, peachy, slightly toasty flavours (from 10 months in French oak, 10 per cent new), finely balanced acidity and lots of drink-young appeal.

Vintage	17	16
WR	7	7
Drink	19-20	P

DRY $19 AV

Mills Reef Reserve Hawke's Bay Chardonnay ★★★★

Made in an upfront style, the 2018 vintage (★★★☆) was fermented in French (mostly) and American oak casks (24 per cent new), and barrel-aged for 10 months. Bright, light yellow/green, it is full-bodied, with fresh, ripe stone-fruit flavours and strong, buttery, toasty notes. It needs a bit more time; best drinking mid-2020+.

Vintage	18	17	16	15	14	13
WR	7	7	6	7	7	7
Drink	19-22	19-21	19-20	P	P	P

DRY $25 AV

Millton Clos de Ste Anne Chardonnay – see Clos de Ste Anne Chardonnay

Millton Opou Vineyard Gisborne Chardonnay ★★★★☆

Certified organic, the highly attractive 2017 vintage (★★★★☆) was hand-picked, fermented with indigenous yeasts in small French oak barrels (10 per cent new), and oak-matured for a year. Pale straw, it is fragrant, full-bodied and sweet-fruited, with generous stone-fruit flavours, slightly biscuity and buttery notes adding complexity, and a very finely balanced, smooth finish. Already drinking well, it should be at its best 2020+.

Vintage	17	16	15	14
WR	5	5	6	6
Drink	19-26	19-25	19-25	19-24

DRY $32 AV

Mission Barrique Reserve Hawke's Bay Chardonnay ★★★★☆

For Mission's classy, upper-tier Chardonnay, the style goal is a wine that 'emphasises fruit characters rather than oak, but offers some of the benefits of fermentation and maturation in wood'. The 2018 vintage (★★★★☆) was fermented and matured for nine months in French oak barriques. Full-bodied and complex, it has rich, peachy, toasty flavours, balanced acidity and a well-rounded finish, in a concentrated, classic regional style. Best drinking 2021+.

 DRY $29 V+

Mission Hawke's Bay Chardonnay ★★★☆

The good-value 2018 vintage (★★★☆) has strong drink-young appeal. Bright, light yellow/green, it is full-bodied and vibrantly fruity, with citrusy, peachy flavours, slightly toasty notes adding complexity, good depth and a fresh, crisp finish.

 DRY $18 V+

Mission Jewelstone Hawke's Bay Chardonnay ★★★★★

Classy stuff. The 2017 vintage (★★★★★) was hand-harvested from vines over 20 years old and fermented and matured for 10 months in French oak barriques (30 per cent new). Bright, light lemon/green, with a fragrant, complex bouquet, it is mouthfilling, rich and rounded, with concentrated, ripe stone-fruit flavours, gentle acidity, a slightly creamy texture and a long, very harmonious finish. Already delicious, it's also well worth cellaring.

Vintage	17	16	15	14	13	12	11	10
WR	7	7	7	7	6	5	NM	7
Drink	19-24	19-23	19-22	19-21	19-20	P	NM	19-20

 DRY $40 AV

Mission Vineyard Selection Hawke's Bay Chardonnay ★★★☆

The 2017 vintage (★★★★) is a single-vineyard wine, grown at Te Awanga and partly barrel-fermented. Offering very good value, it is mouthfilling, fresh and youthful, with strong, peachy, citrusy, slightly toasty flavours, good complexity and lots of current-drinking appeal.

 DRY $19 V+

Misty Cove Marlborough Chardonnay ★★★☆

The 2016 vintage (★★★☆), which is also named 'Signature' on the back label, is drinking well now. Bright, light lemon/green, it is mouthfilling, with generous grapefruit and peach flavours, slightly toasty notes and a well-rounded finish.

 DRY $30 –V

Momo Marlborough Chardonnay ★★★☆

From Seresin, the good-value 2017 vintage (★★★☆) was hand-picked and mostly (80 per cent) fermented and matured in seasoned oak barrels. Light lemon/green, with a citrusy bouquet, it is fresh and mouthfilling, with grapefruit-like flavours, showing some biscuity complexity, and very good depth. Certified organic.

 DRY $19 V+

Monarch Estate Vineyard Kaleidoscope Series Matakana Chardonnay   (★★★★☆)

The powerful 2015 vintage (★★★★☆) was estate-grown and hand-picked north of Auckland, fermented with indigenous yeasts in French oak barriques (50 per cent new), and then wood-aged for 11 months. Bright, light yellow/green, it is weighty and concentrated, with layers of ripe, peachy, biscuity, mealy flavours, showing excellent complexity and richness, and a finely textured, long finish.

 DRY $44 –V

Monowai Hawke's Bay Chardonnay   ★★★☆

Offering good, easy drinking, the 2016 vintage (★★★☆) was grown at Crownthorpe and mostly (60 per cent) barrel-aged. Bright, light lemon/green, with a buttery bouquet, it is mouthfilling and smooth, with vibrant, peachy, slightly citrusy and toasty flavours, revealing very satisfying depth and immediacy.

 DRY $18 V+

Monowai Upper Reaches Hawke's Bay Chardonnay   (★★★★)

The 2015 vintage (★★★★) was estate-grown at Crownthorpe and matured for a year in barrels (partly new). Pale gold, with a toasty bouquet, it is mouthfilling, with balanced acidity and strong, peachy, slightly buttery flavours, showing considerable complexity. Ready.

 DRY $30 –V

Montana Reserve Gisborne Chardonnay   ★★★☆

The 2017 vintage (★★★☆) is bargain-priced. Bright, light lemon/green, it is full-bodied, with generous, ripe, peachy flavours, slightly smoky notes adding a touch of complexity, and a smooth, very harmonious finish.

 DRY $17 V+

Morton Estate [Black Label] Gisborne Chardonnay   ★★★★

This label was for decades indivisibly associated with the Hawke's Bay region, but since 2016 (★★★★) it has been grown in Gisborne. The 2018 vintage (★★★★) is an extroverted style, fresh and full-bodied, with generous, ripe, peachy flavours, seasoned with toasty oak, balanced acidity and a slightly buttery finish. Best drinking 2020+. (From Lion.)

 DRY $20 V+

Mount Brown Estates North Canterbury Chardonnay   ★★★☆

The 2018 vintage (★★★) is a pale, youthful wine, medium to full-bodied, with fresh, citrusy, peachy, gently toasty flavours. Oak-aged for 18 months, the age-worthy 2017 vintage (★★★★) is mouthfilling, fresh and lively, with very good depth of grapefruit and peach flavours, well-integrated oak, balanced acidity and considerable complexity.

Vintage	18	17
WR	5	4
Drink	19-22	19-22

DRY $20 AV

Mount Edward Central Otago Chardonnay   ★★★★

Certified organic, the 'lightly oaked' 2017 vintage (★★★★) is drinking well in its youth. Light lemon/green, it is lemon-scented, with strong, youthful, peachy, slightly toasty and creamy flavours, showing good complexity, and a finely balanced, smooth finish.

DRY $29 AV

Mount Riley Marlborough Chardonnay   ★★★☆

Skilfully balanced for early drinking, the 2017 vintage (★★★☆) was fermented in stainless steel tanks (30 per cent) and French oak barriques (70 per cent). It has a fragrant, slightly buttery bouquet, leading into a full-bodied palate with generous, peachy, citrusy, slightly toasty flavours, balanced acidity and a dry finish. Bargain-priced.

DRY $16 V+

Mount Riley Seventeen Valley Marlborough Chardonnay   ★★★★☆

Priced sharply, the age-worthy 2016 vintage (★★★★☆) was estate-grown and hand-picked at three sites, and fermented and matured in French oak barriques (30 per cent new). Fresh and lively, it has citrusy, biscuity, mealy aromas and flavours, showing excellent delicacy and complexity. Fragrant and creamy-textured, it should be at its best 2020+.

DRY $26 V+

Moutere Hills Nelson Chardonnay   ★★★★☆

The 2018 vintage (★★★★☆) was estate-grown at Upper Moutere, hand-picked and fermented and matured for 11 months in French oak barrels. Pale straw, it is a full-bodied, generous wine, with concentrated, ripe stone-fruit flavours and toasty, buttery notes adding complexity. Already enjoyable, it's a drink-now or cellaring proposition.

Vintage	18
WR	6
Drink	19-24

DRY $35 –V

Moutere Hills Sarau Reserve Nelson Chardonnay   ★★★★★

The powerful 2017 vintage (★★★★★) is an estate-grown, single-vineyard wine, hand-picked at Upper Moutere and fermented and matured for 11 months in French oak barriques. Bright, light yellow/green, it's a full-on style, with highly concentrated stone-fruit flavours, buttery, toasty notes adding richness and complexity, fresh acidity and obvious potential; best drinking 2021+. (Tasted in August 2019, the 2013 vintage (★★★★☆) is maturing gracefully and probably at its peak. Bright, light yellow/green, it is sturdy, vigorous and richly flavoured, with bottle-aged complexity.)

Vintage	17
WR	6
Drink	20-26

DRY $55 AV

Mt Beautiful North Canterbury Chardonnay ★★★★

Estate-grown at Cheviot, north of Waipara, the 2017 vintage (★★★★) is fragrant and full-bodied, with youthful, citrusy, peachy, biscuity flavours, finely integrated oak, good complexity, fresh acidity and a long finish. Best drinking mid-2020+.

Vintage	17	16	15	14
WR	6	7	6	5
Drink	19-24	19-25	19-21	19-20

DRY $27 AV

Mt Difficulty McFelin Ridge Lowburn Valley Chardonnay (★★★★☆)

The vibrant 2018 vintage (★★★★☆) is a single-vineyard wine, grown at around 300 metres above sea level and fermented and matured for 11 months in French oak casks (18 per cent new). Bright, light lemon/green, with a fragrant, gently biscuity bouquet, it's a distinctly cool-climate style, with excellent intensity of grapefruit-evoking flavours, a subtle oak influence, balanced acidity, good complexity and a long finish. Elegant and age-worthy, it's well worth cellaring to 2021+.

Vintage	18
WR	6
Drink	19-26

DRY $37 –V

Mt Difficulty Packspur Lowburn Valley Chardonnay (★★★★★)

The very classy 2018 vintage (★★★★★) is from the oldest vineyard site at Lowburn, in Central Otago, planted in 1992 at 360 to 380 metres above sea level. Fermented and matured for 11 months in French oak casks (12 per cent new), it is elegant and weighty, with deep, vibrant, citrusy, peachy, slightly creamy flavours, a subtle seasoning of oak, and a Chablis-like elegance and length. Already delicious, it's well worth cellaring.

Vintage	18
WR	6
Drink	19-26

DRY $47 AV

Mud House Sub Region Series Omaka Marlborough Chardonnay ★★★★

The attractive 2016 vintage (★★★★) is drinking well now. It has a fragrant, citrusy bouquet, leading into a mouthfilling, sweet-fruited wine with strong, vibrant, citrusy, peachy, slightly buttery flavours and a smooth finish. Fine value.

DRY $20 V+

Muddy Water Waipara Chardonnay ★★★★☆

Still on sale, the elegant 2015 vintage (★★★★☆) was hand-picked from 22-year-old vines and fermented with indigenous yeasts in French oak puncheons (15 per cent new). Light lemon/green, it is weighty, with rich stone-fruit and spice flavours, a subtle seasoning of oak, fresh acidity, and strong personality. Certified organic.

Vintage	15	14	13	12	11	10
WR	7	6	6	6	6	6
Drink	19-26	19-22	19-21	19-20	P	P

DRY $38 AV

Nanny Goat Vineyard Central Otago Chardonnay   ★★★☆

A distinctly cool-climate style, the 2018 vintage (★★★★) is a single-vineyard wine, hand-picked near Cromwell and fermented and matured in French oak casks (10 per cent new). Fresh and crisp, it has grapefruit-like flavours, gently seasoned with oak, firm acid spine, and a youthful, lingering finish. Well worth cellaring, it should be at its best 2021+.

Nautilus Marlborough Chardonnay   ★★★★★

The highly attractive 2018 vintage (★★★★★) was hand-harvested and fermented and lees-stirred in oak casks (25 per cent new). Pale straw, with a fragrant, complex bouquet, it is a very elegant, youthful wine, with deep, vibrant, citrusy, peachy, slightly biscuity flavours, balanced acidity, creamy notes, excellent complexity and a long finish. Best drinking 2021+.

Vintage	18	17	16	15	14	13
WR	7	7	7	7	6	7
Drink	19-24	19-23	19-21	19-20	P	P

DRY $40 AV

Neck of the Woods Hawke's Bay Chardonnay   (★★★★)

The 2017 vintage (★★★★) was hand-picked in the Dartmoor Valley, and fermented and matured for 11 months in French oak barrels (25 per cent new). Light lemon/green, it is medium to full-bodied, with fresh, youthful, citrusy, biscuity flavours, showing good vigour and complexity. Drink 2020+.

Neudorf Moutere Chardonnay   ★★★★★

Superbly rich but not overblown, with arrestingly intense flavours enlivened with fine acidity, this multi-faceted Nelson wine enjoys a reputation second to none among New Zealand Chardonnays. Grown in clay soils threaded with gravel at Upper Moutere, it is hand-harvested from mature vines, fermented with indigenous yeasts, and lees-aged, with regular stirring, for a year in French oak barriques (12 per cent new in 2017). Bright, light lemon/green, the very elegant 2017 vintage (★★★★★) is a fragrant, lemon-scented, tightly structured wine. It has notably concentrated, youthful, grapefruit-like flavours, hints of apple and peach, a subtle seasoning of oak, and an appetisingly crisp, very long finish. Best drinking 2021+. Certified organic.

Vintage	17	16	15	14	13	12	11	10
WR	6	6	7	6	6	7	6	7
Drink	19-24	19-23	19-22	19-21	19-20	19-20	P	P

DRY $79 AV

Neudorf Rosie's Block Chardonnay   ★★★★☆

The stylish 2018 vintage (★★★★) of this Nelson wine was grown mostly at Upper Moutere (including Neudorf's own Rosie's Block), fermented with indigenous yeasts and lees-aged for 10 months in French oak casks (15 per cent new). Pale lemon/green, it is a very lively, medium-bodied wine, with crisp, grapefruit-like flavours, integrated oak, and a very harmonious finish. Best drinking 2021+.

Neudorf Twenty Five Rows Moutere Chardonnay ★★★★☆

'The inspiration is unabashedly Chablis' for this organically certified wine, which is very lightly exposed to oak. The 2016 vintage (★★★★☆), estate-grown and hand-harvested at Upper Moutere, was fermented with indigenous yeasts in tanks and then matured on its yeast lees, with some handling in old oak puncheons. Bright, light lemon/green, it is mouthfilling, fresh and youthful, with ripe, citrusy, peachy flavours to the fore, excellent vibrancy and intensity, mealy notes adding complexity, and a tightly structured finish.

Vintage	16	15	14	13
WR	6	7	6	6
Drink	19-21	19-20	P	P

 DRY $33 AV

Nga Waka Home Block Martinborough Chardonnay ★★★★☆

This single-vineyard wine is from vines planted in 1988. At its best, it is an authoritative wine, weighty and concentrated, with strong personality. Already highly expressive, the 2018 vintage (★★★★★) was fermented and matured for 10 months in French oak casks (30 per cent new), and given a full, softening malolactic fermentation. Pale gold, it is a powerful, lush, weighty style with concentrated, peachy, toasty flavours, showing very good complexity, and a rounded finish.

Vintage	18	17	16	15	14	13	12
WR	6	6	6	6	7	7	6
Drink	19-22	19-22	19-22	19-21	19-20	P	P

 DRY $40 –V

Nga Waka Martinborough Chardonnay ★★★★

This is a consistently rewarding wine. The bright yellow/pale gold 2018 vintage (★★★★☆) was fermented and matured for 10 months in French oak casks (20 per cent new). Already drinking well, it's a powerful, upfront style, with mouthfilling body, generous, peachy, slightly buttery and toasty flavours, showing good complexity, and a creamy-smooth finish.

Vintage	18	17	16	15	14	13
WR	6	6	6	6	7	7
Drink	19-22	19-22	19-20	P	P	P

 DRY $30 –V

Nikau Point Reserve Hawke's Bay Chardonnay ★★☆

Enjoyable now, the 2016 vintage (★★☆) is a full-bodied, easy-drinking wine with lively, ripe stone-fruit flavours, fresh and smooth.

 DRY $16 AV

Nockie's Palette Hawke's Bay Chardonnay ★★★★★

The bold, almost brash 2018 vintage (★★★★☆) was made for Nockie's Palette (in Central Otago) by Clearview Estate, at Te Awanga, in Hawke's Bay. Bright, light yellow/green, it is a powerful wine, crafted in a very upfront style, with concentrated, ripe stone-fruit flavours, buttery and toasty notes adding complexity, balanced acidity, and loads of drink-young appeal.

DRY $46 AV

Novum Marlborough Chardonnay   ★★★★★

An obvious candidate for cellaring, the 2018 vintage (★★★★★) was hand-harvested, fermented with indigenous yeasts in French oak barriques (10 per cent new), and given a full, softening malolactic fermentation. Light lemon/green, it is a weighty, savoury, tightly structured wine, highly refined, with subtle, citrusy, slightly biscuity flavours, showing excellent depth, delicacy and length. Best drinking 2021+.

 DRY $45 AV

Obsidian Reserve Waiheke Island Chardonnay   ★★★★☆

The 2018 vintage (★★★★☆) is a fresh, generous, very age-worthy wine, fermented with indigenous yeasts in French oak barrels (40 per cent new) and wood-aged for 10 months. Weighty and sweet-fruited, with concentrated stone-fruit flavours, balanced acidity, good complexity and a slightly creamy texture, it should be at its best 2021+.

 DRY $48 –V

Odyssey Gisborne Chardonnay   ★★★☆

Drinking well in its youth, the 2018 vintage (★★★☆) is a single-vineyard wine, fermented and matured in seasoned oak casks. Bright, light yellow, it is full-bodied, with strong, peachy, toasty, buttery aromas and flavours. If you prefer a 'full-on' Chardonnay style, try this.

DRY $20 AV

Odyssey Hera Chardonnay   (★★★★★)

Rich and tightly structured, the 2018 vintage (★★★★★) was grown in Gisborne and fermented with indigenous yeasts in French oak barrels (50 per cent new). Bright yellow, it is a stylish wine, still very youthful, with concentrated grapefruit and peach flavours, showing impressive complexity, and a lasting finish. Best drinking mid-2021+.

 DRY $65 AV

Odyssey Reserve Iliad Gisborne Chardonnay   ★★★★☆

Well worth cellaring, the 2018 vintage (★★★★☆) is a single-vineyard wine, hand-harvested and fermented with indigenous yeasts in French oak barriques (30 per cent new). Pale straw, it is fragrant and mouthfilling, with generous stone-fruit and toasty oak flavours, showing good complexity. A 'full-on' style, it's already approachable, but likely to be at its best 2021+.

Vintage	14	13
WR	6	6
Drink	P	P

 DRY $32 AV

Ohinemuri Estate Opou Reserve Poverty Bay Chardonnay   ★★★★

The 2017 vintage (★★★★) is a single-vineyard wine, grown at Opou, in Gisborne, and fermented and lees-aged for nine months in French oak barriques (20 per cent new). Bright, light lemon/green, it is mouthfilling and sweet-fruited, with fresh, generous, peachy, slightly toasty flavours and a well-rounded finish. Enjoyable young, it's also well worth cellaring.

 DRY $25 AV

Old Coach Road Nelson Chardonnay   ★★★

The easy-drinking 2018 vintage (★★☆) was mostly oak-aged (70 per cent of the blend spent several months in French oak). Light straw, with a creamy bouquet, it is full-bodied, with peachy, slightly spicy and honeyed flavours. Drink young.

DRY $15 V+

Old Coach Road Unoaked Nelson Chardonnay   ★★☆

Balanced for early drinking, the 2017 vintage (★★☆) from Seifried is a fresh, fruity, uncomplicated wine, with peachy, slightly buttery flavours and a fully dry finish.

DRY $13 V+

Old House Vineyards One Tree Nelson Chardonnay   ★★★★

The 2018 vintage (★★★★) was estate-grown and hand-picked at Upper Moutere, fermented with indigenous yeasts and matured for 11 months in French oak barrels. Pale straw, with a creamy bouquet, it is fresh and full-bodied, with generous, youthful, citrusy, peachy flavours, mealy and biscuity notes adding complexity, balanced acidity and good potential; best drinking 2021+.

Vintage	18	17
WR	7	6
Drink	19-30	19-30

DRY $35 –V

Omata Estate Russell Chardonnay   (★★★★)

The 2016 vintage (★★★★) was estate-grown at Russell, in Northland, hand-harvested and French oak-aged. Bright yellow, it is mouthfilling, generous and creamy-textured, with strong stone-fruit flavours, full of northern ripeness, toasty oak adding complexity, and a well-rounded finish.

DRY $36 –V

On Giants' Shoulders Martinborough Chardonnay   (★★★★☆)

The stylish 2017 vintage (★★★★☆) is rare – only 900 bottles were produced. Handled in French oak casks (20 per cent new), it is still youthful, with fresh, concentrated, citrusy, slightly mealy and biscuity flavours, showing good complexity, and excellent vigour and length. Best drinking mid-2020+.

DRY $40 –V

Osawa Winemaker's Collection Hawke's Bay Chardonnay   ★★★★☆

Retasted in early 2019, the 2014 vintage (★★★★☆) is maturing gracefully. Grown at Maraekakaho, hand-picked and French oak-aged, it is a light yellow/green, fragrant wine, with concentrated, vibrant stone-fruit flavours, slightly smoky and nutty notes adding complexity, and a long finish. Drink now or cellar.

$85 –V

Oyster Bay Marlborough Chardonnay ★★★★

This huge-selling, moderately priced wine is designed to showcase Marlborough's incisive fruit flavours. About half the blend is handled solely in tanks; the other half is fermented, lees-stirred and matured for nine months in oak barrels, predominantly French. It typically offers strong, ripe, citrusy, peachy flavours, threaded with appetising acidity. The 2018 vintage (★★★★), grown in the Wairau and Awatere valleys, is an excellent example of the 'fruit-driven' style of Chardonnay. Bright, light lemon/green, it is a medium to full-bodied wine, with fresh, vibrant fruit flavours, finely integrated oak adding complexity, balanced acidity and loads of drink-young appeal.

 DRY $20 V+

Pā Road Marlborough Chardonnay ★★★☆

Offering good value, the 2018 vintage (★★★☆) was partly barrel-aged. Light lemon/green, it is full-bodied and vibrantly fruity, with generous, ripe, peachy flavours, and slightly toasty and creamy notes adding complexity. Enjoyable young, it's also worth cellaring. (From te Pā.)

 DRY $18 V+

Paddy Borthwick New Zealand Chardonnay ★★★★

Estate-grown at Gladstone, in the northern Wairarapa, the 2016 vintage (★★★★) was fermented and matured in French oak casks (20 per cent new). A fragrant, medium to full-bodied wine, it has fresh, citrusy flavours, a subtle seasoning of oak, and very good vigour, depth and potential.

DRY $26 AV

Palliser Estate The Great Riddler Martinborough Chardonnay (★★★★★)

Produced in honour of Richard Riddiford (1950–2016), the company's founding managing director, the 2016 vintage (★★★★★) is rare – only 500 bottles exist. Grown in the original Om Santi Vineyard, it was fermented with indigenous yeasts in French oak barriques (20 per cent new), oak-aged for 18 months, given a full, softening malolactic fermentation, and bottled unfiltered. Bright, light lemon/green, it is a full-bodied, slightly creamy wine with concentrated, peachy, slightly toasty flavours, showing excellent vigour, delicacy, harmony and length. Best drinking 2021+.

 DRY $85 AV

Pask Declaration Gimblett Gravels Chardonnay ★★★★☆

The winery's top Chardonnay is estate-grown in the Gimblett Gravels, Hawke's Bay. The 2016 vintage (★★★★☆) was fermented and matured for 11 months in French oak puncheons (100 per cent new). Retasted in May 2019, it is bright, light yellow/green, with a fragrant, complex bouquet. An elegant, tightly structured wine, it is medium to full-bodied, with very good intensity of crisp, citrusy, peachy, slightly toasty flavours, still fresh and youthful. Best drinking 2021+.

Vintage	16	15	14	13	12	11	10
WR	7	7	7	7	5	6	NM
Drink	20-32	20-24	19-21	19-20	P	P	NM

 DRY $40 –V

Pask Gimblett Gravels Chardonnay ★★★☆

This second-tier Hawke's Bay Chardonnay is designed to highlight its vibrant fruit characters, with a subtle wood influence. The elegant 2018 vintage (★★★★) was matured in an even split of new and two-year-old French oak puncheons. Light lemon/green, with a hint of straw, it has a fragrant, fresh, 'fruit-driven' bouquet. Vibrant, with good intensity of delicate, citrusy, peachy flavours, gently seasoned with oak, it's a tightly structured wine, worth cellaring. Best drinking mid-2020+.

DRY $22 AV

Pask Small Batch Wild Yeast Chardonnay ★★★★

Estate-grown in Hawke's Bay, the attractive 2016 vintage (★★★★☆) was fermented with indigenous yeasts and matured for a year in French oak casks (50 per cent new). Retasted in May 2019, it is bright, light yellow, with a fragrant bouquet and strong, citrusy, peachy flavours. Vibrantly fruity, with good freshness and intensity, it's a drink-now or cellaring proposition.

Vintage	16
WR	7
Drink	20-22

DRY $25 AV

Passage Rock Reserve Waiheke Island Chardonnay ★★★★☆

Bright yellow/pale gold, the 2018 vintage (★★★★☆) was hand-harvested and fermented and matured in large French oak casks. Fresh and mouthfilling, it has strong, ripe stone-fruit and toasty oak flavours, showing very good complexity. Already very expressive, it's a drink-now or cellaring proposition.

Vintage	18
WR	5
Drink	19-22

DRY $50 –V

Peacock Sky Waiheke Island Chardonnay ★★★☆

Enjoyable young, the 2018 vintage (★★★☆) was hand-picked and French oak-aged for six months. Bright, light yellow, it is fresh and full-bodied, with lively, ripe, peachy, slightly toasty flavours, showing moderate complexity, and a smooth finish. Very easy drinking.

DRY $42 –V

Pegasus Bay Chardonnay ★★★★★

Strapping yet delicate, richly flavoured yet subtle, this sophisticated North Canterbury wine is one of the country's best Chardonnays grown south of Marlborough. Muscular and taut, it typically offers a seamless array of fresh, crisp, citrusy, biscuity, complex flavours and great concentration and length. Estate-grown at Waipara, it is based on ungrafted, Mendoza-clone vines (about 30 years old), hand-picked and given lengthy oak aging (the 2017 vintage was fermented and lees-aged for a year in French oak puncheons, 30 per cent new). The powerful 2017 vintage (★★★★★) has a definite 'wow' factor. Full of personality, it has a highly fragrant, complex, slightly smoky bouquet, leading into a weighty but elegant palate, with grapefruit-like flavours, finely integrated oak, and lovely depth.

Vintage	17	16	15	14	13	12	11	10
WR	6	6	6	5	7	6	6	6
Drink	19-29	19-28	19-27	19-23	19-23	19-24	19-23	19-20

DRY $43 AV

Pegasus Bay Virtuoso Chardonnay ★★★★★

Blended from the 'best barrels', this wine is hand-harvested from the company's mature, Mendoza-clone vines at Waipara. Fermented with indigenous yeasts, it is lees-aged for a year in French oak puncheons (30 per cent new in 2016), matured in tanks on light lees for several more months before bottling, and then bottle-aged for a year prior to its release. The 2016 vintage (★★★★★) has a fragrant, complex, inviting bouquet. Light lemon/green, it is full-bodied, rich and rounded, with deep stone-fruit and nut flavours, slightly smoky notes, excellent complexity, balanced acidity and a seamless finish. Drink now or cellar.

Vintage	16	15
WR	6	6
Drink	19-29	19-28

 DRY $60 AV

Pukeora Estate Ruahine Range Chardonnay ★★★☆

Grown on limestone slopes in Central Hawke's Bay, the 2016 vintage (★★★★) was hand-picked and fermented with indigenous yeasts in French oak barrels (17 per cent new). Bright, light yellow/green, it is lemon-scented and mouthfilling, with strong, vibrant, citrusy flavours, slightly minerally and buttery, and plenty of personality. Drink now to 2021.

 DRY $27 –V

Pyramid Valley Marlborough Chardonnay (★★★★☆)

Well worth cellaring, the debut 2017 vintage (★★★★☆) was hand-harvested from mature vines at Dog Point Vineyard, in the Southern Valleys, and fermented and matured in seasoned French oak demi-muids. Bright, light yellow/green, it is fragrant, mouthfilling and crisp, with concentrated, peachy, citrusy flavours, firm acid spine, gentle toasty notes adding complexity, and a dry, tightly structured finish. Still very youthful, it should be at its best 2021+.

 DRY $40 –V

Pyramid Valley Vineyards Field of Fire Chardonnay ★★★★★

Full of personality, the 2016 vintage (★★★★★) was estate-grown on an elevated, south-east-facing slope at Waikari, in North Canterbury. Fermented with indigenous yeasts in an even split of clay giare and aged French demi-muids, it was lees-aged for 10 months, then bottled unfined and unfiltered. Bright, light lemon/green, it's a Chablis-like wine, full-bodied, with penetrating, crisp, citrusy flavours, showing impressive vigour and intensity, firm acid spine and a lasting finish. Best drinking 2020+.

 DRY $125 –V

Pyramid Valley Vineyards Growers Collection
Sutherland-Till Vineyard Marlborough Chardonnay ★★★★☆

The 2016 vintage (★★★★☆) was hand-picked from vines planted at Dog Point Vineyard in 1983, handled in old French oak puncheons, and bottled unfined and unfiltered. Light yellow/green, it is fleshy and rich, with a slightly buttery bouquet, substantial body (14.5 per cent alcohol), very good complexity, balanced acidity and generous, ripe, peachy, slightly mealy and biscuity flavours. Drink now onwards.

 DRY $40 –V

Pyramid Valley Vineyards Lion's Tooth Canterbury Chardonnay   ★★★★★

Estate-grown on an east-facing slope at Waikari, in North Canterbury, the distinctive 2016 vintage (★★★★★) was fermented in a 50:50 split of old French oak demi-muids and terracotta clay amphorae from Italy (viewed as a flavour-neutral vessel, compared to barrels). Lees-matured for 10 months and bottled unfined and unfiltered, it is a bright, light lemon/green, sturdy, weighty wine (14.6 per cent alcohol), still unfolding, with deep, youthful, citrusy, slightly peachy flavours, integrated oak, a minerally streak and a tautly structured, lasting finish. Likely to be long-lived, it should be at its best mid-2020+.

Quarter Acre Hawke's Bay Chardonnay   ★★★★★

Instantly inviting, the 2018 vintage (★★★★★) is a multi-site blend, hand-picked and fermented and lees-aged for nine months in French oak casks. Bright, light lemon/green, it has a highly fragrant, complex bouquet, leading into a full-bodied, sweet-fruited wine with concentrated, vibrant stone-fruit flavours, showing excellent complexity, depth and harmony. A classic Hawke's Bay style, it's a drink-now or cellaring proposition.

Ra Nui Marlborough Wairau Valley Chardonnay   ★★★★

Drinking well now, the very harmonious 2016 vintage (★★★★) was fermented and matured in French oak casks (20 per cent new). Bright, light yellow/green, it is mouthfilling, with good concentration of peachy, citrusy, slightly buttery flavours, balanced acidity and a smooth finish.

Rapaura Springs Reserve Marlborough Chardonnay   ★★★★

Enjoyable young, the 2018 vintage (★★★★) is a vibrantly fruity wine, grown in the Southern Valleys and partly barrel-fermented. Bright, light yellow/green, it has rich, peachy, slightly toasty flavours, fresh acidity and a finely balanced finish. Drink now or cellar.

Vintage	18	17	16	15
WR	5	6	6	7
Drink	19-24	19-25	19-23	19-24

DRY $29 AV

Renato Nelson Chardonnay   ★★★★

Drinking well now, but worth cellaring, the 2017 vintage (★★★★) was estate-grown at Kina, on the coast, and fermented and matured for 10 months in French oak barriques (20 per cent new). Bright, light yellow/green, it is full-bodied, with vigorous, ripe stone-fruit flavours, showing good concentration and complexity, slightly toasty notes and well-balanced acidity. Best drinking 2020+.

Vintage	17	16	15	14	13	12
WR	7	6	6	6	NM	7
Drink	19-23	19-22	19-22	19-21	NM	19-20

DRY $26 AV

Rimu Grove Nelson Chardonnay   ★★★★☆

This wine is typically full of personality. Estate-grown near the coast in the Moutere hills and fermented and lees-matured for 11 months in French oak casks, the bright, light yellow/green 2018 vintage (★★★★☆) has a fragrant, slightly creamy and toasty bouquet. Already delicious, it is full-bodied, with strong, vibrant, peachy flavours, finely integrated oak and very good complexity. Best drinking 2021+.

Vintage	18	17	16	15	14	13
WR	7	6	7	7	7	7
Drink	19-32	19-30	19-30	19-30	19-25	19-28

DRY $45 –V

Riverby Estate Marlborough Chardonnay   ★★★★

Tasted in mid-2019, the 2016 vintage (★★★★) was fermented in French oak casks (25 per cent new). Bright yellow/green, with a fragrant, citrusy bouquet, it is full-bodied, with fresh, citrusy, slightly peachy and buttery flavours, showing very good complexity and depth. Maturing very gracefully, the mouthfilling 2015 vintage (★★★★☆) is still fresh and lively, with strong, citrusy, peachy, slightly spicy and buttery flavours, developing excellent complexity, and a lingering finish.

Vintage	16	15
WR	6	7
Drink	19-26	19-25

DRY $27 V+

Riverview Hawke's Bay Chardonnay   (★★★★☆)

Estate-grown at a cool, elevated, inland site, the vigorous 2015 vintage (★★★★☆) was fermented and matured in French oak casks (50 per cent new). An elegant, tightly structured wine, it is bright, light lemon/green, with very good intensity of grapefruit and peach flavours, barrel-ferment complexity, fresh acidity and a lengthy finish. Best drinking 2020+. (From The Wine Portfolio.)

DRY $26 V+

Roaring Meg Central Otago Chardonnay   (★★★☆)

From Mt Difficulty, the very easy-drinking 2018 vintage (★★★☆) was handled in stainless steel tanks, concrete eggs and oak barrels. Bright, light lemon/green, it is full-bodied, with fresh, citrusy fruit flavours to the fore, good depth, creamy notes and a smooth finish.

DRY $30 –V

Rock Ferry 3rd Rock Marlborough Chardonnay   (★★★★☆)

Certified organic, the 2018 vintage (★★★★☆) was estate-grown at Rapaura and matured for 11 months in one barrique and one puncheon. Pale lemon/green, it has a fragrant, slightly biscuity and creamy bouquet. Mouthfilling and fresh, it is still very youthful, with good concentration of citrusy, peachy flavours, mealy, nutty notes adding complexity, balanced acidity and obvious cellaring potential; best drinking 2021+.

DRY $45 –V

Rogue Vine Bay of Islands Chardonnay

(★★★★)

From a Kerikeri-based company, the 2017 vintage (★★★★) is an upfront style – fragrant and sturdy, with loads of flavour. Light lemon/green, it is weighty, fleshy and rich, with a strong surge of peachy, toasty flavours and a creamy-smooth finish. Drink now or cellar.

DRY $30 –V

Rongopai Hawke's Bay Chardonnay

★★☆

The 2017 vintage (★★★) is a 'fruit-driven' style, handled entirely in stainless steel tanks. Bright, light lemon/green, it is very fresh and lively, with peachy, slightly spicy flavours, showing a touch of complexity. Offering good, easy drinking, it's the best vintage yet. (From Babich.)

DRY $19 –V

Ruru Central Otago Chardonnay

(★★★☆)

Enjoyable young, the 2018 vintage (★★★☆) is a single-vineyard, Alexandra wine, matured for nine months in French oak barrels. Bright, light yellow, it is full-bodied and well-rounded, with ripe, peachy, slightly toasty flavours, showing considerable complexity, and a creamy-smooth finish.

DRY $25 –V

Sacred Hill Hawke's Bay Chardonnay

★★★

Lemon-scented, the 2018 vintage (★★★) is a vibrantly fruity wine, estate-grown in the Riflemans Vineyard. Pale lemon/green, it is citrusy and peachy, with fresh acidity, moderate complexity and good, drink-young appeal.

DRY $17 AV

Sacred Hill Riflemans Chardonnay

★★★★★

Sacred Hill's flagship Chardonnay is one of New Zealand's greatest – powerful yet elegant, with striking intensity and outstanding cellaring potential. Grown in the cool, inland, elevated (100 metres above sea level) Riflemans Vineyard in the Dartmoor Valley of Hawke's Bay, it is hand-picked from mature, own-rooted, Mendoza-clone vines and fermented with indigenous yeasts in French oak barriques (new and one year old), with some malolactic fermentation. The 2016 vintage (★★★★★) is an elegant, mouthfilling wine, with concentrated, vibrant grapefruit and peach flavours, seasoned with nutty oak, and lovely freshness, delicacy, poise and complexity. Already delicious, it's a tight-knit wine with obvious potential.

Vintage	16	15	14	13
WR	7	6	7	7
Drink	19-23	19-22	19-20	P

DRY $70 AV

Sacred Hill Single Vineyard Hawke's Bay Chardonnay

(★★★☆)

Enjoyable young, the 2018 vintage (★★★☆) was grown in the Riflemans Vineyard and fermented and lees-aged for 10 months in French oak barriques (30 per cent new). Bright, light yellow/green, with a slightly smoky bouquet, it is fresh and full-bodied, with peachy, slightly toasty flavours, good vigour and a crisp, dry finish.

DRY $25 –V

Sacred Hill Wine Thief Hawke's Bay Chardonnay   ★★★★☆

Designed as a 'richer and toastier' style than the flagship Riflemans Chardonnay (above), this wine is grown in the same vineyard, hand-picked and fermented with indigenous yeasts in new and one-year-old French oak barriques. The 2017 vintage (★★★★☆) is bright, light lemon/green, with a fresh, citrusy bouquet. Full-bodied, it is vibrantly fruity, with toasty, buttery notes adding complexity, lively acidity and lots of upfront, drink-young appeal. Best drinking 2020+.

 DRY $35 –V

Saint Clair James Sinclair Marlborough Chardonnay   ★★★★

The 2016 vintage (★★★★) was grown in the Awatere Valley, fermented and matured in seasoned French and American oak barriques, and given a full, softening malolactic fermentation. Fresh and mouthfilling, with balanced acidity, it has plenty of peachy, slightly toasty flavour, creamy notes, good harmony and lots of early-drinking appeal.

 DRY $24 V+

Saint Clair Marlborough Chardonnay   ★★★☆

Finely balanced for early drinking, the 2016 vintage (★★★☆) is a mouthfilling, moderately complex wine with a slightly creamy texture and generous, citrusy, slightly peachy and toasty flavours. Grown in the Wairau Valley, it was fermented in a mix of tanks and French and American oak barrels.

 DRY $22 AV

Saint Clair Omaka Reserve Marlborough Chardonnay   ★★★★☆

This is typically a fat, creamy wine, weighty and rich, made in a bold, upfront style. Grown in the Southern Valleys – mostly in the company's vineyard in the Omaka Valley – it is hand-picked, fermented and lees-aged for 10 months in American oak casks, and given a full, softening malolactic fermentation. The 2017 vintage (★★★★☆) is invitingly fragrant, with rich stone-fruit flavours, strongly seasoned with toasty oak, slightly smoky notes adding complexity, fresh, balanced acidity and a well-rounded finish.

Vintage	17	16	15	14	13
WR	6	7	7	7	7
Drink	19-21	19-20	P	P	P

 DRY $38 –V

Saint Clair Origin Marlborough Chardonnay   (★★★★)

Skilfully crafted, the 2017 vintage (★★★★) of this 'fruit-driven' Chardonnay was grown in the Wairau Valley and fermented in a mix of tanks and French and American oak barrels. Mouthfilling, it is vibrantly fruity, with very good depth of grapefruit and peach flavours, finely balanced acidity, slightly toasty, buttery notes adding complexity, and a fresh, dry finish.

DRY $22 V+

Saint Clair Pioneer Block 10 Twin Hills Marlborough Chardonnay   ★★★★☆

This powerful wine is grown principally in the company's vineyard in the Omaka Valley, a warm site with clay-based soils. The 2017 vintage (★★★★★) is a lovely young wine, fermented in French oak barriques. It has a fragrant, complex bouquet, leading into a generous, vibrant, very harmonious palate. Fresh and full-bodied, with concentrated, ripe, citrusy, peachy flavours, well-integrated oak, balanced acidity and a very long finish, it should be at its best 2020+.

DRY $38 –V

Sanctuary Marlborough Chardonnay   ★★★

The attractive, easy-drinking 2018 vintage (★★★) was handled in an even split of tanks and old French oak barriques. Full-bodied, it has vibrant, citrusy, slightly appley flavours to the fore, fresh acidity and a smooth finish. (From Grove Mill.)

$20 –V

Seifried Nelson Chardonnay   ★★★

The 2018 vintage (★★☆) was tank-fermented, aged in French oak barriques (one to three years old), and given a full, softening malolactic fermentation. It has golden colour – advanced for its age – in a very 'forward' style, with plenty of peachy, toasty flavour. Drink young.

Vintage	18	17	16	15	14	13
WR	6	6	6	6	6	6
Drink	19-28	19-27	19-26	19-25	19-24	19-21

DRY $18 AV

Seifried Winemaker's Collection Nelson Barrique Fermented Chardonnay
★★★★

This is typically a bold style, concentrated and creamy, with loads of flavour. The powerful 2017 vintage (★★★★☆) was fermented and matured for a year in French oak barriques. Bright, light yellow/green, it is mouthfilling, with strong stone-fruit and spice flavours, toasty oak, good complexity, fresh acidity and obvious potential; best drinking 2021+.

DRY $26 AV

Selaks Founders Limited Edition Hawke's Bay Chardonnay   ★★★★☆

Delicious young, the powerful 2016 vintage (★★★★☆) was barrel-fermented. Light lemon/green, it is a weighty, slightly buttery wine, with strong peach and grapefruit flavours, showing good complexity and harmony, and a fragrant bouquet. Priced right.

Vintage	16
WR	6
Drink	19-21

DRY $25 V+

Selaks The Taste Collection Hawke's Bay Buttery Chardonnay   (★★★★)

If you like soft, buttery Chardonnays, try this. The 2016 vintage (★★★★) was principally (70 per cent) fermented and matured in French oak barriques (30 per cent new); 30 per cent of the blend was handled in tanks. Light lemon/green, with a toasty bouquet, it is mouthfilling, with ripe, peachy flavours, coupled with strong buttery and toasty notes – as you would expect – but also freshness and vivacity. Skilfully crafted for instant appeal, it offers good value.

Seresin Chardonnay Reserve   ★★★★★

Finesse is the keynote quality of this organically certified Marlborough wine. Estate-grown in the Raupo Creek Vineyard, in the Omaka Valley, the 2015 vintage (★★★★★) was hand-picked, fermented with indigenous yeasts and lees-aged for 11 months in French oak barrels (26 per cent new), then blended and matured for a further five months in seasoned oak puncheons. A powerful, tightly structured, concentrated wine, it is very pale gold, with substantial body, fresh acidity, rich, ripe, peachy, citrusy, slightly toasty flavours, showing impressive complexity, and a very harmonious, lasting finish. Drink now or cellar.

Seresin Marlborough Chardonnay   ★★★★☆

This stylish, BioGro-certified wine is designed to 'focus on the textural element of the palate rather than emphasising primary fruit characters'. It is typically a full-bodied and complex wine with good mouthfeel, ripe melon/citrus characters shining through, subtle toasty oak and fresh acidity. The 2016 vintage (★★★★☆) was estate-grown, hand-picked, and fermented with indigenous yeasts and lees-aged for 11 months in French oak barriques and puncheons (6 per cent new), and given a full, softening malolactic fermentation. Lemon-scented, it's a full-bodied, vibrantly fruity wine, with deep, citrusy, peachy flavours, finely integrated oak adding complexity, and a crisp, lengthy finish. Fine value.

Settler Crownthorpe Hawke's Bay Chardonnay   (★★★☆)

Drinking well now, the 2016 vintage (★★★☆) was estate-grown at a cool, elevated site in inland Hawke's Bay, barrel-fermented and oak-aged for nine months. Bright, light yellow/green, it is fresh and mouthfilling, with good vigour and depth of flavour, a touch of complexity, and a crisp finish.

Sileni Cellar Selection Hawke's Bay Chardonnay   ★★★

The 2018 vintage (★★★) is enjoyable young. Made in a 'lightly oaked' style, it is fresh and lively, with ripe, peachy flavours, a touch of complexity, balanced acidity and good depth. Best drinking 2020.

DRY $20 –V

Sileni Grand Reserve Lodge Hawke's Bay Chardonnay ★★★★☆

The 2018 vintage (★★★★☆) is a high-flavoured wine, still unfolding. Bright, light lemon/green, with a fragrant, complex bouquet, it is fresh and youthful, with strong, vigorous, peachy, toasty flavours, balanced acidity and obvious potential; best drinking 2021+.

DRY $35 –V

Sileni Reserve Oaked Hawke's Bay Chardonnay (★★★☆)

The 2018 vintage (★★★☆) is a fresh and lively, medium-bodied wine, with peachy, toasty, slightly buttery flavours. A moderately complex style with balanced acidity and good depth, it's a drink-now or cellaring proposition.

DRY $22 AV

Smith & Sheth Cru Heretaunga Chardonnay ★★★★★

The tightly structured 2017 vintage (★★★★★) was hand-picked in the Howell Vineyard, in the Bridge Pa Triangle, and the Riverview Vineyard, at Mangatahi. Fermented and lees-aged for 11 months in French oak casks (40 per cent new), it is a mouthfilling, concentrated wine, full of youthful vigour. Bright, light lemon/green, it is invitingly fragrant, with fresh acidity and vibrant citrus and stone-fruit flavours, complex, layered and long. Best drinking mid-2020+.

DRY $40 AV

Smith & Sheth Cru Howell Vineyard Chardonnay (★★★★★)

From mature vines in the Bridge Pa Triangle, Hawke's Bay, the debut 2016 vintage (★★★★★) was hand-picked and fermented and matured for 11 months in French oak barriques (67 per cent new). Light lemon/green, it has a fragrant, complex, slightly buttery bouquet. It is full-bodied, fresh, citrusy and peachy, with excellent intensity, well-integrated oak, slightly funky notes adding complexity, appetising acidity and a tightly structured, persistent finish. Well worth cellaring, it should break into full stride 2020+.

DRY $60 –V

Smith & Sheth Cru Mangatahi Chardonnay (★★★★★)

Full of personality, the classy 2015 vintage (★★★★★) was hand-picked from mature vines in the elevated, inland district of Mangatahi, in Hawke's Bay, and fermented and aged for 11 months in French oak barriques (35 per cent new). Drinking well now, but still worth cellaring, it has a fragrant, highly complex bouquet, leading into a weighty, generous wine with layers of grapefruit, peach and biscuity oak flavours. Slightly minerally and earthy, it's a seamless, 'complete' wine, with lovely delicacy and depth.

DRY $60 AV

Soho Carter Waiheke Island Chardonnay ★★★★☆

This estate-grown, single-vineyard wine is hand-picked at Onetangi and fermented and matured in French oak barriques. The 2017 vintage (★★★★☆) has excellent poise and depth. Bright, light lemon/green, it is still youthful, with mouthfilling body, strong, fresh, peachy, slightly nutty flavours, finely balanced acidity, and obvious cellaring potential; best drinking 2020+.

DRY $40 –V

Soljans Estate Fifth Generation Series Kumeu Chardonnay   (★★★★★)

The highly impressive 2016 vintage (★★★★★) was estate-grown and hand-picked at Kumeu, in West Auckland, and matured for 18 months in French oak barriques. Bright, light yellow/green, it is full-bodied, rich and smooth, in a powerful style, with concentrated, complex stone-fruit flavours, gentle acidity, and a finely textured, very harmonious, lasting finish. Already delicious, it's still youthful and likely to be at its best 2021+.

 DRY $48 AV

Spade Oak The Prospect Ormond Gisborne Chardonnay   (★★★★☆)

The softly mouthfilling 2017 vintage (★★★★☆) was hand-picked and fermented and matured for 11 months in French oak barrels (25 per cent new). Bright, light lemon/green, it is full-bodied and well-rounded, with deep, ripe grapefruit and peach flavours, and a less assertive oak influence than the label description ('lashings of toasty vanillin oak') would suggest. Drink now or cellar.

 DRY $25 V+

Spinyback Nelson Chardonnay   ★★☆

From Waimea Estates, the 2017 vintage (★★☆) is medium-bodied, with fresh, peachy, citrusy flavours, woven with crisp acidity. Straightforward, easy drinking, it's enjoyable young and priced right.

 DRY $15 AV

Spy Valley Envoy Johnson Vineyard Marlborough Chardonnay   ★★★★★

This distinguished wine is estate-grown in the Waihopai Valley, hand-picked, fermented with indigenous yeasts and lees-aged in French oak barriques (mostly seasoned) for up to 20 months. Still on sale, the elegant, lively 2014 vintage (★★★★☆) is fragrant and tightly structured, with concentrated, peachy, slightly toasty and creamy flavours, a minerally streak, good acid spine and obvious cellaring potential.

Vintage	14	13	12	11	10
WR	6	6	6	NM	6
Drink	19-22	19-21	P	NM	P

 DRY $35 AV

Spy Valley Marlborough Chardonnay   ★★★★

The distinctive 2016 vintage (★★★★) is a single-vineyard wine, hand-picked, barrel-fermented and oak-aged for nearly a year. Light lemon/green, with a creamy bouquet, it has fresh, vibrant, grapefruit-like flavours to the fore, excellent delicacy, a restrained oak influence, a slightly minerally thread and a dry, smooth finish. Retasted in May 2019, it is unfolding well, with some peachy, spicy notes emerging and considerable complexity.

Vintage	16	15	14	13	12
WR	6	6	7	7	7
Drink	19-26	19-25	19-20	P	P

 DRY $25 AV

Stables Reserve Ngatarawa Hawke's Bay Chardonnay ★★★

Enjoyable young, the 2018 vintage (★★★) is a partly barrel-fermented wine, fresh, vibrant and full-bodied, with peachy, slightly toasty flavours, showing a touch of complexity, balanced acidity, and a slightly creamy finish.

DRY $20 AV

Staete Landt Josephine Marlborough Chardonnay ★★★★☆

This single-vineyard wine is estate-grown at Rapaura, in the Wairau Valley. The 2017 vintage (★★★★☆) was hand-harvested and fermented and matured for 18 months in French oak puncheons (10 per cent new). Bright, light lemon/green, with a fragrant, complex, slightly creamy bouquet, it is mouthfilling, with generous, ripe stone-fruit flavours, finely integrated biscuity oak, balanced acidity and a lengthy, harmonious finish. Drinking well now, it should be at its best mid-2020+.

Vintage	17	16
WR	7	7
Drink	19-24	19-23

DRY $29 V+

Stanley Estates Reserve Single Vineyard
Awatere Valley Marlborough Chardonnay ★★★★

The 2016 vintage (★★★★) was fermented with indigenous yeasts in French oak barrels (25 per cent new), and wood-aged for 10 months. Light lemon/green, it is mouthfilling and vibrant, with strong, citrusy, slightly peachy flavours, well-integrated oak, a minerally streak and a finely balanced, slightly creamy finish.

Vintage	16
WR	6
Drink	19-24

DRY $28 AV

Starborough Family Estate Marlborough Chardonnay ★★★★

The 2018 vintage (★★★☆) is a single-vineyard, Awatere Valley wine, handled in French oak casks (30 per cent new). The bouquet is smoky, with 'struck match' aromas; the palate is full-bodied, with ripe, peachy flavours, showing considerable complexity, but accentuated, sulphide-based, 'gunflint' characters detract. A wine with fresh acidity and youthful vigour, it should be at its best mid-2020+.

DRY $28 AV

Stone Bridge Gisborne Chardonnay ★★★★

Still on sale, the 2015 vintage (★★★★) was hand-picked and fermented and matured for over a year in French oak barrels (25 per cent new). Bright, light yellow, it is mouthfilling and fleshy, with generous, ripe, peachy, toasty flavours and a smooth, slightly buttery finish. A very typical regional style, it's drinking well now.

DRY $25 AV

Stonecroft Gimblett Gravels Hawke's Bay Chardonnay   ★★★★

Certified organic, the 2018 vintage (★★★★) was estate-grown, hand-harvested, and fermented and matured for five months in French oak barriques (35 per cent new). Pale yellow, with a hint of straw, it is full-bodied, with generous, ripe stone-fruit flavours, showing good complexity, hints of butter and toast, balanced acidity, and lots of drink-young appeal. Best drinking 2020+.

Vintage	18	17	16	15	14	13
WR	7	6	5	6	6	6
Drink	19-26	19-24	19-22	19-22	19-21	19-20

 DRY $27 AV

Stonecroft Old Vine Gimblett Gravels Hawke's Bay Chardonnay   ★★★★★

The impressive 2016 vintage (★★★★★) is a rare wine – only two barrels were made. From vines planted in Mere Road in 1992, it was hand-picked, fermented and matured for a year in French oak casks (50 per cent new), and given a full, softening malolactic fermentation. Light lemon/green, it is mouthfilling and highly concentrated, with layers of stone-fruit, grapefruit and biscuity oak flavours, revealing excellent complexity, and a very long, savoury finish. A classy wine, it should be at its peak 2020+.

Vintage	16	15
WR	6	6
Drink	19-25	19-24

 DRY $45 AV

Stoneleigh Rapaura Series Single Vineyard Marlborough Chardonnay   ★★★★

This single-vineyard wine is fermented and matured in new and one-year-old French oak casks. The 2017 vintage (★★★★) is bright, light lemon/green, with a slightly smoky bouquet. Mouthfilling, it has strong, ripe grapefruit and peach flavours, showing good complexity, and a lingering finish.

 DRY $25 AV

Sugar Loaf Marlborough Chardonnay   ★★★★☆

The classy, youthful 2017 vintage (★★★★☆) was estate-grown at Rapaura, hand-harvested and fermented in French oak casks (25 per cent new). Bright, light lemon/green, it is fragrant and smooth, with grapefruit-like flavours to the fore, peachy, nutty notes and a well-rounded finish. A restrained, delicate, finely poised wine, showing excellent complexity and harmony, it's well worth cellaring.

DRY $28 V+

Summerhouse Marlborough Chardonnay   ★★★★

Bargain-priced, the 2017 vintage (★★★☆) is enjoyable young. Made with use of new oak staves and new and second-year barrels, it is freshly scented, full-bodied and vibrantly fruity, with good depth of ripe, peachy flavours, showing a touch of complexity, moderate acidity and a smooth finish.

Vintage	17	16	15	14
WR	7	7	7	7
Drink	19-26	19-25	19-23	19-22

 DRY $17 V+

Tatty Bogler Waitaki Valley North Otago Chardonnay   ★★★★☆

The very elegant, subtle 2018 vintage (★★★★★) was matured for 10 months in old oak barrels. Showing good cellaring potential, it is mouthfilling, fresh and youthful, with vibrant, citrusy, peachy flavours, finely integrated oak and a lasting finish. Best drinking 2022+. (From Forrest Estate.)

 DRY $35 –V

Te Awa Single Estate Hawke's Bay Chardonnay   ★★★★☆

Fragrant, with 'struck-match' aromas, the 2018 vintage (★★★★) is a mouthfilling wine with generous, ripe stone-fruit flavours, balanced acidity, and accentuated, smoky notes adding complexity. A powerful style statement, it is a lively, age-worthy wine, likely to be at its best 2021+.

Vintage	18	17	16	15	14
WR	7	7	7	7	6
Drink	19-29	19-28	19-25	19-25	19-24

 DRY $25 V+

Te Awanga Estate Hawke's Bay Chardonnay   ★★★★

The 2018 vintage (★★★★) was partly hand-picked and partly barrel-fermented. Enjoyable young, it is fresh and lively, with very good depth of citrusy, slightly peachy flavours, a restrained oak influence, appetising acidity and a lengthy finish. Best drinking mid-2020+.

 DRY $25 AV

Te Kairanga John Martin Martinborough Chardonnay   ★★★★☆

Made from the 'best vineyard parcels', this wine is fermented and matured in French oak puncheons (27 per cent new in 2018). The 2018 vintage (★★★★☆) is still very fresh and youthful. Bright, light lemon/green, it has strong, ripe stone-fruit flavours, gently seasoned with toasty oak, and excellent delicacy, harmony and depth. Best drinking 2021+.

Vintage	18	17
WR	7	6
Drink	20-27	20-25

 DRY $40 –V

Te Kairanga Martinborough Chardonnay   ★★★★

The stylish, very harmonious 2018 vintage (★★★★) was fermented and matured in French oak puncheons (19 per cent new). Fresh, mouthfilling and finely balanced, it has strong, ripe stone-fruit flavours, gently seasoned with toasty oak, good complexity and lots of drink-young appeal.

DRY $25 AV

Te Kano Central Otago Chardonnay   (★★★★☆)

A very auspicious debut, the 2017 vintage (★★★★☆) was estate-grown at Bannockburn, hand-picked, barrel-fermented and oak-aged for 10 months. Bright, light lemon/green, it is mouthfilling, fresh and elegant, with ripe, citrusy, peachy flavours, showing excellent depth and complexity, balanced acidity and a persistent finish. A stylish, age-worthy wine, it should be at its best 2020+.

 DRY $35 –V

Te Mata Elston Chardonnay ★★★★★

One of New Zealand's most illustrious Chardonnays, Elston is a stylish, intense, slowly evolving Hawke's Bay wine. At around four years old, it is notably complete, showing concentration and finesse. The grapes are grown and hand-picked principally at two sites in the Te Mata hills at Havelock North, and the wine is fully fermented in French oak barriques (35 per cent new), with full malolactic fermentation. Bright, light lemon/green, the 2017 vintage (★★★★★) is weighty and well-rounded, with ripe stone-fruit flavours, finely integrated oak, and excellent complexity and harmony. A youthful, quietly classy wine, it's already delicious, but should be at its best 2020+.

Vintage	17		
WR	6		
Drink	19-22		

 DRY $40 AV

Te Mata Estate Vineyards Hawke's Bay Chardonnay ★★★★

This good-value, consistently attractive wine is sourced from the company's vineyards at Woodthorpe Terraces, in the Dartmoor Valley, the Bridge Pa Triangle and at Havelock North. Fermented and lees-aged in an even split of tanks and seasoned French oak barrels, it is typically a harmonious wine with fresh, ripe grapefruit characters to the fore, a gentle seasoning of biscuity oak, very good depth and a touch of complexity. The 2017 vintage (★★★★) is bright, light lemon/green, with a fresh, slightly buttery bouquet. Softly mouthfilling, it is moderately complex, with generous, ripe, peachy, gently toasty flavours, balanced acidity and a lingering finish.

Vintage	17	16	15
WR	6	6	6
Drink	19-21	19-20	P

 DRY $20 V+

---

te Pā Marlborough Chardonnay ★★★★

The attractive 2018 vintage (★★★★) was estate-grown and fermented and matured in French oak casks (40 per cent new). A fragrant, generous wine, it has strong, ripe stone-fruit flavours, balanced toasty oak, and good vigour, complexity and harmony. Drink now or cellar.

Vintage	18	17	
WR	6	6	
Drink	19-25	19-22	

DRY $25 AV

---

te Pā The Reserve Collection St Leonard's Marlborough Chardonnay ★★★★★

The impressive 2018 vintage (★★★★★) is a single-vineyard wine, grown in the central Wairau Valley, hand-picked, barrel-fermented (50 per cent new oak), and bottled unfined and unfiltered. It has light lemon/green, not entirely clear, colour. Weighty and rich, it is still very youthful, with concentrated, ripe, peachy, citrusy flavours, showing excellent delicacy, biscuity and mealy notes adding complexity, gentle acidity and a very harmonious, rounded finish. Best drinking 2022+.

 DRY $60 AV

Te Whau Vineyard Waiheke Island Chardonnay ★★★★★

For its sheer vintage-to-vintage consistency, this has been Te Whau's finest wine. Full of personality, it has beautifully ripe fruit characters showing excellent concentration, nutty oak and a long, finely poised finish. Still youthful, the 2017 vintage (★★★★☆) is an elegant wine, well worth cellaring. Light lemon/green, it has ripe, peachy flavours, a hint of pear, a subtle seasoning of oak, excellent delicacy, balanced acidity and a lasting finish. Best drinking 2020+.

Terra Sancta Riverblock Bannockburn Central Otago Chardonnay ★★★★

The 2016 vintage (★★★★) was fermented with indigenous yeasts and matured in French oak puncheons (25 per cent new). Lemon-scented, it is bright, light lemon/green, with fresh, concentrated, citrusy, peachy flavours, a subtle oak influence, slightly buttery notes and a smooth finish. Drink now or cellar.

Vintage	17	16	15	14
WR	6	7	7	7
Drink	19-26	19-23	19-21	19-22

DRY $29 AV

Theory & Practice Hawke's Bay Chardonnay ★★★★

Grown near the coast, the 2017 vintage (★★★★) was mostly hand-picked, all fermented in French oak barrels (30 per cent new), and given a full, softening malolactic fermentation. Made in a fairly upfront style, it's drinking well now, with generous, ripe stone-fruit flavours, toasty and buttery notes adding complexity, fresh acidity and good harmony.

DRY $25 AV

Thornbury Gisborne Chardonnay ★★★☆

Offering great value, the 2018 vintage (★★★☆) is a softly mouthfilling wine, with very satisfying depth of fresh, ripe, peachy, slightly toasty flavour, gentle acidity, a slightly creamy texture and a smooth finish. A typical regional style, it's enjoyable young. (From Villa Maria.)

Vintage	18
WR	6
Drink	19-22

Three Paddles Martinborough Chardonnay ★★★

From Nga Waka, the 2018 vintage (★★★☆) is a lightly oaked, 'fruit-driven' style, enjoyable young. Vibrantly fruity, it has ripe stone-fruit flavours to the fore, with a hint of toasty oak, balanced acidity and a smooth finish.

DRY $18 AV

Vintage	18
WR	6
Drink	19-21

Tiki Estate Waipara Chardonnay   (★★★☆)

The 2016 vintage (★★★☆) was made with some use of barrel fermentation, lees-aging and malolactic fermentation. Bright, light lemon/green, it is a mouthfilling, moderately complex style, with generous, vibrant, peachy flavours, distinct buttery notes, a subtle oak influence, finely balanced acidity and a smooth finish. Enjoyable young.

 DRY $20 AV

Tiki Hawke's Bay Chardonnay   ★★★

Maturing gracefully, the 2017 vintage (★★★☆) is fresh and vibrantly fruity, with good depth of ripe grapefruit-like flavours, slightly buttery and toasty notes, and a well-rounded finish.

Vintage	17
WR	6
Drink	19-21

 DRY $20 –V

Tiki Koro Hawke's Bay Chardonnay   ★★★★☆

Rich but elegant, the 2018 vintage (★★★★★) was hand-picked and fermented and lees-aged in French oak casks (55 per cent new). Bright, light lemon/green, it is a full-bodied, very age-worthy wine, with deep, vibrant stone-fruit flavours, finely balanced acidity, and excellent complexity and length. Best drinking 2021+.

Vintage	18
WR	6
Drink	19-22

 DRY $35 AV

Tiki Single Vineyard Hawke's Bay Chardonnay   ★★★★

The 2018 vintage (★★★★) is a single-vineyard wine, fermented and matured for 10 months in French oak barriques. Already drinking well, it is an upfront style, full-bodied, with ripe stone-fruit, toast and butterscotch flavours, rich and rounded.

Vintage	18
WR	6
Drink	19-20

 DRY $25 AV

Tohu Gisborne Chardonnay   ★★★☆

Enjoyable young, the 2018 vintage (★★★☆) is an easy-drinking, 'fruit-driven' style, tank-fermented with the use of oak. Bright, light lemon/green, it is full-bodied, fresh and vibrant, with ripe, peachy, slightly toasty flavours and a creamy-smooth finish.

DRY $20 AV

Tohu Hemi Reserve Marlborough Chardonnay   ★★★★☆

The 2016 vintage (★★★★) was hand-harvested from estate-grown vines in the Awatere Valley and fermented in old French oak barriques. An elegant, youthful wine, it is bright, light lemon/green, with fresh, citrusy scents. Showing good complexity, it has vibrant grapefruit-like flavours, a slightly minerally streak and a lingering finish. Best drinking 2020+.

 DRY $38 –V

Tohu Marlborough Chardonnay

The 2016 vintage (★★★☆), made without oak, was lees-aged and given a softening malolactic fermentation. Light lemon/green, it is mouthfilling and vibrantly fruity, with ripe, peachy, slightly appley and buttery flavours, showing very good depth.

DRY $22 AV

Tohu Single Vineyard Whenua Awa Awatere Valley
Marlborough Chardonnay

The elegant, youthful 2017 vintage (★★★★★) is a distinctly cool-climate wine, grown in the upper Awatere Valley and French oak-aged. Bright, light lemon/green, with a fragrant, fresh, slightly smoky bouquet, it is vigorous, with intense, peachy, citrusy flavours, oak complexity, and a finely balanced, long finish. Best drinking 2021+.

DRY $36 AV

Tohu Single Vineyard Whenua Matua Upper Moutere Nelson Chardonnay

Well worth cellaring, the 2017 vintage (★★★★☆) is a fresh, elegant, vigorous wine with strong, citrusy, peachy flavours, toasty and smoky notes adding complexity, appetising acidity and a poised, slightly creamy finish. Best drinking 2021+.

DRY $30 AV

Toi Toi Gisborne Chardonnay

Offering easy, early drinking, the 2018 vintage (★★★) is a light yellow wine, mouthfilling, with gentle acidity and soft, ripe, peachy, slightly toasty flavours, showing good depth. Ready to roll.

DRY $17 AV

Toi Toi Reserve New Zealand Chardonnay

Enjoyable young, the 2017 vintage (★★★★) is not labelled by region, but was grown in Gisborne. Bright, light lemon/green, it is fresh and lively, with mouthfilling body, peachy, gently biscuity and toasty flavours, balanced acidity and a rounded, lingering finish.

DRY $26 AV

Tony Bish Golden Egg Hawke's Bay Chardonnay (★★★★★)

Combining power and elegance, the 2017 vintage (★★★★★) was hand-picked in the upper Dartmoor Valley (70 per cent) and at Bay View (30 per cent), and predominantly handled in concrete, egg-shaped fermenters, which 'create natural convection currents, holding the yeast lees in suspension'. Weighty and sweet-fruited, with a citrusy bouquet, it has ripe grapefruit-like flavours, showing excellent concentration and vigour, a slightly creamy texture, and a very harmonious, lasting finish. More subtle than its Heartwood stablemate (see below), with a restrained, toasty oak influence (13 per cent was wood-fermented), it's well worth cellaring.

DRY $40 AV

Tony Bish Heartwood Hawke's Bay Chardonnay ★★★★★

The 2018 vintage (★★★★☆) was hand-picked and fermented and matured in French oak barriques. Fragrant, fresh and youthful, with mouthfilling body, strong, ripe stone-fruit flavours, enriched with toasty oak, balanced acidity, and very good complexity, it's a very age-worthy wine, likely to be at its best 2021+.

DRY $35 AV

Tony Bish Skeetfield Hawke's Bay Chardonnay ★★★★★

The delicious 2017 vintage (★★★★★) is based on mature, Mendoza-clone vines in the Skeetfield Vineyard at Ohiti. Hand-harvested, it was fermented and matured for a year in French oak barriques (60 per cent new). A powerful, very 'complete' wine, it is bright, light yellow/green, mouthfilling and concentrated, with rich, ripe, citrusy, peachy, toasty flavours, showing excellent vigour and complexity, fresh acidity, and a long finish. Best drinking 2021+.

DRY $60 AV

Tony Bish Zen Hawke's Bay Chardonnay (★★★★★)

The debut 2017 vintage (★★★★★) was made in an ovum – an egg-shaped, French oak barrel which creates unique convection currents, keeping the wine's yeast lees in suspension. Grown in the Skeetfield Vineyard and bottled unfined and unfiltered, it is a multi-faceted wine, full-bodied, generous and refined, with deep, vibrant, citrusy, peachy flavours, biscuity notes adding complexity, and a long, savoury finish. A youthful, very harmonious wine, it should be at its best from 2021 onwards.

DRY $140 –V

Trinity Hill Gimblett Gravels Chardonnay ★★★★★

The winery's flagship 'black label' Chardonnay from Hawke's Bay is typically intense and finely structured. Grown in the Gimblett Gravels and fermented and matured for a year in French oak puncheons (30 per cent new), the 2017 vintage (★★★★★) is already drinking well. Bright, light yellow/green, it is fragrant, rich and youthful, in a tight, elegant style, with balanced acidity, vibrant, peachy, slightly toasty flavours, showing excellent complexity and concentration, and a long, harmonious finish.

DRY $40 AV

TW Estate Gisborne Chardonnay ★★★☆

Gisborne in a glass, the generous 2018 vintage (★★★☆) was handled without oak. Bright, light lemon/green, it is full-bodied, sweet-fruited and vibrantly fruity, with fresh, ripe, peachy flavours, showing good depth, and a smooth finish.

DRY $17 V+

TW Platinum Chardonnay (★★★★☆)

Labelled as a 'decadent' style, the 2017 vintage (★★★★☆) was estate-grown in Gisborne and barrel-aged for 18 months. Bright, light yellow/green, with a creamy, toasty bouquet, it is full-bodied, with rich stone-fruit flavours, strongly seasoned with oak, balanced acidity and excellent complexity.

DRY $48 –V

TW Reserve Gisborne Chardonnay   ★★★★☆

Still youthful, the 2018 vintage (★★★★☆) was harvested from estate-grown, mature vines on the Golden Slope and fermented and matured for 10 months in oak barrels. Mouthfilling and sweet-fruited, it shows good complexity, with generous, peachy, slightly spicy and toasty flavours, creamy notes, gentle acidity and a lingering finish. Best drinking 2021+.

 DRY $28 V+

Two Rivers Clos Des Pierres Marlborough Chardonnay   ★★★★☆

From two sites, in the Wairau Valley and Southern Valleys, the 2018 vintage (★★★★☆) was fermented and matured for 11 months in French oak barrels, a new French oak cuve and a concrete egg tank. It has a slightly smoky bouquet, leading into a full-bodied wine with very good intensity of youthful, peachy, citrusy flavours, crisp and long. A vigorous young wine, it should be at its best 2021+.

Vintage	18	17
WR	7	7
Drink	19-24	19-23

 DRY $36 –V

Vavasour Anna's Vineyard Awatere Valley Marlborough Chardonnay   ★★★★★

From a site within the original, terraced vineyard in the lower Awatere Valley, the 2017 vintage (★★★★★) was fermented with indigenous yeasts and matured for 11 months in French oak barriques. A lovely young wine, it is lemon-scented and tightly structured, with layers of citrusy, peachy, slightly biscuity flavours, showing excellent vibrancy, delicacy and depth. Full of vigour and potential, it should break into full stride from 2021 onwards.

Vintage	17
WR	7
Drink	19-28

 DRY $40 AV

Vavasour Awatere Valley Marlborough Chardonnay   ★★★★☆

This typically rich, creamy-textured wine is grown in the Awatere Valley, given a full, softening malolactic fermentation and lees-aged in French oak barrels (18 per cent new in 2018). The 2018 vintage (★★★★★), oak-aged for nine months, is already delicious. Bright, light yellow/green, it is weighty and vibrantly fruity, with generous, ripe, peachy flavours, biscuity notes adding complexity, fresh acidity, and a finely balanced finish. Best drinking mid-2020+.

Vintage	18	17
WR	7	6
Drink	19-25	19-25

 DRY $30 AV

Vidal Anthony Joseph Vidal 1888 Hawke's Bay Chardonnay   ★★★★★

'The absolute pinnacle of Vidal Estate', the 2016 vintage is an extremely rare wine. Only 61 cases were made of the debut 2014 vintage (★★★★★), released in mid to late 2017, and the wine was not produced in 2015, 2017 or 2018. Hand-picked in the Kokako Vineyard, in the Ohiti Valley, the 2016 vintage (★★★★★) was fermented and lees-aged for a year in French oak casks (33 per cent new). From a warm growing season, it has a highly fragrant, complex bouquet, with a hint of gunflint. Bright, light yellow/green, it is very intense and vibrant, with deep, youthful, grapefruit-like flavours, a subtle seasoning of oak, appetising acidity and a lasting finish. Likely to be a 10-year wine, it's well worth cellaring to 2022+.

Vintage	16	DRY $120 –V
WR	7	
Drink	19-26	

Vidal Hawke's Bay Chardonnay ★★★☆

The 2017 vintage (★★★☆) is a top buy. Fermented and lees-stirred in tanks (principally) and seasoned French oak barriques, it has a slightly smoky bouquet, leading into a full-bodied wine with very good depth of fresh grapefruit and peach flavours, lively acidity and a dry, smooth finish. Enjoyable young.

Vintage	18	17	16	15	14	13	DRY $16 V+
WR	7	6	6	6	7	7	
Drink	19-23	19-21	19-20	P	P	P	

Vidal Legacy Hawke's Bay Chardonnay ★★★★★

The 2018 vintage (★★★★★) of Vidal's flagship Chardonnay was grown in two vineyards (Lyons and Kokako), hand-harvested, fermented with indigenous yeasts and matured for 10 months in French oak barriques (45 per cent new). Still extremely youthful, it is bright, light lemon/green, with a highly fragrant, complex, slightly smoky bouquet. Weighty and dry, it is a very elegant and age-worthy wine, with intense, crisp, peachy, citrusy flavours that build to a long finish. Best drinking 2022+.

Vintage	18	DRY $60 AV
WR	7	
Drink	19-26	

Vidal Reserve Hawke's Bay Chardonnay ★★★★

This middle-tier label is a consistently good buy, and the latest release offers irresistible value. The 2018 vintage (★★★★☆) was fermented and matured for 10 months in French oak casks (15 per cent new). Already delicious, it is bright, light lemon/green, with a slightly smoky fragrance. Mouthfilling, fresh and generous, it has citrusy, peachy, slightly toasty flavours, showing excellent richness, delicacy and complexity. Best drinking mid-2020+.

Vintage	18	17	16	15	14	13	12	DRY $20 V+
WR	7	7	7	7	7	7	6	
Drink	19-25	19-21	19-21	19-20	P	P	P	

Vidal Soler Hawke's Bay Chardonnay ★★★★★

The very elegant 2018 vintage (★★★★★) is the second of a range of single-vineyard wines under the Soler brand to be released by Vidal, positioned above Reserve and below Legacy. Grown in the Kokako Vineyard, in the Ohiti Valley, it was fermented and lees-aged for 10 months in French oak barriques (26 per cent new). Bright, light yellow/green, it is fragrant and full-bodied, with a strong surge of youthful, citrusy, peachy flavours, biscuity, smoky notes adding complexity, and a beautifully poised, long finish. A classy, age-worthy wine, it should break into full stride 2021+.

Vintage	18	17
WR	7	7
Drink	19-26	19-24

DRY $35 AV

Villa Maria Cellar Selection Hawke's Bay Chardonnay ★★★★

A top buy. Already drinking well, the 2018 vintage (★★★★) is a full-bodied wine, with strong, ripe stone-fruit flavours to the fore, slightly smoky and toasty notes adding a distinct touch of complexity, fresh acidity and a dry, finely balanced finish. Best drinking 2021+.

Vintage	18	17	16	15	14
WR	6	7	7	7	7
Drink	19-22	19-22	19-21	19-20	P

DRY $18 V+

Villa Maria Cellar Selection Marlborough Chardonnay ★★★★

A stylish, great-value wine. The 2017 vintage (★★★★), grown in the Wairau and Awatere valleys, was partly hand-picked, fully fermented in oak barriques (partly with indigenous yeasts), and barrel-matured for nine months. An elegant, youthful, vibrantly fruity wine, it has citrusy, peachy flavours, woven with fresh acidity, biscuity and buttery notes adding complexity, and good length. Drink now or cellar.

Vintage	18	17	16	15
WR	6	6	6	6
Drink	19-22	19-22	19-20	19-20

DRY $18 V+

Villa Maria Platinum Selection Sur Lie Hawke's Bay Chardonnay (★★★★★)

The very elegant, youthful 2018 vintage (★★★★★) was grown mostly in the Keltern Vineyard, barrel-fermented and aged 'sur lie' (on its yeast lees). Fresh and finely poised, it is sweet-fruited and tightly structured, with citrusy, peachy, mealy flavours, a subtle seasoning of oak, balanced acidity and a lengthy, very harmonious finish. Best drinking 2022+.

Vintage	18
WR	7
Drink	19-23

DRY $25 V+

Villa Maria Private Bin East Coast Chardonnay ★★★☆

Already drinking well, the 2018 vintage (★★★☆) is a good example of 'fruit-driven' Chardonnay. Fresh and vibrant, it is full-bodied, with ripe, peachy, citrusy flavours to the fore, a very subtle seasoning of oak, and very good depth and harmony. Priced sharply.

Vintage	18	17
WR	6	6
Drink	19-22	19-21

DRY $15 V+

Villa Maria Reserve Barrique Fermented Gisborne Chardonnay

This acclaimed wine is usually sourced principally from the company's McDiarmid Hill and Katoa vineyards. The 2018 vintage (★★★★☆) was fermented with indigenous yeasts in French barriques (60 per cent new) and oak-matured for 11 months. A bold, upfront style, it is mouthfilling and sweet-fruited, with concentrated stone-fruit flavours, slightly buttery, toasty notes adding complexity, and a smooth, long finish. Best drinking mid-2020+.

Vintage	18	17	16	15	14	13	12	DRY $40 AV
WR	7	6	7	7	7	7	7	
Drink	19-25	19-24	19-24	19-23	19-22	19-21	P	

Villa Maria Reserve Hawke's Bay Chardonnay

The stylish, tightly structured 2018 vintage (★★★★★) has a fragrant, slightly smoky bouquet. Mouthfilling and youthful, it has vigorous, ripe stone-fruit flavours, gently seasoned with toasty oak, impressive intensity and a long finish. Best drinking 2022+. Retasted in mid-2019, the 2017 vintage (★★★★☆) is still very youthful. An elegant wine with a hint of gunflint, it has strong grapefruit and peach flavours, mealy, biscuity notes adding complexity, and a fresh, tight finish. Best drinking 2021+.

Vintage	18	17	16	15	14	13	12	DRY $32 V+
WR	7	6	7	7	7	7	6	
Drink	19-25	19-24	19-24	19-23	19-22	19-21	P	

Villa Maria Reserve Marlborough Chardonnay

With its rich, slightly mealy, citrusy flavours, this is a distinguished wine, concentrated and finely structured. A marriage of intense, ripe Marlborough fruit with French oak, it is one of the region's greatest Chardonnays. It is typically grown and hand-picked in the warmest sites supplying Chardonnay grapes to Villa Maria, in the Awatere and Wairau valleys. The 2017 vintage (★★★★★) is mouthfilling and vibrantly fruity. Still youthful, it has concentrated, lively grapefruit and peach flavours, slightly smoky notes, a gentle seasoning of oak adding complexity and a lasting finish. Open 2020+. (The 2001 vintage, tasted in mid-2018, was a revelation – still drinking extremely well at 17 years old.)

Vintage	17	16	15	14	13	12	DRY $32 V+
WR	7	7	7	7	7	7	
Drink	19-25	19-22	19-22	19-22	19-20	19-20	

Villa Maria Single Vineyard Ihumatao Chardonnay

This impressive wine is estate-grown at Mangere, in South Auckland. The classy, youthful 2018 vintage (★★★★★) was hand-picked, fermented with indigenous yeasts in French oak barriques (30 per cent new), and oak-aged for 11 months. Bright, light lemon/green, with a fragrant, smoky bouquet, it is weighty and concentrated, with rich, vibrant stone-fruit flavours, finely integrated oak, excellent complexity and a tightly structured finish. Best drinking 2022+.

Vintage	18	17	16	15	14	13	12	DRY $50 AV
WR	7	7	7	NM	7	7	6	
Drink	19-25	19-24	19-22	NM	19-22	19-21	P	

Villa Maria Single Vineyard Keltern Hawke's Bay Chardonnay ★★★★★

Grown in the Keltern Vineyard, a cool, inland site east of Maraekakaho, this classy wine is hand-harvested, fermented with mostly indigenous yeasts and lees-aged in French oak barriques (38 per cent new in 2018). The 2018 vintage (★★★★★) is very youthful. Bright, light lemon/green, with a fragrant, very smoky bouquet, it is weighty, vibrant and tightly structured, with 'struck match' aromas, concentrated, ripe stone-fruit flavours, toasty, savoury notes adding complexity, balanced acidity and obvious cellaring potential. Best drinking 2023+.

Vintage	18	17	16	15	14	13	12
WR	7	7	7	7	7	7	6
Drink	19-25	19-24	19-24	19-23	19-22	19-21	P

Villa Maria Single Vineyard Taylors Pass Chardonnay ★★★★★

Grown in the company's Taylors Pass Vineyard in Marlborough's Awatere Valley, this wine is hand-picked and fermented in French oak barriques (25 per cent new in 2016). Delicious young, the 2016 vintage (★★★★★) is highly refined, with a fragrant, citrusy bouquet, deep, vibrant grapefruit and peach flavours, nutty, smoky notes adding complexity, and a long, dry finish.

Vintage	17	16	15	14	13	12
WR	7	7	7	7	7	7
Drink	19-25	19-22	19-22	19-22	19-20	19-20

Volcanic Hills Hawke's Bay Chardonnay ★★★☆

Enjoyable now, the 2017 vintage (★★★★) was fully barrel-fermented and oak-matured for 10 months. Bright, light yellow/green, it is medium to full-bodied, with strong, citrusy, peachy, slightly toasty flavours, showing good complexity, and a crisp, lively finish.

Waimea Nelson Chardonnay ★★★★

Offering good value, the 2017 vintage (★★★★) was hand-picked and fermented and lees-aged for 11 months in French oak puncheons (45 per cent new). Bright, light yellow/green, it is mouthfilling, with strong, vibrant, peachy, slightly toasty flavours, showing very good balance and depth, fresh acidity and some cellaring potential. Best drinking 2021+.

DRY $22 V+

Waipara Hills Waipara Valley Chardonnay ★★★☆

Enjoyable young, the 2017 vintage (★★★☆) is full-bodied, fresh and smooth, with very good depth of peachy, citrusy flavours, lively acidity and a slightly creamy finish.

DRY $22 AV

Wairau River Reserve Marlborough Chardonnay ★★★★☆

Still youthful, the 2017 vintage (★★★★☆) is a single-vineyard wine, estate-grown at Rapaura, hand-picked and fermented and matured for 10 months in oak barrels. Light lemon/green, with a fresh, slightly smoky bouquet, it is full-bodied, with vibrant peach and grapefruit flavours, finely integrated oak, good delicacy and vigour, and obvious cellaring potential. Best drinking mid-2020+.

DRY $30 AV

Walnut Block Nutcracker Marlborough Chardonnay ★★★★☆

Certified organic, the delicious 2016 vintage (★★★★☆) is a very attractive, harmonious wine, hand-picked and fermented with indigenous yeasts in French oak puncheons (17 per cent new). Light lemon/green, it is full-bodied and vibrant, with generous, ripe stone-fruit flavours to the fore, skilful oak handling contributing a mealy, biscuity complexity, and a dry, slightly buttery finish.

Vintage	16	15
WR	7	6
Drink	19-23	19-22

DRY $32 AV

Whitehaven Marlborough Chardonnay ★★★★☆

The 2018 vintage (★★★★☆) is a fragrant, mouthfilling, slightly creamy-textured wine, drinking well in its youth. Bright, light yellow/green, it has rich stone-fruit and biscuity oak flavours, showing very good complexity, balanced acidity and a very harmonious finish. Best mid-2020+.

DRY $28 V+

Wild Earth Central Otago Chardonnay (★★★★☆)

The 2018 vintage (★★★★☆) is an extroverted but age-worthy wine, grown in the Cromwell Basin and fermented with indigenous yeasts in French oak casks (15 per cent new). Fragrant and full-bodied, it has strong, vibrant, peachy flavours, slightly toasty and creamy notes adding complexity, and fresh acidity. Already highly approachable, it should be at its best 2021+.

DRY $32 AV

Wither Hills Marlborough Chardonnay ★★★☆

Enjoyable young, the 2018 vintage (★★★☆) is fresh and full-bodied, with good depth of peachy, slightly toasty flavours and a smooth, dry, creamy-textured finish. Priced right.

DRY $18 V+

Wither Hills Single Vineyard Benmorven Marlborough Chardonnay ★★★★☆

Hand-harvested and barrel-fermented, the 2018 vintage (★★★★☆) offers fine value. Already delicious, it is a youthful, sweet-fruited wine, with good intensity of ripe, peachy, slightly toasty flavours, fresh acidity, oak-derived complexity and a slightly creamy finish. Best drinking mid-2020+.

DRY $26 V+

Wooing Tree Central Otago Chardonnay ★★★★

The 2016 vintage (★★★★) was estate-grown at Cromwell, hand-picked and fermented and matured for eight months in French oak casks (30 per cent new). Light lemon/green, with a fragrant, slightly biscuity bouquet, it shows good weight and harmony, with mouthfilling body, strong, ripe grapefruit/apple flavours, and a subtle seasoning of oak adding complexity.

DRY $38 –V

Wrights Reserve Organic Gisborne Chardonnay ★★★★☆

Already highly enjoyable, the 2018 vintage (★★★★☆) was grown in the Ormond Valley, matured for a year in new French oak casks, and given a full, softening malolactic fermentation. Pale straw, it is mouthfilling, savoury, ripe and rounded, with good complexity and a creamy-smooth finish. Best drinking mid-2020+. Certified organic.

DRY $38 –V

Zephyr Marlborough Chardonnay ★★★★☆

The classy 2017 vintage (★★★★★) is a single-vineyard wine, grown at Dillons Point, in the lower Wairau Valley, hand-picked and fermented and matured in French oak casks (15 to 20 per cent new). Bright, light lemon/green, with a fragrant, slightly smoky bouquet, it is mouthfilling and vibrant, with strong, citrusy, slightly biscuity and creamy flavours, showing excellent intensity and complexity, and a long, harmonious finish. Best drinking 2021+.

DRY $33 AV

Chenin Blanc

Today's Chenin Blancs are markedly riper, rounder and more enjoyable to drink than the sharply acidic, austere wines of the 1980s, when Chenin Blanc was far more extensively planted in New Zealand. Yet this classic grape variety is still struggling for an identity. In recent years, several labels have been discontinued – not for lack of quality or value, but lack of buyer interest.

A good New Zealand Chenin Blanc is fresh and buoyantly fruity, with melon and pineapple-evoking flavours and a crisp finish. In the cooler parts of the country, the variety's naturally high acidity (an asset in the warmer viticultural regions of South Africa, the United States and Australia) can be a distinct handicap. But when the grapes achieve full ripeness here, this classic grape of Vouvray, in the Loire Valley, yields sturdy wines that are satisfying in their youth yet can mature for many years, gradually unfolding a delicious, honeyed richness.

Only three wineries have consistently made impressive Chenin Blancs over the past decade: Millton, Margrain and Esk Valley. Many growers, put off by the variety's late-ripening nature and the susceptibility of its tight bunches to botrytis rot, have uprooted their vines. Plantings have plummeted from 372 hectares in 1983 to 23 hectares of bearing vines in 2020.

Chenin Blanc is the country's thirteenth most widely planted white-wine variety, with plantings concentrated in Hawke's Bay, Gisborne and Central Otago. In the future, winemakers who plant Chenin Blanc in warm, sunny vineyard sites with devigorating soils, where the variety's vigorous growth can be controlled and yields reduced, can be expected to produce the ripest, most concentrated wines. New Zealand winemakers have yet to get to grips with Chenin Blanc.

Amisfield Central Otago Chenin Blanc ★★★★

Estate-grown at Pisa, in the Cromwell Basin, the 2017 vintage (★★★★) was hand-harvested and mostly (70 per cent) fermented in French oak barriques; the rest was handled in tanks. Light lemon/green, it's a vigorous, youthful wine, with strong pear, apple and lemon flavours, a gentle splash of sweetness (10 grams/litre of residual sugar) and appetising acidity. Finely balanced for easy drinking, it should be at its best 2020+.

MED/DRY $30 –V

Astrolabe Marlborough Chenin Blanc Demi-Sec ★★★★

The 2019 vintage (★★★★☆) was grown in the Wrekin Vineyard, in the Southern Valleys, and handled without oak. Full of drink-young charm, it is attractively scented, fresh and very vibrant, in a medium to full-bodied style, with ripe peach and pear flavours, gentle sweetness (12 grams/litre of residual sugar) and balanced acidity. Still very youthful, it's well worth cellaring.

Vintage	19	
WR	6	MED/DRY $25 AV
Drink	19-30	

Astrolabe Vineyards Wrekin Vineyard Chenin Blanc ★★★★★

The 2018 vintage (★★★★☆) was hand-harvested in the Southern Valleys and partly (40 per cent) fermented with indigenous yeasts in seasoned French oak puncheons. A dry style (2.1 grams/litre of residual sugar), it is very age-worthy. Bright, light lemon/green, it is mouthfilling, with strong, youthful, citrusy, slightly appley flavours, showing good intensity, and slightly biscuity notes adding complexity. Best drinking 2021+.

Vintage	18	
WR	6	DRY $30 V+
Drink	20-30	

Black Estate Home Chenin Blanc   ★★★★

Still youthful, the 2017 vintage (★★★☆) was estate-grown at Omihi, in North Canterbury, hand-picked, barrel-fermented with indigenous yeasts, and bottled unfined and unfiltered. Bright, light yellow, it is medium-bodied, with very good depth of lemony, appley flavours, showing a touch of complexity, and gentle sweetness balanced by steely acidity. Certified organic.

MED/DRY $45 –V

Clos de Ste Anne La Bas Chenin Blanc   ★★★★★

Certified biodynamic, the 2014 vintage (★★★★★) is from a section of the vineyard 'down there' (La Bas). Grown in Millton's Clos de Ste Anne hillside vineyard at Manutuke, in Gisborne, and fermented with indigenous yeasts, it was matured for nine months in large, 600-litre oak barrels ('demi-muids'). A mouthfilling, fleshy wine, it is unusually ripe and well-rounded for Chenin Blanc, with concentrated peach and pineapple flavours, showing excellent complexity, gentle acidity, and a long, dry (2.1 grams/litre of residual sugar) finish. Drink now or cellar.

DRY $75 AV

Forrest Marlborough Chenin Blanc   ★★★★☆

The 2018 vintage (★★★★☆) was handled in a 50:50 split of tanks and barrels. Very harmonious, it is fresh, lively and youthful, with ripe, citrusy, peachy flavours, showing a touch of complexity, balanced acidity, and an off-dry (7.5 grams/litre of residual sugar) finish. Best drinking 2021+.

MED/DRY $25 V+

Maison Noire Hawke's Bay Chenin Blanc   (★★★★☆)

The distinctive, youthful 2018 vintage (★★★★☆) is a dry style, fermented in French oak casks (30 per cent new). Bright, light lemon/green, it is fragrant and mouthfilling, with vibrant, citrusy, peachy, slightly biscuity flavours, showing excellent depth, ripeness and complexity, finely balanced acidity and obvious cellaring potential. Best drinking 2021+.

DRY $30 –V

Margrain Old Vine Martinborough Chenin Blanc   (★★★★★)

The striking 2016 vintage (★★★★★) is based solely on the estate's original, 35-year-old vines. Handled entirely in tanks, it's a highly scented wine, medium-bodied, with gentle sweetness (16 grams/litre of residual sugar), appetising acidity, and rich, vibrant, lemony, appley flavours, showing lovely purity, delicacy and intensity. Already delicious, it should flourish in the bottle for many years.

MED $65 AV

Vintage	16
WR	7
Drink	19-29

Matawhero Church House Single Vineyard Gisborne Chenin Blanc ★★★★

The 2016 vintage (★★★★) was harvested from young vines at Patutahi. Fresh and lively, with strong, citrusy, appley flavours, it's a dryish style (5.2 grams/litre of residual sugar), with moderate acidity for Chenin Blanc and excellent delicacy, poise and depth.

Vintage	16	15
WR	6	7
Drink	P	P

 MED/DRY $26 –V

Millton Te Arai Vineyard Gisborne Chenin Blanc ★★★★★

Certified organic, this Gisborne wine is New Zealand's best-known Chenin Blanc. It's a richly varietal wine with concentrated, fresh, vibrant fruit flavours to the fore in some vintages, nectareous scents and flavours in others. The grapes are hand-picked at up to four stages of ripening, culminating in some years ('It's in the lap of the gods,' says James Millton) in a final harvest of botrytis-affected fruit. Fermentation is in tanks and large 600-litre French oak casks, used in the Loire for Chenin Blanc. Pale gold, the 2017 vintage (★★★★☆) is a full-bodied, dryish wine (5.6 grams/litre of residual sugar), with rich, peachy flavours, hints of honey and toast, excellent varietal character, and moderate acidity for Chenin Blanc. Well worth cellaring.

 MED/DRY $32 AV

Mount Edward Central Otago Chenin Blanc (★★★★)

Labelled as a 'new style of Chenin Blanc', the 2017 vintage (★★★★) is a dry wine (4 grams/litre of residual sugar), half oak-aged. Light lemon/green, with a creamy bouquet, it is full-bodied, fresh and vibrant, with generous, lemony, appley flavours, showing a distinct touch of complexity. Drink now or cellar. Certified organic.

 DRY $29 –V

Moutere Hills Nelson Chenin Blanc ★★★★☆

Forward in its appeal, the 2018 vintage (★★★★☆) is a single-vineyard wine, hand-picked from 25-year-old vines and matured for 11 months in old French oak. Bright, light yellow/green, it is a complex, medium to full-bodied wine, with slightly buttery notes, rich, peachy, slightly spicy flavours, showing good complexity, and a smooth, harmonious finish.

Vintage	18
WR	6
Drink	19-26

 DRY $35 –V

Mt Difficulty Long Gully Bannockburn Chenin Blanc ★★★★☆

Showing obvious potential for cellaring, the 2018 vintage (★★★★☆) is a single-vineyard wine, made in a medium style (21 grams/litre of residual sugar) with finely balanced acidity. Pale lemon/green, it is freshly scented and vibrantly fruity, with strong, peachy, citrusy flavours, showing excellent vigour, delicacy and length. Best drinking 2021+.

MED $34 –V

Queensberry Gardens Central Otago Chenin Blanc   ★★★★

Well worth cellaring, the 2018 vintage (★★★★) was estate-grown at Queensberry – midway between Cromwell and Wanaka – and lees-aged in old barrels. Light lemon/green, it is a medium-bodied, vibrantly fruity wine, with vigorous, peachy, citrusy, appley flavours, showing very good varietal character, and a dryish (9 grams/litre of residual sugar), lengthy finish. Best drinking mid-2020+.

MED/DRY $28 –V

Fiano

A traditional low-yielding variety of Campania, in south-west Italy, Fiano is also grown in Sicily, Argentina and Australia. Only 1 hectare is planted in New Zealand, according to New Zealand Winegrowers' *Vineyard Register Report 2017–2020*, but its age-worthy wines have been praised by UK writer Oz Clarke as 'exciting' and 'distinctive'.

Jenny Dobson Hawke's Bay Fiano (★★★★★)

Well worth discovering, the 2017 vintage (★★★★★) is from vines in the Bridge Pa Triangle that were previously allocated to the Bushhawk Vineyard label. Fermented and lees-aged in stainless steel tanks and barrels, it's a distinctive wine, bright, light yellow/green, with satisfying body (12.5 per cent alcohol), concentrated, peachy, slightly spicy flavours, and a long, dry, finely balanced finish.

DRY $35 AV

Flora

A California crossing of Gewürztraminer and Sémillon, in cool-climate regions Flora produces aromatic, spicy wine. Some of New Zealand's 'Pinot Gris' vines were more than a decade ago positively identified as Flora, but the country's total area of bearing Flora vines in 2020 will be just 2 hectares, almost all in Auckland and Northland.

Shipwreck Bay Northland Flora ★★★

Still on sale, the 2015 vintage (★★★) is a medium-bodied wine, estate-grown in Northland, with lively acidity woven through strong, citrusy, peachy flavours, balanced for easy drinking. (From Okahu Estate.)

MED/DRY $20 –V

Gewürztraminer

Only a trickle of Gewürztraminer is exported (less than 0.1 per cent of our total wine shipments), and the majority of New Zealand bottlings lack the power and richness of the great Alsace model. Yet this classic grape is starting to get the respect it deserves from grape-growers and winemakers here. If you haven't yet discovered the delights of this pungently perfumed, spicy variety, give yourself a treat.

For most of the 1990s, Gewürztraminer's popularity was on the wane. Between 1983 and 1996, New Zealand's plantings of Gewürztraminer dropped by almost two-thirds. A key problem is that Gewürztraminer is a temperamental performer in the vineyard, being particularly vulnerable to adverse weather at flowering, which can decimate grape yields. Now there is proof of a renewal of interest: the area of bearing vines has surged from 85 hectares in 1998 to 227 hectares in 2020. Most of the plantings are in Marlborough (37 per cent of the national total), Hawke's Bay (19 per cent) and Gisborne (17 per cent), but there are also significant pockets in Nelson, Canterbury and Otago. Gewürztraminer is a high-impact wine, brimming with scents and flavours. 'Spicy' is the most common adjective used to pinpoint its distinctive, heady aromas and flavours; tasters also find nuances of gingerbread, freshly ground black pepper, cinnamon, cloves, mint, lychees and mangoes. Once you've tasted one or two Gewürztraminers, you won't have any trouble recognising it in a blind tasting – it's one of the most forthright, distinctive white-wine varieties of all.

Anchorage Family Estate Nelson Gewürztraminer ★★★☆

Offering good value, the 2017 vintage (★★★☆) is fragrant, with a well-spiced bouquet. Medium-bodied, it has fresh, spicy, slightly gingery flavours, a gentle splash of sweetness and very good depth. Enjoyable young.

MED/DRY $19 V+

Askerne Hawke's Bay Gewürztraminer ★★★★☆

Bargain-priced, the 2018 vintage (★★★★☆) is a weighty, medium style (17.5 grams/litre of residual sugar), handled without oak. Bright, light lemon/green, it is a perfumed, softly mouthfilling wine with rich stone-fruit and spice flavours, slightly gingery notes, gentle acidity and loads of drink-young appeal.

MED $23 V+

Askerne Reserve Hawke's Bay Gewürztraminer (★★★★★)

Already lovely, the 2018 vintage (★★★★★) is a medium style (15.4 grams/litre of residual sugar), handled without oak. Bright, light lemon/green, it is weighty, rich, ripe and rounded, with substantial body, concentrated, peachy, slightly spicy, vaguely gingery flavours, showing excellent delicacy and harmony, and a soft, long finish. Drink now or cellar.

MED $32 AV

Ataahua Waipara Gewürztraminer ★★★★☆

Still on sale, the 2016 vintage (★★★★) of this North Canterbury wine is finely textured and perfumed. Weighty, with ripe, citrusy, spicy flavours, showing a touch of complexity, and excellent depth, it should be at its best 2020+.

Vintage	16	15
WR	6	6
Drink	19-22	P

MED/DRY $26 AV

Blackenbrook Vineyard Nelson Gewürztraminer ★★★★

A consistently attractive wine. Estate-grown and hand-picked, the 2019 vintage (★★★★☆) was mostly handled in tanks, but 9 per cent of the blend was matured in old barrels. Light lemon/green, it is gently perfumed and mouthfilling, with peach, pear, lychee and ginger flavours, showing excellent delicacy and freshness, and a distinctly spicy, off-dry (6 grams/litre of residual sugar) finish. Best drinking 2021+.

Vintage	19	18	17	16
WR	7	6	7	5
Drink	19-23	19-22	19-21	19-20

MED/DRY $25 AV

Brennan Gibbston Central Otago Gewürztraminer (★★★★☆)

Finely poised and youthful, the 2018 vintage (★★★★☆) is an estate-grown wine with an invitingly perfumed, floral, spicy bouquet. Mouthfilling and fresh, it is strongly varietal, with rich, yet delicate, peachy, spicy flavours, a slightly oily texture, and obvious potential. Best drinking 2021+.

MED/DRY $40 –V

Cicada Marlborough Gewürztraminer ★★★★

Perfumed and youthful, the 2018 vintage (★★★★) is mouthfilling, with very good depth of fresh peach, spice, lychee and ginger flavours, and a dryish (5 grams/litre of residual sugar), finely balanced finish. Also still available, the lively 2017 vintage (★★★★) has strong, peachy, spicy, slightly gingery flavours, fresh acidity, and an off-dry (5 grams/litre of residual sugar) finish. Best drinking 2020+. (From Riverby Estate.)

Vintage	18	17
WR	7	7
Drink	20-26	19-25

MED/DRY $24 AV

Dry River Lovat Vineyard Gewürztraminer ★★★★★

From mature vines in Martinborough, the bright, light lemon/green 2018 vintage (★★★★★) was mostly handled in tanks; 25 per cent spent 10 months in old oak hogsheads. A powerful, lush, voluptuous wine, it is sturdy and rich, with highly concentrated, youthful, peachy, spicy flavours, balanced acidity and an off-dry (12 grams/litre of residual sugar) finish. Best drinking 2022+.

Vintage	18	17	16	15	14	13
WR	6	6	6	6	6	6
Drink	19-30	19-29	19-28	19-27	19-26	19-25

MED/DRY $50 AV

Falconhead Hawke's Bay Gewürztraminer ★★★

Offering very easy drinking, the 2019 vintage (★★★) is a softly mouthfilling wine, mostly handled in tanks (5 per cent of the blend was barrel-fermented). Light lemon/green, it is gently perfumed, with satisfying depth of peach, lychee and spice flavours, slightly sweet (9 grams/litre of residual sugar) and smooth.

MED/DRY $17 AV

Forrest Marlborough Gewürztraminer   ★★★☆

Still on sale, the 2016 vintage (★★★☆) is full-bodied, with a sliver of sweetness and strong, ripe, peachy, slightly gingery flavours.

MED/DRY $25 –V

Greystone Waipara Valley North Canterbury Gewürztraminer   ★★★★★

An emerging star. Certified organic, the 2018 vintage (★★★★★) was estate-grown and hand-harvested, and part of the blend was fermented and matured for five months in oak barrels. Already delicious, it is highly perfumed and softly mouthfilling, with fresh, deep stone-fruit and spice flavours, gentle sweetness (18 grams/litre of residual sugar) and a rich, well-rounded finish.

MED $33 AV

Hans Herzog Marlborough Gewürztraminer   (★★★★☆)

Certified organic, the 2017 vintage (★★★★☆) was estate-grown in the Wairau Valley, hand-picked, fermented with indigenous yeasts and matured for nine months in French oak puncheons. Deep amber, it's a distinctive, 'full-on' style with concentrated spice and apricot flavours, and a firm, bone-dry finish.

DRY $39 –V

Hunter's Marlborough Gewürztraminer   ★★★★

Estate-grown at Rapaura, on the north side of the Wairau Valley, the 2018 vintage (★★★★) is an enticingly perfumed, fleshy wine with fresh, ripe peach, pear, lychee and ginger flavours, showing good richness, and a dry (2.1 grams/litre of residual sugar) finish. Best drinking 2020+.

DRY $23 AV

Johanneshof Cellars Marlborough Gewürztraminer   ★★★★★

This beauty is one of the country's greatest Gewürztraminers. Hand-picked in the Wairau Valley, the 2018 vintage (★★★★★) has an exotic, highly perfumed bouquet. Already delicious, it is full-bodied, with deep, peachy, spicy, vaguely honeyed flavours, gentle sweetness (17 grams/litre of residual sugar), good complexity and a slightly oily richness. Full of personality, it should be at its best 2020+.

Vintage	18	17	16	15	14	13	12	11	10
WR	7	7	7	6	7	7	7	6	7
Drink	19-27	19-26	19-25	19-24	19-24	19-23	19-21	19-20	19-20

MED $31 AV

Kaimira Estate Brightwater Nelson Gewürztraminer   ★★★★

Maturing gracefully, the 2016 vintage (★★★★☆), certified organic, is an exotically perfumed, strongly varietal wine. Mouthfilling and fleshy, it has excellent delicacy and depth of peachy, peppery flavours, a hint of apricot and a well-spiced, slightly sweet (13 grams/litre of residual sugar), seductively smooth finish.

MED/DRY $24 AV

Lawson's Dry Hills Marlborough Gewürztraminer ★★★★★

One of the country's most impressive Gewürztraminers. Grown in the Home Block and nearby Woodward Vineyard, at the foot of the Wither Hills, it is typically harvested at about 24 brix and mostly fermented in stainless steel tanks; a key part of the blend (about 15 per cent) is given 'the full treatment', with a high-solids, indigenous yeast ferment in seasoned French oak barriques, malolactic fermentation and lees-stirring. The youthful 2018 vintage (★★★★☆) is perfumed and weighty, with vibrant pear, lychee and spice flavours, gentle sweetness (6.7 grams/litre of residual sugar), and excellent delicacy, harmony and length. Best drinking 2021+.

Vintage	18	17	16	15	14	13	12	11	10	MED/DRY $25 V+
WR	7	7	7	7	6	7	7	7	7	
Drink	19-25	19-25	19-24	19-24	19-22	19-20	P	P	P	

Lawson's Dry Hills The Pioneer Marlborough Gewürztraminer ★★★★★

The stunning 2016 vintage (★★★★★) is a weighty (14.5 per cent alcohol), fleshy, Alsace-style wine, estate-grown in the Home Block and barrel-fermented with indigenous yeasts. From 35-year-old vines 'with trunks as thick as thighs', it is a bright, light yellow/green, powerful wine, jam-packed with peachy, spicy flavours, gently sweet (18 grams/litre of residual sugar), finely poised and lasting. Well worth discovering.

Vintage	16	15	14	13	MED $30 AV
WR	7	7	6	7	
Drink	19-26	19-24	19-24	19-20	

Leveret Estate Hawke's Bay Gewürztraminer (★★★☆)

The 2016 vintage (★★★☆) is mouthfilling, with very good depth of peach and pear flavours, hints of spices and ginger, and a slightly sweet finish.

Vintage	16	MED/DRY $23 –V
WR	7	
Drink	19-22	

Main Divide North Canterbury Gewürztraminer ★★★★☆

From a 'great' year for Gewürztraminer, the delicious 2018 vintage (★★★★★) from Pegasus Bay is an irresistible buy. Very open and expressive in its youth, it was fermented in old oak puncheons and then barrel-aged for three months. Bright, light lemon/green, it is richly perfumed and full-bodied, with concentrated, peachy, spicy, slightly gingery flavours, an oily texture and a slightly sweet finish. Showing amazing richness for a $20 wine, it's a drink-now or cellaring proposition.

MED/DRY $21 V+

Matawhero Single Vineyard Gisborne Gewürztraminer ★★★★

Still on sale, the 2016 vintage (★★★☆) is gently perfumed, with a hint of sweetness (7 grams/litre of residual sugar) and vibrant, citrusy, spicy flavours, showing very good balance, delicacy and depth.

 MED/DRY $23 AV

Millton Riverpoint Vineyard Gewürztraminer ★★★★☆

Still available, the 2015 vintage (★★★★★) of this Gisborne wine makes a big statement. Certified organic, it was fermented on its skins for several days, emerging with gold/amber colour and a well-spiced bouquet. Full of personality, it is sturdy (14.5 per cent alcohol), peachy, spicy and slightly honeyed, with hints of ginger and passionfruit, an oily richness and an off-dry (9.5 grams/litre of residual sugar) finish.

Vintage	15	14
WR	6	6
Drink	P	P

 MED/DRY $26 AV

Misha's Vineyard The Gallery Central Otago Gewürztraminer ★★★★☆

The delicious 2016 vintage (★★★★☆) was estate-grown at Bendigo and fermented in seasoned French oak barrels, partly (25 per cent) with indigenous yeasts. Floral, full-bodied and smooth, it has generous, peachy, spicy, slightly citrusy and appley flavours, showing good complexity, gentle acidity and a well-spiced, off-dry (9 grams/litre of residual sugar), very harmonious finish.

Vintage	16	15	14	13	12	11	10
WR	7	7	6	6	7	6	6
Drink	19-29	19-28	19-27	19-26	19-26	19-23	19-22

MED/DRY $32 –V

Mission Hawke's Bay Gewürztraminer ★★★★

Bargain-priced, the 2018 vintage (★★★★) is invitingly perfumed, fresh and full-bodied, with strong, peachy, spicy, slightly gingery flavours, an oily texture and an off-dry finish. Delicious young.

 MED/DRY $16 V+

Mount Riley Marlborough Gewürztraminer ★★★★

Perfumed and full-bodied, the 2019 vintage (★★★★) is a single-vineyard wine, grown in the Southern Valleys and principally handled in tanks; 10 per cent of the blend was barrel-fermented. Enjoyable from the start, it is invitingly scented, with vibrant peach, lychee and spice flavours, showing a distinct touch of complexity, slight sweetness, and excellent depth and harmony. Top value.

MED/DRY $15 V+

Mt Difficulty Growers Series Station Block Pisa Range Gewürztraminer (★★★★)

Drinking well now, the 2016 vintage (★★★★) was grown at Pisa, in the Cromwell Basin. Bright, light lemon/green, it is perfumed and mouthfilling, with concentrated, peachy, spicy, slightly gingery flavours, showing some bottle-aged complexity, and a vaguely honeyed, gently sweet (32 grams/litre of residual sugar) finish.

 MED $27 –V

Ohinemuri Estate Matawhero Gewürztraminer   ★★★☆

Still available, the 2015 vintage (★★★★) was grown in Gisborne and mostly handled in tanks, but 10 per cent of the blend was fermented and matured for four months in oak barrels. It is mouthfilling, slightly sweet (15 grams/litre of residual sugar) and smooth, with fresh, peachy, gently spicy flavours. Finely balanced, it's a strongly varietal wine, enticingly perfumed.

Vintage	15
WR	5
Drink	P

 MED $24 –V

Old Coach Road Nelson Gewürztraminer   ★★★☆

Bargain-priced, the 2019 vintage (★★★☆) is a perfumed, instantly appealing wine. Medium-bodied, it has plenty of fresh, peachy, gently spicy and gingery flavour, with an off-dry (12 grams/litre of residual sugar) finish. Fine value from Seifried Estate.

 MED/DRY $14 V+

Ostler Waitaki Valley North Otago Gewürztraminer   ★★★★☆

The classy 2017 vintage (★★★★☆), part of the 'Grower Selection', was made with a small amount of barrel fermentation. A vibrantly fruity, finely balanced wine, it has a perfumed bouquet and refined palate, showing excellent delicacy and purity. Slightly oily, with gentle sweetness (9 grams/litre of residual sugar), it's a youthful wine, likely to be at its best 2020+.

 MED/DRY $30 –V

Pegasus Bay Gewürztraminer   ★★★★★

Estate-grown at Waipara, in North Canterbury, the delicious 2018 vintage (★★★★★) was handled for six months in old oak puncheons. Bright, light lemon/green, it is a powerful, youthful wine, weighty and rich, with concentrated, peachy, spicy, slightly gingery flavours, a vague hint of honey, and a complex, perfumed bouquet. Made in an off-dry style (14 grams/litre of residual sugar), it's full of personality.

Vintage	18	17	16	15	14	13	12	11	10
WR	6	NM	5	NM	7	7	7	6	6
Drink	19-22	NM	19-22	NM	19-22	19-21	19-20	P	P

 MED/DRY $30 AV

Petane Hawke's Bay Gewürztraminer   (★★★★☆)

Weighty and more complex than most Gewürztraminers, the 2018 vintage (★★★★☆) was hand-harvested at Eskdale and Havelock North, and partly barrel-fermented. Light lemon/green, with a fragrant, gently spicy bouquet, it is full-bodied and concentrated, with strong, ripe pear, lychee and spice flavours, a hint of ginger, and a dryish finish. A subtle, distinctive wine, it's worth discovering.

 MED/DRY $27 AV

Queensberry The Lazy Dog Blown Away Central Otago Gewürztraminer (★★★★☆)

Already enjoyable, the attractive 2018 vintage (★★★★☆) was estate-grown at Queensberry – midway between Cromwell and Wanaka – and fermented and lees-aged in 'pre-loved' barrels. Pale, mouthfilling and finely balanced, it is clearly varietal, with strong pear and lychee flavours, a hint of apricot and distinctly spicy notes. A very harmonious wine with a touch of complexity and a dryish finish (9 grams/litre of residual sugar), it should reward cellaring.

MED/DRY $29 AV

Rimu Grove Nelson Gewürztraminer ★★★★

The 2016 vintage (★★★★☆) is perfumed, weighty and finely textured, in a slightly sweet style (12 grams/litre of residual sugar) with gentle acidity, generous peach, spice and slight ginger flavours, showing excellent depth and harmony, and lots of drink-young appeal.

Vintage	16	15	14
WR	6	7	7
Drink	19-27	19-26	19-25

MED/DRY $26 –V

Ruru Central Otago Gewürztraminer ★★★☆

The perfumed, softly mouthfilling 2018 vintage (★★★★) was grown in the Immigrant's Vineyard, at Alexandra. Bright, light lemon/green, it has strong, ripe, peachy, distinctly spicy flavours, pronounced varietal character, and an off-dry (12 grams/litre of residual sugar), well-rounded finish.

Vintage	18	17	16	15
WR	6	7	NM	6
Drink	19-27	19-26	NM	19-24

MED/DRY $27 –V

Seifried Nelson Gewürztraminer ★★★★

Typically a floral, well-spiced wine, offering excellent value. The 2019 vintage (★★★★☆) is still a baby, but brimful of promise. Perfumed and mouthfilling, it has strong, fresh, peachy, spicy flavours, a hint of apricot, gentle sweetness (14 grams/litre of residual sugar), and a rich, well-spiced finish. Best drinking 2021+.

Vintage	19	18	17	16	15	14	13
WR	7	7	6	6	6	6	6
Drink	19-24	19-23	19-21	19-20	19-20	P	P

MED/DRY $18 V+

Seifried Winemaker's Collection Nelson Gewürztraminer ★★★★★

This is typically a powerful wine with loads of personality. The 2016 vintage (★★★★☆) is richly perfumed and full-bodied, with concentrated, fresh, strongly spicy, slightly gingery flavours and a bone-dry finish.

Vintage	16	15	14	13
WR	7	6	6	6
Drink	19-21	19-21	P	P

DRY $26 V+

Spy Valley Envoy Johnson Vineyard Marlborough Gewürztraminer   ★★★★★

Estate-grown in the lower Waihopai Valley, hand-harvested from mature vines and fermented in small oak vessels, the 2018 vintage (★★★★★) is an arresting wine. Bright, light lemon/green, it is powerful (15 per cent alcohol), bold and youthful, with lovely depth of citrus-fruit, peach, pear and spice flavours, showing notable delicacy, richness and harmony. A sweetish style (68 grams/litre of residual sugar) with a rich, oily texture, it's already irresistible.

Vintage	18	17	16	15	14	13	12
WR	7	6	7	7	6	7	5
Drink	19-25	19-23	19-22	19-20	P	19-20	P

 MED $33 AV

Spy Valley Single Vineyard Marlborough Gewürztraminer   ★★★★☆

Estate-grown in the Waihopai Valley and fermented in tanks and old oak vessels, this wine is consistently impressive. The 2017 vintage (★★★★☆) is perfumed, mouthfilling and soft, with a gentle splash of sweetness (11 grams/litre of residual sugar), rich, peachy, spicy, gingery flavours, showing a touch of complexity, moderate acidity, and excellent delicacy and harmony. Drink now or cellar.

Vintage	17	16	15	14	13
WR	7	6	6	7	6
Drink	19-22	19-22	P	P	P

 MED/DRY $25 V+

Stables Ngatarawa Gewürztraminer   (★★★☆)

Already very open and expressive, the 2018 vintage (★★★☆) of this modestly priced Hawke's Bay wine has a spicy, vaguely honeyed bouquet, leading into a mouthfilling, exuberantly fruity wine with lots of peachy, spicy flavour.

MED/DRY $13 V+

Stonecroft Gimblett Gravels Hawke's Bay Gewürztraminer   ★★★★☆

Certified organic, the 2018 vintage (★★★★) was estate-grown in the Roys Hill Vineyard, hand-picked and tank-fermented. Light gold, it is full-bodied and dryish (6 grams/litre of residual sugar), with strong, ripe, spicy, gingery, vaguely honeyed flavours. A perfumed, sturdy wine, already very expressive, it should be at its best 2020+.

Vintage	18	17
WR	6	5
Drink	19-25	19-24

 MED/DRY $27 AV

Stonecroft Old Vine Gewürztraminer   ★★★★★

The Gewürztraminers from this tiny Hawke's Bay winery are among the finest in the country. This 'Old Vine' wine is made entirely from grapes hand-picked from the original Mere Road plantings of 1983. Certified organic, the 2015 vintage (★★★★★) is a pale gold, mouthfilling (14.5 per cent alcohol), very rich wine, with lush, ripe, peachy, spicy flavours, gentle acidity, and a smooth, gently sweet (20 grams/litre of residual sugar), lasting finish. Drink now or cellar.

Vintage	15	14
WR	6	6
Drink	19-24	19-23

 MED $47 AV

Torlesse Waipara Gewürztraminer   (★★★★)

The 2015 vintage (★★★★), tasted in early 2019, offers great value. Drinking well now, it is fresh and lively, with a bright, light, lemon/green hue and attractively perfumed bouquet. Finely balanced, with plenty of peachy, spicy flavour and an off-dry (14 grams/litre of residual sugar) finish, it offers good, well-priced drinking over the next year or two.

 MED/DRY $18 V+

Universe Hawke's Bay Gewürztraminer   (★★★★☆)

Drinking well in 2019, the 2015 vintage (★★★★☆) is a bright, light yellow/green, richly perfumed wine. Sturdy, with concentrated, peachy, gently spicy and gingery flavours, it's a delicious, off-dry style (8.7 grams/litre of residual sugar), probably at the peak of its powers.

 MED/DRY $28 AV

Villa Maria Private Bin East Coast Gewürztraminer   ★★★★

This regional blend, grown at sites stretching from Auckland to Waipara, typically offers very good value. The 2019 vintage (★★★☆) has a floral, spicy bouquet. Mouthfilling, it has very good depth of peach, pear and spice flavours, slightly sweet (8 grams/litre of residual sugar) and well-rounded. Best drinking mid-2020+.

Vintage	19	18	17	16	15	14	13
WR	6	7	6	7	6	7	7
Drink	19-23	19-22	19-20	P	P	P	P

 MED/DRY $15 V+

Villa Maria Single Vineyard Ihumatao Gewürztraminer   ★★★★★

Estate-grown in South Auckland, the 2017 vintage (★★★★☆) was hand-picked and predominantly (80 per cent) fermented in seasoned French oak puncheons. Mouthfilling and fleshy, it is strongly varietal, with vibrant pear, lychee and spice flavours, showing good complexity, gentle acidity, an off-dry finish (10.8 grams/litre of residual sugar) and an enticingly perfumed bouquet. Drink now or cellar.

Vintage	17
WR	7
Drink	19-23

 MED/DRY $30 AV

Vinoptima Ormond Reserve Gewürztraminer   ★★★★★

The refined 2010 vintage (★★★★★) is from a vineyard founded by Nick Nobilo in Gisborne, devoted exclusively to Gewürztraminer. It was fermented in tanks and large 1200-litre German oak ovals. Dubbed 'Delicatum', it was drinking well in 2019. Bright, light yellow/green, it is fragrant, mouthfilling and well-rounded, with concentrated, peachy, slightly gingery flavours, showing bottle-aged complexity, gentle sweetness and a spicy, very harmonious, lingering finish. (Note: the company was placed in receivership in late 2018 and remaining stocks have been sold at far lower prices than the original $75.)

Vintage	10
WR	7
Drink	19-20

MED $75 –V

Waimea Nelson Gewürztraminer ★★★★

The 2019 vintage (★★★★) is a pale, perfumed wine, fresh and mouthfilling. Strongly varietal, it is already enjoyable, with generous pear, lychee and spice flavours, showing good delicacy, and an off-dry (13 grams/litre of residual sugar) finish. Best drinking mid-2020+.

MED/DRY $22 V+

Waipara Hills Waipara Valley Gewürztraminer (★★★☆)

The 2018 vintage (★★★☆) is highly perfumed. Mouthfilling, it is dryish (7 grams/litre of residual sugar), with plenty of peachy, spicy flavour, in a strongly varietal style, best enjoyed young.

MED/DRY $21 AV

Wairau River Marlborough Gewürztraminer ★★★☆

The 2017 vintage (★★★☆) is a bright, light lemon/green, mouthfilling wine, ripely perfumed, with plenty of peachy, slightly gingery flavour and an off-dry finish.

MED/DRY $20 AV

West Brook Marlborough Gewürztraminer ★★★★

Still on sale, the 2014 vintage (★★★★) was mostly handled in tanks; 9 per cent was fermented in old oak barrels. Maturing gracefully, it is mouthfilling, with ripe peach, lychee and spice flavours, a sliver of sweetness (8 grams/litre of residual sugar), bottle-aged complexity, and a smooth, harmonious finish.

MED/DRY $23 AV

Whitehaven Marlborough Gewürztraminer ★★★★☆

Offering fine value, the 2018 vintage (★★★★☆) has a fragrant, well-spiced bouquet. Bright, light lemon/green, it is weighty and fleshy, with strong, peachy, spicy, slightly gingery flavours and a slightly sweet (11 grams/litre of residual sugar), soft finish. Full of personality, it's delicious young.

MED/DRY $23 V+

Zephyr Marlborough Gewürztraminer ★★★★☆

Well worth cellaring, the 2019 vintage (★★★★★) is a single-vineyard wine, grown at Dillons Point, in the lower Wairau Valley. Richly perfumed, it is full-bodied, with fresh, concentrated, peachy, citrusy, spicy flavours, showing excellent vibrancy and delicacy, a touch of complexity, gentle acidity and a long, off-dry, finely poised finish. A harmonious wine with obvious potential, it should be at its best 2021+.

MED/DRY $28 AV

Grüner Veltliner

Grüner Veltliner, Austria's favourite white-wine variety, is currently stirring up interest in New Zealand, especially in the south. 'Grü-Vee' is a fairly late ripener in Austria, where it yields medium-bodied wines, fruity, crisp and dry, with a spicy, slightly musky aroma. Most are drunk young, but the finest wines, with an Alsace-like substance and perfume, are more age-worthy. Coopers Creek produced New Zealand's first Grüner Veltliner from the 2008 vintage. Of the country's 46 hectares of bearing Grüner Veltliner vines in 2020, most are clustered in Marlborough (31 hectares), with Nelson (8 hectares) a distant second.

Babich Family Estates Headwaters Organic Block Marlborough Grüner Veltliner ★★★☆

Still on sale, the 2016 vintage (★★★★) was estate-grown in the Headwaters Vineyard, near Renwick, in the Wairau Valley. The fermentation, which began in stainless steel tanks, was completed in old oak puncheons. Invitingly aromatic, it's a lively, medium-bodied wine, with vibrant, ripe stone-fruit and spice flavours, a hint of ginger, good intensity, a touch of complexity and a dry (1.8 grams/litre of residual sugar) finish. Certified organic.

Vintage	16	DRY $25 –V
WR	6	
Drink	19-22	

Bannock Brae Marlene's Central Otago Grüner Veltliner ★★★★☆

The impressive 2017 vintage (★★★★★) is highly scented, mouthfilling and dry. Bright, light lemon/green, it has concentrated stone-fruit, peach, ginger and spice flavours, slightly toasty notes, and excellent vigour and complexity.

DRY $25 V+

Blank Canvas Marlborough Grüner Veltliner (★★★★★)

Still on sale and drinking well, the 2013 vintage (★★★★★) was mostly handled in tanks, but 25 per cent of the blend was fermented in oak puncheons (half new). It has a fragrant, spicy, vaguely toasty bouquet. Mouthfilling and crisp, it's a lively, dry style (3.3 grams/litre of residual sugar), with impressive flavour intensity and a lasting finish.

Vintage	13	DRY $26 V+
WR	6	
Drink	19-23	

Forrest Marlborough Grüner Veltliner ★★★★

The 2016 vintage (★★★★) is the last of this label. A single-vineyard wine, it was grown in the Southern Valleys and mostly handled in tanks; 7.5 per cent of the blend was barrel-fermented. Light lemon/green, it is fragrant and medium-bodied, with strong, citrusy, peachy, slightly spicy flavours, showing a touch of bottle-aged complexity, and a finely balanced, basically dry (4.8 grams/litre of residual sugar) finish.

 DRY $25 AV

Hans Herzog Marlborough Grüner Veltliner ★★★★☆

Estate-grown on the north side of the Wairau Valley, the distinctive 2014 vintage (★★★★☆) was fermented and matured for a year in French oak puncheons. A light gold, mouthfilling wine, it has generous, peachy, citrusy flavours, showing good complexity, and a fully dry finish. Ready. Certified organic.

DRY $44 –V

Hunter's Marlborough Grüner Veltliner (★★★★)

The 2018 vintage (★★★★) is a single-vineyard, Awatere Valley wine, hand-picked and fermented and lees-aged for 10 months in seasoned oak puncheons. Bright, light yellow/green, it is mouthfilling and dry (1.8 grams/litre of residual sugar), with strong, peachy, slightly spicy flavours, fresh, balanced acidity and good complexity. It's already very expressive; drink now onwards.

DRY $25 AV

Jules Taylor Marlborough Grüner Veltliner ★★★★☆

Unfolding well, the distinctive 2017 vintage (★★★★☆) is a single-vineyard wine, hand-picked in the Brancott Valley and partly (20 per cent) fermented with indigenous yeasts in French oak casks. Light lemon/green, it is fragrant, full-bodied and bone-dry (0.2 grams/litre of residual sugar), with good intensity of vibrant, peachy, citrusy, slightly spicy flavours, gentle biscuity notes, and a crisp, lingering finish. Drink now or cellar.

Vintage	17	16	15	14
WR	6	6	6	5
Drink	19-21	19-20	P	P

DRY $25 V+

Lime Rock Grüner Veltliner ★★★★☆

Drinking well now, the lively 2017 vintage (★★★★) was estate-grown in Central Hawke's Bay, hand-picked and partly barrel-fermented. Fragrant and vibrantly fruity, it is medium to full-bodied, with ripe-fruit flavours to the fore, slightly spicy notes, a very restrained oak influence, fresh acidity and a finely balanced, dryish finish.

Vintage	17	16
WR	6	7
Drink	19-22	19-21

MED/DRY $28 AV

Lime Rock Single Barrique Ferment Grüner Veltliner (★★★★☆)

Estate-grown in Central Hawke's Bay, the 2017 vintage (★★★★☆) is a rare wine, fermented in a seasoned oak barrel. Gently oaked, it is full-bodied, with good concentration of vibrant, peachy, slightly spicy flavours, and a well-rounded, dry (4.6 grams/litre of residual sugar), harmonious finish.

Vintage	17
WR	7
Drink	19-25

DRY $36 –V

Mount Edward Central Otago Grüner Veltliner   ★★★★☆

Certified organic, the 2016 vintage (★★★★★) was grown in the Morrison Vineyard, at Lowburn. Richly scented, it is mouthfilling and vibrantly fruity, with intense, peachy, citrusy, spicy flavours, showing a distinct touch of complexity, and a finely poised, dryish finish. Well worth cellaring.

MED/DRY $29 AV

Nautilus Marlborough Grüner Veltliner   ★★★★☆

The very youthful 2019 vintage (★★★★☆) is full of promise. Handled without oak, it is fresh and mouthfilling, with strong, peachy, spicy flavours, a vaguely salty streak, balanced acidity, and a dry, lingering finish. Best mid-2020+.

DRY $30 –V

Vintage	19
WR	7
Drink	19-24

Riverby Estate Marlborough Grüner Veltliner   ★★★★

Attractively scented, the 2018 vintage (★★★★☆) was hand-picked at Rapaura, in the Wairau Valley. Bright, light lemon/green, it is full-bodied, with strong, fresh, lively, citrusy flavours, slightly peachy and spicy notes, and a finely balanced, dry (2–3 grams/litre of residual sugar) finish. Best drinking mid-2020+. Maturing well, the 2017 vintage (★★★★) is medium-bodied, with plenty of peachy, spicy flavour, slightly toasty, bottle-aged notes and a dry finish (4 grams/ litre of residual sugar). Drink now or cellar.

DRY $22 V+

Vintage	14	13
WR	6	6
Drink	P	P

Rock Ferry The Corners Vineyard Marlborough Grüner Veltliner   ★★★★☆

Certified organic, the 2017 vintage (★★★★★) is a distinctive, classy wine. Bright, light yellow/ green, it is invitingly fragrant, full-bodied and vibrantly fruity, with deep, citrusy, peachy flavours, a hint of ginger, toasty notes adding complexity and a dry, lasting finish. Full of youthful vigour, it's already drinking well.

DRY $33 –V

Saint Clair Origin Marlborough Grüner Veltliner   ★★★☆

Enjoyable young, the 2017 vintage (★★★☆) is a medium-bodied, dry wine (2.4 grams/litre of residual sugar), grown in the Omaka Valley and made with some use of old oak. It is fragrant, with peachy, spicy, slightly gingery flavours, showing good varietal character, and a well-rounded finish.

DRY $21 AV

Saint Clair Pioneer Block 5 Bull Block Marlborough Grüner Veltliner   ★★★★

The 2015 vintage (★★★★) is a mouthfilling, tightly structured wine, grown in the Omaka Valley. It has generous, peachy, slightly spicy flavours, good freshness and drive through the palate and a dry (2.7 grams/litre of residual sugar), lengthy finish.

DRY $27 –V

Seifried Nelson Grüner Veltliner   ★★★☆

Due for release in early 2020, the 2018 vintage (★★★★) is a good buy. Fragrant and full-bodied, it has plenty of personality, with peachy, slightly spicy flavours, showing excellent vigour and depth, slightly toasty notes, and a dry (2.9 grams/litre of residual sugar) finish.

Vintage	16	15
WR	6	6
Drink	P	P

DRY $18 V+

Soul by Waipara Hills Waipara Valley Grüner Veltliner   (★★★★★)

A very auspicious debut, the classy 2016 vintage (★★★★★) is from first-crop vines in The Mound Vineyard. Hand-picked and lees-aged for eight months, it's an attractively scented, full-bodied wine (14 per cent alcohol), with vibrant, peachy, slightly biscuity flavours, fresh acidity, and a dryish (6 grams/litre of residual sugar), lingering finish. Showing considerable complexity, it's an immaculate, very harmonious wine, likely to reward cellaring.

MED/DRY $28 V+

Waimea Nelson Grüner Veltliner   ★★★★

Grown on the Waimea Plains, the 2018 vintage (★★★★☆) has a real sense of youthful drive. Punchy, crisp and lively, it has strong, citrusy, peachy flavours, hints of spices and ginger, and a dry (3.9 grams/litre of residual sugar) finish. The 2017 vintage (★★★★) tastes ready. Bright yellow/light gold, with a slightly honeyed bouquet, it is medium-bodied, with concentrated, peachy, slightly gingery and spicy flavours, and a dry (3.7 grams/litre of residual sugar), crisp finish.

DRY $23 AV

Wither Hills Cellar Selection Marlborough Grüner Veltliner   (★★★★☆)

The distinctive 2018 vintage (★★★★☆) was estate-grown at Rarangi, near the coast. Light lemon/green, with a highly fragrant, slightly exotic bouquet, it is full-bodied and dryish, with vibrant, youthful, peachy, citrusy, slightly spicy flavours, finely balanced and lingering. Best drinking 2020+.

MED/DRY $25 V+

Marsanne

Cultivated extensively in the northern Rhône Valley of France, where it is often blended with Roussanne, Marsanne yields powerful, sturdy wines with rich pear, spice and nut flavours. Although grown in Victoria since the 1860s, it is extremely rare in New Zealand, with 1 hectare of bearing vines in 2020, clustered mostly in Gisborne.

Coopers Creek SV Gisborne Allison Marsanne ★★★★

The 2015 vintage (★★★☆) is mouthfilling, fleshy and dry, with delicate aromas and fresh, ripe, slightly peachy and spicy flavours, showing good depth.

DRY $24 AV

Hunting Lodge, The, New Zealand Marsanne/Viognier ★★★★

The 2017 vintage (★★★★) was hand-harvested in Gisborne and Hawke's Bay and a small part of the blend (10 per cent) was barrel-fermented. Bright, light lemon/green, it is full-bodied and fleshy, with fresh, ripe stone-fruit flavours to the fore, good vigour, and a tight, dry (2 grams/ litre of residual sugar) finish. Best drinking 2020+.

DRY $25 AV

Trinity Hill Gimblett Gravels Marsanne/Viognier ★★★★☆

The 2016 vintage (★★★★☆) is a weighty, softly seductive blend of Marsanne (51 per cent) and Viognier (49 per cent), hand-picked and fermented and matured for 14 months in seasoned French oak puncheons. It has an inviting floral, ripely scented bouquet. Mouthfilling, it has fresh, peachy, slightly buttery flavours, showing good richness, very gentle acidity, and a smooth (5 grams/litre of residual sugar), persistent finish.

Vintage	16	15	14
WR	6	6	6
Drink	19-21	19-20	19-20

MED/DRY $35 –V

Muscat

Muscat vines grow all over the Mediterranean, but Muscat is rarely seen in New Zealand as a varietal wine, because it ripens late in the season, without the lushness and intensity achieved in warmer regions. Of the country's 25 hectares of bearing Muscat vines in 2020, 22 hectares are clustered in Gisborne. Most of the grapes are used to add an inviting, musky perfume to low-priced sparklings, modelled on the Asti Spumantes of northern Italy.

Brennan Gibbston Central Otago Muscat (★★★★)

Described on the label as a 'playful' wine, the 2018 vintage (★★★★) is clearly varietal, perfumed and full-bodied, with strong, vibrant, peachy, appley flavours, a splash of sweetness and lively acidity. Finely balanced, vigorous and youthful, it should be at its best 2020+.

MED $50 –V

Pegasus Bay Muscat ★★★★★

This rare, estate-grown, North Canterbury wine is made in a sturdy, Alsace style, harvested ultra-ripe (at 28.5 brix in 2016), tank-fermented and matured for six months in old oak puncheons. Retasted in mid-2018, the lovely 2016 vintage (★★★★★) is perfumed and mouthfilling (14 per cent alcohol), with vigorous peach, orange and spice flavours, a gentle splash of sweetness (12 grams/litre of residual sugar) and fresh acidity. The powerful 2017 vintage (★★★★★) was also estate-grown at Waipara and matured for six months in old oak puncheons. Bright, light yellow/green, it is highly perfumed, weighty and fleshy, with concentrated, peachy, slightly spicy flavours, showing a distinct touch of complexity, and a smooth, slightly sweet (18 grams/litre of residual sugar) finish. Already delicious.

Vintage	17	16
WR	7	5
Drink	19-25	19-24

MED $31 AV

Pinot Blanc

If you love Chardonnay, try Pinot Blanc. A white mutation of Pinot Noir, Pinot Blanc is highly regarded in Italy and California for its generous extract and moderate acidity, although in Alsace and Germany the more aromatic Pinot Gris finds greater favour.

With its fullness of weight and subtle aromatics, Pinot Blanc can easily be mistaken for Chardonnay in a blind tasting. The variety is still rare in New Zealand, but in 2020 there will be 10 hectares of bearing vines, mostly in Marlborough and Central Otago.

Blackenbrook Pinot Blanc Nelson (★★★★☆)

The debut 2019 vintage (★★★★☆) is from first-crop vines, estate-grown and hand-picked at Tasman. Handled without oak, it is attractively scented, vibrantly fruity and mouthfilling, with good intensity of peach, pear, lychee and spice flavours, and an off-dry (8 grams/litre of residual sugar) finish. A distinctive, Alsace-style wine, that veers more towards Pinot Gris than Chardonnay in style, it's still extremely youthful; best drinking 2021+.

Vintage	19
WR	7
Drink	19-23

 MED/DRY $28 AV

Gibbston Valley Red Shed Bendigo Single Vineyard
Central Otago Pinot Blanc ★★★★☆

The 2017 vintage (★★★★☆) was estate-grown and hand-picked at Bendigo, fermented with indigenous yeasts in old French barriques, and lees-aged in oak for 10 months. Light lemon/green, it is a mouthfilling wine, with strong, ripe, peachy, citrusy, slightly spicy flavours, subtle and complex, fresh acidity and a tight, bone-dry finish. A youthful wine that could easily be mistaken for Chardonnay, it should be at its best 2020+.

 DRY $39 –V

Greenhough Hope Vineyard Nelson Pinot Blanc ★★★★★

Certified organic, the classy 2016 vintage (★★★★★) was estate-grown, hand-harvested, and fermented and aged for 18 months in seasoned French oak puncheons. Highly refined, it is bright, light yellow/green, with a fresh, fragrant bouquet. Full-bodied, it has rich, vibrant stone-fruit flavours, gently seasoned with oak, moderate acidity and a dry, very harmonious finish.

Vintage	16	15
WR	6	6
Drink	19-21	19-20

DRY $36 AV

Kaimira Estate Brightwater Nelson Pinot Blanc ★★★★

Certified organic, the 2016 vintage (★★★★) was estate-grown and partly wood-aged. Weighty and fleshy, it has strong peachy flavours, showing considerable complexity, a slightly creamy texture and a very harmonious, fully dry finish.

 DRY $25 AV

Mt Rosa Central Otago Pinot Blanc   (★★★★)

Attractively scented, the 2018 vintage (★★★★) was grown at Gibbston and handled in an even split of tanks and old French oak casks. Enjoyable now, but also worth cellaring, it is full-bodied, with vibrantly fruity, pear-like flavours, showing a touch of complexity and very good depth, and a dry (1–2 grams/litre of residual sugar) finish. Best drinking mid-2020+.

DRY $40 –V

Nevis Bluff Merrill's Block Central Otago Pinot Blanc   ★★★★

The full-bodied 2015 vintage (★★★★) was grown at Pisa and fermented and matured in tanks, with no use of oak. Weighty, with delicate, citrusy, appley flavours, hints of pears and spices, and a dry, well-rounded finish, it's a finely textured wine, drinking well now.

DRY $35 –V

Rock Ferry Orchard Vineyard Marlborough Pinot Blanc   ★★★★☆

Full of personality, the powerful 2015 vintage (★★★★★) is a single-vineyard wine, hand-picked at Rapaura, in the Wairau Valley, and fermented in a mix of tanks (80 per cent) and a seasoned oak puncheon (20 per cent). Light lemon/green, it is weighty (14.5 per cent alcohol), fleshy and soft, with rich, ripe stone-fruit flavours to the fore, slightly toasty notes adding complexity, gentle acidity and a fully dry (1.3 grams/litre of residual sugar), well-rounded finish. Best drinking 2020+. Certified organic.

DRY $30 –V

Tohu Single Vineyard Whenua Awa
Upper Awatere Marlborough Pinot Blanc   (★★★★☆)

A drink-now or cellaring proposition, the 2018 vintage (★★★★☆) is a vibrantly fruity, partly barrel-fermented wine. Bright, light lemon/green, with a fragrant, creamy bouquet, it is full-bodied and dry, with fresh, peachy, slightly toasty flavours, balanced acidity and excellent depth.

DRY $36 –V

Pinot Gris

New Zealanders' love affair with Pinot Gris shows no signs of abating, and the wines are also starting to win an international reputation. The variety is spreading like wildfire – from 130 hectares of bearing vines in 2000 to 2519 hectares in 2020 – and accounts for 6.5 per cent of the total producing vineyard area. New Zealand's third most extensively planted white-wine variety, with plantings almost quadruple those of Riesling, Pinot Gris is trailing only Sauvignon Blanc and Chardonnay.

A mutation of Pinot Noir, Pinot Gris has skin colours ranging from blue-grey to reddish-pink, sturdy extract and a fairly subtle, spicy aroma. It is not a difficult variety to cultivate, adapting well to most soils, and ripens with fairly low acidity to high sugar levels. In Alsace, the best Pinot Gris are matured in large casks, but the wood is old, so as not to interfere with the grape's subtle flavour.

What does Pinot Gris taste like? Imagine a wine that couples the satisfying weight and roundness of Chardonnay with some of the aromatic spiciness of Gewürztraminer. A popular and versatile wine, Pinot Gris is well worth getting to know.

In terms of style and quality, however, New Zealand Pinot Gris vary widely. Many of the wines lack the enticing perfume, mouthfilling body, flavour richness and softness of the benchmark wines from Alsace. These lesser wines, typically made from heavily cropped vines, are much leaner and crisper – more in the tradition of cheap Italian Pinot Grigio.

Popular in Germany, Alsace and Italy, Pinot Gris is now playing an important role here too. Well over half of the country's plantings are concentrated in Marlborough (45 per cent) and Hawke's Bay (19 per cent), but there are also significant pockets of Pinot Gris in Gisborne, Otago, Canterbury, Nelson, Wairarapa and Auckland.

12,000 Miles Wairarapa Pinot Gris ★★★☆

From Gladstone Vineyard, the 2018 vintage (★★★☆) was grown in the northern Wairarapa, briefly lees-aged and handled without oak. Attractively scented, it is medium to full-bodied, vibrantly fruity and smooth, with plenty of peachy, slightly spicy flavour, finely balanced for early drinking.

MED/DRY $20 AV

Akarua Bannockburn Central Otago Pinot Gris ★★★★

Full of youthful vigour, the 2018 vintage (★★★★☆) is a complex, basically dry style. Hand-picked and partly (27 per cent) barrel-fermented, it is attractively scented, with mouthfilling body, good intensity of vibrant peach, pear and lychee flavours, showing a distinct touch of complexity, and a fractionally off-dry (5.4 grams/litre of residual sugar) finish. Best drinking 2020+.

MED/DRY $29 –V

Akarua Rua Central Otago Pinot Gris ★★★☆

Hand-harvested at Bannockburn, the 2018 vintage (★★★★) is a basically dry style (5 grams/litre of residual sugar). Bright, light lemon/green, it is sturdy (14.5 per cent alcohol), fragrant and fresh, with very good depth of stone-fruit and pear flavours, full of youthful vigour. Best drinking 2020+.

MED/DRY $24 –V

Allan Scott Marlborough Pinot Gris   ★★★★

Weighty and vibrant, with good depth, the 2018 vintage (★★★★) is delicious young. A full-bodied, Alsace-style wine, it has fresh, strong, pear-like aromas and flavours, hints of peaches and spices, and an off-dry (7 grams/litre of residual sugar) finish. Fine value.

MED/DRY $18 V+

Amisfield Central Otago Pinot Gris   ★★★★

Showing good personality, the 2017 vintage (★★★★☆) was estate-grown and hand-harvested at Pisa, in the Cromwell Basin, and mostly fermented and lees-aged in tanks; 25 per cent of the blend was fermented with indigenous yeasts in large and small seasoned French oak barrels. Full-bodied, it's a medium-dry style (8.7 grams/litre of residual sugar), with generous, ripe, peachy, slightly spicy flavours, showing very good complexity, and a tightly structured, lingering finish.

Vintage	17
WR	5
Drink	19-20

MED/DRY $30 –V

Anchorage Lighter Alcohol Nelson Pinot Gris   (★★★)

Looking for a low-alcohol style of Pinot Gris? The 2018 vintage (★★★) has a fresh, aromatic bouquet, leading into a light (9.5 per cent alcohol) and lively wine, with pear, apple and peach flavours, slightly sweet (10 grams/litre of residual sugar) and crisp. Enjoyable young.

MED/DRY $18 AV

Anna's Way Marlborough Pinot Gris   ★★★☆

Still on sale, the freshly scented 2017 vintage (★★★☆) is a very easy-drinking, medium to full-bodied, dry wine (1.8 grams/litre of residual sugar), with peach, pear and spice flavours, showing good delicacy and depth. The 2018 vintage (★★★☆) is lively and mouthfilling, with satisfying depth of fresh peachy, citrusy, slightly spicy flavours and a smooth, dry (2.1 grams/litre of residual sugar) finish. (From Awatere River Wine Co.)

DRY $17 V+

Archangel Central Otago Pinot Gris   ★★★★

The attractively scented 2018 vintage (★★★★) is a full-bodied, off-dry style. It has pear and lychee aromas and flavours, showing excellent delicacy and harmony, hints of lemons, apples and spices, and obvious potential.

MED/DRY $25 AV

Ash Ridge Hawke's Bay Estate Pinot Gris   ★★★☆

The 2017 vintage (★★★★) is a medium to full-bodied wine, mostly (70 per cent) barrel-fermented. It is finely balanced, with fresh, ripe, peachy, slightly spicy flavours, a sliver of sweetness (5 grams/litre of residual sugar), and very good depth.

MED/DRY $20 AV

Askerne Hawke's Bay Pinot Gris ★★★★

Still unfolding, the 2018 vintage (★★★★) is a pale yellow wine with a fragrant, gently spicy bouquet. Fresh and full-bodied, it has strong, peachy, slightly spicy and gingery flavours, showing a touch of complexity, balanced acidity and a dryish finish. Best drinking mid-2020+.

 MED/DRY $23 AV

Astrolabe Kekerengu Coast Pinot Gris ★★★★

The 2018 vintage (★★★★) is a single-vineyard Marlborough wine, hand-picked at Kekerengu. Full of youthful vigour, it is pale lemon/green, very fresh and vibrant, with generous, peachy, slightly spicy flavours, dry (2.5 grams/litre of residual sugar) and smooth. Still on sale, the 2016 vintage (★★★★) is still very lively, with strong peach, pear and spice flavours, fresh and bone-dry.

 DRY $27 –V

Astrolabe Marlborough Pinot Gris ★★★★

The 2018 vintage (★★★★) was grown mostly (74 per cent) in the Awatere Valley, but also in the Wairau Valley and at Kekerengu. Mostly hand-picked, it is fragrant and fresh, with strong pear-like flavours, hints of peaches and spices, and a dry (3 grams/litre of residual sugar) finish. The 2017 vintage (★★★★), still on sale, is a 50:50 blend of fruit from the Southern Valleys and Awatere Valley. Drinking well now, it has good intensity of vibrant pear and spice flavours, dry (3.9 grams/litre of residual sugar) and lingering.

Vintage	18	17
WR	6	6
Drink	19-23	19-22

 DRY $25 AV

Ata Rangi Lismore Pinot Gris ★★★★☆

Grown in the Lismore Vineyard in Martinborough, 400 metres from the Ata Rangi winery, the impressive 2018 vintage (★★★★★) was handled in old, large oak barrels. Bright, light lemon/green, it is highly fragrant and mouthfilling, with excellent depth of vibrant pear and spice flavours, showing good complexity, and a very harmonious, dry (4.5 grams/litre of residual sugar) finish. A distinctive wine with good aging potential, it should be at its best mid-2020+.

Vintage	18
WR	7
Drink	19-25

 DRY $28 AV

Awatere River by Louis Vavasour Marlborough Pinot Gris ★★★★

The 2018 vintage (★★★★) is already drinking well. Bright, light lemon/green, it is fragrant and fleshy, with very good depth of peachy, spicy, slightly gingery flavours, fresh and dry (3.1 grams/litre of residual sugar).

Vintage	18	17	16	15
WR	6	7	6	7
Drink	19-23	19-22	19-21	19-20

 DRY $20 V+

Babich Black Label Marlborough Pinot Gris   ★★★★

Sold principally in restaurants, the 2017 vintage (★★★★) was mostly handled in tanks; 20 per cent of the blend was fermented in old French oak casks. A full-bodied, age-worthy wine, it has good concentration of ripe stone-fruit flavours, considerable complexity, balanced acidity, and a dry (3.3 grams/litre of residual sugar) finish.

Vintage	17
WR	7
Drink	19-23

 DRY $25 AV

Babich Family Estates Headwaters Organic Marlborough Pinot Gris   (★★★☆)

The 2017 vintage (★★★☆) was estate-grown near Renwick, in the Wairau Valley, fermented with indigenous yeasts and lees-aged for seven months. A fragrant, medium-bodied wine, it is peachy and slightly spicy, with fresh acidity, a touch of complexity, and a fully dry (0.8 grams/litre of residual sugar) finish. Certified organic.

Vintage	17
WR	6
Drink	19-23

DRY $25 –V

Babich Marlborough Pinot Gris   ★★★★

The 2017 vintage (★★★★) was partly (5 per cent) barrel-fermented and made in a dry style (3.4 grams/litre of residual sugar). Fragrant and fleshy, it's an Alsace-style wine, mouthfilling, with generous, peachy, slightly spicy, vaguely honeyed flavours, and a very harmonious, well-rounded finish. Delicious drinking now onwards.

Vintage	18	17
WR	6	6
Drink	19-23	19-22

DRY $22 V+

Bellbird Spring Waipara Valley Block Eight Pinot Gris   ★★★★

Still on sale, the 2015 vintage (★★★★) is a medium style, barrel-matured for five months. Drinking well in 2019, it is a straw-hued, full-bodied wine, with generous, peachy, slightly spicy and gingery flavours, showing good complexity, and a gently sweet, well-rounded finish. Ready.

 MED $32 –V

Bellbird Spring Waipara Valley Dry Pinot Gris   ★★★★

The 2017 vintage (★★★☆) was fermented in old oak barrels. Light lemon/green, it is a distinctive, medium to full-bodied wine with a restrained bouquet, peachy, slightly yeasty and nutty flavours, showing considerable complexity, and a dry finish.

 DRY $32 –V

Black Cottage Marlborough Pinot Gris   ★★★☆

From Two Rivers, the 2018 vintage (★★★☆) is an instantly appealing, freshly scented wine with mouthfilling body and good depth of pear, peach and spice flavours, dryish and lively.

 DRY $18 V+

Black Stilt Waitaki Valley North Otago Pinot Gris   (★★★☆)

Still on sale and drinking well now, the 2016 vintage (★★★☆) was matured on its yeast lees for nine months. Mouthfilling and smooth, it has very good depth of peachy, gently spicy flavours, a slightly creamy texture and a fully dry finish.

DRY $22 AV

Blackenbrook Nelson Pinot Gris   ★★★★

Estate-grown and hand-harvested from 18-year-old vines, the powerful 2019 vintage (★★★★☆) was handled in a mix of tanks (92 per cent) and old oak barrels (8 per cent). Bright, light lemon/green, it is very youthful, with strong yet delicate peach, pear, lychee and spice flavours, showing a distinct touch of complexity, slight sweetness (9 grams/litre of residual sugar) balanced by fresh acidity, and an attractively scented bouquet. Best drinking 2021+.

Vintage	19	18
WR	7	5
Drink	19-23	19-22

MED/DRY $25 AV

Boatshed Bay Marlborough Pinot Gris   ★★★★

Delicious drinking from now onwards, the 2018 vintage (★★★★) is a fleshy, medium-dry style (7.6 grams/litre of residual sugar) from Grove Mill. Bright, light lemon/green, it is mouthfilling and vibrantly fruity, with strongly varietal pear and peach flavours, showing excellent delicacy and depth.

$18 V+

Bohemian The Poet Hawke's Bay Pinot Gris   (★★★★)

Showing good personality, the 2017 vintage (★★★★) was produced by Collaboration Wines for Dhall & Nash, a wine distributor. Fermented in seasoned oak barrels, it is weighty, with fresh, strong peach, pear and spice flavours, balanced acidity and a dry (4–5 grams/litre of residual sugar), harmonious finish.

MED/DRY $22 V+

Brancott Estate Flight Marlborough Pinot Gris   ★★☆

This very easy-drinking, low-alcohol wine is harvested early and made in a slightly sweet style. The freshly scented 2017 vintage (★★☆) is light-bodied (9 per cent alcohol), with gentle pear-like flavours, a hint of lychees, crisp acidity, and a smooth finish.

MED $14 AV

Brancott Estate Identity Awatere Valley Marlborough Pinot Gris   (★★★★)

The Identity range is designed to celebrate Marlborough's sub-regional wine styles. The 'generous, optimistic' 2018 vintage (★★★★) is drinking well young, with mouthfilling body, vibrant pear and spice flavours, gentle sweetness (8.8 grams/litre of residual sugar), and excellent delicacy and length.

MED/DRY $22 V+

Brancott Estate Letter Series 'F' Marlborough Pinot Gris

The 2016 vintage (★★★★☆) is a medium-dry style (12 grams/litre of residual sugar). Estate-grown in the Brancott Vineyard, it was mostly hand-harvested, and fermented in a large, 10,000-litre oak cuve (85 per cent) and French oak puncheons (15 per cent). Mouthfilling and soft, it is vibrantly fruity, with an array of ripe peach, pear, lychee and spice flavours, showing excellent freshness, delicacy and depth.

MED/DRY $33 –V

Brennan Gibbston Central Otago Pinot Grigio

Estate-grown, the 2018 vintage (★★★★) is a freshly aromatic wine, full-bodied, crisp and lively, with strong peach, pear and spice flavours, appetising acidity and a dryish, finely balanced finish. Drink now or cellar.

DRY $27 –V

Brennan Gibbston Central Otago Pinot Gris

Already very enjoyable, the 2018 vintage (★★★★) is full-bodied, with strong stone-fruit and spice flavours, fresh, balanced acidity, a touch of oak-derived complexity and an off-dry finish. Best drinking mid-2020+.

MED/DRY $35 –V

Brick Bay Matakana Pinot Gris ★★★★

At its best, this estate-grown wine is weighty, rich and rounded. Hand-harvested and lees-aged, it is made in an off-dry style. The 2018 vintage (★★★☆) is a vibrant, medium-bodied wine, with strong, pear-like flavours, hints of lemons and apples, slight sweetness balanced by lively acidity, and a freshly scented bouquet.

MED/DRY $36 –V

Brightwater Vineyards Nelson Pinot Gris ★★★★

The 2018 vintage (★★★★) is a fragrant, medium to full-bodied wine, made in an off-dry style (15 grams/litre of residual sugar). Bright, light lemon/green, it is finely poised, with strong peach, pear and spice flavours, gentle acidity and a smooth finish. Already delicious.

Vintage	18	17	16	15	14	13
WR	6	6	6	7	6	6
Drink	19-21	19-20	P	P	P	P

MED $22 V+

Bronte Nelson Pinot Gris ★★★★

Rimu Grove's second-tier label. Hand-harvested in the Moutere hills and mostly handled in tanks (10 per cent oak-aged), the 2018 vintage (★★★★) is an off-dry style (8 grams/litre of residual sugar), freshly scented, mouthfilling and smooth, with a distinct touch of complexity. Already drinking well, with strong peach, pear and spice flavours, showing excellent delicacy and harmony, it should be at its best 2020+.

Vintage	18	17
WR	6	6
Drink	19-24	19-23

MED/DRY $25 AV

Brookfields Robertson Hawke's Bay Pinot Gris   ★★★★

This label originated in the early 1980s. Handled without oak, the 2018 vintage (★★★★) was tank-fermented and lees-aged. Full-bodied and dry (4 grams/litre of residual sugar), with a light touch of tannin, it has good concentration of fresh, ripe stone-fruit and spice flavours, youthful and finely balanced. Best drinking mid-2020+.

Vintage	18
WR	7
Drink	19-25

 DRY $20 V+

Carrick Bannockburn Central Otago Pinot Gris   ★★★★

Certified organic, the 2017 vintage (★★★★) was estate-grown and partly handled in tanks; 60 per cent of the blend was fermented with indigenous yeasts and lees-aged for eight months in old French oak barriques. Bright, light lemon/green, it is a full-bodied wine with lively, peachy, slightly spicy flavours, showing a touch of complexity, and a dry, smooth, lingering finish.

 DRY $27 –V

Catalina Sounds Marlborough Pinot Gris   ★★★★

Grown at two sites in the Waihopai Valley, the stylish 2018 vintage (★★★★☆) was mostly estate-grown (in the Sound of White vineyard), and partly (15 per cent) barrel-fermented. Very pale straw, it is ripely scented, mouthfilling and dry, with concentrated, peachy, citrusy, spicy flavours, showing good complexity, a slightly oily texture and a lingering finish. Best drinking 2020+.

 DRY $25 AV

Ceres Swansong Bannockburn Central Otago Pinot Gris   ★★★★

Invitingly scented, the 2018 vintage (★★★★☆) is a single-vineyard wine, full-bodied and fleshy. It has concentrated, ripe stone-fruit flavours, with gentle spicy notes and an off-dry, creamy-textured finish. Drink now or cellar.

 MED/DRY $28 –V

Chard Farm Sur Lie Central Otago Pinot Gris   ★★★★☆

Delicious young, the 2017 vintage (★★★★☆) of this consistently impressive wine was hand-harvested in the Cromwell Basin. Full-bodied, it is vibrant and sweet-fruited, with generous, ripe peach, pear and spice flavours, balanced acidity, and a dry, well-rounded finish.

 DRY $27 AV

Church Road Hawke's Bay Pinot Gris   ★★★★

Estate-grown in Pernod Ricard NZ's relatively cool, elevated, inland site at Matapiro, this is a consistently impressive and enjoyable, weighty, Alsace-style wine, bargain-priced. Delicious from the start, the 2018 vintage (★★★★☆) has a fragrant, peachy, spicy bouquet. Sturdy, it has strong, vibrant peach, apricot and spice flavours, off-dry, rounded and very harmonious. Forward in its appeal, it's a drink-now or cellaring proposition. Great value.

MED $19 V+

Clark Estate Blackbirch Marlborough Pinot Gris   (★★★★)

The 2018 vintage (★★★★) is a lively, youthful, Awatere Valley wine. Invitingly scented, it is mouthfilling, with ripe stone-fruit flavours, showing good vigour and intensity, fresh acidity and a dryish (5 grams/litre of residual sugar), finely balanced finish. Best drinking 2020+.

 MED/DRY $19 V+

Clericus Wild Pinot Gris   (★★★★☆)

Showing plenty of personality, the 2016 vintage (★★★★☆) of this Awatere Valley wine was made with use of indigenous yeasts and oak. Light lemon/green, it is medium to full-bodied, with concentrated stone-fruit and spice flavours, hints of ginger and honey, good complexity, and a gently sweet (15 grams/litre of residual sugar), finely balanced finish. (From Clark Estate.)

 MED $29 AV

Coopers Creek Kumeu Pinot Gris   ★★★

The 2017 vintage (★★★☆) of this West Auckland wine is less aromatic than southern Pinot Gris, but offers plenty of body and flavour. Fleshy, it has fresh, generous stone-fruit flavours, with hints of honey and spice, and a tight, dryish finish. Priced right.

 MED/DRY $18 AV

Coopers Creek Select Vineyards The Pointer Marlborough Pinot Gris   ★★★★

The Alsace-style 2017 vintage (★★★★) is full-bodied and generous. Pale straw, it is a strongly varietal wine, with very good weight and depth of peachy, slightly spicy flavours and a slightly sweet, rounded, very harmonious finish.

 MED/DRY $23 AV

Crater Rim, The, Waipara Valley Pinot Gris   ★★★★

The 2018 vintage (★★★★) is a sturdy, single-vineyard wine, fermented with indigenous yeasts in seasoned French oak barriques. Light gold, it is mouthfilling and slightly sweet, with a touch of tannin, strong, peachy, spicy flavours, oak complexity, and plenty of drink-young appeal.

 MED/DRY $22 V+

Dancing Petrel Northland Pinot Gris   (★★★★)

Grown on Paewhenua Island, in the Far North, the 2019 vintage (★★★★) was hand-picked and tank-fermented. It has fresh, gently spicy aromas, leading into a mouthfilling, lively wine with strong, youthful pear, lychee and spice flavours, good weight and a finely textured, dryish finish. Best drinking mid-2020+.

 DRY $25 AV

Dashwood by Vavasour New Zealand Pinot Gris   ★★★☆

This is a consistently good buy. The 2019 vintage (★★★☆) doesn't claim on the label to be of Marlborough origin. Full-bodied, fresh and vibrantly fruity, it has plenty of ripe, peachy, slightly spicy flavour and a dryish (5.3 grams/litre of residual sugar) finish.

MED/DRY $16 V+

Delta Marlborough Pinot Gris   ★★★☆

Enjoyable young, the 2018 vintage (★★★☆) is an attractively scented wine, handled entirely in tanks. Finely balanced, it is medium-bodied, with fresh, vibrant, citrusy, peachy flavours, hints of pears and spices, and a slightly off-dry (5.5 grams/litre of residual sugar) finish.

MED/DRY $20 AV

Devil's Staircase Central Otago Pinot Gris   ★★★☆

From Rockburn, the 2018 vintage (★★★★) is drinking well in its youth. Fleshy and mouthfilling, it has very good depth of fresh, ripe stone-fruit and spice flavours, a hint of ginger, and a medium-dry (14 grams/litre of residual sugar), smooth finish.

MED/DRY $26 –V

Domain Road Defiance Bannockburn Central Otago Pinot Gris   (★★★★)

Attractively scented and softly mouthfilling, the 2018 vintage (★★★★) of this single-vineyard wine was mostly handled in tanks; 14 per cent of the blend was fermented in seasoned French oak barriques. Full-bodied, with fresh, generous peach, pear and spice flavours, it is a vividly varietal, off-dry style (11 grams/litre of residual sugar), with a distinct touch of complexity and very good delicacy, depth and harmony.

Vintage	18
WR	6
Drink	19-21

MED/DRY $26 –V

Dragon Bones Waitaki Valley North Otago Pinot Gris   ★★★★☆

The 2016 vintage (★★★★) from Lone Hill Vineyards is still fresh and youthful. Bright, light lemon/green, it is fragrant and weighty, with fresh, vigorous stone-fruit and spice flavours, gentle sweetness (18 grams/litre of residual sugar) and finely balanced acidity. It should be long-lived; best drinking 2020+.

MED $21 V+

Dry River Martinborough Pinot Gris   ★★★★★

From the first vintage in 1986, for many years Dry River towered over other New Zealand Pinot Gris, by virtue of its exceptional body, flavour richness and longevity. A sturdy Martinborough wine, it has peachy, spicy characters that can develop great subtlety and richness with maturity (at around five years old for top vintages, which also hold well for a decade). It is grown in the estate and nearby Craighall vineyards, where the majority of the vines are over 25 years old. In the past, it was not wood-aged, but the 2017 was 15 per cent barrel-fermented and 30 per cent of the 2018 vintage (★★★★★) spent 10 months in old oak hogsheads. Bright, light yellow/green, it is fleshy and well-rounded, with mouthfilling body, gentle sweetness (17 grams/litre of residual sugar) and rich, peachy, slightly spicy flavours. A soft, very harmonious wine with excellent complexity, it's already delicious.

Vintage	18	17	16	15	14	13	12	11	10
WR	7	7	7	7	7	6	7	7	7
Drink	19-30	19-29	19-28	19-27	19-26	19-25	19-22	19-21	19-20

MED $60 AV

Dunnolly North Canterbury Pinot Gris (★★★★)

Offering fine value, the 2017 vintage (★★★★) was grown at three sites and matured on its yeast lees. Light yellow/green, it is mouthfilling, fresh and vibrant, with peachy, spicy flavours, showing a touch of complexity and good richness, and a basically dry (4.8 grams/litre of residual sugar) finish.

DRY $19 V+

Durvillea Marlborough Pinot Gris ★★★☆

Bargain-priced, the 2019 vintage (★★★☆) was mostly (62 per cent) grown in the Awatere Valley, but also in the Southern Valleys and at Kekerengu. Pale and fragrant, it is full-bodied, with good depth of pear and peach flavours, gentle spicy notes, and a dry (3.9 grams/litre of residual sugar), smooth finish. (From Astrolabe.)

Vintage	19
WR	7
Drink	19-22

DRY $15 V+

Eight Ranges Central Otago Pinot Gris (★★★☆)

The tightly structured 2017 vintage (★★★☆) is a single-vineyard wine, hand-picked at Alexandra and tank-fermented. Freshly scented, it has lively pear and spice flavours, showing very good delicacy, firm acid spine and a dryish (6.5 grams/litre of residual sugar) finish. (From Tussock Ridge.)

MED/DRY $27 –V

Elder, The, Martinborough Pinot Gris ★★★★☆

The classy, distinctive 2016 vintage (★★★★★) is a single-vineyard wine, tank-fermented with indigenous yeasts and lees-aged for four months in old oak barrels. Light lemon/green, it is mouthfilling, refined and sweet-fruited, with a fragrant bouquet and rich, vibrant flavours, showing lovely delicacy, vigour and harmony. Slightly Chardonnay-like, with a dry finish (2 grams/litre of residual sugar), it's well worth cellaring.

Vintage	16	15	14	13
WR	7	6	7	6
Drink	19-21	19-20	19-20	P

DRY $42 –V

Elephant Hill Hawke's Bay Pinot Gris ★★★★

The 2017 vintage (★★★★) is a dry style (3 grams/litre of residual sugar). Estate-grown at Te Awanga and lees-stirred in tanks, it is fragrant and full-bodied, with good intensity of vibrant pear, lychee and spice flavours, threaded with fresh acidity, and a lingering finish.

DRY $28 –V

Eradus Awatere Valley Marlborough Pinot Gris

The 2017 vintage (★★★★) is bargain-priced. Fragrant and full-bodied, it was mostly tank-fermented, with a small percentage of oak handling. Bright, light lemon/green, it has generous, ripe, citrusy, peachy, slightly spicy flavours and a well-rounded, dry (1.6 grams/litre of residual sugar) finish.

DRY $17 V+

Esk Valley Hawke's Bay Pinot Gris

Showing strong personality, the 2019 vintage (★★★★☆) was grown at Maraekakaho and partly barrel-fermented. Invitingly scented, it is full-bodied, with strong, vibrant, pear-like flavours, hints of lychees and spices, a touch of complexity, balanced acidity and a dryish, lingering finish. Enjoyable from the start, it offers excellent value.

Vintage	19	18	17
WR	7	6	6
Drink	19-24	19-23	19-20

MED/DRY $20 V+

Falconhead Hawke's Bay Pinot Gris ★★★

The 2019 vintage (★★★) is fresh and lively, with clear-cut varietal characters. Full-bodied, it's an easy-drinking wine with good depth of pear and spice flavours and a basically dry (4 grams/litre of residual sugar) finish. (From The Wine Portfolio.)

Vintage	14
WR	6
Drink	P

DRY $17 AV

Flaxmore Moutere Nelson Pinot Gris (★★★☆)

Estate-grown and hand-picked in the Moutere hills, the 2018 vintage (★★★☆) is a pale, very fresh and lively wine. Medium-bodied, it has youthful pear and spice flavours, showing good delicacy and vibrancy, and a dryish finish. Best drinking mid-2020+.

MED/DRY $24 –V

Flaxmore Moutere Pinot Gris (★★★☆)

Estate-grown and hand-picked in the Moutere hills, the 2018 vintage (★★★☆) is a pale, very fresh and lively, medium-bodied wine, with pear and spice flavours, showing good delicacy and vigour. Still very youthful, it should be at its best mid-2020+.

MED/DRY $24 –V

Forbidden Vines by Babich Marlborough Pinot Gris (★★★)

Offering very easy drinking, the 2017 vintage (★★★) is fresh and lively, with good body and depth of citrusy, slightly spicy flavours and a smooth, off-dry (6 grams/litre of residual sugar) finish. Priced sharply.

MED/DRY $15 V+

Forrest Marlborough Pinot Gris   ★★★☆

Enjoyable young, the 2018 vintage (★★★☆) was mostly tank-fermented; 5 per cent of the blend was handled in old oak casks. Bright, light lemon/green, it is mouthfilling, with fresh, peachy, citrusy, slightly spicy flavours, showing very good depth, and an off-dry (5.9 grams/litre of residual sugar) finish.

MED/DRY $22 AV

Framingham Marlborough Pinot Gris   ★★★★☆

The full-bodied, richly scented 2018 vintage (★★★★☆) was hand-harvested in the Wairau Valley and mostly (65 per cent) fermented in old oak barriques and acacia puncheons. Bright, light yellow/green, it is already open and expressive, with ripe, peachy, vaguely honeyed flavours, slight sweetness (9.8 grams/litre of residual sugar), a slightly oily texture, and excellent richness and texture.

MED/DRY $25 V+

Gale Force Marlborough Pinot Gris   (★★☆)

The low-priced 2017 vintage (★★☆) was grown in the Awatere Valley. Light and crisp, with citrusy aromas, it has lemony, slightly appley flavours and a fully dry (0.6 grams/litre of residual sugar) finish. Verging on three stars, it offers fine value. (From Clark Estate.)

DRY $12 V+

Georges Road Selection Waipara Pinot Gris   ★★★★★

Full of personality, the 2017 vintage (★★★★★) was estate-grown, hand-picked and fermented with indigenous yeasts in seasoned oak barrels. Light yellow/green, it is mouthfilling, with stone-fruit and spice flavours, a vague hint of honey, and excellent complexity and richness. Made in a dry style (4 grams/litre of residual sugar), it's drinking well now.

DRY $26 V+

Gibbston Valley GV Collection Central Otago Pinot Gris   ★★★★

Hand-picked at Bendigo and Lowburn, the 2017 vintage (★★★★) was handled entirely in tanks and made in a dry style (4 grams/litre of residual sugar). Light lemon/green, it is freshly scented, mouthfilling and vibrant, with strong pear and lychee flavours, showing exellent delicacy and harmony.

DRY $28 –V

Gibbston Valley La Dulcinée Bendigo Single Vineyard Pinot Gris   ★★★★☆

Estate-grown and hand-picked at over 350 metres above sea level, in La Dulcinée Vineyard at Bendigo, in Central Otago, the 2016 vintage (★★★★☆) was fermented and lees-aged for a year in stainless steel barriques (85 per cent) and French acacia puncheons (15 per cent). Bright, light lemon/green, it is mouthfilling, with concentrated, vibrant peach and pear flavours, showing good complexity, fresh acidity and a dryish (5 grams/litre of residual sugar), finely poised finish. Certified organic.

MED/DRY $39 –V

Gibbston Valley School House Central Otago Pinot Gris   (★★★★★)

The refined 2017 vintage (★★★★★) was hand-picked at Bendigo, 350 to 400 metres above sea level, and fermented and lees-aged for a year in stainless steel barriques (80 per cent) and French acacia puncheons (20 per cent). A very elegant, youthful wine, it is mouthfilling, with concentrated, vibrant, citrusy, peachy flavours, showing very good complexity, and a long, basically dry (4.6 grams/litre of residual sugar) finish. Certified organic. Best drinking 2020+.

DRY $39 AV

Giesen New Zealand Pinot Gris   ★★★☆

From vineyards in Marlborough (mostly), Waipara and Hawke's Bay, the 2017 vintage (★★★☆) is an attractively scented, medium-bodied wine, with strong, vibrant pear and lychee flavours, a sliver of sweetness (5.3 grams/litre of residual sugar) and balanced acidity. Great value.

MED/DRY $15 V+

Gladstone Vineyard Pinot Gris   ★★★★☆

The 2018 vintage (★★★★) was estate-grown in the northern Wairarapa and handled with some fermentation on skins, barrel fermentation and lees-aging. Already very expressive, it is mouthfilling and smooth, with generous, peachy, spicy, slightly gingery flavours, showing some complexity, and a dry finish.

DRY $27 AV

Greyrock Hawke's Bay Pinot Gris   (★★☆)

The easy-drinking 2018 vintage (★★☆) is pale, light and lively, in a medium-bodied style with fresh peach, pear and spice flavours, and an off-dry (6.5 grams/litre of residual sugar) finish. (From Sileni.)

MED/DRY $19 –V

Greyrock Te Koru Hawke's Bay Pinot Gris   (★★★☆)

Fresh and lively, the pale 2019 vintage (★★★☆) is full-bodied, with good vigour and depth of peach, pear and spice flavours, dry (4.6 grams/litre of residual sugar) and harmonious. (From Sileni.)

DRY $20 AV

Greystone Sand Dollar Waipara Pinot Gris   ★★★★☆

Certified organic, the fragrant, very lively 2018 vintage (★★★★☆) was mostly tank-fermented, with a small portion handled in old oak barrels. Full-bodied, with rich peach, pear and lychee flavours, showing good complexity, and a long, dry (3.9 grams/litre of residual sugar), gently spicy finish, it shows obvious potential; best drinking 2021+.

DRY $28 AV

Greystone Waipara Valley North Canterbury Pinot Gris   ★★★★★

At its best, this is one of the finest Pinot Gris in the country. Estate-grown, it is mostly handled in tanks; a small portion of the blend (5 per cent in 2018) is fermented with indigenous yeasts in old French oak casks. Already delicious, the 2018 vintage (★★★★★) is a pale straw, sturdy

(14.5 per cent alcohol), powerful wine, with highly concentrated stone-fruit flavours, a vague hint of honey, and excellent complexity and harmony. Made in a medium-dry style (12 grams/litre of residual sugar), it's certified organic.

DRY $29 V+

Greywacke Marlborough Pinot Gris ★★★★★

Grown principally in the Southern Valleys, but also at Rapaura, the 2017 vintage (★★★★★) was fermented in a mix of old oak barrels and tanks, blended, and then lees-aged for six months in old barrels. Richly scented, it is a very Alsace-style wine, sturdy and rich, with deep peach, pear and spice flavours, showing good complexity, and an off-dry (10 grams/litre of residual sugar), very harmonious finish. Already delicious, it's also well worth cellaring.

Vintage	17	16	15	14	13	12	11	10
WR	6	6	6	6	6	6	5	5
Drink	19-25	19-24	19-23	19-22	19-22	19-21	P	P

MED/DRY $29 V+

Grove Mill Wairau Valley Marlborough Pinot Gris ★★★★

The 2018 vintage (★★★★) was grown in the Wairau Valley and mostly handled in tanks; 5 per cent of the blend was barrel-fermented. Bright, light yellow/green, it is mouthfilling, with generous peach, pear and spice flavours, fresh and lively, a touch of complexity, and a dryish (7.2 grams/litre of residual sugar), finely poised finish. A full-flavoured, very harmonious wine, it offers good value.

MED/DRY $19 V+

Haha Hawke's Bay Pinot Gris ★★★★

Offering excellent value, the 2019 vintage (★★★★) is attractively scented, mouthfilling, vibrantly fruity and smooth. Bright, light lemon/green, it has generous peach, pear and spice flavours, showing very good vigour and depth, and an off-dry (7.7 grams/litre of residual sugar) finish. A good, all-purpose wine.

MED/DRY $18 V+

Hans Herzog Marlborough Pinot Gris ★★★★★

Prepare for something different! Estate-grown on the northern side of the Wairau Valley, the 2017 vintage (★★★★★) is a thought-provoking wine, like its predecessors. Apricot-coloured, from long skin contact with the juice, it was partly oak-aged (20 per cent of the blend was handled in French oak puncheons). Ripely perfumed, it is weighty, sweet-fruited and bone-dry, with powerful peach, strawberry and apricot flavours, a touch of tannin, and loads of personality. Certified organic.

DRY $39 AV

Hawkshead Central Otago Pinot Gris   ★★★★★

Grown in the elevated Gibbston sub-region, the classy 2018 vintage (★★★★★) was mostly handled in tanks; 15 per cent of the blend was fermented in seasoned American oak barrels. Already delicious, it is pale, invitingly fragrant and fleshy, with concentrated, ripe, peachy, slightly spicy flavours and a very harmonious, dry (2 grams/litre of residual sugar), lasting finish. Best drinking 2020+.

DRY $29 AV

Huntaway Reserve Gisborne Pinot Gris   ★★★☆

The 2018 vintage (★★★☆) is attractive young. Full-bodied, it has ripe stone-fruit flavours, showing very good freshness and depth, and a finely balanced, dryish, smooth finish.

MED/DRY $22 AV

Hunter's Marlborough Pinot Gris   ★★★★

Already drinking well, the weighty, vibrantly fruity 2018 vintage (★★★★) was mostly handled in tanks, but a small part of the blend was fermented in old oak barrels. Made in a dry style (2.9 grams/litre of residual sugar), it is invitingly scented, with mouthfilling body, strong, peachy, citrusy, slightly spicy and gingery flavours, a touch of complexity, and a finely balanced, long finish. Best drinking 2020+.

DRY $20 V+

Hunting Lodge, The, Expressions Marlborough Pinot Gris   (★★★★)

Attractively scented, the 2018 vintage (★★★★) was grown in the Wairau Valley, tank-fermented and lees-aged for four months. Already drinking well, it is a pale straw, full-bodied wine with generous, ripe, peachy, slightly spicy flavours, fresh acidity and an off-dry (9 grams/litre of residual sugar), smooth, harmonious finish. Drink now or cellar.

MED/DRY $22 V+

Hunting Lodge, The, Marlborough Pinot Gris   ★★★★☆

Grown at a coastal site in the Wairau Valley, the 2018 vintage (★★★★☆) was fermented and lees-aged for four months in tanks. A pale straw, full-bodied, Alsace-style wine, already highly appealing, it has generous, peachy, slightly spicy flavours, a touch of complexity, appetising acidity and an off-dry (9.5 grams/litre of residual sugar) finish. A lively, tightly structured wine with cellaring potential, it should break into full stride 2020+.

MED/DRY $24 V+

Invivo Marlborough Pinot Gris   ★★★

The 2019 vintage (★★★) is a very pale straw, full-bodied wine, with fresh, peachy, distinctly spicy flavours, balanced acidity and a dry finish. Already quite open and expressive, it's a slightly Gewürztraminer-like wine, likely to be at its best 2020–21.

DRY $19 AV

Invivo Michelle's Central Otago Pinot Gris   (★★★★☆)

Delicious now and offering great value, the 2017 vintage (★★★★☆) is a highly fragrant, mouthfilling wine, with rich, ripe stone-fruit flavours, slightly spicy notes, good complexity and an off-dry, finely balanced finish.

Johanneshof Marlborough Pinot Gris   ★★★★

The powerful 2018 vintage (★★★★☆) is a pale straw wine, weighty and fleshy, with generous stone-fruit and spice flavours, a touch of complexity and a slightly sweet, smooth finish. Full of personality, it's already drinking well.

Johner Estate Limestone Pinot Gris   (★★★★)

The 2019 vintage (★★★★) was grown in Hawke's Bay. Very pale straw, it's a basically dry style (4 grams/litre of residual sugar), with fresh, strong pear, lychee and spice flavours, crisp acidity, and very good vigour and depth. Best drinking 2021+.

Vintage	19
WR	7
Drink	20-23

Jules Taylor Marlborough Pinot Gris   ★★★★☆

Grown in the Awatere and Wairau valleys, the attractive, light lemon/green 2018 vintage (★★★★☆) was mostly handled in tanks; 5 per cent of the blend was oak-aged. Produced in a dry style (2 grams/litre of residual sugar), it is invitingly scented and full-bodied, with good concentration of vibrant, youthful peach, pear, apple and lychee flavours, gentle spicy notes, balanced acidity, a distinct touch of complexity and a smooth, lingering finish. Best drinking 2020+.

Kahurangi Nelson Pinot Gris   (★★★☆)

Drinking well now, the 2018 vintage (★★★☆) is a light yellow/green, full-bodied wine, with good depth of fresh, peachy, slightly gingery and spicy flavours, and an off-dry finish.

Kim Crawford New Zealand Pinot Gris   ★★★☆

The 2017 vintage (★★★☆) is mouthfilling and vibrantly fruity, with very good depth of ripe peach, pear and lychee flavours, a hint of spice, and a dry (3.3 grams/litre of residual sugar), very harmonious finish. Grown in Marlborough, it offers good value.

DRY $17 V+

Kono Nelson Pinot Gris   (★★★☆)

Offering good value, the 2018 vintage (★★★☆) is enjoyable young. Bright, light lemon/green, it is freshly scented, vibrant and mouthfilling, with lively pear/spice flavours, balanced acidity, and a dryish finish.

MED/DRY $18 V+

Kumeu River Pinot Gris   ★★★★

This consistently attractive wine is grown at Kumeu, in West Auckland, aged on its yeast lees, but not oak-matured. Bright, light lemon/green, the youthful 2018 vintage (★★★★) is a fragrant, medium to full-bodied wine, with good intensity of vibrant peach, pear and spice flavours, and a finely balanced, dryish (5 grams/litre of residual sugar) finish. A good all-purpose wine, it should be at its best mid-2020+.

MED/DRY $25 AV

Lake Chalice The Raptor Marlborough Pinot Gris   (★★★☆)

The 2016 vintage (★★★★), on sale in 2019, is a fragrant, mouthfilling wine, probably at its peak. Estate-grown in the Southern Valleys, it has strong, peachy, slightly spicy and gingery flavours, developing bottle-aged complexity, and a dryish (6 grams/litre of residual sugar), lingering finish.

MED/DRY $23 –V

Lake Hayes Central Otago Pinot Gris   ★★★☆

From Amisfield, the 2017 vintage (★★★★) is invitingly scented and mouthfilling, with vibrant peach, pear, lychee and spice flavours, a gentle splash of sweetness (10 grams/litre of residual sugar), balanced acidity and loads of drink-young charm. Good value.

MED/DRY $20 AV

Landing, The, Bay of Islands Pinot Gris   (★★★★)

Hand-picked in late February, the 2018 vintage (★★★★) is a medium-bodied wine with concentrated peach, pear and spice flavours. Made in an off-dry style, it is freshly scented, with lots of youthful vigour.

MED/DRY $27 –V

Lawson's Dry Hills Marlborough Pinot Gris   ★★★★

Still very youthful, the pale straw 2019 vintage (★★★★) is a basically dry style (4.8 grams/litre of residual sugar). Fresh and full-bodied, it has strong, ripe, peachy, slightly spicy flavours, a touch of complexity and a well-rounded finish. Best drinking mid-2020+.

Vintage	19
WR	6
Drink	19-21

DRY $20 V+

Lawson's Dry Hills Reserve Marlborough Pinot Gris ★★★★☆

The finely textured 2018 vintage (★★★★☆) was mostly estate-grown in the Waihopai Valley and 10 per cent of the blend was fermented with indigenous yeasts in old French oak casks. Pale straw, it is mouthfilling, with concentrated, ripe peach, pear and spice flavours, showing a distinct touch of complexity, and a smooth, dryish (5 grams/litre of residual sugar) finish. Best drinking mid-2020+.

Vintage	18
WR	6
Drink	19-21

 MED/DRY $25 V+

Lawson's Dry Hills The Pioneer Marlborough Pinot Gris ★★★★☆

The 2016 vintage (★★★★) is a single-vineyard wine, grown in the Waihopai Valley, hand-picked and fermented with indigenous yeasts in old French oak barriques. It's a fleshy, full-bodied wine, with a gentle splash of sweetness (14 grams/litre of residual sugar), strong flavours of pears, peaches and spices, and very good complexity and richness.

Vintage	16	15
WR	7	7
Drink	19-25	19-20

 MED/DRY $30 –V

Leo Nelson Pinot Gris (★★★)

From an Auckland-based company, the 2017 vintage (★★★) is a fresh, medium-bodied wine with gentle peachy, slightly spicy flavours and a dryish, smooth finish. An easy-drinking style, it's ready to roll.

 MED/DRY $19 AV

Leveret Estate Marlborough Pinot Gris (★★★★)

The 2019 vintage (★★★★) is fresh and full-bodied, with very good varietal character, delicacy and depth of peach, pear and spice flavours. Made in an off-dry style (8 grams/litre of residual sugar), it has gentle acidity and a very harmonious finish. Best drinking mid-2020+.

 MED/DRY $22 V+

Lime Rock Central Hawke's Bay Pinot Gris ★★★★

Estate-grown near Waipawa, the 2015 vintage (★★★★) was fermented in tanks and old oak barriques. Attractively scented, with pear-like aromas, it is mouthfilling, with strongly varietal pear, lychee and spice flavours, showing very good delicacy and freshness, and a dryish finish.

 MED/DRY $24 AV

Loveblock Marlborough Pinot Gris (★★★★☆)

Delicious young, the 2018 vintage (★★★★☆) is an organically certified wine, estate-grown in the Awatere Valley. Attractively scented, it is fresh and full-bodied, with strong, pure pear, peach and spice flavours, gentle acidity, vague sweetness, a slightly oily texture and a well-rounded finish. Fine value.

MED/DRY $22 V+

Luminary, The, Martinborough Pinot Gris

From Palliser Estate, the 2017 vintage (★★★☆) is an attractively scented, medium-bodied wine with good depth of peach, pear and spice flavours. Crisp and lively, with a sliver of sweetness, it is finely balanced for easy drinking and offers fine value.

MED/DRY $17 V+

Luna Martinborough Pinot Gris

The 2018 vintage (★★★★) was grown at Blue Rock Vineyard, south of the township, and partly handled in tanks; 50 per cent of the blend was fermented and lees-aged for nine months in old French oak barriques. Very pale straw, with a fresh, spicy bouquet, it is mouthfilling, with ripe stone-fruit flavours, balanced acidity and a dry (2.5 grams/litre of residual sugar), slightly creamy finish. Best drinking mid-2020+.

DRY $24 AV

Mahi Marlborough Pinot Gris

The 2018 vintage (★★★★) is a single-vineyard wine, hand-picked near Ward, in the Awatere Valley, and mostly handled in tanks; 10 per cent of the blend was barrel-fermented. It is fermented to dryness (2 grams/litre of residual sugar) 'to produce an elegant, rather than soapy, palate'. Freshly scented, it is lively and mouthfilling, with youthful, citrusy, spicy, slightly peachy and nutty flavours, showing a touch of complexity, and a crisp finish.

Vintage	19	18	17	16
WR	7	6	6	6
Drink	19-22	19-22	19-21	19-20

DRY $22 V+

Main Divide North Canterbury Pinot Gris

From Pegasus Bay, this is a consistently good buy. Tank-fermented and lees-aged, the 2018 vintage (★★★★) is a youthful wine, full-bodied, with good concentration of peachy, slightly spicy, vaguely honeyed flavours, gentle sweetness (10 grams/litre of residual sugar) and balanced acidity. Best drinking mid-2020+.

MED/DRY $21 V+

Main Divide Pokiri Reserve North Canterbury Late Picked Pinot Gris ★★★★☆

Still on sale, the 2014 vintage (★★★★) was fermented and matured for two years in barrels. Gold/amber, with a strong botrytis influence, it is full-bodied, with a fragrant bouquet of honey and spice. A sweetish wine (76 grams/litre of residual sugar), it has concentrated, apricot-like, slightly gingery flavours, showing bottle-aged complexity. Full of personality, it's delicious now.

Vintage	14
WR	5
Drink	19-22

SW $25 V+

Man O' War Exiled Pinot Gris   ★★★★

The 2017 vintage (★★★★) was grown on Waiheke and Ponui islands. Light yellow/pale gold, it is a medium to full-bodied wine, with fresh, concentrated peach, pear and spice flavours, a gentle splash of sweetness (21 grams/litre of residual sugar) and crisp, appetising acidity. Showing good vigour and intensity, it's enjoyable now, but also worth cellaring.

Vintage	17	16	15
WR	5	7	6
Drink	19-22	19-22	P

 MED $34 –V

Man O' War Ponui Island Pinot Gris   ★★★★

Estate-grown and hand-picked on Ponui Island, the 2017 vintage (★★★★) was mostly handled in tanks; 5 per cent of the blend was barrel-fermented. Light to medium-bodied, it has good intensity of vibrant pear, grapefruit and spice flavours, gentle sweetness (18 grams/litre of residual sugar), refreshing acidity and a lingering finish. Drink now or cellar.

 MED $25 AV

Maori Point Central Otago Pinot Gris   ★★★★

Grown in the Cromwell Basin, the 2017 vintage (★★★★) is a single-vineyard wine, fermented with indigenous yeasts and lees-aged in tanks (40 per cent) and old French oak casks (60 per cent). Pale, it is crisp and fully dry (1 gram/litre of residual sugar), with fresh, strong, citrusy flavours to the fore, hints of pears and peaches, good varietal character and vigour, and a long finish.

 DRY $26 –V

Maori Point Grand Reserve Central Otago Pinot Gris   (★★★★☆)

Ensconced in a heavy, punted bottle, the lively 2013 vintage (★★★★☆) was fermented with indigenous yeasts and lees-stirred in French oak barrels (50 per cent new). Still available and maturing very gracefully, it is sturdy and fleshy, with rich stone-fruit flavours to the fore, oak-derived complexity, fresh, balanced acidity, and a long, bone-dry finish. Still full of vigour, it should be at its best 2020+.

DRY $38 –V

Map Maker Marlborough Pinot Gris   ★★★☆

From Staete Landt, the well-priced 2017 vintage (★★★☆) was estate-grown at Rapaura, in the Wairau Valley, hand-picked, and part of the blend was fermented in old French oak puncheons. Pale lemon/green, it is a medium to full-bodied wine with vibrant, delicate pear and spice flavours, showing a touch of complexity, and a finely textured, dry (3.3 grams/litre of residual sugar) finish.

 DRY $19 V+

Marsden Bay of Islands Pinot Gris ★★★★

In favourable seasons, this Kerikeri, Northland winery produces an impressive Pinot Gris. The 2017 vintage (★★★☆) is a pale straw, mouthfilling wine, with good depth of peachy, spicy, vaguely honeyed flavours, a sliver of sweetness (7 grams/litre of residual sugar), and a smooth finish. Good, easy drinking.

Vintage	17
WR	5
Drink	P

MED/DRY $28 –V

Martinborough Vineyard Te Tera Martinborough Pinot Gris ★★★★

Offering good value, the 2019 vintage (★★★★) is an attractively scented wine, fleshy and sweet-fruited. Bright, light lemon/green, it is weighty, with generous, ripe, peachy, slightly spicy flavours and a dry (3.3 grams/litre of residual sugar), slightly creamy finish.

Vintage	19
WR	7
Drink	19-23

DRY $20 V+

Matawhero Gisborne Pinot Gris ★★★☆

Still youthful, the 2018 vintage (★★★☆) is a single-vineyard wine, fragrant, medium-bodied and dryish (6.1 grams/litre of residual sugar), with fresh, balanced acidity and good depth of peachy, slightly spicy flavours. Best drinking 2020+.

MED/DRY $23 –V

Maude Central Otago Pinot Gris ★★★★

The highly attractive 2018 vintage (★★★★☆) was grown at various sites, including the estate's Mt Maude Vineyard at Wanaka, and 40 per cent of the blend was fermented in seasoned oak barrels. Bright, light lemon/green, it is full-bodied, fresh and lively, with strong, peachy, citrusy flavours, hints of pears, apples and spices, a touch of complexity and a finely poised, dry (4 grams/litre of residual sugar) finish. Drink now to 2021.

DRY $27 –V

Maui Marlborough Pinot Gris ★★★☆

The fine-value, easy-drinking 2017 vintage (★★★☆) was estate-grown in the upper Wairau Valley. Light yellow/green, it is full-bodied, with good depth of ripe, peachy flavours, a hint of sweetness, and a smooth, very harmonious finish. (From Tiki.)

MED/DRY $18 V+

Mills Reef Estate Hawke's Bay Pinot Gris ★★★☆

Aromatic and finely balanced, the 2019 vintage (★★★☆) is a fresh, lively, vibrantly fruity wine, with very good depth of pear and spice flavours and an off-dry finish. Offering very easy drinking, it should be at its best from mid-2020+.

MED/DRY $19 V+

Mills Reef Reserve Hawke's Bay Pinot Gris   ★★★★

Enjoyable from the start, the 2019 vintage (★★★★) is a freshly scented, full-bodied wine. Finely balanced, it has very good varietal character and depth of peach, pear and spice flavours, with a smooth, vaguely sweet, very harmonious finish. Drink now or cellar.

 DRY $25 AV

Vintage	19	18	17
WR	7	7	6
Drink	19-22	19-21	19-20

Mischief Waipara Pinot Gris   (★★★★)

From a company based at Amberley, in North Canterbury, the 2018 vintage (★★★★) is enjoyable young. Full-bodied, it has ripe, peachy, vaguely honeyed flavours, a gentle splash of sweetness (8 grams/litre of residual sugar) and a welcoming fragrance.

 MED/DRY $22 V+

Misha's Vineyard Dress Circle Central Otago Pinot Gris   ★★★★★

The refined 2019 vintage (★★★★★) was estate-grown at Bendigo and 42 per cent of the blend was fermented with indigenous yeasts in old French oak hogsheads. Made in an off-dry style (6.3 grams/litre of residual sugar), it is highly scented and strongly varietal. Bright, light lemon/green, it is mouthfilling, with rich, vibrant pear, lychee and spice flavours, a very subtle oak influence, fresh, balanced acidity and a very harmonious finish. Best drinking 2021+.

MED/DRY $28 V+

Vintage	19	18	17	16	15	14	13	12	11	10
WR	6	7	6	7	7	6	6	7	6	6
Drink	19-29	19-29	19-27	19-28	19-27	19-26	19-25	19-24	19-23	19-22

Mission Marlborough Pinot Gris   ★★★

Enjoyable young, the 2019 vintage (★★★) is an attractively scented, mouthfilling wine with vibrant, ripe, peachy flavours and an off-dry (7 grams/litre of residual sugar), distinctly spicy finish.

 MED/DRY $18 AV

Monowai Hawke's Bay Pinot Gris   ★★★☆

Invitingly scented, the 2017 vintage (★★★★) is from an inland, elevated site at Crownthorpe. Already drinking well, it is medium-bodied, with vibrant, peachy, slightly spicy and honeyed flavours, a sliver of sweetness (6 grams/litre of residual sugar), and impressive vigour, varietal character and depth. Fine value.

 MED/DRY $18 V+

Montana Reserve Hawke's Bay Pinot Gris   ★★★☆

Offering good value, the 2018 vintage (★★★☆) is a medium to full-bodied wine. Drinking well from the start, it has good depth of ripe, peachy, slightly spicy flavours, and a slightly sweet, well-rounded finish.

MED/DRY $17 V+

Montford Estate Marlborough Pinot Gris (★★★☆)

The vibrant, finely balanced 2019 vintage (★★★☆) was grown in the Wairau and Awatere valleys. Bright, light lemon/green, it is medium to full-bodied, with good depth of fresh, lively pear and spice flavours, dry (4 grams/litre of residual sugar) and crisp. (From te Pā.)

DRY $20 AV

Morepork Vineyard Northland Pinot Gris ★★★★

Estate-grown and hand-picked at a very small, single-variety vineyard in Kerikeri, the 2019 vintage (★★★★☆) is very age-worthy. Pale and attractively scented, it is full-bodied, with good concentration of ripe peach, pear and spice flavours, a slightly oily texture, balanced acidity and a dryish (5 grams/litre of residual sugar), finely balanced finish. Best drinking 2021+.

Vintage	19	18	17
WR	7	5	7
Drink	19-21	19-20	P

MED/DRY $24 AV

Mount Brown Estates Grand Reserve North Canterbury Pinot Gris ★★★★☆

Delicious young, the 2018 vintage (★★★★☆) is a richly scented wine, fermented and matured in old oak barrels. Bright, light lemon/green, it is strongly varietal and vibrantly fruity, with substantial body, concentrated pear and peach flavours, gentle acidity and an off-dry (10 grams/litre of residual sugar) finish. Bargain-priced.

MED/DRY $20 V+

Mount Brown Estates North Canterbury Pinot Gris ★★★☆

Offering great value, the 2018 vintage (★★★★) is invitingly scented, with mouthfilling body. Delicious from the start, it has very good depth of ripe peach, pear and spice flavours, gentle acidity, a sliver of sweetness (7 grams/litre of residual sugar), and a softly textured, very harmonious finish.

Vintage	18
WR	6
Drink	19-22

MED/DRY $16 V+

Mount Riley Marlborough Pinot Gris ★★★★

Fragrant and full-bodied, the 2018 vintage (★★★★) is a great buy. Grown in the Wairau and Awatere valleys, and made with a small amount of barrel fermentation, it has excellent varietal character, with strong pear and spice flavours, a touch of complexity, and a smooth, off-dry (8.5 grams/litre of residual sugar) finish.

MED/DRY $18 V+

Mount Vernon Marlborough Pinot Gris ★★★☆

Priced right, the easy-drinking 2017 vintage (★★★☆) is fresh and vibrantly fruity, with good depth of peach and pear-like flavours, lively acidity and a basically dry (4.8 grams/litre of residual sugar) finish. (From Lawson's Dry Hills.)

Vintage	17
WR	5
Drink	19-20

DRY $18 V+

Moutere Hills Nelson Pinot Gris ★★★☆

The fresh, medium-bodied 2019 vintage (★★★☆) was mostly handled in tanks; 10 per cent of the blend was oak-aged. Bright, light lemon/green, it is still youthful, with lively pear, apple and spice flavours, and a finely poised, dryish (5 grams/litre of residual sugar) finish. Best drinking mid-2020+.

MED/DRY $25 –V

Mt Beautiful North Canterbury Pinot Gris ★★★★

The 2017 vintage (★★★★☆) was estate-grown and hand-picked at Cheviot. Mouthfilling and fleshy, it has fresh ripe, peach and pear flavours, showing good richness, balanced acidity and a very harmonious, dry (3 grams/litre of residual sugar) finish. The 2018 vintage (★★★★) is sturdy, with generous stone-fruit and spice flavours, showing a distinct touch of complexity, and a dry finish. Best drinking 2020+.

Vintage	15	14
WR	5	6
Drink	P	P

DRY $24 AV

Mt Difficulty Bannockburn Pinot Gris ★★★★☆

Grown and hand-picked at Bannockburn, in Central Otago, the 2018 vintage (★★★★☆) is a fleshy, dry wine (4 grams/litre of residual sugar). Bright, light lemon/green, it is weighty and vibrantly fruity, with concentrated, ripe stone-fruit flavours, hints of ginger and spice, a touch of complexity and a finely textured finish. Drink now or cellar.

DRY $26 AV

Mt Rosa Central Otago Pinot Gris (★★★★)

From a Gibbston-based producer, the 2018 vintage (★★★★) is light lemon/green, with a fragrant, slightly creamy bouquet. Full-bodied and fleshy, it has very good depth of peachy, slightly spicy flavours and a dryish, well-rounded finish. Drink now or cellar.

DRY $30 –V

Mud House Marlborough Pinot Gris ★★★★

Offering great value, the 2018 vintage (★★★★) is drinking well in its youth. Attractively scented, it is full-bodied, with fresh, generous, peachy, slightly spicy flavours, balanced acidity and a dryish finish.

MED/DRY $15 V+

Mud House Single Vineyard Home Block Waipara Valley Pinot Gris   (★★★★☆)

Still youthful, the classy 2018 vintage (★★★★☆) is fresh and vibrant, with obvious potential. Mouthfilling, it has generous stone-fruit flavours, gentle spicy notes, good acidity, and an off-dry, lingering finish. Best drinking 2020+.

 MED/DRY $26 AV

Mud House Sub Region Series Grovetown Marlborough Pinot Gris   ★★★★

The 2018 vintage (★★★★) was grown at Grovetown, north of Blenheim, in the Wairau Valley (and so is a district, rather than sub-regional, wine). Bright, light lemon/green, it is scented, with generous, peachy, distinctly spicy, slightly gingery flavours. Forward in its appeal, it's a rather Gewürztraminer-like wine, ready to roll.

 MED/DRY $20 V+

Nautilus Marlborough Pinot Gris   ★★★★☆

The highly scented 2019 vintage (★★★★☆) was mostly tank-fermented (5 per cent of the blend was fermented in old oak casks). Bright, light lemon/green, it is mouthfilling, with concentrated, peachy, gently spicy flavours, showing excellent freshness, delicacy and harmony, and a dry (4 grams/litre of residual sugar), smooth finish.

Vintage	19
WR	7
Drink	19-24

 DRY $30 –V

Neudorf Moutere Pinot Gris   ★★★★★

The 2017 vintage (★★★★☆) was hand-picked at two sites at Upper Moutere, including the Home Vineyard, and fermented with indigenous yeasts in tanks (80 per cent) and old French oak puncheons (20 per cent). A slightly off-dry style (6.4 grams/litre of residual sugar), it is a tightly structured wine, full-bodied, with concentrated pear, apple, lemon and spice flavours, good acid spine, and obvious cellaring potential; best drinking 2020+.

Vintage	17	16	15	14	13
WR	6	6	7	6	7
Drink	19-22	19-21	19-20	P	P

 MED/DRY $29 V+

Nevis Bluff Oak Aged Central Otago Pinot Gris   ★★★★☆

Maturing well, the 2014 vintage (★★★★☆) was hand-harvested at Pisa, in the Cromwell Basin, and fermented and matured for nine months in seasoned oak casks. It is weighty and generous, with concentrated, ripe, peachy flavours, a subtle seasoning of oak, good complexity and a smooth, fully dry finish.

 DRY $35 –V

Nikau Point Reserve Marlborough Pinot Gris   ★★☆

Estate-grown, the 2019 vintage (★★★) is enjoyable young. Pale lemon/green, it is freshly scented, with mouthfilling body, plenty of ripe, peachy, slightly spicy and gingery flavour, and a basically dry (4.8 grams/litre of residual sugar) finish.

 DRY $16 AV

Nikau Point Select Hawke's Bay Pinot Gris   ★★★

Priced sharply, the 2019 vintage (★★★) offers very easy drinking. Bright, light lemon/green, it is full-bodied and lively, with fresh pear and spice flavours, showing good depth, and an off-dry (5.5 grams/litre of residual sugar) finish. Drink young.

MED/DRY $12 V+

Nobody's Hero Marlborough Pinot Gris   (★★★★)

Priced right, the 2018 vintage (★★★★) from Framingham was tank-fermented and 35 per cent of the blend was aged in old barrels. Light lemon/green, it is fresh, weighty and dryish (5.6 grams/litre of residual sugar), with peachy, slightly spicy flavours, showing good richness, and balanced acidity. A strongly varietal wine, it's already very open and expressive; drink now to 2020.

MED/DRY $20 V+

Obsidian Estate Waiheke Island Pinot Gris   ★★★☆

The attractive 2018 vintage (★★★★) is a single-vineyard wine, made in an off-dry style. Light lemon/green, it is freshly scented and full-bodied, with pear, apple and spice flavours, showing very good delicacy and depth. A finely balanced wine, it should break into full stride 2020+.

MED/DRY $31 –V

Odyssey Marlborough Pinot Gris   ★★★☆

Certified organic, the bright, light gold 2017 vintage (★★★☆) is drinking well now. Estate-grown in the upper Brancott Valley and matured in seasoned oak casks, it is mouthfilling, with peachy, slightly toasty and honeyed flavours, balanced acidity and a dry (2 grams/litre of residual sugar) finish.

DRY $24 –V

Ohau Wines Selected Vines Pinot Gris   (★★★★)

Estate-grown in the Horowhenua, the 2019 vintage (★★★★) was partly oak-aged and made in a medium style (18 grams/litre of residual sugar). Pale straw, it is a vibrantly fruity, gently sweet wine, with mouthfilling body and very good depth of fresh peach, pear and spice flavours, finely balanced for early drinking. Best mid-2020+.

MED $32 –V

Ohinemuri Limestone Pinot Gris   (★★★☆)

Still on sale, the 2016 vintage (★★★☆) was grown in Central Hawke's Bay and mostly handled in tanks, with 10 per cent barrel fermentation. Fresh and full-bodied, it has good depth of peachy, slightly spicy flavours and an off-dry (8 grams/litre of residual sugar) finish.

MED/DRY $27 –V

Old Coach Road Nelson Pinot Gris   ★★☆

From Seifried, the vibrantly fruity 2017 vintage (★★☆) is a fresh, medium-bodied wine with citrusy, peachy flavours, crisp acidity and a dry (3 grams/litre of residual sugar) finish. Priced right.

DRY $15 V+

Opawa Marlborough Pinot Gris

This wine is made in a 'lighter, crisper' style than its Nautilus Estate stablemate. Tank-fermented, the 2019 vintage (★★★☆) is light yellow/green, fresh and full-bodied, with good depth of peachy, spicy, vaguely honeyed flavours, showing a touch of complexity, and a crisp, dry (3 grams/litre of residual sugar) finish. A slightly Gewürztraminer-like wine, it's already enjoyable.

DRY $22 AV

Ostler Audrey's Waitaki Valley Pinot Gris

The powerful 2016 vintage (★★★★★) is a delicious wine, well worth cellaring. Full-bodied and rich, with notably concentrated peach, pear and spice flavours, gentle sweetness, and excellent complexity and harmony, it should be at its best 2020+.

MED/DRY $34 AV

Ostler Lakeside Vines Waitaki Valley Pinot Gris

The characterful 2017 vintage (★★★★☆) was grown at Lake Waitaki and partly (20 per cent) fermented with indigenous yeasts in old oak barriques. A powerful wine, it is full-bodied (14.5 per cent alcohol), with fresh, strong pear and spice flavours, gentle sweetness (14 grams/litre of residual sugar), a distinct touch of complexity and a lingering finish. Best drinking 2020+.

MED/DRY $30 –V

Oyster Bay Hawke's Bay Pinot Gris

Grown mostly at Crownthorpe, a relatively cool, elevated, inland district, this is a good, all-purpose wine, modelled on dry Italian Pinot Grigio rather than the richer, sweeter Pinot Gris of Alsace. Handled without oak, the 2019 vintage (★★★☆) is enjoyable young. Fragrant, it is medium to full-bodied, with fresh, lively peach, pear and spice flavours, and a smooth finish.

DRY $20 AV

Pā Road Marlborough Pinot Gris

From te Pā, the 2019 vintage (★★★) is a very easy-drinking wine, fresh and lively, with satisfying depth of peach, pear and spice flavours, basically dry (4 grams/litre of residual sugar) and crisp.

DRY $18 AV

Pacific Potion Organic Hawke's Bay Pinot Gris (★★★★)

Certified organic, the 2017 vintage (★★★★) was hill-grown in the Tuki Tuki Valley, hand-picked, matured on its yeast lees for three months, and bottled unfined. Attractively scented, it is a vibrantly fruity, medium-bodied wine, with a gentle splash of sweetness (8 grams/litre of residual sugar) and fresh peach, pear and lychee flavours, which show excellent delicacy and richness. A tightly structured, age-worthy wine, it's already drinking well. (From Supernatural Wine Co.)

MED/DRY $25 AV

Paddy Borthwick Wairarapa Pinot Gris

Estate-grown at Gladstone, the 2018 vintage (★★★★) is a full-bodied, partly barrel-fermented wine, with strong, vibrant pear, lychee and spice flavours, and a lingering, dry finish. Showing good varietal character and a distinct touch of complexity, it should be at its best mid-2020+.

DRY $24 AV

Palliser Estate Martinborough Pinot Gris

The full-bodied, generous 2018 vintage (★★★★) was estate-grown and briefly lees-aged in tanks. Vibrantly fruity, it has strong peach and pear flavours, slightly spicy notes, finely balanced acidity and an off-dry (6 grams/litre of residual sugar) finish. Pricey.

MED/DRY $31 –V

Passage Rock Waiheke Island Pinot Gris

Drinking well now, the 2018 vintage (★★★★) was grown at three sites. Bright, light yellow, it is mouthfilling, with strong, peachy, gently spicy, vaguely gingery flavours, and an off-dry (5 grams/litre of residual sugar) finish.

MED/DRY $25 –V

People's, The, Hawke's Bay Pinot Gris

Offering good value, the 2017 vintage (★★★☆) is full-bodied, with good depth of peachy, citrusy, slightly spicy flavours, fresh acidity and a rounded finish. (From Constellation NZ.)

MED/DRY $16 V+

Peregrine Central Otago Pinot Gris

The 2017 vintage (★★★★☆) is a blend of Bendigo (62 per cent) and Pisa (38 per cent) fruit, hand-harvested and partly barrel-fermented (10 per cent). It is a mouthfilling, dryish wine with strong, fresh, peachy, spicy flavours, showing a distinct touch of complexity, and obvious potential; open 2020+.

MED/DRY $30 –V

Prophet's Rock Central Otago Pinot Gris

Estate-grown and hand-harvested at two Bendigo sites, in the Cromwell Basin, the 2017 vintage (★★★★★) is still youthful. Fermented with indigenous yeasts, it is an Alsace-style wine, weighty and rich, with substantial body, concentrated, vibrant stone-fruit and spice flavours and an off-dry (9 grams/litre of residual sugar) finish. Best drinking 2021+.

MED/DRY $36 AV

Vintage	17	16	15
WR	7	7	6
Drink	19-29	19-28	19-22

Providore Central Otago Pinot Gris (★★★★★)

The impressive 2018 vintage (★★★★★) was grown at Gibbston and made in a dry style (3 grams/litre of residual sugar). Pale lemon/green, it is highly scented, mouthfilling and vibrantly fruity, with fresh peach, apple and lychee flavours, lively acidity, and excellent delicacy and depth. Best drinking 2020+.

DRY $25 V+

Quartz Reef Bendigo Estate Single Vineyard Central Otago Pinot Gris ★★★★★

Certified biodynamic, the very classy 2017 vintage (★★★★★) was estate-grown at Bendigo, hand-harvested and fermented and lees-aged in tanks. Bright, light lemon/green, it is highly scented and mouthfilling, with beautifully vibrant, well-ripened pear, lychee and spice flavours, showing excellent intensity, finely balanced acidity and a dry (3 grams/litre of residual sugar), lingering finish.

Vintage	18	17
WR	6	6
Drink	19-22	19-22

 DRY $35 AV

Quest Farm Silver Lining Central Otago Pinot Gris ★★★★

Still on sale, the 2015 vintage (★★★★) is a dry style (2 grams/litre of residual sugar), almost entirely handled in tanks (5 per cent was barrel-aged). It is still fresh and lively, with mouthfilling body, a slightly creamy texture and very good delicacy and depth of peach, pear and lychee flavours. Good value.

 DRY $20 V+

Ra Nui Wairau Valley Marlborough Pinot Gris ★★★★

The youthful 2018 vintage (★★★★) was 20 per cent oak-fermented. Already drinking well, it is medium to full-bodied, with fresh, strong, peachy, slightly spicy flavours, lively acidity and an off-dry (6 grams/litre of residual sugar), finely balanced finish. Best drinking mid-2020+.

 MED/DRY $25 AV

Rabbit Ranch Central Otago Pinot Gris ★★★☆

From Chard Farm, the 2018 vintage (★★★★) is drinking well in its youth. Ripely scented, it is full-bodied, with fresh, strong stone-fruit and spice flavours and a dryish, well-rounded finish.

 MED/DRY $20 AV

Rapaura Springs Marlborough Pinot Gris ★★★☆

The very easy-drinking 2018 vintage (★★★☆) is a freshly scented, exuberantly fruity wine, full-bodied, with ripe, peachy flavours, a sliver of sweetness (8 grams/litre of residual sugar) and gentle acidity. Enjoyable young.

Vintage	18	17	16
WR	6	4	7
Drink	19-21	P	P

MED/DRY $15 V+

Rapaura Springs Reserve Marlborough Pinot Gris ★★★★

The 2019 vintage (★★★☆) was mostly handled in tanks; 5 per cent of the blend was fermented in old barrels. Light lemon/green, it is full-bodied, with vibrant, peachy flavours, hints of spices and ginger, a touch of complexity, and a dryish (6.5 grams/litre of residual sugar) finish.

Vintage	19	18	17	16
WR	6	7	6	7
Drink	19-22	19-23	19-20	19-20

 MED/DRY $19 V+

Renato Nelson Pinot Gris   ★★★★

Enjoyable young but also worth cellaring, the 2018 vintage (★★★★) is a blend of grapes from Upper Moutere and Kina, on the coast. Full-bodied, it has fresh, youthful stone-fruit flavours, showing very good delicacy and depth, and a dryish, finely balanced finish.

Vintage	18	17	16	15	14
WR	6	7	6	7	7
Drink	19-23	19-22	P	19-21	19-21

 MED/DRY $20 V+

Rimu Grove Bronte Pinot Gris – see Bronte Pinot Gris

Riverby Estate Marlborough Pinot Gris   ★★★

The youthful 2018 vintage (★★★☆) was mostly tank-fermented; 10 per cent of the blend was handled in old oak casks. A fresh, medium to full-bodied wine, it has good depth of citrusy, peachy, slightly spicy flavours, showing a touch of complexity, and a dryish (5.8 grams/litre of residual sugar) finish. Best drinking mid-2020+.

Vintage	18
WR	7
Drink	19-24

 MED/DRY $22 AV

Roaring Meg Central Otago Pinot Gris   ★★★☆

From Mt Difficulty, the 2018 vintage (★★★☆) was hand-harvested in the Cromwell Basin and made in a medium-dry style (8.5 grams/litre of residual sugar). Fresh and full-bodied, it has plenty of vibrant, peachy, slightly spicy flavour, in a very easy-drinking style, enjoyable young.

 MED/DRY $20 AV

Rock Ferry 3rd Rock Marlborough Pinot Gris   ★★★★☆

Certified organic, the 2018 vintage (★★★★☆) is an estate-grown wine, fleshy and full-bodied, with good complexity and slightly creamy texture. Still unfolding, it is vibrantly fruity, with strong, ripe stone-fruit flavours to the fore, balanced acidity and a dryish, long finish.

 MED/DRY $27 AV

Rock Ferry Orchard Vineyard Pinot Gris on Skins   (★★★★☆)

Definitely a 'food' wine, the 2017 vintage (★★★★☆) was grown in Marlborough and oak-aged for nine months. Made in a dry style (3.5 grams/litre of residual sugar), it is straw-coloured, with a hint of orange. Full-bodied, it is concentrated, with strong, peachy, spicy flavours, a hint of oranges, a touch of tannin adding slight austerity, and loads of personality.

DRY $39 –V

Rogue Vine Special Blend Hawke's Bay/Bay of Islands Pinot Gris   (★★★★)

The 2018 vintage (★★★★), from a Kerikeri-based company, is a blend of Pinot Gris from 'rogue' (unintentional) plantings in the Bay of Islands with Hawke's Bay Pinot Gris. Pale and fleshy, it is vibrant, with generous, youthful peach, pear and spice flavours, a sliver of sweetness, and good harmony. It's already drinking well.

 MED/DRY $25 AV

Ruru Central Otago Pinot Gris ★★★☆

Grown in the Immigrant's Vineyard at Alexandra, the 2018 vintage (★★★★) was hand-picked and mostly fermented in tanks; 25 per cent of the blend was fermented in a new French oak barrel. Bright, light lemon/green, it is a vibrantly fruity, full-bodied wine with good flavour intensity and a dryish (5.8 grams/litre of residual sugar), crisp, finely balanced finish.

MED/DRY $22 AV

Russian Jack Marlborough Pinot Gris ★★★★

Priced sharply, the 2019 vintage (★★★★) is fresh and mouthfilling, with good concentration of peach, pear and spice flavours, dryish and smooth. A strongly varietal, invitingly scented wine, it's delicious from the start.

MED/DRY $19 V+

Saddleback Central Otago Pinot Gris ★★★★☆

Instantly appealing, the 2018 vintage (★★★★☆) is a tank-fermented wine, blended from Bendigo (39 per cent), Pisa (34 per cent) and Gibbston (27 per cent) grapes. Briefly lees-aged, it is intensely varietal, with mouthfilling body, vibrant, concentrated pear, peach and lychee flavours, fractional sweetness (4.5 grams/litre of residual sugar), finely balanced acidity and a floral bouquet.

DRY $24 V+

Saint Clair Marlborough Pinot Gris ★★★☆

The 2017 vintage (★★★☆) has fresh, pear-like aromas and flavours to the fore. It is fleshy, with very good body and depth, some peachy, spicy notes, and a dryish (5.2 grams/litre of residual sugar) finish.

MED/DRY $21 AV

Saint Clair Origin Marlborough Pinot Gris (★★★☆)

Worth cellaring, the youthful 2017 vintage (★★★☆) is a fragrant, mouthfilling, dryish wine (4.6 grams/litre of residual sugar). Light lemon/green, it is vibrantly fruity, with peachy, slightly spicy flavours, showing very good depth, and a rounded finish.

DRY $22 AV

Saint Clair Pioneer Block 5 Bull Block Marlborough Pinot Gris ★★★★

Full of personality, the 2016 vintage (★★★★☆) was grown in the Omaka Valley. Bright, light lemon/green, it is mouthfilling, rich and smooth, with strong pear and peach flavours, a gentle splash of sweetness (10.6 grams/litre of residual sugar), and a very harmonious finish.

MED/DRY $27 –V

Sanctuary New Zealand Pinot Gris ★★★☆

The 2018 vintage (★★★☆) is not identified by region, but offers good value. Fragrant, it is medium to full-bodied, with very good depth of fresh peach, pear and spice flavours, slight sweetness (7.1 grams/litre of residual sugar), and a smooth, harmonious finish. (From Foley Family Wines.)

MED/DRY $18 V+

Saveé Sea Marlborough Pinot Gris   (★★☆)

Priced right, the 2017 vintage (★★☆) is a fresh, medium-bodied wine, vibrantly fruity, with gentle, pear-like flavours and an off-dry finish. Pleasant, easy drinking. (From Awatere River Wine Co.)

MED/DRY $14 AV

Seifried Nelson Pinot Gris   ★★★

Still very youthful, the 2019 vintage (★★★) is a full-bodied, dry style (2 grams/litre of residual sugar). Fresh and vigorous, it has plenty of peachy, slightly spicy flavour, but needs time; open mid-2020+.

DRY $18 AV

Selaks Reserve Hawke's Bay Pinot Gris   ★★★

The 2017 vintage (★★★) is a good buy – mouthfilling, with good depth of vibrant, ripe, peachy, slightly spicy flavours, well-balanced, slightly sweet and smooth.

Vintage	17
WR	5
Drink	P

MED/DRY $14 V+

Selaks The Taste Collection Hawke's Bay Luscious Pinot Gris   (★★★☆)

The debut 2017 vintage (★★★☆) struck me more as a gently sweet, rather than truly 'luscious', wine. Light lemon/green, it is fragrant and fresh, with pear, lychee and spice flavours, showing good vigour and depth.

MED/DRY $22 AV

Seresin Marlborough Pinot Gris   ★★★★

Certified organic, this is one of the region's most distinctive Pinot Gris. The 2016 vintage (★★★★) was estate-grown and hand-picked at two sites – Raupo Creek Vineyard, in the Omaka Valley (70 per cent), and Noa Vineyard, in the western Wairau Valley (30 per cent). Fermented and lees-aged in a mix of tanks (60 per cent) and old oak barriques (40 per cent), it's a pale straw, complex, dryish wine (6.8 grams/litre of residual sugar), with vibrant pear, citrus-fruit and spice flavours, showing good complexity, fresh acidity and a lively, lingering finish.

MED/DRY $25 AV

Sherwood Estate Stoney Range Waipara Valley Pinot Gris   ★★★☆

Offering good value, the 2019 vintage (★★★☆) was grown in North Canterbury and partly barrel-fermented. Bright, light lemon/green, it is full-bodied, with very good depth of peachy, citrusy, slightly spicy flavours and a crisp, off-dry, finely balanced finish. Best drinking mid-2020+.

MED/DRY $17 V+

Sherwood Waipara Valley Pinot Gris ★★★☆

This is the 'signature' wine of Sherwood Estate. The 2017 vintage (★★★☆) is an off-dry style (6 grams/litre of residual sugar), partly barrel-fermented. Fresh and mouthfilling, with ripe, peachy, slightly spicy flavours, showing very good depth, it's drinking well now.

DRY $20 V+

Sileni Cellar Selection Hawke's Bay Pinot Gris ★★★

The easy-drinking 2019 vintage (★★★) is pale, fresh and full-bodied, with lively, peachy, spicy flavours, and fractional sweetness (4.5 grams/litre of residual sugar) adding to its drink-young charm.

DRY $20 –V

Sileni Grand Reserve Priestess Hawke's Bay Pinot Gris ★★★★

Drinking well now, the 2018 vintage (★★★★) is a full-bodied wine, light yellow/green, with concentrated stone-fruit and spice flavours, a hint of ginger, a distinct touch of complexity, and a basically dry (4 grams/litre of residual sugar) finish. Drink now to 2020.

DRY $22 V+

Soho Jagger Marlborough Pinot Gris ★★★☆

The 2017 vintage (★★★☆) was almost entirely handled in tanks; 5 per cent was fermented in seasoned French oak barrels. Grown in the Awatere Valley and Southern Valleys sub-regions, it is pale straw, with a hint of pink. Mouthfilling, it is fresh and fruity, with peachy, spicy flavours, showing a touch of complexity, a sliver of sweetness (5.3 grams/litre of residual sugar), and very good depth. Slightly 'Gewürz-like'.

MED/DRY $25 –V

Southern Cross Hawke's Bay Pinot Gris (★★★)

Priced right, the 2019 vintage (★★★) is freshly scented and full-bodied. Bright, light lemon/green, it is clearly varietal, with balanced acidity, good depth of pear and spice flavours, and an off-dry (5.5 grams/litre of residual sugar) finish. (From The Wine Portfolio.)

MED/DRY $16 V+

Spinyback Nelson Pinot Gris ★★★

From Waimea Estate, the sharply priced 2018 vintage (★★★) is an aromatic, buoyantly fruity wine, medium-bodied, with citrusy, appley flavours, a hint of passionfruit, and a dryish finish. Good, easy drinking.

MED/DRY $15 V+

Spy Valley Envoy Johnson Vineyard Waihopai Valley
Marlborough Pinot Gris   ★★★★★

Estate-grown in the lower Waihopai Valley, the 2017 vintage (★★★★☆) was harvested from vines planted in 1999 and barrel-aged for 10 months. Still youthful, it is a fresh, medium-bodied wine with concentrated, peachy, spicy flavours, showing good complexity, and abundant sweetness (76 grams/litre of residual sugar). Well worth cellaring to 2020+.

Vintage	17	16
WR	6	6
Drink	19-23	19-22

 SW $32 AV

Spy Valley Single Estate Marlborough Pinot Gris   ★★★★☆

Delicious young, the 2018 vintage (★★★★☆) was hand-harvested at 23.7 to 26.3 brix in the Southern Valleys and fermented in tanks and old oak vessels. Light lemon/green, it is fragrant and weighty, with rich, ripe stone-fruit flavours, a hint of ginger, a distinct touch of complexity, gentle acidity and an off-dry (9.4 grams/litre of residual sugar) finish. A very harmonious wine, it's a drink-now or cellaring proposition.

 MED/DRY $25 V+

Stables Ngatarawa Pinot Gris   ★★★

From Mission, the 2019 vintage (★★★), grown in Hawke's Bay, offers good value. Enjoyable young, it is mouthfilling, fresh and slightly creamy, with peachy, strongly spicy flavours, showing good depth, and a dryish finish.

 MED/DRY $13 V+

Stables Ngatarawa Reserve Hawke's Bay Pinot Gris   (★★★★)

The 2018 vintage (★★★★) is a characterful, single-vineyard wine, grown at Mangatahi. Fragrant and full-bodied, it is pale gold, with generous, peachy, slightly spicy, vaguely honeyed flavours, showing a touch of complexity, and very good depth.

MED/DRY $20 V+

Staete Landt State of Bliss Marlborough Pinot Gris   ★★★★☆

The 2017 vintage (★★★★☆) is a 'serious' style of Pinot Gris, estate-grown, hand-picked and fermented in old French oak puncheons. It is fragrant and weighty, with strong peach, pear and spice flavours, oak complexity and a long, dry (3.2 grams/litre of residual sugar) finish. Best drinking 2020+.

Vintage	17
WR	6
Drink	19-23

 DRY $25 V+

Starborough Family Estate Marlborough Pinot Gris   ★★★★

The attractive 2019 vintage (★★★★) was grown in the Awatere and Wairau valleys and mostly handled in tanks; 15 per cent of the blend was fermented in old oak barrels. Freshly aromatic, it is full of youthful vigour, with strong, peachy, citrusy, spicy flavours, showing a distinct touch of complexity, and a dryish (6.5 grams/litre of residual sugar), crisp finish. Already enjoyable, it should be at its best 2021+.

 MED/DRY $20 V+

Stoneleigh Rapaura Series Marlborough Pinot Gris   ★★★★☆

The 2017 vintage (★★★★☆) of this single-vineyard wine is pale straw, with an inviting fragrance. Full-bodied and very harmonious, it has pear and lychee flavours, hints of apples and ginger, excellent delicacy and depth, and an off-dry finish. Delicious young.

 MED/DRY $28 AV

Stoneleigh Wild Valley Marlborough Pinot Gris   (★★★★)

Priced sharply, the 2018 vintage (★★★★) was fermented with indigenous ('wild') yeasts and handled with some use of oak fermentation. Fragrant and finely balanced, it is delicious young, with pear, peach and spice flavours, showing very good vigour, depth and harmony, and a slightly sweet, crisp finish.

 MED/DRY $18 V+

Sugar Loaf Marlborough Pinot Gris   (★★★★)

The youthful 2018 vintage (★★★★) was handled in tanks (75 per cent) and old French oak (25 per cent). Full-bodied, it is fresh and vibrantly fruity, with ripe, peachy flavours to the fore, citrusy, appley, spicy notes, balanced acidity, and a tightly structured, dryish (6 grams/litre of residual sugar), lingering finish. Open 2020+.

 MED/DRY $20 V+

Summerhouse Marlborough Pinot Gris   ★★★★

The good-value 2019 vintage (★★★★) was grown at Blind River, south of the Awatere Valley. Full of youthful vigour, it is mouthfilling, with strong pear and spice flavours, showing good delicacy and vibrancy, and an off-dry (6.3 grams/litre of residual sugar), very harmonious finish.

Vintage	19	18	17
WR	6	7	7
Drink	19-22	19-23	19-22

MED/DRY $19 V+

Tatty Bogler Waitaki Valley North Otago Pinot Gris   ★★★★

Still very youthful, the 2018 vintage (★★★★) was handled in tanks (90 per cent) and old oak casks (10 per cent). Light lemon/green, it is medium to full-bodied, with fresh, lively pear and apple flavours, hints of peaches and spices, very good delicacy and vigour, and a dryish (6.2 grams/litre of residual sugar), finely balanced finish. Best drinking 2021+. (From Forrest Estate.)

 MED/DRY $25 AV

Te Kairanga Martinborough Pinot Gris ★★★★

Well worth cellaring, the refined 2019 vintage (★★★★☆) was fermented in tanks (75 per cent) and old French oak puncheons (25 per cent). Pale lemon/green, with fragrant, fresh, pear-like aromas, it is mouthfilling and vibrant, with peach, pear and spice flavours, showing excellent delicacy and depth, a distinct touch of complexity, and a dry finish (3 grams/litre of residual sugar).

 DRY $25 AV

Te Kano Central Otago Pinot Gris (★★★★)

Enjoyable young, the 2017 vintage (★★★★) is a single-vineyard wine, hand-picked at Bannockburn. It is highly scented, with mouthfilling body, generous, vibrant pear, lychee and spice flavours, and a dryish (5.8 grams/litre of residual sugar), finely balanced finish.

 MED/DRY $27 –V

te Pā Marlborough Pinot Gris ★★★★

The 2018 vintage (★★★★) was partly barrel-fermented. It is very fresh and lively, with vibrant, peachy, slightly appley and spicy flavours, showing a touch of complexity, and excellent delicacy and length. Well worth cellaring.

 MED/DRY $20 V+

Terra Sancta Lola's Block Bannockburn Central Otago Pinot Gris ★★★★

The distinctive 2017 vintage (★★★★☆) was estate-grown, hand-harvested, and fermented and matured in seasoned French oak puncheons. Pale straw, it is mouthfilling, with concentrated, ripe, peachy, spicy flavours, slightly toasty notes adding complexity, fresh acidity, and a dry (2 grams/litre of residual sugar) finish.

Vintage	18	17	16
WR	7	7	6
Drink	19-26	19-23	19-21

 DRY $28 –V

Terra Sancta Mysterious Diggings Bannockburn Central Otago Pinot Gris ★★★★

Estate-grown, hand-picked and handled in tanks (90 per cent) and seasoned French oak barriques (10 per cent), the 2018 vintage (★★★★) is enjoyable young. Freshly scented, it is full-bodied, vibrant and smooth, with fresh pear and spice flavours, showing clear-cut varietal characters, balanced acidity, and a basically dry (4.6 grams/litre of residual sugar), lingering finish.

Vintage	19	18	17
WR	6	6	7
Drink	19-22	19-21	19-22

DRY $24 AV

Terrace Edge North Canterbury Pinot Gris ★★★★☆

Worth cellaring, the 2018 vintage (★★★★☆) was hand-harvested at Waipara and 60 per cent of the blend was fermented with indigenous yeasts in old oak barrels. Bright, light yellow/green, it is mouthfilling and fleshy, with good intensity of ripe stone-fruit flavours, still very vibrant and youthful, a hint of honey, balanced acidity and an off-dry (14 grams/litre of residual sugar) finish. Certified organic.

MED/DRY $25 V+

Theory & Practice Hawke's Bay Pinot Gris ★★★★

Grown at two coastal sites, the 2018 vintage (★★★★) was fermented in tanks (mostly) and large German oak fuders. Pale straw, it is fresh and lively, with mouthfilling body, generous, peachy, slightly spicy flavours, a touch of complexity and an off-dry, well-rounded finish.

MED/DRY $25 AV

Thomas Legacy Waiheke Island Pinot Gris (★★★★☆)

The rare (450 bottles only) 2018 vintage (★★★★☆) was estate-grown and hand-picked at Batch Winery. Bright, light lemon/green, it is a finely balanced, medium-bodied style, with fresh, concentrated pear, peach and spice flavours, showing excellent delicacy and depth, and a slightly sweet (20 grams/litre of residual sugar), long finish.

MED $76 –V

Thornbury Waipara Pinot Gris ★★★★

A rare example of a low-priced Pinot Gris with personality, the 2018 vintage (★★★★) was grown in the Waiata Vineyard, in North Canterbury, and fermented and lees-aged in tanks. Bright, light lemon/green, it is mouthfilling and vibrantly fruity, with generous stone-fruit and pear flavours, gentle spicy notes, fresh acidity, and an off-dry (9 grams/litre of residual sugar) finish. Delicious young, it offers great value. (From Villa Maria.)

Vintage	19	18	17	16
WR	6	5	4	7
Drink	19-21	19-21	P	P

MED/DRY $15 V+

Tiki Estate Marlborough Pinot Gris ★★★☆

Estate-grown in the upper Wairau Valley, the 2017 vintage (★★★☆) is a fragrant, fresh, full-bodied wine. Made in a very easy-drinking style, it has pear and spice flavours, gentle sweetness (7.7 grams/litre of residual sugar), balanced acidity and some aging potential.

Vintage	17
WR	7
Drink	19-20

MED/DRY $20 AV

Tiki Estate Waipara Pinot Gris (★★★☆)

The lively 2019 vintage (★★★☆) is fresh and mouthfilling, with very youthful, peachy, slightly spicy flavours, showing good depth, and an off-dry (6.5 grams/litre of residual sugar) finish. Best drinking mid-2020+.

Vintage	19
WR	6
Drink	19-21

MED/DRY $20 AV

Tiki Single Vineyard Marlborough Pinot Gris (★★★★)

The 2017 vintage (★★★★) is a single-vineyard wine. Fragrant and full-bodied, it has strong, youthful pear and spice flavours, woven with fresh acidity, a sliver of sweetness (7.6 grams/litre of residual sugar) and obvious potential; best drinking 2020+.

MED/DRY $23 AV

Tohu Awatere Valley Marlborough Pinot Gris ★★★☆

The 2019 vintage (★★★☆) is full-bodied and clearly varietal, with pear and spice aromas, fresh, moderately concentrated flavours and a smooth, dryish (5 grams/litre of residual sugar) finish. Priced right.

Vintage	19
WR	7
Drink	19-24

MED/DRY $18 V+

Tohu Nelson Pinot Gris (★★★☆)

The 2018 vintage (★★★☆) is a mouthfilling, fully dry wine (1.5 grams/litre of residual sugar), with very good depth of fresh, pear-like flavours, slightly spicy notes and a finely balanced, smooth finish.

DRY $18 V+

Toi Toi Brookdale Reserve Marlborough Pinot Gris ★★★★

The 2017 vintage (★★★★☆) is a fragrant, mouthfilling, vibrantly fruity wine, made in an off-dry (6.2 grams/litre of residual sugar) style. Finely poised, with fresh, strong pear, lychee and spice flavours, showing excellent delicacy and depth, it's already delicious, but well worth cellaring.

Vintage	17	16
WR	7	7
Drink	19-21	19-20

MED/DRY $22 V+

Toi Toi Marlborough Pinot Gris ★★★☆

The 2018 vintage (★★★☆) is a fresh, mouthfilling wine, lively and youthful, grown in the Omaka Valley. It has pear and lemon flavours, showing very good delicacy and vibrancy, balanced acidity and a smooth, off-dry (7.7 grams/litre of residual sugar) finish.

Vintage	18
WR	7
Drink	P

MED/DRY $17 V+

Trinity Hill Hawke's Bay Pinot Gris ★★★☆

Ready for drinking when tasted in early 2019, the 2017 vintage (★★★☆) was aged for 10 months in seasoned oak barrels. Pale straw, it's a full-bodied wine, with very good depth of peachy, citrusy, slightly gingery flavours, a vague hint of honey, a touch of complexity, and an off-dry (8.1 grams/litre of residual sugar), smooth finish.

MED/DRY $23 –V

Two Sisters Central Otago Pinot Gris ★★★★☆

The fresh, tightly structured, very age-worthy 2016 vintage (★★★★☆) is a single-vineyard wine, hand-picked at Lowburn, in the Cromwell Basin, and fermented with indigenous yeasts in old French oak casks. Medium to full-bodied, it has concentrated pear-like flavours to the fore, hints of peaches and spices, good complexity, balanced acidity, and a long, dry finish.

DRY $28 AV

Urlar Gladstone Pinot Gris ★★★★

Certified organic, the bright, light lemon/green 2017 vintage (★★★★) was estate-grown and hand-harvested in the northern Wairarapa, and fermented and lees-aged for 10 months in old French oak barrels. Retasted in mid-2019, it is a fully dry style, medium to full-bodied, with strong, still-youthful pear, peach and spice flavours, showing considerable complexity, fresh, balanced acidity, and a slightly creamy finish. Best drinking 2021+. Certified organic.

Vintage	17
WR	6
Drink	19-23

DRY $29 –V

Valli Gibbston Vineyard Central Otago Pinot Gris ★★★★☆

The 2018 vintage (★★★★☆) is a finely scented, youthful wine, estate-grown, hand-picked and handled without oak. Pale lemon/green, it is fresh and weighty, with substantial body, pure stone-fruit, pear, lychee and spice flavours, showing excellent delicacy and depth, and a basically dry finish. Best drinking 2021+.

Vintage	18	17	16
WR	7	7	7
Drink	19-26	19-25	19-24

DRY $30 –V

Vavasour Awatere Valley Marlborough Pinot Gris ★★★★★

A consistently impressive wine, bargain-priced. Partly (10 per cent) fermented and matured for four months in seasoned French oak casks, the 2019 vintage (★★★★★) is bright, light lemon/green, with a fresh, fragrant bouquet. Very finely balanced, with peachy, slightly spicy flavours, showing lovely delicacy and depth, it's an off-dry style (7 grams/litre of residual sugar), already delicious.

MED/DRY $23 V+

Vidal Hawke's Bay Pinot Gris   ★★★☆

The easy-drinking 2018 vintage (★★★☆) was grown at Te Awanga and in the Bridge Pa Triangle, blended with a splash of Gewürztraminer (5 per cent), and made in a basically dry style (4.4 grams/litre of residual sugar). It's a mouthfilling, clearly varietal wine, with good depth of vibrant pear, lychee and spice flavours, fresh acidity and a smooth finish.

Vintage	19	18	17
WR	7	6	6
Drink	19-21	P	P

DRY $16 V+

Vidal Reserve Hawke's Bay Pinot Gris   (★★★☆)

The debut 2018 vintage (★★★☆) was grown mostly at Ohiti and blended with splashes of Gewürztraminer (4 per cent) and Albariño (1 per cent). Lees-aged in tanks, it is fragrant, with good depth of delicate lychee and pear flavours, moderate acidity, and a finely balanced, basically dry (4.5 grams/litre of residual sugar) finish. It's drinking well now.

Vintage	18
WR	6
Drink	19-20

DRY $20 AV

Villa Maria Cellar Selection Marlborough Pinot Gris   ★★★★

Highly fragrant, the 2018 vintage (★★★★) is a full-bodied, finely textured wine, with generous, well-ripened pear and peach flavours, a hint of ginger, and a smooth, slightly sweet, very harmonious finish. Drink now or cellar.

Vintage	18	17	16
WR	6	6	6
Drink	19-20	P	P

MED/DRY $18 V+

Villa Maria Private Bin East Coast Pinot Gris   ★★★★

The great-value 2019 vintage (★★★★) is invitingly scented and mouthfilling, with strong peach, pear and spice flavours, and a dryish (5.5 grams/litre of residual sugar), very fresh and finely balanced finish. Enjoyable from the start.

Vintage	19	18	17	16
WR	7	7	7	6
Drink	19-22	19-21	19-20	P

MED/DRY $15 V+

Villa Maria Private Bin Lighter Gisborne Pinot Gris   (★★★)

The 2017 vintage (★★★) has more character than most 'light' wines. Harbouring 9.5 per cent alcohol, it is fresh and smooth, with crisp acidity, gentle sweetness (13.4 grams/litre of residual sugar), and lively pear-like flavours, showing good balance and depth.

MED/DRY $16 V+

Villa Maria Single Vineyard Seddon Marlborough Pinot Gris   ★★★★★

One of the country's top Pinot Gris, this Awatere Valley wine is typically partly barrel-fermented. The fleshy, finely textured 2018 vintage (★★★★★) was estate-grown and hand-picked. Bright, light yellow/green, it is youthful and concentrated, with excellent weight and mouthfeel, vibrant pear, lychee and spice flavours, a vaguely toasty note adding complexity and a dryish finish. Best drinking 2020+.

Vintage	18	17	16
WR	7	6	7
Drink	19-22	19-20	19-20

 MED/DRY $30 AV

VNO Hawke's Bay Pinot Gris   ★★★☆

Offering good value, the 2017 vintage (★★★☆) is a pale straw wine, fresh and full-bodied. It has pear and spice flavours, showing good vigour and delicacy, a sliver of sweetness, balanced acidity and lots of drink-young appeal.

MED/DRY $17 V+

Waimea Nelson Pinot Gris   ★★★☆

The 2018 vintage (★★★☆) was grown on the Waimea Plains and partly barrel-fermented. Bright, light lemon/green, it's a slightly Gewürztraminer-like wine, fresh, crisp and spicy, with good depth of vibrant, pear-like flavours, and an off-dry (5.7 grams/litre of residual sugar) finish.

MED/DRY $18 V+

Waipara Hills Waipara Valley Pinot Gris   ★★★★

The 2018 vintage (★★★★) was grown in North Canterbury and made in a medium-dry style. A scented, youthful wine, it is fresh and vibrant, with balanced acidity and very good vigour and depth of peachy, citrusy, slightly spicy flavours. Best drinking 2020+.

MED/DRY $22 V+

Wairau River Marlborough Pinot Gris   ★★★★

Estate-grown, the attractive 2017 vintage (★★★★) was handled mostly in tanks, but a small part of the blend was barrel-fermented. It is mouthfilling and vibrant, with strong pear and lychee flavours, hints of peaches and spices, a touch of complexity, fresh acidity, and a dryish (7 grams/litre of residual sugar) finish.

Vintage	17	16	15
WR	6	6	7
Drink	19-21	P	19-20

MED/DRY $20 V+

Whitehaven Marlborough Pinot Gris   ★★★★

The fragrant 2018 vintage (★★★★) is vibrantly fruity and youthful, with very good depth of peachy, slightly spicy and gingery flavours, and an off-dry (5.3 grams/litre of residual sugar), smooth, very harmonious finish. Best drinking mid-2020+.

MED/DRY $22 V+

Wither Hills Early Light Marlborough Pinot Gris ★★★

The attractive, light lemon/green 2018 vintage (★★★) is a light-bodied style (9.5 per cent alcohol), with fresh, vibrant flavours of pears, peaches and spices, and a finely poised, off-dry finish.

MED/DRY $18 AV

Wither Hills Marlborough Pinot Gris ★★★☆

Retasted in mid-2019, the easy-drinking 2018 vintage (★★★☆) is fleshy and clearly varietal, with very good depth of fresh pear, lychee, peach and spice flavours, a sliver of sweetness (7.6 grams/litre of residual sugar) and a smooth, slightly gingery finish. An Alsace-style wine, it offers good value.

MED/DRY $18 V+

Wooing Tree Central Otago Pinot Gris ★★★☆

Fragrant and full-bodied, the charming 2018 vintage (★★★★) is a Cromwell Basin wine, hand-picked and mostly tank-fermented; 26 per cent of the blend was fermented in seasoned French oak barrels. Made in an off-dry style (10.7 grams/litre of residual sugar), it is weighty, with vibrant pear, lychee and spice flavours, showing excellent freshness, delicacy and length.

MED/DRY $32 –V

Woven Stone Ohau Single Vineyard Pinot Gris (★★★☆)

From Ohau, in the Horowhenua, the 2019 vintage (★★★☆) is a faintly pink wine. Fresh and gently spicy, it is an easy-drinking style, with peachy, strawberryish flavours, a distinct touch of tannin, good depth and an off-dry (9.8 grams/litre of residual sugar) finish.

MED/DRY $17 V+

Yealands Estate Single Vineyard Marlborough Pinot Gris ★★★★

Estate-grown in the Seaview Vineyard, in the Awatere Valley, the 2017 vintage (★★★★) was mostly handled in tanks; 30 per cent of the blend was fermented in seasoned French oak barriques. Freshly scented, full-bodied, vibrantly fruity and smooth, it's a basically dry style (4.1 grams/litre of residual sugar), with gentle acidity and clearly varietal pear, lychee and spice flavours, showing very good depth, delicacy and harmony.

Vintage	17	16
WR	6	6
Drink	P	P

DRY $23 AV

Zephyr Marlborough Pinot Gris (★★★★)

Drinking well now, the fleshy 2018 vintage (★★★★) is a single-vineyard wine. Light yellow/ very pale gold, it is mouthfilling, with peachy, citrusy, gently sweet flavours (6 grams/litre of residual sugar), balanced acidity, a touch of complexity and a smooth finish.

MED/DRY $24 AV

Riesling

Riesling isn't yet one of New Zealand's great successes in overseas markets and most New Zealand wine lovers also ignore Riesling. The favourite white-wine variety of many winemakers – especially those in the South Island – Riesling barely registers on the wine sales charts in supermarkets, generating about 1 per cent of the dollar turnover.

Around the world, Riesling has traditionally been regarded as Chardonnay's great rival in the white-wine quality stakes, well ahead of Sauvignon Blanc. So why are wine lovers here slow to appreciate Riesling's stature?

Riesling is usually made in a slightly sweet style, to balance the grape's natural high acidity, but this obvious touch of sweetness runs counter to the fashion for dry wines. And fine Riesling demands time (at the very least, three years) to unfold its full potential; drunk in its infancy, as it so often is, it lacks the toasty, minerally, honeyed richness that is the real glory of Riesling.

After being overhauled by Pinot Gris in 2007, Riesling ranks as New Zealand's fourth most extensively planted white-wine variety. However, between 2007 and 2020, its total area of bearing vines has contracted, from 868 to 665 hectares.

The great grape of Germany, Riesling is a classic cool-climate variety, particularly well suited to the cooler growing temperatures and lower humidity of the South Island. Its two strongholds are Marlborough (where 40 per cent of the vines are clustered) and Canterbury (36 per cent), but the grape is also widely planted in Otago, Nelson and Wairarapa.

Riesling styles vary markedly around the world. Most Marlborough wines are medium to full-bodied (12 to 13.5 per cent alcohol), with just a touch of sweetness. However, a new breed of Riesling has emerged in the past decade – lighter (only 7.5 to 10 per cent alcohol) and markedly sweeter. These refreshingly light, sweet Rieslings offer a more vivid contrast in style to New Zealand's other major white wines, and are much closer in style to the classic German model.

Allan Scott Family Winemakers Estate Marlborough Riesling ★★★★

The 2017 vintage (★★★★) is instantly appealing. It has strong, lively, citrusy, peachy, slightly spicy flavours, gentle sweetness (16 grams/litre of residual sugar), moderate acidity and a smooth, lengthy finish. Good value.

MED $18 V+

Amisfield Dry Central Otago Riesling ★★★★☆

Estate-grown at Pisa, in the Cromwell Basin, the 2017 vintage (★★★★☆) was hand-picked and fermented with cultured and indigenous yeasts. It is scented and lively, in a medium-dry style (10 grams/litre of residual sugar), 10 per cent barrel-fermented, with good intensity of lemony, appley flavours, crisp, harmonious and lingering. Well worth cellaring, it should break into full stride 2020+.

Vintage	17
WR	6
Drink	19-23

 MED/DRY $25 V+

Amisfield Lowburn Terrace Central Otago Riesling ★★★★☆

Estate-grown in the Cromwell Basin, the 2018 vintage (★★★★★) was hand-picked and made in a low-alcohol (9 per cent), medium-sweet style (42 grams/litre of residual sugar). Bright, light lemon/green, it is a Mosel-like wine, light and lovely, with strong, vibrant, citrusy flavours, gentle sweetness, balanced acidity, and excellent depth, delicacy and harmony. Already delicious, it should be at its best 2020+.

Vintage	18
WR	5
Drink	19-23

 MED $30 –V

Astrolabe Astrolabe Farm Marlborough Riesling ★★★★

The 2017 vintage (★★★★☆) was grown at Grovetown, in the lower Wairau Valley, and made in a medium style (42 grams/litre of residual sugar). Light and lively, it has intense, citrusy flavours, a slightly minerally streak, and excellent richness, vigour and harmony. Delicious young, it's a drink-now or cellaring proposition.

Vintage	17
WR	6
Drink	19-30

 MED $25 AV

Astrolabe Farm Marlborough Dry Riesling ★★★★

Grown at Grovetown, in the Wairau Valley, the 2018 vintage (★★★★) is a single-vineyard wine, partly hand-picked. A fresh, medium-bodied wine, it has citrusy, slightly appley flavours, showing very good vigour and depth, and a slightly off-dry (5.3 grams/litre of residual sugar), crisp finish. Still unfolding, it's well worth cellaring to 2021+.

Vintage	18
WR	6
Drink	20-31

 MED/DRY $27 –V

Ata Rangi Martinborough Craighall Riesling ★★★★★

Still available, the 2013 vintage (★★★★☆) is a single-vineyard wine, harvested from mature vines and released after four years. Dry (3 grams/litre of residual sugar) but not austere, it has a fragrant, slightly toasty bouquet. Medium-bodied, it has balanced acidity and good intensity of citrusy, slightly toasty flavours, developing real complexity with bottle-age.

Vintage	13
WR	7
Drink	19-25

DRY $38 AV

Ataahua Waipara Riesling ★★★★☆

Instantly appealing, the 2018 vintage (★★★★☆) is a rich, medium style (44 grams/litre of residual sugar). Attractively scented, it has strong, citrusy, peachy, slightly appley flavours, showing good delicacy, and a lovely balance of sweetness and mouth-watering acidity. Drink now or cellar.

Vintage	18	17
WR	7	6
Drink	19-25	19-25

MED $26 AV

Aurum Central Otago Dry Riesling ★★★★☆

Well worth cellaring, the characterful 2017 vintage (★★★★☆) was hand-picked and handled entirely in stainless steel tanks. Bright, light lemon/green, it is a lemon-scented, vivacious wine, with very good intensity of citrusy, slightly appley and spicy flavours, vague sweetness (7 grams/litre of residual sugar) and firm acid spine. Best drinking 2020+.

Vintage	17
WR	6
Drink	19-27

MED/DRY $28 AV

Babich Family Estates Cowslip Valley Marlborough Riesling ★★★★

Estate-grown in the Waihopai Valley, the 2016 vintage (★★★★) was harvested with some 'noble rot' influence. Full-bodied, with good concentration of lemony, slightly sweet (9.4 grams/litre of residual sugar) and honeyed flavours, it's drinking well now.

MED/DRY $25 AV

Bald Hills Central Otago Riesling ★★★★☆

The classy 2016 vintage (★★★★★), grown at Bannockburn, has a scented, minerally bouquet. Drinking well in its youth, it has concentrated, ripe, citrusy, peachy flavours, gentle sweetness (17 grams/litre of residual sugar), good acid spine, and a very long finish.

Vintage	16
WR	6
Drink	19-23

MED $30 –V

Bannock Brae Central Otago Dry Riesling ★★★★☆

Grown in the Cromwell Basin, the characterful 2017 vintage (★★★★☆) reflects 'traditional practices of German winemakers 200 years ago', including fermentation in old oak barrels. It is lively and minerally, with strong lemon/lime flavours, showing excellent delicacy and complexity, and a crisp, dry (4.6 grams/litre of residual sugar) but not austere finish.

DRY $25 V+

Beach House Stoney Beach Gravels Hawke's Bay Riesling ★★★★

Hand-picked in The Levels Vineyard, at Te Awanga, the 2017 vintage (★★★★) is a light-bodied, medium style (25 grams/litre of residual sugar), with fresh, penetrating, lemony, appley flavours, racy acidity, and good harmony and vigour.

MED $20 V+

Black Ridge Central Otago Old Vine Riesling ★★★★☆

The classy 2017 vintage (★★★★★) was estate-grown at Alexandra and made in a medium-dry style (9 grams/litre of residual sugar). Light lemon/green, with a strong, lemony fragrance, it's a racy, medium-bodied wine with penetrating lemon/apple flavours, appetising acidity, and very impressive delicacy, harmony and length. Drink now or cellar.

Vintage	17	16
WR	5	5
Drink	19-25	19-22

MED/DRY $26 AV

Black Stilt Waitaki Valley Riesling ★★★★

The 2016 vintage (★★★★) is a fragrant, fresh, full-bodied wine (13 per cent alcohol) from North Otago. Light lemon/green, it is slightly sweet (15 grams/litre of residual sugar), with strong, citrusy, appley flavours, youthful vigour, balanced acidity and good harmony. Drink now or cellar.

MED $22 V+

Blank Canvas Marlborough Riesling (★★★★)

The 2018 vintage (★★★★) is a single-vineyard, Awatere Valley wine, light-bodied (8.6 per cent alcohol) and gently sweet (23 grams/litre of residual sugar), with mouth-watering acidity. It has strong, lemony, appley flavours, showing very good delicacy and harmony, and obvious cellaring potential; open 2021+.

Vintage	18
WR	5
Drink	19-25

MED $28 –V

Boneline, The, Hellblock Waipara Riesling ★★★★☆

Already highly appealing, the 2018 vintage (★★★★☆) is a medium style (21 grams/litre of residual sugar). Bright, light lemon/green, it is medium-bodied, with good intensity of citrusy, limey flavours, showing excellent freshness and vigour, and a finely balanced, lingering finish. Best drinking 2021+.

MED $32 –V

Boneline, The, Waipara Dry Riesling (★★★★)

Almost dry (6 grams/litre of residual sugar) but not austere, the 2017 vintage (★★★★) is a light lemon/green, fragrant, medium-bodied wine. Showing good concentration, it has citrusy, slightly appley flavours, balanced acidity, a touch of bottle-aged complexity and good harmony. Drink now or cellar.

MED/DRY $28 –V

Brennan Gibbston Central Otago Riesling

The powerful young 2018 vintage (★★★★☆) is full-bodied, with fresh grapefruit and peach flavours, showing good ripeness and richness. Bright, light lemon/green, with gentle sweetness and lively acidity, it's a generous, finely balanced wine, well worth cellaring.

MED/DRY $33 –V

Brightside Organic Riesling ★★★☆

From Kaimira Estate, in Nelson, the 2016 vintage (★★★☆) is an off-dry style (10 grams/litre of residual sugar). Medium-bodied, it has vibrant, lemony, appley flavours, well balanced for easy drinking, and good depth. Certified organic, it's priced sharply.

MED/DRY $16 V+

Brightwater Vineyards Nelson Natural Light Riesling

Freshly scented, the 2019 vintage (★★★★) is light in terms of alcohol (9 per cent), but there's no shortage of flavour. Bright, light lemon/green, it is tightly structured, with vibrant, lemony, appley flavours, showing good intensity, and a slightly sweet (10 grams/litre of residual sugar), mouth-wateringly crisp finish. Best drinking mid-2020.

Vintage	19
WR	6
Drink	20-23

MED/DRY $22 V+

Brightwater Vineyards Nelson Riesling ★★★★☆

Estate-grown and hand-picked on the Waimea Plains, the 2017 vintage (★★★★☆) is an off-dry style (10 grams/litre of residual sugar). A finely poised, medium-bodied wine, it has strong, fresh, lively, lemony flavours, hints of limes and apricots, good acid spine, and a long finish. Already enjoyable, it should be at its best 2020+.

Vintage	17
WR	6
Drink	19-22

MED/DRY $22 V+

Burn Cottage Central Otago Riesling/Grüner Veltliner ★★★★☆

Certified organic, the 2017 vintage (★★★★★) is an estate-grown, hand-picked blend of Riesling (67 per cent) and Grüner Veltliner (33 per cent), fermented and matured for 11 months in stainless steel barrels and old oak barriques. Bright, light yellow/green, it is mouthfilling, with highly concentrated, peachy, slightly spicy and toasty flavours, showing good complexity, and a finely balanced, dryish (10 grams/litre of residual sugar) finish. Full of personality.

MED/DRY $55 –V

Carrick Bannockburn Central Otago Riesling ★★★★★

Certified organic, the classy 2017 vintage (★★★★★) is a medium style, delicious young. Scented and lively, it has strong, ripe, citrusy, slightly appley and peachy flavours, showing excellent delicacy, harmony and length. Best drinking 2020+.

Vintage	17	16	15	14	13
WR	7	7	6	7	7
Drink	20-30	19-22	19-20	19-20	P

MED $27 V+

Carrick Central Otago Dry Riesling ★★★★☆

Certified organic, the 2017 vintage (★★★★☆) is a bone-dry wine, hand-picked and fermented with indigenous yeasts in old French oak barrels. It is fresh, medium-bodied and vibrantly fruity, with good intensity of lemony, appley flavours, a minerally streak, good acid spine and obvious potential; open mid-2020+.

Vintage	17
WR	6
Drink	20-26

DRY $27 AV

Carrick Josephine Central Otago Riesling ★★★★★

Carrick's 'reserve riesling' is estate-grown in Lot 8 Vineyard at Bannockburn, hand-harvested and made in a low-alcohol (9 per cent), sweetish style. Light lemon/green, the 2017 vintage (★★★★★) has penetrating, citrusy, appley flavours, hints of peaches and apricots, and a poised, racy finish. Certified organic, it's still youthful and best cellared to mid-2020+.

Vintage	17	16	15	14	13
WR	7	7	7	7	7
Drink	20-30	19-21	19-20	P	P

SW $28 V+

Caythorpe Family Estate Marlborough Riesling ★★★☆

The 2018 vintage (★★★☆) is a single-vineyard, Wairau Valley wine. Light lemon/green, it is medium-bodied, with strong, citrusy, peachy, slightly gingery flavours and an off-dry (8.5 grams/litre of residual sugar), crisp finish. Best drinking 2021+.

MED/DRY $20 AV

Ceres Black Rabbit Vineyard Central Otago Riesling ★★★★☆

Grown at Bannockburn, the 2018 vintage (★★★★☆) is attractively scented, with a Mosel-like balance and lightness (10.5 per cent alcohol). Bright, light lemon/green, it is vivacious, with strong lemon/lime flavours, gentle sweetness (34 grams/litre of residual sugar) and fresh acidity. Already delicious, it's age-worthy too.

MED $28 AV

Chard Farm Central Otago Riesling ★★★★☆

Drinking well in its youth, the 2017 vintage (★★★★☆) was hand-picked in the Cromwell Basin. It has a scented, citrusy bouquet. Medium-bodied, with good intensity of fresh, lemony, appley flavours and a slightly minerally streak, it has a gentle splash of sweetness (16 grams/litre of residual sugar) and a long, finely poised finish.

MED $26 AV

Cherry Orchard, The, Bannockburn Single Vineyard Central Otago Riesling   ★★★★

Drinking well now, the 2015 vintage (★★★★) is a single-vineyard wine, lemon-scented, with good intensity of citrusy, slightly spicy flavours, a hint of sweetness and some aging potential.

MED/DRY $22 V+

Clark Estate Classic Marlborough Riesling   (★★★★)

Delicious young, the 2018 vintage (★★★★) is an attractively scented wine, grown in the upper Awatere Valley. Pale straw, it is fresh, medium-bodied and crisp, with a gentle splash of sweetness and generous, ripe, peachy flavours, showing good vigour and depth. Balanced for easy drinking, it should also reward cellaring.

MED $19 V+

Coopers Creek Marlborough Riesling   ★★★☆

Finely balanced for early enjoyment, the 2018 vintage (★★★☆) is a fresh, medium-bodied wine with vibrant, lemony, appley flavours, showing good depth, a gentle splash of sweetness and lively acidity. Drink now or cellar.

MED/DRY $18 V+

Crater Rim, The, Waipara Riesling   ★★★★☆

Tasted in mid-2018, the 2012 to 2014 vintages, all from a single vineyard, showed impressive quality and value. The 2014 vintage (★★★★☆) is a medium style (30 grams/litre of residual sugar), with strong, ripe, peachy, slightly spicy flavours, building bottle-aged complexity. The 2013 vintage (★★★★☆) has excellent drive and depth, with peachy, spicy flavours, low alcohol (9.5 per cent), gentle sweetness and lovely harmony. Maturing well, the 2012 vintage (★★★★) is slightly more restrained, with a pale lemon/green hue, good weight, a splash of sweetness and strong, lemony, appley flavours. It's drinking well now.

MED $22 V+

Dashwood by Vavasour Marlborough Riesling   ★★★★

The 2019 vintage (★★★★) offers top value. Light-bodied, it is attractively scented, with vibrant, citrusy, slightly appley flavours, gentle sweetness (19 grams/litre of residual sugar), appetising acidity, and very good delicacy, depth and harmony. Already enjoyable, it should be at its best 2021+.

Vintage	19
WR	7
Drink	19-25

MED $16 V+

Doctors', The Marlborough Riesling   ★★★★

Light and lively, the 2019 vintage (★★★★) is already very enjoyable. Crafted in a low-alcohol style (9 per cent), it is strongly varietal, with fresh, citrusy, appley flavours, a distinct splash of sweetness (37 grams/litre of residual sugar), and finely balanced acidity. Good summertime sipping. (From Forrest Estate.)

MED $22 V+

Domain Road Duffers Creek Bannockburn Central Otago Riesling   ★★★★☆

Approachable now, the 2017 vintage (★★★★☆) is a medium style, hand-picked at two sites. Bright, light lemon/green, it is invitingly scented, with strong, vibrant, citrusy, slightly appley flavours, a gentle splash of sweetness (14.7 grams/litre of residual sugar), appetising acidity and a long finish. Full of youthful vigour, it should be at its best 2021+.

 MED/DRY $25 V+

Domain Road The Water Race Bannockburn Central Otago Dry Riesling   ★★★★

Highly scented, the 2017 vintage (★★★★☆) is a vigorous, youthful wine, dryish (5.5 grams/litre of residual sugar) rather than bone-dry. Bright, light lemon/green, it is medium-bodied, with penetrating, vibrant, citrusy flavours, firm acid spine and obvious potential; open 2021+.

 MED/DRY $25 AV

Dragon Bones Waitaki Valley North Otago Riesling   (★★★★★)

From Lone Hill Vineyard, the 2016 vintage (★★★★★) is a delicious wine, bargain-priced. Described as a 'spatlese trocken style', it is a single-vineyard, hand-picked wine, with a bright light lemon/green hue and highly scented bouquet. Full of personality, it has intense, peachy, lemony flavours, gentle sweetness (7 grams/litre of residual sugar), crisp acidity, slightly toasty, bottle-aged notes adding complexity, and a poised, long finish. Great value.

 MED/DRY $22 V+

Dry River Craighall Vineyard Martinborough Riesling   ★★★★★

One of the finest Rieslings in the country, this is typically a wine of exceptional purity, delicacy and depth, with a proven ability to flourish in the cellar for many years. The grapes are sourced from a small block of mature vines, mostly over 20 years old, in the Craighall Vineyard, with yields limited to an average of 6 tonnes per hectare, and the wine is stop-fermented just short of dryness – the 2018 vintage (★★★★★) has 5 grams/litre of residual sugar. Bright, light lemon/green, it is invitingly scented, with intense, lemony, appley flavours, hints of spices and ginger, a minerally streak, good acid spine, and a long, tight finish. Best drinking 2023+.

 MED/DRY $50 AV

Dry River Craighall Vineyard Selection Martinborough Riesling   ★★★★★

This consistently classy wine is late-harvested to 'produce a Riesling with low alcohol, high residual sugar and high acidity, in order to create a tension between these components'. The gently botrytis-affected 2018 vintage (★★★★★) is already a lovely mouthful. Bright, light gold, it has a fragrant, slightly honeyed bouquet, concentrated, ripe, peachy flavours, abundant sweetness (120 grams/litre of residual sugar) and a crisp, lasting finish. Drink now or cellar.

SW $69 –V

Esk Valley Marlborough Riesling ★★★★

Grown at two sites, in the Awatere and Wairau valleys, the freshly scented, finely balanced 2018 vintage (★★★★) is medium-bodied, with citrusy, slightly sweet flavours (8.1 grams/litre of residual sugar) that linger well. Showing very good intensity, vigour and harmony, it's enjoyable young, but well worth cellaring.

Vintage	18	17
WR	6	6
Drink	19-25	19-23

MED/DRY $20 V+

Felton Road Bannockburn Central Otago Riesling ★★★★★

Estate-grown in The Elms Vineyard, this gently sweet style has deep flavours woven with fresh acidity. It offers more drink-young appeal than its Dry Riesling stablemate, but invites long-term cellaring. Hand-picked and tank-fermented with indigenous yeasts, it is bottled with a high level of residual sugar (50 grams/litre in 2019). The 2019 vintage (★★★★★) is a Mosel-like wine, still very youthful. Bright, light lemon/green, it is intense and vibrant, with strong peach, lemon and apple flavours and a crisp, lasting finish. Best drinking 2022+.

Vintage	19	18
WR	7	7
Drink	19-39	19-38

SW $39 AV

Felton Road Block 1 Riesling – see Sweet White Wines

Felton Road Dry Riesling ★★★★★

Based on low-yielding vines in schisty soils at Bannockburn, in Central Otago, this wine is hand-picked in The Elms Vineyard and fermented with indigenous yeasts. The 2019 vintage (★★★★★) is well worth cellaring. Bright, light lemon/green, it is attractively scented, medium-bodied and youthful, with intense, lemony, slightly appley and spicy flavours, dry (4 grams/litre of residual sugar), finely balanced and long. Not at all austere in its infancy, it should be at its best 2022+.

Vintage	19	18
WR	7	7
Drink	19-34	19-33

DRY $39 AV

Forrest Marlborough Riesling ★★★★

Drinking well now, but also worth cellaring, the 2017 vintage (★★★★) is light to medium-bodied (10.5 per cent alcohol), with fresh, strong, citrusy flavours, a splash of sweetness (8 grams/litre of residual sugar), and very good depth and harmony.

MED/DRY $20 V+

Framingham Classic Marlborough Riesling ★★★★★

Top vintages of this Marlborough wine are strikingly aromatic, richly flavoured and zesty. The classy 2016 vintage (★★★★★), from a frost-affected year, is not certified organic (unlike the 2015). Light lemon/green, it is invitingly scented, with strong, youthful, citrusy, limey flavours, showing excellent vigour, delicacy and intensity, and a very harmonious, lingering finish. Best drinking 2020+.

Framingham F-Series Old Vine Marlborough Riesling ★★★★★

From estate vines planted at Renwick 35 years ago, this organically certified wine is promoted as an 'Old World style, with more texture and complexity'. Powerful but elegant, the 2016 vintage (★★★★★) was partly (10 per cent) barrel-fermented and all of the wine was lees-aged. A dryish style (7.7 grams/litre of residual sugar), it is fragrant and mouthfilling, with intense, vibrant, citrusy flavours, peachy, spicy, toasty notes adding complexity, good acid spine, and a finely balanced, enduring finish. Full of personality, it's drinking well now, but likely to be long-lived.

Framingham Jack Frost Marlborough Riesling (★★★★)

In a growing season when 'your organic Riesling vineyard gets frosted for the first time in 35 years, what do you do?' Framingham checked with mates next door, to see what else was available. Delicious in its youth, the 2016 vintage (★★★★) is mouthfilling, ripe and rounded, with gentle sweetness, moderate acidity and strong, peachy, vaguely honeyed flavours.

Gemstone by Giesen Marlborough Riesling ★★★★☆

Full of interest, the 2018 vintage (★★★★) is a single-vineyard, Awatere Valley wine, fermented in a mix of large granite tanks (made from a 'giant slab of volcanic rock'), seasoned French oak puncheons, and stainless steel tanks. Fragrant and light-bodied, it has citrusy, slightly appley flavours, gentle sweetness (39 grams/litre of residual sugar), balanced acidity, a distinct touch of complexity, and notable harmony. Already enjoyable, it's well worth trying.

Georges Road Block Three Waipara Riesling ★★★★☆

The 2017 vintage (★★★★☆) was estate-grown in North Canterbury, hand-picked, fermented with indigenous yeasts and lees-aged. A tightly structured, medium-bodied wine, it is highly scented, with strong, peachy, citrusy, slightly spicy and gingery flavours, crisp, lively acidity and an off-dry (8 grams/litre of residual sugar), lasting finish. Already very expressive, it should also be long-lived.

MED/DRY $25 V+

Gibbston Valley GV Collection Central Otago Riesling   ★★★★

The youthful 2018 vintage (★★★★) was grown at Bendigo and Pisa, hand-picked and cool-fermented in tanks. It is a medium-bodied, vibrantly fruity wine, with strong, lemony, limey, slightly appley flavours, gentle sweetness (9.5 grams/litre of residual sugar) and appetising acidity. Best drinking 2020+.

MED/DRY $28 –V

Gibbston Valley Red Shed Central Otago Riesling   (★★★★★)

The lovely 2018 vintage (★★★★★) is a single-vineyard, Bendigo wine, hand-harvested and tank-fermented with indigenous yeasts. Medium-bodied, it has intense, vibrant, citrusy, limey flavours, and a gently sweet (15 grams/litre of residual sugar), finely poised, lasting finish. Still youthful, it's well worth cellaring to 2021+. (From the same vines, this wine replaces Gibbston Valley's former Le Fou Riesling.)

MED $39 AV

Gladstone Vineyard Wairarapa Riesling   (★★★★☆)

Certified organic, the stylish 2016 vintage (★★★★☆) was hand-picked from 25-year-old, estate-grown vines and matured for six months on its full yeast lees. Light-bodied, it's a medium-dry style (11 grams/litre of residual sugar), with youthful lemon/lime flavours, showing excellent freshness, delicacy, poise and length.

MED/DRY $25 V+

Greenhough Apple Valley Nelson Riesling   ★★★★★

Instantly appealing, the 2019 vintage (★★★★★) was grown and hand-picked at Upper Moutere. Light-bodied (9.5 per cent alcohol) and gently sweet, it is attractively scented, with intense peach, lemon and apple flavours, showing excellent freshness, delicacy and harmony.

MED $22 V+

Greenhough Hope Vineyard Nelson Riesling   ★★★★☆

This wine is hand-harvested from vines that average over 20 years old. Certified organic, the 2015 vintage (★★★★☆) was handled entirely in tanks. An attractively scented, medium-bodied wine, it has strong, vigorous, citrusy, limey flavours, a minerally streak, a touch of complexity and a dryish (6 grams/litre of residual sugar), crisp finish. Still developing, it should be at its best 2020+.

Vintage	15	14	13
WR	7	7	6
Drink	19-23	19-21	19-20

MED/DRY $26 AV

Greystone Sea Star Waipara Valley Riesling ★★★★☆

A top example of dry Riesling, the 2016 vintage (★★★★★) was estate-grown, hand-picked, fermented and lees-stirred in tanks, and bottled unfined. Fleshy and full-bodied (13 per cent alcohol), with moderate acidity for Riesling, it has penetrating, peachy, lemony, slightly limey flavours, that build to a very finely balanced, dry (4.7 grams/litre of residual sugar), lasting finish.

Vintage	16
WR	6
Drink	19-25

DRY $28 AV

Greystone Waipara Valley Riesling ★★★★★

Greystone sees this wine as 'the truest expression of the variety for us'. Certified organic, the 2017 vintage (★★★★☆) was hand-picked, with some botrytis ('noble rot') influence. It is medium-bodied, with fresh, strong, citrusy, slightly peachy and honeyed flavours, a distinct splash of sweetness (22 grams/litre of residual sugar), crisp acidity and lots of drink-young appeal.

Vintage	17
WR	4
Drink	19-25

MED $27 V+

Greywacke Marlborough Riesling ★★★★★

The 2018 vintage (★★★★☆) is a single-vineyard wine, grown at Fairhall. Hand-harvested, it was 50 per cent fermented in old oak casks and fully oak-matured. Still unfolding, it is weighty, with good concentration of vigorous lemon/lime flavours, gentle sweetness (20 grams/litre of residual sugar) and appetising acidity. Best drinking 2021+. The 2017 vintage (★★★★★) is a very refined, youthful wine, likely to be long-lived. Light lemon/green, it has strong, peachy, citrusy flavours, showing excellent delicacy and depth, a splash of sweetness (16 grams/litre of residual sugar), and a finely balanced, persistent finish.

Vintage	18	17	16	15	14	13	12	11	10
WR	6	6	6	5	5	6	5	6	5
Drink	19-27	19-26	19-25	19-24	19-23	19-23	P	P	P

MED $29 V+

Grove Mill Wairau Valley Marlborough Riesling ★★★☆

Maturing gracefully, the 2016 vintage (★★★☆) is full-bodied, with gentle sweetness (6 grams/litre of residual sugar) and plenty of citrusy, peachy, slightly spicy flavour.

Vintage	16
WR	6
Drink	19-26

MED/DRY $20 AV

Hans Herzog Marlborough Riesling ★★★★★

Certified organic, the fragrant 2014 vintage (★★★★) was estate-grown in the Wairau Valley and matured for nine months in French oak puncheons. Bright, light yellow, it is a powerful, full-bodied style, delicious now, with deep, vibrant grapefruit-like flavours and a fully dry finish. Sure to be long-lived, it's best opened 2020+.

DRY $44 AV

Hawkshead Central Otago Riesling ★★★★☆

The 2018 vintage (★★★★☆) was grown at Lowburn, in the Cromwell Basin. Bright, light lemon/green, it is ripely scented and mouthfilling, with strong, peachy, slightly spicy flavours, a hint of apricot, and a gentle splash of sweetness (11 grams/litre of residual sugar), balanced by lively acidity. Already very open and expressive, it should be at its best 2020+.

MED/DRY $29 AV

Highfield Marlborough Riesling ★★★★

Still on sale, the 2015 vintage (★★★★) is a gently sweet style (24 grams/litre of residual sugar), medium-bodied and vaguely honeyed, with ripe, peachy, slightly limey and toasty flavours, showing good concentration.

Vintage	15
WR	6
Drink	P

MED $21 V+

Hunter's Marlborough Riesling ★★★★

This wine is consistently good and bargain-priced. Grown at two sites at Rapaura, the attractively scented 2018 vintage (★★★★) is fresh, medium-bodied and lively, with very good depth of citrusy, slightly appley flavours, a sliver of sweetness (6.9 grams/litre of residual sugar) and appetising acidity. Open 2021+.

Vintage	18
WR	6
Drink	19-28

MED/DRY $20 V+

Jackson Estate Homestead Marlborough Dry Riesling ★★★★

Starting to break into full stride, the 2016 vintage (★★★★☆), partly barrel-aged, is a very good buy. Bright, light lemon/green, it has a lemony, slightly toasty, inviting fragrance. Medium-bodied, it is citrusy, with bottle-aged complexity and a crisp, dry (3.8 grams/litre of residual sugar), long finish.

Vintage	16
WR	6
Drink	20-26

DRY $20 V+

Johanneshof Marlborough Riesling Medium-Dry   ★★★★

Vibrantly fruity and tightly structured, the 2016 vintage (★★★★☆) is a full-bodied, medium style (19.5 grams/litre of residual sugar). It has strong, crisp, citrusy flavours, a vague hint of honey, and excellent poise and persistence.

MED $25 AV

Johner Estate Wairarapa Riesling   ★★★★

The 2017 vintage (★★★★☆) is a good buy. Bright, light lemon/green, it is crisp, strong and lively, with good intensity of lemony, limey flavours, gentle sweetness (12 grams/litre of residual sugar), and a finely poised finish. Best drinking 2021+.

Vintage	17	16	15
WR	5	6	7
Drink	19-23	19-22	19-25

MED/DRY $20 V+

Kahurangi Estate Mt Arthur Reserve Nelson Riesling   (★★★★★)

Already drinking well, the 2017 vintage (★★★★★) is fragrant, tightly structured and very age-worthy. Bright, light lemon/green, it has excellent intensity and vigour, with strong lemon/apple flavours, gentle sweetness, lively acidity and a long finish. A good buy.

MED/DRY $25 V+

Kahurangi Estate Nelson Riesling   (★★★★)

The tightly structured 2017 vintage (★★★★) is still unfolding. Bright, light lemon/green, it is fresh and vigorous, with good intensity of citrusy, slightly appley flavours and an off-dry, crisp finish. Well worth cellaring.

MED/DRY $22 V+

Kaimira Estate Brightwater Nelson Riesling   ★★★☆

This estate-grown Nelson wine typically matures well. The 2015 vintage (★★★☆) is fresh and vibrant, with lemon/lime flavours, slightly peachy notes, good depth, and a finely balanced, dry (4.9 grams/litre of residual sugar) finish. Starting to develop bottle-aged complexity, it's certified organic.

DRY $22 AV

Kaimira Estate Iti Selection Brightwater Riesling   ★★★☆

Made in a fairly low-alcohol style ('Iti' is Maori for 'Small'), the 2016 vintage (★★★☆), retasted in March 2018, is light-bodied (10.5 per cent), with lively, lemony, appley, slightly sweet flavours (15.4 grams/litre of residual sugar), showing good depth, and an appetisingly crisp, harmonious finish. It's certified organic.

Vintage	16
WR	5
Drink	19-23

MED $22 AV

Kalex Alex Kaufman Single Vineyard Bendigo Terraces
Central Otago Riesling   (★★★☆)

Still on sale, the 2015 vintage (★★★☆ was grown in the Mondillo Vineyard, at Bendigo. Although not highly fragrant, it has good intensity and vigour. Made in an off-dry style (11.5 grams/litre of residual sugar), it is medium-bodied, citrusy and crisp, with very good balance and depth. Drink now or cellar.

 MED/DRY $26 –V

Kalex Alex Kaufman Single Vineyard Pisa Terrace Central Otago Riesling (★★★★☆)

Grown at Lowburn, the attractive 2015 vintage (★★★★☆) was made in an off-dry style (12.3 grams/litre of residual sugar). It is fresh and lively, with good intensity of citrusy, slightly limey flavours, a touch of bottle-aged complexity, and a long, racy finish.

 MED/DRY $26 AV

Konrad Dry Marlborough Riesling   ★★★☆

Estate-grown in the Waihopai Valley, the 2015 vintage (★★★★) has a scented, slightly toasty bouquet. Showing good personality, it has moderate alcohol (10.5 per cent) and strong, lemony, appley, minerally flavours, crisp, dryish and finely balanced for current drinking.

 MED/DRY $23 –V

Lawson's Dry Hills Marlborough Riesling   ★★★★

The youthful 2018 vintage (★★★★) is a single-vineyard, Waihopai Valley wine. Worth cellaring, it is medium-bodied, with strong, citrusy, slightly spicy flavours, and an off-dry (7 grams/litre of residual sugar), crisp finish.

Vintage	18	17	16	15	14
WR	7	7	6	7	6
Drink	19-30	19-28	19-24	19-22	19-20

MED/DRY $20 V+

Loveblock Bone Dry Marlborough Riesling   ★★★★

Still on sale, the 2014 vintage (★★★★) was estate-grown in the lower Awatere Valley. Showing some toasty, bottle-aged development, it is full-bodied, with tangy acidity, a minerally streak and a strong surge of ripe, peachy, slightly spicy, fully dry (1.4 grams/litre of residual sugar) flavours. Certified organic.

Vintage	14	13	12	11
WR	6	NM	NM	6
Drink	19-22	NM	NM	P

DRY $25 AV

Luna Martinborough Riesling   (★★★☆)

Already enjoyable, the 2018 vintage (★★★☆) is a single-vineyard wine, medium-bodied, with strong, lemony, slightly peachy and appley flavours, showing good vigour, and an off-dry, crisp finish. Best drinking 2020+.

MED/DRY $24 –V

Main Divide North Canterbury Riesling ★★★★

Enjoyable now, the 2016 vintage (★★★★) of this good-value Waipara wine is a distinctly medium style. Bright, light yellow/green, it has generous, citrusy, slightly spicy flavours, a hint of honey, fresh acidity, and excellent immediacy and harmony. (From Pegasus Bay.)

MED $21 V+

Maori Point Single Vineyard Central Otago Riesling (★★★★☆)

Already highly enjoyable, the 2018 vintage (★★★★☆) was hand-picked in the Mondillo Vineyard at Bendigo. It is attractively scented, with fresh, punchy, citrusy, slightly appley and peachy flavours, gentle sweetness (11 grams/litre of residual sugar), appetising acidity and a lengthy finish. An intense, harmonious wine, it should reward cellaring, but is very expressive in its youth.

Vintage	18
WR	6
Drink	19-22

MED/DRY $28 AV

Martinborough Vineyard Manu Martinborough Riesling ★★★★☆

The 2018 vintage (★★★★★) is delicious in its youth, but well worth cellaring. Finely scented, it has intense, lemony, appley flavours, gentle sweetness (23 grams/litre of residual sugar), fresh acidity and lovely vibrancy, depth and harmony.

MED $28 AV

Maude Mt Maude Vineyard East Block Wanaka Riesling ★★★★★

From vines planted in 1994 on a steep, north-facing slope at Wanaka, in Central Otago, the 2019 vintage (★★★★★) is light and racy, with an attractively scented bouquet. Bright, light lemon/green, it is a Mosel-like wine, with intense lemon/apple flavours, gentle sweetness (41 grams/litre of residual sugar), lively acidity and a long finish. Best drinking 2022+.

Vintage	19	18	17	16	15
WR	7	7	7	7	5
Drink	19-29	19-26	19-26	19-26	19-22

MED $32 AV

Maude Mt Maude Vineyard Wanaka Dry Riesling ★★★★★

Hand-harvested from vines planted in Central Otago in 1994, the 2018 vintage (★★★★★) is a great candidate for cellaring. Fresh, tight, intense and minerally, it is medium-bodied, with citrusy, appley flavours, showing lovely delicacy, vibrancy and length. The 2019 vintage (★★★★★) is very youthful and intense. Full of potential, it is a crisp, medium-bodied wine, with strong lemon/lime flavours, a sliver of sweetness (6 grams/litre of residual sugar), and a racy, lasting finish.

Vintage	19	18	17	16	15
WR	7	7	6	7	5
Drink	19-29	19-26	19-26	19-29	19-25

MED/DRY $32 AV

Millton Opou Vineyard Riesling   ★★★★☆

Typically scented, with rich, lemony, often honeyed flavours, this is the country's northernmost fine-quality Riesling. Harvested from Gisborne vines of varying ages – the oldest planted in 1981 – it is gently sweet, in a less racy style than South Island wines. The grapes, grown in the Opou Vineyard at Manutuke, are hand-picked over a month at three stages of ripening, usually culminating in a final pick of botrytis-affected fruit. Still on sale, the 2015 vintage (★★★★☆) is a low-alcohol (8.5 per cent), gently sweet wine (36 grams/litre of residual sugar). Bright, light lemon/green, it is light and tangy, with intense, vibrant lemon/lime flavours, appetising acidity, and excellent poise and vigour. Certified organic.

Vintage	15	14	13	12
WR	6	6	7	6
Drink	19-25	19-25	19-22	19-20

 MED $28 AV

Misha's Vineyard Limelight Riesling   ★★★★★

This single-vineyard wine is hand-harvested at Bendigo, in Central Otago. Lovely now, the 2016 vintage (★★★★★) was made in a medium style (29 grams/litre of residual sugar), with complexity gained by fermenting 24 per cent of the blend with indigenous yeasts in old French oak barrels. Bright, light lemon/green, it is richly scented and vivacious, with deep, lemony, appley, slightly peachy flavours, gentle sweetness balanced by mouth-watering acidity, and a finely poised, lasting finish. Best drinking 2021+.

Vintage	15	14	13	12	11	10
WR	7	6	7	7	6	6
Drink	19-27	19-26	19-25	19-23	19-23	19-22

 MED $28 V+

Misha's Vineyard Lyric Riesling   ★★★★★

This is the sort of 'dry' Riesling New Zealand needs a lot more of. Estate-grown and hand-harvested at Bendigo, in Central Otago, the youthful 2016 vintage (★★★★★) is fractionally off-dry (4.5 grams/litre of residual sugar). It was mostly handled in tanks, but 14 per cent of the blend was fermented with indigenous yeasts in old French oak barrels. Bright, light lemon/green, it is finely scented, mouthfilling and vibrantly fruity, with penetrating, citrusy, limey flavours, dry but not austere, appetising acidity, a distinct touch of complexity and a finely poised, long finish. Likely to be long-lived, it should be at its best 2021+.

Vintage	16	15	14	13	12	11	10
WR	7	7	NM	7	7	6	6
Drink	19-29	19-27	NM	19-25	19-23	19-23	19-22

 DRY $28 V+

Mission Hawke's Bay Riesling   ★★★☆

Still youthful, the 2016 vintage (★★★☆) is a great-value, single-vineyard wine, grown at Ohiti. Bright, light lemon/green, with a scented bouquet and emerging toasty, bottle-aged aromas, it is medium-bodied, with strong, crisp, citrusy, limey flavours and an off-dry, tangy finish.

MED/DRY $16 V+

Mondillo Central Otago Riesling   ★★★★☆

Estate-grown at Bendigo, the impressive 2018 vintage (★★★★★) has lovely freshness, delicacy, drive and harmony. Light lemon/green, it is an attractively scented, medium-bodied wine, with concentrated, ripe, citrusy flavours, hints of peaches and spices, slightly minerally notes and a long, basically dry (5.7 grams/litre of residual sugar) finish. Best drinking 2020+.

MED/DRY $28 AV

Mount Brown Estates Grand Reserve Waipara Valley Riesling   (★★★★)

The 2016 vintage (★★★★) is a late-picked, medium style (18 grams/litre of residual sugar), with a scented, slightly honeyed bouquet. Citrusy, with moderate acidity, it is full-flavoured, with a vague hint of botrytis and very good balance and depth.

MED $23 AV

Mount Brown Estates North Canterbury Riesling   ★★★☆

Delicious young, the 2018 vintage (★★★★) is a distinctly medium style (30 grams/litre of residual sugar). Light lemon/green, it is medium-bodied and vibrantly fruity, with good intensity of citrusy, peachy flavours, hints of apricot and honey, and appetising acidity. Great value.

MED $16 V+

Mount Edward Central Otago Riesling   ★★★★★

Certified organic, the classy 2017 vintage (★★★★★) was grown at Lowburn. Full of personality, it is invitingly scented, crisp and dryish (7 grams/litre of residual sugar), with excellent intensity of peachy, slightly spicy flavours, a minerally thread, and a finely balanced, very long finish. A dynamic young wine, it should be long-lived.

MED/DRY $27 V+

Mount Riley Marlborough Riesling   ★★★☆

Still a baby, the 2019 vintage (★★★☆) is an attractively scented wine, grown in the central Wairau Valley. Pale lemon/green, it is fresh and medium-bodied, with a gentle splash of sweetness, balanced acidity, good depth of citrusy, slightly appley and spicy flavours, and lots of youthful vigour. Fine value.

MED/DRY $15 V+

Moutere Hills Single Vineyard Nelson Riesling   ★★★★

The 2018 vintage (★★★★) was estate-grown at Upper Moutere. Still very youthful, it is fresh and lively, with strong lemon, apple and spice flavours, a slightly minerally streak, gentle sweetness (16 grams/litre of residual sugar) and a crisp, finely balanced finish. Best drinking 2021+.

MED $29 –V

Mt Beautiful North Canterbury Riesling ★★★★☆

Estate-grown at Cheviot, the 2017 vintage (★★★★★) has a strong presence. Already very expressive, it is a highly scented, medium-bodied wine, with concentrated, citrusy, appley flavours, showing excellent drive and immediacy, gentle sweetness, a touch of complexity and a long, minerally finish.

Vintage	17	16	15
WR	5	7	7
Drink	19-23	19-25	19-25

 MED/DRY $28 AV

Mt Difficulty Bannockburn Central Otago Dry Riesling ★★★★☆

Estate-grown, the 2018 vintage (★★★★☆) is a mouthfilling, bone-dry wine, but not at all austere. Fleshy, with generous, ripe grapefruit and lime flavours, it's a distinctive wine, fresh and finely balanced. Very age-worthy, it's already drinking well.

Vintage	18
WR	6
Drink	19-28

 DRY $27 V+

Mt Difficulty Packspur Lowburn Valley Riesling ★★★★☆

Already delicious, the 2017 vintage (★★★★★) is a single-vineyard, Central Otago wine, from an elevated site (360 to 380 metres above sea level), planted in 1992. Bright, light yellow/green, it is mouthfilling and fleshy, with highly concentrated, peachy, citrusy flavours, woven with fresh acidity, gentle sweetness (29 grams/litre of residual sugar), and a long, very harmonious finish. Drink now or cellar.

 MED $39 –V

Mt Difficulty Target Bannockburn Medium Riesling ★★★★☆

From Central Otago, the 2017 vintage (★★★★☆) is already delicious. Made in a medium style (37 grams/litre of residual sugar), it is attractively scented and lively, with very good intensity of lemony, slightly appley and peachy flavours, balanced acidity, and excellent vibrancy and harmony. Drink now or cellar.

Vintage	17
WR	6
Drink	19-28

 MED $26 AV

Mud House The Mound Vineyard Waipara Valley Riesling ★★★★

Made in a 'medium-sweet' style, the 2018 vintage (★★★★) is a single-vineyard wine, estate-grown in North Canterbury. It is light (8.5 per cent alcohol) and lively, with crisp, lemony, appley flavours, showing good intensity, and firm acid spine. Best drinking 2021+.

MED $23 AV

Mud House Waipara Valley Riesling   ★★★☆

Priced sharply, the 2018 vintage (★★★☆) is a medium style. Enjoyable young, it is bright, light lemon/green, with good depth of citrusy, peachy, gently sweet flavours, in a fresh, medium-bodied style, balanced for smooth, easy drinking.

 MED $15 V+

Neudorf Moutere Riesling Dry   ★★★★☆

The very age-worthy 2016 vintage (★★★★☆) was estate-grown at Upper Moutere, in Nelson, hand-harvested and fermented in tanks (81 per cent) and old oak puncheons (19 per cent). A medium-bodied wine, it has searching, delicate, lemony and appley flavours, biscuity and minerally notes, and a dryish (7.5 grams/litre of residual sugar), long finish.

Vintage	16	15	MED/DRY $27 AV
WR	6	7	
Drink	19-26	19-25	

Nga Waka Martinborough Dry Riesling   ★★★★☆

Still available, the 2015 vintage (★★★★☆) is an attractively scented wine with strong, citrusy flavours, dryish (5 grams/litre of residual sugar) and harmonious, and some toasty, bottle-aged notes. An intensely varietal wine, it shows good personality.

Vintage	15	MED/DRY $25 V+
WR	6	
Drink	19-28	

Old Coach Road Nelson Riesling   ★★★

From Seifried, the 2018 vintage (★★★) is priced very sharply. Bright, light yellow/green, it has good depth of lemony, slightly spicy flavours, a hint of honey, gentle sweetness (16 grams/litre of residual sugar), and plenty of drink-young charm.

Vintage	15	MED $14 V+
WR	6	
Drink	19-22	

Omeo Blackman's Gully Single Vineyard Central Otago Riesling   ★★★★

Past releases have been impressive, but the 2018 vintage (★★), grown at Alexandra, was disappointing when I tasted it in September 2019. Made in a medium-dry style (8 grams/litre of residual sugar), it lacked fragrance and delicacy, with strong, but slightly hard and austere, flavours.

Vintage	18	17	MED/DRY $23 AV
WR	7	6	
Drink	19-26	19-25	

Ostler Lakeside Riesling Spätlese (★★★★★)

Grown in the Waitaki Valley, North Otago, the 2015 vintage (★★★★★) is a lovely wine. Light-bodied, it is vivacious, with penetrating, citrusy, peachy flavours, gently sweet (29 grams/litre of residual sugar) and mouth-wateringly crisp, and a very long finish.

Paddy Borthwick Wairarapa Riesling ★★★★

Drinking well in its youth, the 2018 vintage (★★★★) is a single-vineyard wine, scented and full-bodied, with lively acidity, good intensity of citrusy, limey flavours and an appetisingly crisp, dry (3 grams/litre of residual sugar) finish.

Palliser Estate Martinborough Riesling ★★★★

The tightly structured, youthful 2018 vintage (★★★★) was estate-grown at two sites. Bright, light lemon/green, it is vigorous, with good intensity of fresh, lemony, slightly spicy flavours, woven with appetising acidity, and an off-dry (6.6 grams/litre of residual sugar) finish.

MED/DRY $25 AV

Pegasus Bay Aria Late Picked Riesling – see Sweet White Wines

Pegasus Bay Bel Canto Riesling Dry ★★★★★

Bel Canto means 'Beautiful Singing'. Based on the estate's mature, ungrafted vines at Waipara, in North Canterbury, late-harvested with 'a good portion of noble botrytis', the 2017 vintage (★★★★★) is a very powerful, weighty wine (14.5 per cent alcohol), with concentrated, peachy flavours, hints of oranges and honey, good delicacy and a dry (5.2 grams/litre of residual sugar), lasting finish. It should be long-lived; open 2021+.

Pegasus Bay Riesling Aged Release ★★★★★

This 'Aged Release' label is a re-release of the Waipara Valley, North Canterbury classic when it is 10 years old. The 2009 vintage (★★★★★), currently on sale, is powerful, with a strong presence. Bright yellow/pale gold, it is richly scented, with concentrated, peachy, limey, vaguely honeyed flavours, gentle sweetness and a rich, harmonious finish.

MED $40 AV

Pegasus Bay Waipara Valley North Canterbury Riesling ★★★★★

Classy stuff. Estate-grown at Waipara, in North Canterbury, in top vintages it is richly fragrant and thrillingly intense, with flavours of citrus fruits and honey, complex and luscious. Based on mature vines and stop-fermented in a distinctly medium style, it breaks into full stride at about three years old and can mature well for a decade. The 2016 vintage (★★★★★) makes a powerful statement. Showing lovely richness and poise, it has concentrated, peachy, citrusy, slightly spicy flavours, moderate sweetness (21.7 grams/litre of residual sugar), lively acidity, and a very harmonious, lasting finish. The 2017 vintage (★★★★★) is bright, light yellow/

green, with a gently honeyed bouquet. Concentrated, with gentle sweetness (21 grams/litre of residual sugar), it has lush stone-fruit flavours, a hint of honey and good acid spine. Best drinking 2021+.

Vintage	16	15
WR	5	6
Drink	19-32	19-32

Prophet's Rock Central Otago Dry Riesling ★★★★★

Estate-grown and hand-picked at Bendigo, in the Cromwell Basin, the 2017 vintage (★★★★☆) was fermented with indigenous yeasts in old oak barrels. Light lemon/green, it is a very youthful, tightly structured wine, with strong, citrusy, limey flavours and a crisp, dryish (6.7 grams/litre of residual sugar), persistent finish. Best drinking 2021+.

Rimu Grove Nelson Riesling ★★★★

The 2018 vintage (★★★★) is a light-bodied style (10 per cent alcohol), fresh and fragrant. Vibrantly fruity, it is youthful, with generous, citrusy, slightly spicy flavours, a splash of sweetness (20 grams/litre of residual sugar), balanced acidity, and excellent depth and harmony. Best drinking 2021+.

Vintage	18	17	16	15	14	13	12	11
WR	6	6	6	7	6	7	7	6
Drink	20-30	19-30	19-27	19-26	19-25	19-21	19-20	P

Rippon Mature Vine Riesling ★★★★★

This single-vineyard, Lake Wanaka, Central Otago wine is a distinctly cool-climate style, steely, long-lived and penetratingly flavoured. Based on mature vines, it is fermented with indigenous yeasts and given extended lees-aging. The 2015 vintage (★★★★★) has a slightly yeasty fragrance. Full-bodied, it is weighty, deep and unusually complex, with fresh, concentrated, citrusy, slightly spicy flavours that build across the palate to a dryish, resounding finish. It should be long-lived; best drinking 2020+.

Riverby Estate Marlborough Riesling ★★★☆

Still very youthful, the 2018 vintage (★★★☆) is a single-vineyard wine, grown at Rapaura. Medium-bodied, it has good depth of citrusy, slightly appley flavours and a crisp, dryish (5 grams/litre of residual sugar) finish. Unfolding well, the 2017 vintage (★★★★) is fresh and medium-bodied, with strong, lemony flavours, slightly toasty, bottle-aged notes adding complexity, balanced acidity and a finely balanced (6 grams/litre of residual sugar), lengthy finish.

Vintage	18	17
WR	7	7
Drink	19-28	20-30

Riverby Estate Sali's Block Marlborough Riesling   ★★★☆

Estate-grown at Rapaura, the 2018 vintage (★★★☆) is still unfolding. Made in a medium style (20 grams/litre of residual sugar), it is light-bodied (10 per cent alcohol), with fresh, youthful, lemony, appley flavours, showing good depth. Open mid-2020+. Enjoyable now, but also worth cellaring, the attractive 2017 vintage (★★★★) is scented and vigorous, with strong, citrusy, appley flavours and an off-dry (12 grams/litre of residual sugar), appetisingly crisp finish.

Vintage	18	17
WR	6	7
Drink	19-23	19-25

 MED $22 AV

Roaring Meg Central Otago Riesling   ★★★★

From Mt Difficulty, the 2017 vintage (★★★★) is a good buy. A distinctly medium style (19 grams/litre of residual sugar), it is fresh and lively, with citrusy, slightly limey flavours, showing excellent vigour, harmony and depth. It's drinking well now.

 MED $20 V+

Rock Ferry 3rd Rock Marlborough Riesling   ★★★★

Still on sale, the attractively scented 2014 vintage (★★★★) was hand-picked in The Corners Vineyard, at Rapaura, in the Wairau Valley, fermented in tanks and given extended lees contact. Fleshy, it has ripe stone-fruit and spice flavours, showing good concentration, and a finely textured, off-dry (7.5 grams/litre of residual sugar) finish. Certified organic.

 MED/DRY $27 –V

Rock Ferry Trig Hill Vineyard Central Otago Riesling   ★★★★☆

Still on sale, the powerful 2014 vintage (★★★★☆) is a sturdy (14 per cent alcohol), dryish style (6.3 grams/litre of residual sugar), with strong personality. It is scented and weighty, with good intensity of ripe grapefruit and peach flavours, moderate acidity, and bottle-aged notes adding complexity. Certified organic.

 MED/DRY $33 –V

Rockburn Central Otago Tigermoth Riesling   ★★★★☆

Estate-grown at Parkburn, in the Cromwell Basin, and made in a low-alcohol (8.5 per cent) style, the delicious 2016 vintage (★★★★☆) was 'inspired by the spätlese wines of Germany'. It is light and lively, with excellent vibrancy, delicacy and depth, and a gently sweet (59 grams/litre of residual sugar), mouth-wateringly crisp finish.

Vintage	16	15	14	13	12	11
WR	6	6	6	6	6	7
Drink	19-30	19-30	19-30	19-30	19-25	19-25

SW $39 –V

Saint Clair Pioneer Block 9 Big John Marlborough Riesling ★★★★★

Already delicious, but well worth cellaring, the 2017 vintage (★★★★☆) is a Mosel-like wine, grown in the lower Brancott Valley and stop-fermented to make a medium-sweet style. Vivacious, light (9 per cent alcohol) and appetisingly crisp, with citrusy, appley flavours, showing excellent freshness, delicacy and intensity, it is a youthful, very harmonious wine with a lasting finish. Best drinking 2020+.

MED $27 V+

Saving Grace Dry Riesling (★★★★★)

From Waipara Hills, the 2018 vintage (★★★★★) is a shining example of deliciously drinkable, yet basically dry (5 grams/litre of residual sugar) Riesling. Estate-grown at Waipara, in North Canterbury, it was hand-picked, fermented with indigenous yeasts and lees-aged for six months. Bright, light lemon/green, it has a fragrant, citrusy, appley, inviting bouquet. Finely poised, with rich fruit flavours, a slightly minerally thread, and a real sense of youthful drive, it's already delicious.

MED/DRY $28 V+

Seifried Nelson Riesling ★★★★

From a pioneer of Riesling in New Zealand, the 2019 vintage (★★★★) is typically good value. Well worth cellaring, it is full-bodied, crisp and dry (3.8 grams/litre of residual sugar), with vigorous, citrusy, slightly appley flavours, showing very good depth. Open 2021+.

MED/DRY $18 V+

Vintage	17	16	15	14	13	12
WR	4	5	6	6	6	6
Drink	19-21	19-21	19-25	19-21	19-20	P

Sherwood Estate Stoney Range Waipara Valley Riesling (★★★☆)

Priced sharply, the 2019 vintage (★★★☆) is a distinctly medium style (19 grams/litre of residual sugar). It has punchy, youthful, citrusy flavours, hints of apples and limes, and a crisp, tangy finish. Best drinking mid-2020+.

MED $17 V+

Sherwood Estate Stratum Waipara Valley Riesling ★★★☆

Bargain priced, the 2016 vintage (★★★★) is a distinctly medium style (20.5 grams/litre of residual sugar). Bright, light yellow/green, it is medium-bodied, with generous, peachy, vaguely honeyed flavours. Delicious young.

MED $15 V+

Soho Betty Marlborough Riesling Spätlese (★★★☆)

Light and lively, the 2017 vintage (★★★★) is a low-alcohol (9.5 per cent), medium style (41 grams/litre of residual sugar), enjoyable young. It has very good depth of citrusy, appley flavours, threaded with appetising acidity, and impressive freshness and harmony.

MED $22 V+

Soho Maren Marlborough Riesling   ★★★★

Very 'open' and expressive in its youth, the 2017 vintage (★★★★☆) is a freshly scented, medium-bodied wine with incisive, citrusy, slightly peachy and gingery flavours, gentle sweetness (12.9 grams/litre of residual sugar) and firm acid spine. Best drinking 2020+.

MED/DRY $25 AV

Spinyback Nelson Riesling   ★★★

Invitingly scented, the 2017 vintage (★★★☆) is a slightly sweet style, with good depth of citrusy, gently spicy flavours, finely balanced for easy drinking. (From Waimea Estates.)

MED/DRY $15 V+

Spy Valley Envoy Johnson Vineyard Waihopai Valley
Marlborough Dry Riesling   ★★★★★

Estate-grown and hand-picked from the oldest vines, the 2017 vintage (★★★★★) was initially fermented in old oak barrels, then transferred to stainless steel tanks. Light lemon/green, it is finely scented, intense and youthful, with tightly structured, citrusy, slightly peachy and toasty flavours that build across the palate to a crisp, dry (4.5 grams/litre of residual sugar), harmonious finish. A distinctive, classy wine, already enjoyable, it's well worth cellaring to 2020+.

Vintage	17	16
WR	6	6
Drink	19-27	19-26

DRY $33 AV

Spy Valley Envoy Single Vineyard Marlborough Riesling   ★★★★★

Estate-grown in the lower Waihopai Valley, the 2012 vintage (★★★★★), released in 2018, was hand-picked, with no botrytis influence, and barrel-fermented. Bright, light lemon/green, it is highly scented. Light and lovely, it is low in alcohol (9 per cent), with searching, citrusy, limey flavours, sweet (65 grams/litre of residual sugar) and tangy, poised and persistent. Acquiring excellent bottle-aged complexity, with a strong sense of depth, delicacy and drive, it should be long-lived; drink now or cellar.

Vintage	12	11
WR	7	7
Drink	19-22	19-21

SW $33 AV

Spy Valley Single Vineyard Marlborough Riesling   ★★★★

The 2016 vintage (★★★★☆) is a full-bodied, off-dry style (6.2 grams/litre of residual sugar), fermented in tanks and barrels. Bright, light lemon/green, it is attractively scented, with very good intensity of citrusy, limey flavours, lively acidity, slightly toasty notes adding complexity, and a crisp, long finish. Very finely balanced for current drinking, it should also reward cellaring.

MED/DRY $25 AV

Stoneleigh Marlborough Riesling ★★★☆

The 2018 vintage (★★★) is a very easy-drinking style. Bright, light lemon/green, it has fresh, lively, citrusy, appley flavours, gentle sweetness, and a finely poised finish. Enjoyable young.

MED/DRY $16 V+

Sugar Loaf Marlborough Riesling (★★★★☆)

Delicious young, the 2018 vintage (★★★★☆) from this Rapaura-based producer is a regional blend. Attractively scented, it is light and lively, with gentle sweetness (28 grams/litre of residual sugar), finely balanced acidity and strong, yet delicate, peachy, lemony, appley flavours. Already very harmonious, it's a drink-now or cellaring proposition, offering excellent value.

MED $20 V+

Te Kairanga Martinborough Riesling ★★★★

Estate-grown, the 2018 vintage (★★★★) is a finely poised wine, still unfolding. Bright, light lemon/green, it has fresh lemon/lime flavours, a gentle splash of sweetness (8.6 grams/litre of residual sugar), balanced acidity and excellent depth. Best drinking 2021+.

Vintage	18
WR	6
Drink	20-25

MED/DRY $25 AV

Terrace Edge Liquid Geography North Canterbury Riesling ★★★★☆

As a medium style of Riesling for drinking young, the 2018 vintage (★★★★☆) is hard to beat, especially at the price. Hand-picked at Waipara, it is bright, light yellow/green, with a slightly honeyed fragrance. Medium-bodied, it has concentrated, ripe, peachy, gently spicy flavours, gentle sweetness (34 grams/litre of residual sugar), finely balanced acidity, and a rich, long finish. A top buy. Certified organic.

Vintage	18
WR	7
Drink	19-26

MED $20 V+

Thomas Martinborough Riesling (★★★★☆)

From Batch Winery, based on Waiheke Island, the 2018 vintage (★★★★☆) is youthful and well worth cellaring. Bright, light lemon/green, it is medium-bodied, with strong, vibrant flavours of peaches and grapefruit, a gentle splash of sweetness (14 grams/litre of residual sugar), good acid spine, and excellent drive, harmony and length.

MED/DRY $38 –V

Three Miners Central Otago Riesling (★★★★)

Invitingly scented, the 2017 vintage (★★★★) is a lively, light-bodied, estate-grown wine, hand-picked at Earnscleugh, near Alexandra. Pale lemon/green, it has citrusy, slightly appley flavours, showing excellent delicacy and depth, and a slightly sweet, finely balanced finish. Drink now or cellar.

MED/DRY $23 AV

Three Paddles Martinborough Riesling ★★★☆

The 2016 vintage (★★★☆) from Nga Waka is medium-bodied, with good depth of fresh, ripe, citrusy, peachy, slightly limey flavours, gentle sweetness (10 grams/litre of residual sugar) and an easy-drinking balance. Enjoyable young.

Vintage	16
WR	6
Drink	19-22

 MED/DRY $18 V+

Tohu Single Vineyard Marlborough Riesling ★★★★

Estate-grown in the upper Awatere Valley, the vigorous 2017 vintage (★★★★) is a dryish style (7 grams/litre of residual sugar). Bright, light lemon/green, it is fresh and youthful, with strong, lemony, appley, slightly peachy flavours, threaded with crisp acidity, and obvious potential; open mid-2020+.

 MED/DRY $22 V+

Tohu Single Vineyard Whenua Awa Awatere Valley Marlborough Riesling   (★★★★)

Attractively scented and lively, the 2018 vintage (★★★★) is a fresh, generous, estate-grown wine, already drinking well. Bright, light lemon/green, it has peachy, slightly gingery flavours, with a sliver of sweetness balanced by appetising acidity, and excellent vibrancy, harmony and depth.

 MED/DRY $28 –V

Torlesse Waipara Riesling   (★★★★)

Drinking well in 2019, the 2016 vintage (★★★★) is an off-dry style (15 grams/litre of residual sugar). Bright, light yellow/green, it is medium-bodied, with fresh, lively acidity and strong, citrusy, limey, slightly honeyed flavours. Good value.

 MED $20 V+

Tupari Awatere Valley Riesling   (★★★★)

Still on sale and delicious young, the 2016 vintage (★★★★) is a medium style (25 grams/litre of residual sugar), with excellent depth of fresh, citrusy, limey flavour, woven with appetising acidity. Drink now or cellar.

 MED $23 AV

Two Paddocks Picnic Central Otago Riesling ★★★★

Certified organic, the 2017 vintage (★★★★☆) was estate-grown and hand-picked in the Red Bank Vineyard, at Earnscleugh, near Alexandra. Made in an off-dry style, it has excellent intensity of vigorous, citrusy flavours, a sliver of sweetness and a long, crisp finish. Already drinking well, it should be at its best 2020+.

MED/DRY $25 AV

Two Sisters Central Otago Riesling ★★★★★

Estate-grown on a steeply sloping site at Lowburn, the lovely 2011 vintage (★★★★★), available now, is a medium style (18 grams/litre of residual sugar). A distinctive wine that tastes half its age, it has a youthful, bright, light lemon/green hue. Finely scented, with deep, vibrant, citrusy, limey flavours, it has excellent delicacy, poise and depth. Well worth discovering.

MED $30 AV

Urlar Gladstone Riesling ★★★★☆

The very age-worthy 2017 vintage (★★★★☆) was estate-grown and hand-harvested in the northern Wairarapa. Retasted in mid-2019, it is a bright, light lemon/green, invitingly scented, medium-bodied wine, with fresh, strong, delicate, citrusy, appley flavours, slightly toasty, bottle-aged notes emerging, good acid spine and a long, unusually dry (2.7 grams/litre of residual sugar), steely finish. Best drinking 2021+. Certified organic.

Vintage	17
WR	5
Drink	19-26

DRY $25 V+

Valli Waitaki North Otago Riesling ★★★★☆

The arresting 2018 vintage (★★★★★) is already delicious. Bright, light lemon/green, it is notably fragrant, vibrant and intense, with excellent weight and depth of citrusy, appley, peachy flavours, gentle sweetness (14.4 grams/litre of residual sugar), and a racy, very harmonious finish. Likely to be at its best from 2020 onwards, it's well worth discovering.

Vintage	18
WR	7
Drink	19-33

MED/DRY $30 –V

Vavasour Marlborough Riesling ★★★☆

The 2017 vintage (★★★☆) is a medium-bodied wine with strong, citrusy, slightly peachy flavours, a minerally streak, and a sliver of sweetness (6.1 grams/litre of residual sugar), balanced by crisp acidity. Best drinking 2020+.

Vintage	19
WR	7
Drink	19-25

MED/DRY $25 –V

Vidal Marlborough Riesling ★★★★

Offering top value, the 2017 vintage (★★★★) was grown in the Wairau and Waihopai valleys. Strongly varietal, it is a fresh, medium-bodied wine with strong, citrusy flavours, a minerally streak, gentle sweetness (10 grams/litre of residual sugar), and a crisp, long finish.

Vintage	17
WR	6
Drink	19-25

MED/DRY $16 V+

Villa Maria Cellar Selection Marlborough Dry Riesling ★★★★☆

Offering great value, the 2017 vintage (★★★★☆) was grown at three sites in the Wairau Valley. A medium-bodied, vibrantly fruity wine, it has penetrating grapefruit and lime flavours, a slightly minerally thread, and a dryish (7.5 grams/litre of residual sugar), very harmonious finish. Drink now or cellar.

Vintage	18	17	16	15	14	13
WR	6	6	6	7	7	6
Drink	19-22	19-22	19-22	19-22	19-20	P

 MED/DRY $19 V+

Villa Maria Private Bin Marlborough Riesling ★★★★

The 2019 vintage (★★★★) is enjoyable from the start. Made in a slightly sweet style (12 grams/litre of residual sugar), it is attractively scented, with strong, crisp, lemony, appley flavours, showing excellent delicacy and length. Great value.

Vintage	19	18
WR	6	5
Drink	19-22	19-22

 MED/DRY $15 V+

Waimea Estates Nelson Riesling ★★★★

This luscious wine, balanced for easy drinking, is consistently impressive and offers good value. Delicious young, the 2017 vintage (★★★★) is a bright, light, yellow/green wine, made in a medium-dry style. It has rich, citrusy, peachy, limey flavours, a hint of honey, and a fragant bouquet.

 MED/DRY $18 V+

Waipara Hills Waipara Valley Riesling ★★★★

Finely balanced for early enjoyment, the 2018 vintage (★★★★) is medium-bodied, very fresh and lively. Bright, light lemon/green, it has vibrant, citrusy, peachy flavours, a gentle splash of sweetness, appetising acidity, and excellent depth and harmony. Drink now or cellar.

 MED/DRY $22 V+

Wairau River Summer Marlborough Riesling ★★★★

The 2016 vintage (★★★★) was made 'to be supped with frivolous frivolity'. Fresh and light-bodied (9.5 per cent alcohol), it is medium-sweet (41 grams/litre of residual sugar), with good intensity of peachy, citrusy flavours, fresh and tangy. Delicious young.

Vintage	16	15
WR	6	7
Drink	P	P

MED $20 V+

Whitehaven Marlborough Riesling ★★★★

The 2018 vintage (★★★★) is a highly aromatic, very finely balanced wine, with lots of youthful impact. Light lemon/green, it has strong, citrusy, slightly spicy flavours, gentle sweetness (10.7 grams/litre of residual sugar) and a moderately crisp finish. Enjoyable young, it should break into full stride mid-2020+.

MED/DRY $22 V+

Wild Earth Central Otago Riesling (★★★★☆)

The 2017 vintage (★★★★☆) is a single-vineyard wine, hand-picked at Bendigo. Fragrant, it is medium-bodied, with strong, vibrant grapefruit and lime flavours, a hint of spice, and a finely balanced, off-dry, lingering finish. Best drinking 2021+.

MED/DRY $27 AV

Wither Hills Cellar Release Kerseley Marlborough Riesling (★★★★★)

Currently on sale, the delicious 2011 vintage (★★★★★) is bright, light lemon/green, with a highly forthcoming, scented bouquet. A medium-dry style, it is rich, with an array of ripe-fruit flavours, bottle-aged complexity and a very harmonious, long finish.

MED/DRY $25 V+

Wither Hills Cellar Release Rarangi Marlborough Riesling ★★★★☆

Currently on sale, the 2011 vintage (★★★★☆), tasted in 2019, is probably near its peak. Light lemon/green, it is invitingly fragrant, with concentrated, vigorous, citrusy flavours, threaded with appetising acidity, slight sweetness, bottle-aged complexity and a finely balanced finish. The 2012 vintage (★★★★☆) is very similar. Bright, light lemon/green, it is richly scented, with deep, lemony, limey flavours, good sugar/acid balance, slightly toasty, bottle-aged notes emerging, and a tightly structured finish. Drink now or cellar.

MED/DRY $25 V+

Wither Hills Marlborough Riesling ★★★★

Instantly appealing, the 2018 vintage (★★★★) is scented, youthful and vibrantly fruity. Light lemon/green, it is medium-bodied, with very good depth of fresh lemon/lime flavours, a sliver of sweetness, appetising acidity, and excellent delicacy and harmony. Well worth cellaring, it offers good value.

MED/DRY $18 V+

Zephyr Marlborough Riesling (★★★★)

Still very youthful, the 2019 (★★★★) is a single-vineyard wine, grown at Dillons Point, in the lower Wairau Valley. Fresh and medium-bodied, it has very good depth of citrusy, appley flavours and an off-dry (7 grams/litre of residual sugar), appetisingly crisp finish. Best drinking 2022+.

MED/DRY $24 AV

Roussanne

Roussanne is a traditional ingredient in the white wines of France's northern Rhône Valley, where typically it is blended with the more widely grown Marsanne. Known for its fine acidity and 'haunting aroma', likened by some tasters to herbal tea, it is also found in the south of France, Italy and Australia, but this late-ripening variety is extremely scarce in New Zealand, with 0.2 hectares bearing in 2020, north of Auckland.

Mahurangi River Winery Roussanne/Viognier ★★★★☆

Still on sale, the 2015 vintage (★★★★☆) was estate-grown and hand-picked near Matakana. A blend of two Rhône Valley varieties, Roussanne and Viognier, it is a powerful wine, weighty and fleshy, with peachy, slightly spicy flavours, a gentle seasoning of oak, and a dry, lengthy finish.

DRY $34 AV

Sauvignon Blanc

Sauvignon Blanc is New Zealand's major calling card in the wine markets of the world, often – but not always, due to the rising challenge from Chile – winning trophies at big competitions in the UK. For countless wine lovers overseas, New Zealand 'is' Sauvignon Blanc, almost invariably from Marlborough. The rise to international stardom of New Zealand Sauvignon Blanc was remarkably swift. Government Viticulturist Romeo Bragato imported the first Sauvignon Blanc vines from Italy in 1906, but it was not until 1974 that Matua Valley marketed New Zealand's first varietal Sauvignon Blanc, grown in West Auckland. Montana first planted Sauvignon Blanc vines in Marlborough in 1975; its first bottling of Marlborough Sauvignon Blanc flowed in 1979. In 2018, 86 per cent by volume of New Zealand's wine exports were based on Sauvignon Blanc.

Sauvignon Blanc is by far New Zealand's most extensively planted variety, in 2020 comprising 61 per cent of the bearing national vineyard. Almost 90 per cent of the vines are concentrated in Marlborough, with further significant plantings in Hawke's Bay, Nelson, Canterbury and Wairarapa. Between 2005 and 2020, the area of bearing Sauvignon Blanc vines will surge from 7277 hectares to 23,799 hectares.

The flavour of New Zealand Sauvignon Blanc varies according to fruit ripeness. At the herbaceous, under-ripe end of the spectrum, vegetal and fresh-cut grass aromas hold sway; riper wines show capsicum, gooseberry and melon-like characters; very ripe fruit displays tropical-fruit flavours.

Intensely herbaceous Sauvignon Blancs are not hard to make in the viticulturally cool climate of the South Island and the lower North Island (Wairarapa). 'The challenge faced by New Zealand winemakers is to keep those herbaceous characters in check,' says Kevin Judd, of Greywacke Vineyards, formerly chief winemaker at Cloudy Bay. 'It would be foolish to suggest that these herbaceous notes detract from the wines; in fact I am sure that this fresh edge and intense varietal aroma are the reason for its international popularity. The better of these wines have these herbaceous characters in context and in balance with the more tropical-fruit characters associated with riper fruit.'

There are two key styles of Sauvignon Blanc produced in New Zealand. Wines handled entirely in stainless steel tanks – by far the most common – place their accent squarely on their fresh, direct fruit flavours. Alternatively, many top labels are handled principally in tanks, but 5 to 15 per cent of the blend is barrel-fermented, adding a touch of complexity without subduing the wine's fresh, punchy fruit aromas and flavours.

Another major style difference is regionally based: the crisp, incisively flavoured wines of Marlborough contrast with the softer, less pungently herbaceous Hawke's Bay style. These are wines to drink young (traditionally within 18 months of the vintage) while they are irresistibly fresh, aromatic and tangy, although the oak-matured, more complex wines can mature well for several years.

The swing since the 2001 vintage from corks to screwcaps has also boosted the longevity of the wines. Rather than running out of steam, many are still highly enjoyable at two years old.

Allan Scott Marlborough Sauvignon Blanc   ★★★☆

Offering good value, the 2018 vintage (★★★★) is a fresh, full-bodied, strongly varietal Wairau Valley wine, with good vigour and intensity of tropical-fruit and herbaceous flavours, crisp, dry and lingering.

DRY $18 V+

Amisfield Central Otago Sauvignon Blanc ★★★★☆

The classy 2018 vintage (★★★★★), estate-grown at Pisa, was mostly handled in tanks, but a small portion of the blend (4 per cent) was fermented with indigenous yeasts in old French oak barriques. Ripely scented, it is full-bodied and vibrantly fruity, with fresh, concentrated tropical-fruit flavours, showing good complexity, tangy acidity, and a finely balanced, long, dry (3.4 grams/litre of residual sugar) finish. Well worth discovering.

Vintage	18
WR	4
Drink	19-20

DRY $25 V+

Anchorage Lighter Alcohol Nelson Sauvignon Blanc (★★☆)

The easy-drinking 2018 vintage (★★☆) is a light-bodied (10.5 per cent alcohol), off-dry style. Grown mostly in the original Anchorage vineyard, it is tangy, with fresh, green capsicum-like flavours, a hint of passionfruit, a splash of sweetness (8 grams/litre of residual sugar) and lively acidity.

MED/DRY $18 –V

Anna's Way Marlborough Sauvignon Blanc (★★★★)

Drinking well in late 2019, the 2018 vintage (★★★★) was grown at two sites in the Awatere Valley and partly French oak-fermented. Bright, light lemon/green, it is highly aromatic, with mouthfilling body, strong tropical-fruit and herbaceous flavours, showing a touch of complexity, and a smooth, lingering finish. (From Awatere River.)

DRY $19 V+

Aotea by Seifried Nelson Sauvignon Blanc ★★★★☆

The classy 2019 vintage (★★★★★) is based on 'the very best fruit harvested from our family vineyard'. Due for release in early 2020, it is a powerful, punchy wine, weaving tropical-fruit and herbaceous flavours, crisp and intense. Highly aromatic and full of youthful vigour, with a long, basically dry finish (4.5 grams/litre of residual sugar), it should be at its best mid-2020+.

Vintage	19	18
WR	7	6
Drink	19-21	19-20

DRY $29 AV

Ashwell Martinborough Sauvignon Blanc ★★★☆

Estate-grown on the Martinborough Terraces, the youthful 2019 vintage (★★★★) is ripely scented, with strong tropical-fruit flavours, showing good freshness and vigour, finely balanced acidity and a lengthy finish.

DRY $20 AV

Askerne Hawke's Bay Sauvignon Blanc (★★★★)

The weighty, full-bodied 2018 vintage (★★★★) has generous passionfruit and pineapple aromas and flavours. It's a distinctly non-herbaceous style, fresh and dry, in the ripe, rounded style typical of Hawke's Bay.

DRY $20 V+

Askerne Hawke's Bay Sauvignon Blanc/Sauvignon Gris/Sémillon   (★★★★☆)

The distinctive 2018 vintage (★★★★☆) is a blend of Sauvignon Blanc (73 per cent), Sauvignon Gris (20 per cent) and Sémillon (7 per cent), partly barrel-fermented. Already drinking well, but worth cellaring, it is full-bodied, with fresh, strong tropical-fruit flavours, showing very good complexity, and a long, dry finish. Good value.

DRY $23 V+

Astrolabe Awatere Valley Marlborough Sauvignon Blanc   ★★★★☆

A typical sub-regional style, the 2018 vintage (★★★★☆) has clearly herbaceous aromas and flavours. Crisp and full-bodied, it has excellent weight and depth, with strong, vigorous, nettley, slightly leesy flavours, a minerally streak, and a long, crisp, fully dry finish.

DRY $25 V+

Astrolabe Marlborough Sauvignon Blanc   ★★★★☆

The skilfully crafted 2018 vintage (★★★★☆) is a regional blend, grown in the Awatere Valley (58 per cent), Southern Valleys (26 per cent), the Lower Wairau (5 per cent) and at Kekerengu (11 per cent). Full-bodied, with strong tropical-fruit and herbaceous flavours, it has lees-aging notes adding complexity and a dry (1.6 grams/litre of residual sugar), very harmonious finish.

DRY $23 V+

Astrolabe Valleys Kekerengu Coast Marlborough Sauvignon Blanc   ★★★★☆

Grown at Kekerengu, south of the Awatere Valley, the distinctive 2018 vintage (★★★★☆) was mostly handled in tanks, but part of the blend was fermented and matured in seasoned French oak puncheons. Fresh, lively and mouthfilling, it shows very good complexity, vigour and intensity of tropical-fruit and herbaceous flavours, with a dry, long finish.

Vintage	18
WR	6
Drink	19-24

DRY $27 AV

Astrolabe Vineyards Taihoa Vineyard Marlborough Sauvignon Blanc   ★★★★★

Grown at Kekerengu, south of the Awatere Valley, the classy, very age-worthy 2017 vintage (★★★★★) was hand-picked and fermented and matured for 11 months in old French oak barrels. Bright, light lemon/green, it is concentrated and tightly structured, with deep, ripely herbaceous flavours, a subtle seasoning of oak adding complexity, and a long, crisp, bone-dry finish.

DRY $32 AV

Ata Rangi Martinborough Raranga Sauvignon Blanc   ★★★★

The youthful, lively 2018 vintage (★★★★) was hand-picked and 45 per cent barrel-fermented. Bright, light lemon/green, it is medium to full-bodied, with strong, ripely herbaceous flavours, a distinct touch of complexity, and a tightly structured finish. Best drinking mid-2020+.

Vintage	18
WR	6
Drink	19-23

DRY $24 AV

Auntsfield Single Vineyard Southern Valleys Marlborough Sauvignon Blanc   ★★★★★

Estate-grown on the south side of the Wairau Valley, on the site where the region's first wines were made in the 1870s, the 2018 vintage (★★★★★) was mostly handled in tanks; 5 per cent was fermented in old French oak casks. Still youthful, it is mouthfilling and dry (2.9 grams/ litre of residual sugar), with excellent weight and depth of ripely herbaceous, grapefruit/lime flavours. A powerful, finely poised wine with a long finish, it should age well.

Vintage	18	17
WR	6	6
Drink	19-22	19-21

 DRY $25 V+

Auntsfield South Oaks Southern Valleys Marlborough
Barrel-Fermented Sauvignon Blanc   ★★★★☆

Still youthful, the weighty 2016 vintage (★★★★☆) was estate-grown and fermented and matured for 10 months in seasoned French oak casks. Bright, light lemon/green, it is mouthfilling and tightly structured, with ripely herbaceous flavours, well-integrated oak, good complexity, and a dry (2 grams/litre of residual sugar), finely textured finish. Best drinking 2021+.

Vintage	16
WR	5
Drink	19-26

 DRY $38 –V

Awatere River Marlborough Sauvignon Blanc   ★★★★

Offering good value, the 2019 vintage (★★★★) was grown in the Awatere Valley and partly hand-picked. Light lemon/green, it is fresh and aromatic, mouthfilling and lively, with melon and green-capsicum flavours, showing good vigour and intensity, and a dry (3.2 grams/litre of residual sugar) finish.

 DRY $20 V+

Babich Marlborough Sauvignon Blanc   ★★★★

Babich favours 'a fuller, riper, softer' Sauvignon Blanc. 'It's not a jump out of the glass style, but the wines develop well.' The latest releases reflect a rising input of grapes from the company's Cowslip Valley Vineyard in the Waihopai Valley, which gives less herbaceous fruit characters than its other Marlborough vineyards. The 2018 vintage (★★★★) is ripely scented, full-bodied and dry, with passionfruit/lime flavours, fresh, tight and strong.

 DRY $20 V+

Babich Winemakers' Reserve Barrel Fermented
Marlborough Sauvignon Blanc   ★★★★★

A stylish example of age-worthy, gently oak-influenced Sauvignon Blanc. The classy 2017 vintage (★★★★★) was fermented and lees-aged for eight months in French oak casks (25 per cent new). Bright lemon/green, it is complex and concentrated, with deep, dry tropical-fruit flavours to the fore, a seasoning of nutty, toasty oak adding complexity, and a tight, lasting finish.

Vintage	17
WR	7
Drink	19-24

 DRY $35 AV

Bel Echo by Clos Henri Marlborough Sauvignon Blanc   ★★★★☆

This well-priced, distinctive wine is grown in the more clay-based soils at Clos Henri (the top wine, sold as 'Clos Henri', is from the stoniest blocks). The 2017 vintage (★★★★★) was hand-picked, tank-fermented and matured on its yeast lees. Bright, light lemon/green, it is weighty, ripely herbaceous and well-rounded, in a fleshy style with excellent depth of grapefruit/lime flavours, a minerally streak, and good complexity and texture. Certified organic.

Vintage	17
WR	6
Drink	19-23

 DRY $26 AV

Bellbird Spring Block Eight Waipara Sauvignon Blanc   ★★★★☆

This distinctive wine is hand-picked and fermented with indigenous yeasts in old oak barriques. The 2016 vintage (★★★★☆), barrel-matured for five months, is a light yellow/green, mouthfilling wine with strong, ripely herbaceous flavours. A fleshy, generous wine, with well-integrated oak adding richness and complexity, slightly buttery notes and excellent harmony, it's drinking well now.

 DRY $32 –V

Black Cottage Marlborough Sauvignon Blanc   ★★★☆

From Two Rivers, the 2019 vintage (★★★☆) is priced sharply. Bright, light lemon/green, it is freshly aromatic and strongly varietal, with good depth of lively melon and green-capsicum flavours, dry (3 grams/litre of residual sugar) and crisp.

Vintage	19	18
WR	6	6
Drink	19-20	P

 DRY $18 V+

Blackenbrook Nelson Sauvignon Blanc   ★★★☆

Estate-grown at Tasman, the 2019 vintage (★★★★) was hand-picked and fermented in tanks (mostly) and old oak barrels (4 per cent). Freshly aromatic, it is mouthfilling and tangy, with vibrant tropical-fruit flavours to the fore, a herbaceous undercurrent, good intensity, and a basically dry (4 grams/litre of residual sugar) finish. Best drinking mid-2020+.

Vintage	19	18
WR	6	6
Drink	19-20	P

DRY $21 AV

Blank Canvas Abstract Marlborough Sauvignon Blanc   ★★★★★

Currently delicious, but still developing, the 2017 vintage (★★★★☆), tasted in March 2019, is a single-vineyard wine, grown at Dillons Point, in the lower Wairau Valley. It was fermented with indigenous yeasts and matured for over a year in seasoned French oak puncheons. Bright, light lemon/green, it is weighty and complex, with ripe tropical-fruit flavours, a gentle seasoning of toasty oak, and a rounded, bone-dry, lengthy finish. Best drinking 2020+.

 DRY $38 AV

Blank Canvas Marlborough Sauvignon Blanc (★★★★☆)

The highly aromatic 2018 vintage (★★★★☆) is a single-vineyard wine, grown at Dillons Point. It is weighty, with ripe tropical-fruit flavours, showing excellent delicacy and depth, a slightly minerally streak, and a dry (2 grams/litre of residual sugar), lingering finish.

DRY $26 AV

Blind River Awatere Valley Marlborough Sauvignon Blanc ★★★★☆

This classy, single-vineyard wine is partly (10 per cent) barrel-fermented. The 2019 vintage (★★★★☆) is bright, light lemon/green, fresh and punchy, with a touch of complexity and lively tropical-fruit and herbaceous flavours that build to a long, crisp, dry (1.5 grams/litre of residual sugar) finish. Best drinking mid-2020+.

DRY $25 V+

Blind River Tekau Awatere Valley Marlborough Sauvignon Blanc ★★★★★

The 2018 vintage (★★★★☆) is a single-vineyard wine, fermented with indigenous yeasts in French oak barrels (partly new). Light gold, it is weighty, fleshy and dry (1.5 grams/litre of residual sugar), with concentrated tropical-fruit flavours, slightly toasty notes adding complexity, and a rich, rounded finish. It's already drinking well.

Vintage	18
WR	7
Drink	19-25

DRY $30 AV

Boneline, The, Waipara Sauvignon Blanc ★★★★☆

The distinctive 2018 vintage (★★★★☆) is a clearly varietal but not pungent wine, grown in North Canterbury. Bright, light lemon/green, it is weighty and mouthfilling, with fresh, ripely herbaceous flavours, showing excellent vigour, a minerally streak, and a well-rounded, dryish (7 grams/litre of residual sugar), very finely textured finish. Delicious drinking now onwards.

MED/DRY $25 V+

Brancott Estate Chosen Rows Marlborough Sauvignon Blanc ★★★★★

From the company that planted the region's first Sauvignon Blanc vines in 1975, Chosen Rows is promoted as 'the ultimate expression of Marlborough Sauvignon Blanc'. The goal is to create 'an age-worthy wine with great palate weight and texture . . . a sophisticated, thought-provoking wine'. The 2013 vintage (★★★★★) was grown in the historic Brancott Vineyard, hand-picked from 15 to 17-year-old vines, fermented with indigenous yeasts in large French oak cuves, and lees-aged for eight months. Bottled in June 2014 and released in December 2015, it is a powerful (14.5 per cent alcohol) wine, weighty and fleshy, with firm acid spine, very ripe melon/lime flavours, showing excellent concentration and complexity, and a dry, lasting finish. The third, 2015 vintage (★★★★★) was released in late 2019. Fermented and matured mostly in large oak cuves (19 per cent of the blend was handled in one-year-old French oak puncheons), it is a powerful, very weighty wine, bright, light yellow/green, with deep, ripe passionfruit/lime flavours, gently seasoned with toasty oak, finely balanced acidity and a very long finish. Best drinking mid-2020+.

Vintage	13	12	11	10
WR	7	NM	NM	7
Drink	19-20	NM	NM	P

DRY $80 –V

Brancott Estate Identity Awatere Valley Marlborough Sauvignon Blanc   (★★★★)

The debut 2018 vintage (★★★★) was mostly handled in tanks; 12 per cent of the blend was fermented in French oak cuves. Still youthful, it is full-bodied, with ripely herbaceous flavours – more subtle, less green-edged than many Sauvignon Blancs from the Awatere Valley – and a crisp, dry (4.6 grams/litre of residual sugar), lingering finish.

DRY $22 V+

Brancott Estate Letter Series 'B' Brancott Marlborough Sauvignon Blanc   ★★★★★

This wine is promoted by Pernod Ricard NZ as 'our finest expression of Marlborough's most famous variety' – and lives up to its billing. 'Palate weight, concentration and longevity' are the goals. It has traditionally been grown in the company's sweeping Brancott Vineyard, on the south, slightly cooler side of the Wairau Valley, and a significant portion (14 per cent in 2018) is fermented and lees-aged in large French oak vessels, to add 'some toast and spice as well as palate richness'. The delicious 2018 vintage (★★★★★) has rich, ripe tropical-fruit aromas, leading into a fleshy, sweet-fruited wine with strong passionfruit/lime flavours, showing considerable complexity, and a dry, very harmonious finish.

DRY $25 V+

Brancott Estate Marlborough Sauvignon Blanc   ★★★☆

This famous wine is promoted as 'the original Marlborough Sauvignon Blanc', since it is descended directly from the pioneering label, Montana Marlborough Sauvignon Blanc, launched in 1979. It is usually aromatic and medium-bodied, with strong, freshly herbaceous flavours of melons and green capsicums, lively and balanced for early drinking.

DRY $17 V+

Brancott Estate Reflection Limited Edition Marlborough
Sauvignon Blanc/Sauvignon Gris   (★★★★★)

Modelled on the great dry whites of Bordeaux, the 2016 vintage (★★★★★) was mostly (92 per cent) hand-picked and fermented and matured in an array of oak vessels – cuves, foudres and puncheons. Mouthfilling, it is fresh and complex, with substantial body (14.7 per cent alcohol), ripely herbal flavours, and a long, dry (4.2 grams/litre of residual sugar) finish. Powerful but not heavy, it's a wine to ponder.

DRY $60 AV

Brightside New Zealand Sauvignon Blanc   ★★★☆

The 2018 vintage (★★★☆) from Kaimira Estate offers good value. Light lemon/green, it's a brisk, medium to full-bodied, clearly herbaceous Nelson wine, with some riper tropical-fruit notes, very good depth, and a racy, dry (2.7 grams/litre of residual sugar) finish.

DRY $18 V+

Brightwater Vineyards Lord Rutherford Nelson Sauvignon Blanc ★★★★☆

Grown at Hope, on the Waimea Plains, the 2017 vintage (★★★★) is a single-vineyard wine, from mature vines. Most of the blend was tank-fermented and briefly lees-aged, but 30 per cent was fermented and aged in seasoned French oak barrels. Full-bodied, it is sweet-fruited, with ripe tropical-fruit flavours to the fore, a subtle seasoning of oak adding complexity, and a dry (1.5 grams/litre of residual sugar), harmonious finish.

Vintage	17	16	15
WR	6	6	6
Drink	19-22	19-21	19-20

 DRY $25 V+

Brightwater Vineyards Nelson Sauvignon Blanc ★★★★

Grown at Hope, on the Waimea Plains, and briefly lees-aged, this is a consistently attractive wine, fresh and punchy. Bright, light lemon/green, the 2019 vintage (★★★★☆) is mouthfilling and dry (3 grams/litre of residual sugar), with very good vigour and intensity of youthful, ripe tropical-fruit flavours. Best drinking mid-2020+.

Vintage	19	18
WR	6	5
Drink	20-21	19-20

 DRY $20 V+

Carrick Wild Ferment Central Otago Sauvignon Blanc (★★★☆)

Still on sale, the 2017 vintage (★★★☆) was estate-grown, hand-picked, and then fermented (with 'wild' yeasts) and matured for eight months in seasoned oak barrels (60 per cent) and tanks (40 per cent). A fresh, lively, medium-bodied wine, it has citrusy, slightly appley and nettley flavours, with a very restrained touch of oak and a crisp finish. Certified organic.

 DRY $22 AV

Catalina Sounds Marlborough Sauvignon Blanc ★★★★☆

Intensely aromatic, the 2018 vintage (★★★★★) was grown partly at growers' sites in the Wairau Valley, but the 'backbone' of the wine was estate-grown in the Sound of White vineyard, in the upper Waihopai Valley. Made with a small amount of barrel fermentation, it is a refined, intense wine, with excellent weight, vigour and depth of tropical-fruit flavours, a herbaceous undercurrent, good complexity, and a dry (1.9 grams/litre of residual sugar), crisp, sustained finish. Best drinking 2020.

 DRY $24 V+

Catalina Sounds Sound of White Marlborough Sauvignon Blanc ★★★★☆

The complex 2017 vintage (★★★★★) was estate-grown in the Sound of White vineyard, in the upper Waihopai Valley, and fermented in large French oak foudres. Mouthfilling and youthful, it has concentrated, ripely herbaceous flavours, gently seasoned with oak, excellent delicacy and complexity, and a well-rounded, long finish. A savoury and subtle, finely textured, very harmonious wine, it should be at its best for drinking 2020+.

DRY $32 –V

Caythorpe Family Estate Marlborough Sauvignon Blanc ★★★☆

Grown in the 'heart of the Wairau Plains', the very youthful 2019 vintage (★★★) is a single-vineyard, estate-grown wine. Light lemon/green, it has good weight and depth of fresh tropical-fruit and herbaceous flavours, dry (2.5 grams/litre of residual sugar) and crisp. Open mid-2020+.

DRY $20 AV

Church Road Grand Reserve Barrel Fermented
Hawke's Bay Sauvignon Blanc ★★★★★

The impressive 2016 vintage (★★★★★) was estate-grown in the Redstone Vineyard, in the Bridge Pa Triangle, hand-picked and barrel-fermented with indigenous yeasts. It has a fragrant, ripely scented, slightly biscuity bouquet. Weighty and fleshy, with highly concentrated tropical-fruit flavours, finely integrated oak adding complexity, gentle acidity, and a well-rounded finish, it's delicious now.

DRY $44 AV

Church Road Hawke's Bay Sauvignon Blanc ★★★★

Aiming for a style that is 'more refined and softer than a typical New Zealand Sauvignon Blanc', this wine is based principally on fruit from Pernod Ricard NZ's inland, elevated, cool site at Matapiro (300 metres above sea level); a minor part of the blend is estate-grown in the Redstone Vineyard, in the Bridge Pa Triangle. It is typically lees-aged, with some use of barrel fermentation. The 2017 vintage (★★★★) is medium-bodied, with vibrant, ripe passionfruit/lime aromas and flavours, showing very good depth, and a dry finish.

DRY $19 V+

Church Road McDonald Series Hawke's Bay
Barrel Fermented Sauvignon Blanc ★★★★☆

The 2017 vintage (★★★★☆) was designed as a 'more complex style of Sauvignon Blanc without relying on new oak'. A single-vineyard wine, it was hand-picked in the Matapiro Vineyard, at Crownthorpe, and fermented with indigenous yeasts in French oak barrels. Mouthfilling and sweet-fruited, it has generous tropical-fruit flavours, a subtle seasoning of oak, balanced acidity, and a very harmonious, long finish. Drink now or cellar.

DRY $25 V+

Churton Best End Marlborough Sauvignon Blanc ★★★★★

This is Churton's 'single block, organic Sauvignon Blanc'. From a north-facing slope, 185 metres above sea level, in the Waihopai Valley, the 2017 vintage (★★★★★) was fermented and lees-aged for a year in French oak puncheons (20 per cent new), and bottled unfined and unfiltered. Weighty and tightly structured, it has vigorous, intense, ripely herbaceous flavours, showing good complexity, a minerally streak, very finely integrated oak, and a sustained, dry (1.4 grams/litre of residual sugar) finish. Best drinking 2020+. Certified organic.

Vintage	17	16	15	14	13
WR	6	NM	7	NM	7
Drink	19-25	NM	19-28	NM	19-28

DRY $47 AV

Churton Marlborough Sauvignon Blanc ★★★★★

This producer aims for a style that 'combines the renowned flavour and aromatic intensity of Marlborough fruit with the finesse and complexity of fine European wines'. Estate-grown on an elevated site in the Waihopai Valley, it is hand-harvested and a small part of the blend (15 per cent in 2017) is fermented and lees-aged in seasoned and new French oak puncheons. Certified organic, the fleshy 2017 vintage (★★★★★) is a distinctive wine, fragrant and mouthfilling, with intense, ripely herbaceous flavours, subtle, biscuity notes adding complexity, and a lingering, fully dry, finely textured finish.

Vintage	17	16	15	14	13
WR	5	6	7	5	7
Drink	19-22	19-25	19-28	19-20	19-25

 DRY $27 V+

Clark Estate Upper Awatere Marlborough Sauvignon Blanc (★★★★)

Full of youthful impact, the 2018 vintage (★★★★) is a vibrant, punchy wine with incisive, freshly herbaceous flavours and a dry (3.5 grams/litre of residual sugar), appetisingly crisp finish. Drink now to 2020.

DRY $19 V+

Clericus Wild Sauvignon Blanc (★★★★★)

Maturing gracefully, the 2016 vintage (★★★★★) is a distinctive wine, grown in the Awatere Valley and made with indigenous yeasts and 'intelligent use of oak'. Bright, light yellow/green, it is full-bodied, with deep, still lively tropical-fruit flavours, some herbal notes, finely integrated oak, excellent complexity and a finely textured, lasting finish. Drink now to 2020. (From Clark Estate.)

DRY $29 V+

Clos Henri Marlborough Sauvignon Blanc ★★★★★

The Clos Henri Vineyard near Renwick is owned by Henri Bourgeois, a leading, family-owned producer in the Loire Valley, which feels this wine expresses 'a unique terroir . . . and French winemaking approach'. A sophisticated and distinctive Sauvignon Blanc, in top years it's a joy to drink. Certified organic, the 2017 vintage (★★★★★) was hand-picked and mostly fermented and matured on its yeast lees in tanks; 12 per cent was fermented and aged for nine months in French oak barrels. A highly satisfying wine, it is fragrant and weighty, with excellent body and depth of ripely herbaceous flavours, a subtle seasoning of oak and a crisp, dry, sustained finish.

Vintage	17	16	15	14	13	12
WR	4	7	7	6	7	7
Drink	20-21	19-25	19-22	19-21	19-21	19-20

DRY $33 AV

Clos Henri Petit Clos Marlborough Sauvignon Blanc   ★★★★

From this Wairau Valley estate's youngest vines, the 2018 vintage (★★★★) is a good buy. Certified organic, it has a fresh, ripe bouquet, leading into a mouthfilling, sweet-fruited wine with generous tropical-fruit flavours, crisp, dry and lively.

Vintage	18
WR	4
Drink	19-20

DRY $21 V+

Clos Marguerite Marlborough Sauvignon Blanc   ★★★★★

Estate-grown at Seaview, in the Awatere Valley, this wine is consistently classy. The 2018 vintage (★★★★☆) was mostly lees-aged for six months in tanks; 14 per cent of the blend was barrel-fermented. Bright, light lemon/green, it is mouthfilling, fresh and sweet-fruited, with tropical-fruit and herbaceous flavours, showing good richness and complexity, lively acidity, and a dry (3.4 grams/litre of residual sugar), finely balanced finish. Drink now or cellar.

DRY $29 V+

Cloudy Bay Sauvignon Blanc   ★★★★★

New Zealand's most internationally acclaimed wine is sought after from Sydney to New York and London. Its irresistibly aromatic and zesty style and intense flavours stem from 'the fruit characters that are in the grapes when they arrive at the winery'. It is sourced from company-owned and several long-term contract growers' vineyards in the Rapaura, Fairhall, Renwick and Brancott districts of the Wairau Valley, Marlborough. The juice is mostly cool-fermented with cultured and indigenous yeasts in stainless steel tanks and aged on its yeast lees, and a small percentage of the blend (5 per cent in 2019) is fermented at warmer temperatures in old French barriques and large-format vats. Bright, light lemon/green, the 2019 vintage (★★★★★) is ripely scented, weighty and intensely varietal, with rich, ripe tropical-fruit flavours to the fore, a herbaceous undercurrent, a very subtle seasoning of oak adding complexity, and a crisp, dry (2.2 grams/litre of residual sugar) finish. Best drinking mid-2020+.

Vintage	19	18	17	16	15
WR	7	6	6	6	7
Drink	19-21	19-20	P	P	P

DRY $37 AV

🍇🍇🍇

Cloudy Bay Te Koko – see the Branded and Other White Wines section

Coal Pit Central Otago Sauvignon Blanc   ★★★☆

Well worth discovering, the 2018 vintage (★★★★☆) is a weighty wine, hand-picked from mature vines at Gibbston and lees-aged in tanks. Fresh and full-bodied, it has strong, lively, grapefruit-like flavours, hints of apples and limes, a minerally streak and a crisp, basically dry (4.4 grams/litre of residual sugar), sustained finish.

DRY $27 –V

Coal Pit Proprietor's Reserve Central Otago Sauvignon Blanc

The 2018 vintage (★★★★☆) is a fragrant, weighty wine, full of youthful vigour. Estate-grown and hand-picked at Gibbston, it was fermented in French oak barrels (30 per cent new). Full-bodied and ripely herbaceous, with savoury, leesy notes adding complexity, fresh acidity and a powerful finish, it's a distinctive wine, likely to be at its best from 2020+.

DRY $38 –V

Coopers Creek Marlborough Sauvignon Blanc   ★★★☆

The 2018 vintage (★★★☆) is a crisp and lively, medium-bodied wine, with fresh, ripely herbaceous aromas and flavours, firm acid spine and good depth.

DRY $19 V+

Craggy Range Marlborough Sauvignon Blanc   ★★★★

The attractive 2018 vintage (★★★★) is a mouthfilling, dry wine with passionfruit and lime flavours, tight and lingering. Freshly scented, it shows good delicacy and vibrancy.

DRY $20 V+

Crater Rim, The, Waipara Valley Sauvignon Blanc   ★★★★

Retasted in 2019, the partly barrel-fermented 2017 vintage (★★★★) is still fresh and lively, with a bright, light, yellow/green hue and fragrant tropical-fruit aromas and flavours. Mouthfilling, with good richness, balanced acidity and a subtle seasoning of oak, it's drinking well now.

DRY $18 V+

Crater Rim, The, Woolshed Block Waipara Valley Sauvignon Blanc

On sale now, the distinctive, delicious 2013 vintage (★★★★★) is a single-vineyard wine, partly French oak-aged. Currently in full stride, it is a bright, light yellow/green wine, ripely scented, fresh, mouthfilling and lively, with concentrated tropical-fruit flavours, bottle-aged complexity, and a crisp, lasting finish. Drink now to 2020.

DRY $24 V+

Dashwood by Vavasour Marlborough Sauvignon Blanc   ★★★★

This regional blend offers consistently good value. The 2019 vintage (★★★★) is punchy, with strong, fresh tropical-fruit and herbaceous flavours, and a basically dry (4.6 grams/litre of residual sugar), crisp finish. Marlborough in a glass.

DRY $16 V+

Delegat Awatere Valley Sauvignon Blanc   ★★★★

The 2019 vintage (★★★★☆) is a top buy. Bright, light lemon/green, it is fresh, mouthfilling and dry, with good vigour and intensity of ripe melon and green-capsicum flavours, lees-aging notes adding complexity, and a lingering finish. Best drinking mid-2020+.

DRY $20 V+

Delta Hatters Hill Marlborough Sauvignon Blanc

The classy, intense 2017 vintage (★★★★★) was grown in the Dillons Point district and handled without oak. Light lemon/green, it is mouthfilling and dry (2.6 grams/litre of residual sugar), with pure, penetrating passionfruit and lime flavours, appetisingly crisp and very long.

DRY $27 V+

Delta Marlborough Sauvignon Blanc ★★★★

The 2018 vintage (★★★★☆) is a full-on, intensely varietal style, offering fine value. A single-vineyard wine, it was grown in the lower Wairau Valley and handled entirely in tanks. The bouquet is punchy and slightly leafy; the palate is tightly structured and vibrant, with a salty streak, fresh, pungent tropical-fruit and herbaceous flavours, and a dry, crisp, lengthy finish.

DRY $20 V+

Doctors', The, Marlborough Sauvignon Blanc ★★★

A good example of the low-alcohol style, the easy-drinking 2019 vintage (★★★) is light (9.5 per cent alcohol) and lively. Vibrantly fruity, it is clearly varietal, with fresh, citrusy, green-edged flavours and an off-dry (5.4 grams/litre of residual sugar), smooth finish. (From Forrest Estate.)

MED/DRY $22 –V

Dog Point Vineyard Marlborough Sauvignon Blanc ★★★★★

This classic wine offers a clear style contrast to Section 94, Dog Point's complex, barrel-aged Sauvignon Blanc (see the Branded and Other White Wines section). Hand-picked at several sites in the Wairau Valley, it is lees-aged in tanks but handled without oak. The classy 2019 vintage (★★★★★) is highly aromatic, weighty and sweet-fruited, with intense, ripely herbaceous flavours and a crisp, dry, very long finish. Best drinking mid-2020+. Certified organic.

Vintage	19	18	17	16	15	14	13
WR	7	5	4	7	7	6	7
Drink	19-26	19-22	19-21	19-21	19-20	P	P

DRY $28 V+

Domain Road Vineyard Bannockburn Central Otago Sauvignon Blanc ★★★★

The lively 2017 vintage (★★★★) was estate-grown, hand-picked and partly (42 per cent) French oak-fermented. It has good intensity of citrusy, herbaceous flavours, with a subtle seasoning of oak adding complexity, and a slightly nettley bouquet.

DRY $23 AV

Eaton Fortissimo Marlborough Sauvignon Blanc (★★★★)

The 2018 vintage (★★★★) is rare – 648 bottles were produced. Hand-picked at two sites, in the Awatere Valley and further south, at Flaxbourne, it was fermented with indigenous yeasts and matured for 11 months in oak barrels (40 per cent new). Pale gold, it is a powerful wine, weighty, ripe and rounded, with tropical-fruit flavours, hints of nutty oak, balanced acidity and a dry finish.

Vintage	18
WR	7
Drink	20-25

DRY $48 –V

Eaton Marlborough Sauvignon Blanc   (★★★★☆)

The distinctive 2018 vintage (★★★★☆) was grown in the Awatere Valley and at Flaxbourne, hand-picked, and fermented and matured for 11 months in oak casks (30 per cent new). Bright, light yellow/green, it is mouthfilling and dry, with generous tropical-fruit flavours, showing good complexity, and a finely textured finish.

Vintage	18
WR	7
Drink	19-22

 DRY $39 –V

Eaton Thistle Hill Flaxbourne Marlborough Sauvignon Blanc   ★★★★☆

The 2018 vintage (★★★★) is rare – only 378 bottles were produced. A single-vineyard wine, it was hand-picked in southern Marlborough, barrel-fermented with indigenous yeasts and oak-aged for 11 months. Pale gold, it is less vibrant than most of the region's Sauvignon Blancs, but weighty, with ripe tropical-fruit flavours, showing good concentration and complexity.

Vintage	18	17
WR	7	7
Drink	20-25	19-25

 DRY $59 –V

Eradus Awatere Valley Marlborough Sauvignon Blanc   ★★★★

Offering good value, the 2019 vintage (★★★★) is an aromatic, intensely varietal wine, mouthfilling and smooth, with punchy, freshly herbaceous flavours, crisp and lively.

 DRY $17 V+

Esk Valley Marlborough Sauvignon Blanc   ★★★★

The punchy, youthful 2019 vintage (★★★★) was grown in the Awatere and Wairau valleys. Mouthfilling and vibrantly fruity, it has strong tropical-fruit flavours, a herbaceous undercurrent, and a dry (2.8 grams/litre of residual sugar), long finish. Best drinking mid-2020+.

Vintage	19	18
WR	6	6
Drink	19-22	19-20

DRY $20 V+

Fairbourne Marlborough Sauvignon Blanc   ★★★★★

From elevated, north-facing slopes in the Wairau Valley, the 2017 vintage (★★★★★) of this single-vineyard wine was hand-picked and fermented to full dryness. It was mostly handled in tanks, but a small portion of the blend (2 per cent) was French oak-fermented. Fragrant and full-bodied, it has concentrated, ripe tropical-fruit flavours to the fore, a herbaceous undercurrent, balanced acidity, and excellent complexity, drive and length.

Vintage	17	16	15	14	13
WR	6	7	6	7	7
Drink	19-21	19-22	19-21	19-20	P

 DRY $30 AV

Fairhall Downs Family Estate Marlborough Sauvignon Blanc   ★★★★

Estate-grown in the Brancott Valley, the full-bodied 2018 vintage (★★★★☆) was mostly handled in tanks; 4 per cent of the blend was wood-fermented. Bright, light lemon/green, it has concentrated, ripe tropical-fruit flavours to the fore, a herbaceous undercurrent, a touch of complexity, and a crisp, dry (3.4 grams/litre of residual sugar), sustained finish.

 DRY $24 AV

Falconhead Marlborough Sauvignon Blanc   ★★★

The good-value 2018 vintage (★★★☆) is an aromatic, full-bodied, lively wine, in a clearly varietal style with ripe passionfruit and lime flavours, finely balanced, dry and crisp.

 DRY $17 AV

Folium Reserve Marlborough Sauvignon Blanc   ★★★★★

The impressive 2018 vintage (★★★★★) was hand-picked in the Brancott Valley and handled entirely in tanks. A distinctive wine, it is fragrant, fresh and full-bodied, with concentrated tropical-fruit flavours, a herbaceous undercurrent, and a long finish. An age-worthy wine, it is full of personality.

Vintage	18	17	16
WR	4	5	6
Drink	19-25	19-25	19-30

 DRY $32 AV

Folium Vineyard Marlborough Sauvignon Blanc   ★★★★★

The 2018 vintage (★★★★☆) was hand-harvested in the Brancott Valley and handled entirely in tanks. Bright, light lemon/green, it is fresh and lively, with very good weight and intensity of tropical-fruit and herbaceous flavours, crisp, dry and lingering.

Vintage	18	17
WR	4	5
Drink	19-21	19-20

 DRY $26 V+

Forbidden Vines by Babich Marlborough Sauvignon Blanc   (★★★)

Offering very good value, the easy-drinking 2018 vintage (★★★) is freshly scented, with ripe-fruit aromas. Medium-bodied, it has good depth of tropical-fruit flavours, balanced acidity, and a smooth finish.

Vintage	18
WR	7
Drink	19-21

 MED/DRY $15 V+

Forrest Marlborough Sauvignon Blanc   ★★★★

The 2019 vintage (★★★★) is enjoyable from the start. Bright, light lemon/green, it is a medium to full-bodied, finely balanced wine, with very good depth of lively tropical-fruit and herbaceous flavours, dry (3.3 grams/litre of residual sugar) and lingering.

 DRY $22 V+

Gale Force Marlborough Sauvignon Blanc   (★★★)

Grown in the Awatere Valley, the 2017 vintage (★★★) is an aromatic, strongly herbaceous style, still fresh and lively. Crisp, with punchy, dry (2.4 grams/litre of residual sugar), green capsicum-like flavours, it's ready to roll. Fine value. (From Clark Estate.)

 DRY $12 V+

Giesen Marlborough Sauvignon Blanc   ★★★☆

This huge-volume wine from Giesen enjoys major export success. Grown in estate-owned and contract growers' vineyards, mostly in the Wairau Valley, with a smaller portion from the Awatere Valley, it is typically medium to full-bodied, with ripely herbaceous flavours, showing very good freshness, vigour and depth.

 DRY $17 V+

Gladstone Vineyard Sauvignon Blanc   ★★★★

The 2018 vintage (★★★★) was grown in the northern Wairarapa and 50 per cent barrel-fermented; the rest was handled in tanks. It is mouthfilling, with fresh, ripe tropical-fruit flavours to the fore, hints of toasty oak adding complexity, and a dry (1.5 grams/litre of residual sugar), smooth finish. Drink now or cellar.

Vintage	18
WR	6
Drink	19-22

 DRY $25 AV

Goldwater Wairau Valley Marlborough Sauvignon Blanc   ★★★★☆

The 2019 vintage (★★★★☆) is delicious from the start. Light lemon/green, it has concentrated, ripe tropical-fruit flavours to the fore, mingled with fresh, herbaceous notes, excellent delicacy and vibrancy, and a smooth (4.7 grams/litre of residual sugar), persistent finish.

 DRY $25 V+

Graham Norton's Own Marlborough Sauvignon Blanc   ★★★★

From 'chief winemaker Graham Norton', Invivo's instantly appealing 2019 vintage (★★★★☆) is ripely scented and full-bodied, with strong, fresh tropical-fruit flavours to the fore, a herbal undercurrent, moderate acidity and great drinkability.

 DRY $19 V+

Green Songs Funky Sauvignon Blanc   (★★★★)

Grown on a north-facing hillside at Atamai Village, in the Motueka district of Nelson, the fresh and punchy 2017 vintage (★★★★) was fermented and matured for 10 months in French oak casks (20 per cent new), and given a full, softening malolactic fermentation. Pale lemon/green, it is mouthfilling, crisp and youthful, with strong, lively, clearly herbaceous flavours, appetising acidity and good complexity.

DRY $30 –V

Greenhough Hope Vineyard Nelson Sauvignon Blanc   ★★★★☆

Certified organic, the 2017 vintage (★★★★★) was estate-grown, hand-picked and fermented with indigenous yeasts in French oak barrels (17 per cent new). Wood-aged for eight months, it is a notably complex, very harmonious wine, with a fragrant, inviting bouquet. Mouthfilling, it is vibrant and concentrated, with deliciously ripe flavours, fresh but not high acidity, and a sustained finish. Retasted in August 2019, it's probably at its peak now.

 DRY $32 –V

Greenhough River Garden Nelson Sauvignon Blanc   ★★★★☆

Certified organic, this consistently rewarding wine is mostly handled in tanks, but a small portion is fermented with indigenous yeasts and lees-aged in French oak casks. The 2019 vintage (★★★★★) is the first to be labelled 'River Garden'. Fresh and mouthfilling, it is sweet-fruited, with generous, ripe tropical-fruit flavours, a subtle seasoning of oak, good drive through the palate, finely balanced acidity, and a rounded finish. Already delicious, it offers excellent drinking now to 2021.

 DRY $22 V+

Greyrock Te Koru Marlborough Sauvignon Blanc   (★★★★)

Priced right, the 2019 vintage (★★★★) is medium-bodied and finely balanced, with very good depth of tropical-fruit and herbaceous flavours, and a crisp, dry (3.1 grams/litre of residual sugar), lingering finish.

 DRY $20 V+

Greystone Sauvignon Blanc Barrel Fermented   ★★★★☆

Showing good complexity, the 2018 vintage (★★★★☆) of this Waipara, North Canterbury wine was fermented and lees-aged for eight months in old French oak barrels. Bright, light yellow/green, it is mouthfilling, sweet-fruited and smooth, with well-ripened tropical-fruit flavours, finely integrated oak, and a long, very harmonious finish.

 DRY $26 AV

Greywacke Marlborough Sauvignon Blanc   ★★★★★

Grown in the central Wairau Valley and the Southern Valleys, the 2019 vintage (★★★★★) was handled principally in tanks (a small percentage was fermented with indigenous yeasts in old barrels). Pale lemon/green, it is fleshy, sweet-fruited and rounded, with generous, ripe tropical-fruit flavours, showing a distinct touch of complexity, and a dry, long finish. It's already very open and expressive.

Vintage	19	18	17	16	15	14	13	12
WR	6	6	5	6	6	6	6	5
Drink	20-25	19-24	19-22	19-22	19-21	19-20	P	P

 DRY $27 V+

Greywacke Marlborough Wild Sauvignon ★★★★★

This is a leading example of Marlborough Sauvignon Blanc from well outside the mainstream. Fermented with indigenous yeasts in old French oak barriques, the highly refined 2017 vintage (★★★★★) is fleshy, with impressively concentrated, ripe tropical-fruit flavours, showing excellent complexity, and a very harmonious, long finish. Already delicious, it's a drink-now or cellaring proposition.

Vintage	17	16	15	14	13	12	11	10
WR	6	6	6	6	6	4	6	6
Drink	19-27	19-26	19-25	19-24	19-23	19-22	19-21	19-21

 DRY $37 AV

Grove Mill Wairau Valley Marlborough Sauvignon Blanc ★★★★

Offering good value, the 2019 vintage (★★★★) was mostly handled in tanks; 5 per cent of the blend was fermented in old French oak casks. Richly fragrant, with tropical-fruit aromas, it is vibrantly fruity, with strong, ripely herbaceous flavours, a touch of complexity and a dry, lingering finish.

 DRY $19 V+

Haha Marlborough Sauvignon Blanc ★★★☆

This is a good buy. Very fresh and lively, the 2019 vintage (★★★★) is medium-bodied, with a punchy, aromatic bouquet. Strongly varietal, it is tangy, with very good vigour and depth of passionfruit, lime and green-capsicum flavours, dry (1.4 grams/litre of residual sugar) and crisp.

 DRY $18 V+

Hans Herzog Marlborough Sauvignon Blanc Barrel Fermented Sur Lie ★★★★★

Outside the regional mainstream, the 2016 vintage (★★★★★) was estate-grown and hand-picked on the north side of the Wairau Valley, fermented with indigenous yeasts in French oak puncheons, and wood-aged for 15 months. Light yellow/green, it has good weight and mouthfeel, with concentrated, ripe tropical-fruit flavours, impressive complexity and a dry, finely textured finish. Retasted in 2019, it's delicious now. Certified organic.

 DRY $44 AV

Huntaway Reserve Marlborough Sauvignon Blanc ★★★★

Grown in the Wairau Valley, the 2018 vintage (★★★★) is bright, light lemon/green, with a very fresh, aromatic bouquet. Medium-bodied, it has strong, vibrant passionfruit/lime flavours, with an appetisingly crisp finish. (From Lion.)

 DRY $22 V+

Hunter's Kaho Roa Marlborough Sauvignon Blanc ★★★★

The 2017 vintage (★★★☆) was grown in the Omaka Valley, and fermented and matured for six months in seasoned French oak puncheons. Fragrant, it is medium-bodied, with youthful, ripe flavours, a slightly minerally streak, and an appetisingly crisp, dry (1.8 grams/litre of residual sugar) finish. Restrained in its youth, it is worth cellaring to 2020+.

Vintage	17
WR	4
Drink	19-25

 DRY $24 AV

Hunter's Marlborough Sauvignon Blanc ★★★★

Hunter's fame rests on this wine. The goal is 'a strong expression of Marlborough fruit – a bell-clear wine with a mix of tropical and searing gooseberry characters'. The grapes are sourced from numerous sites in the Wairau Valley, and to retain their fresh, vibrant characters they are processed quickly, with some use of indigenous yeasts and lees-aging. The wine is usually at its best between one and two years old. The 2018 vintage (★★★★) was mostly handled in tanks, but 10 per cent of the blend was barrel-fermented. Crisp and vibrantly fruity, it is full-bodied and dry (1.6 grams/litre of residual sugar), with ripe tropical-fruit flavours to the fore, slightly minerally notes, and very good drive and depth.

Vintage	18
WR	5
Drink	19-21

 DRY $20 V+

Hunting Lodge, The, Expressions Marlborough Sauvignon Blanc ★★★★

Full of youthful vigour, the 2019 vintage (★★★★) was tank-fermented and matured on its yeast lees. Light lemon/green, it is vividly varietal, with strong, vibrant green-capsicum and passionfruit-like flavours, showing very good freshness, delicacy and length.

 DRY $22 V+

Hunting Lodge, The, Marlborough Sauvignon Blanc ★★★★☆

The 2018 vintage (★★★★☆) is a blend of Awatere Valley (70 per cent) and Wairau Valley (30 per cent) grapes, tank-fermented and lees-aged for four months. Bright, light lemon/green, it is highly aromatic, with penetrating, vibrant tropical-fruit and herbaceous flavours, dry (3.2 grams/litre of residual sugar) and appetisingly crisp. An intensely varietal wine, it shows excellent weight, vigour and depth.

DRY $22 V+

Hunting Lodge, The, Waimauku Homeblock Wild Ferment Sauvignon Blanc ★★★★☆

Estate-grown in West Auckland, the second, 2018 vintage (★★★★☆) was hand-picked (from vines principally planted in 2008, but dating back to 1979), and fermented and matured for four months in French oak barriques (25 per cent new). Bright, light lemon/green, it is full-bodied and vibrant, with concentrated tropical-fruit flavours, gently seasoned with toasty oak, good acid spine, excellent complexity and obvious potential. A tightly structured young wine, it should be at its best 2020+.

 DRY $33 –V

Invivo Marlborough Sauvignon Blanc

The 2019 vintage (★★★★) is fresh and aromatic, with very good body and depth of ripe tropical-fruit flavours, lees-aging notes adding complexity, moderate acidity, and a finely balanced, lingering finish.

DRY $19 V+

Invivo SJP Sarah Jessica Parker Marlborough Sauvignon Blanc

Aimed principally at the US market, the debut 2019 vintage (★★★★☆) is a good buy. Bright, light lemon/green, it is fresh and lively, with good weight, delicacy and intensity of passionfruit/ lime flavours. An elegant, tightly structured wine, it is very harmonious, with balanced acidity and a long, dry finish.

DRY $19 V+

Jackson Estate Grey Ghost Barrique Wairau Valley
Marlborough Sauvignon Blanc

On sale now, the 2015 vintage (★★★★☆) was hand-harvested from vines planted in 1988 and 50 per cent barrel-fermented. Tightly structured, it is a light yellow/green, medium to full-bodied wine, with ripe tropical-fruit flavours, balanced acidity, slightly toasty notes adding complexity, and a crisp, dry (1.9 grams/litre of residual sugar), long finish.

Vintage	15
WR	5
Drink	20-25

DRY $29 AV

Jackson Estate Somerset Block 2 Single Vineyard
Waihopai Valley Marlborough Sauvignon Blanc

Currently in full stride, the concentrated 2017 vintage (★★★★★) was grown in the Waihopai Valley and handled entirely in tanks. An aromatic, intensely varietal wine, it is full-bodied and ripe, with strong tropical-fruit flavours, bottle-aged notes adding a toasty complexity, and a crisp, dry (3 grams/litre of residual sugar), lasting finish.

Vintage	17
WR	6
Drink	20-22

DRY $29 –V

Jackson Estate Stich Marlborough Sauvignon Blanc

The 2018 vintage (★★★★) is a typical Wairau Valley style, with good body and fresh, ripely herbaceous aromas and flavours. Light lemon/green, it is aromatic, with strong passionfruit/ lime flavours, balanced acidity, and a dry (2.5 grams/litre of residual sugar), lingering finish. Priced right.

Vintage	18
WR	5
Drink	20-23

DRY $21 V+

Johanneshof Cellars Marlborough Sauvignon Blanc ★★★☆

Still on sale, the 2017 vintage (★★★★) is drinking well now. Bright, light lemon/green, it is medium-bodied and smooth, with good intensity of fresh tropical-fruit and herbaceous flavours, and a finely balanced, slightly off-dry (5 grams/litre of residual sugar) finish.

MED/DRY $24 –V

Johner Estate Wairarapa Sauvignon Blanc ★★★☆

Still youthful, the 2018 vintage (★★★☆) is a fresh, medium-bodied wine with good depth of ripe tropical-fruit flavours of passionfruit and lime, crisp and dry (3 grams/litre of residual sugar). Drink over the summer of 2019–20.

Vintage	18	17
WR	6	5
Drink	19-20	P

DRY $20 AV

Joiy Marlborough Sauvignon Blanc (★★★★)

The non-vintage wine (★★★★) I tasted in late 2019 is packaged in a 250-ml can, designed to be 'enjoiyed' at picnics or at the beach. Crisp and lively, with strong, ripely herbaceous flavours of melons and green capsicums, it's as good as most bottled wines, and priced sharply.

DRY $6 (250ML) V+

Jules Taylor Marlborough Sauvignon Blanc ★★★★☆

The 2019 vintage (★★★★☆) was grown in the lower Wairau, Southern and Awatere valleys, and made in a fully dry style (1.3 grams/litre of residual sugar). Full-bodied, sweet-fruited and lively, it has good intensity of tropical-fruit and herbaceous flavours, with a finely balanced, crisp finish.

DRY $23 V+

Jules Taylor OTQ Limited Release Single Vineyard
Marlborough Sauvignon Blanc ★★★★★

Made 'On The Quiet', the 2018 vintage (★★★★★) is a single-vineyard wine, fermented and matured in old French oak barriques. Still youthful, but already delicious, it is bright, light yellow/green with a fragrant, complex bouquet. Fleshy, rich and rounded, it has well-ripened tropical-fruit flavours, finely integrated oak, and a long, fully dry (1.3 grams/litre of residual sugar) finish. Drink now or cellar.

Vintage	18
WR	5
Drink	19-24

DRY $33 AV

Kahurangi Estate Mt Arthur Reserve Nelson Fumé Blanc   (★★★★☆)

Drinking well now, the distinctive 2018 vintage (★★★★☆) was fermented and matured in French oak casks (partly new), and most of the wine went through a softening malolactic fermentation. Bright, light yellow/green, with a creamy, slightly toasty bouquet, it's a slightly Chardonnay-like wine, fleshy and smooth, with rich, ripe tropical-fruit and stone-fruit flavours, showing good complexity.

DRY $25 V+

Kaimira Estate Brightwater Sauvignon Blanc   ★★★★

Certified organic, the 2018 vintage (★★★★) was estate-grown in Nelson and mostly handled in tanks; 10 per cent of the blend was fermented in seasoned oak casks. Bright, light lemon/green, it is freshly herbaceous, with strong, ripe tropical-fruit flavours to the fore, subtle toasty notes adding a touch of complexity, and a dry (2.5 grams/litre of residual sugar), appetisingly crisp finish. Drink now or cellar to 2020.

DRY $21 V+

Koha Marlborough Sauvignon Blanc   (★★★)

Light and lively, the 2019 vintage (★★★) is a strongly varietal wine, with fresh, herbaceous aromas and flavours, dry (3.5 grams/litre of residual sugar) and crisp. (From te Pā.)

DRY $19 AV

Kono Marlborough Sauvignon Blanc   ★★★

The 2018 vintage (★★★☆) is a fresh, lively, medium-bodied wine, with citrusy and herbaceous flavours that linger well to a dry finish.

DRY $18 AV

Kōparepare Marlborough Sauvignon Blanc   (★★★★)

Still very fresh and lively, the 2017 vintage (★★★★) was made by Whitehaven for LegaSea, to help fund its work to restore inshore fisheries to abundance. Tasted in mid-2019, it is bright, light lemon/green, with punchy tropical-fruit and herbaceous flavours, and a crisp, finely balanced finish. Priced sharply.

DRY $16 V+

Kumeu River Sauvignon Blanc   (★★★★☆)

The very age-worthy 2018 vintage (★★★★☆) is from the company's newly purchased vineyard on an elevated, north-facing site in Hawke's Bay. Hand-picked and fermented with indigenous yeasts, it is a distinctive, medium-bodied, youthful wine, with an array of fruit flavours – citrusy, limey, appley – showing good intensity, a minerally streak, a touch of complexity, and a long finish. Best drinking 2020+.

DRY $25 V+

Lake Chalice The Falcon Marlborough Sauvignon Blanc ★★★☆

Still on sale, the 2017 vintage (★★★☆) was grown in the lower Wairau Valley. A lively, medium-bodied wine with freshly herbaceous aromas, it has very good depth of green capsicum-like flavours, some tropical-fruit notes, and a finely balanced, basically dry (4.2 grams/litre of residual sugar), crisp finish.

 DRY $19 V+

Lake Chalice The Raptor Marlborough Sauvignon Blanc ★★★★

Drinking well now, the 2016 vintage (★★★★) is a weighty, dry wine, grown at Dillons Point, in the lower Wairau Valley. Light lemon/green, it is mouthfilling, with generous, ripely herbaceous flavours, bottle-aged complexity and a long, dry (2.4 grams/litre of residual sugar), well-rounded finish.

 DRY $23 AV

Lawson's Dry Hills Marlborough Sauvignon Blanc ★★★★★

One of the region's best, widely available Sauvignon Blancs, this stylish wine is vibrant, intense and finely structured. The grapes are grown at several sites, mostly in the Southern Valleys, and to add a subtle extra dimension, part of the blend (7 per cent in 2019) is fermented with indigenous yeasts in old French oak barrels. The wine typically has strong impact in its youth, but also has a proven ability to age, acquiring toasty, minerally complexities. Light lemon/green, the punchy 2019 vintage (★★★★) is freshly aromatic, with strong, very youthful tropical-fruit and herbaceous flavours, showing a distinct touch of complexity, and a dry (2.9 grams/litre of residual sugar), appetisingly crisp finish. Best drinking mid-2020+.

Vintage	19
WR	7
Drink	19-23

 DRY $20 V+

Lawson's Dry Hills Reserve Marlborough Sauvignon Blanc ★★★★★

The 2019 vintage (★★★★☆), grown in the Waihopai, Awatere and Wairau valleys, was made with some use of indigenous yeasts and barrel fermentation. Light lemon/green, it is a vigorous young wine, mouthfilling, with strong, freshly herbaceous flavours, oak complexity, and a dry (1.8 grams/litre of residual sugar), crisp finish. Best drinking mid-2020+.

Vintage	19
WR	7
Drink	19-23

 DRY $25 V+

Leveret Estate Marlborough Sauvignon Blanc ★★★☆

The 2018 vintage (★★★☆) is fresh and full-bodied, with tropical-fruit and herbaceous flavours, lively, crisp and strong, and a basically dry (4.2 grams/litre of residual sugar), finely balanced finish.

Vintage	17
WR	7
Drink	P

DRY $22 AV

Leveret Estate Reserve Barrel Aged Marlborough Sauvignon Blanc   (★★★★)

Drinking well now, the 2017 vintage (★★★★) was partly (50 per cent) barrel-fermented. Fresh and full-bodied, it is sweet-fruited, with tropical-fruit flavours, gently seasoned with oak, considerable complexity, and a dry (2 grams/litre of residual sugar), crisp finish.

DRY $26 –V

Linden Estate Hawke's Bay Sauvignon Blanc   ★★★☆

Barrel-fermented, the 2018 vintage (★★★★) is a finely balanced wine with ripe tropical-fruit aromas. Medium-bodied, it is sweet-fruited and vibrantly fruity, with fresh acidity, a touch of complexity and very good flavour depth.

DRY $20 AV

Loveblock Marlborough Sauvignon Blanc   ★★★★

Certified organic, the attractive 2018 vintage (★★★★) was estate-grown in the lower Awatere Valley and a third of the blend was hand-picked and fermented in old French oak barrels. Bright, light lemon/green, it is a ripely scented, medium to full-bodied wine, with generous, ripely herbaceous flavours, dry (3.5 grams/litre of residual sugar) and crisp. Showing good complexity and harmony, it's drinking well now.

DRY $22 V+

Loveblock Orange Marlborough Sauvignon Blanc   (★★★☆)

Estate-grown in the lower Awatere Valley, the distinctive 2018 vintage (★★★☆) has 'zero added sulphur', with green tea used as the only preserving agent. Pale straw-coloured, it is a medium to full-bodied, fresh, herbaceous wine, with vibrant, green-edged aromas and flavours, some tropical-fruit notes, and a crisp, lingering finish.

DRY $22 AV

Luna Martinborough Sauvignon Blanc   (★★★☆)

The crisp, strongly varietal 2018 vintage (★★★☆) was grown in the Blue Rock Vineyard and partly handled in tanks; 70 per cent of the blend was fermented and lees-aged for nine months in old, neutral oak barriques. Pale, it has good depth of lively, citrusy, slightly appley flavours, leesy notes adding complexity, firm acidity and lots of youthful vigour; best drinking 2020+.

DRY $24 –V

Mahi Marlborough Sauvignon Blanc   ★★★★★

Drinking superbly in 2019, the 2018 vintage (★★★★★) was grown at seven sites, principally at the western end of the Wairau Valley, and mostly handled in tanks; the ripest, hand-harvested fruit (11 per cent of the blend) was barrel-fermented with indigenous yeasts. Pale lemon/green, it is a freshly scented, weighty wine, with ripe tropical-fruit flavours to the fore, a herbaceous undercurrent, good complexity, and excellent intensity, delicacy and poise. Fine value.

Vintage	18	17	16	15
WR	6	6	7	6
Drink	19-23	19-22	19-20	P

DRY $22 V+

Mahi Single Vineyard Boundary Farm Marlborough Sauvignon Blanc   ★★★★★

Still unfolding, the impressive 2017 vintage (★★★★★) was grown on the lower slopes of the Wither Hills, on the south side of the Wairau Valley, hand-picked, and fermented and matured for 11 months in French oak barriques. Bright, light yellow/green, it is mouthfilling, fresh and youthful, with vibrant tropical-fruit flavours, showing excellent complexity, that build to a fully dry, very long finish. Full of potential, it should be at its best 2021+.

Vintage	17
WR	5
Drink	19-24

 DRY $34 AV

Mahi Single Vineyard The Alias Marlborough Sauvignon Blanc   (★★★★★)

Still on sale, the 2015 vintage (★★★★★) is maturing very gracefully. Grown at Conders Bend, near Renwick, in the Wairau Valley, hand-picked, barrel-fermented and oak-aged for 15 months, it is bright, light yellow/green, weighty and lively, with substantial body and deep, ripely herbaceous flavours, showing excellent complexity and richness. A thought-provoking wine, it's well worth trying.

 DRY $30 AV

Main Divide North Canterbury Sauvignon Blanc   ★★★★

Looking good for the summer of 2019–20, the 2019 vintage (★★★★) is full-bodied and freshly scented, with good intensity of ripely herbaceous flavours, crisp, dry and punchy. (From Pegasus Bay.)

Vintage	19
WR	5
Drink	19-21

 DRY $21 V+

Map Maker Marlborough Sauvignon Blanc   ★★★★

Priced sharply, the 2019 vintage (★★★★) was estate-grown at Rapaura, in the Wairau Valley. It has a punchy, aromatic bouquet, leading into a lively, intensely varietal wine, with strong tropical-fruit and herbaceous flavours, crisp, bone-dry and lingering. (From Staete Landt.)

 DRY $18 V+

Marlborough Vines Marlborough Sauvignon Blanc   ★★★

From Toi Toi, the 2018 vintage (★★★) offers good value. It is punchy and racy, with fresh, herbaceous aromas and flavours, and lots of youthful impact.

DRY $15 V+

Martinborough Vineyard Martinborough Sauvignon Blanc   ★★★★

The 2018 vintage (★★★☆) was mostly handled in tanks; 10 per cent of the blend was fermented and matured in old oak barrels. Bright, light lemon/green, it is ripely scented, fresh and lively, with tropical-fruit flavours, showing a distinct touch of complexity, and a dry, crisp finish. It's drinking well now.

 DRY $24 AV

Martinborough Vineyard Te Tera Sauvignon Blanc   ★★★★

The 2019 vintage (★★★★) is a ripely scented, lively, medium-bodied wine, with good intensity of tropical-fruit flavours, a herbaceous undercurrent and a basically dry (4 grams/litre of residual sugar), crisp finish. Good value.

Vintage	19	18	17
WR	7	7	7
Drink	19-23	19-23	19-22

DRY $20 V+

Matahiwi Estate Wairarapa Sauvignon Blanc   ★★★★

The strongly varietal 2019 vintage (★★★★) is medium-bodied, very fresh and vibrant, with penetrating melon, green-capsicum and passionfruit flavours, appetising acidity, and a dry (1.9 grams/litre of residual sugar), tangy finish.

Vintage	19
WR	5
Drink	19-20

DRY $20 V+

Maui Waipara Sauvignon Blanc   (★★★☆)

Already enjoyable, the 2019 vintage (★★★☆) is a lively, herbaceous style, with some riper tropical-fruit notes. Medium-bodied, it is fresh and finely balanced, with a basically dry (4 grams/litre of residual sugar), crisp finish. Fine value. (From Tiki.)

DRY $14 V+

Mills Reef Estate Marlborough Sauvignon Blanc   ★★★

The 2019 vintage (★★★) is medium to full-bodied, fresh and lively, with tropical-fruit and herbaceous flavours, crisp and finely balanced for easy drinking, with a basically dry (4 grams/litre of residual sugar) finish.

DRY $19 AV

Mills Reef Reserve Hawke's Bay Sauvignon Blanc   ★★★☆

The 2019 vintage (★★★☆) is a medium-bodied, vibrantly fruity wine, with very good depth of melon, passionfruit and lime flavours, fresh, dry (2 grams/litre of residual sugar) and smooth.

Vintage	19	18	17	16
WR	7	7	5	7
Drink	19-21	19-20	P	P

DRY $23 –V

Misha's Vineyard The Starlet Central Otago Sauvignon Blanc   ★★★★☆

The 2018 vintage (★★★★) was estate-grown at Bendigo, in the Cromwell Basin. Hand-harvested, it was mostly handled in tanks, but 23 per cent of the blend was fermented with indigenous yeasts in seasoned French oak casks. Bright, light lemon/green, it is ripely scented, fresh and weighty, with vibrant passionfruit and citrus-fruit flavours, showing a touch of complexity, very good depth, and a finely balanced, basically dry (5 grams/litre of residual sugar) finish. Best drinking 2020+.

Vintage	18	17	16	15	14	13
WR	7	6	7	7	6	7
Drink	19-26	19-25	19-24	19-23	19-22	19-23

MED/DRY $27 AV

Mission Marlborough Sauvignon Blanc   ★★★★

Priced sharply, the 2019 vintage (★★★★) is instantly likeable. Estate-grown in the Awatere Valley, it has fresh, strong, ripely herbaceous aromas. Medium-bodied, it is very lively and zesty, with passionfruit and lime flavours, showing excellent delicacy, purity and depth, and a finely balanced, dryish (5 grams/litre of residual sugar), crisp finish.

MED/DRY $16 V+

Mission Vineyard Selection Marlborough Sauvignon Blanc   ★★★★

The 2018 vintage (★★★★) was estate-grown in the Cable Station Vineyard, in the Awatere Valley. Fresh and full-bodied, it has strong, ripe passionfruit and lime flavours to the fore, inconspicuous sweetness (6 grams/litre of residual sugar), a touch of complexity, and strong drink-young appeal.

MED/DRY $20 V+

Montana Reserve Marlborough Sauvignon Blanc   ★★★☆

The 2018 vintage (★★★☆) offers good value. Aromatic, it has fresh, strong passionfruit and green-capsicum flavours, and a dry, appetisingly crisp finish.

DRY $17 V+

Montford Estate Marlborough Sauvignon Blanc   (★★★☆)

The attractive 2019 vintage (★★★☆) was grown in the Wairau and Awatere valleys. Full-bodied, it is fresh and lively, with ripe tropical-fruit and herbaceous flavours, showing good vigour and depth, and a finely balanced, dry (3.5 grams/litre of residual sugar) finish. (From te Pā.)

DRY $20 AV

Morton Estate [Black Label] Marlborough Sauvignon Blanc   ★★★★

The tightly structured 2017 vintage (★★★★☆) was partly barrel-fermented. Retasted in mid-2019, it is a light lemon/green, freshly aromatic, sweet-fruited wine. Full-bodied, with concentrated, ripe tropical-fruit flavours, and toasty, bottle-aged notes adding complexity, it's drinking well now. (From Lion.)

DRY $20 V+

Morton Estate Marlborough Sauvignon Blanc   (★★★)

The 2018 vintage (★★★) is a strongly varietal wine, with good body and depth of tropical-fruit and herbaceous flavours, still fresh and lively.

DRY $17 AV

Mount Brown Estates North Canterbury Sauvignon Blanc   ★★★☆

Bargain priced, the 2018 vintage (★★★☆) is pale lemon/green, with fresh, lifted, herbaceous aromas. A vibrant, medium-bodied wine, it has tropical-fruit and herbaceous flavours, very fresh and lively, and a crisp, dry (4 grams/litre of residual sugar) finish.

Vintage	18
WR	6
Drink	19-20

DRY $16 V+

Mount Riley Limited Release Marlborough Sauvignon Blanc   ★★★★

Offering great value, the 2019 vintage (★★★★) was substantially (55 per cent) grown in the lower Wairau Valley, blended with fruit from the central Wairau Valley (40 per cent) and the Awatere Valley (5 per cent). Lees-aged for three months, it is fresh and full-bodied, with very good vigour and concentration of tropical-fruit flavours, a herbaceous undercurrent, and a lingering finish.

DRY $17 V+

Mount Riley Marlborough Sauvignon Blanc   ★★★☆

Priced sharply, the 2019 vintage (★★★☆) is a 4:1 blend of Wairau Valley and Awatere Valley grapes. Highly aromatic, it's a medium-bodied wine with very good depth of fresh, lively tropical-fruit and herbaceous flavours, and a crisp, tangy finish.

DRY $15 V+

Mount Vernon Marlborough Sauvignon Blanc   ★★★☆

From Lawson's Dry Hills, the light lemon/green 2019 vintage (★★★☆) is a lively, medium-bodied wine, with herbaceous flavours, fresh and direct, a crisp, dry (2.7 grams/litre of residual sugar) finish, and lots of youthful impact.

Vintage	19	18
WR	5	5
Drink	19-21	19-20

DRY $18 V+

Moutere Hills Nelson Sauvignon Blanc   ★★★★

The 2019 vintage (★★★★) is a single-vineyard wine, grown at Hope, on the Waimea Plains. Still very youthful, it is crisp and lively, with ripely herbaceous flavours, showing good vigour and intensity, and a dry, lingering finish.

DRY $21 V+

Mt Beautiful North Canterbury Sauvignon Blanc ★★★★

Estate-grown at Cheviot, north of Waipara, the 2018 vintage (★★★★☆) is ripely scented, fresh and full-bodied. Fleshy and finely textured, it's a distinctly tropical fruit-flavoured, non-herbaceous style, with balanced acidity and strong passionfruit/lime characters. A distinctive wine, it's a drink-now or cellaring proposition.

DRY $21 V+

Mt Difficulty Bannockburn Central Otago Sauvignon Blanc ★★★★

The impressive 2018 vintage (★★★★☆) is delicious young. Handled solely in tanks, it is a mouthfilling wine, fresh and sweet-fruited, with excellent vigour and depth of ripe tropical-fruit flavours, a touch of complexity, and a crisp, fully dry (under 1 gram/litre of residual sugar) finish. If you haven't discovered just how good the region's Sauvignon Blancs can be, try this.

DRY $27 –V

Mud House Marlborough Sauvignon Blanc ★★★☆

This is typically a lively, aromatic wine, offering top value. Estate-grown in the upper Wairau Valley, the 2018 vintage (★★★☆) is fresh and medium-bodied, with very good depth of crisp tropical-fruit and herbaceous flavours.

DRY $15 V+

Mud House Single Vineyard The Woolshed Marlborough Sauvignon Blanc ★★★★

Estate-grown in the upper Wairau Valley, the 2018 vintage (★★★★) is a mouthfilling wine, with good intensity of vibrant melon, grapefruit, lime and green-capsicum flavours, dry and crisp.

DRY $23 AV

Nautilus Marlborough Sauvignon Blanc ★★★★

This is typically a fragrant, sweet-fruited wine with crisp, concentrated flavours. The 2019 vintage (★★★★☆) is pungently aromatic, fresh and full-bodied, with strong passionfruit/lime flavours, showing very good vigour and intensity, and a dry (2 grams/litre of residual sugar), crisp finish. Best drinking 2020+.

Vintage	19	18	17	16
WR	7	7	7	7
Drink	19-22	19-21	19-20	P

DRY $25 AV

Nautilus The Paper Nautilus Marlborough Sauvignon Blanc ★★★★★

Named after a paper-thin shell, the 2017 vintage (★★★★★) was estate-grown, hand-picked and fermented in a single, seasoned French oak cuve. Bright, light lemon/green, it is a distinctive, weighty wine, with ripe tropical-fruit flavours, showing lovely delicacy and depth, and a dry (2 grams/litre of residual sugar), ultra-smooth finish. A delicious mouthful.

DRY $34 AV

Neudorf Nelson Sauvignon Blanc

Grown on the Waimea Plains, the 2018 vintage (★★★★) is a single-vineyard wine, mostly handled in tanks; 40 per cent of the blend was fermented and matured in old French oak barrels. Bright, light lemon/green, it is full-bodied and fresh, with good intensity of tropical-fruit and herbaceous flavours, crisp and dry (2.9 grams/litre of residual sugar), and a distinct touch of complexity.

DRY $25 AV

Nga Waka Martinborough Sauvignon Blanc

Still on sale, the 2017 vintage (★★★★) is a softly mouthfilling, dry wine, fermented in tanks (80 per cent) and seasoned oak barrels (20 per cent). Weighty and rounded, with generous, ripe tropical-fruit flavours and gentle acidity, it's drinking well now.

DRY $25 AV

Nikau Point Reserve Marlborough Sauvignon Blanc

Priced sharply, the 2019 vintage (★★★☆) is a medium-bodied wine, fresh and lively, with good depth of passionfruit/lime flavours, and a finely balanced, dry (3 grams/litre of residual sugar) finish.

DRY $16 V+

Nikau Point Select Marlborough Sauvignon Blanc

Enjoyable young, the very low-priced 2019 vintage (★★☆) is a medium-bodied wine with fresh, ripely herbaceous flavours, and a smooth, basically dry (4.9 grams/litre of residual sugar) finish.

DRY $12 V+

Odyssey Marlborough Sauvignon Blanc

(★★★★)

Estate-grown at the top of the Brancott Valley, the 2018 vintage (★★★★) is certified organic. Bright, light lemon/green, it is a medium to full-bodied, fresh and lively wine, sweet-fruited, with tropical-fruit flavours, good acid spine, and a dry (2.5 grams/litre of residual sugar), lasting finish.

DRY $20 V+

Ohau Gravels Selected Vines Sauvignon Blanc

(★★★★☆)

Grown in the Horowhenua, the 2014 vintage (★★★★☆), now on sale, was fermented with indigenous yeasts and barrel-aged. Bright, light gold, it's a distinctive, mature wine, with tropical-fruit flavours, some herbaceous notes, oak richness and very good complexity. Drink now.

DRY $30 –V

Old Coach Road Lighter Alcohol Nelson Sauvignon Blanc ★★☆

The 2018 vintage (★★☆) from Seifried is light-bodied (10.5 per cent alcohol) and tangy, with fresh, grassy, citrusy aromas and flavours, dry (3.5 grams/litre of residual sugar) and crisp.

Vintage	18	17	DRY $13 V+
WR	6	6	
Drink	19-20	P	

Old Coach Road Nelson Sauvignon Blanc ★★★

This is Seifried Estate's lowest-tier Sauvignon, priced sharply and enjoyable young. The 2019 vintage (★★★☆) offers great value. It has fresh, punchy herbaceous and tropical-fruit aromas and flavours, and a basically dry (4.3 grams/litre of residual sugar), tangy finish. A top vintage.

DRY $14 V+

Old House Vineyards Kaho Nelson Sauvignon Blanc ★★★★☆

The 2018 vintage (★★★★) is a single-vineyard, Upper Moutere wine, fermented and matured for eight months in French oak casks (12 per cent new). Bright, light lemon/green, it has a creamy, slightly toasty bouquet. Weighty, it's an age-worthy wine, clearly oak-influenced, with ripe tropical-fruit flavours, showing good complexity. Best drinking mid-2020+.

Vintage	18	17	DRY $30 –V
WR	7	6	
Drink	19-26	19-25	

Old House Vineyards Nelson Sauvignon Blanc ★★★★

Estate-grown at Upper Moutere, the 2018 vintage (★★★★) is a tank-fermented wine. Drinking well now, it is sweet-fruited, fresh and vigorous, with good intensity of ripely herbaceous flavours and a crisp, fully dry finish.

Vintage	18	17	DRY $21 V+
WR	7	6	
Drink	19-23	19-22	

Opawa Marlborough Sauvignon Blanc ★★★★

Already highly enjoyable, the 2019 vintage (★★★★☆) was grown in the Wairau Valley and principally handled in tanks; 5 per cent of the blend was fermented with indigenous yeasts in large oak cuves. Bright, light lemon/green, it is aromatic, with good intensity of ripely herbaceous flavours, a touch of complexity, and a finely balanced, dry (2 grams/litre of residual sugar), crisp finish. A top vintage. (From Nautilus.)

DRY $22 V+

Oyster Bay Marlborough Sauvignon Blanc ★★★★

Oyster Bay is a Delegat brand, focused mostly on Marlborough wines and enjoying huge success in global markets. Two-thirds estate-grown, this wine is grown at a multitude of sites around the Wairau (mostly) and Awatere valleys, handled entirely in stainless steel tanks, and made in a dry style with tropical-fruit and herbaceous flavours, crisp and punchy. Bright, light lemon/green, the 2019 vintage (★★★★) is mouthfilling and lively, with fresh, tangy tropical-fruit and herbaceous flavours, showing good intensity, and a dry, appetisingly crisp finish.

Pā Road Marlborough Sauvignon Blanc ★★★☆

The 2019 vintage (★★★☆) is full of youthful vigour, with good depth of fresh, lively tropical-fruit and herbaceous flavours, dry (3 grams/litre of residual sugar) and crisp. (From te Pā.)

Paddy Borthwick Wairarapa Sauvignon Blanc ★★★★

Full of personality, the explosively flavoured 2019 vintage (★★★★★) is a single-vineyard wine, with a pungently, ripely aromatic, very fresh and lively bouquet. Mouthfilling and racy, it is sweet-fruited, with penetrating, ripely herbaceous flavours, threaded with crisp acidity, and a dry, persistent finish. A top buy.

Passage Rock Waiheke Island Sauvignon Blanc (★★★★★)

Already delicious, the 2019 vintage (★★★★★) was estate-grown and hand-picked at Te Matuku Bay. Weighty, fleshy and sweet-fruited, it is attractively aromatic, with balanced acidity and fresh, concentrated, distinctly tropical-fruit flavours. A top example of the North Island style of Sauvignon Blanc.

Pegasus Bay Sauvignon/Sémillon ★★★★★

This distinctive Waipara, North Canterbury wine is concentrated and complex, with loads of personality. It is typically a 70:30 blend of Sauvignon Blanc and Sémillon, partly (35 per cent) fermented and matured in French oak barrels. From vines over 30 years old, the 2017 vintage (★★★★★) is bright, light yellow/green, with a complex bouquet. Crisp, full-bodied and dry (0.9 grams/litre of residual sugar), it is a youthful, very vigorous wine, with ripe tropical-fruit flavours, a subtle seasoning of oak, fresh acidity, and a tightly structured, lasting finish. Best drinking 2021+.

Vintage	17	16	15	14
WR	7	6	6	6
Drink	19-27	19-26	19-27	19-25

Pruner's Reward, The, Waipara Sauvignon Blanc ★★★☆

From Bellbird Spring, the 2016 vintage (★★★★) was fermented in tanks (80 per cent) and old oak casks (20 per cent). Retasted in August 2019, it is medium to full-bodied, with very good depth of ripe tropical-fruit flavours, showing a touch of complexity, and a dry, now-softening finish.

DRY $22 AV

Pyramid Valley Marlborough Sauvignon Blanc   (★★★★★)

Full of potential, the debut 2018 vintage (★★★★★) was hand-harvested in the Churton Vineyard, an elevated site between the Waihopai and Omaka valleys, and fermented and lees-aged for six months in seasoned French oak demi-muids. Bright, light lemon/green, it is scented and mouthfilling, with penetrating, ripe tropical-fruit flavours, and a long, tightly structured finish. Still a baby, it's a distinctive, subtle, minerally wine, finely poised and likely to be at its best mid-2020+.

 DRY $35 AV

Pyramid Valley North Canterbury Sauvignon Blanc   (★★★★★)

Showing strong personality, the bright, light lemon/green 2019 vintage (★★★★★) is mouthfilling and sweet-fruited, with concentrated, ripe tropical-fruit flavours and a finely balanced, lingering finish. An impressive debut.

 DRY $28 V+

Quarter Acre Hawke's Bay Sauvignon Blanc   ★★★★☆

The stylish 2017 vintage (★★★★☆) was hand-picked at Maraekakaho and fermented and lees-aged for nine months in seasoned puncheons and barriques. Bright, light lemon/green, it is medium to full-bodied, with vigorous, ripely herbaceous flavours, a subtle seasoning of oak, good complexity and a long, dry finish. Drink now to 2020.

DRY $28 AV

Ra Nui Marlborough Sauvignon Blanc   ★★★★

Grown in the lower Wairau Valley, the 2018 vintage (★★★★) is a single-vineyard wine, mostly handled in tanks; 5 per cent was barrel-fermented. Light lemon/green, it is weighty, with fresh, ripe tropical-fruit flavours, a touch of complexity, fresh acidity and very good vigour and depth.

DRY $25 AV

Rapaura Springs Bull Paddock Marlborough Sauvignon Blanc   (★★★★★)

The classy 2019 vintage (★★★★★) was grown at Dillons Point, in the lower Wairau Valley. An age-worthy wine, it is ripely scented and weighty, with strong tropical-fruit flavours, gentle herbaceous notes, excellent delicacy and vibrancy, and a dry (3.1 grams/litre of residual sugar), lingering finish. Best drinking mid-2020+.

Vintage	19
WR	7
Drink	19-22

 DRY $33 AV

Rapaura Springs Classic Marlborough Sauvignon Blanc   ★★★☆

Priced sharply, the 2019 vintage (★★★☆) is fresh and lively with very good depth of tropical-fruit and herbaceous flavours, crisp acidity, and a dryish (4.9 grams/litre of residual sugar), smooth finish.

Vintage	19
WR	7
Drink	19-22

 DRY $17 V+

Rapaura Springs Reserve Marlborough Sauvignon Blanc   ★★★★

Offering good value, the 2019 vintage (★★★★) was grown in the Wairau Valley. It is mouthfilling and vibrantly fruity, with strong tropical-fruit flavours, a herbaceous undercurrent, and a finely balanced, dry (3.6 grams/litre of residual sugar), lingering finish.

Vintage	19	18	17
WR	7	6	6
Drink	19-22	19-21	19-20

 DRY $19 V+

Rapaura Springs Rohe Blind River Marlborough Sauvignon Blanc   (★★★★)

Grown in the Blind River district, south of the Awatere Valley, the 2019 vintage (★★★★) is a mouthfilling, lively, freshly herbaceous wine, with very good depth of green capsicum-like flavours, some tropical-fruit notes, and a finely balanced, dry (3.3 grams/litre of residual sugar) finish.

 DRY $25 AV

Rapaura Springs Rohe Dillons Point Marlborough Sauvignon Blanc   (★★★★★)

Grown in the lower Wairau Valley, the youthful 2019 vintage (★★★★★) is mouthfilling and lively, with punchy, ripe tropical-fruit and herbaceous flavours, a slightly salty streak and a long, dry (3.2 grams/litre of residual sugar) finish. A classic Dillons Point style.

 DRY $25 V+

Renato Nelson Sauvignon Blanc   ★★★★

Priced sharply, the 2018 vintage (★★★★) is a blend of fruit from Moutere and the Waimea Plains. Highly aromatic, it is very fresh and vibrant, with strong passionfruit and green-capsicum flavours, and a finely balanced (4 grams/litre of residual sugar), tangy finish.

Vintage	18	17	16	15
WR	6	6	6	6
Drink	19-21	19-21	19-20	19-20

DRY $18 V+

Riverby Estate Marlborough Sauvignon Blanc   (★★★)

The 2018 vintage (★★★) is a single-vineyard wine, grown at Rapaura. Fresh and lively, it is medium-bodied, with gently herbaceous flavours, and a crisp, dry (3 grams/litre of residual sugar) finish.

Vintage	18
WR	6
Drink	19-21

 DRY $20 -V

Roaring Meg Central Otago Sauvignon Blanc   ★★★☆

The attractive 2019 vintage (★★★★) is mouthfilling, with a freshly herbaceous bouquet. Vibrantly fruity, it has very good depth of tropical-fruit and herbaceous flavours, crisp and dry (3 grams/litre of residual sugar), and lots of drink-young appeal. (From Mt Difficulty.)

 DRY $20 AV

Rock Ferry The Corners Vineyard Marlborough Sauvignon Blanc   ★★★★☆

Retasted in late 2018, the 2014 vintage (★★★★☆) was estate-grown at Rapaura, in the Wairau Valley, and mostly tank-fermented; 15 per cent of the blend was fermented with indigenous yeasts and lees-aged in seasoned French oak cuves. Bright, light lemon/green, it has a complex, ripely herbal bouquet. Maturing very gracefully, it is a distinctive wine, with good body, richness and drive, crisp acidity, and a basically dry (4.2 grams/litre of residual sugar), long finish. Certified organic.

 DRY $30 –V

Rockburn Central Otago Fumé Blanc   ★★★★☆

Still on sale, the bright, light yellow/green 2015 vintage (★★★★★) is a rare beast – a memorable Sauvignon Blanc from Central Otago. Estate-grown at Parkburn, in the Cromwell Basin, it is a single-vineyard wine, barrel-fermented with indigenous yeasts, oak-aged for 18 months, and bottled unfined and unfiltered. Retasted in November 2018, it is fragrant, weighty, concentrated and complex, with deep, ripely herbaceous flavours and a dry, well-rounded, lasting finish. Full of personality.

 DRY $40 –V

Rockburn Central Otago Sauvignon Blanc   ★★★☆

Retasted in late 2018, the 2016 vintage (★★★★) currently on sale is maturing very gracefully. A vibrant, medium-bodied wine, it was fermented in a 2:1 mix of tanks and seasoned French oak barrels. Bright, light yellow/green, it has crisp, dry tropical-fruit and herbaceous flavours, with a gentle seasoning of oak adding complexity, and excellent depth and harmony.

 DRY $25 –V

Roys Hill Hawke's Bay Sauvignon Blanc   (★★☆)

Still on sale and priced sharply, the 2017 vintage (★★☆) was grown in the Gimblett Gravels. Bright, light yellow/green, it is medium-bodied, with solid depth of tropical-fruit and herbaceous flavours, slightly honeyed notes emerging, and a crisp, dry (2 grams/litre of residual sugar) finish. Ready.

 DRY $13 V+

Russian Jack Marlborough Sauvignon Blanc   ★★★

Priced right, the 2019 vintage (★★★☆) is a medium-bodied wine, aromatic, with ripely herbaceous flavours, showing good vigour and depth, and a finely balanced, crisp, dry finish.

DRY $19 AV

Saint Clair Barrique Marlborough Sauvignon Blanc   ★★★★☆

Currently in full stride, the 2016 vintage (★★★★☆) is a weighty, dry wine, fermented with indigenous yeasts in seasoned oak barriques and lees-aged for 11 months. Bright, light lemon/green, it has a fragrant, complex bouquet, leading into a rich palate with ripe, non-herbaceous fruit flavours, enriched but not dominated by a slightly nutty oak influence, and a well-rounded, very harmonious finish.

 DRY $27 AV

Saint Clair James Sinclair Marlborough Sauvignon Blanc ★★★★

The 2018 vintage (★★★★☆) was grown at Dillons Point, in the lower Wairau Valley. Bright, light lemon/green, it is mouthfilling and vigorous, with excellent intensity of ripely herbaceous flavours, a slightly salty streak, balanced acidity and a finely poised, dry (2.7 grams/litre of residual sugar), lingering finish.

DRY $25 AV

Saint Clair Origin Marlborough Sauvignon Blanc ★★★★

The 2018 vintage (★★★★) is fresh, full-bodied and vibrantly fruity. Finely balanced, it has tropical-fruit and herbaceous flavours, a slightly salty streak, and good intensity and length.

DRY $22 V+

Saint Clair Pioneer Block 21 Bell Block Marlborough Sauvignon Blanc (★★★★★)

Showing excellent weight and depth, the 2018 vintage (★★★★★) of this Dillons Point wine is highly aromatic. Mouthfilling, it has pure, searching grapefruit and lime flavours, some tropical-fruit notes, good intensity and a long, dry finish.

DRY $27 V+

Saint Clair Pioneer Block 27 Buzz Block Marlborough Sauvignon Blanc (★★★★)

Very fresh and lively, the 2018 vintage (★★★★) of this Dillons Point wine is medium-bodied, with punchy, incisive melon, lime and green-capsicum flavours that linger well.

DRY $27 –V

Saint Clair Pioneer Block 3 43 Degrees Marlborough Sauvignon Blanc ★★★★☆

Full of youthful vigour, the 2018 vintage (★★★★☆) was grown at Dillons Point, in the lower Wairau Valley. Fresh, crisp and dry, it has incisive melon, lime and green-capsicum flavours, lees-aging notes, a slightly salty streak and a lasting finish.

DRY $27 AV

Saint Clair Wairau Reserve Marlborough Sauvignon Blanc ★★★★★

Marlborough's largest family-owned wine producer has an extensive array of Sauvignon Blancs. This is not the region's most complex Savvy, but in terms of sheer pungency, it's a star, having won countless gold medals and trophies since the first, 2001 vintage. Grown in the cooler, coastal end of the Wairau Valley and handled entirely in stainless steel tanks, it is typically super-charged, in an exuberantly fruity, very pure and zesty style. The 2018 vintage (★★★★★) is a single-vineyard wine, grown at Dillons Point. It has fresh, strong, herbaceous aromas and flavours, with pure, penetrating grapefruit and green-capsicum notes, a minerally streak and a long, dry (2.3 grams/litre of residual sugar) finish.

DRY $34 AV

Sanctuary Marlborough Sauvignon Blanc ★★★

Enjoyable young, the 2019 vintage (★★★) is fresh, lively and crisp, with tropical-fruit flavours to the fore, gentle herbaceous notes, and lots of youthful impact. (From Grove Mill.)

DRY $20 –V

Saveé Sea Marlborough Sauvignon Blanc ★★★

Priced sharply, the 2019 vintage (★★★) is a very easy-drinking style, with faint sweetness (5.5 grams/litre of residual sugar) and good depth of ripe tropical-fruit and herbaceous flavours, fresh and crisp. (From Awatere River.)

MED/DRY $14 V+

Saving Grace Sauvignon Blanc (★★★★☆)

Designed principally for sale in restaurants, the subtle, satisfying 2018 vintage (★★★★☆) is a single-vineyard wine, hand-picked at Waipara, in North Canterbury, and fermented in seasoned oak barrels. Bright, light lemon/green, it is mouthfilling, complex and dry, with strong, well-ripened fruit flavours, a very subtle seasoning of oak, balanced acidity, and plenty of personality. Best drinking 2020. (From Waipara Hills.)

DRY $30 –V

Seifried Nelson Sauvignon Blanc ★★★★

Priced right, the 2019 vintage (★★★★) is very fresh, crisp and punchy, with ripely herbaceous flavours, showing good vigour and intensity, and a basically dry (4.5 grams/litre of residual sugar), appetisingly crisp finish.

DRY $18 V+

Vintage	19	18	17	16
WR	7	6	6	6
Drink	19-21	19-20	P	P

Seresin Marlborough Sauvignon Blanc ★★★★★

This is one of the region's most sophisticated, subtle and satisfying Sauvignons. It's also one of the most important, given its widespread international distribution and certified BioGro status. The wine (which includes 5 to 9 per cent Sémillon) is mostly fermented in tanks with indigenous yeasts, but 15 to 20 per cent of the blend is fermented and lees-aged in seasoned French oak casks. The refined, subtle 2016 vintage (★★★★☆) is weighty and sweet-fruited, with deep, ripely herbaceous flavours, showing good complexity, and a dry, finely textured finish.

DRY $24 V+

Sherwood Estate Sherwood Waipara Valley Sauvignon Blanc ★★★☆

The easy-drinking 2019 vintage (★★★☆) is fresh and full-bodied, with lively, ripe passionfruit/lime flavours, showing good depth, balanced acidity and a smooth finish.

DRY $20 AV

Sherwood Estate Stoney Range Waipara Valley Sauvignon Blanc   ★★★

The 2019 vintage (★★★) is a fresh, medium-bodied, youthful wine, with tangy tropical-fruit and herbaceous flavours, crisp and lively.

DRY $17 V+

Sherwood Estate Waipara Valley Sauvignon Blanc   (★★★★)

Drinking well now, the 2018 vintage (★★★★) was grown in the Waipara Valley, North Canterbury, and handled entirely in tanks. Light lemon/green, it is vibrantly fruity, with fresh, strong, ripely herbaceous flavours and a crisp, finely balanced (4.3 grams/litre of residual sugar) finish. Priced right.

DRY $19 V+

Sileni Cellar Selection Marlborough Sauvignon Blanc   ★★★

The 2019 vintage (★★★) is an easy-drinking wine, fresh and lively, with tropical-fruit and herbaceous flavours, showing good depth, and a dry (3.5 grams/litre of residual sugar), crisp finish.

DRY $20 –V

Sileni Estate Selection Straits Marlborough Sauvignon Blanc   ★★★★

The 2018 vintage (★★★★☆) is a classy wine, with lots of youthful impact. Medium to full-bodied, with incisive melon, lime, capsicum and passionfruit flavours, showing a distinct touch of complexity, it has a finely balanced, dry (4 grams/litre of residual sugar) finish.

DRY $25 AV

Sileni Grand Reserve Cape Hawke's Bay Sauvignon Blanc   (★★★★)

The tightly structured, youthful 2018 vintage (★★★★) is a fresh, lively, medium to full-bodied wine, with tropical-fruit flavours, showing excellent delicacy and vigour, and a dry (2.5 grams/litre of residual sugar) finish. Best drinking mid-2020+.

DRY $25 AV

Sisters Ridge North Canterbury Sauvignon Blanc   (★★★★)

Sold mostly in the US, the 2018 vintage (★★★★) is priced sharply. Bright, light lemon/green, it is mouthfilling and fleshy, with generous, ripe peach and passionfruit flavours, balanced acidity, and a dry (3 grams/litre of residual sugar) finish. (From Mt Beautiful.)

DRY $15 V+

Smith & Sheth Cru Wairau Sauvignon Blanc   ★★★★★

The classy 2019 vintage (★★★★★) is a richly fragrant, weighty wine, sweet-fruited and tightly structured. Bright, light lemon/green, it is highly concentrated, with lively tropical-fruit flavours, pure, focused and long. Already delicious, it should be at its best mid-2020+.

DRY $28 V+

Soho Caviar Jomara Vineyard Marlborough Sauvignon Blanc   (★★★★★)

Hand-picked in the Southern Valleys, the delicious 2017 vintage (★★★★★) was fermented and lees-aged for eight months in seasoned French oak barrels. Light lemon/green, with a ripely fragrant bouquet, it is full-bodied, sweet-fruited and dry, with rich, ripely herbaceous flavours, showing excellent delicacy, a subtle seasoning of biscuity oak adding complexity, balanced acidity, and very impressive vigour and depth.

 DRY $38 AV

Soho Pink Sheep Marlborough Sauvignon Blanc   (★★★☆)

From two sites in the Wairau and Awatere valleys, the 2018 vintage (★★★☆) is fresh, vibrant and medium-bodied, with tropical-fruit and herbaceous flavours, crisp and strong.

DRY $26 –V

Soho Stella Marlborough Sauvignon Blanc   ★★★★

The 2018 vintage (★★★★) is a generous, zesty blend of Wairau Valley and Awatere Valley grapes. Mouthfilling, it has strong tropical-fruit flavours to the fore, a herbaceous undercurrent, and a dry (3 grams/litre of residual sugar), lingering finish.

Vintage	16	15
WR	6	5
Drink	P	P

 DRY $25 AV

Soljans Marlborough Sauvignon Blanc   ★★★

The highly aromatic 2019 vintage (★★★☆) is a fresh and lively, medium-bodied wine, with tropical-fruit and herbaceous flavours, showing good depth and lots of youthful vigour.

DRY $19 AV

Spinyback Nelson Sauvignon Blanc   ★★★

From Waimea Estates, the 2019 vintage (★★☆) is fresh and lively, with melon and green-capsicum flavours, and a smooth, basically dry (4 grams/litre of residual sugar) finish.

DRY $15 V+

Spy Valley E Block Marlborough Sauvignon Blanc   (★★★★☆)

The debut 2017 vintage (★★★★☆) was harvested from estate-grown vines in the Waihopai Valley, planted in 1995, and matured for seven months on its yeast lees in tanks. Showing strong personality, it is highly aromatic, punchy and crisp, in a medium-bodied style with penetrating, citrusy, limey flavours, full of youthful vigour, and a long, dry (1.8 grams/litre of residual sugar) finish.

Vintage	17
WR	5
Drink	19-22

 DRY $25 V+

Spy Valley Marlborough Sauvignon Blanc ★★★★

Typically a very good buy. The 2018 vintage (★★★★), grown in the Wairau and Waihopai valleys, was partly barrel-fermented and made in a dry style (1.3 grams/litre of residual sugar). Light lemon/green, it is vibrantly fruity and tangy, with passionfruit, lime and green-capsicum flavours, showing a touch of complexity, good intensity, and a crisp, racy finish.

Vintage	18	17	16	15
WR	5	5	7	6
Drink	19-21	P	P	P

 DRY $20 V+

Staete Landt Annabel Marlborough Sauvignon Blanc ★★★★★

Estate-grown at Rapaura, on the relatively warm north side of the Wairau Valley, the youthful 2018 vintage (★★★★☆) was partly hand-picked and 30 per cent barrel-fermented. Bright, light lemon/green, it is medium to full-bodied, with good intensity of fresh, ripe tropical-fruit flavours, showing a distinct touch of complexity, and a fully dry, crisp finish. Best drinking mid-2020+.

 DRY $22 V+

Starborough Family Estate Marlborough Sauvignon Blanc ★★★★

This label typically offers good value. Estate-grown in the Awatere (60 per cent) and Wairau (40 per cent) valleys, the 2019 vintage (★★★★) is punchy and freshly herbaceous, with strong passionfruit, lime and green-capsicum flavours, dry (3.5 grams/litre of residual sugar) and crisp.

 DRY $20 V+

Stoneleigh Marlborough Sauvignon Blanc ★★★☆

From Pernod Ricard NZ, this very large-volume but typically satisfying wine flows from the stony, relatively warm Rapaura district of the Wairau Valley, which produces a ripe style of Sauvignon Blanc, yet retains good acidity and vigour. The 2018 vintage (★★★☆) is mouthfilling, with good depth of vibrant passionfruit/lime flavours, dry and crisp. Priced sharply.

DRY $16 V+

Stoneleigh Rapaura Series Single Vineyard Marlborough Sauvignon Blanc ★★★★

This richly flavoured wine is grown in the relatively warm, shingly soils of the Rapaura district and partly fermented in large oak cuves. The 2018 vintage (★★★★☆) is light lemon/green, mouthfilling and crisp, with good intensity of ripe tropical-fruit flavours, lively, dry (4.2 grams/litre of residual sugar) and lingering.

 DRY $27 –V

Sugar Loaf Marlborough Sauvignon Blanc   ★★★★

Offering excellent value, the pale green 2018 vintage (★★★★☆) from this Rapaura-based producer is a regional blend. A stylish young wine, it has strong, ripe passionfruit/lime flavours, showing good delicacy, a slightly minerally streak, and an appetisingly crisp, dry (3 grams/litre of residual sugar), long finish. Well worth discovering.

DRY $20 V+

Summerhouse Marlborough Sauvignon Blanc   ★★★★

The 2019 vintage (★★★★) was grown in the Blind River district, south of the Awatere Valley. Bright, light lemon/green, it is mouthfilling and punchy, with ripely herbaceous, tropical-fruit flavours, finely balanced, dry (4.3 grams/litre of residual sugar) and lively.

DRY $19 V+

Vintage	19	18	17
WR	7	7	6
Drink	19-22	19-21	19-21

Supernatural, The, Hawke's Bay Sauvignon Blanc   ★★★★☆

Closed with a crown seal, the 2017 vintage (★★★★) is certified organic. Handled without oak, it was grown on a hill site in the Tuki Tuki Valley, held on its skins for six hours before pressing, fermented with indigenous yeasts, and matured on its yeast lees, with stirring, for six months before bottling. Bright, light yellow/green, it is a distinctive, medium to full-bodied wine, ripe and rounded, with tropical-fruit flavours to the fore, some herbal notes, good complexity and a fully dry finish. Drink now to 2020.

DRY $30 –V

Te Awanga Estate Hawke's Bay Sauvignon Blanc   (★★★★☆)

Full of youthful vigour, the 2018 vintage (★★★★☆) is a crisp, medium-bodied wine with punchy capsicum and lime flavours, slightly yeasty notes adding complexity, and a long, tangy finish. Showing greater intensity and complexity than many of the region's Sauvignon Blancs, it's a characterful wine, well worth tracking down.

DRY $22 V+

Te Kairanga Estate Martinborough Sauvignon Blanc   ★★★★

The 2019 vintage (★★★★) is a partly (12 per cent) barrel-fermented wine. Light lemon/green, it is still very youthful. Medium to full-bodied, it is fresh and vigorous, with good intensity of ripely herbaceous flavours, dry (3.3 grams/litre of residual sugar) and lingering.

DRY $25 AV

Te Mata Cape Crest Sauvignon Blanc   ★★★★★

This oak-aged Hawke's Bay label is impressive for its ripely herbal, complex, sustained flavours. Most of the grapes are hand-picked in the company's relatively warm Bullnose Vineyard, inland from Hastings (the rest is grown at Woodthorpe, in the Dartmoor Valley), and the blend includes small proportions of Sémillon (to add longevity) and Sauvignon Gris (which contributes weight and mouthfeel). The wine is fully fermented and lees-aged for about eight months in French oak barriques (partly new). In a vertical tasting, the two to four-year-old wines look best – still fresh, but very harmonious. Already delicious, the pale lemon/green 2018 vintage (★★★★★) has a fragrant, ripely herbal bouquet. Weighty, sweet-fruited and complex, it shows excellent concentration, in an open, already highly expressive style.

Vintage	18
WR	7
Drink	19-30

DRY $30 AV

Te Mata Estate Vineyards Hawke's Bay Sauvignon Blanc ★★★★

The 2018 vintage (★★★★) is a highly aromatic, medium-bodied wine, grown in the Bridge Pa Triangle and at the Woodthorpe Terraces Vineyard, in the Dartmoor Valley. Made without oak, it is punchy, with passionfruit, melon and lime flavours, dry and tightly structured. It's drinking well now.

Vintage	18
WR	6
Drink	19-20

DRY $20 V+

te Pā Marlborough Sauvignon Blanc ★★★★

The 2019 vintage (★★★☆) is mouthfilling, with generous tropical-fruit and herbaceous flavours, slightly spicy notes, and a dry (3 grams/litre of residual sugar), finely balanced finish.

DRY $20 V+

te Pā Oke Marlborough Sauvignon Blanc ★★★★☆

Estate-grown in the lower Wairau Valley, the age-worthy 2018 vintage (★★★★) was hand-picked and fermented and lees-aged in French oak barrels (50 per cent new). Bright, light yellow/green, it is mouthfilling, with strong, ripe tropical-fruit flavours, oak-derived complexity, fresh acidity and a fully dry, long finish. Best drinking 2021+.

Vintage	18	17
WR	6	6
Drink	19-23	19-22

DRY $25 V+

te Pā Reserve Collection Seaside Marlborough Sauvignon Blanc (★★★★☆)

The 2019 vintage (★★★★☆) was hand-picked in the lower Wairau Valley. Light lemon/green, it is mouthfilling, with good intensity of melon, passionfruit and capsicum flavours, vigorous, dry (2 grams/litre of residual sugar) and lingering.

DRY $25 V+

te Pā The Reserve Collection Hillside Marlborough Sauvignon Blanc (★★★★)

The very youthful 2019 vintage (★★★★) is a single-vineyard wine, hand-picked in the Awatere Valley. Pale, very fresh and delicate, it has subtle, green capsicum-like flavours, vigorous, dry (2 grams/litre of residual sugar) and crisp. Best drinking mid-2020+.

DRY $25 AV

Thornbury Marlborough Sauvignon Blanc   ★★★★

Offering fine value, the 2019 vintage (★★★★) is fresh, full-bodied and sweet-fruited, with ripe passionfruit-like flavours to the fore, a herbaceous undercurrent, and a dry (3.2 grams/litre of residual sugar), crisp, lingering finish. Good drinking for the summer of 2019–20.

Vintage	19	18	17
WR	5	5	4
Drink	19-20	19-20	P

 DRY $16 V+

Three Paddles Martinborough Sauvignon Blanc   ★★★☆

Still on sale, the 2016 vintage (★★★☆) from Nga Waka is medium to full-bodied, with good depth of melon and green-capsicum flavours, dry and slightly minerally.

Vintage	16	15	14
WR	6	7	7
Drink	P	P	P

 DRY $18 V+

Tiki Estate Marlborough Sauvignon Blanc   ★★★☆

The 2019 vintage (★★★★) is mouthfilling, fresh and punchy, with vigorous passionfruit, lime and green-capsicum flavours, crisp and basically dry (4.7 grams/litre of residual sugar). The 2018 vintage (★★★) is full-bodied and ripely flavoured, with a very smooth (4.2 grams/litre of residual sugar), rounded finish.

Vintage	19	18	17
WR	6	6	7
Drink	19-21	19-20	19-20

 DRY $20 AV

Tiki Single Vineyard Waipara Sauvignon Blanc   (★★★☆)

Drinking well now, the 2018 vintage (★★★☆) is vibrantly fruity, with good depth of tropical-fruit flavours, gentle herbal notes, and a dryish (5.1 grams/litre of residual sugar), smooth finish.

 MED/DRY $25 –V

Toa Marlborough Sauvignon Blanc   (★★★★)

Offering good value, the 2018 vintage (★★★★) is fresh and punchy, with good intensity of ripe pineapple and passionfruit flavours, crisp and tightly structured, and a fully dry finish. (From Ra Nui.)

DRY $18 V+

Tohu Awatere Valley Marlborough Sauvignon Blanc   ★★★★

Offering good value, the 2019 vintage (★★★★) is an aromatic, lively, medium-bodied wine, with passionfruit, capsicum and lime flavours, showing excellent delicacy and vibrancy, balanced acidity, and a dry (3.5 grams/litre of residual sugar) finish. Best drinking mid-2020+.

Vintage	19
WR	7
Drink	19-22

 DRY $18 V+

Tohu Mugwi Reserve Marlborough Sauvignon Blanc   ★★★★☆

Maturing gracefully, the 2016 vintage (★★★★) was estate-grown in the upper Awatere Valley and fermented with indigenous yeasts in old French oak barriques. Light lemon/green, with a complex bouquet, it is medium-bodied, with fresh, ripely herbaceous flavours, slightly toasty notes adding complexity, a minerally streak and a lingering finish. Drink now.

DRY $27 AV

Tohu Single Vineyard Whenua Awa Awatere Valley
Marlborough Sauvignon Blanc   (★★★★☆)

The punchy, highly aromatic 2018 vintage (★★★★☆) was estate-grown in the upper Awatere Valley. Bright, light lemon/green, it is crisp and mouthfilling, with excellent vigour and depth of tropical-fruit and herbaceous flavours, lively and long.

DRY $28 AV

Toi Toi 8.5 Marlborough Sauvignon Blanc   (★★★☆)

Designed as a 'perfect no glass option', the non-vintage wine (★★★☆) released in late 2018 is a low-alcohol (8.5 per cent by volume) style, packaged in a slim 250-ml can. Highly aromatic, it is strongly varietal, with appetising acidity and fresh, punchy passionfruit, lime and green-capsicum flavours. By offering greater body and flavour depth, it's superior to most other low-alcohol Sauvignon Blancs.

DRY $8 –V

Toi Toi Marlborough Sauvignon Blanc   ★★★☆

The vigorous 2019 vintage (★★★☆) of this regional blend is a strongly varietal, medium-bodied style with youthful melon and green capsicum-like flavours, crisp and lively. Good value.

DRY $16 V+

Toi Toi Reserve Marlborough Sauvignon Blanc   ★★★★☆

Grown in the Wairau Valley, the pale lemon/green 2019 vintage (★★★★☆) is a weighty wine with strong, ripe tropical-fruit flavours and a finely balanced, smooth finish. Full of youthful impact, it's already drinking well. Fine value.

DRY $22 V+

Toi Toi Single Vineyard Loddon Lane Marlborough Sauvignon Blanc   (★★★☆)

Grown in the upper Wairau Valley, the bright, light lemon/green 2018 vintage (★★★☆) is fresh and full-bodied, with good depth of clearly herbaceous flavours, crisp and lively.

DRY $23 –V

Toi Toi Winemakers Selection Marlborough Sauvignon Blanc   (★★★★)

The punchy, very youthful 2019 vintage (★★★★) is full-bodied and vibrant, with fresh, strong passionfruit and green-capsicum flavours, lively acidity and a finely balanced finish. Good value.

DRY $21 V+

Twin Islands Marlborough Sauvignon Blanc   ★★★☆

Bright, light lemon/green, the sweet-fruited 2019 vintage (★★★★) is already drinking well. Crisp and dry (3 grams/litre of residual sugar), it is medium to full-bodied, with lively, ripe tropical-fruit flavours and a lingering finish. (From Nautilus.)

DRY $20 V+

Two Rivers Marlborough Convergence Sauvignon Blanc   ★★★★☆

The aromatic 2019 vintage (★★★★☆) is from three sites in the Awatere and Wairau valleys. Matured for three months on its yeast lees in stainless steel tanks and concrete, egg-shaped vessels, it is mouthfilling and vibrantly fruity, with very good intensity of tropical-fruit and herbaceous flavours, a touch of complexity, and a dry (2.7 grams/litre of residual sugar), lingering finish.

Vintage	19
WR	7
Drink	19-22

DRY $24 V+

Urlar Gladstone Sauvignon Blanc   ★★★★

The highly aromatic 2018 vintage (★★★★☆) was mostly handled in tanks; 10 per cent was fermented in old oak barrels. Bright, light lemon/green, it is a fresh, medium to full-bodied wine, with vigorous peach, lime and herb flavours, barrel-ferment notes adding richness, crisp acidity, and excellent intensity and complexity. Tightly structured, it should break into full stride mid-2020+. Certified organic.

DRY $25 AV

Urlar Select Parcels Gladstone Sauvignon Blanc   ★★★★☆

Developing good complexity with age, the 2017 vintage (★★★★☆) was estate-grown in the northern Wairarapa and fermented and lees-aged for 10 months in seasoned French oak barrels. Retasted in mid-2019, it is a light yellow, medium to full-bodied wine, sweet-fruited, with generous, ripe tropical-fruit flavours to the fore, some herbal notes, a subtle seasoning of toasty oak, balanced acidity, and impressive harmony. Drink now or cellar. Certified organic.

Vintage	17
WR	6
Drink	19-25

DRY $29 AV

Vavasour Awatere Valley Marlborough Sauvignon Blanc   ★★★★☆

The tightly structured 2019 vintage (★★★★☆) is still very youthful. A fresh, medium to full-bodied wine, it is strongly varietal, with very good intensity of melon and green-capsicum flavours, showing excellent delicacy, and a crisp, dry (3.5 grams/litre of residual sugar), lingering finish. Best drinking mid-2020+.

DRY $23 V+

Vidal Marlborough Sauvignon Blanc ★★★☆

The lively 2019 vintage (★★★☆) was grown in the Awatere and Wairau valleys. Light lemon/green, it has very good depth of fresh passionfruit, melon and capsicum flavours, dry (2.7 grams/litre of residual sugar) and crisp. Top value.

Vintage	19	18	17
WR	6	7	6
Drink	19-21	19-20	P

 DRY $16 V+

Vidal Reserve Marlborough Sauvignon Blanc ★★★★

Offering great value, the 2019 vintage (★★★★☆) was grown in the Wairau Valley (85 per cent) and the Awatere Valley (15 per cent), and matured for four months on its yeast lees. Light lemon/green, it is mouthfilling and sweet-fruited, with youthful, passionfruit-like flavours, showing a distinct touch of complexity, and a dry (2.4 grams/litre of residual sugar), lengthy finish. Best drinking mid-2020+.

Vintage	19	18
WR	6	7
Drink	19-21	19-20

 DRY $20 V+

Villa Maria Cellar Selection Marlborough Sauvignon Blanc ★★★★☆

An intensely flavoured wine, typically of a high standard, blended from Wairau Valley and Awatere Valley grapes, and fermented and lees-aged in tanks. The 2019 vintage (★★★★☆) is ripely scented and weighty, with concentrated, vibrant passionfruit/lime flavours and a crisp, dry (3.5 grams/litre of residual sugar), long finish. As usual, a great buy (especially on special at under $15).

 DRY $18 V+

Villa Maria Cellar Selection Organic Marlborough Sauvignon Blanc ★★★★

Certified organic, the 2019 vintage (★★★★) is a bright, light lemon/green, medium-bodied wine, fresh and vibrant, with strong, ripe tropical-fruit and herbaceous flavours, dry (3.1 grams/litre of residual sugar) and crisp.

 DRY $18 V+

Villa Maria Platinum Selection Sur Lie Marlborough Sauvignon Blanc (★★★★☆)

'This is not your usual Sauvignon Blanc', notes the back label on the 2018 vintage (★★★★☆), handled in an even split of tanks and seasoned French oak barrels. Fleshy and sweet-fruited, it has strong, ripe tropical-fruit flavours, good complexity from lees-aging in oak, and a dry, rounded finish.

 DRY $25 V+

Villa Maria Private Bin Marlborough Sauvignon Blanc ★★★☆

This huge-volume label consistently offers very good quality and value. The 2019 vintage (★★★☆) is crisp and lively, with melon and green-capsicum flavours, showing very good depth, and a finely balanced, dry (3.3 grams/litre of residual sugar) finish.

DRY $15 V+

Villa Maria Private Bin Organic Marlborough Sauvignon Blanc   ★★★☆

Priced sharply, the 2019 vintage (★★★☆) is mouthfilling, fresh and ripe, with tropical-fruit flavours, crisp and dry (3.3 grams/litre of residual sugar), and very good depth. Certified organic.

Villa Maria Reserve Clifford Bay Awatere Valley
Marlborough Sauvignon Blanc   ★★★★★

Named after Clifford Bay, into which the Awatere River empties, this is a very classy Marlborough wine. Seddon Vineyards and the Taylors Pass Vineyard – both managed but not owned by Villa Maria – are the key sources of fruit. Handled entirely in stainless steel tanks and aged on its light yeast lees for several months, the wine typically exhibits the leap-out-of-the-glass fragrance and zingy, explosive flavour of Marlborough Sauvignon Blanc at its best. The outstanding 2019 vintage (★★★★★) is a powerful, punchy wine, with lifted, freshly herbaceous aromas. Already delicious, it is weighty and vibrant, with pure, penetrating flavours of passionfruit, lime and green capsicums, that build across the palate to a dry (2.5 grams/litre of residual sugar), lasting finish. A great buy.

Vintage	19
WR	7
Drink	19-22

Villa Maria Reserve Wairau Valley Sauvignon Blanc   ★★★★★

An authoritative wine, it is typically ripe and zingy, with impressive weight and length of flavour, and tends to be fuller in body, less herbaceous and rounder than its Clifford Bay stablemate (above). The contributing vineyards vary from vintage to vintage, but Peter and Deborah Jackson's warm, stony vineyard in the heart of the valley has long been a key source of grapes, and sometimes a small part of the blend is barrel-fermented, to enhance its complexity and texture. The 2019 vintage (★★★★★) was handled entirely in tanks. Weighty, it is highly concentrated, with rich, well-ripened tropical-fruit flavours, fresh, dry (3.2 grams/litre of residual sugar), crisp and long.

Vintage	19
WR	7
Drink	19-21

Villa Maria Single Vineyard Southern Clays Marlborough Sauvignon Blanc   ★★★★☆

From north-facing clay slopes on the south side of the Wairau Valley, the delicious 2018 vintage (★★★★★) has ripe, tropical-fruit aromas and flavours. Weighty and sweet-fruited, it's a very non-herbaceous style, dry (3.8 grams/litre of residual sugar) and crisp, with a lasting finish.

DRY $30 –V

Villa Maria Single Vineyard Taylors Pass Marlborough Sauvignon Blanc   ★★★★★

Taylors Pass Vineyard lies 100 metres above sea level in the Awatere Valley. This is typically a classic example of the sub-regional style – vibrant, punchy, minerally and herbal, with intense capsicum and 'tomato stalk' aromas and a long, dry, racy finish. The 2019 vintage (★★★★★)

is still very youthful. Handled entirely in tanks, it is mouthfilling, fresh and lively, with strong, herbaceous flavours, some riper, tropical-fruit notes, a minerally streak and a tightly structured, dry (2.8 grams/litre of residual sugar), sustained finish. Best drinking mid-2020+.

Vintage	19
WR	7
Drink	19-22

 DRY $30 AV

Waimea Nelson Sauvignon Blanc ★★★☆

Always a good buy. The easy-drinking 2019 vintage (★★★☆), grown on the Waimea Plains and lees-aged in tanks, is fresh and lively, with very good depth of melon, green-capsicum and passionfruit flavours, and a dry (3.7 grams/litre of residual sugar), smooth finish.

 DRY $18 V+

Waipara Hills Marlborough Sauvignon Blanc ★★★★

The 2018 vintage (★★★☆) is full-bodied, fresh and lively, with good depth of ripe passionfruit/lime flavours, balanced acidity and a dry finish.

 DRY $22 V+

Wairau River Marlborough Sauvignon Blanc ★★★★

The 2019 vintage (★★★★) is a fresh, punchy, medium-bodied wine, with ripe passionfruit-like flavours to the fore, a herbaceous undercurrent, good intensity and a crisp, dry finish. Good drinking for the summer of 2019–20.

 DRY $20 V+

Wairau River Reserve Marlborough Sauvignon Blanc ★★★★☆

The 2017 vintage (★★★★☆) was grown in the Longbend Vineyard, on the warm, stony north side of the Wairau Valley. It is weighty, sweet-fruited and ripely herbaceous, with concentrated tropical-fruit flavours, moderate acidity, and a finely textured, dry, lingering finish.

Vintage	17	16	15
WR	7	6	6
Drink	19-21	P	P

 DRY $30 –V

Walnut Block Nutcracker Marlborough Sauvignon Blanc ★★★★☆

Certified organic, the 2018 vintage (★★★★☆) is a Wairau Valley wine, hand-picked from mature vines and 30 per cent barrel-fermented. Sweet-fruited, it is a youthful, medium to full-bodied wine, with ripe tropical-fruit flavours, a subtle seasoning of oak adding complexity, and a crisp, fully dry (0.2 grams/litre of residual sugar) finish. A restrained, age-worthy style, it should break into full stride 2020+.

DRY $25 V+

Whitehaven Greg Awatere Valley Single Vineyard Marlborough Sauvignon Blanc ★★★★★

The 2019 vintage (★★★★☆) is a mouthfilling, punchy, tangy wine, very fresh and forthright, with good intensity of ripely herbaceous flavours, dry (4.2 grams/litre of residual sugar) and mouth-wateringly crisp.

Whitehaven Marlborough Sauvignon Blanc ★★★★

Still very youthful, the 2019 vintage (★★★★) is mouthfilling and dry (3.7 grams/litre of residual sugar), with strong, ripely herbaceous flavours, tightly structured and crisp. Best drinking mid-2020+.

Wither Hills Early Light Marlborough Sauvignon Blanc ★★★

A good example of the low-alcohol style (9.5 per cent), the 2018 vintage (★★★) is freshly scented. Light and lively, it is well balanced, with crisp acidity and good depth of citrusy, green-edged flavours.

Wither Hills Marlborough Sauvignon Blanc ★★★☆

The attractive 2018 vintage (★★★★) is a mouthfilling, vibrantly fruity wine. Tasted in mid-2019, it has strong passionfruit/lime flavours, lively, finely balanced and lingering. (From Lion.)

Wither Hills Rarangi Marlborough Sauvignon Blanc ★★★★☆

From a coastal site at the north-east edge of the Wairau Valley, the distinctive 2016 vintage (★★★★☆), retasted in mid-2019, is still drinking well. Pale lemon/green, it is fragrant, mouthfilling, crisp and dry, with a slightly salty streak running through its melon/lime flavours, which show excellent vigour, intensity and length.

Woven Stone Single Vineyard Ohau Sauvignon Blanc (★★★)

Grown in the Horowhenua, the strongly varietal 2019 vintage (★★★) is a fresh and lively, medium-bodied wine with a fairly restrained bouquet, but good depth of melon, lime and green-capsicum flavours. Bargain-priced. (From Ohau Wines.)

DRY $14 V+

Yealands Estate M2 Organic Single Block Wairau Valley
Marlborough Sauvignon Blanc   (★★★★)

Grown in the lower Wairau Valley, the 2018 vintage (★★★★) is a fresh, medium to full-bodied wine. Drinking well now, it has fresh, ripe tropical-fruit flavours, dry and well-rounded, with an inviting fragrance. Certified organic.

DRY $25 AV

Zephyr Marlborough Sauvignon Blanc   (★★★★★)

The classy 2018 vintage (★★★★★) is a single-vineyard wine, grown at Dillons Point, in the lower Wairau Valley. Light lemon/green, it is aromatic, weighty and punchy, with deep lime and passionfruit flavours, good acid spine, and a tightly structured, dry, lasting finish. A label worth discovering.

DRY $24 V+

Zephyr MKIII Marlborough Sauvignon Blanc   (★★★★☆)

Wood-aged, the bright, light yellow/green 2018 vintage (★★★★☆) is a refined wine, fragrant and weighty, with ripe tropical-fruit flavours, showing good complexity, and a long, dry, harmonious finish. Still unfolding, it should be at its best mid-2020+.

DRY $33 –V

Sauvignon Gris

Pernod Ricard NZ launched New Zealand's first commercial bottlings of an old French variety, Sauvignon Gris, from the 2009 vintage. Also known as Sauvignon Rosé – due to its pink skin – Sauvignon Gris typically produces less aromatic, but more substantial, wines than Sauvignon Blanc.

Sauvignon Gris is not a blend of Sauvignon Blanc and Pinot Gris; nor is it a new vine, bred by crossing those grapes. Sauvignon Gris is a variety in its own right.

In Bordeaux, Sauvignon Gris is commonly used as a minority partner in dry white blends dominated by Sauvignon Blanc, but in Chile – like New Zealand – producers are bottling and exporting Sauvignon Gris as a varietal wine. In Marlborough, Sauvignon Gris has proved to be fairly disease-resistant, ripening in the middle of the Sauvignon Blanc harvest. Of New Zealand's 101 hectares of bearing vines in 2020, 99 hectares are in Marlborough.

Brancott Estate Letter Series 'R' Sauvignon Gris ★★★★☆

Still on sale, the 2015 vintage (★★★★) is instantly appealing. Mouthfilling (14.5 per cent alcohol), it is very smooth, with ripely herbaceous aromas and flavours, stone-fruit notes and some oak-derived complexity.

MED/DRY $33 –V

Loveblock Marlborough Sauvignon Gris (★★★★)

Maturing gracefully, the 2014 vintage (★★★★) is an estate-grown, Awatere Valley wine, fermented and matured in old French oak casks. Bright, light yellow/green, it is mouthfilling and dry, with good intensity of ripely herbaceous flavours, slightly toasty notes adding complexity and a finely textured, lingering finish. It's a distinctive wine, priced right.

DRY $22 V+

Villa Maria Cellar Selection Marlborough Sauvignon Gris (★★★★)

Aromatic, mouthfilling and dry (4 grams/litre of residual sugar), the 2015 vintage (★★★★) is a single-vineyard wine, grown in the Wairau Valley and mostly handled in tanks; a small part of the blend was barrel-fermented. Fruit-driven, it has a touch of complexity and strong, ripely herbaceous flavours, crisp and refreshing.

DRY $18 V+

Waimea Nelson Sauvignon Gris ★★★★

The 2015 vintage (★★★★) was estate-grown at Hope. Full-bodied and fleshy, it has strong, ripe tropical-fruit flavours to the fore, a herbal undercurrent, fresh acidity, and a dryish (4.8 grams/litre of residual sugar), finely balanced finish.

DRY $23 AV

Sémillon

You'd never guess it from the tiny selection of labels on the shelves, but Sémillon is New Zealand's eighth most widely planted white-wine variety. The few winemakers who once played around with Sémillon could hardly give it away, so aggressively stemmy and spiky was its flavour. Now, there is a new breed of riper, richer, rounder Sémillons on the market – and they are ten times more enjoyable to drink.

The Sémillon variety is beset by a similar problem to Chenin Blanc. Despite being the foundation of outstanding white wines in Bordeaux and Australia, Sémillon is out of fashion in the rest of the world, and in New Zealand its potential is still largely untapped. The area of bearing Sémillon vines has contracted markedly between 2007 and 2020, from 230 to 46 hectares.

Sémillon is highly prized in Bordeaux, where as one of the two key varieties both in dry wines, most notably white Graves, and the inimitable sweet Sauternes, its high levels of alcohol and extract are perfect foils for Sauvignon Blanc's verdant aroma and tartness. With its propensity to rot 'nobly', Sémillon forms about 80 per cent of a classic Sauternes.

Cooler climates like those of New Zealand's South Island, however, bring out a grassy-green character in Sémillon which, coupled with its higher acidity in these regions, can give the variety strikingly Sauvignon-like characteristics.

Grown principally in Hawke's Bay (over half of the variety's plantings) and Marlborough (29 per cent), Sémillon is mostly used in New Zealand not as a varietal wine but as a minor (and anonymous) partner in wines labelled Sauvignon Blanc, contributing complexity and aging potential. By curbing the variety's natural tendency to grow vigorously and crop bountifully, winemakers are now overcoming the aggressive cut-grass characters that in the past plagued the majority of New Zealand's unblended Sémillons. The spread of clones capable of giving riper fruit characters has also contributed to quality advances.

However, very few wineries in New Zealand are exploring Sémillon's potential to produce complex, long-lived dry whites.

Askerne Hawke's Bay Sémillon (★★★★)

Riper and more complex than most New Zealand Sémillons, the 2016 vintage (★★★★) was partly (45 per cent) barrel-fermented. Light lemon/green, it is full-bodied and ripely herbaceous, with very good flavour depth, a touch of complexity, balanced acidity and good aging potential; best drinking 2020+.

DRY $23 AV

Kaimira Estate Brightwater Sémillon (★★★★)

Currently on sale, the 2009 vintage (★★★★) offers a rare chance to buy a decade-old New Zealand white wine. Estate-grown and hand-harvested on the Waimea Plains, in Nelson, it is still very lively, with bright, light, yellow/green colour. Highly fragrant, it is medium-bodied, with citrusy, limey, lingering flavours, toasty, bottle-aged notes adding complexity, and a fully dry finish. Ready; no rush.

DRY $25 AV

Sileni Estate Selection The Circle Sémillon ★★★★

Maturing very gracefully, the 2013 vintage (★★★★☆) is still on sale. Grown in the Bridge Pa Triangle, Hawke's Bay, it was hand-picked and mostly handled in tanks; 20 per cent of the blend was fermented in old French oak barriques. Bright, light lemon/green, it is mouthfilling, with strong, ripe tropical-fruit flavours, bottle-aged complexity, and a finely balanced, dry (4.6 grams/litre of residual sugar), lasting finish. Probably at its peak, it's well worth trying.

DRY $24 V+

Verdelho

A Portuguese variety traditionally grown on the island of Madeira, Verdelho preserves its acidity well in hot regions, yielding enjoyably full-bodied, lively, lemony table wines in Australia. It is still extremely rare in New Zealand, with only 7 hectares of bearing Verdelho vines in 2020, mostly in Hawke's Bay and Auckland.

Esk Valley Gimblett Gravels Verdelho ★★★★

The 2018 vintage (★★★★) was grown in the company's Omahu Gravels and Joseph Soler vineyards, and 30 per cent of the blend was barrel-fermented with indigenous yeasts; the rest was handled in tanks. Full-bodied and vigorous, it has strong, lively, citrusy flavours, a sliver of sweetness (5.1 grams/litre of residual sugar), appetising acidity, minerally notes and lots of youthful impact.

Vintage	18	17	16	15
WR	6	5	7	7
Drink	19-22	P	P	P

 MED/DRY $20 V+

Hans Herzog Marlborough Verdelho (★★★★★)

Certified organic, the 2018 vintage (★★★★★) has a powerful personality. Estate-grown, handled without oak, and bottled unfined and unfiltered, it is light gold, mouthfilling and fleshy, with rich, ripe tropical-fruit flavours, balanced acidity and a dry, well-rounded finish.

 DRY $39 AV

Summerhouse Marlborough Verdelho ★★★★

Offering fine value, the 2016 vintage (★★★★) was fermented and matured for nine months in seasoned oak barriques. It is weighty and vibrant, with ripe tropical-fruit flavours, a subtle seasoning of oak, balanced acidity, considerable complexity, and a dry (1.7 grams/litre of residual sugar), lingering finish.

Vintage	16	15	14
WR	6	7	7
Drink	19-23	19-21	19-20

 DRY $19 V+

TW Verdelho (★★★★)

The light yellow 2014 vintage (★★★★) was grown in Gisborne. Full-bodied and fleshy, it has strong, vibrant tropical-fruit flavours to the fore, slightly buttery notes, appetising acidity, and very good depth and complexity.

 DRY $25 AV

Villa Maria Single Vineyard Ihumatao Vineyard Auckland Verdelho ★★★★★

Estate-grown at Mangere, in South Auckland, the organically certified 2014 vintage (★★★★★) is a notably varietal wine. Highly fragrant and mouthfilling, it has concentrated tropical-fruit flavours, with hints of pears and spices, and a long, dry finish.

DRY $30 AV

Vermentino

Extremely rare in New Zealand, this aromatic variety is grown extensively on Sardinia and Corsica, and is also well known in north-west Italy and southern France. Often compared to Sauvignon Blanc, it yields dry, light-bodied wines, with peach, lemon and dried-herb flavours, woven with fresh acidity. According to New Zealand Winegrowers' *Vineyard Register Report 2017–2020*, only 0.1 hectares will be bearing in 2020, planted in Northland.

Doubtless Vermentino ★★★☆

Grown at Doubtless Bay, in Northland, this is New Zealand's only example of a variety associated with coastal European wine regions. The 2016 vintage (★★★☆) is a freshly scented, medium-bodied wine, with strong, lively, peachy, slightly citrusy flavours, firm acid spine and a dry, persistent finish. A good food wine.

DRY $23 AV

Viognier

A classic grape of the Rhône Valley, in France, Viognier is renowned for its exotically perfumed, substantial, peach and apricot-flavoured dry whites. A delicious alternative to Chardonnay, Viognier (pronounced *Vee-yon-yay*) is an internationally modish variety, popping up with increasing frequency in shops and restaurants here.

Viognier accounts for only 0.2 per cent of the national vineyard, but the area of bearing vines has expanded from 15 hectares in 2002 to 93 hectares in 2020. Over two-thirds of the vines are clustered in Hawke's Bay and Gisborne, with further significant plantings in Marlborough (15 per cent) and Auckland (6 per cent).

As in the Rhône, Viognier's flowering and fruit set have been highly variable here. The deeply coloured grapes go through bud-burst, flowering and 'veraison' (the start of the final stage of ripening) slightly behind Chardonnay and are harvested about the same time as Pinot Noir.

The wine is often fermented in seasoned oak barrels, yielding scented, substantial, richly alcoholic wines with gentle acidity and subtle flavours. If you enjoy mouthfilling, softly textured, dry or dryish white wines, but feel like a change from Chardonnay and Pinot Gris, try Viognier. You won't be disappointed.

Ash Ridge Premium Hawke's Bay Viognier ★★★★

The 2016 vintage (★★★★), grown inland at Mangatahi, was fermented and matured for 10 months in seasoned French oak barriques. Attractively scented, it is a medium to full-bodied wine, sweet-fruited and slightly oily-textured, with fresh, ripe peach, pear and lychee flavours, dry and harmonious.

DRY $30 –V

Askerne Hawke's Bay Viognier ★★★★

The 2018 vintage (★★★★☆) is a great buy. Fully barrel-fermented, it is a fragrant, generous, strongly varietal wine, with substantial body. Sweet-fruited and finely textured, it has ripe stone-fruit flavours, gently seasoned with toasty oak, fresh acidity, and a smooth, dryish (5 grams/litre of residual sugar), well-rounded finish.

MED/DRY $23 AV

Black Barn Vineyards R & D Hawke's Bay 'Sur Lie' Viognier (★★★★★)

The impressive 2015 vintage (★★★★★) is a single-vineyard wine, matured on its yeast lees and bottled straight from the barrel, without fining or filtering. A notably powerful and fleshy wine (14.5 per cent alcohol), it shows excellent complexity, with concentrated, ripe stone-fruit flavours, enriched with finely integrated oak, balanced acidity, and a finely textured, lasting finish. It should be long-lived.

DRY $39 –V

Brookfields Barrique Fermented Hawke's Bay Viognier (★★★★)

Still unfolding, the 2018 vintage (★★★★) was estate-grown, hand-picked and barrel-fermented (25 per cent new oak). It's a rather Chardonnay-like wine, fleshy, with generous, ripe stone-fruit flavours, oak complexity and gentle acidity. Best drinking 2021+.

Vintage	18
WR	7
Drink	19-25

DRY $25 AV

Byrne Northland Waingaro Viognier ★★★★

The 2016 vintage (★★★★), grown at Kerikeri, was fermented and matured in seasoned French oak barriques. It is full-bodied and soft, with generous, peachy, slightly toasty flavours, a creamy-smooth texture, and lots of drink-young appeal.

 DRY $32 –V

Churton Marlborough Viognier ★★★★☆

The 2015 vintage (★★★★☆) is maturing gracefully. Estate-grown and hand-picked in the Waihopai Valley, it was fermented and matured for 10 months in large, 600-litre French oak casks. Sturdy and fleshy, it is still fresh, with peachy, gently spicy, slightly biscuity and toasty flavours, showing good richness and complexity, balanced acidity and a bone-dry, lingering finish.

Vintage	15	14	13	12	'11	10
WR	7	6	7	NM	5	6
Drink	19-23	19-21	19-22	NM	P	P

 DRY $37 –V

Clos de Ste Anne Viognier Les Arbres ★★★★★

This biodynamically certified Gisborne wine from Millton shows impressive richness and complexity. Hill-grown, it is hand-harvested and fermented with indigenous yeasts in large, 600-litre oak barrels. The 2015 vintage (★★★★★) is instantly seductive. Weighty and fleshy, it is rich, sweet-fruited and soft, with generous, peachy flavours, a creamy texture, and a very harmonious, dry (4 grams/litre of residual sugar), lasting finish.

 DRY $60 AV

Coopers Creek Select Vineyards Chalk Ridge Hawke's Bay Viognier ★★★★

Fresh, mouthfilling and sweet-fruited, the 2018 vintage (★★★★) was hand-picked near Havelock North and barrel-fermented. It has very good vigour and depth of stone-fruit flavours, a subtle seasoning of biscuity oak adding complexity, balanced acidity and some cellaring potential; best drinking mid-2020+.

 DRY $25 AV

Dancing Petrel Paewhenua Island Mangonui Northland Viognier (★★★★)

From a coastal vineyard in the Far North, the 2018 vintage (★★★★) is a freshly scented, full-bodied, vibrantly fruity wine, with generous, ripe, peachy, slightly spicy flavours and a dry finish. Still youthful, it should be at its best 2020+.

DRY $22 V+

De La Terre Reserve Hawke's Bay Viognier ★★★★☆

The 2015 vintage (★★★★☆) was grown on limestone terraces at Havelock North, hand-picked, and fermented in seasoned French oak barriques. It is fleshy, with rich stone-fruit flavours, showing good complexity, a slightly minerally thread, and a dry, lingering finish.

Vintage	15	14
WR	6	6
Drink	19-24	19-20

DRY $40 –V

De La Terre Ridgeline Hawke's Bay Viognier ★★★★☆

Handled without oak, the refined 2016 vintage (★★★★☆) was estate-grown at Havelock North. Weighty, fresh and vibrant, it has concentrated, ripe stone-fruit flavours, slightly spicy and minerally, and a dry, long finish. Well worth discovering.

DRY $40 –V

Decibel Bridge Pa Hawke's Bay Viognier (★★★★)

Enjoyable young, the 2018 vintage (★★★★) was handled without oak. Fragrant, with good varietal character, it is fruity and softly mouthfilling, with good weight, ripe stone-fruit flavours, gentle acidity and a very harmonious finish.

DRY $26 –V

Dry River Martinborough Viognier ★★★★☆

The 2016 vintage (★★★★☆) is delicious young. Handled without oak, it is a fragrant, full-bodied, fleshy wine, vibrantly fruity, with rich, ripe, citrusy, peachy flavours, a sliver of sweetness (7 grams/litre of residual sugar) and a rounded finish.

MED/DRY $55 –V

Elephant Hill Hawke's Bay Sea Viognier ★★★★☆

Still unfolding, the 2018 vintage (★★★★) was estate-grown at Te Awanga and partly (60 per cent) barrel-fermented. Bright, light lemon/green, it is mouthfilling and very vibrant, with fresh, citrusy, slightly biscuity flavours, showing good vigour and complexity, and a smooth finish. Best drinking mid-2020+.

DRY $34 –V

Gladstone Vineyard Viognier ★★★★

A 'floral tease', the 2018 vintage (★★★★☆) was hand-picked in the northern Wairarapa and fermented in oak barrels (50 per cent new). Fragrant and softly mouthfilling, it is fresh and vibrant, with peachy, citrusy flavours, a subtle seasoning of oak adding complexity, and a fully dry (0.5 grams/litre of residual sugar), slightly creamy finish. Best drinking 2020+.

DRY $27 –V

Hans Herzog Marlborough Viognier   ★★★★★

Certified organic, the 2017 vintage (★★★★★) was hand-harvested from mature, estate-grown vines on the north side of the Wairau Valley, fermented and matured for 18 months in French oak puncheons, and bottled unfined and unfiltered. Bright, light yellow, it has a fragrant, slightly toasty bouquet. Sturdy, with fresh, ripe stone-fruit flavours, it shows excellent concentration, with oak complexity and a long, dry, savoury finish.

 DRY $44 AV

Hopesgrove Estate Single Vineyard Hawke's Bay Viognier   ★★★★

A drink-now or cellaring proposition, the 2018 vintage (★★★★☆) was hand-harvested and oak-aged for seven months. A fresh, medium to full-bodied wine, it has balanced acidity and rich, vibrant, peachy, slightly spicy and toasty flavours, showing good complexity.

Vintage	18
WR	5
Drink	19-23

 DRY $30 –V

Johner Estate Gladstone Viognier   (★★★★☆)

Enjoyable young, but still youthful, the 2018 vintage (★★★★☆) was matured for nine months in seasoned oak casks. Fresh and mouthfilling, it is vibrantly fruity, with good intensity of stone-fruit flavours, a subtle twist of oak, and a fully dry, very harmonious finish. Best drinking mid-2020+.

Vintage	18
WR	6
Drink	19-22

 DRY $26 AV

Leveret Estate Hawke's Bay Viognier   ★★★★

The 2016 vintage (★★★★) is drinking well now. Bright, light lemon/green, it is mouthfilling, fresh and smooth, with generous, ripe stone-fruit flavours, gently seasoned with oak, and a well-rounded, very harmonious finish.

 DRY $23 AV

Linden Estate Hawke's Bay Viognier   ★★★★

The 2014 vintage (★★★★) was grown in the Dartmoor Valley and fermented in tanks and barrels. It is full-bodied, with strong, peachy, slightly spicy flavours, creamy and buttery notes adding a touch of complexity, gentle acidity and a slightly off-dry (6 grams/litre of residual sugar), finely balanced finish. Ready.

MED/DRY $25 AV

Marsden Bay of Islands Viognier   ★★★☆

The 2017 vintage (★★★☆) was hand-picked and aged in seasoned oak barrels. Attractively scented and mouthfilling, with ripe, peachy, slightly spicy flavours, showing very good depth, it's enjoyable young.

 DRY $27 –V

Millton Clos de Ste Anne Viognier Les Arbres – see Clos de Ste Anne Viognier Les Arbres

Millton Riverpoint Vineyard Gisborne Viognier   ★★★★☆

The very characterful 2016 vintage (★★★★☆) was hand-picked and fermented with indigenous yeasts in tanks and French oak hogsheads. Marsanne was added to the blend (6 per cent), for 'depth and richness', and a splash of Muscat (2 per cent) for a 'fruity lift'. Certified organic, it is a medium-bodied, fully dry style (1.6 grams/litre of residual sugar), yellow/pale gold, with gentle acidity and strong, peachy, slightly spicy, vaguely honeyed flavours, showing excellent richness and complexity.

Moutere Hills Nelson Viognier   ★★★☆

Estate-grown at Upper Moutere, the 2018 vintage (★★★☆) is a rare wine – only 47 cases were produced. Hand-picked and matured for 11 months in old French oak barrels, it is a light gold, fleshy wine, with strong, peachy, slightly spicy and honeyed flavours, oak complexity and a well-rounded finish. Showing considerable development, it's probably best drunk young.

Obsidian Reserve Waiheke Island Viognier   ★★★★

Hand-harvested at Onetangi, the 2015 vintage (★★★☆) is a vibrantly fruity wine, mouthfilling, with peachy, slightly appley flavours and hints of apricot and spice, in a fresh, uncomplicated style.

Pask Gimblett Gravels Small Batch Hawke's Bay Viognier   (★★★★)

Well worth cellaring, the youthful 2018 vintage (★★★★) was cool-fermented in stainless steel tanks and barriques, then matured and lees-aged in oak puncheons. Very pale straw, it is fresh and mouthfilling, with generous, ripe stone-fruit flavours, showing a distinct touch of complexity, and a dry, finely poised finish. Best drinking 2020+.

Passage Rock Reserve Waiheke Island Viognier   ★★★★☆

Full of personality, the 2019 vintage (★★★★★) was barrel-matured. Bright, light lemon/green, it has a complex, slightly creamy and nutty bouquet. Weighty and fleshy, it is still very youthful, with concentrated, ripe stone-fruit flavours, oak complexity and a rich, fully dry (2 grams/litre of residual sugar) finish. Best drinking mid-2021+.

Vintage	19
WR	7
Drink	19-25

DRY $50 –V

Petane Tracks Block Hawke's Bay Viognier   (★★★☆)

A strongly oak-influenced style, the 2018 vintage (★★★☆) was grown at Eskdale and barrel-fermented. Very pale straw, with coconut-like aromas, it is full-bodied and fleshy, with very good depth of ripe stone-fruit flavours, showing considerable complexity. It needs time; open 2020+.

DRY $27 –V

Quarter Acre Hawke's Bay Viognier   ★★★★☆

The classy 2018 vintage (★★★★★) is a single-vineyard wine, grown in the Bridge Pa Triangle, hand-harvested and mostly barrel-fermented. Seductively weighty and rich, it has lush stone-fruit flavours, finely integrated oak, gentle acidity and a long, well-rounded finish. Already delicious.

DRY $35 –V

Saint Clair Origin Hawke's Bay Viognier   (★★★★)

Instantly appealing, the 2017 vintage (★★★★) is a single-vineyard, Gimblett Gravels wine. It shows good varietal character, in a medium-bodied style, with strong, fresh, peachy, gently spicy flavours, dry and smooth.

DRY $22 V+

Sileni Estate Selection Hedonist Hawke's Bay Viognier   (★★★★)

The 2015 vintage (★★★★) was grown at Te Awanga, hand-picked and fermented in old French oak barriques. Fleshy and generous, it has citrusy, peachy, slightly nutty flavours, showing good delicacy, a touch of complexity, faint sweetness (4.7 grams/litre of residual sugar), fresh acidity and a floral bouquet.

Vintage	15
WR	6
Drink	19-22

DRY $25 AV

Staete Landt State of Surrender Marlborough Viognier   ★★★★☆

Still youthful, the 2016 vintage (★★★★★) was estate-grown at Rapaura, hand-harvested, and fermented and lees-aged for eight months. Fresh and full-bodied, it is vibrantly fruity, with concentrated, peachy, slightly spicy flavours, showing good complexity, and a dry (2 grams/litre of residual sugar) finish. Best drinking mid-2020+.

Vintage	16	15	14	13	12
WR	6	7	6	6	6
Drink	19-26	19-25	19-20	P	P

DRY $39 –V

Stonecroft Gimblett Gravels Hawke's Bay Viognier ★★★★

Certified organic, the 2018 vintage (★★★★☆) was estate-grown in the Roys Hill Vineyard, hand-harvested and fermented and matured for six months in seasoned French oak barrels. Already highly enjoyable, it has a floral, slightly buttery fragrance. Full-bodied and sweet-fruited, it is well-rounded, with generous, ripe stone-fruit flavours, showing good complexity, and a dry, softly textured finish.

Vintage	18	17	16
WR	6	5	5
Drink	19-23	19-22	19-21

 DRY $27 –V

Te Mata Estate Zara Hawke's Bay Viognier ★★★★★

This estate-grown wine is from Woodthorpe Terraces, on the south side of the Dartmoor Valley. Hand-picked, in 2018 it was fermented and lees-aged for seven months in French oak barrels (partly new). Delicious young, the 2018 vintage (★★★★★) is fragrant and fleshy, with good weight and intensity of fresh, ripe stone-fruit flavours, finely integrated biscuity oak, gentle acidity and a long, savoury, dry finish. Seductively rich and soft, it should break into full stride 2020+.

 DRY $30 AV

Turanga Par Nature Viognier (★★★★)

Still on sale, the attractive 2014 vintage (★★★★) was estate-grown and hand-picked at Whitford, in Auckland. Full-bodied, it has vibrant stone-fruit flavours, showing very good ripeness and depth, a slightly oily texture, and a fully dry finish. Certified organic.

 DRY $25 AV

TW Viognier (★★★☆)

Estate-grown in Gisborne, the 2016 vintage (★★★☆) is fragrant, fresh and full-bodied. Vibrantly fruity, with pear and peach flavours, gentle acidity and a soft finish, it's enjoyable young.

 DRY $25 –V

Villa Maria Cellar Selection Hawke's Bay Viognier ★★★★

Weighty and sweet-fruited, the youthful, partly (20 per cent) barrel-fermented 2018 vintage (★★★★) offers good value. Fresh, full-bodied and vibrantly fruity, it has stone-fruit flavours, showing a distinct touch of complexity, and a dry, well-rounded finish. Best drinking mid-2020+.

DRY $19 V+

Wairau River Reserve Marlborough Viognier ★★★★

The youthful 2018 vintage (★★★★) was estate-grown in The Angler Vineyard, on the banks of the Wairau River, hand-picked and fermented in a seasoned French oak barrique. Vibrantly fruity, it is freshly scented and weighty, with strong pear and citrus-fruit flavours, lively acidity, and a dry (1.8 grams/litre of residual sugar) finish. Open 2020+.

 DRY $30 –V

Würzer

A German crossing of Gewürztraminer and Müller-Thurgau, Würzer is extremely rare in New Zealand, with 0.4 hectares of bearing vines in 2020, all in Nelson, where Seifried has 'a few rows' at its Redwood Valley Vineyard.

Seifried Nelson Würzer ★★★☆

The attractive 2018 vintage (★★★★) has a floral, musky perfume. A fresh, medium-bodied wine, it is slightly sweet (10 grams/litre of residual sugar), with strong, lively, citrusy, spicy flavours, and loads of summer-drinking appeal.

Vintage	18	MED/DRY $18 V+
WR	7	
Drink	19-21	

Sweet White Wines

New Zealand's sweet white wines (often called dessert wines) are hardly taking the world by storm, with only a few thousand cases exported each year. Yet around the country, winemakers work hard to produce some ravishingly beautiful, honey-sweet white wines that are worth discovering and can certainly hold their own internationally. New Zealand's most luscious, concentrated and honeyish sweet whites are made from grapes which have been shrivelled and dehydrated on the vines by 'noble rot', the dry form of the *Botrytis cinerea* mould. Misty mornings, followed by clear, fine days with light winds and low humidity, are ideal conditions for the spread of noble rot, but in New Zealand this favourable interplay of weather factors occurs irregularly.

Some enjoyable but rarely exciting dessert wines are made by the 'freeze-concentration' method, whereby a proportion of the natural water content in the grape juice is frozen out, leaving a sweet, concentrated juice to be fermented.

Marlborough has so far yielded a majority of the finest sweet whites. Most of the other wine regions, however, can also point to the successful production of botrytised sweet whites in favourable vintages.

Riesling has been the foundation of the majority of New Zealand's most opulent sweet whites, but Sauvignon Blanc, Sémillon, Gewürztraminer, Pinot Gris, Chenin Blanc, Viognier and Chardonnay have all yielded fine dessert styles. With their high levels of extract and firm acidity, most of these wines mature well for two to three years, although few are very long-lived.

Alpha Domus AD Noble Selection ★★★★★

A pale gold beauty, the botrytis-affected 2015 vintage (★★★★★) was made from Sémillon grapes, grown in the Bridge Pa Triangle and mostly harvested with soaring sugar contents (45 to 47 brix). French oak-aged, it is fresh and full-bodied (although only 10 per cent alcohol), with rich, ripe flavours, showing good complexity, plentiful sweetness (248 grams/litre of residual sugar), and an oily, honeyed richness.

Askerne Hawke's Bay Noble Sémillon (★★★★☆)

Delicious now, the light gold 2016 vintage (★★★★☆) was barrel-aged. Medium-bodied, it is honeyed, with rich, ripe stone-fruit flavours, oak complexity, excellent freshness and vigour, and a finely balanced, sweet (128 grams/litre of residual sugar) finish.

Askerne Late Harvest Hawke's Bay Gewürztraminer (★★★★☆)

Ready to roll, the highly expressive 2017 vintage (★★★★☆) is a gold/amber wine, handled without oak. It has a honeyed, gently spicy bouquet, leading into a rich wine with concentrated peach, apricot and honey flavours, a slightly oily texture and a sweet (122 grams/litre of residual sugar), finely balanced finish. Fine value.

Astrolabe Wrekin Vineyard Late Harvest Marlborough Chenin Blanc   ★★★★☆

The 2018 vintage (★★★★) was grown in the Wrekin Vineyard, in the Southern Valleys, hand-picked and 50 per cent barrel-fermented. Made from 'lightly botrytised' grapes, it is a fresh, medium-bodied wine, attractively scented, with rich, ripe, peachy, slightly honeyed flavours, abundant sweetness (108 grams/litre of residual sugar), balanced acidity, and a smooth finish. A gentle, very harmonious wine, it's a drink-now or cellaring proposition.

Vintage	18
WR	7
Drink	19-30

 SW $30 (375ML) AV

Ata Rangi Kahu Martinborough Botrytis Riesling   ★★★★★

Already hard to resist, the 2018 vintage (★★★★★) is golden, with a rich, honeyed fragrance. Strongly botrytis-affected, it has highly concentrated peach, apricot and honey flavours, lush, sweet (120 grams/litre of residual sugar) and crisp, with lovely depth and harmony.

Vintage	18
WR	7
Drink	19-27

 SW $34 (375ML) V+

Ataahua Waipara Late Harvest Gewürztraminer   (★★★★★)

Still on sale, the pale gold 2014 vintage (★★★★★) is packed with personality. From grapes hand-harvested in early winter and barrel-fermented with indigenous yeasts, it is perfumed and weighty, with sweet, concentrated stone-fruit and spice flavours, showing lovely complexity, richness and harmony.

 SW $26 (375ML) V+

Babich Family Estates Cowslip Valley Marlborough Noble Riesling   (★★★★☆)

A strong candidate for cellaring, the 2016 vintage (★★★★☆) was harvested at 32 brix, with a 70 per cent botrytis infection, and fermented in tanks (80 per cent) and new oak casks (20 per cent). Light yellow/green, it is mouthfilling (12 per cent alcohol) and sweet (101 grams/litre of residual sugar), with vibrant, pure, citrusy, gently honeyed flavours, showing lovely delicacy and harmony.

SW $35 (375ML) –V

Babich Winemakers' Reserve Late Harvest Marlborough Riesling   (★★★★)

Drinking well from the start, the 2017 vintage (★★★★) was estate-grown in the Cowslip Valley Vineyard, in the Waihopai Valley, and partly (16 per cent) barrel-fermented. Bright, light lemon/green, it's a sweet but not super-sweet wine (51 grams/litre of residual sugar), medium to full-bodied, with ripe, citrusy, peachy flavours, showing good complexity, gentle acidity and a very harmonious, well-rounded finish.

 SW $35 (375ML) –V

Beach House Hawke's Bay Noble Chardonnay   (★★★★)

The delicious 2016 vintage (★★★★) is a single-vineyard wine, hand-harvested when the grapes were 'botrytis laden', and tank-fermented. Light gold, with a slightly oily richness, it has concentrated peach, apricot and honey flavours, sweet (120 grams/litre of residual sugar) and smooth.

SW $20 (375ML) V+

Beach House Hawke's Bay Noble Sauvignon Blanc   (★★★★☆)

The impressive 2016 vintage (★★★★☆) is a single-vineyard wine, hand-picked at 35 brix, when the grapes were 'botrytis laden', and tank-fermented. Light gold, it is full-bodied, with deep, ripe peach and passionfruit flavours, fresh and honeyed, abundant sweetness (126 grams/litre of residual sugar), balanced acidity, and a long finish.

SW $35 (375ML) –V

Bellbird Spring Muté 'L'Alouette'   (★★★★☆)

The powerful 2016 vintage (★★★★) was made from late-picked Sauvignon Blanc, estate-grown at Waipara, in North Canterbury, fermented in old barrels and fortified with the estate's own pot still brandy. Retasted in August 2019, it is weighty (17.5 per cent alcohol) and very harmonious, with rich, ripe pear-like flavours, showing good complexity. A moderately sweet wine (81 grams/litre of residual sugar), it's well worth trying.

SW $35 (375ML) –V

Bellbird Spring Muté 'Les Epices'   (★★★★★)

The delicious, pale gold 2016 vintage (★★★★★) is a Waipara blend of Riesling, Gewürztraminer and Muscat, late-picked, fermented in old barrels and fortified with the estate's own pot still brandy. It's a distinctive wine, sturdy (17.5 per cent alcohol), rich and rounded, with pear, peach and spice flavours, sweet (85 grams/litre of residual sugar), complex and harmonious. Worth discovering.

SW $35 (375ML) AV

Blank Canvas Marlborough Meta Riesling   (★★★★★)

For sheer hedonistic pleasure, the botrytised 2018 vintage (★★★★★) is hard to beat. Hand-picked in the Wairau Valley and fermented and aged in seasoned French oak puncheons, it is pale gold, with a highly fragrant, honeyed bouquet. Showing lovely concentration and harmony, it has rich, sweet apricot and honey flavours, good acid spine, an oily texture, and delicious vibrancy, poise and depth.

SW $40 (375ML) AV

Brancott Estate Letter Series 'B' Late Harvest Marlborough Sauvignon Blanc   ★★★★

The 2017 vintage (★★★★) is a seductive mouthful, light-bodied (9 per cent alcohol), rich and soft, with ripe pear-like flavours, a hint of honey, and a sweet, very harmonious finish. Ready.

SW $25 (375ML) AV

Brookfields Indulgence Hawke's Bay Viognier   ★★★★☆

The highly seductive 2017 vintage (★★★★☆) was made from botrytis-affected grapes, handled without oak. Pale gold, it is deliciously rich and sweet (over 250 grams/litre of residual sugar), with an oily texture and a strong surge of peach, apricot and honey flavours.

Vintage	17	16
WR	7	7
Drink	P	19-20

SW $25 (375ML) V+

Churton Marlborough Petit Manseng   ★★★★★

The lovely 2016 vintage (★★★★★) of this traditional variety of Jurancon, in south-west France, was estate-grown in the Waihopai Valley and fermented in seasoned oak casks of various sizes. Revealing great personality, it is light gold, with highly concentrated, honey-sweet flavours (93 grams/litre of residual sugar), threaded with appetising acidity, and lots of youthful vigour. More forward than the 2016, the highly seductive 2017 vintage (★★★★★), designated 'passerillé', is the first to be made from raisined, botrytis-affected grapes. Green/gold, it is full-bodied, rich, peachy and honeyed, in an instantly appealing style, threaded with mouth-watering acidity. Certified organic.

Vintage	17	16	15	14	13	12
WR	7	7	7	NM	6	7
Drink	19-30	19-35	19-30	NM	19-28	19-30

SW $49 (500ML) AV

Coopers Creek Coopers Gold   ★★★☆

The 2017 vintage (★★★☆) was made from Gisborne Chardonnay, partly freeze-concentrated to intensify its natural grape sugars. Light lemon/green, it is fresh and smooth, with citrusy, peachy flavours, gentle sweetness (105 grams/litre of residual sugar) and an easy-drinking charm.

SW $22 (375ML) AV

De La Terre Noble Hawke's Bay Viognier   ★★★★☆

Estate-grown at Havelock North, the 2016 vintage (★★★★☆) is weighty and smooth, with ripe, peachy, slightly honeyed flavours, gentle sweetness (100 grams/litre of residual sugar), and a well-rounded, very harmonious finish. Delicious drinking now onwards.

SW $34 (375ML) AV

Domain Road Central Otago Bannockburn Symposium   (★★★★)

The estate-grown, hand-picked 2018 vintage (★★★★) is a late-harvested Sauvignon Blanc, partly (40 per cent) barrel-fermented. Light lemon/green, it has vibrant, ripe, peachy, citrusy, limey flavours, showing good delicacy, a touch of complexity, moderate acidity and a sweet (121 grams/litre of residual sugar), very harmonious finish. Delicious young.

SW $32 (375ML) –V

Dragon Bones Waitaki Valley North Otago Riesling Beerenauslese   (★★★★★)

Ensconced in a full (750-ml) bottle, the 2014 vintage (★★★★★) from Lone Hill Vineyards is a single-vineyard wine, hand-picked and made in a sweet (135 grams/litre of residual sugar) style with steely acidity and low alcohol (9.5 per cent). Light gold, with a gently honeyed bouquet, it shows lovely intensity, vibrancy and harmony, with deep, peachy flavours, enriched but not dominated by botrytis. Tasted in mid-2018, it's a wine of rare beauty, with lovely poise and depth.

 SW $45 (750ML) V+

Dry River Martinborough Gewürztraminer
Botrytis Bunch Selection Lovat Vineyard   (★★★★★)

Sweet but not super-sweet, the 2018 vintage (★★★★★) is a very 'complete' wine, already delicious but also well worth cellaring. Made from 100 per cent botrytis-infected grapes and handled without oak, it is light gold, with a spicy, honeyed fragrance. It has rich stone-fruit, spice and honey flavours, a hint of ginger, and a sweet (160 grams/litre of residual sugar), very harmonious finish. Hard to resist. (750 ml.)

 SW $59 (750ML) V+

Esk Valley Late Harvest Hawke's Bay Chenin Blanc   ★★★★★

Already hard to resist, the 2018 vintage (★★★★★) is a pale gold wine with an intense, honeyed fragrance. Showing lovely depth and harmony, it has concentrated, vibrant, peachy, botrytis-enriched flavours, abundant sweetness, finely poised acidity, and excellent vigour and richness.

Vintage	18
WR	6
Drink	19-29

SW $30 (375ML) V+

Felton Road Block 1 Central Otago Riesling   ★★★★★

Estate-grown in The Elms Vineyard, from mature vines on a 'steeper slope' which yields 'riper fruit' without noble rot, this Bannockburn wine is made in a style 'similar to a late-harvest, Mosel spätlese'. The 2019 vintage (★★★★★) is a very Mosel-like wine. Bright, light lemon/green, it is light and vivacious, with lemony, appley, slightly spicy flavours, sweet (57 grams/litre of residual sugar) and crisp, and excellent delicacy, harmony and length. Best drinking 2023+.

Vintage	19	18
WR	7	7
Drink	19-44	19-43

 SW $49 (750ML) V+

Folium Late Harvest Marlborough Sauvignon Blanc   (★★★★★)

The distinctly Sauternes-style 2018 vintage (★★★★★) is a lovely young wine, handled in French oak casks (10 per cent new). Bright, light yellow/green, it is mouthfilling and sweet (140 grams/litre of residual sugar), with ripe, vibrant tropical-fruit flavours, gentle honeyed notes, a hint of apricot and a subtle seasoning of oak adding complexity. The producer suggests cellaring up to 2050, but it's already delicious. (750 ml.)

Vintage	18
WR	7
Drink	19-50

 SW $52 (750ML) V+

Forrest Botrytised Marlborough Riesling   ★★★★★

The 2018 vintage (★★★★★) is a richly botrytised style with a fragrant, honeyed bouquet. Bright, light gold/green, it has concentrated, peachy, honeyed flavours, abundant sweetness (213 grams/litre of residual sugar), balanced acidity, and a slightly oily richness. Drink now or cellar.

 SW $30 (375ML) V+

Forrest Marlborough Petit Manseng   ★★★★

Forrest Estate says this is their most popular wine at the cellar door over summer. The tangy 2018 vintage (★★★★) is delicious young. Light-bodied, it is gently sweet (80 grams/litre of residual sugar), with peachy flavours, a hint of apricot and lots of youthful impact. (750 ml.)

 SW $20 (750Ml) V+

Framingham F-Series Riesling Auslese   ★★★★★

The 2016 vintage (★★★★★) is light gold, vibrantly fruity and rich, with low alcohol (8.5 per cent), good acid spine, and concentrated, citrusy, honeyed flavours. Showing lovely freshness, depth and poise, it's already delicious, but very age-worthy.

Vintage	16	15
WR	7	7
Drink	19-21	19-20

 SW $45 (375ML) AV

Framingham F-Series Riesling Trockenbeerenauslese   ★★★★★

The 2016 vintage (★★★★★) is a ravishing wine. Light gold, it is highly scented and vibrantly fruity, with bottomless depth of sweet, lemony, honeyed flavours, perfectly pitched acidity, a distinct hint of apricot and a very long finish. A memorable mouthful, it's a drink-now or cellaring proposition.

Vintage	16	15
WR	7	7
Drink	19-21	19-20

 SW $70 (375ML) AV

Framingham Noble Riesling ★★★★★

Delicious young, the 2017 vintage (★★★★★) is an oily-rich, sweet (176 grams/litre of residual sugar), vibrantly fruity wine, handled in a mix of tanks (55 per cent) and barrels (45 per cent). Pale gold, with a green tinge, it has fresh, concentrated lemon, apple, apricot and honey flavours, enriched but not swamped by botrytis, good acid spine and a very harmonious, lasting finish. Drink now or cellar.

 SW $40 (375ML) AV

Framingham Select Marlborough Riesling ★★★★★

'Inspired by the German Spätlese style', the 2017 vintage (★★★★★) is light-bodied (9 per cent alcohol) and highly scented. Vibrantly fruity, it is a gently sweet (62 grams/litre of residual sugar) style, with penetrating, citrusy, appley flavours, showing lovely purity, delicacy and harmony. A very age-worthy wine, it should break into full stride from 2020 onwards.

 SW $35 (750ML) V+

Greywacke Botrytis Marlborough Pinot Gris ★★★★★

Lovely now, the 2015 vintage (★★★★★) is a single-vineyard wine, grown in the Wairau Valley, and fermented and matured for a year in old barrels. Pale gold, it is mouthfilling, rich and complex, with concentrated stone-fruit and spice flavours, sweet (105 grams/litre of residual sugar), rounded and lasting. Drink now or cellar.

Vintage	15
WR	6
Drink	20-25

 SW $37 (375ML) AV

Greywacke Marlborough Botrytis Gewürztraminer (★★★★☆)

Delicious now, the 2014 vintage (★★★★☆) is a single-vineyard wine, grown in the Wairau Valley. Light green/gold, with a spicy fragrance, it is generous, with strong, peachy, spicy, slightly gingery and honeyed flavours, sweet and rounded.

Vintage	14
WR	6
Drink	20-24

 SW $37 (375ML) –V

Grove Mill Wairau Valley Marlborough Botrytis Riesling (★★★★★)

Delicious now, the 2017 vintage (★★★★★) is a strongly botrytised style, with a richly honeyed fragrance and flavours. Light gold, it has concentrated peach and apricot flavours, showing a slightly oily richness, abundant sweetness (215 grams/litre of residual sugar), finely balanced acidity, and a long finish.

Vintage	17
WR	7
Drink	19-29

 SW $50 (375ML) AV

Jackson Estate Botrytis Marlborough Riesling   ★★★★★

The lovely 2018 vintage (★★★★★) was estate-grown in the heart of the Wairau Valley. Light gold, it is fresh and lively, with concentrated peach and apricot flavours, enriched by botrytis-derived honey notes, abundant sweetness (216 grams/litre of residual sugar), balanced acidity and a slightly oily texture. Drink now or cellar.

SW $45 (375ML) AV

Johanneshof Noble Late Harvest Marlborough Riesling   (★★★★★)

Still on sale in 2019, the striking 2011 vintage (★★★★★) is amber-hued, with a honeyed, rich, complex bouquet and flavours. Probably at its peak, it has highly concentrated apricot and honey flavours, crisp, sweet (150 grams/litre of residual sugar) and finely poised. A very 'complete' wine.

SW $40 (375ML) AV

Johner Estate Gladstone Noble Pinot Noir   ★★★☆

Estate-grown in the northern Wairarapa, the 2017 vintage (★★★★) has a pale straw colour. Delicious young, it is sweet (130 grams/litre of residual sugar) and soft, with strong, peachy flavours, botrytis-derived honey characters adding richness, and loads of drink-young charm.

SW $22 (375ML) AV

Johner Estate Gladstone Noble Sauvignon Blanc   ★★★☆

Estate-grown in the northern Wairarapa, the 2017 vintage (★★★★) is well worth cellaring. It is mouthfilling, with fresh, ripe tropical-fruit flavours, a hint of honey, gentle sweetness (120 grams/litre of residual sugar), and excellent delicacy and depth.

SW $22 (375ML) AV

Jules Taylor Late Harvest Marlborough Sauvignon Blanc   ★★★★

Enjoyable from the start, the 2018 vintage (★★★★) is a rich, youthful wine, fresh and full-bodied. Bright, light yellow/green, it has well-ripened tropical-fruit flavours, a hint of honey, gentle sweetness, balanced acidity and excellent harmony. Best drinking 2020+.

Vintage	18
WR	5
Drink	19-23

SW $30 (375ML) –V

Leveret Hawke's Bay Late Harvest   (★★★★☆)

Delicious young, the 2016 vintage (★★★★☆) was made from Viognier. A fragrant wine, it has vibrant, peachy, honeyed flavours, sweet (140 grams/litre of residual sugar), rich and oily-textured. Fine value.

Vintage	16
WR	5
Drink	19-25

SW $22 (375ML) V+

Leveret Reserve Hawke's Bay Late Harvest   (★★★★★)

The classy 2016 vintage (★★★★★) is difficult to resist. Made from Viognier, it is a golden, honey-sweet beauty (200 grams/litre of residual sugar), strongly botrytis-influenced, with lively acidity, an oily texture, and lush, peachy, honeyed flavours.

Vintage	16
WR	7
Drink	19-30

 SW $26 (375ML) V+

Loop Road Central Otago Noble Riesling   (★★★★★)

The memorable 2016 vintage (★★★★★) will be a 'oncer', unfortunately, as the producer (Quartz Reef) no longer has access to the grapes. An exquisite wine, showing lovely richness, vibrancy, vigour and poise, it was made from botrytis-affected grapes, grown in the Torr Vineyard at Pisa, in the Cromwell Basin. Beautifully scented, it's a classic sweet style (186 grams/litre of residual sugar), intense and likely to be long-lived – but already hard to resist.

 SW $35 (375ML) AV

Loveblock Marlborough Noble Chenin Blanc   (★★★★★)

The delicious 2014 vintage (★★★★★) was estate-grown and hand-picked in the Awatere Valley at 42 brix, with 100 per cent botrytis infection. Light gold, deliciously peachy and honeyed, it has abundant sweetness (230 grams/litre of residual sugar), balanced by firm acidity, and a slightly oily, lasting finish.

 SW $30 (500ML) V+

Loveblock Marlborough Sweet Moscato   (★★★★)

Estate-grown in the Awatere Valley, the 2014 vintage (★★★★) is a full-bodied (13.5 per cent alcohol), sweet but not super-sweet wine, fortified with grain alcohol, 'in true Muscat de Beaumes-de-Venise style'. It is invitingly perfumed, with fresh, pure Muscat aromas and strong, vibrant peach, lemon, orange and grape flavours.

 SW $30 (500ML) V+

Marsden Bay of Islands Late Harvest Muscat   ★★★

The 2017 vintage (★★☆) is a blend of Northland (mostly) and Gisborne grapes. An easy-drinking wine, it has peachy, gently sweet flavours (180 grams/litre of residual sugar) and a soft finish.

Vintage	17
WR	5
Drink	19-20

SW $20 (375ML) –V

Millton Clos Samuel Special Berry Selection Viognier   (★★★★★)

The arresting 2015 vintage (★★★★★), estate-grown in the Te Arai Vineyard, at Gisborne, was made from 'golden, fluffy, raisined', botrytis-affected grapes. Amber-hued, with a soaring bouquet of apricots and honey, it is full-bodied, with a rich, oily texture and lovely concentration of peach and apricot-like flavours, sweet (188 grams/litre of residual sugar) and complex. A super-charged wine with a powerful presence, it's well worth discovering. Certified organic.

 SW $80 (750ML) AV

Misha's Vineyard The Cadenza Late Harvest Gewürztraminer   ★★★★☆

The 2019 vintage (★★★★☆) was estate-grown and hand-picked on 6 June at Bendigo, in Central Otago, at 30.2 brix, with 15 per cent of the fruit botrytis-affected, and handled without oak. Pale lemon/green, with an invitingly perfumed, gently spicy bouquet, it is an elegant, light-bodied style (9.5 per cent alcohol), with very youthful, vibrant, citrusy, spicy flavours, showing excellent delicacy and depth, and a sweet (120 grams/litre of residual sugar), smooth finish. A very harmonious wine, it is well worth cellaring; best drinking 2021+.

Vintage	19	18	17	16	15	14
WR	6	7	6	7	7	6
Drink	19-29	19-28	19-26	19-26	19-25	19-24

 SW $32 (375ML) AV

Mission Late Harvest   (★★★☆)

Still very youthful, the 2018 vintage (★★★☆) was made from botrytis-affected Riesling, grown in Hawke's Bay. Bright, light yellow/green, it is fresh, lively and crisp, with citrusy, slightly spicy flavours, a hint of apricot and good sugar/acid balance (90 grams/litre of residual sugar). Best drinking 2021+.

 SW $16 (375ML) V+

Mondillo Central Otago Nina   ★★★★★

Already a delicious mouthful, the 2018 vintage (★★★★★) was made from late-harvested Riesling, hand-picked at Bendigo. Beautifully perfumed, it has notable depth of vibrant, citrusy, peachy, slightly honeyed flavours, and a hint of apricot, and a finely poised, sweet (126 grams/litre of residual sugar), very rich finish. Well worth discovering.

SW $38 (375ML) AV

Mt Difficulty Growers Series Silver Tussock Tinwald Burn Noble Riesling   (★★★★)

Retasted in 2019, the 2016 vintage (★★★★) is from a site at the head of Lake Dunstan, in the Cromwell Basin. Bright, light yellow/green, it is sweet (137 grams/litre of residual sugar), with lively acidity, strong, peachy, limey, gently honeyed flavours, and slightly toasty, bottle-aged notes adding complexity. Drink now or cellar.

Vintage	16
WR	7
Drink	19-28

 SW $70 (750ML) –V

Mt Difficulty Single Vineyard Long Gully Bannockburn
Late Harvest Riesling

Still developing, the vigorous 2016 vintage (★★★★☆) is bright, light yellow/green, with strong, peachy, citrusy flavours, a hint of honey, gentle sweetness (72 grams/litre of residual sugar), lively acidity, and complex, bottle-aged notes emerging. Best drinking mid-2020+.

Vintage	16	SW $70 (750ML) –V
WR	5	
Drink	19-28	

Nevis Bluff Selection De Grains Noble Pinot Gris ★★★★★

The 2015 vintage (★★★★★) is a truly memorable Central Otago wine. Bright, light yellow/green, it is enticingly scented, with lovely vibrancy and intensity of peach, pear and honey flavours. Unabashedly sweet (338 grams/litre of residual sugar), it is oily-textured, with balanced acidity, and notable concentration and harmony. Drink now.

SW $35 (375ML) AV

O:TU Sweet Marlborough Sauvignon Blanc (★★★)

The 2017 vintage (★★★) has fresh, direct, clearly varietal aromas and flavours. Light-bodied, it is lively, with grapefruit, lime and green-capsicum fruit characters in a gently sweet style, with appetising acidity and plenty of flavour. Drink young.

SW $18 (375ML) AV

Palliser Estate Martinborough Noble Riesling ★★★★★

Gold/amber, the 2016 vintage (★★★★★) has a richly honeyed, enticing fragrance. Showing strong personality, it is highly concentrated, with rich, vibrant peach, apricot and honey flavours, a powerful botrytis influence, good acid spine and lots of drink-young appeal.

SW $30 (375ML) V+

Pegasus Bay Aria Late Picked Riesling ★★★★★

Estate-grown at Waipara, the exquisite 2016 vintage (★★★★★) is packaged in a full-sized (750-ml) bottle (the 2014 is in a half bottle). Bright yellow/green, it is beautifully harmonious, with rich, vibrant, citrusy, peachy flavours, showing good complexity, abundant sweetness (84.5 grams/litre of residual sugar), and a fresh, lasting finish. Hard to resist.

Vintage	16	15	14	13	12	SW $40 (750ML) V+
WR	5	NM	6	7	6	
Drink	19-32	NM	19-37	19-25	19-25	

Pegasus Bay Encore Noble Riesling   ★★★★★

Grown at Waipara, in North Canterbury, this beauty is from hand-selected, botrytised bunches and berries, harvested late in the season in multiple passes through the vineyard. The 2016 vintage (★★★★★) has a scented, honeyed bouquet. A very elegant wine, it has concentrated, citrusy, peachy, honeyed flavours, sweet (177 grams/litre of residual sugar), crisp, finely balanced and lasting. Drink now or cellar.

Vintage	16
WR	6
Drink	19-42

 SW $40 (375ML) AV

Pegasus Bay Finale Noble Barrique Matured Sauvignon Blanc/Sémillon   ★★★★★

A wine of strong presence, the 2017 vintage (★★★★★) is a golden, honey-sweet North Canterbury wine, made in the classic Sauternes style. French oak-aged for 18 months, it has a fragrant, gently honeyed bouquet. Full-bodied, it has rich, apricot-like flavours, showing lovely complexity, poise and vigour. Best drinking 2022+.

 SW $42 (375ML) AV

Pegasus Bay Fortissimo Waipara Muscat   (★★★★★)

The very rare 2016 vintage (★★★★★) was estate-grown in North Canterbury. Modelled on Muscat de Beaumes de Venise, a traditional fortified Muscat from the Rhône Valley, it is richly perfumed and full-bodied (17 per cent alcohol), with lovely, vibrant, pure lemon and orange flavours, sweet (142 grams/litre of residual sugar) and strong. Finely balanced, with gentle acidity, it's delicious now.

Vintage	16
WR	7
Drink	19-32

SW $40 (375ML) AV

Prophet's Rock Vin de Paile   (★★★★★)

The distinctive 2016 vintage (★★★★★) was made from Pinot Gris grapes, estate-grown at Bendigo, in Central Otago, and dried for 45 days in the loft of the vineyard barn. Fermented with indigenous yeasts in old oak barrels, it is a pale yellow/gold, medium-bodied wine, with rich, very intense, pear-like flavours, fresh and sweet (168 grams/litre of residual sugar). Worth trying.

SW $70 (375ML) –V

Queensberry The Lazy Dog Sweet on Chenin
Central Otago Chenin Blanc/Gewürztraminer   (★★★★)

From 'later harvest' grapes, the 2018 vintage (★★★★) was estate-grown at Queensberry – midway between Cromwell and Wanaka – and fermented in 'pre-loved' barrels. It is very fresh and vibrant, with gentle sweetness (70 grams/litre of residual sugar), strong, citrusy, spicy flavours, a hint of apricot, and a finely balanced, crisp finish. Already delicious, it should be at its best 2020+.

 SW $29 (750 ML) V+

Riverby Estate Marlborough Noble Riesling   ★★★★★

Tasted together in mid-2019, the 2016 to 2018 vintages were an impressive trio. Estate-grown at Rapaura, the 2018 (★★★★★) is golden, with rich, peachy, honeyed aromas and flavours, a strong botrytis influence, and a sweet (187 grams/litre of residual sugar), finely poised finish. Best drinking mid-2020+. The 2017 vintage (★★★★) shows some development, with very good flavour depth, gentle honeyed notes and a sweet (157 grams/litre of residual sugar) finish. Delicious now, the 2016 vintage (★★★★★) is amber-hued, with apricot and honey flavours, sweet (200 grams/litre of residual sugar) and highly concentrated.

Vintage	17	16
WR	6	7
Drink	19-30	19-29

 SW $35 (375ML) AV

Rock Ferry Botrytised Riesling   ★★★★☆

Certified organic, the delicious 2017 vintage (★★★★★) was hand-harvested in Marlborough and 50 per cent of the blend was fermented and matured for six months in barrels. Golden, with an inviting, richly honeyed bouquet, it has concentrated, apricot-like flavours, abundant sweetness (129 grams/litre of residual sugar), finely balanced acidity, good complexity and a very harmonious, lasting finish. Drink now or cellar.

 SW $30 (375ML) AV

Seifried Winemaker's Collection Sweet Agnes Nelson Riesling   ★★★★★

Seifried's most celebrated wine. The 2018 vintage (★★★★★) was hand-picked in the company's Redwood Valley Vineyard, when a large portion of the fruit was shrivelled and raisined. Bright, light yellow/green, it is rich and finely poised, with excellent concentration of citrusy, peachy, gently honeyed flavours, and a sweet (153 grams/litre of residual sugar), crisp, finely balanced finish. The 2019 vintage (★★★★★) is already delicious. Light yellow/green, it is lively and intense, with rich, peachy, citrusy, gently honeyed flavours, sweet (198 grams/litre of residual sugar), crisp and harmonious. Drink now or cellar. (In a tasting of the 2011, 2010 and 2008 vintages, held in September 2019, the star was the golden 2011 (★★★★★), which shows lovely richness, vigour and harmony.)

Vintage	19	18	17	16	15
WR	7	7	5	7	5
Drink	19-29	19-28	19-25	19-27	19-23

 SW $29 (375ML) V+

Sherwood Estate Waipara Collection Huntaway
Late Pick Waipara Valley Riesling   (★★★★★)

Delicious now, the 2013 vintage (★★★★★) is a great buy. Bright, light yellow/green, it's a sweet but not super-sweet wine (100 grams/litre of residual sugar), long and lovely, with rich, peachy, gently honeyed flavours, fresh acidity, bottle-aged complexity, and a lasting, very harmonious finish.

SW $26 (750ML) V+

Sileni Estate Selection Late Harvest Hawke's Bay Sémillon   ★★★☆

The 2018 vintage (★★★☆) was handled without oak. Well worth cellaring, it is light and youthful, with fresh, delicate pear, lemon and apple flavours, a vague hint of honey, gentle sweetness (91 grams/litre of residual sugar) and moderate acidity. Best drinking 2020+.

Vintage	18
WR	6
Drink	19-23

SW $20 (375ML) AV

Sileni Exceptional Vintage Marlborough Pourriture Noble   ★★★★☆

The lovely 2014 vintage (★★★★★) is light gold, very honeyed and rich, with lush stone-fruit flavours, advanced sweetness (245 grams/litre of residual sugar), an oily texture and good acid spine. (Although not labelled by variety, it was made from botrytised Sauvignon Blanc grapes, picked in Marlborough at a super-ripe 46 brix.)

Vintage	14
WR	7
Drink	19-22

SW $32 (375ML) AV

Spy Valley Iced Marlborough Sauvignon Blanc   ★★★★☆

The golden 2015 vintage (★★★★) was hand-picked at 34 brix, with a noble rot infection, and fermented in tanks and barrels. It is fresh and sweet (157 grams/litre of residual sugar), with vibrant, citrusy, peachy flavours, balanced acidity, and a rich, harmonious finish. Delicious young.

Vintage	15	14
WR	6	6
Drink	19-20	P

SW $23 (375ML) V+

Stonecroft Gimblett Gravels Hawke's Bay Late Harvest Gewürztraminer   (★★★★★)

The lovely 2016 vintage (★★★★★) is from two passes through the vineyard, when 80 per cent of the grapes were botrytis-affected. It is full-bodied, with ripe, peachy, spicy, gently honeyed flavours, in a sweet but not super-sweet style (80 grams/litre of residual sugar), with strong personality. It should be long-lived.

Vintage	16
WR	6
Drink	19-25

SW $35 (375ML) AV

te Pā Marlborough Noble Sauvignon Blanc (★★★☆)

The 2017 vintage (★★★☆) is a single-vineyard, botrytised wine, late-picked in the Awatere Valley and partly (30 per cent) barrel-fermented. Light gold/green, with a slightly herbal fragrance, it is medium-bodied, with very good depth of apricot, honey and herb flavours, and plentiful sweetness (150 grams/litre of residual sugar).

 SW $30 (375ML) –V

Terra Sancta Late Harvest Bannockburn Central Otago Mysterious White (★★★★★)

The delicious 2015 vintage (★★★★★) is a blend of Muscat, Gewürztraminer and Riesling, estate-grown at Bannockburn, harvested in June, and aged in old French oak barrels. Softly seductive, it is perfumed, with concentrated peach and orange flavours, a hint of honey, abundant sweetness (112 grams/litre of residual sugar), and lovely balance, roundness and richness.

Vintage	15
WR	6
Drink	19-28

 SW $37 (375ML) AV

Tohu Raiha Reserve Limited Release Marlborough Noble Riesling ★★★★☆

The classy 2016 vintage (★★★★★) is an estate-grown, Awatere Valley wine. Bright yellow/green, with a scented, gently honeyed bouquet, it is delicious now, with intense, peachy, honeyed flavours, a slightly oily richness, and lovely balance of sweetness and acidity. Drink now or cellar.

 SW $28 (375ML) V+

Urlar Select Parcels Gladstone Noble Riesling ★★★★☆

Estate-grown in the northern Wairarapa and hand-picked, the 2017 vintage (★★★★☆) was partly barrel-aged. Bright, light yellow/green, it has a rich, honeyed bouquet. Well worth cellaring, but already drinking well, it has concentrated, peachy, citrusy flavours, firm acid spine, and a sweet (131 grams/litre of residual sugar), slightly oily finish.

Vintage	17
WR	6
Drink	19-25

 SW $30 (375ML) AV

Valli Late Harvest Waitaki North Otago Riesling ★★★★☆

The 2015 vintage (★★★★) is light-bodied (9 per cent alcohol), with strong, gently sweet flavours (85 grams/litre of residual sugar), citrusy, appley, and woven with appetising acidity. It should mature well.

 SW $45 (750ML) V+

Villa Maria Reserve Marlborough Noble Riesling Botrytis Selection ★★★★★

One of New Zealand's top sweet wines on the show circuit. It is typically stunningly perfumed, weighty and oily, with intense, very sweet honey/citrus flavours and a lush, long finish. The grapes are grown mainly in the Fletcher Vineyard, in the centre of Marlborough's Wairau Plains, where trees create a 'humidity crib' around the vines and sprinklers along the vines' fruit zone create ideal conditions for the spread of noble rot. The luscious 2015 vintage (★★★★★), hand-harvested in mid-May, is a pale gold wine, light (10 per cent alcohol), peachy, sweet (240 grams/litre of residual sugar), oily-textured and long, with instant appeal.

Vintage	15
WR	7
Drink	19-25

SW $37 (375ML) AV

Wairau River Botrytised Reserve Riesling   ★★★★☆

The 2017 vintage (★★★★☆) is golden, with apricot and honey aromas and flavours, rich and sweet. A lush wine with a powerful botrytis ('noble rot') influence, it's delicious young.

Vintage	17	16	15
WR	7	6	6
Drink	19-21	19-20	P

SW $30 (375ML) AV

Whitehaven Marlborough Noble Riesling   (★★★★★)

Already delicious, the 2018 vintage (★★★★★) is light green/gold, with a scented, honeyed bouquet. Light (9.5 per cent alcohol) and lovely, it has concentrated peach and apricot flavours, sweet (192 grams/litre of residual sugar) and crisp, and a slightly oily richness.

SW $30 (375ML) V+

Wooing Tree Tickled Pink   ★★★★

The pale red 2018 vintage (★★★★) is hard to resist in its youth. Made from Central Otago Pinot Noir, it was late-harvested and stop-fermented with 146 grams per litre of residual sugar. Deliciously fruity, sweet and smooth, with rich, berryish, plummy flavours, it's a distinctive wine, well worth trying.

SW $38 (375ML) –V

Sparkling Wines

Fizz, bubbly, *méthode traditionnelle*, sparkling – whatever name you call it by (the word Champagne is reserved for the wines of that most famous of all wine regions), wine with bubbles in it is universally adored.

How good are Kiwi bubblies? Good enough for the industry to export about 130,000 cases in 2018, although that accounts for less than 0.5 per cent of New Zealand's overseas wine shipments.

The selection of New Zealand bubblies is not wide, but has been boosted in recent years by an influx of low-priced sparkling Sauvignon Blancs, sparkling Pinot Gris and the like. Most small wineries find the production of bottle-fermented sparkling wine too time-consuming and costly, and the domestic demand for premium bubbly is limited. The vast majority of purchases are under $15.

New Zealand's sparkling wines can be divided into two key classes. The bottom end of the market is dominated by sweet, simple wines which acquire their bubbles by simply having carbon dioxide pumped into them. Upon pouring, the bubbles race out of the glass. A few other sparklings are made by the 'Charmat' method, which involves a secondary fermentation in a sealed tank.

At the middle and top end of the market are the much drier, bottle-fermented *méthode traditionnelle* (formerly *méthode Champenoise*, until the French got upset) labels, in which the wine undergoes its secondary, bubble-creating fermentation not in a tank but in the bottle, as in Champagne itself. Ultimately, the quality of any fine sparkling wine is a reflection both of the standard of its base wine and of its later period of maturation in the bottle in contact with its yeast lees. Only bottle-fermented sparkling wines possess the additional flavour richness and complexity derived from extended lees-aging.

Pinot Noir and Chardonnay, both varieties of key importance in Champagne, are also the foundation of New Zealand's top sparkling wines. Pinot Meunier, also extensively planted in Champagne, is still rare here, with 23 hectares of bearing vines in 2020.

Marlborough, with its cool nights preserving the grapes' fresh natural acidity, has emerged as the country's premier region for bottle-fermented sparkling wines (10 producers launched a promotional group, Méthode Marlborough, in 2013), but there are also some very stylish examples flowing from Central Otago.

The vast majority of sparkling wines are ready to drink when marketed, and need no extra maturation. A short spell in the cellar, however, can benefit the very best bottle-fermented sparklings.

Akarua Central Otago Brut NV ★★★★

This non-vintage wine has evolved over the past five years from a Pinot Noir-predominant style to a 2:1 blend of Chardonnay and Pinot Noir. Designed as an apéritif style, it is estate-grown at Bannockburn and disgorged after at least 18 months on its yeast lees. It is typically vivacious and smooth, with a fragrant, yeasty bouquet, citrusy, slightly appley and biscuity flavours, showing good complexity, and a crisp, harmonious finish.

MED/DRY $33 –V

Alpha Domus AD Cumulus Méthode Traditionnelle   (★★★★)

The 2015 vintage (★★★★) is a 'blanc de blancs' style, estate-grown and hand-picked in the Bridge Pa Triangle, Hawke's Bay. Partly barrel-fermented and closed with a crown seal, rather than a cork, it is light lemon/green, with a fragrant, citrusy, yeasty bouquet. Fresh, lemony, yeasty and dry (1 gram/litre of residual sugar), it is vivacious, with very good depth and complexity, and a smooth finish.

DRY $35 –V

Amisfield Central Otago Méthode Traditionnelle Brut   (★★★★★)

The classy 2015 vintage (★★★★★) was disgorged from its yeast lees in May 2018. Pale straw, with a complex, yeasty fragrance, it is crisp and lively, with excellent vigour and intensity of citrusy, yeasty, biscuity flavours, and a dry (2 grams/litre of residual sugar), lasting finish.

DRY $45 AV

Aurum Rosé Vintage   (★★★★)

The pale pink 2011 vintage (★★★★) was blended from estate-grown, Central Otago Pinot Gris and Pinot Noir, and disgorged after three years on its yeast lees. Mouthfilling and dryish (5 grams/litre of residual sugar), it has good complexity, vigour and intensity of berryish, gently spicy and yeasty flavours.

MED/DRY $34 –V

Brancott Estate New Zealand Brut Cuvée   ★★★☆

There's a lot to like about this bottle-fermented blend of Pinot Noir and Chardonnay, including its sharp price. A non-vintage wine from unidentified regions, it is typically pale pink and lively, with fresh peach and strawberry flavours, biscuity, yeasty notes adding complexity, and a smooth, dryish finish.

MED/DRY $14 V+

Clos Henri La Chappelle Blanc de Noirs   (★★★★)

This non-vintage wine is made entirely from Pinot Noir, estate-grown in the Wairau Valley, Marlborough, bottle-fermented and disgorged after 'long' lees-aging. Pale, crisp and lively, it's a dryish style (6 grams/litre of residual sugar), with citrusy, slightly appley, yeasty, lingering flavours and an invitingly scented bouquet.

MED/DRY $39 –V

Cloudy Bay Pelorus NV   ★★★★★

Cloudy Bay's non-vintage Marlborough bubbly is a Chardonnay-dominant style, with 30 per cent Pinot Noir, grown in the Wairau Valley and hand-picked. The base wines are fermented and aged in tanks, large oak vats and small French oak barrels, and the bottle-fermented blend is matured for at least two years on its yeast lees, before it is disgorged. Refined, tightly structured and elegant, it typically has strong, citrusy, peachy, yeasty flavours, showing excellent depth and harmony. The sample I tasted in late 2018 (★★★★★) is invitingly scented, with a yeasty, citrusy bouquet. Bright, light lemon/green, it is tightly structured and vivacious, with excellent richness and complexity, and a finely balanced, persistent finish.

MED/DRY $35 AV

Cloudy Bay Pelorus Rosé ★★★★★

This classy, non-vintage wine is a blend of Pinot Noir (mostly) and Chardonnay, hand-picked in the Wairau Valley, partly fermented in old oak vats and French oak barrels, and disgorged after at least two years maturing on its yeast lees. Pink/very pale red, the wine I tasted in mid to late 2018 (★★★★★) is mouthfilling and rich, 'serious' yet vivacious, with a strong surge of strawberryish, yeasty, complex flavours and a dryish, very harmonious and persistent finish.

Cloudy Bay Pelorus Vintage (★★★★★)

Now on sale, the classy 2010 vintage (★★★★★) is a very intensely flavoured blend of Pinot Noir and Chardonnay, estate-grown in Marlborough. It was disgorged after seven years' maturation on its yeast lees. Bright, light lemon/green, it is highly fragrant, with a complex, yeasty bouquet. Vivacious, with citrusy, peachy, biscuity flavours, crisp and complex, it's a real mouthful of flavour. Well worth discovering.

Daniel Le Brun Blanc de Blancs Méthode Traditionnelle ★★★★★

Disgorged after at least five years' maturation on its yeast lees, the very fresh, elegant, still youthful 2012 vintage (★★★★★) now on sale was made entirely from Chardonnay, grown in Marlborough. Light lemon/green, it is highly scented, citrusy, yeasty, crisp and lively, with a hint of cashew nuts, excellent complexity and a racy, dryish, lingering finish.

Daniel Le Brun Méthode Traditionnelle Brut NV ★★★★☆

This non-vintage blend of Chardonnay and Pinot Noir is grown in Marlborough and disgorged after at least two years on its yeast lees. The batch I tasted in June 2019 (★★★★☆) is vivacious, with very good intensity of citrusy, peachy, appley, slightly nutty flavours. A very attractive and harmonious wine, it's produced by Lion, owner of Wither Hills.

Daniel Le Brun Méthode Traditionnelle Rosé NV ★★★★☆

The pale pink, non-vintage wine I tasted in June 2019 (★★★★☆) was made from Pinot Noir grapes, hand-picked in Marlborough. Lively, with gentle strawberry, watermelon and peach flavours, it has yeasty notes adding complexity and a finely balanced, very harmonious finish.

MED/DRY $30 AV

Daniel Le Brun Vintage Méthode Traditionnelle   ★★★★★

The 2010 vintage (★★★★★), currently on sale, is a blend of Marlborough Pinot Noir and Chardonnay, disgorged after six years on its yeast lees. Bright, light lemon/green, it is very refined and vigorous, with a fresh, complex bouquet, yeasty and slightly nutty. A very 'complete' wine, it has generous, peachy, yeasty flavours, with a distinct hint of cashew nuts, and a long, rich finish.

MED/DRY $40 AV

De La Terre Cuvée 11 Hawke's Bay Méthode Traditionnelle   (★★★★☆)

The stylish 2015 vintage (★★★★☆) was estate-grown at Havelock North. Invitingly scented and vivacious, it is appetisingly crisp, with citrusy, gently yeasty flavours, showing excellent intensity, good complexity and a lasting finish.

MED/DRY $40 –V

Deutz Marlborough Cuvée Blanc de Blancs   ★★★★★

New Zealand's most awarded bubbly on the show circuit. This Chardonnay-predominant blend is hand-harvested on the south side of the Wairau Valley, at Renwick Estate and in the Brancott Vineyard, and matured for up to three years on its yeast lees. It is typically a very classy wine with delicate, piercing, lemony, appley flavours, well-integrated yeastiness, and a slightly creamy finish. The 2015 vintage (★★★★★) is a light lemon/green, vivacious wine with a scented, lemony, yeasty bouquet. It has fresh, citrusy, yeasty flavours, showing excellent intensity, delicacy and complexity, that build across the palate to a dryish, lasting finish.

MED/DRY $30 V+

Deutz Marlborough Cuvée Brut NV   ★★★★☆

The marriage of Pernod Ricard NZ's fruit at Marlborough with the Champagne house of Deutz's 150 years of experience created an instant winner. Bottled-fermented and matured on its yeast lees for two to three years, this non-vintage wine has evolved over the past decade into a less overtly fruity, more delicate and flinty style. The Pinot Noir grapes are drawn principally from Kaituna Estate, on the north side of the Wairau Valley; the Chardonnay comes mostly from Renwick Estate, in the middle of the valley. Before being bottled, the base wine is lees-aged for up to three months and given a full malolactic fermentation. Reserve wines, a year or two older than the rest, are added to each batch, contributing consistency and complexity to the final blend. The wine I tasted in 2018 (★★★★☆) was vivacious and smooth, with vibrant, citrusy, biscuity, yeasty flavours, showing excellent complexity and harmony.

MED/DRY $27 V+

Deutz Marlborough Prestige Cuvée ★★★★★

Well worth discovering, this is typically a very classy wine. The outstanding 2015 vintage (★★★★★) is a 2:1 blend of Chardonnay and Pinot Noir. Pale straw, it is notably complex and tight-knit, with searching, citrusy, yeasty, slightly peachy flavours that float across the palate to a crisp, lasting finish. A 'complete' wine, it offers top value.

MED/DRY $33 V+

Deutz Marlborough Cuvée Rosé ★★★★

Offering easy drinking, this non-vintage wine (★★★★) is a pale pink sparkling, made principally from Pinot Noir. Lively and finely balanced, it typically has peachy, strawberryish, yeasty flavours, showing good freshness and complexity, and an off-dry, crisp finish.

MED/DRY $27 AV

Dulcét Brut (★★★☆)

This easy-drinking, non-vintage wine is a blend of Gisborne Chardonnay and Pinot Noir, given its secondary, bubble-inducing fermentation in tanks. Fresh, crisp, peachy and citrusy, with a touch of complexity, it is vibrantly fruity, with good depth, and a slightly sweet (7.3 grams/litre of residual sugar) finish. (From Villa Maria.)

MED/DRY $20 AV

En Rose ★★★★☆

This Martinborough sparkling is based entirely on Pinot Noir. The 2014 vintage (★★★★), disgorged after three years on its yeast lees, is an orange/very pale red wine, showing good complexity. Crisp and basically dry (5 grams/litre of residual sugar), it has strong, strawberryish flavours, hints of oranges and nuts, and a long finish. (From Margrain.)

MED/DRY $45 –V

Gibbston Valley NV Méthode Traditionnelle ★★★★★

This classy wine, from grapes hand-picked in Central Otago, is disgorged after 26 to 29 months on its yeast lees. Pale straw, it's typically a hugely drinkable wine, crisp and vivacious, with intense, citrusy, slightly peachy and appley flavours, good yeast-derived complexity, and a smooth, very finely balanced, lasting finish.

MED/DRY $50 AV

Gibbston Valley Rosé Méthode Traditionnelle (★★★★★)

Disgorged in late 2016, the distinctive 2011 vintage (★★★★★) was made from barrel-fermented base wine, bottle-fermented and matured on its yeast lees for four and a half years. Pink-hued, with a hint of orange, it is a highly complex wine, with peach, strawberry and spice flavours, showing lovely depth, and a long, yeasty, dry (4 grams/litre of residual sugar), very harmonious finish. It's ready to roll.

DRY $120 –V

Gold Digger Frizzante Naturally Sparkling Pinot Gris ★★★

Ensconced in a beer bottle with a crown seal, this non-vintage wine is from Maori Point Vineyard, at Tarras, in Central Otago. Based on Pinot Gris, it is tank-fermented and made in a gently sparkling, dryish style (8 grams/litre of residual sugar). Very easy to enjoy, it is fresh, light and zesty, with crisp, peachy flavours, hints of pears and apples, and a smooth finish.

MED/DRY $11 (330ML) AV

Gold Digger Frizzante Naturally Sparkling Rosé (★★★★)

From Maori Point, in Central Otago, this non-vintage wine is instantly appealing. Bright, light pink, it is light and lively, with vibrant strawberry and watermelon flavours, yeasty notes, and a crisp, off-dry (8 grams/litre of residual sugar), lingering finish.

MED/DRY $12 (330ML) AV

Haha Brut Cuvée ★★★★

The non-vintage wine (★★★★) I tasted in April 2019 offers good value. Blended from Chardonnay (56 per cent) and Pinot Noir (44 per cent), grown in Marlborough, it is an elegant wine, fragrant and lively, with fresh, strong, citrusy, appley, yeasty flavours and a dryish (6.6 grams/litre of residual sugar), crisp finish.

MED/DRY $22 V+

Haha Brut Rosé ★★★★

Offering good value, the non-vintage (★★★★) sparkling I tasted in 2019 is a blend of Chardonnay and Pinot Noir, grown in Marlborough and Hawke's Bay. Pale pink, with fresh, strawberryish, slightly yeasty aromas, it is vivacious, with strong peach, strawberry and spice flavours, and a dry (4.9 grams/litre of residual sugar), gently yeasty, crisp finish. Very lively and likeable.

DRY $22 V+

Hans Herzog Cuvée Therese Rosé Méthode Traditionnelle Brut ★★★★★

Tasted in early 2019, the 2014 vintage (★★★★★) was barrel-aged for 18 months, bottle-fermented and made in a bone-dry style. Light red, with a fragrant, complex bouquet, it is crisp and very lively, with strawberryish, slightly spicy flavours, showing excellent intensity. A highly distinctive wine, it's well worth discovering. The 2015 vintage (★★★★☆) was also barrel-aged for 18 months and bottle-fermented. Light red, it has strong strawberry and spice flavours, showing good complexity, and a dry (4 grams/litre of residual sugar), smooth finish.

DRY $64 AV

Hunter's Miru Miru NV ★★★★☆

'Miru Miru' means 'Bubbles'. This Marlborough wine is disgorged after a minimum of 18 months on its yeast lees (earlier than its Reserve stablemate, below), has a lower Pinot Noir content and a crisper finish. The very lively, non-vintage wine (★★★★☆) I tasted in mid-2019 is a blend of Chardonnay (50 per cent), Pinot Noir (46 per cent) and Pinot Meunier (4 per cent). Pale lemon/green, it has rich, peachy, slightly citrusy and appley flavours, toasty notes adding complexity, and a crisp, dryish finish. Good value.

MED/DRY $29 V+

Hunter's Miru Miru Reserve ★★★★★

This has long been one of Marlborough's best sparklings, full and lively, with loads of citrusy, yeasty, nutty flavour and a creamy, long finish. It is matured on its yeast lees for an average of three and a half years. The 2013 vintage (★★★★★) is a blend of Pinot Noir, Chardonnay and Pinot Meunier. It's a very elegant and tight-knit wine, with crisp, citrusy, yeasty flavours, a dry impression (6 grams/litre of residual sugar), and a very long, harmonious finish.

Vintage	13
WR	6
Drink	19-22

MED/DRY $50 AV

Hunter's Miru Miru Rosé NV (★★★★★)

The very classy, non-vintage wine (★★★★★) now on sale was blended from Pinot Noir (55 per cent), Chardonnay (41 per cent) and Pinot Meunier (4 per cent), and disgorged after three years on its yeast lees. Pink/pale orange, it is highly scented, vivacious, complex and smooth, with strawberry, peach and yeast flavours, and a long, dryish (7.5 grams/litre of residual sugar), very finely balanced finish. Well worth trying.

MED/DRY $39 AV

Hunter's Offshoot Marlborough Sauvignon Blanc (★★☆)

The distinctive 2018 vintage (★★☆) was grown in the Wairau Valley and bottled while still fermenting in tanks, 'to create a naturally carbonated sparkling wine'. Medium-bodied, with cloudy sediment in the bottle, it is gently bubbly, with lively, appley flavours and a slightly sweet, crisp finish, but basically simple, lacking richness and complexity. (Cellar door and website sales only.)

MED/DRY $25 –V

Johanneshof Cellars Blanc de Blancs NV ★★★★☆

Released after a minimum of five years' maturation on its yeast lees, this Chardonnay-based Marlborough wine is hand-picked and barrel-fermented. The very refreshing, non-vintage batch (★★★★☆) I tasted in 2018 has a lemony, gently yeasty fragrance. Crisp, lively and tightly structured, it is vivacious, with strong, citrusy, moderately yeasty flavours and a very persistent finish.

MED/DRY $38 –V

Johanneshof Cellars Emmi ★★★★☆

Now on sale, the 2009 vintage (★★★★★) is a blend of Pinot Noir and Chardonnay, hand-picked in Marlborough and disgorged after at least five years on its yeast lees. Very pale straw, it shows excellent complexity, with rich, peachy, citrusy, yeasty, gently toasty flavours and a smooth, very harmonious finish. It's delicious now.

MED/DRY $40 –V

Johanneshof Cellars New Dawn Marlborough Brut   (★★★★★)

Still on sale, the classy, deliciously smooth 2010 vintage (★★★★★) was made from Pinot Noir, hand-harvested in Marlborough and disgorged after a minimum of five years on its yeast lees. Very pale pink, it is highly scented, with gentle strawberry, peach and spice flavours, showing lovely delicacy and complexity. Yeasty and dryish, with excellent harmony, it's well worth discovering.

MED/DRY $38 AV

Johner Estate Wairarapa Méthode Traditionnelle Brut   (★★★★☆)

The characterful 2016 vintage (★★★★☆) is a blend of Pinot Noir (55 per cent) and Chardonnay (45 per cent), oak-aged for six months, then bottle-fermented and lees-aged. Bright, light yellow, it is crisp and lively, with peachy, citrusy, yeasty flavours, showing excellent vigour, complexity and intensity, and a finely balanced, dryish finish.

MED/DRY $36 –V

June Nelson Méthode Traditionnelle   (★★★☆)

Still on sale, the 2009 vintage (★★★☆) is from Kaimira Estate. A pale straw blend of Chardonnay (78 per cent) and Pinot Noir (22 per cent), it was grown at Brightwater and disgorged after six years aging on its yeast lees. The bouquet is citrusy; the palate is tightly structured, crisp and lemony, with considerable complexity, and a dryish (6 grams/litre of residual sugar), smooth finish.

MED/DRY $39 –V

Kahurangi Estate Vintage Reserve Blanc de Blancs   (★★★★☆)

The crisp, elegant 2016 vintage (★★★★☆) was grown in Nelson. Bright, light lemon/green, with fragrant, citrusy, yeasty aromas, it is very lively, with strong, citrusy, gently yeasty flavours, showing excellent intensity and vigour.

MED/DRY $36 –V

Kalex Pinot Noir Rosé Brut   ★★★★

Showing good complexity, the 2012 vintage (★★★★), currently on sale, was estate-grown in Central Otago. Pale pink/orange, with a fragrant, yeasty bouquet, it is crisp and lively, with peachy, strawberryish, yeasty flavours, and a dry (4.3 grams/litre of residual sugar) finish. Ready.

DRY $40 –V

Kumeu River Kumeu Crémant   (★★★★★)

Bottled in early 2015 and disgorged in December 2018, the non-vintage wine (★★★★★) I tasted in mid to late 2019 is impressive. Light lemon/green, it is crisp and dry, with strong, citrusy, slightly nutty flavours, showing excellent vigour, intensity and complexity. Fragrant, it's a highly distinctive wine, well worth trying.

DRY $50 AV

La Michelle ★★★★☆

From Margrain, the 2014 vintage (★★★★☆) is a bottle-fermented bubbly, blended from Pinot Noir (66 per cent) and Chardonnay (34 per cent), grown in Martinborough and made in an unusually dry style (4 grams/litre of residual sugar). Disgorged after a minimum of 30 months on its yeast lees, it is pale yellow, with a fragrant, very yeasty bouquet. It has strong, lively, citrusy, yeasty flavours, showing excellent vigour and complexity, and a lengthy finish.

 DRY $45 –V

Leveret IQ Premium Brut NV ★★★☆

This vivacious Hawke's Bay sparkling is a blend of Pinot Noir, Chardonnay and Pinot Meunier, disgorged after a minimum of 18 months on its yeast lees. The non-vintage wine I tasted in mid-2019 (★★★★) is bright, light yellow and invitingly scented, with fresh, lively grapefruit and peach flavours, biscuity, yeasty characters adding complexity, and a crisp, finely balanced finish.

 MED/DRY $22 AV

Leveret IQ Rosé Méthode Traditionnelle ★★★

The non-vintage wine (★★★) I tasted in mid to late 2019 is a Hawke's Bay blend of Pinot Noir, Chardonnay and Pinot Meunier. Orange/slight amber, it is gently yeasty, with plenty of mature, peachy, spicy flavour and an off-dry (9.5 grams/litre of residual sugar), crisp finish.

 MED/DRY $22 –V

Leveret IQ3 Méthode Traditionnelle ★★★☆

The non-vintage wine (★★★) I tasted in late 2018 was made from Chardonnay grapes, grown in Hawke's Bay, and disgorged after a minimum of three years on its yeast lees. Bright, light yellow/green, it is a mature wine, distinctly citrusy, with yeasty, toasty notes adding complexity and a smooth, off-dry finish.

 MED/DRY $25 –V

Lindaeur Special Reserve Cuvée Riche ★★★☆

The non-vintage wine (★★★☆) I tasted in late 2018 was grown in Hawke's Bay and Gisborne. Straw-coloured, with a hint of orange, it is a sweetish style, with good depth of strawberryish, peachy flavours, showing some yeasty complexity, and a crisp, smooth finish.

 MED $16 V+

Lindauer Brut Cuvée NV ★★★

Given its track record of good quality, low price and huge volumes (batch variation is inevitable), this non-vintage bubbly has been a miracle of modern winemaking for several decades. Made from Pinot Noir and Chardonnay, grown in Gisborne and Hawke's Bay, it is matured for a year on its yeast lees, and blended with some reserve wine from past vintages. Fractionally sweet (12 grams/litre of residual sugar), it typically has good vigour and depth, with moderate complexity and lively, lemony, slightly nutty and yeasty flavours.

MED/DRY $10 V+

Lindauer Enlighten Moscato Rosé ★★★

'Enlighten' is – you guessed it – a range of light wines, and this charmer is just 8.5 per cent alcohol. Based on Muscat grapes, grown in Gisborne, it was blended with a splash of Pinotage (hence its enticing, pale pink hue). Deliciously light and lively, it is unabashedly sweet (60 grams/litre of residual sugar), but very crisp, fruity and well-balanced, in a simple but vivacious style that offers plenty of pleasure.

SW $13 V+

Lindauer Enlighten Pinot Gris (★★☆)

Offering easy drinking, the lively non-vintage wine (★★☆) I tasted in 2018 is low in alcohol (8.5 per cent), with a gentle stream of bubbles and fresh, peachy, citrusy flavours, fruity and smooth.

MED $13 AV

Lindauer Enlighten Sauvignon Blanc ★★

The non-vintage wine (★★) I tasted in 2018 is light-bodied (8.5 per cent alcohol), with slightly appley aromas and lively, green-edged flavours, fresh and smooth.

MED/DRY $13 –V

Lindauer Fraise (★★)

The non-vintage wine (★★) I tasted in 2018 is labelled 'Lindauer and Strawberry', meaning it has been 'infused with natural strawberry essence'. It offers crisp, easy drinking, with – you guessed it – fresh, strawberryish aromas and flavours.

MED $13 –V

Lindauer Pinot Gris ★★★

The non-vintage wine (★★★) I tasted in 2018 is fresh and lively, with good depth of peach and pear-like flavours, gentle sweetness, balanced acidity, and lots of easy-drinking charm.

MED/DRY $13 V+

Lindauer Rosé ★★★

The non-vintage wine (★★☆) I tasted in 2018 is a blend of Chardonnay and Pinot Noir, grown in Gisborne and Hawke's Bay. Pink/orange, with a hint of development, it is dryish, with peachy, strawberryish flavours.

MED/DRY $13 V+

Lindauer Sauvignon Blanc (★★☆)

The non-vintage wine (★★☆) I tasted in 2018 is aromatic, with herbaceous, uncomplicated flavours, fresh and lively.

MED/DRY $13 AV

Lindauer Special Reserve Blanc de Blancs   ★★★★

The non-vintage wine (★★★★) I tasted in 2019 was made from Gisborne Chardonnay and bottle-fermented. Very pale straw, with a yeasty fragrance, it is lively and lemony, with very good intensity and a finely balanced, dryish finish. Great value.

MED/DRY $15 V+

Lindauer Special Reserve Brut Cuveé   ★★★★

The non-vintage wine (★★★★) I tasted in late 2018 is a bottle-fermented blend of Pinot Noir and Chardonnay, grown in Hawke's Bay and Gisborne. Pale pink, it looks like a sparkling rosé, with fresh, strawberryish, yeasty aromas and flavours, a hint of apricot, and impressive intensity and length. A great buy.

MED/DRY $16 V+

Lindauer Special Reserve Rosé   ★★★★

The non-vintage wine (★★★★) I tasted in 2018 offers fine value. Bottle-fermented, it is pink/pale red, with a fresh, yeasty bouquet, lively, strawberryish flavours, yeasty notes adding complexity and a finely balanced, dryish finish.

MED/DRY $15 V+

Lindauer Summer Blush   (★★★)

The non-vintage wine (★★★) I tasted in 2018 is a 'sparkling rosé', made from Pinot Noir and other varieties. Pale pink, it is fresh and crisp, with gentle peach, strawberry and spice flavours, a touch of complexity and a dryish finish.

MED/DRY $13 V+

Lindauer White Moscato   (★★★☆)

'Perfect for lunching with the girls', this recent addition to the Lindauer range (★★★☆) is from Muscat grapes grown in Gisborne. Light lemon/green, it is perfumed, frothy, very lively and light (9 per cent alcohol), with fresh, ripe, peachy, slightly appley flavours and a sweetish finish. Asti Spumante-like, it's priced sharply.

SW $14 V+

LV by Louis Vavasour Marlborough Méthode Traditionnelle NV   (★★★★★)

Rich but refined, the non-vintage wine (★★★★★) I tasted in late 2018 is a blend of Pinot Noir (principally) and Chardonnay, disgorged after more than two years on its yeast lees. Light lemon/green, with a rich, yeasty fragrance, it is lively, with strong, peachy, complex flavours, balanced acidity and a smooth, very long finish. Full of personality, it makes a powerful statement. (From Awatere River Wine Co.)

MED/DRY $49 AV

Morton [Black Label] Brut ★★★★

The non-vintage wine (★★★★) I tasted in late 2018 was produced from Chardonnay and Pinot Noir, grown in Hawke's Bay and Marlborough. Pale straw, it is fresh, yeasty, crisp and dry, with strong, biscuity, toasty flavours, showing good complexity, and a sustained finish. Fine value.

MED/DRY $20 V+

Morton Brut ★★★☆

The non-vintage wine (★★★☆) I tasted in 2018 is a blend of Chardonnay, Pinot Noir and Pinot Meunier, disgorged after at least 18 months on its yeast lees. Pale straw, it has peachy, yeasty, toasty flavours, showing considerable complexity, and a dryish finish. Good value.

MED/DRY $18 V+

Nautilus Cuvée Marlborough ★★★★★

Recent releases of this non-vintage, bottle-fermented sparkling have generally revealed an intensity and refinement that positions the label among the finest in the country. Made with Pinot Noir (mostly) and Chardonnay, it is blended with older, reserve stocks held in old oak barriques and disgorged after a minimum of three years aging on its yeast lees. Lean and crisp, piercing and long, it's a beautifully tight, vivacious and refined wine, its Marlborough fruit characters enriched with intense, bready aromas and flavours. The sample I tasted in August 2019 (★★★★★) was – as the back label indicates helpfully – bottled in October 2015 and disgorged in May 2019. A blend of Pinot Noir (73 per cent) and Chardonnay (27 per cent), it was blended with 12 per cent reserve stocks. Refined and complex, it has intense, citrusy, peachy, yeasty, nutty flavours and a smooth, finely poised, dryish (6 grams/litre of residual sugar), lingering finish.

MED/DRY $43 AV

Nautilus Cuvée Marlborough Vintage Rosé ★★★★★

The vivacious 2016 vintage (★★★★★), made entirely from Pinot Noir, was bottle-fermented and disgorged after two and a half years on its yeast lees in May 2019. Pale pink, it is elegant and tightly structured, with intense, strawberryish, peachy, yeasty flavours, showing excellent complexity, and an inviting fragrance.

MED/DRY $49 AV

Nikau Point Gold Méthode Traditionnelle ★★★

The non-vintage wine (★★★) I tasted in late 2019 is a blend of Chardonnay, Pinot Noir and Pinot Meunier. Pale straw, it's a crisp, gently sweet style (12 grams/litre of residual sugar), with a touch of complexity and plenty of citrusy, peachy, gently yeasty flavour.

MED/DRY $16 AV

No 1 Cuvée Virginie   ★★★★★

Currently on sale, the 2009 vintage (★★★★★) is very classy. A Marlborough blend of
Chardonnay (80 per cent) and Pinot Noir (20 per cent), it was disgorged after more than four
years on its yeast lees. Bright yellow, with an inviting, complex bouquet, it has vibrant, citrusy,
yeasty flavours, showing notable intensity, vigour and harmony. A lovely mouthful.

 MED/DRY $95 –V

Osawa Prestige Collection Méthode Traditionnelle NV   (★★★★☆)

The non-vintage wine (★★★★☆) I tasted in 2018 is a stylish sparkling, matured for three and
a half years on its yeast lees, with base wine dating back to 2009. Made from equal portions
of Chardonnay and Pinot Noir, grown at Maraekakaho, in Hawke's Bay, it has an invitingly
fragrant, lively, yeasty bouquet. Crisp and lively, with citrusy, biscuity flavours, it shows excellent
vigour, complexity and length.

 MED/DRY $55 –V

Oyster Bay Sparkling Cuvée Brut   ★★★☆

Chardonnay-based, this Hawke's Bay wine is a blanc de blancs style, with fresh, citrusy fruit
flavours to the fore. Made by the Charmat method (where the secondary, bubble-inducing
fermentation occurs in tanks, rather than in the individual bottles), the wine I tasted in mid
to late 2019 (★★★★) is instantly likeable. Bright, light lemon/green, it has a fragrant, fresh,
citrusy, gently yeasty bouquet. Vivacious, it has good vigour and intensity, with a distinct touch
of complexity and a dryish finish.

MED/DRY $22 AV

Oyster Bay Sparkling Cuvée Rosé   ★★★☆

The non-vintage wine (★★★★) I tasted in mid to late 2019 was blended from Hawke's
Bay Chardonnay (mostly) and Marlborough Pinot Noir. Pale pink, it is lively, with strong,
strawberryish, peachy, spicy flavours, gentle yeasty notes adding complexity, and a dryish, finely
balanced finish.

MED/DRY $22 AV

Palliser Estate The Griffin Martinborough Méthode Traditionnelle   (★★★★★)

The 2015 vintage (★★★★★) is an elegant, bottle-fermented blend of Pinot Noir (50 per
cent) and Chardonnay (50 per cent), disgorged in March 2018. It has a highly scented, yeasty
bouquet, leading into a vivacious wine with citrusy, slightly appley, distinctly yeasty flavours,
very harmonious, delicate, racy and long.

 MED/DRY $52 AV

Pask Declaration Gimblett Gravels Méthode Traditionnelle   (★★★★☆)

Still on sale, the 2010 vintage (★★★★☆) is mature, but still extremely lively. Closed with a
crown seal, it is a blend of barrel-fermented Chardonnay (80 per cent) and Pinot Noir (20 per
cent), disgorged after seven years on its yeast lees. Released in late 2018, it is pale straw, fragrant
and full-bodied, with very toasty, biscuity aromas and flavours, rich and complex, and a dry,
smooth, lingering finish.

 MED/DRY $30 AV

Porters Reserve Martinborough Cuvée Zoe (★★★★☆)

Drinking well now, the 2012 vintage (★★★★☆) was handled in old oak casks. Pale straw, with a biscuity, yeasty fragrance, it's a distinctive wine, with strong, citrusy, peachy flavours, showing excellent vigour and complexity, and a basically dry (5 grams/litre of residual sugar) finish.

MED/DRY $60 –V

Quartz Reef Méthode Traditionnelle Brut NV ★★★★☆

This increasingly Champagne-like, non-vintage bubbly is estate-grown at Bendigo, in Central Otago, and lees-aged for at least two years. The batches vary in their varietal composition, but the release I tasted in 2018 (★★★★☆) is a blend of Pinot Noir (62 per cent) and Chardonnay (38 per cent), disgorged from autumn 2018 onwards. Very pale straw, with a refined, yeasty bouquet, it has very harmonious, citrusy, biscuity, yeasty flavours and a smooth, dry (4 grams/litre of residual sugar), lingering finish. Certified biodynamic.

DRY $35 –V

Quartz Reef Méthode Traditionnelle Rosé ★★★★☆

Instantly appealing, the vivacious, non-vintage wine (★★★★★) I tasted in 2018 was estate-grown at Bendigo, in Central Otago. Made entirely from Pinot Noir and disgorged in autumn 2018, it is bright pink, with a fragrant, berryish, gently yeasty bouquet. Crisp and tightly structured, it has lively peach, strawberry and apricot flavours, showing impressive depth and complexity, and a finely textured, smooth, dry (4 grams/litre of residual sugar) finish.

DRY $45 –V

Quartz Reef Méthode Traditionnelle Vintage Blanc de Blancs ★★★★★

Top vintages are outstanding, showing great vigour and complexity in a Champagne-like style, intense and highly refined. A wine of great presence, the vivacious 2013 vintage (★★★★★) is promoted as the 'crown jewel' of Quartz Reef's Central Otago sparklings. A blend of Chardonnay (91 per cent) and Pinot Noir (9 per cent), estate-grown at Bendigo, it is pale straw, with very intense, citrusy, yeasty, biscuity flavours, crisp acidity, and a lasting, dry (4 grams/litre of residual sugar) finish.

DRY $75 AV

Rock Ferry Blanc de Blancs ★★★★☆

Currently on sale, the classy 2012 vintage (★★★★★) was made entirely from Chardonnay, estate-grown in The Corners Vineyard at Rapaura, in Marlborough. Hand-picked and fermented in a mix of old oak and stainless steel barrels, it was disgorged after four years on its yeast lees. Light lemon/green, it has a richly scented, citrusy, yeasty bouquet. A distinctive wine, it is crisp and intense, with penetrating, lively, lemony, yeasty flavours, slightly toasty notes adding complexity, and an unusually dry (3.5 grams/litre of residual sugar), lasting finish. Certified organic.

DRY $45 –V

Saint Clair Dawn Méthode Traditionnelle ★★★★☆

An elegant 2:1 blend of Marlborough Chardonnay and Pinot Noir, the 2013 vintage (★★★★) was disgorged after nearly three years on its yeast lees. Light lemon/green, it is lively and medium-bodied, with good intensity of citrusy, appley flavours, yeasty, biscuity notes adding complexity, and a crisp, dryish finish.

MED/DRY $45 –V

Saint Clair Vicar's Choice Marlborough Sauvignon Blanc Bubbles (★★☆)

The 2017 vintage (★★☆) is crisp and lively, in a refreshing, simple style with clearly varietal, herbaceous flavours and an off-dry (9.9 grams/litre of residual sugar) finish.

MED/DRY $18 –V

Selaks Reserve Sparkling Marlborough Sauvignon Blanc (★★★)

The 2017 vintage (★★★) is a fresh, strongly varietal wine, balanced for easy drinking, with ripely herbaceous flavours, showing good depth, and a slightly sweet, crisp finish.

MED $15 AV

Soljans Fusion Sparkling Moscato ★★★★

This 'Asti-style' bubbly has a long, proud history. The wine I tasted in 2019 (★★★★) is perfumed and light (8.5 per cent alcohol), with vivacious, crisp, sweetly seductive flavours, simple but full of charm.

SW $15 V+

Soljans Legacy Méthode Traditionnelle ★★★★☆

Now on sale, the 2013 vintage (★★★★☆) is a blend of Hawke's Bay Chardonnay (60 per cent) and Marlborough Pinot Noir (40 per cent), disgorged after three years on its yeast lees. Light yellow/green, it is rich and lively, with peachy, yeasty, toasty flavours, showing very good complexity, and a finely balanced, smooth (9.5 grams/litre of residual sugar) finish.

MED/DRY $33 AV

Te Hana Reserve Cuvée (★★★★)

Offering great value, the non-vintage wine (★★★★) I tasted in late 2018 is a Gisborne sparkling, blended from Chardonnay (mostly) and Pinot Noir. Pale straw, with a yeasty fragrance, showing good complexity, it is vivacious, with strong, citrusy, biscuity flavours and a crisp, dryish finish. (From Lion.)

MED/DRY $17 V+

Te Hana Rosé Cuvée (★★★★)

Bargain-priced, the non-vintage wine (★★★★) I tasted in late 2018 is a Gisborne bubbly, bright pink, fresh and lively. It has strawberry and watermelon flavours, yeasty notes adding complexity and a finely poised finish. (From Lion.)

MED/DRY $17 V+

Thomas Waiheke Island Blanc De Gris ★★★★

The vivacious 2017 vintage (★★★★) of this Waiheke Island sparkling is a distinctive blend of Pinot Gris (78 per cent) and Flora (22 per cent). Very fresh and aromatic, it is crisp and lively, with vibrant, pear-like flavours, slightly citrusy and spicy, lees-aging notes adding a touch of complexity, and an off-dry, finely balanced finish.

MED $46 –V

Tohu Rewa Marlborough Blanc de Blancs Méthode Traditionnelle ★★★★☆

The attractive 2015 vintage (★★★★☆) is a very fresh, elegant sparkling, from hand-picked Chardonnay grapes. Disgorged after 27 months on its yeast lees, it is bright, light lemon/green, with a fragrant, citrusy, yeasty bouquet. Crisp and lively, it is a tight-knit, complex wine with lemony, slightly appley flavours, showing good intensity and harmony, and a lingering finish.

DRY $34 AV

Tohu Rewa Marlborough Rosé Méthode Traditionnelle (★★★★☆)

The 2015 vintage (★★★★☆) was made from Pinot Noir, disgorged after two years on its yeast lees. Bright, light pink, it is fragrant, fresh and vivacious, with crisp, strawberryish, yeasty flavours, showing excellent delicacy, harmony and length.

MED/DRY $34 AV

Twin Islands Pinot Noir/Chardonnay Brut NV ★★★★

'A great bottle to be seen with in some of the classiest bars and restaurants', Nautilus's sparkling is a bottle-fermented, non-vintage style. The batch I tasted in mid to late 2018 (★★★★) is dryish (10 grams/litre of residual sugar), crisp and vivacious, with strong, citrusy, slightly appley, gently yeasty flavours, showing considerable complexity.

MED/DRY $25 AV

Wither Hills Cellar Selection Marlborough Frivoli (★★★★)

A 'new perspective of Marlborough in a glass', the 2018 vintage (★★★★) is from Gewürztraminer vines, estate-grown in the Taylor River Vineyard. Pale pink, it is an instantly appealing, vivacious wine, light-bodied (8 per cent alcohol), with gentle, peachy, strawberryish flavours, showing excellent delicacy and freshness, and a smooth, sweetish finish.

SW $25 AV

Rosé Wines

The number of rosé labels on the market has exploded recently, as drinkers discover that rosé is not an inherently inferior lolly water, but a worthwhile and delicious wine style in its own right. The rising popularity of '2 o'clock lunches' is believed to have helped sales. New Zealand rosé is even finding offshore markets (over 400,000 cases in 2018) and collecting overseas awards.

In Europe many pink or copper-coloured wines, such as the rosés of Provence, Anjou and Tavel, are produced from red-wine varieties. (Dark-skinned grapes are even used to make white wines: Champagne, heavily based on Pinot Meunier and Pinot Noir, is a classic case.) To make a rosé, after the grapes are crushed, the time the juice spends in contact with its skins is crucial; the longer the contact, the greater the diffusion of colour, tannin and flavour from the skins into the juice.

'Saignée' (bled) is a French term that is seen occasionally on rosé labels. A technique designed to produce a pink wine or a more concentrated red wine – or both – it involves running off or 'bleeding' free-run juice from crushed, dark-skinned grapes after a brief, pre-ferment maceration on skins. An alternative is to commence the fermentation as for a red wine, then after 12 or 24 hours, when its colour starts to deepen, drain part of the juice for rosé production and vinify the rest as a red wine.

Pinot Noir and Merlot are the grape varieties most commonly used in New Zealand to produce rosé wines. Regional differences are emerging. South Island and Wairarapa rosés, usually made from Pinot Noir, are typically fresh, crisp and often slightly sweet, while those from the middle and upper North Island – Hawke's Bay, Gisborne and Auckland – tend to be Merlot-based, fuller-bodied and drier.

These are typically charming, 'now-or-never' wines, peaking in their first 12 to 18 months with seductive strawberry/raspberry-like fruit flavours. Freshness is the essence of the wines' appeal.

Alchemy Hawke's Bay Rosé (★★★★)

The highly attractive 2018 vintage (★★★★) was made from hand-picked Merlot grapes and aged on its yeast lees in tanks. Pale pink, it is mouthfilling and lively, with peach, strawberry and spice flavours, showing very good delicacy and freshness, and a finely balanced, smooth finish. Priced right.

DRY $20 V+

Alexander Raumati Martinborough Pinot Noir Rosé ★★★★

Tasted in mid to late 2019, the 2018 vintage (★★★★) was estate-grown, hand-picked and made in a fully dry (1.4 grams/litre of residual sugar) style. Pale pink, it is fresh and full-bodied, with strong watermelon and spice flavours, hints of peaches and apricots, and lots of current-drinking appeal.

DRY $24 AV

Allan Scott Marlborough Rosé ★★★☆

Released as early as May, the very easy-drinking 2019 vintage (★★★) is pale pink, scented and lively, with peachy, strawberryish flavours, a gentle splash of sweetness (11 grams/litre of residual sugar), balanced acidity, and a fresh, smooth finish.

MED/DRY $18 V+

Amisfield Central Otago Pinot Noir Rosé   ★★★★

Estate-grown and hand-harvested in the Cromwell Basin, and mostly handled in tanks (4 per cent barrel-fermented), the delicious 2018 vintage (★★★★☆) has an inviting, bright pink hue. Made in a slightly off-dry style (6.1 grams/litre of residual sugar), it has fresh, lively strawberry, watermelon, plum and spice flavours, showing a distinct touch of complexity, balanced acidity, and excellent depth and harmony.

Vintage	18
WR	6
Drink	P

 MED/DRY $30 –V

Anchorage Nelson Pinot Rosé   (★★★)

Fresh, light (10 per cent alcohol) and lively, the 2018 vintage (★★★) is an easy-drinking, Pinot Gris-based wine, blended with Pinot Noir. Pale pink, it has peach, strawberry and watermelon flavours, with an off-dry (5.7 grams/litre of residual sugar) finish.

 MED/DRY $18 AV

Aronui Single Vineyard Nelson Pinot Rosé   ★★★☆

Esate-grown at Upper Moutere, the lively 2018 vintage (★★★☆) is a light pink, fresh, medium-bodied wine, with strawberry and spice flavours, a hint of apricot, and good depth.

DRY $20 AV

Astrolabe Comelybank Vineyard Marlborough Pinot Rosé   ★★★★★

The classy 2019 vintage (★★★★★) was grown in the lower Waihopai Valley. A blend of Pinot Noir (85 per cent) and Pinot Gris (15 per cent), it is a bright, light pink, very fragrant and fleshy wine, with strong peach, strawberry and spice flavours, and a smooth, fully dry finish. Delicious young.

Vintage	19
WR	7
Drink	19-20

DRY $25 V+

Aurum Organic Central Otago Pinot Gris Rosé   ★★★★

The delicious 2018 vintage (★★★★☆) was made from estate-grown, hand-harvested Pinot Gris. Very pale pink, it is mouthfilling, fresh and smooth, with concentrated stone-fruit and spice flavours, showing excellent delicacy and depth, and a dry (3 grams/litre of residual sugar), well-rounded finish. Certified organic.

 DRY $28 –V

Babich Marlborough Pinot Noir Rosé   ★★★☆

The highly attractive 2018 vintage (★★★★) is bright pink, fragrant and lively. It has good intensity of strawberry, peach and spice flavours, fresh and persistent, and a dry finish.

 DRY $20 AV

Bellbird Spring Pinot Noir Rosé   ★★★★

Still on sale, the 2017 vintage (★★★★☆) is a 'serious', flavour-packed style of rosé from Waipara, fermented in old oak barrels and made in a dry style. Pale pink/slight orange, it is medium-bodied, with fresh, peachy, spicy flavours, showing unusual depth and complexity.

DRY $27 –V

Black Cottage Marlborough Rosé   ★★★☆

The bright, light pink 2019 vintage (★★★☆) has fresh, slightly spicy aromas. Blended from Pinot Noir and Pinot Gris, grown in the Wairau Valley and lees-aged for two months, it is a medium-bodied wine, with lively strawberry, watermelon and spice flavours, slightly peachy notes, and a crisp, basically dry (4.9 grams/litre of residual sugar) finish.

DRY $18 V+

Blackenbrook Nelson Pinot Rosé   ★★★★

Instantly appealing, the vivacious 2019 vintage (★★★★☆) was made from hand-picked Nelson Pinot Noir, 10 per cent oak-aged. Made in a basically dry style (4.5 grams/litre of residual sugar), it is bright pink/very pale red, with finely balanced, vibrant, berryish, slightly spicy flavours, showing excellent vigour and intensity.

Vintage	19	18	17
WR	6	7	6
Drink	19-21	19-20	P

DRY $25 AV

Boulder Bay Rosé   ★★★★

The highly attractive 2018 vintage (★★★★☆) was made from Syrah, estate-grown on Moturoa Island, in the Bay of Islands. Pink, with a hint of orange, it is very fresh and lively, with good intensity of peach, watermelon, strawberry and spice flavours, a hint of apricot, and a crisp, off-dry, finely balanced finish. Drink now to mid-2020.

MED/DRY $25 AV

Brancott Estate Identity Wairau Valley Marlborough Pinot Noir Rosé   (★★★★)

Rosé, the label states, is 'more than a colour', it's 'a lifestyle'. The debut 2018 vintage (★★★★) is a pale pink, vivacious wine, with peachy, strawberryish, slightly spicy flavours, showing very good delicacy and harmony, and a dryish (5.9 grams/litre of residual sugar) finish.

MED/DRY $22 V+

Brennan Gibbston Central Otago Rosé   (★★★★)

Offering easy drinking, the 2018 vintage (★★★★) is a fresh and lively blend of Tempranillo (70 per cent) and Zinfandel (30 per cent). Light pink/orange, it is medium-bodied, with a sliver of sweetness, a touch of tannin, and strong, peachy, slightly spicy flavours.

MED/DRY $40 –V

Brick Bay Matakana Rosé

Estate-grown, this is a blend of traditional Bordeaux varieties, especially Cabernet Sauvignon. Attractively scented, the vivacious 2018 vintage (★★★★) is pale pink, fresh and full-bodied, with good intensity of lively, strawberryish flavours, hints of apricot and spice, and an off-dry finish.

MED/DRY $30 –V

Brightside Organic Blush

Certified organic, the 2018 vintage (★★★★) is a light pink, very attractive Nelson wine. Freshly scented, it is full-bodied and lively, with strawberry, watermelon and peach flavours, showing excellent delicacy and vibrancy, and a dry (4.5 grams/litre of residual sugar) finish. Fine value. (From Kaimira Estate.)

DRY $17 V+

Brightwater Vineyards Sophie's Kiss Nelson Rosé

Delicious young, the 2019 vintage (★★★★☆) is Pinot Noir-based. Bright pink, it is full-bodied, with fresh watermelon and spice flavours, showing excellent vibrancy and depth, and a finely balanced, off-dry (9 grams/litre of residual sugar) finish.

Vintage	19	18
WR	6	6
Drink	20-21	19-20

MED/DRY $22 V+

Church Road Gwen Hawke's Bay Rosé

The debut 2018 vintage (★★★★☆) is a blend of Merlot (92 per cent), Tempranillo (7 per cent) and Malbec (1 per cent), grown predominantly in the Bridge Pa Triangle and lees-aged for over four months. Very pale pink, it has excellent lightness and delicacy, with gentle peach, strawberry and spice flavours, fresh acidity, and a long, dry (1.5 grams/litre of residual sugar) finish.

DRY $27 AV

Church Road Hawke's Bay Rosé

Offering very easy drinking, the 2018 vintage (★★★★) was blended from Merlot and Syrah. Pink/very pale red, it is mouthfilling, with strong, fresh strawberry, peach and spice flavours, showing a touch of complexity, and a slightly sweet, smooth finish.

MED/DRY $19 V+

Clark Estate Dayvinleigh Marlborough Pinot Noir Rosé

Tasted in early 2019, the 2018 vintage (★★☆) is a single-vineyard wine, grown in the upper Wairau Valley. Pink/orange, it has pleasant, peachy, spicy, crisp, slightly sweet flavours (6 grams/litre of residual sugar), showing considerable development. Ready.

MED/DRY $20 –V

Clos Marguerite Marlborough Rosé ★★★★

Drinking well from the start, the 2018 vintage (★★★★) was made from Pinot Noir, estate-grown in the Awatere Valley. Pink-hued, with a hint of orange, it is full-bodied, with generous peach, strawberry and watermelon flavours, and a well-rounded finish.

DRY $28 –V

Collaboration Impression Rosé (★★★★)

Tasted in July 2019, the 2018 vintage (★★★★) is a pale pink, very fresh and lively rosé, produced from Cabernet Franc grapes, hand-picked in Hawke's Bay. Lees-aged for three months in old French oak barrels, it is light-bodied, with gentle strawberry, watermelon and spice flavours, slightly peachy notes, good delicacy, a touch of complexity and a basically dry (4 grams/litre of residual sugar) finish. Good drinking for the summer of 2019–20.

DRY $25 AV

Coopers Creek Kumeu Rosé ★★★☆

Pale pink, fresh and lively, the 2018 vintage (★★★☆) is a finely balanced, West Auckland blend of Malbec and Merlot. Medium-bodied, it has good depth of peach, watermelon, apricot and spice flavours, fresh, balanced acidity, and a fully dry (2 grams/litre of residual sugar) finish.

DRY $18 V+

Dancing Petrel Mangonui Northland Rosé (★★★★)

Grown in the Far North, the 2019 vintage (★★★★) was blended from Syrah and Cabernet Franc. Bright, light pink, it is lively and full-bodied, with strong, fresh berry and spice flavours, a touch of tannin, and a smooth, dryish finish.

MED/DRY $25 AV

Dashwood by Vavasour New Zealand Rosé ★★★☆

The 2019 vintage (★★★☆) makes no claims about regional origin or varieties, but was grown in Marlborough and offers great value. Bright pink, it is a charming, vibrantly fruity wine with watermelon and peach flavours, hints of strawberry and spices, and an ultra-smooth finish.

MED/DRY $16 V+

Decibel Hawke's Bay Rosé (★★☆)

Tasted in April 2019, the 2017 vintage (★★☆) is now slightly past its best. A single-vineyard wine, grown at Crownthorpe, it is mouthfilling, with mature colour. A dryish style (5 grams/litre of residual sugar), it has peachy, slightly strawberryish and spicy flavours, and a smooth finish.

MED/DRY $24 –V

Doctors', The, Marlborough Rosé ★★★

The 2019 vintage (★★★) was crafted as 'a lower alcohol rosé' (9.5 per cent). Pale pink, it is fresh and lively, with youthful, gentle watermelon and strawberry flavours, and a slightly sweet (6 grams/litre of residual sugar), crisp finish.

MED/DRY $22 –V

Domain Road Bannockburn Central Otago Rosé

Delicious from the start, the 2018 vintage (★★★★) of this Pinot Noir rosé is freshly scented, with an inviting, light pink hue. Vibrantly fruity, it has gentle strawberry, peach, apricot and spice flavours, with a smooth, dry (2.7 grams/litre of residual sugar), finely poised finish.

Vintage	18
WR	5
Drink	19-21

`DRY $25 AV`

Durvillea Marlborough Rosé

Offering great value, the 2019 vintage (★★★★), grown in the Awatere Valley, is a 50:50 blend of Pinot Noir and Pinot Gris. Bright, light pink, it is crisp and lively, with good body, strong watermelon and spice flavours, and a crisp, fully dry (1.3 grams/litre of residual sugar) finish.

`DRY $15 V+`

Elder, The, Martinborough Rosé

The vivacious 2018 vintage (★★★★☆) was made from Pinot Noir grapes, estate-grown at Te Muna. Bright pink, it is very fresh and vibrant, with strong, cherryish, plummy flavours, hints of watermelon and strawberry, appetising acidity, and a fully dry (1.5 grams/litre of residual sugar) finish.

`DRY $31 –V`

Elephant Hill Hawke's Bay Tempranillo Rosé

The distinctive, full-flavoured 2018 vintage (★★★★☆) was made from Tempranillo, hand-picked in the Bridge Pa Triangle. and held briefly on its skins (for one hour) to extract its pale pink hue. A 'serious' but very approachable wine, it is fragrant, fresh and smooth, with strong, strawberryish, peachy, slightly spicy flavours, a hint of apricot, and a long, fully dry finish.

`DRY $29 AV`

Esk Valley Hawke's Bay Rosé   ★★★★

For many years, this was New Zealand's most successful rosé on the show circuit. The 2019 vintage (★★★★) is a Merlot-based wine, bright, pale pink, fragrant and lively. Vibrantly fruity, it is medium-bodied, with very good depth of fresh strawberry and spice flavours, a hint of peaches, and a smooth, dry finish. Good drinking for the summer of 2019–20.

Vintage	19	18
WR	7	6
Drink	20-21	19-20

`DRY $20 V+`

Falconhead Hawke's Bay Rosé

Enjoyable young, the 2019 vintage was mostly handled in tanks, but 25 per cent of the blend was barrel-fermented. Pale pink, it is mouthfilling, with generous, fresh peach, watermelon and spice flavours, and a dryish (5 grams/litre of residual sugar) finish. Good value.

`MED/DRY $17 AV`

Flaxmore Moutere Rosé (★★★★)

The distinctive 2018 vintage (★★★★) was made from hand-picked Pinot Noir, grown in the Moutere hills. Pale pink, it is a fresh and lively, medium-bodied wine, with very satisfying depth of watermelon, peach and spice flavours, dry and lingering. A 'serious' style of rosé, it's looking good for the summer of 2019–20.

DRY $21·V+

Forbidden Vines Marlborough Pinot Noir Rosé ★★★

Enjoyable from the start, the sharply priced 2018 vintage (★★★) is a pale pink, lively, medium-bodied wine, with fresh strawberry and peach flavours, a sliver of sweetness, and a smooth finish. Good value. (From Babich.)

MED/DRY $15 V+

Forrest Marlborough Rosé ★★★★

The 2019 vintage (★★★★☆) is already delicious. Bright pink, it is vibrantly fruity, with strong watermelon and strawberry flavours, a hint of spice, fresh acidity, a sliver of sweetness (5.4 grams/litre of residual sugar), and a lively, long finish.

MED/DRY $22 V+

Georges Road Les Terrasses Waipara Rosé ★★★★☆

The classy 2018 vintage (★★★★★) was made from Syrah grapes, hand-picked, fermented with indigenous yeasts and lees-aged in tanks. Pink, with a fresh, spicy fragrance, it is medium-bodied and vibrantly fruity, with strong plum and watermelon flavours, a hint of apricot, excellent delicacy and a crisp, dry (2 grams/litre of residual sugar) finish. A wine with lots of personality, it's well worth discovering.

DRY $25 V+

Gibbston Valley GV Collection Central Otago Rosé ★★★★

The bright pink, vivacious 2018 vintage (★★★★) was hand-picked and cool-fermented in tanks. Fragrant and fresh, it has strong, strawberryish, slightly peachy flavours, a gentle splash of sweetness (7 grams/litre of residual sugar), and a finely balanced, smooth finish.

MED/DRY $28 –V

Gillman Clairet ★★★★

Labelled as 'slightly darker than a modern rosé, with more fruit richness and structure', the distinctive 2017 vintage (★★★★) was made from Cabernet Franc and Merlot, grown at Matakana, and barrel-aged for a year. A rare wine (only 294 bottles were made), it has light red colour and a fragrant, spicy bouquet. A complex, dry style, it is ready now, with a gentle touch of tannin and strong, berryish, nutty, slightly earthy flavours. (The 2014 vintage, tasted in December 2018, has matured well, developing a savoury, leathery complexity.)

DRY $46 –V

Gladstone Vineyard Wairarapa Rosé

Showing greater complexity than many rosés, the 2018 vintage (★★★★☆) was blended from Merlot, Cabernet Franc and Pinot Noir. Pale pink, it is mouthfilling, with peachy, strawberryish flavours, balanced acidity and a fragrant bouquet.

`DRY $27 AV`

Graham Norton's Own Pink by Design Rosé

The 2018 vintage (★★★☆) was made from Pinot Gris, Pinot Noir and Sauvignon Blanc, grown in Marlborough, Gisborne and Hawke's Bay. Very pale pink, it is aromatic, light and lively, with gentle strawberry, peach and spice flavours, and a dry (2.5 grams/litre of residual sugar) finish.

`DRY $19 V+`

Greyrock Hawke's Bay Rosé

The 2018 vintage (★★☆), tasted in September 2019, is a pale pink, basically dry wine (4 grams/litre of residual sugar), with peach, strawberry and spice flavours, just starting to lose its youthful freshness and charm. Drink now. (From Sileni.)

`DRY $19 AV`

Grove Mill Wairau Valley Marlborough Rosé

The 2018 vintage (★★★★) offers good value. Made from Pinot Noir, it is bright pink, freshly scented and lively, with gentle strawberry and spice flavours, showing excellent vibrancy and harmony, and a basically dry (3.5 grams/litre of residual sugar) finish.

`DRY $19 V+`

Haha Hawke's Bay Rosé

The bright pink 2019 vintage (★★★★) is a blend of Merlot and Malbec. It has a fragrant, fresh bouquet, leading into a vivacious, dry (3 grams/litre of residual sugar) wine with strong, lively watermelon and spice flavours. Good drinking now and through the summer of 2019–20.

`DRY $18 V+`

Hancock & Sons Lillies Hawke's Bay Rosé   (★★★☆)

From winemaker John Hancock and his son, Willy, the debut 2018 vintage (★★★☆) was made from Cabernet Franc grapes, hand-picked at Bridge Pa. Pale, it is light-bodied and lively, with gentle, delicate, peachy flavours, hints of spices and strawberries, and a dry (3 grams/litre of residual sugar) finish.

Vintage	18
WR	4
Drink	19-21

`DRY $22 AV`

Hawke's Bay Estate Rosé   (★★★☆)

From Pask, the 2018 vintage (★★★☆) is a good buy. Made from Syrah, it is bright pink, lively and smooth, with very good body and depth of peach, berry, plum and spice flavours, and a crisp, dryish (5 grams/litre of residual sugar) finish. It's drinking well now.

 MED/DRY $14 V+

Hawkshead Central Otago Rosé   ★★★☆

The 2018 vintage (★★★★) is 'a sexy little number', according to the back label. Bright pink, it is mouthfilling, fresh and smooth, with attractive, berryish, plummy flavours, showing good delicacy and vibrancy, appetising acidity, and a fully dry (1.5 grams/litre of residual sugar) finish.

 DRY $29 –V

Hopesgrove Single Vineyard Hawke's Bay Estate Rosé   (★★★★★)

Delicious now, the classy 2018 vintage (★★★★★) was hand-picked and barrel-fermented. Bright pink, it is floral and vibrantly fruity, with good weight, fresh acidity and strong berry and watermelon flavours that build well to a very harmonious, dry (2 grams/litre of residual sugar) finish.

 DRY $25 V+

Hunting Lodge, The, Expressions Marlborough Pinot Noir Rosé   (★★★★)

Drinking well in mid-2019, the 2018 vintage (★★★★) was grown in the Wairau Valley and lees-aged in tanks for four months. Picked slightly early for 'aromatic expression', it is a pale pink, lively, medium-bodied wine with strong peach, strawberry and spice flavours, a sliver of sweetness (4.8 grams/litre of residual sugar) and fresh, finely balanced acidity.

 DRY $22 V+

Jackson Estate Alayna Marlborough Pinot Noir Rosé   (★★★☆)

Pink/orange, the 2018 vintage (★★★☆) is a full-bodied, basically dry style (4 grams/litre of residual sugar), with strong, peachy, strawberryish, slightly spicy flavours and a rounding finish. Ready to roll.

DRY $21 AV

Johanneshof Marlborough Pinot Noir Rosé Maybern Single Vineyard   ★★★★☆

Still on sale, the distinctive, pink/pale orange 2017 vintage (★★★★) is from a hillside vineyard at Koromiko. Mouthfilling, it has strong, peachy, spicy flavours, hints of strawberry and apricot, a touch of complexity and a dryish (5.6 grams/litre of residual sugar) finish.

 MED/DRY $25 V+

Johner Estate Pinot Noir Rosé   ★★★★

The 2019 vintage (★★★★) was grown at Gladstone, in the Wairarapa. Pink/pale red, with floral, berryish scents, it is fresh and full-bodied, with vibrant berry and plum flavours, vague sweetness (5 grams/litre of residual sugar) and fresh acidity. Good drinking for the summer of 2019–20.

MED/DRY $20 V+

Jules Taylor Gisborne Rosé

★★★★

The 2018 vintage (★★★★) is a bright pink/very pale red blend of Gisborne Merlot (predominantly) and Pinot Noir, grown in Marlborough. Delicious young, it is vibrantly fruity, with strong plum and strawberry flavours, a hint of spice, and a smooth, dry (1.1 grams/litre of residual sugar) finish.

DRY $23 AV

Jules Taylor OTQ Single Vineyard Marlborough Rosé

★★★★☆

Strikingly packaged, the 2018 vintage (★★★★☆) was produced 'OTQ' (On The Quiet) from Pinot Noir, mostly handled in tanks, but 10 per cent was barrel-fermented. Pale pink, it is fresh and mouthfilling, with strong peach, strawberry and spice flavours, a hint of apricot, good complexity, and a dry (1.1 grams/litre of residual sugar), lingering finish.

DRY $34 –V

Kahurangi Estate Nelson Pinot Noir Rosé

(★★★☆)

The 2019 vintage (★★★☆) is bright pink/pale red, fresh and lively, with berryish, plummy flavours and an off-dry finish. It's already drinking well.

MED/DRY $22 AV

Kono Nelson Pinot Rosé

(★★★☆)

The pale pink 2018 vintage (★★★☆) was made from Pinot Noir. Enjoyable young, it has fresh strawberry, watermelon, peach and spice flavours, showing good depth, and a dryish, finely balanced finish.

MED/DRY $18 V+

Kōparepare Marlborough Pinot Noir Rosé

(★★★)

Ready to roll, the 2017 vintage (★★★), tasted in mid-2019, was made by Whitehaven for LegaSea, to help fund its work to restore inshore fisheries to abundance. Light pink, it is still fresh, with gentle strawberryish flavours, slightly peachy and spicy notes, and an off-dry, crisp finish.

MED/DRY $16 V+

Lake Chalice The Falcon Marlborough Pinot Noir Rosé

(★★☆)

The 2017 vintage (★★☆) was harvested from estate-grown Pinot Noir, picked early to produce a light (10.5 per cent alcohol) style. Bright, light pink, it is fresh and crisp, with lively watermelon and spice flavours, and a basically dry (4 grams/litre of residual sugar) finish.

DRY $16 AV

Landing, The, Bay of Islands Rosé

(★★★☆)

Drinking well from the start, the 2018 vintage (★★★☆) was blended from Northland Syrah, Merlot and Cabernet Franc. Pale pink, it is a fresh, medium-bodied wine with peachy, slightly spicy flavours, and a well-rounded, dryish (8 grams/litre of residual sugar) finish.

MED/DRY $27 –V

Lawson's Dry Hills Pink Pinot   (★★★★☆)

The 2019 vintage (★★★★☆) is a characterful Marlborough rosé, brimful of flavour. Bright pink, it has generous strawberry and watermelon flavours, slightly spicy notes, and excellent vigour and length, with a dry (2.9 grams/litre of residual sugar) finish.

Vintage	19
WR	6
Drink	19-20

 DRY $25 V+

Left Field Hawke's Bay Rosé   ★★★☆

The 2018 vintage (★★★☆) is a pale pink, fragrant, off-dry style (5.3 grams/litre of residual sugar), with vibrant strawberry and spice flavours, woven with fresh acidity. Lively, fruity and smooth, it offers very easy drinking. (From Te Awa.)

Vintage	18	17	16
WR	6	6	6
Drink	19-20	P	P

 MED/DRY $18 V+

Leveret Estate Hawke's Bay Rosé   (★★★☆)

Bright, light pink, the 2019 vintage (★★★☆) was 30 per cent barrel-fermented and made in a basically dry (4.5 grams/litre of residual sugar) style. Fresh and lively, it has finely balanced acidity and very good depth of watermelon and peach flavours.

 DRY $22 AV

Luna Martinborough Pinot Meunier Rosé   (★★★★☆)

From Pinot Meunier vines in the Blue Rock Vineyard, the 2018 vintage (★★★★☆) was made with some use of old oak barrels. Pale pink, it is a medium-bodied, fully dry style (1 gram/litre of residual sugar), with fresh, strong strawberry, peach and spice flavours, showing a touch of complexity, a hint of apricot, and a lingering finish.

 DRY $24 V+

Madam Sass Central Otago Pinot Noir Rosé   (★★★★)

Full of drink-young charm, the 2018 vintage (★★★★) is a bright pink, freshly scented wine. Lively, it is medium-bodied, with strawberry, watermelon, peach and spice flavours, showing very good vibrancy and delicacy, and a crisp, dryish (5.1 grams/litre of residual sugar) finish.

 MED/DRY $25 AV

Mahi Marlborough Rosé   ★★★★☆

The impressive 2018 vintage (★★★★☆) was made from Pinot Noir, grown at two sites in the Wairau Valley, and briefly lees-aged. Bright, pale pink, it is floral, with strong, delicate strawberry, watermelon and spice flavours, and a dry (1.8 grams/litre of residual sugar), lingering finish.

Vintage	19	18
WR	6	7
Drink	19-22	19-21

DRY $23 V+

Main Divide North Canterbury Rosé ★★★★

The fresh, vivacious 2019 vintage (★★★★) is a blend of Pinot Noir, Cabernet Sauvignon and Cabernet Franc. Bright, light pink, it has strong, yet delicate, flavours of peaches, srawberries and watermelon, and a slightly sweet (6 grams/litre of residual sugar), crisp finish.

Vintage	19	18
WR	5	6
Drink	19-20	19-20

 MED/DRY $21 V+

Maison Noire Hawke's Bay Rosé ★★★

Deep pink, the 2018 vintage (★★★☆) is fresh and crisp, in a light to medium-bodied style with strawberryish flavours, hints of spices and apricots, slightly earthy notes adding a touch of complexity, and a dryish finish. Tasted in July 2019, it's ready to roll.

Vintage	17
WR	6
Drink	P

 MED/DRY $20 –V

Maori Point Barrel Reserve Central Otago Pinot Noir Rosé (★★★★★)

Still on sale, the delicious 2016 vintage (★★★★★) is a single-vineyard wine, hand-harvested, fermented to full dryness in French oak barrels, and wood-aged for two years. Pink/pale orange, it is full-bodied, in a 'serious' style that is maturing very gracefully. Showing unusual complexity for a rosé, it has strawberry, peach and spice flavours, woven with fresh acidity, and a long finish.

 DRY $36 AV

Maori Point Central Otago Pinot Noir Rosé ★★★★

Estate-grown at Tarras, in the Cromwell Basin, the 2019 vintage (★★★★☆) is instantly likeable. Bright pink, it has strong, vivacious strawberry and spice flavours, and a finely balanced, slightly sweet (9 grams/litre of residual sugar) finish.

 MED/DRY $26 –V

Margrain Martinborough Pinot Rosé ★★★☆

The attractive 2018 vintage (★★★★) was made from Pinot Noir. Bright pink, it is fresh and full-bodied, with good intensity of delicate strawberry, watermelon and spice flavours, lively acidity, and an off-dry (6 grams/litre of residual sugar), lingering finish.

Vintage	18	17	16
WR	7	6	7
Drink	19-20	P	P

MED/DRY $26 –V

Matawhero Single Vineyard Gisborne Pinot Rosé ★★★☆

The pale pink 2018 vintage (★★★★) is a very good example of slightly sweet rosé (9 grams/litre of residual sugar). Full of drink-young charm, it has lively, peachy, slightly spicy flavours, appetising acidity, and excellent depth and harmony.

 MED/DRY $23 –V

Maui Waipara Rosé

The 2019 vintage (★★☆) was blended from Pinot Noir (70 per cent) and Pinot Gris (30 per cent). Pink/pale red, it has fresh, berryish flavours, which show a slight lack of delicacy, some earthy notes, and an off-dry (6 grams/litre of residual sugar) finish. Solid but plain.

$20 –V

Mills Reef Reserve Hawke's Bay Rosé ★★★★

The 2019 vintage (★★★★), made from Merlot, looks good for the summer of 2019–20. Bright pink, it is lively and generous, with strong, fresh watermelon and spice flavours, dry and lingering.

DRY $25 AV

Misha's Vineyard The Soloist Central Otago Pinot Rosé ★★★★☆

The 2019 vintage (★★★★☆) was made from Pinot Noir, estate-grown at Bendigo. Bright pink, it has vibrant strawberry, watermelon, peach and spice flavours, showing excellent freshness, delicacy and depth, balanced acidity, and a finely poised, dry (4 grams/litre of residual sugar) finish.

Vintage	19	18	17	16
WR	6	7	6	7
Drink	19-23	19-22	19-21	19-20

DRY $27 AV

Mission Hawke's Bay Rosé ★★★☆

The bright pink, very pale red 2019 vintage (★★★☆) was blended from red-wine varieties. Very fresh and lively, it has good depth of vibrant strawberry, watermelon and spice flavours, slightly peachy notes, and a finely balanced, dryish finish. Good value.

MED/DRY $16 V+

Mondillo Central Otago Rosé (★★★★☆)

The very lively 2018 vintage (★★★★☆) was made from Pinot Noir, estate-grown at Bendigo. Freshly scented, with a pink/pale red hue, it is full-bodied and vibrantly fruity, with strong red-berry and watermelon flavours, a sliver of sweetness (7 grams/litre of residual sugar), appetising acidity, and a smooth finish. Delicious young.

MED/DRY $28 AV

Montana Reserve Marlborough Rosé (★★★★)

A staff member at Pernod Ricard NZ (owner of the Montana brand) told me the charming 2018 vintage (★★★★) is their 'go to' wine at home – and I can see why. Bright, light pink, it is fragrant, with fresh, vibrant strawberry, apricot and spice flavours, a sliver of sweetness, a slightly creamy texture, and loads of drink-young appeal. Bargain-priced.

MED/DRY $17 V+

Mount Brown Estates Grand Reserve North Canterbury Pinot Noir Rosé   (★★★★)

The pale, lively 2018 vintage (★★★★) was estate-grown and fermented with indigenous yeasts in seasoned French oak barrels. Full of youthful impact, it is medium-bodied, with strong, peachy, spicy flavours, woven with fresh acidity, and an off-dry (10 grams/litre of residual sugar) finish.

Vintage	18
WR	6
Drink	19-20

 MED/DRY $20 V+

Mount Brown Estates North Canterbury Pinot Noir Rosé   ★★★

Priced sharply, the charming 2018 vintage (★★★☆) is a bright pink wine, freshly scented and smooth. It has vibrant, delicate strawberry and watermelon flavours, with a sliver of sweetness (7 grams/litre of residual sugar) adding to its drink-young appeal.

Vintage	18
WR	5
Drink	19-20

 MED/DRY $16 V+

Mount Riley The Bonnie Marlborough Pinot Rosé   ★★★☆

The 2019 vintage (★★★☆) is a bright pink, highly scented wine, blended from Pinot Noir and Pinot Gris. Briefly lees-aged, it is vibrantly fruity, with strawberry, watermelon and spice flavours, a hint of peaches, and a slightly sweet, smooth finish. Priced sharply.

 MED/DRY $17 V+

Moutere Hills Nelson Pinot Rosé   ★★★☆

The 2018 vintage (★★★☆) is a light pink/pale orange wine, made in a 'serious' style, rather than for easy, no-fuss sipping. It has gentle watermelon and spice flavours, with a touch of tannin and dry finish (3 grams/litre of residual sugar), that combine to make it a good 'food' wine.

DRY $25 –V

Mt Beautiful North Canterbury Rosé   (★★★★)

The distinctive 2018 vintage (★★★★) was fermented in tanks and barrels. Full-bodied (14.5 per cent alcohol) and dry, it has strong, ripe, peachy, slightly spicy flavours, a hint of apricot and a smooth finish. Ready.

 DRY $22 V+

Mud House Sub Region Series Burleigh Marlborough Pinot Rosé   ★★★☆

The very pretty 2018 vintage (★★★★) was grown in the Burleigh district, just west of Blenheim, in the Wairau Valley sub-region. Bright, light pink, it is a fresh, medium-bodied wine, with lively strawberry and spice flavours, showing excellent delicacy and vivacity, and an off-dry finish.

 MED/DRY $20 AV

Neudorf Pinot Rosé ★★★★☆

The distinctive, very pale pink 2018 vintage (★★★★★) was made from Pinot Noir, hand-harvested at two sites at Upper Moutere, in Nelson. Fermented with indigenous yeasts in tanks (80 per cent) and barrels (20 per cent), it's a 'serious' but delicious rosé, fully dry, with peachy, slightly spicy and strawberryish flavours, showing notable depth, complexity and harmony.

 $25 V+

Nga Waka Martinborough Rosé ★★★★

From Pinot Noir grapes, the 2018 vintage (★★★★) is a lively, medium-bodied wine, light pink, with strong strawberry, watermelon, peach and spice flavours, a gentle touch of tannin and a dry finish. It's drinking well now.

Vintage	18	17	16
WR	7	6	6
Drink	19-20	P	P

 DRY $25 AV

Nockie's Palette Georgetown Central Otago Pinot Rosé (★★★★★)

The 2018 vintage (★★★★★) is strikingly packaged – and the wine is very classy too. Estate-grown in Georgetown Vineyard, at the eastern end of the Kawarau Gorge, it was partly (18 per cent) fermented in old French oak barriques. A pale pink, 'serious' but delicious wine, showing lovely delicacy and harmony, it is mouthfilling and dry (2.9 grams/litre of residual sugar), with vibrant strawberry and spice flavours, a hint of apricot, and a long finish. Drinking well now, it should offer top drinking into 2020.

 DRY $39 AV

Obsidian Estate Waiheke Island Rosé ★★★★

A hand-harvested, Merlot-based wine, the 2018 vintage (★★★★) is bright pink, fresh, full-bodied and dry, with lively strawberry, spice and peach flavours, appetising acidity and good harmony.

 DRY $29 –V

Opawa Marlborough Pinot Noir Rosé ★★★★

The lively 2019 vintage (★★★☆) offers very easy drinking. Pale pink, it is light-bodied, with vibrant, peachy, slightly spicy flavours, dryish (5 grams/litre of residual sugar) and smooth.

 MED/DRY $22 V+

Oyster Bay Marlborough Rosé ★★★★

The fresh, medium-bodied 2019 vintage (★★★★) was made from Pinot Noir. Bright, pale pink, it is vibrantly fruity, with watermelon and spice flavours, slightly peachy notes, good intensity and a dry finish.

DRY $20 V+

Pā Road Marlborough Rosé ★★★

Balanced for easy drinking, the pale pink 2019 vintage (★★★) is fresh and light, with gentle strawberry and spice flavours, hints of peaches and watermelon, and a crisp, smooth finish. (From te Pā.)

 MED/DRY $16 V+

Paddy Borthwick New Zealand Pinot Rosé (★★★★)

The instantly appealing 2018 vintage (★★★★) was estate-grown at Gladstone, in the Wairarapa. Pale pink, it is fresh and lively, with peach, strawberry and spice flavours, appetising acidity, and a dry (3 grams/litre of residual sugar), lengthy finish.

 DRY $24 AV

Palliser Estate Martinborough Rosé ★★★★

Delicious young, the 2018 vintage (★★★★) is a vibrantly fruity, easy-drinking rosé, made from Pinot Noir, matured on its yeast lees for three months. Pale pink, it has fresh, strong strawberry and spice flavours, a hint of apricot, and a dryish (6 grams/litre of residual sugar), smooth finish.

MED/DRY $25 AV

Pinot 3 – The Pink Edition (★★★★)

Offering good value, the 2019 vintage (★★★★) is a blend of Pinot Noir, Pinot Gris and Pinot Blanc, grown in Marlborough and Gisborne, and handled in old oak barriques. Bright, light pink, it is highly fragrant, with generous peach, watermelon and spice flavours, showing a distinct touch of complexity, and a smooth finish. (From Untitled Wines, based in West Auckland.)

MED/DRY $20 V+

Providore Central Otago Rosé (★★★★☆)

The highly attractive 2018 vintage (★★★★☆) was grown mostly at Gibbston, supplemented by fruit from the Cromwell Basin. Pale pink, it is scented and mouthfilling (14 per cent alcohol), with strong peach, strawberry and spice flavours, fresh acidity and a dry finish.

 DRY $25 V+

Rabbit Ranch Central Otago Rosé ★★★★

The 2018 vintage (★★★★) is a pale pink, mouthfilling rosé, made from hand-picked Pinot Noir. It has strong, ripe, peachy, slightly spicy flavours, a hint of apricot, and a dry, well-rounded finish. (From Chard Farm.)

 DRY $23 AV

Rapaura Springs Reserve Marlborough Pinot Rosé   ★★★★

Enjoyable from the start, the 2019 vintage (★★★★) is pale pink, fresh and mouthfilling, with very good depth of peachy, spicy flavours, a hint of apricot, and an off-dry (6.8 grams/litre of residual sugar) finish. Fine value.

Vintage	19
WR	6
Drink	19-21

 MED/DRY $19 V+

Redmetal Vineyards Bridge Pa Triangle Hawke's Bay Cabernet Franc Rosé   ★★★★

Full of personality, the classy 2018 vintage (★★★★★) is a bright, light-pink wine, fresh, fragrant, mouthfilling and lively. It has strong yet delicate flavours of strawberry and watermelon, and a crisp, dry (3.2 grams/litre of residual sugar), slightly peachy, poised, persistent finish.

 DRY $22 V+

Ruru Central Otago Rosé   ★★★★

From Immigrant's Vineyard, at Alexandra, the 2018 vintage (★★★★) was made from hand-harvested Pinot Noir. Pale pink/slight orange, it is a 'serious' style, mouthfilling and dry (4 grams/litre of residual sugar), with good concentration of peachy, spicy flavours, enlivened by fresh acidity.

 DRY $21 V+

Saint Clair Origin Marlborough Pinot Gris Rosé   (★★★☆)

The 2018 vintage (★★★☆) is fragrant, fresh and smooth, with bright, light pink colour, lively strawberry and watermelon flavours, and a crisp, dry (3.5 grams/litre of residual sugar) finish.

 DRY $22 AV

Scott Base Central Otago Rosé   ★★★★☆

Showing lots of personality, the 2018 vintage (★★★★☆) is a bright pink, invitingly scented wine, made solely from Pinot Noir. Mouthfilling and vibrantly fruity, it has good concentration of peachy, strawberryish, spicy flavours, with a dry (3 grams/litre of residual sugar) finish. (From Allan Scott.)

DRY $26 AV

Seifried Nelson Pinot Noir Rosé   (★★★★)

Scheduled for release in early 2020, the very charming 2019 vintage (★★★★) is pale pink, with a floral, scented bouquet. A vivacious young wine, it has vibrant plum, red-berry, strawberry and spice flavours, with an off-dry (5.6 grams/litre of residual sugar) finish. Fine value.

 MED/DRY $18 V+

Sexy Rexy Marlborough Rosé   (★★★★)

Drinking well now, the 2018 vintage (★★★★) is deep pink, fresh, lively and smooth. Vibrantly fruity, it has berryish, plummy, peachy flavours, a touch of tannin, and a finely balanced, dry (4 grams/litre of residual sugar) finish. (From Ra Nui.)

 DRY $20 V+

Sherwood Estate Stoney Range Waipara Valley Rosé ★★★★

Priced sharply, the 2019 vintage (★★★★) was blended from Pinot Noir, Pinot Gris and Syrah. Very pale pink, it has strong peach, strawberry, watermelon and spice flavours, a hint of apricot, and a crisp, dry finish. Showing plenty of personality, it looks good for the summer of 2019–20.

DRY $18 V+

Sileni Cellar Selection Hawke's Bay Cabernet Franc Rosé ★★★☆

The 2019 vintage (★★★☆) is a pale pink, fresh and lively wine, with peach, spice and watermelon flavours, a slightly earthy streak adding interest, gentle tannins, and a basically dry (4.2 grams/litre of residual sugar) finish.

DRY $20 AV

Spy Valley Pinot Noir Marlborough Rosé ★★★★

The distinctive, pale pink 2018 vintage (★★★★☆) is from estate-grown grapes, hand-harvested in the Waihopai Valley, and was made with some use of barrel fermentation. A characterful wine, full of interest, it is very vibrant, with delicate, peachy, spicy flavours, showing a distinct touch of complexity, fresh acidity, and a long, dry (1.7 grams/litre of residual sugar) finish.

DRY $23 AV

Stables Ngatarawa Rosé (★★☆)

Pale pink, the 2019 vintage (★★☆) is a blend of Sauvignon Blanc (55 per cent) and red varieties, grown in Hawke's Bay. It has moderate depth of fresh watermelon and spice flavours, slightly sweet and crisp. Priced right. (From Mission.)

MED/DRY $13 V+

Staete Landt Nude Marlborough Rosé (★★★★☆)

Drinking well in late 2019, the 2018 vintage (★★★★☆) is a dry style (1.5 grams/litre of residual sugar), barrel-fermented and given prolonged contact with its yeast lees. Bright, light pink, it is a characterful wine, with peachy, spicy, strawberryish flavours, fresh and strong, a touch of tannin, and greater complexity than most rosés.

DRY $25 V+

Stonecroft Gimblett Gravels Hawke's Bay Rosé ★★★☆

Still on sale, the easy-drinking 2017 vintage (★★★☆) is a single-vineyard wine, made from hand-picked Syrah. Matured for four months on its yeast lees, it is medium-bodied and smooth, with pale red colour, plenty of fresh, lively, berryish, slightly spicy flavour, a sliver of sweetness (5 grams/litre of residual sugar) and balanced acidity.

MED/DRY $22 AV

Stoneleigh Latitude Marlborough Rosé (★★★★)

Drinking well from the start, the 2018 vintage (★★★★) was grown at Rapaura, on the north side of the Wairau Valley. Bright pink, it is vibrantly fruity, with gentle strawberry and spice flavours, dryish, harmonious and lingering.

MED/DRY $20 V+

Stoneleigh Wild Valley Marlborough Rosé   (★★★★)

The attractive 2018 vintage (★★★★) was produced from Pinot Noir, fermented with indigenous yeasts (hence the 'Wild Valley'). Bright pink, it is fragrant and vibrantly fruity, with excellent depth of peach, strawberry, watermelon and spice flavours, showing a touch of complexity, and a lengthy, dryish (6.5 grams/litre of residual sugar) finish.

MED/DRY $18 V+

Sugar Loaf Harriet Marlborough Pinot Noir Rosé   (★★★★☆)

The vivacious 2018 vintage (★★★★☆) is pale pink, with strong, peachy, spicy aromas. Very fresh and lively, it has excellent intensity of peach, strawberry and spice flavours, a sliver of sweetness (5.5 grams/litre of residual sugar) balanced by appetising acidity, and a long finish. Drink now to 2020.

MED/DRY $20 V+

Summerhouse Marlborough Pinot Rosé   ★★★★

The 2019 vintage (★★★★) is labelled 'Pinot', rather than Pinot Noir, suggesting the inclusion of Pinot Gris. Bright pink, it is fresh and mouthfilling, with very good depth of lively watermelon, peach and spice flavours, a splash of sweetness (6.1 grams/litre of residual sugar), and a very easy-drinking balance. Good value.

Vintage	19
WR	6
Drink	19-20

MED/DRY $19 V+

Tatty Boggler Waitaki Valley Rosé   ★★★★

Bright pink, the 2018 vintage (★★★★) is freshly scented and mouthfilling, with lively strawberry, peach and spice flavours, balanced acidity and a basically dry (4.7 grams/litre of residual sugar) finish. (From Forrest Estate.)

DRY $25 AV

Te Kairanga Martinborough Pinot Rosé   ★★★★☆

Full of drink-young charm, the 2019 vintage (★★★★☆) is a bright pink, full-bodied wine. It has watermelon and spice flavours, showing excellent vibrancy, delicacy and depth, and an off-dry (9.9 grams/litre of residual sugar) finish.

MED/DRY $25 V+

te Pā Marlborough Pinot Noir Rosé   ★★★☆

The 2019 vintage (★★★★) is a refined wine, pale pink, with fresh strawberry, peach and spice flavours, a touch of tannin, very good delicacy and depth, and a dry finish.

DRY $20 AV

Terra Sancta Bannockburn Central Otago Pinot Noir Rosé   ★★★★★

From one vintage to the next, this is one of the country's leading rosés. The 2018 vintage (★★★★★) was mostly handled in tanks, but a significant 30 per cent of the blend was fermented and aged in seasoned French oak barriques. Bright, light pink, it is fragrant, mouthfilling and smooth, with lovely depth of fresh, vibrant strawberry, watermelon and spice flavours, hints of peaches and apricots, and a finely textured, basically dry (4.2 grams/litre of residual sugar) finish.

Vintage	19	18	17
WR	7	7	7
Drink	19-22	19-21	19-20

DRY $28 V+

Terra Sancta Special Release First Vines Pinot Noir Rosé (★★★★★)

New Zealand's highest-priced rosé to date is the debut 2017 vintage (★★★★★) of this unusually complex wine, estate-grown in Central Otago. From ungrafted vines at Bannockburn, planted in 1991 and 1995, it was hand-harvested, fermented with indigenous yeasts in old French oak puncheons, and bottled with a cork closure. Deep pink, it is full-bodied, sweet-fruited, smooth and dry (3.3 grams/litre of residual sugar), with layers of strawberry, watermelon, spice and apricot flavours, gentle acidity, and a very harmonious, long finish. A 'serious', age-worthy wine, beautifully packaged, it's a drink-now or cellaring proposition.

Vintage	18
WR	7
Drink	19-26

DRY $49 AV

Terrace Edge North Canterbury Rosé (★★★★★)

Offering loads of flavour, the distinctive 2018 vintage (★★★★★) was made from Syrah grapes, grown at Waipara and held on their skins for four hours 'to extract colour, tannin and spice'. Pink/very pale red, it is highly fragrant, with strong, lively, strawberryish, spicy flavours, and a long, slightly sweet (8 grams/litre of residual sugar), smooth finish. Delicious young, it offers great value. Certified organic.

MED/DRY $22 V+

Theory & Practice Hawke's Bay Rosé (★★★★)

The refreshing 2018 vintage (★★★★) was made from Pinot Noir, grown at Maraekakaho. Pink/pale red, it is mouthfilling, vibrant and smooth, with strong, strawberryish, slightly peachy and spicy flavours, and an off-dry (6 grams/litre of residual sugar), lingering finish.

MED/DRY $21 V+

Three Miners Rocker Box Central Otago Pinot Noir Rosé (★★★★)

The vivacious 2018 vintage (★★★★) is a single-vineyard rosé, hand-picked near Alexandra. Bright, pale pink, it is freshly scented, with strawberryish, slightly peachy and spicy flavours, and a finely balanced, dry (1.6 grams/litre of residual sugar) finish.

DRY $26 –V

Tiki Estate Waipara Pinot Noir Rosé ★★★☆

The 2019 vintage (★★★★) is a real charmer. Bright pink/very pale red, it is finely balanced, with strong, vibrant plum, red-berry and watermelon flavours, and an off-dry (6 grams/litre of residual sugar), smooth finish.

Vintage	19
WR	6
Drink	19-21

 MED/DRY $24 –V

Tohu Nelson Pinot Rosé ★★★★

Estate-grown at Upper Moutere, the 2019 vintage (★★★★) was made from Pinot Noir. Bright pink/pale red, it has fresh, berryish scents and flavours, in a very lively, buoyantly fruity style with a dry (4.4 grams/litre of residual sugar) finish. Fine value.

Vintage	19
WR	6
Drink	19-22

 DRY $18 V+

Toi Toi Sara's Marlborough Rosé ★★★☆

Offering good value, the 2018 vintage (★★★☆) was made from Pinot Noir and Pinot Gris. Pale pink, it is fresh and mouthfilling, with good depth of peach, strawberry and spice flavours, appetising acidity, and a dryish (5.6 grams/litre of residual sugar) finish.

 MED/DRY $18 V+

Two Rivers New Zealand Isle of Beauty Rosé ★★★★

Grown at three sites in the Southern Valleys of Marlborough, the appealing 2018 vintage (★★★★☆) is a unique blend of Pinot Noir, Syrah, Viognier, Pinot Gris, Riesling and Roussanne. Bright, pale pink, it is fragrant, with excellent depth of fresh strawberry, spice and watermelon flavours, hints of peach and apricot, and a crisp, dry (3 grams/litre of residual sugar), persistent finish.

 DRY $24 AV

Two Sisters Central Otago Pinot Rosé (★★★★)

The vivacious 2019 vintage (★★★★) is a single-vineyard wine, hand-picked at Lowburn, in the Cromwell Basin. Bright pink, it is medium-bodied, with fresh, strong watermelon and spice flavours, crisp, dry and finely balanced.

Vintage	19
WR	7
Drink	19-21

DRY $30 –V

Untitled Pink Blend (★★★★)

Drinking well now, the 2018 vintage (★★★★) was grown in Auckland and Marlborough, and handled in old oak barriques. Bright, light pink, it is lively, with strong, peachy, spicy flavours, showing a touch of complexity, gentle tannins and a dry finish. (From Untitled Wines, based in West Auckland.)

 DRY $20 V+

Vavasour Awatere Valley Marlborough Rosé ★★★★★

The classy 2019 vintage (★★★★★) is pink/pale red, with loads of youthful vigour and charm. It has fresh, strong strawberry, watermelon and spice flavours, with a dry (3.6 grams/litre of residual sugar), lasting finish. Top drinking for the summer of 2019–20.

 DRY $23 V+

Vidal Reserve Hawke's Bay Rosé (★★★★☆)

The attractive 2018 vintage (★★★★☆) is Merlot-based (94 per cent), with splashes of Pinot Noir (5 per cent) and Syrah (1 per cent). Pale pink, it is full-bodied, with vibrant peach, apricot, spice and watermelon flavours, showing excellent depth, and a very harmonious, dry (4.2 grams/litre of residual sugar) finish.

Vintage	19	18
WR	7	7
Drink	19-21	19-20

 DRY $20 V+

Villa Maria Private Bin Hawke's Bay Rosé ★★★★

Merlot-based, the 2018 vintage (★★★★) is a bright pink, charming rosé, with vibrant strawberryish flavours, hints of spices and apricots, and very good delicacy and depth. A basically dry style (4.8 grams/litre of residual sugar), it is finely poised and priced sharply.

Vintage	18	17
WR	7	7
Drink	19-20	P

 DRY $16 V+

Villa Maria Single Vineyard Braided Gravels Hawke's Bay Rosé (★★★★★)

Full of flavour, the 2017 vintage (★★★★★) was made from Merlot harvested in the Joseph Soler Vineyard, in the Gimblett Gravels. Pale pink, it is a fragrant, fresh, medium to full-bodied wine, with very generous, strawberryish flavours, hints of spices and peaches, and a dry (3 grams/litre of residual sugar) finish. Certified organic.

DRY $30 AV

Waipara Hills Waipara Valley Pinot Noir Rosé ★★★★

Looking good for this summer, the 2019 vintage (★★★★) is a bright pink, vivacious wine, grown in the Home Block (mostly) and briefly lees-aged. Medium-bodied, it is fresh and vibrant, with lively strawberry and spice flavours, a touch of tannin, and a basically dry (4.2 grams/litre of residual sugar), appetisingly crisp finish. Fine value.

 DRY $18 V+

Wairau River Marlborough Rosé ★★★☆

Pale pink, the 2018 vintage (★★★☆) was made from Pinot Noir. A fresh, medium-bodied wine, it has peach, strawberry, watermelon and spice flavours, and a dry (3 grams/litre of residual sugar), crisp finish.

Vintage	16	15	14	13
WR	6	7	7	4
Drink	P	P	P	P

 DRY $20 AV

Whitehaven Marlborough Pinot Noir Rosé ★★★★

Showing plenty of personality, the attractively scented 2019 vintage (★★★★☆) is a light pink, mouthfilling wine, with strawberryish, spicy flavours, peachy notes, a touch of tannin and a dry, lasting finish. A 'serious' but vivacious wine, it's already delicious.

 DRY $23 AV

Wither Hills Early Light Marlborough Pinot Noir Rosé (★★★)

The 2018 vintage (★★★) is an attractive, light style (9.5 per cent alcohol). Pale pink, it is fresh and lively, with crisp, strawberryish, slightly spicy flavours, finely balanced for easy drinking.

 MED/DRY $18 AV

Wither Hills Marlborough Pinot Noir Rosé ★★★★

Bright pink, the 2018 vintage (★★★★) is a skilfully balanced wine. Retasted in mid-2019, it is fresh and medium-bodied, with lively flavours of watermelon and strawberry, hints of peach and apricot, and a dry (3.5 grams/litre of residual sugar), finely poised finish. A good buy.

 DRY $18 V+

Wooing Tree Central Otago Rosé ★★★★

From estate-grown Pinot Noir grapes, hand-picked in the Cromwell Basin, the 2018 vintage (★★★★) is a bright pink, vivacious wine. Finely balanced, it has fresh, strong strawberry and spice flavours, dry (3.7 grams/litre of residual sugar) and lasting.

 DRY $27 –V

Zaria Hawke's Bay Rosé (★★★★)

The very charming 2018 vintage (★★★★) is a single-vineyard wine, from Malbec grapes grown in the Bridge Pa Triangle. Bright pink, it is fresh and medium-bodied, with vibrant watermelon, strawberry and spice flavours, finely balanced, dry (1.5 grams/litre of residual sugar) and lingering. Priced right.

 DRY $20 V+

Zephyr MK I Rosé (★★★★☆)

A single-vineyard Marlborough wine, the debut 2019 vintage (★★★★☆) is bright pink, crisp and vivacious, with watermelon, strawberry and spice flavours, showing excellent intensity, and a long, dry finish. A top pick for the summer of 2019–20. (From Glover Family Wines.)

DRY $28 AV

Red Wines

Barbera

One of Italy's most widely planted red-wine varieties – particularly in Piedmont, in the north-west – Barbera is known for its generous yields of robust, full-coloured reds, typically with lively acidity. Although increasingly popular in California, it is extremely rare in New Zealand and is not listed separately in New Zealand Winegrowers' *Vineyard Register Report 2017–2020*.

De La Terre Hawke's Bay Barbera ★★★★

The 2014 vintage (★★★★) was hand-picked at Havelock North and matured for 18 months in seasoned French oak barriques. Full-coloured, it is mouthfilling, with concentrated, ripe, plummy, gently spicy flavours, firm tannins beneath, and good complexity.

Vintage	14	13
WR	6	5
Drink	19-20	P

`DRY $40 –V`

Branded and Other Red Wines

Most New Zealand red wines carry a varietal label, such as Pinot Noir, Syrah, Merlot or Cabernet Sauvignon (or blends of the last two). Those not labelled prominently by their principal grape varieties – often prestigious wines such as Esk Valley Heipipi The Terraces or Destiny Bay Magna Praemia – can be found here. Although not varietally labelled, these wines are mostly of high quality and sometimes outstanding.

Alpha Domus AD The Aviator ★★★★★

Estate-grown in the Bridge Pa Triangle, this is a blend of classic Bordeaux varieties. The outstanding 2015 vintage (★★★★★) is a marriage of Cabernet Sauvignon (50 per cent), Cabernet Franc (22 per cent), Merlot (21 per cent) and Malbec (7 per cent). Matured in French oak barriques (46 per cent new), it is deeply coloured, with a fragrant, very refined bouquet. Full-bodied, it is youthful, with concentrated, deliciously ripe blackcurrant, plum and spice flavours, excellent complexity and a long finish. A very elegant, rich wine, showing lovely delicacy and depth, it's already very approachable, but likely to be at its best 2020+.

Vintage	15	DRY $98 AV
WR	7	
Drink	19-25	

Alpha Domus The Navigator ★★★★☆

The deeply coloured, generous 2014 vintage (★★★★☆) is a blend of Merlot (46 per cent), Malbec (24 per cent), Cabernet Sauvignon (16 per cent) and Cabernet Franc (14 per cent), estate-grown in the Bridge Pa Triangle, Hawke's Bay, and matured in seasoned oak barrels (mostly French). Full-bodied, it has fresh, strong, well-ripened blackcurrant, plum and spice flavours, hints of nuts, leather and coffee, excellent complexity and good tannin backbone. A full-on style, with a slightly sweet oak influence, it's drinking well now.

Vintage	14	DRY $32 AV
WR	7	
Drink	19-22	

Ash Ridge Hawke's Bay Reserve The Blend ★★★★☆

Grown in the Bridge Pa Triangle, the 2015 vintage (★★★★) was blended from five varieties, mostly Merlot and Cabernet Sauvignon, and matured in French and American oak casks. Full-coloured, with a youthful, slightly spicy bouquet, it is a medium to full-bodied style, with strong, vibrant, plummy, spicy flavours, showing good complexity. Best drinking 2019+. (This label will be replaced by a top Cabernet Sauvignon/Merlot.)

 DRY $45 –V

Ata Rangi Martinborough Célèbre ★★★★☆

Pronounced 'say-lebr', this is a blend of Merlot, Syrah and Cabernet Sauvignon. It typically has excellent weight and depth of plummy, spicy flavours in a complex style that matures well.

Vintage	14	13	12	11	10	DRY $40 –V
WR	7	7	NM	6	NM	
Drink	19-26	19-25	NM	19-20	NM	

Babich Heritage Anniversary Label Hawke's Bay Premium Red Blend   (★★★★★)

Clad in the company's Cabernet Sauvignon label from the 1970s, the classy 2016 vintage (★★★★★) is a celebration of Babich's 100-year history, produced in quite large volumes (about 1000 cases). French oak-matured for 15 months, it is a blend of Cabernet Sauvignon, Merlot and Cabernet Franc, grown in the Gimblett Gravels and French oak-aged for 16 months. A very elegant, 'complete' wine, it is deeply coloured, with concentrated blackcurrant, plum and spice flavours, showing excellent complexity, fine-grained tannins, and impressive vigour and harmony.

 DRY $80 AV

Babich The Patriarch   ★★★★★

This is promoted as Babich's greatest red, regardless of the variety or region of origin, but all vintages have been grown in the company's shingly Irongate Vineyard in Gimblett Road, Hawke's Bay (in other words, they have been Cabernet Sauvignon or Merlot-based blends, rather than Pinot Noirs from further south). It is typically a dark, ripe and complex, deliciously rich red. The 2016 vintage (★★★★★) is a boldly coloured blend of Merlot (40 per cent), Malbec (33 per cent) and Cabernet Sauvignon (27 per cent), matured for 16 months in French oak barriques. A powerful young wine, it is sturdy, with concentrated, ripe berry, plum and spice flavours, finely integrated oak, good tannin backbone and obvious potential. Retasted in April 2019, it is still very fresh and youthful; open 2022+.

Vintage	16	15	14	13	12	11	10
WR	6	7	7	7	5	5	7
Drink	19-26	19-25	19-25	19-25	19-21	19-20	19-22

 DRY $90 AV

Boneline, The, Waipara Iridium   (★★★★★)

Deeply coloured, the 2016 vintage (★★★★★) is a commanding North Canterbury red, blended from Cabernet Franc, Merlot and Cabernet Sauvignon. Matured in French oak casks (35 per cent new), it has a fragrant, slightly herbal bouquet, leading into a sturdy wine (15 per cent alcohol), with notable density. Youthful, it has highly concentrated blackcurrant, plum, herb and spice flavours, with a firmly structured, lasting finish. A very distinctive red, it's well worth cellaring to 2022+.

DRY $50 AV

Brick Bay Martello Rock   ★★★★

The 2015 vintage (★★★★) is a blend of Malbec (40 per cent), Merlot (22 per cent), Cabernet Sauvignon (22 per cent) and Cabernet Franc (16 per cent), estate-grown at Matakana and barrel-aged. It has deep, youthful colour and a very fresh, fragrant bouquet. Full-bodied, it is youthful and sweet-fruited, with strong, berryish, plummy, spicy flavours, and ripe, supple tannins. Best drinking 2020+.

 $30 –V

Brick Bay Pharos ★★★★☆

Likely to be long-lived, the 2014 vintage (★★★★☆) is a dark blend of Petit Verdot, Malbec, Cabernet Franc and Merlot, estate-grown at Matakana and matured in French oak barriques (mostly new). Mouthfilling and vibrantly fruity, it has strong, ripe berry, plum and spice flavours, firm and complex, and obvious cellaring potential; best drinking 2021+.

DRY $48 –V

Cable Bay Five Hills ★★★★

This Waiheke Island red has traditionally been a blend of Merlot and Malbec, but the 2016 vintage (★★★★) was made entirely from Malbec. Hand-harvested and matured in seasoned French oak barriques, it is full-coloured, fresh and mouthfilling, with generous, berryish, spicy flavours, oak complexity, fine-grained tannins and a spicy fragrance. Best drinking 2020+.

Vintage	16
WR	6
Drink	19-22

DRY $48 –V

Clearview Hawke's Bay Enigma ★★★★★

Entirely estate-grown at Te Awanga, the lovely 2016 vintage (★★★★★) is a deeply coloured blend of Merlot (70 per cent), Malbec (20 per cent) and Cabernet Franc (10 per cent), matured for 16 months in French oak casks (40 per cent new). Sturdy, rich and youthful, it has concentrated blackcurrant, plum and spice flavours, savoury and complex, a hint of dark chocolate, fine-grained tannins and obvious cellaring potential. Already drinking well, it's a very 'complete' wine, likely to be at its best 2021+.

DRY $55 AV

Clearview Old Olive Block ★★★★★

This Hawke's Bay red is named after the estate vineyard at Te Awanga, which has an old olive tree in the centre. It is grown there and in the Gimblett Gravels. Still very youthful, the 2016 vintage (★★★★★) is a deeply coloured blend of Cabernet Sauvignon (63 per cent), Malbec (20 per cent) and Cabernet Franc (17 per cent), matured for 16 months in French oak casks (25 per cent new). Grown principally (70 per cent) in the Gimblett Gravels, it is well worth cellaring, with a fragrant, slightly herbal bouquet and concentrated blackcurrant, herb and spice flavours. Complex, savoury and nutty, it is an elegant, very finely structured red, likely to break into full stride from 2021 onwards.

Vintage	16	15
WR	6	6
Drink	21-26	20-25

DRY $45 AV

Clearview The Basket Press ★★★★★

The distinguished 2013 vintage (★★★★★) is a blend of 35 per cent Cabernet Sauvignon, grown in the Gimblett Gravels, with coastal Te Awanga fruit: Merlot (30 per cent), Cabernet Franc (30 per cent) and Malbec (5 per cent). Hand-picked and matured for over two years in all-new French oak barriques, it is deeply coloured, with dense, pure blackcurrant, plum and spice flavours that build to a lasting, finely poised finish. Weighty and highly concentrated, with a backbone of ripe, supple tannins, it has lapped up the new oak influence, creating a savoury, multi-faceted red. Already delicious, it should flourish for a decade – or longer.

Vintage	13
WR	7
Drink	19-25

DRY $165 –V

Craggy Range Aroha ★★★★★

The delicious 2017 vintage (★★★★★) is a single-vineyard Pinot Noir, estate-grown at Te Muna, on the edge of Martinborough. Hand-picked, it was fermented with indigenous yeasts and matured for 11 months in French oak barriques (28 per cent new). Deep, bright ruby, it is mouthfilling and savoury, with generous cherry, plum and spice flavours, oak complexity and ripe, supple tannins. A very refined, youthful, harmonious red, it's well worth cellaring to 2022+.

Vintage	17	16	15	14	13	12	11	10
WR	6	7	7	7	7	7	7	NM
Drink	19-27	19-27	19-26	19-25	19-25	19-24	19-23	NM

DRY $150 –V

Craggy Range Le Sol ★★★★★

This famous Syrah impresses with its lovely fragrance and finesse. Estate-grown in the Gimblett Gravels of Hawke's Bay, the densely packed 2016 vintage (★★★★★) was hand-picked and matured for 17 months in French oak barriques (35 per cent new). Still very youthful, it is dark and purple-flushed, mouthfilling and supple, with highly concentrated plum and black-pepper flavours, refined tannins and a lasting finish. It needs time; open 2021+. (There is no 2017.)

Vintage	17	16	15	14	13	12	11	10
WR	NM	7	7	7	7	NM	7	7
Drink	NM	19-31	19-30	19-30	19-30	NM	19-25	19-27

DRY $150 AV

Craggy Range Sophia ★★★★★

This is Craggy Range's premier Merlot-based red. The 2016 vintage (★★★★★) is a Gimblett Gravels, Hawke's Bay blend of Merlot, Cabernet Sauvignon, Cabernet Franc and Petit Verdot, hand-picked and matured for 18 months in French oak barriques (45 per cent new). Dark and purple-flushed, it is weighty and highly concentrated, with youthful, very vibrant plum, spice and blackcurrant flavours, oak complexity, and a finely textured finish. It's still very youthful; open 2021+. (There is no 2017.)

Vintage	17	16	15	14	13	12	11	10
WR	NM	7	7	7	7	NM	7	7
Drink	NM	19-31	19-30	19-30	19-30	NM	19-25	19-27

DRY $140 AV

Craggy Range Te Kahu ★★★★☆

Estate-grown in the Gimblett Gravels, the youthful 2017 vintage (★★★★☆) of this Hawke's Bay red is Merlot-based (66 per cent), with smaller portions of Cabernet Franc and Cabernet Sauvignon and splashes of Petit Verdot and Malbec. Matured for 17 months in oak barriques (20 per cent new), it is full-coloured, fresh and mouthfilling, with generous, ripe blackcurrant, plum and spice flavours, firm tannins, and the depth and structure to mature well. Best drinking 2022+.

 DRY $30 AV

Craggy Range The Quarry ★★★★★

The impressive 2016 vintage (★★★★★) is the first since 2011. From hand-harvested Cabernet Sauvignon grapes, estate-grown in the Gimblett Gravels, it was matured for 18 months in French oak barriques (50 per cent new). Densely coloured, it is a sturdy, very youthful red, sweet-fruited, with highly concentrated, pure blackcurrant-like flavours, very finely structured and set for the long haul. Open 2023+.

 DRY $150 AV

Crazy by Nature Gisborne Cosmo Red ★★★☆

Certified organic, the 2016 vintage (★★★☆) from Millton is a blend of Malbec, Syrah and Viognier, matured for 15 months in large oak barrels, and bottled unfined and unfiltered. Full-coloured, with a fresh, slightly rustic bouquet, it is a medium-bodied, youthful red, fruity, plummy, slightly spicy and smooth, with some savoury notes, balanced acidity and very good flavour depth.

 DRY $26 –V

Crossroads Hawke's Bay Talisman ★★★★★

A blend of several red varieties whose identities the winery long delighted in concealing (I saw Malbec and Syrah as prime suspects), Talisman was at first estate-grown in the Origin Vineyard at Fernhill, in Hawke's Bay, and has recently also included grapes from sites in the Gimblett Gravels (a spy tells me that the key 'mystery' varieties are in fact Tannat and Petite Syrah). The 2014 vintage (★★★★★) has bold, inky-red colour. Sturdy and rich, it is a powerful, very youthful red, with dense plum, spice, liquorice and dark chocolate flavours, buried tannins and a smooth, long finish.

Vintage	14	13	12	11	10
WR	7	7	5	5	7
Drink	19-25	19-23	19-23	19-22	19-22

 DRY $56 AV

Destiny Bay Destinae ★★★★★

The 2013 vintage (★★★★★) is a perfect introduction to the Destiny Bay range. Estate-grown on Waiheke Island, it is a blend of Cabernet Sauvignon (38 per cent), Merlot (36 per cent), Cabernet Franc (12 per cent), Malbec (8 per cent) and Petit Verdot (6 per cent), harvested at 24 to 25.6 brix and matured in a 50:50 split of French and American oak casks (40 per cent new). A distinguished but very approachable red, it is deeply coloured, fleshy, rich and softly textured, with blackcurrant, plum, dried-herb and spice flavours, showing excellent concentration, complexity and harmony.

DRY $125 –V

Destiny Bay Magna Praemia ★★★★★

The powerful, lush 2013 vintage (★★★★★), harvested at 24 to 25.6 brix, is a blend of Cabernet Sauvignon (71 per cent) and Merlot (16 per cent), with minor portions of Cabernet Franc, Petit Verdot and Malbec. Matured for up to 15 months in an even split of French and American oak casks (60 per cent new), it is dark and full-bodied (14.5 per cent alcohol), with deliciously dense, ripe blackcurrant, plum and spice flavours, fine-grained tannins, excellent complexity and a lasting finish. A classy, savoury, highly concentrated red, it's already approachable, but likely to be long-lived; best drinking 2020+.

DRY $355 –V

Destiny Bay Mystae ★★★★★

The 2013 vintage (★★★★★) of this Waiheke Island blend is Cabernet Sauvignon-based (52 per cent), with Merlot (25 per cent), Cabernet Franc (9 per cent), Malbec (8 per cent) and Petit Verdot (6 per cent). Harvested at 24 to 25.6 brix, it was matured in an even split of French and American oak casks (60 per cent new). Dark and youthful in colour, it is a powerful red (14.5 per cent alcohol), fleshy and rich, sweet-fruited and lush, with concentrated blackcurrant and spice flavours, a hint of sweet oak, and fine-grained tannins. A very age-worthy wine, it should be at its best 2020+.

DRY $155 –V

Dry River The Twelve Spies (★★★★☆)

The debut 2017 vintage (★★★★☆) is an estate-grown, Martinborough blend of Pinot Noir, Tempranillo, Syrah and Viognier, matured for a year in oak hogsheads (15 per cent new). Full-coloured, it is fresh, vibrant and youthful, with good concentration of plummy, spicy flavours, savoury notes adding complexity, and a spicy fragrance. Best drinking 2021+.

DRY $70 –V

Elephant Hill Hawke's Bay Hieronymus ★★★★★

The powerful, sturdy, rich 2015 vintage (★★★★★) is a blend of Cabernet Sauvignon (41 per cent), Merlot (22 per cent), Cabernet Franc (17 per cent), Malbec (12 per cent) and Tempranillo (8 per cent), estate-grown in the Gimblett Gravels (58 per cent) and the Bridge Pa Triangle (42 per cent). Matured for 26 months in French oak casks (50 per cent new), it is a boldly coloured, fruit-packed red, with a fragrant, spicy bouquet. Still youthful, it is full-bodied, with dense, well-ripened blackcurrant, plum, spice and nut flavours, hints of pepper and liquorice, good tannin backbone, and a long, very harmonious finish. Best drinking 2022+.

DRY $120 AV

Elephant Hill Hawke's Bay Le Phant Rouge ★★★★

The 2015 vintage (★★★★) is a deeply coloured, Merlot-based red (70 per cent), with minor portions of Cabernet Sauvignon, Syrah, Malbec and Cabernet Franc. Hand-picked in the Gimblett Gravels, at Te Awanga and in the Bridge Pa Triangle, it was oak-aged for a year.

Fragrant and fresh, with generous, ripe blackcurrant, plum and spice flavours, tinged with sweet oak, it has a solid foundation of tannin, and nutty, savoury notes adding complexity. Enjoyable young, it's also well worth cellaring.

DRY $24 V+

Esk Valley Heipipi The Terraces ★★★★★

Grown on the steep, terraced, north-facing hillside flanking the winery at Bay View, in Hawke's Bay, this is a strikingly bold, dark wine with bottomless depth of blackcurrant, plum and strongly spicy flavour. Malbec (43 per cent of the vines) and Merlot (35 per cent) are typically the major ingredients, supplemented by Cabernet Franc; the Malbec gives 'perfume, spice, tannin and brilliant colour'. Yields in the 1-hectare vineyard are very low, and the wine is matured for 17 to 22 months in French oak barriques (50 per cent new in 2016). 'En primeur' (payment at a reduced price, in advance of delivery) has been the best way to buy. It typically matures well, developing a beautiful fragrance and spicy, Rhône-like complexity. The 2016 vintage (★★★★★) is a terrific wine. Densely coloured, it is powerful, with lovely concentration of blackcurrant, plum and spice flavours, a hint of liquorice, refined tannins, and a fragrant, spicy bouquet. Set for a long life, it's already delicious.

Vintage	16	15	14	13	12	11	10
WR	7	7	7	7	NM	NM	NM
Drink	19-30	19-30	19-30	19-35	NM	NM	NM

DRY $160 AV

Four Daughters Hawke's Bay Red Wine ★★★

Probably at its peak, the 2013 vintage (★★★☆) is an unusual blend of Hawke's Bay Malbec (29 per cent), Cabernet Franc (26 per cent), Syrah (25 per cent) and Merlot (20 per cent), grown in the Bridge Pa Triangle and the Gimblett Gravels. Maturing well, it is fullish in colour, with very good depth of plummy, spicy flavours, a hint of herbs, and a savoury, moderately firm finish. (From Coopers Creek.)

DRY $18 AV

Frenchmans Hill Estate Waiheke Island Blood Creek 8 ★★★★★

The fragrant, highly concentrated 2014 vintage (★★★★★) is a blend of eight varieties – principally Cabernet Sauvignon (36 per cent), Merlot (17 per cent) and Petit Verdot (15 per cent), plus smaller portions of Cabernet Franc, Tannat, Syrah, Viognier and Koler. Matured for 16 months in all-new French oak barriques, it is dark, fresh and full-bodied, with dense, ripe blackcurrant, plum and spice flavours, good tannin backbone, and impressive power through the palate. Still youthful, it should be at its best from 2021 onwards.

DRY $125 –V

Gillman ★★★★★

This rare, estate-grown Matakana red is a blend of Cabernet Franc, Merlot and Malbec, matured in French oak barrels. In late 2018, I tasted the 2016, 2015, 2014 and 2012 vintages. Fleshy, savoury and full-coloured, the 2016 (★★★★★) is a classy young red, likely to be long-lived, with deep blackcurrant/spice flavours, leathery notes adding complexity, good tannin support, and a very harmonious finish. Drinking well now, the 2015 vintage (★★★★☆) is elegant, with good but not great intensity of plum, spice, herb and nut flavours, a hint of coffee, and supple tannins. The 2014 (★★★★★), oak-aged for two years (50 per cent new), is a powerful, almost robust red, very fragrant, savoury and concentrated, with a long future ahead; open 2021+. The 2012 vintage (★★★★★), still fairly youthful in colour, has an earthy streak running through its savoury, complex flavours, which are fresh, smooth and strong. Drink now or cellar.

Vintage	12	11	10
WR	6	6	7
Drink	19-24	19-23	19-30

DRY $85 AV

Kaimira Estate Brightwater Hui Whero ★★★☆

The 2016 vintage (★★★☆) is a Nelson 'blend of classic varieties', matured for 10 months in oak casks (15 per cent new). Full-coloured, with a spicy bouquet, it is a medium-bodied, vibrantly fruity, slightly Syrah-like red, fresh, plummy and distinctly peppery, with lively acidity and very good flavour depth. Certified organic.

Vintage	16
WR	5
Drink	19-28

DRY $28 –V

Kemp Road Whenua (★★★★☆)

Released in late 2018, the 2009 vintage (★★★★☆) is a blend of Cabernet Sauvignon (40 per cent), Merlot (38 per cent) and Malbec (22 per cent), grown in vineyards 'around Gimblett Road', in Hawke's Bay, and matured for 18 months in French and American oak barriques. It has deep, moderately developed colour and a fragrant, spicy bouquet. Mouthfilling, it is still lively, with generous blackcurrant, herb and spice flavours, slightly earthy and nutty notes adding complexity, and a firm finish. It's drinking well now. (From Great Little Vineyards.)

DRY $45 –V

Linden Estate Hawke's Bay Dam Block ★★★★☆

Already drinking well, the 2017 vintage (★★★★☆) is a blend of Cabernet Sauvignon, Merlot and Cabernet Franc. Full-coloured, it is savoury and complex, with mouthfilling body, deep, berryish, spicy, nutty flavours, and the structure to age well.

DRY $55 –V

Little Brother (★★★☆)

The attractive, easy-drinking 2016 vintage (★★★☆) was grown at two sites in Kerikeri, Northland. Syrah is the principal variety, 'spiked with Viognier and a touch of Chambourcin'. Matured in old oak barriques, it is full-coloured, mouthfilling and smooth, in a vibrantly fruity style with fresh, ripe, plummy, juicy flavours to the fore. A good summer red. (From Byrne.)

DRY $19 V+

Man O' War Ironclad ★★★★☆

This powerful red, grown at the eastern end of Waiheke Island, is typically based on Cabernet Franc and Merlot, with minor portions of Cabernet Sauvignon, Petit Verdot and Malbec. The classy 2013 vintage (★★★★★) is a blend of Cabernet Franc (32 per cent), Merlot (29 per cent), Petit Verdot (16 per cent), Malbec (12 per cent) and Cabernet Sauvignon (11 per cent). Densely coloured, it is sturdy and bold, with very generous blackcurrant and plum flavours, showing excellent ripeness and concentration, good tannin support, and plenty of cellaring potential; best drinking 2020+.

Vintage	13	12	11
WR	5	5	4
Drink	19-28	19-25	19-23

 DRY $49 –V

Man O' War Warspite ★★★★☆

The 2014 vintage (★★★★) is a Ponui Island (Auckland) blend of Cabernet Franc, Merlot and Malbec, matured in French oak casks (45 per cent new). Deeply coloured, with slightly herbal aromas, it is a powerful, sturdy (15 per cent alcohol) red, with generous plum, spice and herb flavours, seasoned with nutty oak, good complexity and a well-rounded finish. Drink now or cellar.

Vintage	14
WR	5
Drink	19-20

 DRY $47 –V

Messenger ★★★★★

After the lovely debut 2008 (★★★★★), Messenger is established as one of Auckland's greatest reds. It is estate-grown at Stillwater, north of the city. French oak-matured for two years, the 2013 vintage (★★★★☆) is a blend of Merlot, Cabernet Franc and Malbec. Dense and inky in colour, it's a robust (14.8 per cent alcohol), almost super-charged red, very sweet-fruited, with highly concentrated plum, spice and slight liquorice flavours. Notable for its power and richness, rather than finesse, it is full of personality.

 DRY $85 AV

Mills Reef Elspeth One (★★★★★)

The 2013 vintage (★★★★★) is the first for many years. Likely to be long-lived, it is a Gimblett Gravels, Hawke's Bay blend of estate-grown Syrah (41 per cent), Cabernet Franc (23 per cent), Merlot (18 per cent) and Cabernet Sauvignon (18 per cent), matured for 20 months in French oak casks (35 per cent new). Full-coloured, it has deep, plummy, spicy flavours – in which the Syrah makes its presence well felt – finely balanced tannins, excellent complexity, and a long, very persistent finish. Best drinking 2020+.

 DRY $150 –V

Mission Jewelstone Gimblett Gravels Hawke's Bay Antoine ★★★★★

Named after pioneer winemaker Father Antoine Gavin, the 2016 vintage (★★★★★) is a classy blend of Cabernet Sauvignon (41 per cent), Cabernet Franc (33 per cent) and Merlot (26 per cent), matured for 18 months in French oak barriques. Deeply coloured, it is fragrant and youthful, with deep blackcurrant, red-berry and spice flavours, and fine-grained tannins. Showing excellent delicacy and finesse, it's a very age-worthy wine, likely to be at its best 2023+.

DRY $50 AV

Mokoroa   ★★★☆

From Puriri Hills, the 2016 vintage (★★★☆) was estate-grown at Clevedon, in South Auckland. Promoted as 'a good lunchtime wine', it is a blend of Merlot (71 per cent), Cabernet Sauvignon (15 per cent), Cabernet Franc (8 per cent), Carménère (5 per cent) and Malbec (1 per cent). Deep ruby, it is a medium-bodied red with vibrant, berryish, plummy flavours, slightly earthy and savoury notes adding complexity, and a smooth, very harmonious finish.

Vintage	16
WR	5
Drink	19-23

 DRY $30 –V

Moutere Hills Nelson Rumer   (★★★☆)

The 2016 vintage (★★★☆) is a blend of Syrah, Merlot and Cabernet Sauvignon, hand-picked and matured for 10 months in French and American oak casks. Enjoyable young, it is full-coloured, mouthfilling, fresh and smooth, with plum and blackcurrant flavours, a hint of herbs, fresh acidity and very good depth.

 DRY $55 –V

Newton Forrest Estate Cornerstone   ★★★★★

Grown in the Cornerstone Vineyard, on the corner of Gimblett Road and State Highway 50 – where the first vines were planted in 1989 – this is a distinguished Hawke's Bay blend of Cabernet Sauvignon, Merlot and Malbec, matured in French (principally) and American oak barriques. The highly refined 2015 vintage (★★★★★) is dark, full-bodied and tightly structured, with concentrated, ripe blackcurrant, plum and spice flavours, complex and savoury, fine-grained tannins, and a very harmonious finish. Already delicious, it's well worth cellaring.

 DRY $60 AV

Obsidian Reserve The Obsidian   ★★★★★

The Obsidian Vineyard at Onetangi produces one of the most stylish Waiheke Island reds. Blended from classic Bordeaux red varieties – Cabernet Franc, Merlot, Cabernet Sauvignon, Petit Verdot and Malbec – it is matured in French oak barriques. The 2014 vintage (★★★★★) has deep, youthful colour. Fragrant and supple, it has deep blackcurrant, plum, herb and spice flavours, showing excellent complexity, fine-grained tannins, and a rich, harmonious finish. A graceful wine, it's already delicious, but well worth cellaring.

Vintage	14	13	12	11	10
WR	7	7	6	6	7
Drink	19-24	19-23	19-20	P	19-20

 DRY $68 AV

Obsidian Reserve Waiheke Island The Mayor ★★★★☆

Still very youthful, the 2018 vintage (★★★★☆) is a bold, vibrantly fruity blend of Cabernet Franc (50 per cent), Petit Verdot (25 per cent) and Malbec (25 per cent), matured in new French and seasoned American oak barrels. Full-coloured, it has fresh, berryish, spicy aromas and flavours, showing excellent depth and complexity, fine-grained tannins and good aging potential.

DRY $58 –V

Obsidian Waiheke Island Vitreous (★★★★)

Grown at Onetangi, the debut 2015 vintage (★★★★) is a blend of Cabernet Sauvignon (28 per cent), Merlot (25 per cent), Cabernet Franc (23 per cent), Petit Verdot (19 per cent) and Malbec (5 per cent). Matured in French oak casks (20 per cent new), it is full-coloured, mouthfilling and smooth, with fresh, generous, slightly spicy and herbal flavours, nutty, savoury and showing good complexity.

DRY $32 –V

Paritua 21:12 ★★★★★

The powerful, still youthful 2015 vintage (★★★★★) is a blend of Cabernet Sauvignon (52 per cent), Merlot (31 per cent) and Cabernet Franc (17 per cent), estate-grown in the Bridge Pa Triangle, Hawke's Bay, and matured for 20 months in French oak barriques (50 per cent new). A classic, claret-style red, it is dark and highly concentrated, with substantial body and rich blackcurrant, plum, spice and nut flavours. A dense, firmly structured wine, it should flourish for at least 15 years.

DRY $130 –V

Pask Small Batch Trilliant (★★★☆)

The 2016 vintage (★★★☆) is a full-coloured Hawke's Bay red, blended from Merlot (53 per cent), Cabernet Sauvignon (20 per cent) and Malbec (27 per cent). Matured for 14 months in American oak casks (50 per cent new), it is medium-bodied, with fresh acidity, good depth of berryish, plummy flavours and a smooth finish.

Vintage	16
WR	6
Drink	19-28

 DRY $35 –V

Passage Rock Waiheke Island Magnus ★★★★★

The impressive 2017 vintage (★★★★★) is a rare blend of Syrah, Cabernet Sauvignon, Montepulciano, Merlot and Malbec, grown on Waiheke Island and matured for a year in French oak casks (30 per cent new). A rich, very 'complete' wine, it's already delicious. Deeply coloured and sturdy, with concentrated blackcurrant, plum, berry and spice flavours, hints of liquorice and nuts, and good tannin backbone, it should be at its best 2022+.

Vintage	17
WR	6
Drink	19-25

 DRY $98 AV

Pegasus Bay Maestro ★★★★★

The 2016 vintage (★★★★★) is a Waipara, North Canterbury blend of Merlot, Cabernet Sauvignon and Malbec, from vines over 30 years old. Barrel-aged for two years (60 per cent new), it is a powerful, dense, youthful red, set for a very long life. Dark and still purple-flushed, it has rich, harmonious plum, blackcurrant, herb and spice flavours, fine-grained tannins and an enticingly fragrant bouquet. One of the South Island's greatest 'Bordeaux-style' reds, it should flourish for a decade.

Vintage	16	15
WR	7	6
Drink	19-34	19-28

 DRY $50 AV

Pinot 3 – The Red Edition (★★★☆)

Floral and fresh, the 2019 vintage (★★★☆) is an unusual blend of Pinot Noir, Pinot Gris and Pinot Blanc, grown in Marlborough and Gisborne, and handled without oak. Bright pink/pale red, it is light and lively, with fruity, berryish flavours, in a highly enjoyable, smooth, drink-young style with a Beaujolais-like charm. (From Untitled Wines, based in West Auckland.)

 DRY $20 AV

Prophet's Rock Central Otago Cuvée Aux Antipodes ★★★★★

The 2017 vintage (★★★★★) is a Pinot Noir, estate-grown at an elevated site (320 to 400 metres above sea level) at Bendigo, in Central Otago, and matured in French oak casks. Deeply coloured, it is a powerful red, with substantial body and concentrated, vibrant, plummy, spicy flavours, showing real depth through the palate. Still extremely youthful, it should break into full stride 2023+.

 DRY $118 –V

Prophet's Rock Retrospect (★★★★★)

Only 736 bottles were made of the powerful yet elegant 2013 vintage (★★★★★), released in early 2018. Estate-grown at Bendigo, in Central Otago, it is a Pinot Noir, barrel-aged for 17 months. Still youthful, it is rich and savoury, with cherry, plum and spice flavours, a hint of liquorice, and excellent vigour, complexity and length. Best drinking 2020+.

 DRY $140 –V

Pukeora Estate Ruahine Ranges The Benches (★★★★☆)

The 2013 vintage (★★★★☆) is the best 'Bordeaux-style' red I've tasted from Central Hawke's Bay. A blend of Merlot (70 per cent), Malbec (17 per cent), Syrah (7 per cent) and Cabernet Sauvignon (6 per cent), it was hand-picked and matured for 22 months in American and French oak barriques (33 per cent new). Deep and bright in colour, it is fragrant and vibrantly fruity, with substantial body and deep, ripe blackcurrant, plum and spice flavours, still fresh and youthful. Best drinking 2020+. Fine value.

 DRY $28 V+

Puriri Hills Estate   ★★★★☆

Estate-grown at Clevedon, in South Auckland, this is a classy, Merlot-based blend. The 2013 vintage (★★★★★) is the best since 2010. Dark and highly fragrant, it is a very elegant, poised, youthful wine, with deep, plummy, spicy, nutty flavours and a long life ahead. The youthful 2014 vintage (★★★★☆) is a blend of Merlot (77 per cent), Cabernet Sauvignon (13 per cent), Cabernet Franc (7 per cent) and Malbec (3 per cent). Deeply coloured, it is a sweet-fruited, medium to full-bodied red, with concentrated, ripe plum, berry and spice flavours, refined tannins and obvious cellaring potential. Best drinking 2021+.

Vintage	14	13	12	11	10
WR	7	7	6	6	7
Drink	19-31	19-30	19-28	P	19-27

 DRY $45 –V

Puriri Hills Harmonie Du Soir   ★★★★★

Formerly called 'Puriri Hills Reserve' (up to and including the 2010 vintage), this regional classic has been labelled as 'Harmonie Du Soir' since 2012 (there was no 2011 vintage). Estate-grown at Clevedon, in South Auckland, it is blended from varying proportions of Merlot (principally), Cabernet Franc, Carménère, Cabernet Sauvignon and Malbec, and typically matured for two years in French oak barriques (a high percentage new). The 2012 vintage (★★★★★), currently on sale, is a blend of Merlot (50 per cent), Carménère (25 per cent), Cabernet Franc (13 per cent) and Malbec (12 per cent). Full-coloured, it is mouthfilling, savoury, complex and supple, with concentrated blackcurrant, plum, spice, herb and nut flavours, finely balanced and long. A highly Bordeaux-like red, it's delicious now, but will also reward cellaring. (The benchmark 2013 vintage (★★★★★) is notably refined, beautifully rich and silky-textured, and the dark, youthful 2014 vintage (★★★★★) also shows impressive density and complexity.)

 DRY $85 AV

Puriri Hills Pope   ★★★★★

Named after Ivan Pope, who planted and tended the vines at this Clevedon, South Auckland vineyard. Full of youthful promise, the 2013 vintage (★★★★★) is a classy blend of Merlot (70 per cent), Cabernet Franc (10 per cent), Carménère (10 per cent), Cabernet Sauvignon (5 per cent) and Malbec (5 per cent), matured in French oak casks (100 per cent new). Deeply coloured, it has a fragrant, berryish, spicy bouquet, leading into a full-bodied, already very approachable wine, with densely packed, complex plum, blackcurrant and spice flavours, savoury and persistent. Best drinking 2020+. The very elegant 2014 vintage (★★★★★) is a blend of Merlot (41 per cent), Cabernet Franc (31 per cent), Carménère (18 per cent) and Malbec (10 per cent). Fragrant, rich and youthful, with deep, bright colour, it is concentrated and finely structured, with deep, plummy, spicy flavours, savoury, silky and long. Best drinking 2022+.

Vintage	14	13	12	11	10
WR	6	7	NM	NM	7
Drink	19-31	19-31	NM	NM	19-28

 DRY $160 –V

Sacred Hill Brokenstone ★★★★★

Merlot-based, this is a typically outstanding Hawke's Bay red from the Gimblett Gravels (principally the company's Deerstalkers Vineyard). The highly attractive 2015 vintage (★★★★★), matured for 19 months in French oak casks (22 per cent new), is Merlot-dominant (87 per cent), with minor portions of Malbec (4 per cent), Syrah (4 per cent), Cabernet Sauvignon (3 per cent) and Cabernet Franc (2 per cent). Full-coloured, it is vibrantly fruity, with concentrated, ripe, plummy, spicy flavours, well-integrated oak, savoury notes adding complexity, and supple tannins. Already delicious, it should be at its best 2020+.

Vintage	15	14	13	12	11	10
WR	7	7	7	NM	6	7
Drink	19-30	19-26	19-23	NM	P	19-20

 DRY $50 AV

Sacred Hill Helmsman ★★★★★

This is a classy, single-vineyard Gimblett Gravels red from Hawke's Bay. The powerful 2015 vintage (★★★★★), blended from Cabernet Sauvignon (76 per cent), Merlot (19 per cent) and Cabernet Franc (5 per cent), was hand-picked and matured for 20 months in French oak barriques (50 per cent new). A classic, youthful, Cabernet-based red, it is fragrant and deeply coloured, with highly concentrated blackcurrant, plum and herb flavours, seasoned with nutty oak. Dense and firmly structured, it's a stylish, very age-worthy wine, likely to be at its best 2022+.

 DRY $85 AV

Sileni Ruber Grand Reserve Hawke's Bay Red Blend ★★★★☆

The attractive 2018 vintage (★★★★☆) is a distinctive blend of Merlot, Syrah and Cabernet Franc, grown in the Bridge Pa Triangle. Full-coloured, it is mouthfilling and sweet-fruited, with concentrated, plummy, spicy flavours, showing good backbone and complexity, and a fragrant bouquet. Best drinking 2021+.

DRY $37 AV

Smith & Sheth Cru Omahu Cantera ★★★★★

The youthful 2017 vintage (★★★★★) is a Hawke's Bay blend of Cabernet Sauvignon (55 per cent), Tempranillo (26 per cent) and Cabernet Franc (19 per cent), hand-picked in the Gimblett Gravels and matured for 18 months in oak barriques (40 per cent new). Named after the Spanish word for quarry (cantera), it has deep, purple-flushed colour. Fragrant, with fresh, berryish, spicy aromas, it is mouthfilling, with deep blackcurrant, plum, berry and spice flavours that build to a long, smooth finish. A very graceful red, it should be at its best 2022+.

 DRY $60 AV

Soho Blue Blood Zabeel Reserve ★★★★★

The powerful 2015 vintage (★★★★★) is a distinctive Waiheke Island blend of Syrah (51 per cent), Petit Verdot (35 per cent) and Malbec (14 per cent), estate-grown at Onetangi and matured for nine months in French oak casks (75 per cent new). Deeply coloured, with a fragrant, spicy bouquet, it's a full-on, bold style, weighty and fruit-packed, with fresh, highly concentrated, still youthful plum, spice and blackcurrant flavours, rich, savoury and long. It's crying out for time; open 2020+.

 DRY $99 AV

Soho Revolver ★★★★

Estate-grown at Onetangi, on Waiheke Island, the 2015 vintage (★★★☆) is a blend of Merlot (44 per cent), Malbec (27 per cent), Cabernet Franc (20 per cent) and Cabernet Sauvignon (9 per cent). French and American oak-aged, it is fragrant and lively, with moderately rich, berryish, spicy flavours, fresh acidity and gentle tannins.

Vintage	15	14	13	12	11	10
WR	6	5	7	6	NM	7
Drink	19-23	19-22	19-20	P	NM	P

 DRY $38 –V

Stonyridge Larose ★★★★★

Typically a stunning Waiheke Island wine. Dark and seductively perfumed, with smashing fruit flavours, at its best it is a magnificently concentrated red that matures superbly for a decade or longer, acquiring great complexity. The vines – Cabernet Sauvignon, Merlot, Cabernet Franc, Malbec and Petit Verdot – are grown in free-draining clay soils on a north-facing slope, a kilometre from the sea at Onetangi, and are very low-yielding (4 tonnes/hectare). The wine is matured for a year in French (80 to 90 per cent) and American oak barriques (half new, half one year old), and is sold largely on an 'en primeur' basis, whereby the customers, in return for paying for their wine about nine months in advance of its delivery, secure a substantial price reduction. The 2015 vintage (★★★★★) is a classic young claret-style red, dense but not tough, with power through the palate and obvious potential. Dark and purple-flushed, it is sturdy, rich and supple, with very ripe blackcurrant, plum and spice flavours, showing lovely freshness, harmony and length. Needing five years to unfold, it should mature gracefully for decades.

Vintage	15	14	13	12	11	10
WR	5	6	7	6	5	7
Drink	23-33	23-33	23-33	19-25	19-23	20-30

 DRY $280 –V

Tantalus Waiheke Island Écluse Reserve ★★★★

The powerful, concentrated and classy 2015 vintage (★★★★★) is a blend of Cabernet Sauvignon, Cabernet Franc, Merlot and Malbec. Estate-grown at Onetangi, it was matured for a year in French oak barriques. Deep and youthful in colour, it is very youthful, with dense, firm blackcurrant, plum and spice flavours, complex, well-structured and likely to be long-lived. Well worth discovering, it should be at its best 2022+.

 DRY $95 –V

Tantalus Waiheke Island Évoque Reserve ★★★★★

The impressive 2015 vintage (★★★★★), estate-grown at Onetangi, is a blend of Merlot, Malbec, Cabernet Sauvignon and Cabernet Franc, matured for a year in French oak barriques. A powerful but approachable red, it is dark, fragrant and full-bodied, with highly concentrated, plummy, spicy flavours, showing excellent ripeness and complexity, good tannin backbone, and a rich, harmonious finish. Already delicious, it's well worth cellaring to 2022+.

DRY $90 AV

Tantalus Waiheke Island Voilé Reserve   (★★★★☆)

The deeply coloured, powerful 2015 vintage (★★★★☆) is a very age-worthy Syrah. Estate-grown at Onetangi and matured for a year in French oak barriques, it is fragrant, with concentrated, ripe blackcurrant, plum, spice and nut flavours – less overtly peppery than southern styles – and a well-structured, harmonious finish. Best drinking 2021+.

DRY $80 –V

Te Mata Coleraine   ★★★★★

Breed, rather than brute power, is the hallmark of Coleraine (correctly pronounced Cole-raine rather than Coler-aine), which since its first vintage in 1982 has carved out an illustrious reputation among New Zealand's claret-style reds. In all vintages since 2007, Cabernet Sauvignon has been the predominant variety. At its best, it is a magical Hawke's Bay wine, with a depth, complexity and subtlety on the level of a top-class Bordeaux. The grapes are grown and hand-picked in the Havelock North hills, in the company's warm, north-facing Buck and 1892 vineyards, and the wine is matured for 17 to 20 months in French oak barriques, predominantly new. The 2017 vintage (★★★★★) is a blend of Cabernet Sauvignon (73 per cent) and Merlot (27 per cent). Still very youthful, it is deeply coloured and full-bodied, with highly concentrated blackcurrant, plum and spice flavours, complex, finely structured and very harmonious. Best drinking 2024+. (Tasted in late 2017, the 1982 vintage had a beguiling fragrance and notable complexity; the lovely 1998 vintage is a star, with superb concentration and complexity.)

Vintage	17	16	15	14	13	12	11	10
WR	6	7	7	7	7	NM	7	7
Drink	19-32	20-30	19-30	19-28	19-33	NM	19-23	19-22

DRY $130 AV

Te Motu   ★★★★☆

This Waiheke Island red is grown at Onetangi, over the fence from Stonyridge. Compared to its neighbour, it has typically been less opulent than Larose, in a more earthy, slightly leafy style. Cabernet Sauvignon-predominant, with Merlot and Cabernet Franc, the youthful, fruit-packed 2013 vintage (★★★★★) is a standout. It was matured for 20 months in French oak casks (30 per cent new). Deep and youthful in colour, it is highly fragrant, with concentrated blackcurrant, plum and spice flavours, complex, savoury, supple and finely poised. An elegant rather than powerful red, it's already delicious, but likely to be long-lived.

DRY $140 –V

Te Motu Kokoro   ★★★★★

Estate-grown at Onetangi, on Waikehe Island, the 2014 vintage (★★★★★) was blended from Merlot (principally), with smaller amounts of Cabernet Sauvignon, Cabernet Franc, Malbec and Syrah. Made 'in a more forward style' (meaning not requiring lengthy cellaring), it is deeply coloured, fragrant and softly mouthfilling. Rich, savoury and complex, with ripe, berryish, spicy, nutty flavours, showing excellent depth and harmony, it's drinking well now.

DRY $85 –V

Te Motu Tipua

'Within any vintage, there is always a varietal that transcends', according to the back label on this Waiheke Island red. The 2008 (★★★★★) was a powerful Syrah, but the 2013 vintage (★★★★★) is one of New Zealand's best-yet Cabernet Francs. Grown at Onetangi and matured for 20 months in French oak casks (30 per cent new), it has fragrant red-berry and spice aromas. A lovely, mouthfilling, silky-textured red, it is sweet-fruited, with youthful, ripe berry, spice and nut flavours, oak complexity, and excellent depth and harmony. Best drinking 2020+.

DRY $115 AV

Te Whau The Point

This classy Waiheke Island red flows from a steeply sloping vineyard at Putiki Bay. The outstanding 2014 vintage (★★★★★) was blended from Cabernet Sauvignon (50 per cent), Merlot (31 per cent), Cabernet Franc (12 per cent), Malbec (5 per cent) and Petit Verdot (2 per cent), matured in French oak casks for 18 months. Deeply coloured and ripely fragrant, it is a powerful, weighty red, dense and savoury, with concentrated blackcurrant, plum and spice flavours, seasoned with nutty oak, and good tannin backbone. A top vintage that reminded me of a fine Pauillac, it should be long-lived, but is already a delicious mouthful. The 2015 vintage (★★★★☆) is a full-coloured, youthful red with a fragrant bouquet and strong blackcurrant, plum, spice and herb flavours. Showing good concentration, it is earthy, savoury and complex, with good tannin backbone. Best drinking 2020+.

Vintage	15	14	13	12	11	10
WR	6	7	7	6	NM	7
Drink	19-26	19-26	19-25	19-20	NM	19-25

DRY $75 AV

Trinity Hill Gimblett Gravels The Gimblett

The deeply coloured 2017 vintage (★★★★★) is a Hawke's Bay blend of Cabernet Sauvignon (64 per cent), Merlot (25 per cent), Cabernet Franc (4 per cent), Malbec (4 per cent) and Petit Verdot (3 per cent). Matured for 16 months in French oak casks (almost all new), it is fragrant and mouthfilling, with concentrated, youthful blackcurrant, plum and spice flavours, finely structured, savoury and complex. Likely to be long-lived, it should be at its best 2022+. (To be released in 2020.)

Vintage	15	14	13	12	11	10
WR	6	6	7	4	5	6
Drink	19-27	19-25	19-25	19-25	19-25	19-20

DRY $40 AV

TW Makauri   (★★★☆)

Grown in Gisborne, the 2014 vintage (★★★☆) is a blend of Malbec and Merlot. Full-coloured, it is full-bodied, with plummy, spicy flavours, oak complexity and good depth.

DRY $27 –V

Vergence Red by Pegasus Bay

The Vergence label is used by Pegasus Bay for 'experimental, non-traditional wines'. The 2017 vintage (★★★★☆) is a Central Otago Pinot Noir, fermented with indigenous yeasts, barrel-aged for a year, and bottled unfined and unfiltered. Deeply coloured, it is fragrant, fresh and full-bodied, with concentrated, ripe, plummy, spicy, slightly nutty flavours, firm but balanced tannins, and good complexity. A powerful, fruit-packed, very bold style of Pinot Noir, it should be long-lived. The 2018 vintage (★★★★★) has a real sense of lightness and elegance. Full-coloured, with a spicy fragrance, it is generous and supple, with plummy, spicy flavours, deep and complex, refined tannins and a long finish. Already very enjoyable, it's a distinctive red, well worth trying.

DRY $40 AV

Villa Maria Ngakirikiri The Gravels ★★★★★

The debut 2013 vintage (★★★★★) is promoted as the company's 'icon' Bordeaux-style red. From vines planted in the Gimblett Gravels between 1998 and 2000, it is Cabernet Sauvignon-based (97 per cent), with a splash of Merlot (3 per cent). Matured for 18 months in French oak barrels (52 per cent new), it is densely coloured, with substantial body (14 per cent alcohol) and bold, still extremely youthful, blackcurrant and plum-evoking flavours, showing lovely richness, purity and complexity. It should flourish for decades; open 2020 onwards. The 2014 vintage (★★★★★), made entirely from Cabernet Sauvignon, was matured for 18 months in French oak barriques (40 per cent new). A powerful, lush red, it is sturdy, boldly coloured and fleshy, with dense, very ripe blackcurrant and plum flavours, hints of nuts, spices and liquorice, and a rich, harmonious finish. Combining power and grace, it will be very long-lived; best drinking 2022+.

Vintage	14	13
WR	7	7
Drink	20-30	20-30

DRY $150 AV

Cabernet Franc

New Zealand's sixth most widely planted red-wine variety, Cabernet Franc is probably a mutation of Cabernet Sauvignon, the much higher-profile variety with which it is so often blended. Jancis Robinson's phrase, 'a sort of claret Beaujolais', aptly sums up the nature of this versatile and underrated red-wine grape.

As a minority ingredient in the recipe of many of New Zealand's top reds, Cabernet Franc lends a delicious softness and concentrated fruitiness to its blends with Cabernet Sauvignon and Merlot. However, admirers of Château Cheval Blanc, the illustrious St Émilion (which is two-thirds planted in Cabernet Franc), have long appreciated that Cabernet Franc need not always be Cabernet Sauvignon's bridesmaid, but can yield fine red wines in its own right. The supple, fruity wines of Chinon and Bourgueil, in the Loire Valley, have also proved Cabernet Franc's ability to produce highly attractive, soft light reds.

According to the latest national vineyard survey, the bearing area of Cabernet Franc will be 96 hectares in 2020 – well below the 213 hectares in 2004. Over two-thirds of the vines are clustered in Hawke's Bay and most of the rest are in Auckland. As a varietal red, Cabernet Franc is lower in tannin and acid than Cabernet Sauvignon; or as Michael Brajkovich, of Kumeu River, has put it: 'more approachable and easy'.

Askerne Hawke's Bay Cabernet Franc   (★★★★☆)

Priced sharply, the characterful 2016 vintage (★★★★☆) was matured for 18 months in oak barrels (38 per cent new). Promisingly deep in colour, it is mouthfilling and vibrantly fruity, with strong, ripe berry, plum and spice flavours, finely integrated oak, gentle tannins and good complexity. Well worth cellaring.

DRY $23 V+

Black Estate Home North Canterbury Cabernet Franc   ★★★★

The age-worthy 2017 vintage (★★★★) was estate-grown, hand-harvested, fermented with indigenous yeasts, matured for seven months in old barrels, and bottled unfined and unfiltered. Full-coloured, it is a graceful, medium-bodied red, with youthful berryish, plummy, slightly spicy flavours, cool-climate freshness and vibrancy, savoury notes adding complexity, gentle tannins, and excellent vigour and harmony. Certified organic.

DRY $45 –V

Clearview Reserve Hawke's Bay Cabernet Franc   ★★★★★

From mature vines, around 30 years old, the 2015 vintage (★★★★★) was estate-grown at Te Awanga and matured for 17 months in barrels (30 per cent new). Deep and youthful in colour, it is floral and rich, with fresh, dense blackcurrant, plum and spice flavours, hints of herbs and dark chocolate, and a very harmonious, finely textured, lasting finish.

DRY $45 AV

Elephant Hill Reserve Cabernet Franc/Cabernet/Merlot   (★★★★★)

The powerful, weighty, youthful 2016 vintage (★★★★★) is a blend of Cabernet Franc (34 per cent), Cabernet Sauvignon (32 per cent) and Merlot (26 per cent), with a splash of Malbec. Hand-harvested in the Gimblett Gravels (75 per cent) and the Bridge Pa Triangle (25 per cent), it was matured for 21 months in French oak casks (48 per cent new). Dark and purple-flushed, it is fragrant, with substantial body, concentrated blackcurrant, plum and spice flavours, and firm tannin backbone. Set for a long life, it should be at its best 2023+.

DRY $54 AV

Lime Rock Central Hawke's Bay Cabernet Franc   ★★★★

The highly attractive 2015 vintage (★★★★☆) was estate-grown, hand-picked and matured in seasoned French oak barriques. Full and bright in colour, it is fresh, fragrant and full-bodied, with strong, ripe berry, plum and spice flavours, showing excellent complexity. A savoury, finely structured red, it should be at its best 2020+. The youthful 2016 vintage (★★★★) is medium to full-bodied, with fresh, vibrant plum, spice and herb flavours, oak complexity, gentle tannins and a lingering finish.

Vintage	16	15
WR	7	7
Drink	19-23	19-22

 DRY $28 AV

Maison Noire Hawke's Bay Cabernet Franc   ★★★☆

The 2015 vintage (★★★☆) was matured in French oak barrels (25 per cent new). A medium-bodied style with fullish colour, it has moderately concentrated, plummy, spicy, slightly herbal flavours, showing some savoury complexity, fresh acidity and a fairly firm finish.

 DRY $25 –V

Maison Noire Hawke's Bay Cabernet/Merlot   (★★★★)

The 2016 vintage (★★★★) is maturing gracefully. A medium-bodied style, it is a blend of Cabernet Franc (48 per cent), Merlot (45 per cent) and Cabernet Sauvignon (7 per cent), matured for a year in French oak barrels (25 per cent new). Youthful and savoury, it has very satisfying depth of ripe, berryish, plummy, slightly spicy flavours, showing good complexity, and a smooth, finely textured finish.

Vintage	16
WR	5
Drink	19-20

 DRY $25 AV

Man O'War Waiheke Island Cabernet Franc/Merlot/Malbec/Petit Verdot   ★★★☆

The 2015 vintage (★★★☆) is Cabernet Franc-based (64 per cent), with Merlot, Malbec, Petit Verdot and Cabernet Sauvignon in the blend. Matured for 18 months in French oak casks (25 per cent new), it has fullish, slightly developed colour and a slightly herbaceous bouquet. Mouthfilling, with generous blackcurrant, spice and herb flavours, and a smooth finish, it's ready to roll.

DRY $29 –V

Mills Reef Elspeth Gimblett Gravels Hawke's Bay Cabernet Franc   ★★★★

Revealing good personality, the elegant 2016 vintage (★★★★☆) is a full-coloured, sweet-fruited red, matured for 17 months in French oak barrels (24 per cent new). Rich and supple, with red-berry, plum and spice flavours, good complexity and fine-grained tannins, it shows obvious potential; best drinking 2020+.

Vintage	16
WR	7
Drink	19-24

 DRY $50 –V

Ohinemuri Esk River Valley Cabernet Franc/Merlot/Malbec   (★★★☆)

The 2015 vintage (★★★☆) is a full-coloured, mouthfilling, fruity Hawke's Bay red, French oak-aged, with berryish, plummy, slightly nutty flavours, a hint of tamarillo, balanced tannins and good depth. It should be at its best from 2020+.

Vintage	15	
WR	5	
Drink	19-21	

DRY $28 –V

Peacock Sky Waiheke Island Pure Franc   (★★★☆)

Still on sale, the 2014 vintage (★★★☆) is a fresh, smooth wine, like a very light Bordeaux. Fullish in colour, it has berry, plum, spice and herb flavours, savoury notes adding complexity, and some elegance.

DRY $50 –V

Pyramid Valley Vineyards Growers Collection Howell
Family Vineyard Hawke's Bay Cabernet Franc   ★★★★☆

The classy 2015 vintage (★★★★★) was hand-picked from 30-year-old vines in the Bridge Pa Triangle, matured in seasoned French oak barrels, and bottled unfined and unfiltered. Sturdy (14.5 per cent alcohol), with deep, bright, purple-flushed colour, it is concentrated, with lovely ripeness and depth of blackcurrant and plum flavours, buried tannins, and excellent vigour and harmony. Drink now to 2023.

DRY $45 –V

Sileni Grand Reserve Pacemaker Hawke's Bay Cabernet Franc   ★★★★

Grown in the Bridge Pa Triangle, the 2018 vintage (★★★★☆) is full-coloured and fleshy, with mouthfilling body and deep, berryish, plummy, spicy, slightly nutty flavours, showing good complexity. A youthful, very age-worthy red, it's well worth cellaring to 2021+.

DRY $40 –V

Sileni Reserve Hawke's Bay Cabernet Franc/Merlot   (★★★☆)

Grown mostly in the Bridge Pa Triangle and briefly oak-aged, the easy-drinking 2018 vintage (★★★☆) has fullish colour and fresh berry and spice aromas. Mouthfilling, it is vibrantly fruity, with very good depth of berryish, slightly spicy flavours and a smooth finish. Best drinking 2020–21.

DRY $22 AV

Te Rata Cabernet Franc/Merlot   (★★★☆)

Grown at Matakana, the characterful 2014 vintage (★★★☆) has full, fairly mature colour and a fragrant, slightly herbaceous bouquet. Full-bodied, it is gutsy, with strong, berryish, spicy, nutty, slightly earthy flavours, showing considerable complexity, and a firm finish. (From Free Range Wines.)

DRY $34 –V

Thomas Cabernet Franc/Merlot   ★★★★☆

The 2014 vintage (★★★★☆) is a blend of Cabernet Franc (48 per cent) and Merlot (45 per cent), with splashes of Syrah (4 per cent) and Cabernet Sauvignon (3 per cent). Hand-harvested at Onetangi, on Waiheke Island, it was matured for 15 months in French oak barriques (26 per cent new). Full-coloured, it is mouthfilling, fresh and smooth, with strong, ripe plum, red-berry and spice flavours, seasoned with nutty oak. An elegant, supple red, it should be at its best 2020+. (From Batch Winery.)

DRY $46 –V

Waimea Estates Nelson Cabernet Franc/Syrah   (★★★)

A drink-young charmer, the 2017 vintage (★★★) is a medium-bodied blend with fullish colour and fresh, berryish flavours. Fruity and smooth, it's a very easy-drinking style.

DRY $18 AV

Cabernet Sauvignon and Cabernet-predominant blends

Cabernet Sauvignon has proved a tough nut to crack in New Zealand. Mid-priced models were – until recently – usually of lower quality than a comparable offering from Australia, where the relative warmth suits the late-ripening Cabernet Sauvignon variety. Yet a top New Zealand Cabernet-based red from a favourable vintage can hold its own in illustrious company and the overall standard of today's middle-tier, $20 bottlings is far higher than many wine lovers realise – which makes for some great bargains.

Cabernet Sauvignon was widely planted here in the nineteenth century. The modern resurgence of interest in the great Bordeaux variety was led by Tom McDonald, the legendary Hawke's Bay winemaker, whose string of elegant (though, by today's standards, light) Cabernet Sauvignons under the McWilliam's label, from the much-acclaimed 1965 vintage to the gold medal-winning 1975, proved beyond all doubt that fine-quality red wines could be produced in New Zealand.

During the 1970s and 1980s, Cabernet Sauvignon ruled the red-wine roost in New Zealand. Since then, as winemakers – especially in the South Island, but also Hawke's Bay – searched for red-wine varieties that would ripen more fully and consistently in our relatively cool grape-growing climate than Cabernet Sauvignon, it has been pushed out of the limelight by Merlot, Pinot Noir and Syrah. Between 2003 and 2020, the country's total area of bearing Cabernet Sauvignon vines will contract from 741 to 255 hectares. Growers with suitably warm sites have often retained faith in Cabernet Sauvignon, but others have moved on to less challenging varieties.

Over 87 per cent of the country's Cabernet Sauvignon vines are clustered in Hawke's Bay, and Auckland also has significant plantings. In the South Island, Cabernet-based reds have typically lacked warmth and richness. This magnificent but late-ripening variety's future in New Zealand clearly lies in the warmer vineyard sites of the north.

What is the flavour of Cabernet Sauvignon? When newly fermented a herbal character is common, intertwined with blackcurrant-like fruit aromas. New oak flavours, firm acidity and taut tannins are other hallmarks of young, fine Cabernet Sauvignon. With maturity the flavour loses its aggression and the wine develops roundness and complexity, with assorted cigar-box, minty and floral scents emerging. It is unwise to broach a Cabernet Sauvignon-based red with any pretensions to quality at less than three years old; at about five years old the rewards of cellaring really start to flow.

Ash Ridge Premium Cabernet/Merlot (★★★★)

Grown in the Bridge Pa Triangle, Hawke's Bay, the 2016 vintage (★★★★) is a blend of Cabernet Sauvignon (80 per cent) and Merlot (20 per cent). Deep ruby, it is drinking well now, with mouthfilling body, berry, plum and spice flavours, showing good complexity, and a supple, very harmonious finish.

DRY $30 –V

Ashwell Martinborough Cabernet Sauvignon ★★★

Still on sale, the French oak-matured 2013 vintage (★★★) is full-coloured. It shows a slight lack of ripeness and richness, but is vibrantly fruity, with blackcurrant, plum and spice flavours, and a smooth finish.

Vintage	13
WR	5
Drink	19-23

 DRY $28 –V

Awaroa Requiem Waiheke Island Cabernet/Merlot/Malbec ★★★★★

The 2016 vintage (★★★★★) is a powerful blend of Cabernet Sauvignon (50 per cent), Merlot (30 per cent) and Cabernet Franc (20 per cent), matured in French oak barriques (70 per cent new). Dark and fragrant, it is mouthfilling, with deep, youthful blackcurrant, plum and spice flavours, savoury, nutty notes adding complexity, and supple tannins. It's already quite expressive; drink now or cellar.

Vintage	16	15	14
WR	6	7	7
Drink	20-25	20-25	20-25

DRY $75 AV

Awaroa Waiheke Island Cabernet/Merlot/Malbec ★★★★

The fragrant, fleshy 2016 vintage (★★★★☆) is a blend of Cabernet Sauvignon (50 per cent), Merlot (30 per cent) and Cabernet Franc (20 per cent), matured in French oak barriques. Deep and youthful in colour, it is full-bodied, with strong blackcurrant, plum and spice flavours, showing excellent ripeness and complexity, and a firm tannin grip. Best drinking 2022+.

DRY $45 –V

Babich Irongate Gimblett Gravels Hawke's Bay Cabernet/Merlot/Franc ★★★★★

Grown in the Irongate Vineyard and aged in French oak barriques (40 per cent new in 2016), this elegant, complex, firmly structured red is designed for cellaring. Retasted in April 2019, the 2016 vintage (★★★★★) has promisingly deep, youthful colour. Fragrant and mouthfilling, it is well-structured, with deep blackcurrant, plum and spice flavours, oak complexity, good tannin backbone and excellent cellaring potential; open 2022+.

Vintage	16	15	14	13	12	11	10
WR	6	7	7	7	5	4	7
Drink	19-26	19-27	19-25	19-25	19-22	19-20	19-22

DRY $40 AV

Babich Limited Edition 100 Years Cabernet Sauvignon (★★★★★)

Launched in 2016 – a century after Babich's first vintage in 1916 – the rare 2013 vintage (★★★★★) was not shown to critics. Estate-grown in the Gimblett Gravels, Hawke's Bay, and French oak-aged, it is deeply coloured and weighty, sweet-fruited and savoury, with youthful, complex flavours of blackcurrant, plums and spices, and a tight, exceptionally long finish.

DRY $399 –V

Babich The Patriarch – see the Branded and Other Red Wines section

Bespoke Mills Reef Gimblett Gravels Hawke's Bay
Cabernet Sauvignon/Cabernet Franc (★★★★☆)

The debut 2015 vintage (★★★★☆) is a blend of Cabernet Sauvignon (63 per cent) and Cabernet Franc (37 per cent), harvested from 20-year-old vines in Mere Road and matured for over a year in a 2:1 mix of French and American oak casks (39 per cent new). Full-coloured, it is fresh, mouthfilling and vibrantly fruity, with ripe blackcurrant, plum and spice flavours, oak-derived complexity and finely balanced tannins. Drinking well now, it should be in peak form from 2020 onwards.

DRY $40 –V

Brookfields Ohiti Estate Cabernet Sauvignon ★★★★

Hawke's Bay winemaker Peter Robertson says the shingly Ohiti Estate, inland from Fernhill, yields 'sound Cabernet Sauvignon year after year – which is a major challenge to any vineyard'. The youthful 2017 vintage (★★★★) was oak-aged for a year. Full-bodied, with deep, purple-flushed colour, it shows good concentration of vibrant, plummy, spicy, slightly nutty flavours, with a smooth finish. Best drinking 2020+.

Vintage	17
WR	7
Drink	19-28

 DRY $20 V+

Brookfields Reserve Vintage Hawke's Bay Cabernet/Merlot ★★★★★

Brookfields' top red is one of the most powerful, long-lived reds in Hawke's Bay. At its best, it is a thrilling wine – robust, tannin-laden and overflowing with very rich cassis, plum and mint flavours. The grapes are sourced from the Lyons family's sloping, north-facing vineyard at Bridge Pa, and the wine is matured for a year in predominantly new French oak barriques. The 2016 vintage (★★★★★) is fragrant, with deep, purple-flushed colour. Full-bodied, it has fresh, notably concentrated, ripe blackcurrant, plum and spice flavours, firm tannins, and obvious potential. A powerful young red, set for a long life, it's best opened 2021+.

DRY $59 AV

Church Road Cabernet/Merlot – see Church Road Merlot/Cabernet Sauvignon

Church Road McDonald Series Hawke's Bay Cabernet Sauvignon ★★★★★

This consistently impressive red is grown principally in the company's Redstone Vineyard, in the Bridge Pa Triangle, and matured in French and Hungarian oak barrels (30 to 35 per cent new). The 2015 vintage (★★★★☆) is a powerful, bold style of Cabernet Sauvignon, with dense, still purple-flushed colour. Robust, with concentrated, well-ripened blackcurrant, red-berry and spice flavours, rich and smooth, it's approachable now, but set for a long life. Best drinking 2022+.

 DRY $28 V+

Church Road Tom Cabernet Sauvignon/Merlot ★★★★★

Pernod Ricard NZ's top Hawke's Bay red honours pioneer winemaker Tom McDonald, a driving force behind New Zealand's first prestige red, McWilliam's Cabernet Sauvignon (first vintage 1965). The early releases of Tom in the mid-1990s were Cabernet Sauvignon-predominant, but from 1998 onwards, Merlot emerged as an equally crucial part of the recipe. Typically a wine of great finesse, it is savoury, complex and more akin to a quality Bordeaux than other New World reds. Released in September 2019, the 2015 vintage (★★★★★) is arguably one of the greatest reds ever crafted in New Zealand. A very dark blend of Cabernet Sauvignon (66 per cent), estate-grown in the Redstone Vineyard, in the Bridge Pa Triangle, and Merlot (34 per cent), estate-grown in the Gimblett Vineyard and Redstone Vineyard, it was matured for 20 months in French oak barriques (74 per cent new). A commanding wine, it is dark and sturdy, but not heavy, with rich, lush blackcurrant, plum and spice flavours, showing lovely vibrancy, depth, complexity and harmony. Already delicious, it should flourish in the cellar for a couple of decades.

DRY $220 –V

Collaboration Argent Cabernet Sauvignon ★★★★☆

The distinctive, skilfully crafted 2013 vintage (★★★★★) is the finest yet. Hand-harvested at 'select vineyard sites' in Hawke's Bay and matured in French oak barrels (25 per cent new), it is deeply coloured, with a ripely fragrant bouquet. A refined, mouthfilling, generous red, it is a pure expression of Cabernet Sauvignon, with strong, vibrant blackcurrant, plum and spice flavours, fine-grained tannins, and excellent length.

DRY $40 –V

Collaboration Impression Cabernet/Cabernet Franc/Merlot (★★★★)

Drinking well now, the 2014 vintage (★★★★) is a Hawke's Bay blend, matured for 16 months in seasoned French oak barrels, and bottled unfined and unfiltered. Full-coloured, it is mouthfilling, with generous, plummy, berryish, slightly earthy and nutty flavours, showing good freshness and complexity, and a well-rounded finish.

DRY $28 AV

Coopers Creek Reserve Gimblett Gravels Hawke's
Bay Cabernet Sauvignon ★★★★★

Still very youthful, the 2016 vintage (★★★★★) is a dark, purple-flushed red, maturing very gracefully. A single-vineyard wine, it has a dense, structured palate. Full-bodied and highly concentrated, with cassis, plum and spice flavours, oak complexity and a well-structured finish, it should be at its best 2022+.

DRY $60 AV

Coopers Creek Select Vineyards Gimblett Gravels
Hawke's Bay Cabernet/Merlot ★★★★☆

Retasted in 2019, the age-worthy 2016 vintage (★★★★☆) was blended from almost equal portions of Cabernet Sauvignon (51 per cent) and Merlot (49 per cent). A full-coloured, youthful red with good substance, it is mouthfilling, fresh, vibrantly fruity and firmly structured, with strong, ripe blackcurrant, berry, plum and spice flavours. Open 2021+.

DRY $28 V+

Cornerstone Cabernet/Merlot/Malbec – see Newton Forrest Estate Cornerstone in the Branded and Other Red Wines section

Esk Valley Winemakers Reserve Gimblett Gravels
Cabernet Sauvignon/Merlot/Malbec ★★★★★

This wine has previously been Merlot-predominant (see the Merlot section), but the 2016 vintage (★★★★★) is Cabernet Sauvignon-based. Matured for 16 months in French oak barriques (50 per cent new), it is a very elegant, youthful red, set for a long life. Dark and purple-flushed, it is mouthfilling, with vibrant, well-ripened blackcurrant, plum and spice flavours, showing excellent density, and a seamless, persistent finish. Open 2022+.

Vintage	16	15
WR	7	NM
Drink	19-30	NM

 DRY $60 AV

Johner Wairarapa Cabernet/Merlot ★★★★

Priced right, the muscular 2014 vintage (★★★★) was wood-aged for a year and bottled unfiltered. Deep and bright in colour, it is mouthfilling and supple, with generous, ripe plum, berry and spice flavours, hints of blackcurrants, herbs and spices, and oak-derived complexity.

DRY $26 AV

Kidnapper Cliffs Gimblett Gravels Hawke's Bay
Cabernet Sauvignon/Merlot (★★★★★)

From Te Awa, the estate-grown 2013 vintage (★★★★★) was hand-harvested from vines averaging 25 years old and matured for 21 months in French oak barriques (35 per cent new). A blend of Cabernet Sauvignon (73 per cent), Merlot (24 per cent) and Cabernet Franc (3 per cent), it is full-coloured and ripely scented, with mouthfilling body and very generous blackcurrant, plum, spice and nut flavours. Delicious now, but also age-worthy, it's a very finely textured red, savoury, complex and smooth, with strong personality.

 DRY $65 AV

Linden Estate Reserve Hawke's Bay Cabernet Sauvignon (★★★★)

The full-coloured 2017 vintage (★★★★) was matured in French oak barriques. It has a fragrant, savoury bouquet, leading into a mouthfilling wine with strong, berryish, spicy flavours, showing considerable complexity, and good tannin backbone. Best drinking 2021+.

 DRY $65 –V

Mahurangi River Cabernet Sauvignon/Merlot/Malbec (★★★★)

The full-coloured 2014 vintage (★★★★) is a savoury Matakana red, Cabernet Sauvignon-based (67 per cent), with equal parts of Merlot and Malbec, matured for over a year in French and American oak casks (30 per cent new). It has fresh, concentrated blackcurrant, plum, herb and spice flavours, showing good complexity. Best drinking 2020+.

 DRY $29 AV

Maison Noire Hawke's Bay Cabernet Sauvignon   (★★★★☆)

The 2015 vintage (★★★★☆) was grown in the Gimblett Gravels and matured for 16 months in barrels (35 per cent new). Full-coloured, with a fragrant, spicy bouquet, it is mouthfilling, with generous, ripe plum and spice flavours, finely integrated oak, savoury, earthy notes adding complexity, and gentle tannins. A very harmonious red, highly approachable in its youth, it also shows good potential and should be at its best 2020+. Priced sharply.

Vintage	15
WR	5
Drink	19-22

DRY $25 V+

Mills Reef Arthur Edward Gimblett Gravels Cabernet/Merlot   (★★★★★)

After tasting the debut 2013 vintage (★★★★★) 'blind' (identity hidden) against acclaimed French reds, Mills Reef decided they were of similar quality. Released in late 2018 at an eye-catching $350, it was hand-picked from the oldest vines, pruned to extremely low yields, and matured for 20 months in 100 per cent new French oak hogsheads. A 50:50 blend of Cabernet Sauvignon and Merlot, it is deeply coloured, fragrant, mouthfilling, elegant and supple, with rich blackcurrant, plum and spice flavours, in a classic Bordeaux style. Best drinking 2023+.

DRY $350 –V

Mills Reef Elspeth Gimblett Gravels Hawke's Bay Cabernet Sauvignon   ★★★★★

Fragrant, fresh and full-bodied, the 2016 vintage (★★★★☆) was hand-picked from mature, 21-year-old vines in the company's Mere Road Vineyard, and matured for 17 months in French (90 per cent) and American oak hogsheads (48 per cent new). Likely to be at its best from 2021 onwards, it has strong, vibrant, well-ripened blackcurrant and plum flavours, spicy and nutty characters adding complexity, and obvious potential for cellaring.

Vintage	16	15	14	13	12	11	10
WR	7	7	7	7	NM	7	7
Drink	19-25	19-25	19-24	19-25	NM	P	P

DRY $50 AV

Mills Reef Elspeth Gimblett Gravels Hawke's Bay Cabernet/Merlot   ★★★★★

Grown and hand-picked at the company's close-planted Mere Road site, this is a consistently impressive wine. The 2016 vintage (★★★★☆) was matured for 17 months in French oak hogsheads (37 per cent new). It is a youthful, full-coloured, medium to full-bodied red. Fresh and vibrant, it is sweet-fruited, with concentrated blackcurrant, plum and slight nut flavours, oak complexity and refined tannins. Best drinking 2021+.

Vintage	16
WR	7
Drink	19-26

DRY $50 AV

Mills Reef Reserve Gimblett Gravels Hawke's Bay Cabernet/Merlot   ★★★★

The 2018 vintage (★★★★) was matured for 15 months in French oak hogsheads (36 per cent new). Full-coloured, it is mouthfilling and supple, with ripe blackcurrant, plum and spice flavours. A generous wine, finely balanced for early enjoyment, it should be at its best 2021+.

Vintage	18	DRY $25 AV
WR	7	
Drink	19-25	

Mission Gimblett Gravels Barrique Reserve Cabernet Sauvignon   ★★★★☆

The 2017 vintage (★★★★☆), a blend of Cabernet Sauvignon (96 per cent) and Cabernet Franc (4 per cent), was matured for a year in French oak barrels (30 per cent new). Deeply coloured, it is fresh, mouthfilling and finely structured, with concentrated blackcurrant, plum and spice flavours, braced by firm tannins. Best drinking 2022+.

Vintage	15	14	13	DRY $30 AV
WR	6	5	7	
Drink	19-23	19-22	19-25	

Mission Hawke's Bay Cabernet Sauvignon   ★★★

The bargain-priced 2016 vintage (★★★) was partly (20 per cent) barrel-aged for 18 months. Full-coloured, it is mouthfilling, with fresh, berryish, slightly herbal and spicy flavours, showing good depth.

DRY $16 V+

Osawa Prestige Collection Hawke's Bay Cabernet Sauvignon/Merlot   (★★★★☆)

Grown at Mangatahi and maturing gracefully, the 2013 vintage (★★★★☆) is a 50:50 blend of Cabernet Sauvignon and Merlot, matured for 20 months in French oak casks (65 per cent new). Still moderately youthful, it is concentrated, with blackcurrant and plum characters, savoury and complex, and good tannin backbone. Drink now or cellar.

DRY $55 –V

Pask Declaration Gimblett Gravels Hawke's Bay Cabernet/Merlot/Malbec   ★★★★☆

Retasted in April 2019, the 2013 vintage (★★★★☆) was matured for 19 months in a mix of French and American oak casks (85 per cent new). Deep and still fairly youthful in colour, it is fragrant, with generous, ripe flavours, a hint of sweet oak, good complexity and a smooth finish. It's drinking well now. The 2014 vintage (★★★★☆) was matured for two years in French and American oak puncheons (100 per cent new). Full-coloured, it shows good concentration, with fresh, ripe blackcurrant, plum and spice flavours, complex and savoury, and fine-grained tannins.

Vintage	14	13	12	11	10	DRY $50 –V
WR	7	7	NM	NM	6	
Drink	19-25	20-25	NM	NM	19-20	

Pask Gimblett Gravels Cabernet/Merlot ★★★★

The fresh, supple, medium to full-bodied 2016 vintage (★★★☆) is a blend of Cabernet Sauvignon (71 per cent) and Merlot (29 per cent). Full-coloured, it has very good depth of blackcurrant, plum and herb flavours, a gentle seasoning of French oak (14 months in seasoned barrels) adding complexity, and plenty of current-drinking appeal.

 DRY $22 V+

Pask Small Batch Cabernet Sauvignon ★★★★

Estate-grown in the Gimblett Gravels, Hawke's Bay, the 2014 vintage (★★★★) was matured for 17 months in French and American oak casks (20 per cent new). Full-coloured, it is ripe and savoury, with concentrated blackcurrant, plum and spice flavours, a hint of herbs, good complexity and a finely poised finish. Still youthful, it should be at its best 2020+.

Vintage	14
WR	5
Drink	20-26

 DRY $29 AV

Passage Rock Reserve Waiheke Island Cabernet Sauvignon/Merlot ★★★★☆

The sturdy 2015 vintage (★★★★★) was matured for a year in French oak barrels (30 per cent new). Highly fragrant and deeply coloured, it is built to last, with deep, fairly youthful blackcurrant, plum, spice and nut flavours, showing excellent structure and complexity. Best drinking 2022+.

Vintage	15
WR	6
Drink	19-25

 DRY $55 –V

Saint Clair James Sinclair Gimblett Gravels Hawke's Bay Cabernet/Merlot ★★★☆

Well worth cellaring, the 2017 vintage (★★★☆) is a deeply coloured, vibrantly fruity red, medium-bodied, with a slightly earthy bouquet. Moderately firm, with oak complexity and very good depth, it should be at its best 2020+.

DRY $28 –V

Saint Clair Pioneer Block 17 Plateau Gimblett Gravels Cabernet/Merlot ★★★★

The 2015 vintage (★★★★☆) is an estate-grown, deeply coloured blend of Cabernet Sauvignon (78 per cent) and Merlot (22 per cent), matured for 11 months in French oak casks (55 per cent new). Vibrantly fruity, it is generous and supple, with fresh, strong blackcurrant, plum, herb and spice flavours that have easily lapped up the new oak influence. Enjoyable in its youth, it should also reward cellaring.

 DRY $38 –V

Squawking Magpie SQM Gimblett Gravels Cabernets/Merlot   ★★★★★

The very age-worthy 2017 vintage (★★★★★) is a classy Hawke's Bay blend of Cabernet Sauvignon (66 per cent), Merlot (23 per cent) and Cabernet Franc (11 per cent), matured for 15 months in French oak casks (22 per cent new). Mouthfilling, with deep, purple-flushed colour, it has rich, ripe blackcurrant, plum and spice flavours, good tannin backbone, and excellent complexity and cellaring potential. Best drinking 2022+.

DRY $79 AV

Stolen Heart, The, Hawke's Bay Cabernet Sauvignon/Merlot   (★★★★☆)

Certified organic, the 2014 vintage (★★★★☆) was grown in the Gimblett Gravels and matured for a year in French oak casks (30 per cent new). Deep and youthful in colour, it is medium-bodied and savoury, in a distinctly Bordeaux-like style, with fresh, ripe blackcurrant, plum, spice and herb flavours, seasoned with nutty oak, good complexity, firm tannins and obvious cellaring potential. (From Crown Range Cellar.)

DRY $50 –V

Stonecroft Gimblett Gravels Hawke's Bay Cabernet Sauvignon   ★★★★★

Well worth cellaring, the classy 2016 vintage (★★★★★) is an unblended Cabernet Sauvignon, estate-grown in Mere Road. Hand-harvested from mature vines (planted in 2000 and 2001), it was matured for over 18 months in French oak barrels (35 per cent new). Dark and still purple-flushed, it is ripely fragrant, rich and supple, with fresh, concentrated blackcurrant, plum and spice flavours, finely integrated oak, gentle tannins and obvious potential; open 2021+. Certified organic.

Vintage	16	15	14
WR	7	7	7
Drink	20-30	19-28	19-26

DRY $45 AV

Stonecroft Ruhanui Gimblett Gravels Hawke's Bay
Cabernet Sauvignon/Merlot   ★★★★☆

The youthful 2017 vintage (★★★★☆) is a blend of Cabernet Sauvignon (90 per cent) and Merlot (10 per cent), matured for 20 months in seasoned French oak barrels. Deeply coloured, it is medium-bodied, with good density of blackcurrant, plum and spice flavours, savoury notes adding complexity, and fine-grained tannins. A very harmonious young red, well worth cellaring, it should be at its best 2022+. (The 2015 (★★★★☆) and 2016 (★★★★) vintages of Ruhanui are Merlot-predominant.)

Vintage	17
WR	4
Drink	20-25

DRY $31 AV

Te Mata Awatea Cabernets/Merlot   ★★★★★

Positioned below its Coleraine stablemate in Te Mata's hierarchy of Hawke's Bay, claret-style reds, since 1995 Awatea has been grown at Havelock North and in the Bullnose Vineyard, inland from Hastings. A blend of Cabernet Sauvignon, Merlot and Cabernet Franc – with a splash of Petit Verdot in most years since 2001 – it is hand-harvested and matured for 15 to 18 months in French oak barriques (partly new). Compared to Coleraine, in its youth Awatea is more seductive, more perfumed, and tastes more of sweet, ripe fruit, but it is more forward and slightly less concentrated. The wine can mature gracefully for many years, but is also typically delicious in its youth. The 2017 vintage (★★★★☆) is a blend of Cabernet Sauvignon (56 per cent), Merlot (39 per cent) and Cabernet Franc (5 per cent). Fragrant and full-coloured, it is medium to full-bodied, with strong, ripe berry, plum and spice flavours, good tannin backbone, and excellent structure and complexity. A refined, youthful red, it should be at its best 2022+.

Vintage	17	16	15	14	13	12	11	10	DRY $40 AV
WR	6	7	7	6	7	6	7	7	
Drink	19-27	19-26	19-25	19-25	19-23	P	P	P	

Te Mata Coleraine – see the Branded and Other Red Wines section

Te Mata Estate Vineyards Hawke's Bay Cabernets/Merlot   (★★★☆)

The 2017 vintage (★★★☆) is a blend of Cabernet Sauvignon, Merlot and Cabernet Franc, matured for 11 months in French oak barrels (partly new). Full-coloured, with a fresh, berryish bouquet, it is medium-bodied, with vibrant, ripe red-berry and plum flavours, showing moderate complexity, fresh acidity and gentle tannins. Enjoyable young, it offers good drinking now to 2021.

Vintage	18	DRY $20 AV
WR	6	
Drink	19-23	

Thomas Legacy Waiheke Island Cabernet Sauvignon   (★★★★★)

Promisingly dark, the 2013 vintage (★★★★★) was made solely from Cabernet Sauvignon, hand-harvested at Onetangi and matured for 18 months in French oak barrels (33 per cent new). Fragrant, with blackcurrant and herb aromas and flavours, it is sturdy, with excellent structure, density and complexity. Approachable now, it should be long-lived. (From Batch Winery.)

DRY $90 –V

Thomas Legacy Waiheke Island Cabernet/Merlot/Franc   (★★★★★)

Set for the long haul, the fragrant, youthful 2013 vintage (★★★★★) is a blend of Cabernet Sauvignon (72 per cent), Merlot (23 per cent) and Cabernet Franc (5 per cent), matured for 18 months in French oak barriques (62 per cent new). Deeply coloured, it is full-bodied and fresh, with generous blackcurrant, plum, spice and herb flavours, seasoned with nutty oak, excellent complexity, good tannin backbone and a lasting finish.

DRY $120 –V

Vidal Legacy Gimblett Gravels Hawke's Bay Cabernet Sauvignon/Merlot   ★★★★★

The distinguished 2016 vintage (★★★★★) is a blend of Cabernet Sauvignon (80 per cent) and Merlot (20 per cent), matured for 20 months in French oak barriques (60 per cent new). Recommended by Vidal for cellaring up to 20 years, it has dark, purple-flushed colour and a fragrant, ripe blackcurrant-evoking bouquet. Densely packed, it has vibrant cassis, plum and spice flavours, a hint of dark chocolate, and fine-grained tannins. A complex, savoury, finely structured red, it's a star of the 2016 vintage in Hawke's Bay. Best drinking 2021+.

Vintage	16	DRY $65 AV
WR	7	
Drink	19-28	

Vidal Soler Gimblett Gravels Hawke's Bay Cabernet Sauvignon   (★★★★★)

Offering fine value, the debut 2017 vintage (★★★★★) was estate-grown in the Gimblett Gravels and matured for 18 months in French oak barriques (45 per cent new). Still very youthful, with dark, purple-flushed colour, it is mouthfilling and tightly structured, but not austere, with concentrated blackcurrant, plum and spice flavours, seasoned with nutty oak, and a welcoming fragrance. An elegant, rich, finely balanced red, it's well worth cellaring to 2022+. (Opened in mid-2018, Vidal Joseph Soler Cabernet Sauvignon 1998 is maturing magnificently and should live for another decade.)

Vintage	17
WR	6
Drink	19-27

 DRY $35 V+

Villa Maria Library Release Gimblett Gravels Hawke's Bay Cabernet Sauvignon   (★★★★★)

Released in 2017, the 2009 vintage (★★★★★) is a still-youthful red, to savour over the next decade. Matured for 20 months in French oak barriques (67 per cent new), it has deep, moderately youthful colour, rich, ripe blackcurrant-like flavours to the fore, hints of plums and spices, and savoury, nutty notes adding complexity. An elegant, tightly structured, classic Cabernet Sauvignon, it's set for the long haul.

 DRY $70 AV

Villa Maria Reserve Gimblett Gravels Hawke's Bay Cabernet Sauvignon/Merlot   ★★★★★

Densely coloured, the 2018 vintage (★★★★★) is a blend of Cabernet Sauvignon (78 per cent), Merlot (14 per cent) and Malbec (8 per cent), matured for 16 months in French oak barriques (35 per cent new). A refined, very youthful red, it is fragrant and full-bodied, with deep, well-ripened blackcurrant, plum and spice flavours, finely integrated oak, excellent complexity and a long life ahead. Best drinking 2023+.

Vintage	18	17	16	15	14	13	12	10
WR	7	NM	7	7	7	7	6	7
Drink	20-30	NM	20-28	19-25	19-25	19-25	19-22	19-25

DRY $70 AV

🍇🍇🍇

Villa Maria Reserve Library Release Gimblett Gravels Hawke's Bay Cabernet Sauvignon/Merlot   (★★★★★)

Released in 2017, the very elegant, still age-worthy 2009 vintage (★★★★★) is a blend of Cabernet Sauvignon (55 per cent) and Merlot (45 per cent), matured for 20 months in French oak barrels (70 per cent new). Delicious now, it has deep, fairly youthful colour, beautifully ripe, still fresh blackcurrant/plum flavours, and spicy, leathery notes adding complexity. Notably rich and savoury, it is developing superbly, but the best is yet to come; open 2020+. (Note: most 'Library Release' reds have been – and in future will be – labelled as a stand-alone range, without the 'Reserve' designation.)

 DRY $70 AV

Carménère

Ransom, at Matakana, in 2007 released New Zealand's first Carménère. Now virtually extinct in France, Carménère was once widely grown in Bordeaux and still is in Chile, where, until the 1990s, it was often mistaken for Merlot. In Italy it was long thought to be Cabernet Franc.

In 1988, viticulturist Alan Clarke imported Cabernet Franc cuttings here from Italy. Planted by Robin Ransom in 1997, the grapes ripened about the same time as the rest of his Cabernet Franc, but the look of the fruit and the taste of the wine were 'totally different'. So Ransom arranged DNA testing at the University of Adelaide. The result? His Cabernet Franc vines are in fact Carménère.

Only 1 hectare of Carménère has been recorded in New Zealand, and the variety is not listed separately in New Zealand Winegrowers' *Vineyard Register Report 2017–2020*.

Ransom Carménère ★★★☆

Estate-grown at Mahurangi, north of Auckland, the 2013 vintage (★★★☆) is deeply coloured, with a fresh, slightly herbal bouquet. Mouthfilling, it shows good density, with vibrant plum and herb flavours, a hint of nuts, and fine-grained tannins. Drink now or cellar.

DRY $29 –V

Chambourcin

Chambourcin is one of the more highly rated French hybrids, well known in Muscadet for its good disease-resistance and bold, crimson hue. Rare in New Zealand (with 4 hectares of bearing vines in 2020), it is most often found as a varietal red in Northland.

Ake Ake Organic Northland Chambourcin ★★★☆

The 2016 vintage (★★★★) was matured in seasoned French and American oak barrels. Bright and youthful in colour, it is a generous, age-worthy red, medium to full-bodied, with fresh, vibrant, plummy, spicy flavours, lively acidity and lots of youthful vigour.

DRY $35 –V

Byrne Northland Chambourcin ★★★★☆

Byrne is the region's finest producer of Chambourcin. The 2016 vintage (★★★★), matured in old oak barriques, is full-coloured, with fresh, berryish, spicy aromas and flavours. Vibrantly fruity, with the slightly rustic note typical of the variety, gentle tannins and a lingering finish, it's a highly attractive, drink-young style.

DRY $21 V+

Marsden Bay of Islands Chambourcin ★★★★

Top vintages of this Northland red are generous, deeply coloured and crammed with flavour. The 2015 vintage (★★★★) was matured for 16 months in French oak casks. Dark and purple-flushed, it is fresh, vibrantly fruity and concentrated, with youthful blackcurrant and plum flavours, fresh acidity, and good structure and density.

DRY $26 –V

Vintage	15	14	13
WR	6	6	6
Drink	19-23	19-20	P

Dolcetto

Grown in the north of Italy, where it produces purple-flushed, fruity, supple reds, usually enjoyed young, Dolcetto is extremely rare in New Zealand. Only 2 hectares of bearing vines have been recorded in New Zealand, mostly in Auckland, and the variety is not listed separately in New Zealand Winegrowers' *Vineyard Register Report 2017–2020*.

Milcrest Estate Nelson Dolcetto ★★★☆

Tasted in mid to late 2018, the 2013 vintage (★★★☆) is very youthful, with purple-flushed colour. Medium-bodied, it is fresh and vibrant, with plummy, berryish, slightly spicy flavours, lively acidity and a smooth finish. French oak-aged for 11 months, the 2014 vintage (★★★★) is also very youthful, with strong, plummy, spicy flavours, showing good density and backbone. Best drinking 2020+.

DRY $30 –V

Gamay Noir

Gamay Noir is single-handedly responsible for the seductively scented and soft red wines of Beaujolais. The grape is still very rare in New Zealand, with 10 hectares of bearing vines in 2020, mostly in Hawke's Bay. In the Omaka Springs Vineyard in Marlborough, Gamay ripened later than Cabernet Sauvignon (itself an end-of-season ripener), with higher levels of acidity than in Beaujolais, but at Te Mata's Woodthorpe Terraces Vineyard in Hawke's Bay, the crop is harvested as early as mid-March.

Te Mata Estate Vineyards Hawke's Bay Gamay Noir ★★★★

A sort of red wine for white-wine lovers, the 2018 vintage (★★★★) is delicious young. Estate-grown in the inland Woodthorpe Terraces Vineyard and matured for 11 weeks in seasoned French oak barrels, it is bright, light ruby, with fresh, berryish aromas. Medium-bodied, it is vibrantly fruity and smooth, with strong, plummy, slightly spicy flavours, gentle tannins, and lots of youthful impact.

DRY $20 V+

Grenache

Grenache, one of the world's most extensively planted grape varieties, thrives in the hot, dry vineyards of Spain and southern France. It is also yielding exciting wines in Australia, especially from old, unirrigated, bush-pruned vines, but is exceedingly rare in New Zealand, with a total producing area in 2020 of 1 hectare, all in Hawke's Bay.

Villa Maria Cellar Selection Hawke's Bay Grenache ★★★★☆

The 2018 vintage (★★★★☆) of this very late-ripening variety was blended with Syrah (7 per cent) and matured in small and large French oak vessels. Deep ruby, with a fragrant, berryish, spicy bouquet, it is sturdy and supple, with strong, ripe berry and spice flavours, oak complexity and gentle tannins. A powerful young red, it's well worth cellaring to 2021+.

DRY $25 V+

Lagrein

Cultivated traditionally in the vineyards of Trentino-Alto Adige, in north-east Italy, Lagrein yields deeply coloured, slightly astringent reds with fresh acidity and plum/cherry flavours, firm and strong. The area of bearing vines in New Zealand will leap from 2 hectares in 2015 to 10 hectares in 2020, mostly in Hawke's Bay (8 hectares), but also in Marlborough and Nelson.

Hunting Lodge, The, Marlborough Lagrein (★★★★★)

Worth tracking down, the powerful 2018 vintage (★★★★★) is described on the back label as 'an Italian hillbilly on OE in Marlborough'. From a variety related to Syrah and Pinot Noir, it is a deeply coloured, single-vineyard red, grown in the Awatere Valley and matured for 10 months in French oak barriques (20 per cent new). Bold, vibrant and fruit-packed, it has concentrated, youthful, plummy, distinctly spicy flavours, good tannin backbone, and loads of personality. New Zealand's finest Lagrein to date, it's well worth cellaring to 2021+.

DRY $32 AV

Stanley Estates Awatere Valley Marlborough Lagrein ★★★★

The lively 2015 vintage (★★★☆) was estate-grown, hand-picked and matured for 10 months in French oak casks (24 per cent new). Deeply coloured, it is mouthfilling and vibrantly fruity, with strong, plummy, spicy flavours, showing considerable complexity, and a lingering finish.

Vintage	15	
WR	6	
Drink	19-25	

DRY $28 –V

Malbec

With a rise from 25 hectares of bearing vines in 1998 to 120 hectares in 2020, this old Bordeaux variety is starting to make its presence felt in New Zealand, where nearly 75 per cent of all plantings are clustered in Hawke's Bay (most of the rest are in Auckland). It is often used as a blending variety, adding brilliant colour and rich, sweet-fruit flavours to its blends with Merlot, Cabernet Sauvignon and Cabernet Franc. Numerous unblended Malbecs have also been released recently, possessing loads of flavour and often the slight rusticity typical of the variety (or at least some of the clones established here).

Brookfields Hawke's Bay Sun Dried Malbec ★★★★

Promoted as 'Malbec on steroids', the 2018 vintage (★★★★) was made from grapes sun-dried to concentrate their sugars and flavours, then matured for a year in French and American oak casks. Full-bodied, with deep, purple-flushed colour, it is vibrantly fruity and supple, with strong plum and spice flavours, oak complexity and a smooth finish. Highly approachable in its youth, it should be at its best 2020+.

Vintage	18
WR	7
Drink	19-29

DRY $25 AV

Clearview Two Pinnacles Reserve Hawke's Bay Malbec ★★★★

The 2015 vintage (★★★★☆) is a boldly coloured red, estate-grown on the coast, at Te Awanga, and matured for 17 months in oak barrels (14 per cent new). Gutsy and fruit-packed, it's a full-on style, with strong, fresh plum, spice and blackcurrant flavours, showing good ripeness, tannin backbone, and obvious cellaring potential.

DRY $26 AV

Coopers Creek Gisborne Malbec ★★★☆

The 2016 vintage (★★★☆) was barrel-aged for a year. An easy-drinking red, offering good value, it is full-coloured and mouthfilling, with satisfying depth of fresh, vibrant, berryish, slightly spicy flavours, a subtle seasoning of oak, and a smooth finish.

DRY $18 V+

Decibel Gimblett Gravels Malbec (★★★☆)

The 2017 vintage (★★★☆) is deeply coloured, with strong, fresh, fruity aromas. Handled with old oak, it is full-bodied and vibrant, with very good depth of plummy, spicy flavours and lots of youthful vigour.

 DRY $28 –V

Fromm Malbec Fromm Vineyard ★★★★☆

Estate-grown in Marlborough and hand-picked from mature vines, this red is recommended by winemaker Hätsch Kalberer for drinking with 'a large piece of wild venison'. The 2017 vintage (★★★★☆) is rare – only four barrels were made. Oak-aged for 19 months, it has deep, purple-flushed colour. Fresh, spicy aromas lead into a full-bodied, very youthful wine, with strong plum, spice and blackcurrant flavours, good tannin backbone and a long finish. Unusually refined for Malbec, it should break into full stride 2021+. Certified organic.

 DRY $65 –V

Mahurangi River Winery Matakana Reserve Malbec   (★★★★☆)

The powerful 2015 vintage (★★★★☆) is boldly coloured. Full-bodied, it is packed with plum, red-berry, spice and slight liquorice flavours, fresh and strong. Showing considerable complexity, with good density and tannin backbone, it should reward cellaring.

 DRY $54 –V

Matawhero Church House Single Vineyard Gisborne Malbec   ★★★☆

The easy-drinking 2018 vintage (★★☆) is bright ruby (light for Malbec), with fresh, berryish aromas. Fruity and smooth, with berryish, slightly spicy flavours, it's an uncomplicated red with an off-dry (5 grams/litre of residual sugar) finish.

 MED/DRY $26 –V

Saint Clair James Sinclair Hawke's Bay Malbec   ★★★☆

The easy-drinking 2017 vintage (★★★☆) is a medium-bodied, supple red with strong, fresh, berryish, plummy, slightly earthy flavours, and oak-derived complexity. Drink now or cellar.

 DRY $28 –V

Saint Clair Pioneer Block 17 Plateau Gimblett Gravels Hawke's Bay Malbec   ★★★★

The smooth, easy-drinking 2015 vintage (★★★★) was estate-grown and French oak-aged. Full-coloured, with fresh, berryish, plummy flavours, some earthy notes, gentle tannins and good depth, it's a drink-now proposition.

 DRY $38 –V

Stonyridge Luna Negra Waiheke Island Hillside Malbec   ★★★★★

Promoted as 'like going on an energetic dance with a Cuban beauty queen', this bold, classy red is estate-grown in the Vina del Mar Vineyard at Onetangi and matured in American oak barriques. The 2015 vintage (★★★★★) has dense, inky, purple-flushed colour. A powerful, sturdy wine, it has concentrated, well-ripened blackcurrant and plum flavours, in a structured, age-worthy style, already delicious, but likely to be at its best 2020+.

 DRY $95 –V

Te Aotea Vineyard South Kaipara Malbec   ★★★★☆

The delicious 2014 vintage (★★★★☆), labelled 'Angels', was matured for 16 months in new American and seasoned French oak barrels. Full-coloured, it is mouthfilling, with strong, ripe berry, plum and spice flavours, a hint of liquorice, good complexity and a finely balanced, long finish.

DRY $60 –V

Testify by Decibel Hawke's Bay Malbec   (★★★★)

Drinking well in 2019, but also worth cellaring, the 2016 vintage (★★★★) was grown in the Gimblett Gravels and matured in French oak barrels (partly new). Deep and youthful in colour, it is fresh, fragrant and vibrantly fruity, with a seasoning of nutty oak adding complexity. It's not a blockbuster (unlike many Malbecs), but skilfully crafted.

DRY $56 –V

Tironui Hawke's Bay Malbec/Merlot/Cabernet   ★★★★☆

From an elevated site at Taradale, the single-vineyard 2016 vintage (★★★★) is a blend of Malbec (70 per cent), Merlot (18 per cent) and Cabernet Sauvignon (12 per cent). Matured for 20 months in seasoned French oak barrels, it is very fresh and youthful, with generous, plummy, spicy flavours, gentle tannins and good harmony.

DRY $35 AV

Villa Maria Reserve Gimblett Gravels Hawke's Bay Malbec   ★★★★★

The dark, rich 2015 vintage (★★★★☆) was estate-grown in the Omahu Gravels Vineyard and matured for 18 months in French oak barriques (25 per cent new). It is vibrantly fruity, with deep, plummy, berryish flavours, woven with fresh acidity, and fine-grained tannins.

DRY $50 AV

Marzemino

Once famous, but today rare, Marzemino is cultivated in northern Italy, where it typically yields light, plummy reds. Established in New Zealand in 1995, Marzemino has been made commercially by Pernod Ricard NZ under the Church Road brand since 2005, but is not listed separately in New Zealand Winegrowers' *Vineyard Register Report 2017–2020*.

Church Road McDonald Series Hawke's Bay Marzemino ★★★★

Grown in the company's Redstone Vineyard, in the Bridge Pa Triangle, this rare wine is matured in French oak barriques. The 2015 vintage (★★★★☆) is dark and buoyantly fruity, with fresh berry, plum and spice flavours, showing excellent ripeness and density, gentle tannins and obvious potential.

DRY $28 AV

Merlot

Pinot Noir is New Zealand's red-wine calling card on the world stage, but our Merlots are also proving competitive. Interest in this most extensively cultivated red-wine grape in Bordeaux is especially strong in Hawke's Bay. Everywhere in Bordeaux – the world's greatest red-wine region – except in the Médoc and Graves districts, the internationally higher-profile Cabernet Sauvignon variety plays second fiddle to Merlot. The elegant, fleshy wines of Pomerol and St Émilion bear delicious testimony to Merlot's capacity to produce great, yet relatively early-maturing, reds.

In New Zealand, after initial preoccupation with the more austere and slowly evolving Cabernet Sauvignon, the rich, rounded flavours and (more practically) earlier-ripening ability of Merlot are now fully appreciated. Poor set can be a major drawback with the older clones, reducing yields, but Merlot ripens ahead of Cabernet Sauvignon, a major asset in cooler wine regions, especially in vineyards with colder clay soils. Merlot grapes are typically lower in tannin and higher in sugar than Cabernet Sauvignon's; its wines are thus silkier and a shade stronger in alcohol.

Hawke's Bay has 87.5 per cent of New Zealand's bearing Merlot vines in 2020; the rest are clustered in Gisborne, Auckland and Marlborough. The country's fifth most widely planted variety, Merlot covers well over four times the area of Cabernet Sauvignon. Between 2003 and 2020, the total area of bearing Merlot vines barely changed, from 1249 to 1197 hectares, but in most vintages, the wines offer terrific value.

Merlot's key role in New Zealand was traditionally that of a minority blending variety, bringing a soft, mouthfilling richness and floral, plummy fruitiness to its marriages with the predominant Cabernet Sauvignon. Now, with a host of straight Merlots and Merlot-predominant blends on the market, this aristocratic grape is fully recognised as a top-flight wine in its own right.

Alexander Martinborough Merlot ★★★★

The 2018 vintage (★★★★) was estate-grown, hand-picked and matured for 11 months in French oak barriques (33 per cent new). Full-coloured, it is fragrant and sturdy, with strong, ripe berry, plum and spice flavours, showing good complexity, and a firmly structured finish. Best drinking 2022+.

Alpha Domus The Fox Moth Hawke's Bay Merlot ★★★☆

The highly attractive 2015 vintage (★★★★) was estate-grown in the Bridge Pa Triangle and oak-aged for a year. The colour is full and bright; the palate is mouthfilling and supple, with fresh, ripe plum, spice and nut flavours, generous and smooth.

Ash Ridge Estate Hawke's Bay Merlot/Cabernet ★★★☆

The 2017 vintage (★★★☆), estate-grown in the Bridge Pa Triangle, was blended from Merlot (85 per cent) and Cabernet Sauvignon (15 per cent), matured for a year in French oak casks. The winery's only 'Bordeaux-style' red from the vintage, it is medium to full-bodied, with youthful, berryish, slightly spicy and nutty flavours, showing considerable complexity, and a fairly firm finish. Best drinking mid-2020+.

DRY $22 AV

Askerne Hawke's Bay Merlot/Cabernet Sauvignon/Cabernet Franc ★★★☆

The 2016 vintage (★★★☆) is a youthful blend of Merlot (66 per cent), Cabernet Sauvignon (15 per cent), Cabernet Franc (12 per cent) and Malbec (7 per cent), matured for 18 months in barrels (40 per cent new). Full-coloured, it is mouthfilling, with fresh plum, spice and herb flavours, savoury notes adding complexity, smooth tannins and very good depth. Verging on four stars, it's a finely textured red, worth cellaring.

Askerne Reserve Hawke's Bay Merlot/Cabernet Sauvignon/Cabernet Franc ★★★★

Deeply coloured, the youthful 2018 vintage (★★★★) is a blend of Merlot (43 per cent), Cabernet Sauvignon (36 per cent), Cabernet Franc (11 per cent), Petit Verdot (7 per cent) and Malbec (3 per cent). Mouthfilling and sweet-fruited, it has generous, plummy, spicy flavours, a hint of herbs, and a very smooth finish. Best drinking 2021+.

Ataahua Waipara Merlot ★★★★

The 2015 vintage (★★★★☆) proves that you can make excellent Merlot in the South Island. Hand-picked from 20-year-old vines and barrel-aged for over a year, it has deep, moderately youthful colour. Sturdy, it's a powerful wine with well-ripened plum, red-berry and spice flavours, vibrant and concentrated, and good tannin backbone. Drinking well now, it's also worth cellaring.

Babich Hawke's Bay Merlot/Cabernet ★★★☆

Priced right, the 2017 vintage (★★★☆) is full-coloured, mouthfilling and smooth. Wood-aged for a year, it has good depth of fresh, berryish, slightly spicy flavours, finely balanced tannins and some savoury complexity. Best drinking mid-2020+.

Vintage	17
WR	5
Drink	19-23

Babich Winemakers' Reserve Hawke's Bay Merlot ★★★★☆

Likely to be long-lived, the classy 2015 vintage (★★★★★) is a full-coloured Gimblett Gravels red, estate-grown in the Irongate Vineyard. Fragrant, with a warm, ripe, savoury bouquet, it is mouthfilling, with deep, plummy, spicy, nutty flavours, showing excellent structure and complexity, and good tannin backbone. Retasted in April 2019, it offers fine value and should be at its best 2021+. The elegant, slightly lighter 2016 vintage (★★★★☆) was French oak-aged for a year. Full-coloured and fragrant, it is fresh and full-bodied, with strong berry, plum and spice flavours, savoury and complex, supple tannins and obvious potential; best drinking 2020+.

Vintage	16	15
WR	6	7
Drink	19-22	19-22

DRY $35 AV

Brookfields Burnfoot Hawke's Bay Merlot   ★★★★

Typically great value. The 2015 vintage (★★★☆), grown in the Tuki Tuki Valley, was matured for a year in seasoned French and American oak casks. A mouthfilling red with fullish, bright colour, it is vibrantly fruity, with fresh acidity and strong, plummy, slightly herbal flavours, gently seasoned with oak.

Vintage	15
WR	7
Drink	19-21

 DRY $20 V+

Brookfields Highland Hawke's Bay Merlot/Cabernet   ★★★★☆

The 2015 vintage (★★★★☆) is a blend of Merlot and Cabernet Sauvignon, matured for a year in new and one-year-old French and American oak casks. Deeply coloured, with plenty of personality, it has mouthfilling body and rich, vibrant plum, cassis and spice flavours, with a hint of coffee. Complex and savoury, it should be at its best 2020+.

Vintage	15	14
WR	7	7
Drink	20-26	19-25

 DRY $45 –V

Church Road 1 Single Vineyard Gimblett Gravels Merlot   (★★★★★)

The very classy 2016 vintage (★★★★★) is a youthful Hawke's Bay red, matured for 18 months in French oak barriques (54 per cent new). Deeply coloured, with a fragrant, inviting bouquet, it is mouthfilling and sweet-fruited, but not heavy, with highly concentrated red-berry and plum flavours, well-integrated oak and a very harmonious, seductively smooth finish. Best drinking 2022+. (Note: only available in 'travel retail and cellar door/online'.)

 DRY $90 AV

Church Road Grand Reserve Hawke's Bay Merlot/Cabernet Sauvignon   ★★★★☆

The powerful, classy, fragrant 2015 vintage (★★★★★) was blended from Merlot (86 per cent) and Cabernet Sauvignon (14 per cent), grown in the Bridge Pa Triangle and Gimblett Gravels, and was French oak-aged for 20 months. The colour is dark and youthful; the palate is robust and well-structured, with blackcurrant, plum and spice flavours, showing excellent freshness, ripeness and concentration, good tannin backbone, and a long future ahead. Best drinking 2022+.

 DRY $40 AV

Church Road Hawke's Bay Merlot/Cabernet Sauvignon   ★★★★

This full-flavoured, Bordeaux-like red from Pernod Ricard NZ can offer wonderful value. Merlot-based, it is typically estate-grown in the Redstone Vineyard, in the Bridge Pa Triangle, and matured in French and Hungarian oak barrels. The 2015 vintage (★★★★) is a blend of Merlot (74 per cent) and Cabernet Sauvignon (26 per cent), oak-aged for a year. Dark, it's a fresh, 'fruit-driven' style, with substantial body, very generous, ripe blackcurrant/plum flavours, gentle tannins and excellent depth. It's already delicious.

DRY $20 V+

Church Road McDonald Series Hawke's Bay Merlot ★★★★★

Estate-grown in the Gimblett Vineyard, in the Gimblett Gravels (75 per cent), and the Redstone Vineyard, in the Bridge Pa Triangle (25 per cent), the 2014 vintage (★★★★☆) was matured for 20 months in French and Hungarian oak barrels (39 per cent new), and bottled unfined and unfiltered. A powerful, very ripe-tasting, sturdy red, it is deeply coloured. Fragrant, rich and supple, it has very generous plum/spice flavours, hints of liquorice and nuts, well-integrated oak and gentle tannins.

 DRY $27 V+

Clearview Cape Kidnappers Hawke's Bay Merlot ★★★★☆

Offering irresistible value, the 2016 vintage (★★★★☆) is Merlot-based, with 14 per cent Malbec in the blend. Grown at Te Awanga and matured for 14 months in French oak barrels (18 per cent new), it is fragrant, dark and weighty, with strong, ripe blackcurrant, plum and spice flavours, hints of liquorice and dark chocolate, good complexity and a seductively smooth finish. Unexpectedly rich for a wine in its moderate price category, it will reward cellaring but is already delicious.

 DRY $22 V+

Collaboration Impression Merlot/Cabernet/Cabernet Franc ★★★★☆

The distinctive, attractive 2016 vintage (★★★★☆) is a blend of Merlot, Cabernet Sauvignon and Cabernet Franc. Matured for 18 months in seasoned French oak barrels, and bottled unfined and unfiltered, it is full-coloured, with a fragrant, berryish, slightly herbal bouquet. Medium to full-bodied, it is vibrantly fruity, with strong plum, red-berry and spice flavours, showing good complexity, and fine-grained tannins. Already highly enjoyable, it should also reward cellaring; best drinking 2021+.

DRY $30 AV

Coopers Creek Select Vineyards Gimblett Gravels
Hawke's Bay Merlot/Malbec ★★★★

Well worth cellaring, the 2016 vintage (★★★★) is a blend of Merlot (54 per cent) and Malbec (46 per cent), matured in French oak casks. Full-coloured, it is fresh and vibrant, with strong, ripe plum and spice flavours, finely balanced tannins and savoury notes adding complexity. Best drinking 2020+.

 DRY $25 AV

Craggy Range Gimblett Gravels Vineyard Hawke's Bay Merlot ★★★★☆

The 2016 vintage (★★★★☆) was matured for 17 months in French oak barriques (30 per cent new). Dark and purple-flushed, it is mouthfilling and vibrantly fruity, with fresh, ripe, concentrated, plummy, spicy flavours that build across the palate to a long finish. A stylish, youthful red, it's well worth cellaring to 2021+.

 DRY $40 –V

Delegat Crownthorpe Terraces Merlot   ★★★★

Bargain-priced, the 2016 vintage (★★★★) was estate-grown in the company's cool, elevated, inland vineyard at Crownthorpe, in Hawke's Bay, and matured for a year in French oak barriques (new and one year old). Deeply coloured, with a fragrant bouquet of berries and herbs, it is mouthfilling, vibrantly fruity and supple, with generous, plummy flavours, fine-grained tannins, and loads of drink-young appeal. (Note: there is no 2017 vintage and this label is being replaced by Delegat Gimblett Road Merlot – see below.)

`DRY $20 V+`

Delegat Gimblett Road Merlot   (★★★★☆)

Offering outstanding value, the debut 2018 vintage (★★★★☆) was grown in the Gimblett Gravels, Hawke's Bay, and matured for 14 months in oak barriques (new and one year old). Richly coloured, with fresh, spicy aromas, it is mouthfilling and vibrantly fruity, with concentrated, plummy, spicy flavours, finely integrated oak, good tannin support, and obvious cellaring potential. A distinctive, youthful wine, it should be at its best 2021+.

`DRY $20 V+`

Delta Hawke's Bay Merlot   (★★★★)

Offering good value, the youthful 2017 vintage (★★★★) is a single-vineyard red, French and American oak-aged. Deeply coloured, it is fragrant and full-bodied, with concentrated, plummy, spicy flavours and a moderately firm finish. Best drinking 2020+.

`DRY $19 V+`

Eaton Marlborough Merlot/Malbec/Cabernet   ★★★★☆

The classy 2015 vintage (★★★★☆) was grown in the Eaton Family Vineyard, in the Omaka Valley. A blend of Merlot, Malbec and Cabernet Sauvignon, it was fermented with indigenous yeasts, matured for 20 months in French oak barrels (one year old), and bottled unfined and unfiltered. Already drinking well, it is full-coloured, sturdy, fragrant and complex, with deep, ripe blackcurrant, plum and spice flavours, leathery and nutty notes adding complexity, and good tannin backbone. Best drinking 2021+.

Vintage	15	14
WR	7	6
Drink	19-30	19-25

 `DRY $48 –V`

Elephant Hill Hawke's Bay Merlot/Malbec   ★★★★☆

The 2015 vintage (★★★★☆) is a deeply coloured blend of Merlot and Malbec, estate-grown and hand-picked in the Gimblett Gravels and the Bridge Pa Triangle. Matured in French oak casks, it is a full-bodied, generous red with concentrated, ripe plum, red-berry and spice flavours, gently seasoned with oak, hints of dark chocolate and liquorice, and excellent harmony and potential.

Vintage	15
WR	6
Drink	19-25

`DRY $34 AV`

Elephant Hill Reserve Hawke's Bay Merlot/Malbec ★★★★★

Already delicious, the 2015 vintage (★★★★★) is a blend of Merlot (72 per cent), Malbec (20 per cent) and Cabernet Sauvignon (8 per cent). Hand-harvested in the company's vineyards in the Gimblett Gravels and Bridge Pa Triangle, it was matured for two years in French oak casks (42 per cent new). Deep and youthful in colour, it has a fresh, fragrant bouquet. The palate is full-bodied, sweet-fruited and lush, with concentrated blackcurrant and spice flavours, hints of dark chocolate and nuts, fine-grained tannins and a long, smooth-flowing finish. Highly enjoyable now, but well worth cellaring, it should break into full stride 2020+.

 DRY $54 AV

Esk Valley Gimblett Gravels Merlot/Cabernet Sauvignon/Malbec ★★★★

Offering irresistible value, the 2017 vintage (★★★★☆) is a blend of Merlot (49 per cent), Malbec (26 per cent), Cabernet Sauvignon (19 per cent) and Cabernet Franc (6 per cent), matured for a year in French oak barriques (10 per cent new). Possessing more muscle, density, structure and complexity than most reds in its price category, it is mouthfilling, fleshy and savoury, with strong, ripe, plummy, berryish, spicy flavours, good complexity, and a well-rounded, very harmonious finish. Drink now or cellar.

Vintage	18	17	16	15	14	13	12	11
WR	6	5	6	6	7	7	6	5
Drink	19-27	19-23	19-22	19-21	19-21	19-20	P	P

 DRY $20 V+

Esk Valley The Hillside Merlot/Cabernet Franc/Malbec ★★★★★

The first, 2010 vintage (★★★★★) was Malbec-predominant, but the 2013 vintage (★★★★★) is a blend of Merlot (66 per cent), Cabernet Franc (30 per cent) and Malbec (4 per cent). Estate-grown at The Terraces Vineyard in Bay View, Hawke's Bay, it was matured for 18 months in French oak barriques (50 per cent new). A powerful, sturdy, very savoury wine, it is boldly coloured, with lush, plummy, spicy flavours, hints of liquorice and nuts, and excellent complexity. Still youthful, it should be long-lived, but is already a memorable mouthful.

Vintage	13
WR	7
Drink	19-25

 DRY $90 AV

Esk Valley Winemakers Reserve Merlot/Malbec/Cabernet Franc ★★★★★

This powerful, classy wine is typically one of Hawke's Bay's greatest reds (it is almost always Merlot-based, but the proportions of minor varieties vary). Grown in the company's Ngakirikiri Vineyard and the Cornerstone Vineyard, both in the Gimblett Gravels, it is matured for up to 20 months in French oak barriques (40 per cent new in 2014). The 2014 vintage (★★★★☆) is a concentrated blend of Merlot (54 per cent) with Malbec (31 per cent), Cabernet Franc (10 per cent) and Cabernet Sauvignon (5 per cent). Very full-bodied, with a strong surge of ripe dark berry and plum flavours, it has savoury notes adding complexity, supple tannins, and a rich, rounded finish. (There is no 2015.) The 2016 vintage (★★★★★) is Cabernet Sauvignon-based (see the Cabernet Sauvignon and Cabernet-predominant blends section).

Vintage	16	15	14	13	12	11	10
WR	7	NM	7	7	NM	7	7
Drink	19-33	NM	19-30	19-30	NM	19-25	19-25

 DRY $60 AV

Falconhead Hawke's Bay Merlot/Cabernet ★★★☆

Priced sharply, the 2016 vintage (★★★) was barrel-aged for two years. It has full, moderately youthful colour, mouthfilling body, plenty of fresh, berryish, spicy, slightly earthy flavour, and a fairly firm finish.

Vintage	16
WR	5
Drink	19-22

 DRY $17 V+

Greyrock Hawke's Bay Merlot ★★☆

Fullish in colour, the 2017 vintage (★★☆) is medium-bodied, with fresh berry, herb and spice flavours, showing a touch of complexity. An easy-drinking style, it's ready to roll. (From Sileni.)

 DRY $19 –V

Greyrock Te Koru Hawke's Bay Merlot (★★★☆)

The 2018 vintage (★★★☆) is full-coloured, fresh and fragrant, with very good depth of berry, plum and spice flavours. A youthful, firmly structured red with considerable complexity, it should be at its best 2021+. (From Sileni.)

 DRY $20 AV

Gunn Estate Reserve Hawke's Bay Merlot/Cabernet ★★★☆

The 2016 vintage (★★★☆) is a very fruit-driven style, but was French oak-aged for a year. It has full, bright, youthful colour. Fresh and full-bodied, it has very good depth of plum and blackcurrant-like flavours, gentle tannins, and lots of drink-young appeal.

Vintage	16	15
WR	6	6
Drink	19-22	19-20

 DRY $17 V+

Haha Hawke's Bay Merlot ★★★☆

The 2018 vintage (★★★☆) is an instantly appealing, vibrantly fruity red. Full-coloured, it is mouthfilling and smooth, with very gentle acidity, a restrained oak influence, and fresh, generous berry, plum and spice flavours to the fore. Offering good value, it's an uncomplicated but highly attractive wine, likely to be at its best during 2020–21.

 DRY $18 V+

Hans Herzog Spirit of Marlborough Merlot/Cabernet ★★★★★

Who says you can't make outstanding claret-style reds in the South Island? Estate-grown on the banks of the Wairau River, matured for at least two years in new and one-year-old French oak barriques, and then bottle-aged for several years, this is typically a densely coloured wine with a classy fragrance, substantial body and notably concentrated blackcurrant, plum, herb and spice flavours. The 2014 vintage (★★★★★) is a blend of equal portions of Merlot, Cabernet

Franc and Cabernet Sauvignon. Fragrant, with deep, fairly youthful colour, it is sturdy, with concentrated blackcurrant, plum and spice flavours, showing excellent ripeness and depth, good complexity, and a well-structured, long finish. Best drinking 2022+. Certified organic.

Vintage	14	13
WR	7	7
Drink	19-28	19-28

DRY $69 AV

Hunter's Marlborough Merlot ★★★

Estate-grown at Rapaura, in the Wairau Valley, the 2016 vintage (★★★☆) is a single-vineyard red, hand-picked from mature vines, matured for a year in French oak barrels (50 per cent new), and bottled unfined and unfiltered. Fullish in colour, it is mouthfilling and youthful, with good depth of vibrant red-berry, plum, spice and herb flavours, showing considerable complexity, an earthy streak, and a fairly firm finish. Best drinking 2020+.

Vintage	16
WR	5
Drink	19-25

DRY $35 –V

Karikari Estate Hell Hole Merlot/Cabernet Franc (★★☆)

The 2016 vintage (★★☆) is an estate-grown, Far North blend of Merlot (75 per cent) and Cabernet Franc (25 per cent), hand-harvested and matured in old oak barrels, mostly American. 'Honest, raucous and a little rough' (according to the back label), it has mature colour. Full-bodied, it's a slightly gutsy, easy-drinking red, with red-berry, herb and spice flavours, and a smooth finish. Ready.

DRY $27 –V

Karikari Estate Toa Iti Merlot/Cabernet Franc/Tannat (★★★)

Tasted in early 2019, this distinctive, non-vintage wine (★★★) is a blend of 2016 and 2017 vintages. Merlot-based (50 per cent), with Cabernet Franc (40 per cent) and Tannat (10 per cent), it was hand-picked in the Far North and matured for two years in old oak barrels, French and American. Very developed in colour, it is a distinctive, full-flavoured wine, with hints of liquorice and spices, and moderately firm tannins. Savoury and mellow, it tastes ready.

DRY $30 –V

Kumeu River Melba's Vineyard Merlot ★★★★

Still available, the 2013 vintage (★★★★) was estate-grown at Kumeu, in West Auckland, and barrel-aged for a year. Deeply coloured, it is an elegant rather than powerful red, sweet-fruited, with vibrant, plummy flavours, showing some savoury complexity, and a finely poised finish.

DRY $25 AV

Lake Chalice The Falcon Gimblett Gravels Hawke's Bay Merlot (★★★☆)

The 2017 vintage (★★★☆) is a slightly gutsy red, matured for 10 months in French oak casks. Full-coloured, it is mouthfilling and vibrantly fruity, with strong, plummy, slightly spicy and earthy flavours, and a moderately smooth finish.

DRY $19 V+

Left Field Hawke's Bay Merlot ★★★★

Offering good value, the 2017 vintage (★★★☆) is a blend of Merlot (86 per cent) and Malbec (14 per cent), barrel-aged for a year. It is full-bodied and very smooth, with youthful, vibrant, plummy, berryish flavours, savoury notes adding a touch of complexity, gentle tannins, and lots of drink-young charm. (From Te Awa.)

Vintage	17	16	15	14
WR	5	6	6	5
Drink	19-23	19-23	19-20	19-20

DRY $19 V+

Leveret Estate Hawke's Bay Merlot/Cabernet ★★★☆

Drinking well now, the 2015 vintage (★★★☆) is a single-vineyard red, grown in the Bridge Pa Triangle and barrel-aged for two years (10 per cent new). Full-coloured, it is fresh, mouthfilling and supple, with generous, berryish, slightly spicy and nutty flavours.

Vintage	15	14	13
WR	5	7	7
Drink	19-25	19-20	19-20

DRY $22 AV

Leveret Estate Reserve Hawke's Bay Merlot Cabernet ★★★★

Full-bodied and youthful, the 2015 vintage (★★★★) is a single-vineyard red, grown in the Bridge Pa Triangle and barrel-aged for two years. Deeply coloured, it has generous, ripe, plummy, spicy flavours, woven with fresh acidity, and gentle tannins. Best drinking 2020+.

Vintage	15	14	13
WR	7	6	7
Drink	19-25	19-24	19-25

DRY $27 AV

Lime Rock Central Hawke's Bay Merlot (★★★★)

Maturing gracefully, the 2013 vintage (★★★★) was grown in Central Hawke's Bay, hand-harvested and matured in seasoned French oak casks. An attractive red, it is fragrant, full-coloured and mouthfilling, with very good depth of ripe, plummy, spicy flavours, nutty and leathery notes adding complexity, and supple tannins. Drink now or cellar.

Vintage	13
WR	6
Drink	19-21

DRY $24 V+

Linden Estate Reserve Hawke's Bay Merlot ★★★★

Estate-grown and hand-picked in the Esk Valley, the age-worthy 2015 vintage (★★★★) was matured in French oak casks. Full-coloured, it is mouthfilling and savoury, with youthful plum/ spice flavours, hints of nuts and liquorice, good concentration and a firm finish. Best drinking 2020+.

Vintage	15
WR	5
Drink	19-25

DRY $38 –V

Mahurangi River Winery Merlot/Cabernet Sauvignon/Malbec ★★★★

Still available, the 2014 vintage (★★★★) is a blend of Merlot (54 per cent), Cabernet Sauvignon (31 per cent) and Malbec (15 per cent), grown at Matakana and matured for 14 months in French and American oak barrels (50 per cent new). Deeply coloured, with plum/ spice aromas, it is weighty and generous, with ripe blackcurrant, plum, herb and spice flavours, finely integrated oak, and savoury notes adding complexity.

DRY $29 AV

Main Divide North Canterbury Merlot/Cabernet ★★★☆

Offering good value, the 2017 vintage (★★★★) from Pegasus Bay was grown at Waipara and matured for over a year in French oak barriques (10 per cent new). It is a blend of Merlot (50 per cent), Cabernet Sauvignon (40 per cent), Malbec (5 per cent) and Cabernet Franc (5 per cent). Fragrant and full-coloured, it is mouthfilling, with strong, vibrant plum, spice and blackcurrant flavours, showing excellent ripeness and depth, oak complexity, and a very harmonious finish. Drink now or cellar.

Vintage	17
WR	6
Drink	19-24

DRY $21 AV

Matawhero Single Vineyard Gisborne Merlot ★★★☆

The 2018 vintage (★★★☆) is a 'fruit-driven' style, mouthfilling and full-coloured, with strong, fresh, plummy, spicy flavour. An uncomplicated but attractive red, it's delicious young.

DRY $23 AV

Milcrest Estate Nelson Merlot (★★★☆)

Still on sale, the 2014 vintage (★★★☆) is a single-vineyard red, aged for 10 months in seasoned French oak barrels. Medium to full-bodied, with good colour depth, it is vibrantly fruity, with strong plum/spice flavours, a hint of herbs, fresh acidity and considerable complexity.

DRY $34 –V

Mills Reef Bespoke Gimblett Gravels Merlot/Cabernet Franc (★★★★)

The very approachable 2016 vintage (★★★★) is a blend of Merlot (66 per cent) and Cabernet Franc (34 per cent), matured for 17 months in French (mostly) hogsheads (44 per cent new). Full-coloured, it is mouthfilling, with generous, well-ripened plum, spice and blackcurrant flavours, and hints of liquorice and nuts, in a smooth, moderately complex style, with lots of upfront appeal.

DRY $40 –V

Mills Reef Elspeth Gimblett Gravels Hawke's Bay Merlot ★★★★☆

The age-worthy 2016 vintage (★★★★☆) was hand-picked in the company's Mere Road Vineyard and matured for 17 months in French oak hogsheads (34 per cent new). Deep ruby, it is fragrant and vibrant, with strong, youthful blackcurrant, plum and spice flavours, seasoned with quality oak, and good tannin support. Best drinking 2020+.

Vintage	16	DRY $50 –V
WR	7	
Drink	19-26	

Mills Reef Estate Hawke's Bay Merlot/Cabernet ★★★☆

Deeply coloured, with a fresh, slightly herbal bouquet, the 2018 vintage (★★★☆) is a blend of Merlot (54 per cent), Cabernet Sauvignon (33 per cent) and Cabernet Franc (13 per cent), French oak-aged for a year. Mouthfilling, it is vibrantly fruity and supple, with generous blackcurrant, plum, herb and spice flavours, a distinct touch of complexity and good tannin support. Best mid-2020+.

DRY $19 V+

Mills Reef Reserve Gimblett Gravels Hawke's Bay Merlot ★★★★

The 2018 vintage (★★★★) was hand-picked and matured for a year in French oak barrels (25 per cent new). Boldly coloured, it is freshly scented and fruit-packed, with mouthfilling body, strong, plummy, spicy flavours, well-integrated oak and good cellaring potential. Best drinking 2021+.

Vintage	18	17	16	15	14	13	12	DRY $25 AV
WR	7	5	7	7	6	7	6	
Drink	20-24	19-23	19-22	19-21	19-20	P	P	

Mills Reef Reserve Gimblett Gravels Hawke's Bay Merlot/Malbec ★★★☆

The very easy-drinking 2017 vintage (★★★☆) was matured for 13 months in French (mostly) and American oak hogsheads (33 per cent new). Full-coloured, it has good youthful impact, with vibrant, plummy, berryish, spicy flavours, woven with fresh acidity, slightly earthy notes, and a very smooth finish. The 2018 vintage (★★★☆) was barrel-aged for 14 months (35 per cent new). Full-coloured and fresh, it has very good depth of plummy, spicy, slightly earthy flavours, in a medium to full-bodied style with some savoury complexity. Best drinking 2021+.

Vintage	18	17	16	15	14	13	12	11	10	DRY $25 –V
WR	7	7	7	7	7	7	6	7	7	
Drink	19-25	19-22	19-22	19-21	19-20	P	P	P	P	

Mission Gimblett Gravels Barrique Reserve Merlot ★★★★

The 2015 vintage (★★★★☆) is a generous, single-vineyard red from the Gimblett Gravels, matured for a year in French oak barriques. Deep and bright in colour, it is fragrant and supple, with concentrated blackcurrant and plum flavours, nutty, savoury elements adding complexity, and obvious cellaring potential.

Vintage	15	14	13	12	11	10	DRY $29 AV
WR	7	7	7	5	5	6	
Drink	19-26	19-25	19-25	P	P	P	

Mission Hawke's Bay Merlot   ★★★

The 2018 vintage (★★★) is a very easy-drinking red, full-coloured and mouthfilling, with fresh, vibrant, berryish, spicy flavours, gentle tannins and a smooth finish. It's not a complex style, but enjoyable young and priced right.

DRY $16 V+

Mission Hawke's Bay Merlot/Cabernet Sauvignon   ★★★

The 2018 vintage (★★★☆) of this sharply priced red is based on Merlot (77 per cent) and Cabernet Sauvignon (19 per cent), with splashes of Malbec and Cabernet Franc. Full-coloured, with a fragrant, slightly herbal bouquet, it is mouthfilling and supple, with generous, berryish, slightly spicy and herbal flavours, underlying tannins, and some aging potential.

DRY $16 V+

Mission Vineyard Selection Hawke's Bay Merlot   ★★★☆

The 2015 vintage (★★★★) was mostly matured for over a year in French oak casks. Deeply coloured, it is full-bodied and smooth, with strong blackcurrant and plum flavours, a hint of herbs, and very good vigour and depth.

DRY $20 AV

Monowai Hawke's Bay Merlot   (★★★)

The 2016 vintage (★★★) is a medium-bodied, easy-drinking red, grown at Crownthorpe. Fullish in colour, it has fresh, berryish, plummy aromas and flavours, in a 'fruit-driven' style with a hint of herbs, good depth and a smooth finish.

DRY $18 AV

Montford Estate Hawke's Bay Merlot/ Cabernet   (★★☆)

The debut 2017 vintage (★★☆) is a blend of Merlot (79 per cent) and Cabernet Sauvignon (21 per cent.) Fullish in colour, it has a slightly rustic bouquet, leading into a fresh, firm palate with plenty of berryish, spicy, slightly earthy flavour. (From te Pā.)

DRY $25 –V

Morton Estate [Black Label] Hawke's Bay Merlot   (★★★★)

The 2016 vintage (★★★★) offers good value. Full-coloured, it is mouthfilling, with generous, ripe blackcurrant, plum and spice flavours, savoury and nutty notes adding complexity, and a fresh, smooth finish. Best drinking 2020–21.

DRY $20 V+

Mount Riley Marlborough Merlot/Malbec   ★★★☆

Offering fine value, the 2016 vintage (★★★★) is a blend of Merlot (93 per cent) and Malbec (7 per cent), grown in the central Wairau Valley and matured for 10 months in French and American oak barriques (10 per cent new). Full-coloured, it is fresh and mouthfilling, with generous, ripe, berryish, slightly spicy and nutty flavours, finely textured and smooth. Delicious young.

DRY $17 V+

Moutere Hills Nelson Merlot   (★★★☆)

Estate-grown at Upper Moutere, the 2016 vintage (★★★☆) is a single-vineyard red, hand-harvested from 23-year-old vines and matured for 10 months in French oak casks. Made in a 'fruit-driven' style, it is fresh and youthful, with good depth of plummy, berryish, gently spicy flavours, lively acidity and some cellaring potential.

DRY $32 –V

Moutere Hills Sarau Reserve Nelson Merlot   ★★★☆

The 2018 vintage (★★★☆) is a single-vineyard red, estate-grown at Upper Moutere, hand-picked and matured for 11 months in French oak barriques. A rare wine (only 35 cases were produced), it has lightish, moderately youthful colour. Mouthfilling, with plenty of berryish, slightly herbal and spicy flavour, fresh acidity and some savoury complexity, it should be at its best mid-2020+.

Vintage	18
WR	6
Drink	20-28

DRY $55 –V

Music Bay Winter Hawke's Bay Merlot/Cabernet/Malbec   (★★★☆)

Enjoyable young, the generous 2016 vintage (★★★☆) is a fresh, mouthfilling red with full, bright, youthful colour. It has very good depth of ripe, plummy, spicy flavours, with gentle tannins and lots of upfront appeal. (From Otuwhero.)

DRY $20 AV

Nikau Point Reserve Hawke's Bay Merlot   ★★☆

Estate-grown and barrel-aged for two years, the 2015 vintage (★★☆) is drinking solidly now. Full-coloured, it is mouthfilling, in a slightly gutsy style, with fresh, plummy, spicy flavours and a firm finish.

DRY $16 AV

Oyster Bay Hawke's Bay Merlot   ★★★☆

From Delegat, this red accounts for a huge slice of New Zealand's exports of 'Bordeaux-style' wines (Merlot and/or Cabernet Sauvignon). Winemaker Michael Ivicevich aims for a wine with 'sweet fruit and silky tannins. The trick is – not too much oak.' Grown in the Gimblett Gravels and at Crownthorpe, it is typically fragrant and mouthfilling, with strong blackcurrant, herb and dark chocolate flavours, supple tannins, and plenty of drink-young appeal. The 2018 vintage (★★★☆) is deeply coloured, mouthfilling and smooth, with generous, berryish, plummy flavours, ripe and rounded.

DRY $20 AV

Paritua Red Hawke's Bay Merlot/Cabernets ★★★★☆

The 2015 vintage (★★★★★) is a blend of Merlot (74 per cent), Cabernet Sauvignon (19 per cent) and Cabernet Franc (7 per cent), matured for 18 months in French oak barriques (40 per cent new). Deepy coloured, it has a fragrant, complex, nutty bouquet. A powerful, well-structured red, it has concentrated, berryish, spicy flavours, showing excellent complexity, and good tannin backbone. Still youthful, it should mature well for a decade.

 DRY $49 –V

Paritua Stone Paddock Scarlet Merlot/Cabernet Franc/Cabernet Sauvignon/Malbec (★★★★☆)

Offering excellent value, the deeply coloured 2016 vintage (★★★★☆) is a Hawke's Bay blend of Merlot (42 per cent), Cabernet Franc (30 per cent), Cabernet Sauvignon (20 per cent) and Malbec (8 per cent), matured for a year in seasoned oak barrels. Fragrant, with a gently spicy bouquet, it is mouthfilling, with generous plum, berry and spice flavours, oak complexity, and good freshness and vigour. Drinking well now, it should be at its best 2021+.

DRY $26 V+

Pask Declaration Gimblett Gravels Hawke's Bay Merlot ★★★★☆

Retasted in April 2019, the 2013 vintage (★★★★☆) was estate-grown and matured for 18 months in French oak casks (80 per cent new). It has deep, still fairly youthful colour. Mouthfilling and savoury, with deep plum and red-berry flavours, strongly seasoned with oak, and a smooth finish, it's drinking well now but still youthful; best drinking 2021+. The 2014 vintage (★★★★☆) is deeply coloured, mouthfilling, rich and smooth. Finely poised, with good varietal character, it has strong, youthful plum and spice flavours, showing very good complexity, and a finely balanced finish.

Vintage	13
WR	7
Drink	20-25

 DRY $50 –V

Pask Gimblett Gravels Merlot ★★★☆

Retasted in mid-2019, the 2016 vintage (★★★☆) was matured for over a year in French and American oak barrels (one and two years old). Still unfolding, it is mouthfilling, with very good depth of vibrant plum, spice and herb flavours, finely balanced tannins and some savoury complexity. Best drinking mid-2020+.

Vintage	16
WR	6
Drink	20-26

DRY $22 AV

Peacock Sky Waiheke Island Pure Merlot ★★★☆

Still on sale, the sturdy 2014 vintage (★★★☆) was matured for over a year in French oak barrels. Full-coloured, it has strong, ripe, plummy, slightly spicy and nutty flavours, and a firm backbone of tannin.

 DRY $40 –V

Pegasus Bay Waipara Valley Merlot/Cabernet ★★★★☆

The very impressive 2016 vintage (★★★★★) is a blend of Merlot (40 per cent), Cabernet Sauvignon (40 per cent), Malbec (15 per cent) and Cabernet Franc (5 per cent), estate-grown in North Canterbury and matured for two years in French oak barriques (25 per cent new). Dense and youthful in colour, it's a classy young red, with concentrated, ripe blackcurrant and plum flavours, oak complexity, and lovely richness and suppleness. Best drinking 2020+. Fine value.

Vintage	16	DRY $32 AV
WR	7	
Drink	19-28	

Quarter Acre Hawke's Bay Merlot/Malbec ★★★★☆

Still youthful, the fruit-packed 2016 vintage (★★★★☆) was matured for nine months in French oak barriques. Full-coloured, it is fragrant and mouthfilling, with strong, vibrant, plummy, spicy flavours, showing good complexity, and a firm, long finish. Well worth cellaring, it should be at its best 2021+.

 DRY $35 AV

Redmetal Vineyards Basket Press Bridge Pa
Triangle Merlot/Cabernet Franc ★★★★☆

Retasted in April 2019, the 2016 vintage (★★★★☆) was made almost entirely (99.5 per cent) from Merlot and matured for 14 months in oak barrels (25 per cent new). Deeply coloured, it is mouthfilling, sweet-fruited and supple, with generous, vibrant, plummy, nutty flavours, a hint of liquorice and a smooth finish. Drink now or cellar.

Vintage	16	DRY $36 AV
WR	5	
Drink	19-26	

Redmetal Vineyards Bridge Pa Triangle Hawke's Bay Merlot/Cabernet Franc ★★★☆

Retasted in May 2019, the 2016 vintage (★★★☆) was matured in tanks and barrels. Full and still fairly youthful in colour, it is fresh and vibrantly fruity, with smooth, ripe blackcurrant, plum and spice flavours, in an uncomplicated but generous style.

 DRY $22 AV

Regent of Tantallon, The, Hawke's Bay Limited Edition Merlot/Cabernet ★★★★☆

Set for a long life, the 2015 vintage (★★★★☆) was matured for 30 months in oak barrels (36 per cent new). A sturdy, fleshy, youthful red, it is deeply coloured, with concentrated blackcurrant, plum and spice flavours, nutty, savoury notes adding complexity, and a firm foundation of tannin. Best drinking 2022+.

DRY $45 –V

Renato Estate Nelson Merlot ★★★★

From mature, very low-cropped (3 tonnes/hectare) vines at Kina, the 2015 vintage (★★★★) was hand-picked and matured for 11 months in French oak casks (15 per cent new). Full-coloured, it is fresh and full-bodied, with generous, ripe, plummy, spicy flavours, a hint of liquorice, considerable complexity and good potential. Best drinking 2020+.

Vintage	15	14	13	12
WR	6	6	5	6
Drink	19-20	P	P	P

DRY $25 AV

Rongopai Hawke's Bay Merlot/Cabernet ★★★

From Babich, the 2016 vintage (★★★☆) is enjoyable now. Full-coloured, it is mouthfilling and vibrantly fruity, with very good depth of fresh, plummy, slightly spicy flavours and a smooth finish.

DRY $18 AV

Roys Hill Hawke's Bay Merlot/Cabernet (★★★)

From Pask, the 2017 vintage (★★★) was grown in the Gimblett Gravels and partly barrel-aged. Enjoyable young, it has fullish colour, with ripe plum, berry and spice flavours, a touch of savoury complexity and a smooth finish.

DRY $18 AV

Sacred Hill Brokenstone Merlot – see Sacred Hill Brokenstone in the Branded and Other Red Wines section

Sacred Hill Hawke's Bay Merlot/Cabernet Sauvignon ★★★☆

The good-value 2016 vintage (★★★☆) was French oak-matured for 10 months. A 'fruit-driven' style, it is full-coloured, with mouthfilling body and strong, berryish, slightly herbal flavours, fresh and smooth.

Vintage	16	15
WR	6	6
Drink	19-22	19-20

DRY $17 V+

Sacred Hill Reserve Hawke's Bay Merlot/Cabernet Sauvignon ★★★☆

Delicious young, the 2016 vintage (★★★★) was French oak-aged for a year. Full, bright and youthful in colour, it is rich and flowing, with generous, plummy flavours, hints of herbs, spices and nuts, and fine-grained tannins.

Vintage	16
WR	6
Drink	19-26

DRY $25 –V

Saint Clair Origin Hawke's Bay Merlot   (★★★★)

The powerful young 2017 vintage (★★★★) was grown in the Gimblett Gravels and matured in seasoned French oak casks. Deeply coloured, it has good concentration of plummy, berryish, spicy flavours, a hint of dark chocolate, and good tannin backbone. Best drinking 2020+.

Saint Clair Pioneer Block 17 Plateau Block Hawke's Bay Merlot   ★★★★☆

The deeply coloured, purple-flushed 2016 vintage (★★★★★) was estate-grown at Omahu Road, in the Gimblett Gravels, and matured in French oak casks (26 per cent new). Delicious young, it is fragrant and vibrantly fruity, with very generous plum, blackcurrant, red-berry and spice flavours, gentle tannins, and a very harmonious, rich finish. Forward in its appeal, it's likely to be at its best 2020+.

Selaks Founders Limited Edition Hawke's Bay Merlot/Cabernet   ★★★★

The estate-grown, barrel-matured 2015 vintage (★★★★) is a powerful red, drinking well now. Mouthfilling, it has rich, ripe berry and plum flavours, hints of herbs, spices and liquorice, a slightly nutty oak influence, and a smooth finish. Drink now or cellar.

Vintage	15
WR	5
Drink	19-21

DRY $25 AV

Selaks Reserve Hawke's Bay Merlot/Cabernet   ★★★

Priced right, the 2016 vintage (★★★) is enjoyable young. Mouthfilling, with fullish, youthful colour, it is vibrantly fruity, with satisfying depth of plummy, berryish flavours, hints of spices and herbs, and a well-rounded finish.

Vintage	16
WR	5
Drink	P

DRY $16 V+

Selaks The Taste Collection Silky Smooth Hawke's Bay Merlot   (★★★)

The 2016 vintage (★★★) is a gutsy red, full-coloured and mouthfilling. It has plenty of fresh, ripe, plummy, spicy, slightly nutty flavour, with some rustic, earthy notes, and a fairly firm (rather than 'silky smooth') finish.

DRY $22 –V

Sileni Cellar Selection Hawke's Bay Merlot   ★★★☆

The 2018 vintage (★★★☆) is full-coloured, with fresh, plummy, spicy aromas. Medium to full-bodied, it is vibrantly fruity and flavoursome, with finely balanced tannins and lots of drink-young appeal. Best drinking mid-2020+.

Vintage	18	17	16	15	14	13
WR	7	5	6	7	7	6
Drink	19-24	19-23	19-23	19-23	19-22	P

DRY $19 V+

Sileni Exceptional Vintage Hawke's Bay Merlot ★★★★☆

The 2014 vintage (★★★★☆), estate-grown in the Bridge Pa Triangle, was matured for 14 months in French oak barriques (50 per cent new). A powerful, strapping red (15 per cent alcohol), it is deeply coloured and jam-packed with very ripe plum, spice and liquorice flavours. A super-charged style, it will appeal strongly to fans of 'big reds'. Best drinking 2020+.

Vintage	14	13
WR	7	7
Drink	19-25	19-25

 DRY $70 –V

Sileni Grand Reserve Cut Cane Hawke's Bay Merlot ★★★★☆

The 2018 vintage (★★★★☆) is a powerful red (15.5 per cent alcohol), made by 'cutting the bunch canes and allowing the fruit to shrivel prior to harvest [which] concentrated the juice within'. Deeply coloured, it is robust, with fresh, very ripe-tasting, berryish, plummy flavours and a hint of liquorice. If you like 'big' reds, try this.

 DRY $50 –V

Sileni Grand Reserve Triangle Hawke's Bay Merlot ★★★★☆

The very youthful 2018 vintage (★★★★☆) was grown in the Bridge Pa Triangle. Deeply coloured, it is fresh and rich, with mouthfilling body, concentrated plum and spice flavours, seasoned with nutty oak, good complexity and the structure to age well. Best drinking 2022+.

DRY $35 AV

Soljans Tribute Hawke's Bay Merlot/Malbec ★★★★

The 2016 vintage (★★★★) is a blend of Merlot (70 per cent) and Malbec (30 per cent), matured for 18 months in French oak barriques (partly new). Fresh and mouthfilling, with full, moderately youthful colour, it has generous, berryish, spicy flavours, with earthy, savoury notes adding complexity. Drink now onwards.

Vintage	16	15
WR	6	7
Drink	19-23	19-22

DRY $40 –V

Stables Reserve Ngatarawa Hawke's Bay Merlot ★★☆

Made with 'light oak aging', the 2018 vintage (★★☆) is full-coloured, fresh and vibrantly fruity, with decent depth of berryish, slightly herbal flavours and a smooth finish. (From Mission.)

DRY $20 –V

Stolen Heart Merlot/Malbec (★★★★☆)

Densely packed, the 2014 vintage (★★★★☆) is a Gimblett Gravels, Hawke's Bay blend of Merlot (78 per cent) and Malbec (16 per cent), with splashes of Cabernet Franc (3 per cent) and Syrah (3 per cent). Deeply coloured, it is full-bodied, with vibrant, plummy, spicy flavours, finely integrated oak, good tannin backbone, and excellent ripeness and depth. (From Crown Range Cellar.)

 DRY $50 –V

Stonecroft Ruhanui Gimblett Gravels Hawke's Bay
Merlot/Cabernet Sauvignon   ★★★★☆

Still very youthful, the 2016 vintage (★★★★) is a blend of Merlot (55 per cent) and Cabernet Sauvignon (45 per cent), estate-grown at Roys Hill and matured for 20 months in seasoned French oak barrels. Full-coloured, it is mouthfilling, with fresh, ripe plum and blackcurrant flavours, showing very good depth and considerable complexity, and a smooth, tightly structured finish. Best drinking 2020+.

Vintage	16	15	14	13
WR	5	6	7	7
Drink	20-27	19-26	19-26	18-25

DRY $31 AV

Stoneleigh Latitude Marlborough Merlot   ★★★☆

Grown in the relatively warm Rapaura district, on the north side of the Wairau Valley, the 2016 vintage (★★★) is full-coloured, with a slightly earthy bouquet and good depth of plummy, spicy flavours, woven with fresh acidity.

DRY $22 AV

Tantalus Estate Waiheke Island Merlot/Cabernet Franc   ★★★★☆

Estate-grown at Onetangi, the 2015 vintage (★★★★☆) was matured for 10 months in American and French oak casks. Full-coloured, it is fragrant, with rich, plummy, slightly spicy and nutty flavours, showing excellent freshness, vigour and complexity, and a supple, lingering finish. Best drinking 2021+.

Vintage	15	14
WR	6	6
Drink	19-21	19-20

DRY $45 –V

Te Awa Single Estate Gimblett Gravels Hawke's Bay
Merlot/Cabernet Sauvignon   ★★★★☆

The 2016 vintage (★★★★☆) was matured in French oak casks (35 per cent new). A refined, generous, youthful red with full, purple-flushed colour, it is fresh and full-bodied, with concentrated plum and blackcurrant flavours, a subtle seasoning of oak and fine-grained tannins. Well worth cellaring, it should be at its best 2020+.

DRY $35 AV

Te Awanga Estate Hawke's Bay Merlot/Cabernet Franc   (★★★★☆)

The stylish 2015 vintage (★★★★☆) was estate-grown near the coast and oak-aged for nine months. Full-coloured, it is mouthfilling, with strong, ripe berry, plum and spice flavours, a hint of herbs, fresh acidity and very good complexity. Tasted in April 2019, it is still youthful, with obvious potential; best drinking 2021+.

DRY $28 V+

Theory & Practice Hawke's Bay Merlot ★★★★

The 2016 vintage (★★★☆) is a blend of Merlot (85 per cent), Malbec (13 per cent) and Cabernet Sauvignon (2 per cent), hand-picked at two sites in the Bridge Pa Triangle, fermented with indigenous yeasts and matured for a year in French oak casks (20 per cent new). Full-coloured, it has a ripe, slightly raisiny bouquet, leading into a mouthfilling, sweet-fruited wine with a hint of liquorice and a smooth, easy-drinking appeal.

 DRY $25 AV

Thornbury Hawke's Bay Merlot ★★★☆

The 2017 vintage (★★★) is a good-value, drink-young red. Fullish in colour, with fresh, plummy, slightly spicy aromas, it is medium-bodied, with very satisfying depth of dark berry and plum flavours, offering smooth, easy drinking. (From Villa Maria.)

Vintage	18	17	16	15	14	13
WR	5	3	5	5	6	7
Drink	19-21	19-21	19-21	19-20	P	P

 DRY $16 V+

Tiki Koro Hawke's Bay Merlot/Cabernet Sauvignon (★★★★☆)

The age-worthy 2015 vintage (★★★★☆) was hand-picked and matured for 10 months in French oak barriques. Full-coloured, it is mouthfilling and youthful, with concentrated, ripe plum, spice, blackcurrant and nut flavours, oak complexity and a fairly firm finish. Best drinking 2022+.

Vintage	15
WR	6
Drink	19-21

DRY $35 AV

Tironui Above & Beyond Single Vineyard Hawke's Bay Merlot (★★★☆)

The 2015 vintage (★★★☆) was estate-grown at Taradale, hand-picked and matured for 20 months in French oak barrels. Fullish in colour, it is mouthfilling and smooth, with good depth of plummy, spicy flavours and a subtle seasoning of oak adding complexity. Drink now or cellar.

 DRY $25 –V

Tohu Hawke's Bay Merlot ★★★☆

An excellent drink-young style, the 2018 vintage (★★★★) was matured for eight months in French oak barriques (15 per cent new). Full-coloured, with a fragrant, gently spicy bouquet, it is mouthfilling and supple, with very good depth of berryish, plummy flavours and a smooth finish. Fine value.

Vintage	18
WR	5
Drink	19-24

DRY $18 V+

Toi Toi Hawke's Bay Merlot   ★★★

The 2017 vintage (★★★) is a very easy-drinking red, ruby-hued and vibrantly fruity, with decent depth of berry, plum and spice flavours, some savoury notes adding complexity, and a dry, well-rounded finish.

DRY $17 AV

Vidal Hawke's Bay Merlot/Cabernet Sauvignon   ★★★☆

The good-value 2017 vintage (★★★☆) is a blend of Merlot (95 per cent) and Cabernet Sauvignon (5 per cent), partly barrel-matured. Full-bodied, it has very good depth of plummy, spicy flavours, showing some savoury complexity, and a smooth finish.

Vintage	18	17	16	15
WR	6	5	6	6
Drink	19-23	19-21	19-21	19-20

DRY $16 V+

Vidal Reserve Gimblett Gravels Merlot/Cabernet Sauvignon   ★★★★

A consistently good buy. Matured for 18 months in French oak barriques (20 per cent new), the 2017 vintage (★★★★) is a blend of Merlot (68 per cent) and Cabernet Sauvignon (32 per cent). Fragrant, full-coloured and fruit-packed, it has very good body and depth of vibrant, plummy, spicy flavours. An elegant, still-youthful red, it should be at its best from 2021 onwards.

Vintage	17	16	15	14	13	12	11	10
WR	5	7	7	7	7	5	6	7
Drink	19-23	19-23	19-23	19-23	19-22	P	P	P

DRY $20 V+

Villa Maria Cellar Selection Hawke's Bay Merlot   ★★★★

Offering great value, the 2018 vintage (★★★★) was matured for a year in French and Hungarian oak barriques (18 per cent new). It has deep, purple-flushed colour. Fresh and full-bodied, with youthful plum, berry and spice flavours, oak complexity and good density, it needs time; open 2021+.

Vintage	18	17
WR	7	6
Drink	19-24	19-23

DRY $18 V+

Villa Maria Cellar Selection Hawke's Bay Merlot/Cabernet Sauvignon   ★★★★

Sharply priced, the 2018 vintage (★★★★) is a blend of Merlot (63 per cent) and Cabernet Sauvignon (25 per cent), with minor portions of Malbec and Cabernet Franc, matured for a year in French, American and Hungarian oak barriques (10 per cent new). Still very youthful, it is mouthfilling, with good concentration of vibrant plum and spice flavours, a hint of herbs, and obvious cellaring potential. Open 2022+.

Vintage	18
WR	6
Drink	19-24

DRY $18 V+

Villa Maria Cellar Selection Hawke's Bay Organic Merlot   ★★★★

The good-value 2016 vintage (★★★★) was grown in the Joseph Soler Vineyard and matured for 17 months in French and Hungarian oak barriques (20 per cent new). It's a full-bodied, vibrant red with excellent depth of plum/spice flavours, rich and smooth.

Vintage	16	15	14	13
WR	7	6	6	7
Drink	19-23	19-22	19-20	19-20

 DRY $19 V+

Villa Maria Library Release Gimblett Gravels
Merlot/Cabernet Sauvignon   (★★★★★)

The 2010 vintage (★★★★★), released in 2017, is a classy, very refined blend of Merlot (62 per cent) and Cabernet Sauvignon (38 per cent), matured in French oak barriques (60 per cent new) for 18 months. Currently delicious, it is deeply coloured, with concentrated, beautifully ripe blackcurrant and spice flavours, showing good, savoury complexity, and fine-grained tannins. Built to last, it should be at its best 2020+.

Vintage	10
WR	7
Drink	19-22

 DRY $70 AV

Villa Maria Private Bin Hawke's Bay Merlot   ★★★

Enjoyable young, the full-coloured 2018 vintage (★★★) is a partly barrel-aged red, mouthfilling, with good depth of plummy, slightly spicy flavours, fresh and smooth.

Vintage	18	17	16	15	14	13
WR	6	6	7	7	7	6
Drink	19-22	19-21	19-21	19-20	P	P

 DRY $15 V+

Villa Maria Private Bin Hawke's Bay Merlot/Cabernet Sauvignon   ★★★☆

The 2016 vintage (★★★☆) is a generous, fruity style, matured in tanks and seasoned barrels. Full-coloured, with strong plum and blackcurrant flavours, a hint of herbs and a well-rounded finish, it offers fine value.

Vintage	16	15	14	13
WR	6	6	7	7
Drink	19-21	19-20	P	P

DRY $15 V+

Villa Maria Private Bin Organic Hawke's Bay Merlot   ★★★☆

Certified organic, the 2017 vintage (★★★) is a ruby-hued, medium-bodied red, with berryish, slightly spicy flavours, showing a touch of complexity, and a fresh, smooth finish.

 DRY $16 V+

Villa Maria Reserve Hawke's Bay Merlot ★★★★★

This consistently outstanding wine is estate-grown and matured in French oak barriques. The 2016 vintage (★★★★★) was grown in the Te Awa Vineyard and matured for 18 months in French oak casks (37 per cent new). Deep and bright in colour, it is mouthfilling and concentrated, with excellent depth of very ripe, plummy, spicy flavours, a hint of liquorice, and fine-grained tannins. (Note: there is no reference to the Gimblett Gravels on the label of the 2016 vintage.)

Vintage	16
WR	7
Drink	20-26

 DRY $50 AV

Wairau River Marlborough Merlot ★★★

The easy-drinking 2017 vintage (★★★) is full-coloured and mouthfilling, with vibrant, plummy, spicy flavours, fresh and smooth.

Vintage	14
WR	6
Drink	19-20

 DRY $20 –V

Woodside Hill Reserve Merlot/Cabernet Franc (★★★★☆)

Grown on Waiheke Island, the 2014 vintage (★★★★☆) is a blend of Merlot (73 per cent), Cabernet Franc (23 per cent) and Petit Verdot (4 per cent), matured for 15 months in French oak casks (50 per cent new). Sturdy and full-coloured, it has generous, plummy, berryish, spicy flavours, showing good structure and complexity. Drink now or cellar.

 DRY $45 –V

Zaria Hawke's Bay Merlot ★★★★

The 2015 vintage (★★★★) is a single-vineyard red, grown in the Bridge Pa Triangle and matured for 15 months in seasoned French oak barrels. Full-coloured and fragrant, it is mouthfilling and savoury, with strong, plummy, spicy flavours, a hint of dark chocolate and good complexity.

DRY $25 AV

Montepulciano

Montepulciano is widely planted across central Italy, yielding deeply coloured, ripe wines with good levels of alcohol, extract and flavour. In the Abruzzi, it is the foundation of the often superb-value Montepulciano d'Abruzzo, and in the Marches it is the key ingredient in the noble Rosso Conero. In New Zealand, Montepulciano is a rarity and there has been confusion between the Montepulciano and Sangiovese varieties. Some wines may have been incorrectly labelled. According to the latest national vineyard survey, between 2005 and 2020, New Zealand's area of bearing Montepulciano vines will expand slightly from 6 to 8 hectares (mostly in Auckland, Hawke's Bay, Nelson and Marlborough).

Blackenbrook Family Reserve Nelson Montepulciano   (★★★★)

Showing good personality, the 2016 vintage (★★★★) was matured for a year in seasoned French oak barriques. Full-coloured, it is mouthfilling, with strong, fresh plum and spice flavours, earthy, savoury notes adding complexity, and finely balanced tannins. Drink now or cellar.

Vintage	16
WR	7
Drink	19-25

 DRY $43 –V

Coopers Creek SV Guido In Velvet Pants Huapai Montepulciano   ★★★★

Estate-grown at Huapai, in West Auckland, the 2016 vintage (★★★★) is still youthful. Full-coloured, with a berryish, spicy fragrance, it is mouthfilling and smooth, with strong, vibrant berry, plum and spice flavours, savoury notes adding complexity, supple tannins and a lingering finish. Drink now to 2021.

Vintage	16	15	14	13
WR	6	6	6	6
Drink	19-21	19-20	P	P

 DRY $28 AV

De La Terre Hawke's Bay Montepulciano   ★★★★★

The classy, youthful 2015 vintage (★★★★☆) is rare, but well worth tracking down. Hand-harvested at Havelock North and matured for 16 months in French oak barriques (50 per cent new), it's a worthy follow-up to the delicious 2014 vintage (★★★★★). Deeply coloured, it is concentrated and vibrantly fruity, with generous plum, spice and slight liquorice flavours, oak complexity, and a moderately firm, long finish.

Vintage	15	14	13
WR	6	7	6
Drink	19-27	19-25	19-28

 DRY $45 AV

Hans Herzog Marlborough Montepulciano   ★★★★★

This classy, estate-grown red is typically overflowing with sweet-fruit flavours. The 2015 vintage (★★★★☆) was hand-picked on the north side of the Wairau Valley, fermented with indigenous yeasts, matured for two and a half years in French oak barriques (partly new), and bottled unfined and unfiltered. Fragrant, with deep, youthful colour, it is mouthfilling, with fresh, youthful plum and spice flavours, showing excellent depth, refined tannins and obvious potential; best drinking 2022+.

DRY $64 AV

Kahurangi Estate Monte Nelson Montepulciano   (★★★★)

Worth cellaring, the 2018 vintage (★★★★) is full-coloured, mouthfilling, fruit-packed and firmly structured. It has concentrated, fresh, plummy, spicy flavours, fresh acidity, oak complexity and obvious potential. Best drinking 2021+.

DRY $25 AV

Milcrest Estate Nelson Montepulciano   ★★★☆

Grown in a single vineyard at Hope and French oak-aged for 10 months, the 2014 vintage (★★★☆) is still fresh and youthful. Medium-bodied, it is lively, with very good depth of plummy, slightly spicy flavours. Drink now or cellar.

DRY $32 –V

Obsidian Estate Waiheke Island Montepulciano   ★★★★☆

The highly attractive 2018 vintage (★★★★☆) was grown at Onetangi and matured for 10 months in French oak casks (30 per cent new). Full of drink-young charm, it is deeply coloured, fresh and full-bodied, with vibrant, ripe plum and red-berry flavours, showing good concentration, oak-derived complexity and a smooth finish. Best drinking 2021+.

DRY $42 –V

Nebbiolo

Nebbiolo is the foundation of Piedmont's most majestic red wines – Barolo, Barbaresco and Gattinara – renowned for their complex leather and tar flavours, powerful tannins and great longevity. In New Zealand, only 1 hectare of vines will be bearing in 2020, mostly in Marlborough.

Hans Herzog Marlborough Nebbiolo ★★★★☆

Currently on sale, the rare 2013 vintage (★★★★) was estate-grown on the north side of the Wairau Valley and matured for 30 months in French oak puncheons (100 per cent new). Fullish and moderately developed in colour, it is savoury, with fresh, berryish, slightly nutty flavours, woven with fresh acidity, and good depth. Certified organic.

DRY $125 –V

Rock Ferry The Corners Vineyard Marlborough Nebbiolo (★★★★☆)

Set for a long life, the 2016 vintage (★★★★☆) is certified organic. Barrel-aged for 17 months, it is full-coloured, with an earthy bouquet. Mouthfilling, it has concentrated, vigorous berry, plum, spice and nut flavours, fresh and firmly structured. Very much a 'food' wine, it has obvious cellaring potential; best drinking 2021+.

DRY $65 –V

Pinot Noir

New Zealand Pinot Noir enjoys strong overseas demand and there are now countless Pinot Noir labels, as producers launch second and even third-tier labels, as well as single-vineyard bottlings (and others under 'buyer's own' and export-only brands you and I have never heard of). The wines are enjoying notable success in international competitions, but you need to be aware that most of the world's elite Pinot Noir producers, especially in Burgundy, do not enter. Between 2000 and 2020, New Zealand's area of bearing Pinot Noir vines is expanding from 1126 hectares to 5719 hectares, makng it the country's most widely planted red-wine variety (far ahead of Merlot, with 1197 hectares).

Pinot Noir is the princely grape variety of red Burgundy. Cheaper wines typically display light, raspberry-evoking flavours, but great Pinot Noir has substance, suppleness and a gorgeous spread of flavours: cherries, fruit cake, spice and plums.

Pinot Noir is now New Zealand's most internationally acclaimed red-wine style. Nearly half of the country's total Pinot Noir plantings are in Marlborough, and the variety is also well established in Otago (27 per cent), Wairarapa (9 per cent), Canterbury (7.5 per cent), Hawke's Bay and Nelson.

Yet Pinot Noir is a frustrating variety to grow. Because it buds early, it is vulnerable to spring frosts; its compact bunches are also very prone to rot. One crucial advantage is that it ripens early, well ahead of Cabernet Sauvignon. Low cropping and the selection of superior clones are essential aspects of the production of fine wine.

Martinborough (initially) and Central Otago have enjoyed the highest profile for Pinot Noir over the past 30 years. As their output of Pinot Noir has expanded, average prices have fallen, reflecting the arrival of a tidal wave of 'entry-level' (drink-young) wines.

Of the other small regions, Nelson and Canterbury (especially Waipara) are also enjoying success. Marlborough's potential for the production of outstanding – but still widely underrated – Pinot Noir, in sufficient volumes to supply the burgeoning international demand, has also been tapped.

12,000 Miles Gladstone Pinot Noir ★★★☆

Enjoyable young, but age-worthy too, the 2016 vintage (★★★☆) was grown in the northern Wairarapa. Bright ruby, with a fragrant, gently herbal bouquet, showing a touch of complexity, it is fresh, full-bodied and smooth, with lively acidity and very good depth of plum, spice and herb flavours. (From Gladstone Vineyard.)

DRY $27 AV

Akarua Bannockburn Central Otago Pinot Noir ★★★★★

Estate-grown, hand-picked from mature vines and aged for 11 months in French oak barriques (27 per cent new), the 2017 vintage (★★★★★) is a bold, finely textured red. Fragrant, mouthfilling and supple, it is crammed with concentrated, ripe plum, cherry and spice flavours, showing great vigour and potential. Still youthful, it's best cellared to 2021+.

Vintage	17
WR	6
Drink	19-25

DRY $45 AV

Akarua Rua Central Otago Pinot Noir   ★★★★

For a third-tier label, known for its 'vivaciousness and soft, silky tannins', this regional blend can be very seductive. Matured for eight months in French oak casks (10 per cent new), the deep ruby 2017 vintage (★★★★) is floral, with strong, fresh plum and cherry flavours, rich and smooth.

Akarua The Siren Bannockburn Central Otago Pinot Noir   ★★★★★

The 2016 vintage (★★★★★) of Akarua's top Pinot Noir was estate-grown and selected from the best eight barrels out of 800. Deep ruby, it is a powerful, sturdy, very ripe-tasting wine, lush and smooth, with concentrated plum, cherry and spice flavours, and very gentle tannins. Youthful, with a complex bouquet, it should break into full stride 2020+.

Vintage	16
WR	7
Drink	19-28

Akin Central Otago Pinot Noir   (★★★★)

From Te Kano, the very charming 2016 vintage (★★★★) was estate-grown at Bannockburn and matured for 10 months in French oak barrels. Bright ruby, it is fragrant, full-bodied and supple, with vibrant, plummy, slightly nutty flavours, showing considerable complexity, fresh acidity, and lots of current-drinking appeal.

Akitu A1 Central Otago Pinot Noir   ★★★★★

Estate-grown 380 metres above sea level at Mt Barker, in the Wanaka sub-region, the 2016 vintage (★★★★★) was matured in French oak barrels (25 per cent new). Deep ruby, with a fragrant, savoury bouquet, it is a very graceful, mouthfilling red with concentrated plum, cherry and spice flavours, fine-grained tannins, and lovely poise and depth. Best drinking 2021+.

Akitu A2 Central Otago Pinot Noir   ★★★★

Grown at high altitude at Mt Barker, in the Wanaka sub-region, the 2016 vintage (★★★★☆) was designed as a 'highly drinkable wine of unthinkable quality'. Matured in French oak casks (12 per cent new), it is bright ruby, floral, buoyantly fruity and supple, with mouthfilling body, strong, ripe, cherryish, plummy flavours, woven with fresh acidity, and gentle tannins. A refined, age-worthy red, it should be at its best from 2020 onwards.

DRY $40 –V

Alex Gold Central Otago Pinot Noir ★★★★

From the Alexandra Wine Co., in Central Otago, the 2017 vintage (★★★★) has lots of youthful impact. Made in a 'fruit-driven' (lightly oaked) style, it is deep ruby, with a floral, fresh, fruity bouquet. Mouthfilling, it has strong, plummy, spicy flavours, vibrant and concentrated, with good tannin backbone and obvious potential; best drinking 2020+.

 DRY $30 AV

Alexander Dusty Road Martinborough Pinot Noir ★★★★☆

Designed for early drinking, but typically age-worthy, this second-tier red consistently offers great value. The 2018 vintage (★★★★☆) is an estate-grown, single-vineyard wine, hand-picked and matured for 11 months in French oak barriques (20 per cent new). Bright ruby, with a fragrant, savoury bouquet, it is mouthfilling, with concentrated, ripe, plummy, spicy flavours, showing good complexity, and the structure to mature well. Approachable now, it should be at its best 2022+.

Vintage	18	17	16	15	14
WR	6	6	6	6	6
Drink	19-24	19-23	19-22	19-21	19-20

 DRY $27 V+

Alexander Martinborough Pinot Noir ★★★★★

Offering top value, the 2018 vintage (★★★★★) was estate-grown in Martinborough, hand-picked and matured for 11 months in French oak barriques (25 per cent new). Deep ruby, it has rich, well-ripened, plummy, spicy, nutty flavours, complex and savoury, and a well-structured, long finish. A powerful young red, still very youthful, it's well worth cellaring to 2023+.

Vintage	18	17	16	15	14
WR	7	7	7	7	7
Drink	22-26	21-25	20-24	19-23	19-22

 DRY $38 V+

Amisfield Central Otago Pinot Noir ★★★★★

Estate-grown at Pisa, in the Cromwell Basin, the classy 2016 vintage (★★★★☆) was hand-harvested, fermented with indigenous yeasts and matured in French oak barriques (22 per cent new). Bright ruby, it is fragrant, full-bodied and sweet-fruited, with vibrant cherry, plum and spice flavours, a subtle seasoning of oak, and a finely textured, very harmonious finish. A very graceful red, it's well worth cellaring; best drinking 2020+.

Vintage	16
WR	5
Drink	19-23

 DRY $50 AV

Amisfield RKV Reserve Central Otago Pinot Noir ★★★★★

Estate-grown and hand-picked from selected blocks in the Rocky Knoll Vineyard at Pisa, in the Cromwell Basin, the 2015 vintage (★★★★★) was fermented with indigenous yeasts and matured in French oak barriques (30 per cent new). Deeply coloured, it is a powerful, full-bodied red, very savoury and complex, with highly concentrated plum, spice and nut flavours, good tannin backbone and a lasting finish. Set for a long life, it's well worth cellaring.

Vintage	15
WR	6
Drink	19-23

 DRY $120 AV

Anna's Way Marlborough Pinot Noir

Enjoyable now, the 2017 vintage (★★★☆) was matured for 10 months in French oak barrels. Lightish in colour, with a hint of development, it is medium-bodied, with gentle, plummy, spicy, slightly nutty flavours, showing some complexity, and a smooth finish. (From Awatere River Wine Co.)

DRY $23 V+

Archangel Central Otago Pinot Noir ★★★★

Estate-grown south of Wanaka, at the northern end of the Cromwell Basin, the stylish 2015 vintage (★★★★☆) of this single-vineyard red was matured for a year in French oak casks (28 per cent new). Tasted in early 2019, it is still unfolding. Deep ruby, with mouthfilling body, it has vibrant, ripe plum/spice flavours, balanced acidity, and excellent harmony and depth. The 2016 (★★★★) was matured for a year in French oak casks (25 per cent new). Full, bright ruby, it is floral and sweet-fruited, with fine-grained tannins and very satisfying depth of plummy, spicy flavours. A supple, youthful red, it's well worth cellaring to 2020+.

DRY $37 AV

Aronui Single Vineyard Nelson Pinot Noir ★★★★

From Kono (which also owns the Tohu brand), the 2016 vintage (★★★★) was estate-grown at Upper Moutere, hand-picked and French oak-aged. Drinking well now, it is light ruby, savoury and sweet-fruited. Made with a gentle touch, it has delicate cherry, plum, spice and nut flavours, velvety tannins, and very good complexity and harmony.

DRY $25 V+

Ashwell Martinborough Pinot Noir ★★★★

The youthful 2018 vintage (★★★★☆) was barrel-matured for a year. Full, bright ruby, it's a very age-worthy, full-bodied red, with concentrated, ripe plum and spice flavours, nutty and savoury, and a moderately firm finish. Best drinking 2021+.

Vintage	18	17
WR	6	5
Drink	19-28	19-27

DRY $40 –V

Askerne Hawke's Bay Pinot Noir ★★★

The 2017 vintage (★★★) is light ruby, with a hint of development. A moderately concentrated, savoury, supple red, it shows considerable complexity. Drink now to 2020.

DRY $23 AV

Astrolabe Comelybank Vineyard Marlborough Pinot Noir (★★★★☆)

The delicious 2015 vintage (★★★★☆) was grown in the lower Waihopai Valley, hand-harvested and fermented with indigenous yeasts. Matured for nine months in French oak casks (33 per cent new), it was then barrel-selected and matured for another nine months in older barrels, before bottling, without fining or filtering, in March 2017. Bright ruby, it is fragrant, mouthfilling, sweet-fruited and supple, with concentrated, plummy, spicy flavours, finely textured and lingering. Drink now to 2021.

Vintage	15
WR	7
Drink	19-24

DRY $60 –V

Astrolabe Marlborough Pinot Noir ★★★★☆

The 2017 vintage (★★★★) was grown in the Southern Valleys (85 per cent) and at Kekerengu (15 per cent), hand-picked, fermented with indigenous yeasts and matured for 10 months in French oak barriques. Bright ruby, it is a powerful, full-bodied red, with strong, plummy, spicy flavours, an earthy streak, good complexity and a fairly firm finish. Best drinking 2021+.

Vintage	17	16
WR	7	7
Drink	20-25	19-24

 DRY $35 V+

Astrolabe Sleepers Vineyard Marlborough Pinot Noir (★★★★)

The 2016 vintage (★★★★) was grown on the Kekerengu Coast, hand-harvested and matured for 10 months in French oak barrels (33 per cent new). Following barrel selection, it then spent another 10 months in seasoned French oak casks, before it was bottled, unfined and unfiltered, in December 2017. Bright ruby, it is mouthfilling and vibrantly fruity, with generous, ripe, plummy, gently spicy flavours, showing good complexity, gentle acidity, and a well-rounded finish.

 DRY $60 –V

Astrolabe Vineyards Wrekin Vineyard Pinot Noir ★★★★★

The very generous 2016 vintage (★★★★★) was hand-picked in Marlborough's upper Brancott Valley, fermented with indigenous yeasts, matured for 10 months in French oak barriques (33 per cent new), and bottled unfined and unfiltered. Full-coloured, it is rich and supple, with concentrated, youthful, plummy, slightly spicy flavours, showing excellent vigour and complexity. Best drinking 2021+.

Vintage	16
WR	7
Drink	19-24

DRY $60 AV

Ata Rangi Martinborough Pinot Noir ★★★★★

One of the greatest of all New Zealand wines, this Martinborough red is powerfully built and concentrated, yet seductively fragrant and supple. 'Intense, opulent fruit with power beneath' is founder Clive Paton's goal. 'Complexity comes with time.' The grapes are drawn from numerous sites, including the estate vineyard, planted in 1980, and the vines, up to 39 years old, have a very low average yield of 4.5 tonnes of grapes per hectare. The wine is fermented with indigenous yeasts and maturation is for 11 months in French oak barriques (35 per cent new in 2017). The 2017 vintage (★★★★★) is a very 'complete', highly perfumed wine. Full-coloured, it is savoury and supple, with deep, vigorous plum and spice flavours, seasoned with nutty oak, and a long, finely structured finish. A complex, very age-worthy red, it should be at its best 2022+.

Vintage	17	16	15	14	13	12	11	10
WR	6	7	7	7	7	7	7	7
Drink	20-30	19-28	19-27	19-26	19-25	19-24	19-23	19-22

DRY $75 AV

Ataahua Waipara Pinot Noir ★★★★

The very age-worthy 2016 vintage (★★★★☆) was estate-grown, hand-picked and matured for over a year in seasoned oak barrels. Deeply coloured, it is fragrant and full-bodied, with strong, youthful cherry, plum and spice flavours, finely balanced tannins and very good complexity. Best drinking 2021+.

Vintage	16	15	
WR	6	6	
Drink	21-27	19-25	

DRY $37 AV

Auntsfield Hawk Hill Southern Valleys Marlborough Pinot Noir ★★★★☆

Currently on sale, the powerful, lush 2012 vintage (★★★★★) is an estate-grown, single-block red, matured for 14 months in French oak barrels (38 per cent new). Deep and still youthful in colour, it is sturdy (14.5 per cent alcohol), with a fragrant, rich bouquet of spices and a hint of liquorice. Highly concentrated, it has deep, berryish, plummy, spicy flavours, good tannin backbone, and real power through the palate. A wine to ponder over, it should be at its best 2020+.

Vintage	12	
WR	7	
Drink	19-22	

DRY $58 –V

Auntsfield Heritage Marlborough Pinot Noir ★★★★★

A rare wine with a 'wow' factor, the 2013 vintage (★★★★★), currently on sale, was blended from the top seven barrels of the year. Matured for 18 months in French oak barrels (28 per cent new), it has deep, youthful colour and a highly fragrant bouquet. A lovely wine, it is very rich, sweet-fruited and harmonious, with mouthfilling body, concentrated plum and spice flavours, a hint of liquorice, and a finely poised, very persistent finish. Still youthful, it's well worth cellaring to 2021+.

Vintage	13	
WR	7	
Drink	19-23	

DRY $95 AV

Auntsfield Single Vineyard Southern Valleys Marlborough Pinot Noir ★★★★★

Grown on north-facing slopes at Auntsfield, on the south side of the Wairau Valley, the 2017 vintage (★★★★★) is impressive. Matured for 10 months in French oak casks (28 per cent new), it is a powerful wine with bold, purple-flushed colour. Mouthfilling and very sweet-fruited, it is overflowing with ripe, plummy, spicy flavours, with good tannin backbone, and obvious cellaring potential; open 2021+.

Vintage	17	16	
WR	6	6	
Drink	19-32	19-27	

DRY $45 AV

Aurum Madeleine Organic Central Otago Pinot Noir ★★★★☆

Named after the winemaker's daughter, the 2016 vintage (★★★★★) was estate-grown at Lowburn, hand-picked, fermented with indigenous yeasts, matured for a year in seasoned French oak casks, and bottled unfined and unfiltered. Full (and not entirely clear) in colour, it is mouthfilling and silky-textured, with deep cherry, plum and spice flavours, supple and savoury, and excellent complexity and harmony. A thought-provoking wine, it should be at its best 2020+. Certified organic.

Vintage	16
WR	6
Drink	22-28

 DRY $88 –V

Aurum Mathilde Organic Central Otago Pinot Noir ★★★★★

Estate-grown at Lowburn, in the Cromwell Basin, the 2016 vintage (★★★★☆) was hand-picked, fermented with indigenous yeasts, matured for a year in French oak casks (18 per cent new), and bottled unfined and unfiltered. Deep ruby, it is fragrant, mouthfilling and sweet-fruited, with concentrated, vibrant, cherryish, plummy, spicy flavours, showing excellent complexity and length. Already delicious, it should be at its best for drinking 2021+.

Vintage	16
WR	6
Drink	20-26

 DRY $55 AV

Aurum Organic Central Otago Pinot Noir ★★★★☆

Estate-grown at Lowburn, in the Cromwell Basin, and matured for 12 months in French oak casks (20 per cent new), the very age-worthy 2017 vintage (★★★★☆) was hand-picked, fermented with indigenous yeasts, and bottled unfined and unfiltered. Deep and youthful in colour, it is sturdy and concentrated, with deep, plummy, spicy flavours, savoury notes adding complexity, and finely balanced tannins. Best drinking 2020+. Certified organic.

Vintage	17
WR	6
Drink	20-24

 DRY $38 V+

Awatere River Marlborough Pinot Noir ★★★☆

The 2018 vintage (★★★☆) was matured in French oak barriques. Ruby-hued, it is a fresh, medium-bodied, supple red, with ripe cherry, plum and spice flavours, hints of herbs and nuts, considerable complexity and gentle tannins. Best drinking 2020–21.

 DRY $30 –V

Babich Black Label Marlborough Pinot Noir ★★★★

Designed for sale principally in restaurants, the 2017 vintage (★★★★) was matured for 10 months in French and Hungarian oak casks (25 per cent new). Full, bright ruby, it is mouthfilling, with generous, youthful, plummy, gently spicy flavours, showing good complexity, gentle tannins, and a harmonious, lingering finish. Best drinking 2020+.

DRY $25 V+

Babich Family Estates Marlborough Pinot Noir ★★★★

Certified organic, the 2017 vintage (★★★★) was grown in the Headwaters Vineyard and matured for 11 months in French and Hungarian oak casks (30 per cent new). Bright ruby, it is fragrant and supple, in an elegant style with ripe, cherryish, spicy flavours, showing very good depth and complexity, and a supple, lingering finish.

DRY $40 –V

Babich Marlborough Pinot Noir ★★★

The 2017 vintage (★★★), barrel-matured for seven months, is light ruby, with ripe cherry and spice flavours, showing a touch of complexity, and a smooth finish. A fairly light style of Pinot Noir, it is clearly varietal, with drink-young appeal.

DRY $25 –V

Babich Winemakers' Reserve Marlborough Pinot Noir ★★★★☆

The 2017 vintage (★★★★☆) was estate-grown in the Cowslip Valley Vineyard, in the Waihopai Valley, and matured for 10 months in barrels (35 per cent new). Full, bright ruby, it is a very graceful, sweet-fruited, savoury and supple red, with cherry, plum and spice flavours, showing good complexity, and a long, harmonious finish. Best drinking 2021+.

Vintage	17
WR	6
Drink	19-24

DRY $45 –V

Baby Doll Marlborough Pinot Noir (★★☆)

The 2018 vintage (★★☆) is ruby-hued and floral, in a fresh, vibrantly fruity, uncomplicated style with drink-young charm. (From Yealands.)

DRY $20 –V

Bald Hills 3 Acres Central Otago Pinot Noir ★★★★

The 2016 vintage (★★★★) was estate-grown at Bannockburn and matured for a year in French oak barriques (31 per cent new). Full, bright ruby, it is mouthfilling and vibrantly fruity, with fresh cherry, plum and spice flavours, well-integrated oak, and very good complexity and depth.

DRY $35 AV

Bald Hills Bannockburn Single Vineyard Central Otago Pinot Noir ★★★★☆

A proven performer in the cellar. The 2016 vintage (★★★★★) was estate-grown and matured for a year in French oak barriques (33 per cent new). Full, bright ruby, it is mouthfilling, savoury and structured, with well-ripened cherry, plum, spice and nut flavours, youthful and complex, and a moderately firm finish. Best drinking mid-2021+.

DRY $46 –V

Ballasalla Central Otago Pinot Noir

The 2016 vintage (★★★★☆) is a single-vineyard Bendigo red, matured for 10 months in French oak barriques (20 per cent new). Bright ruby, with a fragrant, savoury bouquet, it is mouthfilling and sweet-fruited, with concentrated, ripe cherry, plum and spice flavours, showing very good complexity, and a supple, harmonious finish. Fine value. Best drinking mid-2020+. (From Folding Hill.)

DRY $32 V+

Bannock Brae Central Otago Pinot Noir ★★★★★

This Bannockburn red is typically outstanding. The 2016 vintage (★★★★☆) is a refined, youthful wine, ruby-hued, with ripe cherry, plum, spice and nut flavours, showing good complexity, and a very harmonious, savoury, lengthy finish. Best drinking mid-2021+.

Vintage	16	15	14	13	12	11	10
WR	7	7	7	7	NM	7	6
Drink	19-26	19-26	19-25	19-25	NM	19-25	19-24

DRY $60 AV

Bannock Brae Goldfields Central Otago Pinot Noir ★★★★

The 2017 vintage (★★★★) is deep ruby, with a fresh, fragrant bouquet. Mouthfilling, it is vibrantly fruity, with strong cherry, plum and spice flavours, finely integrated oak and ripe, supple tannins. Best drinking mid-2020+.

Vintage	17	16	15	14	13	12
WR	7	6	6	7	6	7
Drink	19-25	19-24	19-23	19-23	19-22	19-22

DRY $35 AV

Bel Echo by Clos Henri Marlborough Pinot Noir ★★★★

The 2016 vintage (★★★★) was estate-grown on the stonier, less clay-bound soils at Clos Henri, in the Wairau Valley, and matured in a mix of large oak vats and old French oak barrels. Ruby-hued, with a hint of development, it is drinking well now. Savoury and complex, it has good concentration of plummy, cherryish, slightly herbal and nutty flavours, gentle tannins and good harmony. Certified organic.

Vintage	16	15	14	13	12
WR	6	6	6	6	6
Drink	19-25	19-22	19-20	P	P

DRY $32 AV

Bell Hill Pinot Noir ★★★★★

From a small vineyard on a limestone slope at Waikari, inland from Waipara, in North Canterbury, this is a rare, distinguished red. It is typically a generous wine, powerful yet silky, with sweet cherry, plum and spice flavours, complex, very harmonious and graceful. Tasted 'blind' in 2017, the notably powerful 2006 vintage was dark, rich and still in full stride. The most recent vintage I have tasted was the 2011 (★★★★★), in late 2014. Full-coloured, with lovely ripeness and harmony, it was youthful, plummy, spicy and savoury, with excellent complexity, and a very finely textured, long finish.

DRY $120 AV

Bellbird Spring Block Eight Waipara Valley North Canterbury Pinot Noir   (★★★★☆)

Drinking well now, the 2015 vintage (★★★★☆) was matured for a year in French oak barrels (50 per cent new). Ruby-hued, with some development showing, it has a fragrant, savoury bouquet. Mouthfilling, with cherry, plum, spice and nut flavours, it shows excellent complexity, with good tannin backbone. Best drinking 2020+.

 DRY $45 –V

Bellbird Spring Waipara Valley North Canterbury Pinot Noir   (★★★★)

Still unfolding, the 2016 vintage (★★★★) was matured for a year in French oak casks (20 per cent new). Ruby-hued, it is fragrant, with fresh, youthful cherry, plum, spice and nut flavours, showing good complexity. Best drinking 2021+.

 DRY $37 AV

Big Sky Te Muna Road Martinborough Pinot Noir   ★★★★★

Offering very good value, the 2018 vintage (★★★★★) was estate-grown and matured in French oak casks (15 per cent new). Full-coloured, it is fragrant, mouthfilling and sweet-fruited, with generous, ripe cherry, plum, spice and nut flavours, good tannin support, and a savoury, finely structured finish. A very age-worthy wine, it's well worth cellaring to mid-2021+. The 2017 vintage (★★★★☆) is ruby-hued, with strong, berryish, spicy, nutty flavours, savoury notes adding complexity, and a firm finish. It shows a slight lack of fruit sweetness, compared to the 2018, but needs time; open 2021+.

 DRY $40 V+

Bird Big Barrel Marlborough Pinot Noir   ★★★☆

Matured in large, 900-litre barrels, the 2017 vintage (★★★☆) is ruby-hued, with a savoury, slightly earthy bouquet. Full-bodied, it has youthful, ripe, slightly spicy and nutty flavours and a fairly firm finish. Best drinking 2020+.

 DRY $38 –V

Black Cottage Marlborough Pinot Noir   ★★★☆

A very enjoyable drink-young style, the 2018 vintage (★★★☆) is a blend of Wairau Valley (mostly) and Awatere Valley grapes, partly oak-aged. Light ruby, it is medium-bodied, vibrant, sweet-fruited and supple, with gentle cherry, plum and spice flavours, fresh acidity and a touch of complexity. (From Two Rivers of Marlborough.)

 DRY $20 V+

Black Cottage Reserve Central Otago Pinot Noir   ★★★☆

Delicious young, the 2016 vintage (★★★★) was aged for 10 months in tanks and seasoned French oak barrels. Deep ruby, it is fragrant, full-bodied, fruit-packed and supple, with generous, ripe plum, red-berry and spice flavours, showing a distinct touch of complexity, and a finely textured finish. A real charmer.

DRY $25 AV

Black Estate Damsteep North Canterbury Pinot Noir   ★★★★★

The outstanding 2016 vintage (★★★★★) was estate-grown in the Damsteep Vineyard, planted in 1999 'at the top of Waipara Valley', fermented with indigenous yeasts, barrel-aged, and bottled unfined and unfiltered. Deeply coloured, it is mouthfilling, very savoury, ripe and deep, with finely balanced tannins and lovely plum, berry, spice and nut flavours. Likely to flourish for a decade, it's full of personality. Best drinking 2020+.

DRY $45 AV

Black Estate Home North Canterbury Pinot Noir   ★★★★☆

The 2016 vintage (★★★★☆) was grown in the Home Vineyard at Omihi, planted in 1994. Hand-picked, it was fermented with indigenous yeasts, matured for a year in French oak barriques, and bottled unfined and unfiltered. Full, bright ruby, it is savoury and supple, in a medium to full-bodied style with ripe, plummy, spicy flavours, hints of herbs and nuts, finely balanced tannins and excellent complexity. Drink now or cellar. Certified organic.

DRY $45 –V

Black Estate Netherwood North Canterbury Pinot Noir   ★★★★☆

The 2015 vintage (★★★★☆) is from the first hill-grown vineyard in North Canterbury, established in 1986. Hand-harvested from ungrafted, unirrigated vines, it was fermented with indigenous yeasts, matured for a year in seasoned oak barrels, and bottled unfined and unfiltered. Unfolding well, it is a bright ruby, medium-bodied wine with good vigour and concentration of ripe, cherryish, plummy flavours, distinctly savoury notes adding complexity, fresh acidity, and a very harmonious finish. It should be at its best 2020+.

DRY $60 –V

Black Peak Wanaka Central Otago Pinot Noir   (★★★★★)

The classy, distinctive 2017 vintage (★★★★★) is deeply coloured, youthful and fruit-packed. A powerful young red, it is mouthfilling, with rich cherry, plum and spice flavours, finely integrated oak, good complexity, and a supple, persistent finish. Already delicious, it should be at its best mid-2021+.

DRY $42 V+

Black Stilt Waitaki Valley Pinot Noir   ★★★

Grown in the Waitaki Valley, North Otago, and barrel-matured, the 2014 vintage (★★★☆) shows signs of early development, with mature colour. Mouthfilling, it has strong plum, spice and nut flavours, slightly leafy notes, fresh acidity, and some savoury complexity. Drink now.

DRY $39 –V

Blackenbrook Family Reserve Nelson Pinot Noir   ★★★★☆

The youthful 2017 vintage (★★★★☆) was estate-grown, hand-picked and matured for a year in French oak barriques (31 per cent new). Deep ruby, it is mouthfilling and savoury, with concentrated cherry, plum and spice flavours, good tannin backbone, and excellent complexity. A powerful wine, it's well worth cellaring to 2021+.

Vintage	17
WR	6
Drink	19-25

DRY $40 AV

Blackenbrook Nelson Pinot Noir (★★★★)

The graceful, estate-grown 2017 vintage (★★★★) was hand-harvested from 16-year-old vines and matured for a year in French oak barriques (10 per cent new). Full-coloured, it is mouthfilling, sweet-fruited and supple, with very good depth of plummy, slightly spicy flavours, showing considerable complexity, gentle tannins, and lots of drink-young appeal.

Vintage	17	DRY $29 V+
WR	6	
Drink	19-20	

Blank Canvas Marlborough Pinot Noir (★★★★★)

The youthful, very age-worthy 2015 vintage (★★★★★) is a single-vineyard wine, grown in the Waihopai Valley, hand-picked, fermented with indigenous yeasts and matured for 10 months in French oak barriques (35 per cent new). Full-coloured, it is mouthfilling, with impressive density of fresh, plummy, spicy, slightly nutty flavours, fine-grained tannins, excellent complexity, and a long, finely structured finish. Best drinking 2021+.

Vintage	15	DRY $45 AV
WR	6	
Drink	19-24	

Blank Canvas Upton Downs Marlborough Pinot Noir (★★★★☆)

The 2016 vintage (★★★★☆) is a single-vineyard, Awatere Valley red, hand-picked and matured in French oak barriques (30 per cent new). Ruby-hued, it is highly fragrant, savoury and sweet-fruited, with mouthfilling body, cherryish, plummy, spicy flavours and good texture. A complex style, it's a drink-now or cellaring proposition.

Vintage	16	DRY $49 –V
WR	6	
Drink	19-28	

Blind River Awatere Valley Marlborough Pinot Noir ★★★★

Estate-grown in the Awatere Valley, the 2017 vintage (★★★★) is bright ruby and mouthfilling, with strong, vibrant, plummy, spicy, slightly nutty flavours. Youthful, with good complexity and a floral bouquet, it should be at its best 2020+.

Vintage	17	DRY $35 AV
WR	7	
Drink	19-25	

Boneline, The, Waimanu Waipara Pinot Noir ★★★★☆

Hand-picked from 'old' vines, the 2016 vintage (★★★★☆) was barrel-matured for a year. Deep ruby, it is full-bodied and concentrated, with strong cherry, plum and spice flavours, nutty, savoury notes adding complexity, finely balanced tannins, and a long, harmonious finish. Drink now or cellar.

 DRY $40 AV

Boneline, The, Waipara Wai-Iti Pinot Noir   (★★★★)

Already open and expressive, the 2017 vintage (★★★★) was hand-picked and given 'judicious' wood handling (one year in barrels, 5 per cent new). Full, bright ruby, it is mouthfilling, supple and savoury, with cherry, plum, spice and nut flavours, showing very good complexity and harmony. Best drinking 2021+.

DRY $40 –V

Brancott Estate Identity Awatere Valley Marlborough Pinot Noir   (★★★☆)

The new Identity range was designed to celebrate Marlborough's sub-regions. Enjoyable young, the 2017 vintage (★★★☆) is ruby-hued, with generous, plummy, spicy flavours, a hint of herbs, some savoury complexity and a smooth finish. Drink now onwards.

DRY $22 V+

Brancott Estate Letter Series 'T' Marlborough Pinot Noir   ★★★★

Still youthful, the 2017 vintage (★★★★) is a savoury red, barrel-aged for nine months. Ruby-hued, it is fragrant and full-bodied, with ripe, plummy, spicy flavours, showing good complexity, and a fairly firm finish. Best drinking mid-2020+.

DRY $25 V+

Brancott Estate Reflection Limited Edition Marlborough Pinot Noir   (★★★★★)

The 2015 vintage (★★★★★) is Pinot Noir on a grand scale. Hand-picked from 15-year-old vines in the Brancott Vineyard, it was fermented with indigenous yeasts and matured for 18 months in French oak barriques (36 per cent new). Deeply coloured, with a fragrant, slightly earthy bouquet, it is powerful and sturdy (14.4 per cent alcohol), with concentrated cherry, plum, spice and nut flavours, very harmonious, rich and supple. Already delicious, it should break into full stride 2020+.

DRY $80 AV

Brennan B2 Central Otago Pinot Noir   ★★★★

Estate-grown at Gibbston, the 2015 vintage (★★★★☆) is a savoury, finely poised red, drinking well now. Full-coloured, with a hint of development, it is fragrant and vibantly fruity, with ripe cherry, plum and spice flavours, a hint of herbs, good tannin backbone and excellent depth.

DRY $35 AV

Brennan Gibbston Central Otago Pinot Noir   ★★★★☆

Still moderately youthful, the 2014 vintage (★★★★★) is an impressively fragrant, rich and complex red. Full-coloured, it is mouthfilling, with concentrated, ripe cherry, plum, herb and spice flavours, savoury, nutty notes, and a long, harmonious finish. Still on sale, the 2012 vintage (★★★★☆) is probably at or near its peak. Fragrant and full-coloured, it is mouthfilling, savoury and supple, with strong, plummy, spicy, nutty, slightly herbal flavours, showing excellent complexity, and a well-rounded finish.

DRY $65 –V

Brightside Organic New Zealand Pinot Noir

Certified organic, the 2017 vintage (★★★☆) was grown in Nelson. Full, bright ruby, it is mouthfilling and vibrantly fruity, with strong, plummy, spicy flavours, an earthy streak, fresh acidity and good density. Priced sharply. (From Kaimira Estate.)

DRY $17 V+

Brightwater Vineyards Lord Rutherford Nelson Pinot Noir ★★★★☆

The youthful 2017 vintage (★★★★☆) was estate-grown, fermented with indigenous yeasts, matured for 11 months in French oak barriques (25 per cent new), and bottled unfined and unfiltered. Fragrant, rich and complex, it is sweet-fruited and vibrant, with deep cherry, plum and spice flavours, fine-grained tannins, and a lengthy finish. Best drinking 2020+.

Vintage	17	16	15
WR	7	NM	NM
Drink	19-24	NM	NM

DRY $50 –V

Brightwater Vineyards Nelson Pinot Noir ★★★★☆

Still youthful, the 2017 vintage (★★★★) was matured for 11 months in French oak casks (20 per cent new), and bottled unfined and unfiltered. Bright ruby, with mouthfilling body, it is sweet-fruited, with good concentration of cherry, plum and spice flavours, a gentle seasoning of oak adding complexity, and a smooth finish. Open 2020+.

Vintage	17	16	15	14	13	12	11	10
WR	6	NM	6	7	6	6	7	6
Drink	19-22	NM	19-20	P	P	P	P	P

DRY $40 AV

Bristol Farm Central Otago Pinot Noir ★★★★☆

Grown at Bannockburn, the 2015 vintage (★★★★) was matured for 11 months in French oak barrels (22 per cent new), and bottled unfined and unfiltered. Ruby-hued, with some development showing, it is fragrant and savoury, with fresh acidity, an array of cherry, plum, spice and herb flavours, showing good complexity, and finely balanced tannins. Drink now to 2021.

DRY $45 –V

Bronte Nelson Pinot Noir ★★★★

From Rimu Grove, the 2018 vintage (★★★★) was estate-grown and matured for 11 months in French oak casks. Bright ruby, it is mouthfilling and supple, with very good depth of ripe, cherryish, slightly nutty flavours, savoury notes adding complexity, and a finely textured, very harmonious finish. Best drinking mid-2020+.

Vintage	18	17
WR	6	6
Drink	19-26	19-25

DRY $30 AV

Burn Cottage Burn Cottage Vineyard Central Otago Pinot Noir ★★★★★

Estate-grown in the foothills of the Pisa Range, in the Cromwell Basin, the powerful, youthful 2017 vintage (★★★★★) was hand-harvested and matured in French oak barriques (25 per cent new). Deeply coloured, it is mouthfilling, with notably rich, ripe cherry, plum and spice flavours, finely integrated oak, good tannin backbone and a well-rounded finish. Best drinking 2022+. Certified organic.

Vintage	17	16	15	14	13	12	11	10
WR	7	7	6	7	7	7	6	6
Drink	19-27	19-26	19-25	19-25	19-25	19-21	P	P

Burn Cottage Moonlight Race Central Otago Pinot Noir ★★★★★

The classy, distinctive 2016 vintage (★★★★★) was grown at three sites (including Burn Cottage Vineyard) in the Cromwell Basin, fermented with indigenous yeasts and matured in French oak casks (19 per cent new). Bright ruby, it is fragrant and very sweet-fruited, with generous cherry, plum and spice flavours, earthy, savoury notes adding complexity, and gentle tannins, giving a well-rounded finish. Delicious young.

Burn Cottage Valli Vineyard Gibbston Central Otago Pinot Noir ★★★★★

Since the debut 2014 vintage (★★★★★), Burn Cottage, based in the Cromwell Basin, has drawn grapes from the more elevated Valli Vineyard, at Gibbston (for their reverse swap, see Valli Burn Cottage Vineyard Central Otago Pinot Noir). Matured in French oak barriques (29 per cent new), the 2017 vintage (★★★★★) is rich and finely textured. From 18-year-old vines, it is deeply coloured and highly fragrant. A powerful red, it has notably dense, plummy, slightly herbal and spicy flavours, youthful vigour and ripe, supple tannins. Best drinking 2022+.

Burnt Spur Martinborough Pinot Noir ★★★★

Drinking well now, the 2016 vintage (★★★★) was French oak-aged for 10 months. Full, bright ruby, it is mouthfilling and sweet-fruited, with generous, ripe cherry, plum and spice flavours, showing good complexity, and supple tannins. Priced right.

Vintage	16
WR	6
Drink	19-23

DRY $28 V+

Cable Bay Awatere Valley Marlborough Pinot Noir ★★★

Ruby-hued, the 2016 vintage (★★★) is a single-vineyard red, medium-bodied, vibrantly fruity and supple. It has cherry/plum flavours, a restrained oak influence, fresh acidity and drink-young appeal.

Vintage	16
WR	6
Drink	19-22

DRY $36 –V

Carrick Bannockburn Central Otago Pinot Noir ★★★★★

A regional classic. Certified organic, the very age-worthy 2017 vintage (★★★★★) was estate-grown and matured in French oak barriques. Full-coloured, it is mouthfilling, concentrated, savoury and structured, with ripe cherry, plum, spice and nut flavours, slightly earthy notes adding complexity, real depth through the palate and a long finish. Best drinking mid-2021+.

Vintage	17	16
WR	7	7
Drink	21-27	20-26

DRY $47 AV

Carrick Crown and Cross Central Otago Pinot Noir (★★★★)

The 2016 vintage (★★★★) from this Bannockburn-based winery was grown in Alexandra. Full-coloured, it was matured for 11 months in French oak barrels (20 per cent new). A mouthfilling, sweet-fruited wine, it has generous, plummy, spicy flavours, showing some savoury complexity. An upfront style, it's drinking well now.

DRY $36 AV

Carrick Excelsior Central Otago Pinot Noir ★★★★★

Likely to be long-lived, the very classy 2014 vintage (★★★★★) was harvested from mature, estate-grown vines at Bannockburn. A full-coloured, powerful but approachable wine, it was matured for 16 months in barrels (15 per cent new). It has substantial body, fresh, deep cherry, plum and spice flavours, nutty oak adding complexity, fine-grained tannins and a resounding finish. Best drinking 2020+.

Vintage	14
WR	7
Drink	20-30

DRY $95 AV

Carrick The Magnetic Central Otago Pinot Noir (★★★★☆)

Showing good personality, the 2016 vintage (★★★★☆) is based on the Abel clone of Pinot Noir, estate-grown at Bannockburn and matured for 11 months in seasoned oak barrels. Ruby-hued, it is a distinctive wine, with concentrated cherry, plum and spice flavours, a gentle seasoning of oak, good complexity, smooth tannins, and loads of drink-young appeal. Certified organic.

Vintage	16
WR	6
Drink	19-23

DRY $48 –V

Carrick Unravelled Central Otago Pinot Noir ★★★★

The 2018 vintage (★★★★) of this organically certified red doesn't claim Bannockburn origin on its labels, but is 'essentially a declassification of wine from the Carrick vineyards'. Full, bright ruby, it has very good depth of vibrant, ripe, plummy, spicy flavours, savoury notes adding complexity, supple tannins and lots of drink-young appeal.

DRY $29 V+

Catalina Sounds Marlborough Pinot Noir ★★★★

Attractive young, but also worth cellaring, the 2018 vintage (★★★★) was partly estate-grown in the Sound of White Vineyard, in the upper Waihopai Valley. Bright ruby, it has moderately rich cherry, plum, spice and nut flavours, showing good complexity, fresh acidity and a smooth, harmonious finish.

 DRY $30 AV

Catalina Sounds Sound of White Marlborough Pinot Noir ★★★★☆

Estate-grown in the Sound of White Vineyard, in the upper Waihopai Valley, the 2017 vintage (★★★★★) is a very classy young red. Deeply coloured, it is mouthfilling, sweet-fruited and savoury, with concentrated, ripe fruit flavours, excellent complexity, and a well-structured, lasting finish. Best drinking 2022+.

 DRY $50 –V

Ceres Composition Bannockburn Central Otago Pinot Noir ★★★★☆

Weighty and supple, the 2017 vintage (★★★★☆) is a ruby-hued, fruit-packed red, mouthfilling and youthful. Fresh and sweet-fruited, it has vibrant cherry, plum and spice flavours, good tannin support, and obvious potential; best drinking 2021+.

 DRY $40 AV

Ceres The Artists Collection Black Rabbit Vineyard Bannockburn Central Otago Pinot Noir (★★★★☆)

Ruby-hued, with a hint of development, the 2016 vintage (★★★★☆) is a 'serious' style, still unfolding. Savoury, with cherry, plum, spice and nut flavours, oak complexity and a fairly firm finish, it should be at its best 2021+.

 DRY $79 –V

Ceres The Artists Collection Inlet Vineyard Bannockburn Central Otago Pinot Noir (★★★★★)

Delicious now, the 2016 vintage (★★★★★) is ruby-hued, fragrant and sweet-fruited, in a slightly softer style than its Black Rabbit Vineyard stablemate (above). Savoury, nutty and complex, it has generous cherry, plum, spice and nut flavours, that build well to a powerful finish.

DRY $79 AV

Charcoal Gully Sally's Pinch Central Otago Pinot Noir ★★★★

Still on sale, the deeply coloured 2014 vintage (★★★★) is a single-vineyard red, hand-harvested at Pisa, in the Cromwell Basin, and matured for 10 months in French oak casks (32 per cent new). Fragrant, mouthfilling and sweet-fruited, it has generous, well-ripened cherry, plum and spice flavours, and a firm finish.

Vintage	14	13
WR	7	5
Drink	19-27	19-24

 DRY $32 AV

Chard Farm Mason Vineyard Central Otago Pinot Noir ★★★★

The 2017 vintage (★★★★) is a tightly structured, single-vineyard Parkburn red, matured in French oak casks (20 per cent new). Ruby-hued, it is invitingly fragrant, full-bodied and fresh, with a hint of herbs, savoury, nutty notes adding complexity, and firm tannins. It needs time; open 2022+.

Vintage	14	
WR	6	
Drink	19-22	

Chard Farm Mata-Au Central Otago Pinot Noir ★★★★

Chard Farm's 'signature' red is estate-grown in the Lowburn and Parkburn districts, in the Cromwell Basin, and barrel-aged (20 per cent new in 2017). The generous, youthful 2017 vintage (★★★★☆) is ruby-hued, savoury and supple, with strong cherry, plum, spice and nut flavours, oak complexity and obvious potential; best drinking 2021+.

Chard Farm River Run Central Otago Pinot Noir ★★★★

Delicious young, the 2017 vintage (★★★★) is a fresh, elegant red, estate-grown and barrel-aged (15 per cent new). Bright ruby, it is sweet-fruited and supple, with youthful, ripe, moderately concentrated cherry, plum and spice flavours, oak-derived complexity and some tannin backbone. A very graceful red, it should be at its best mid-2020+.

Chard Farm The Tiger Lowburn Central Otago Pinot Noir ★★★★☆

This is my pick of Chard Farm's reds from the 2017 vintage (★★★★★). A single-vineyard Lowburn wine, it was hand-picked and barrel-aged (20 per cent new). Deep ruby, it is mouthfilling and supple, with generous, youthful cherry, plum, spice and nut flavours, oak-derived complexity and a long, very harmonious finish. A very age-worthy, graceful young red, it should break into full stride 2021+.

Vintage	17	
WR	7	
Drink	19-25	

Chard Farm The Viper Parkburn Central Otago Pinot Noir ★★★★

Invitingly perfumed and finely textured, the 2017 vintage (★★★★☆) is a single-vineyard Parkburn red, hand-harvested and barrel-aged (20 per cent new). Mouthfilling, it is ruby-hued, with strong, ripe cherry, plum and spice flavours, nutty oak adding complexity, and a very harmonious finish. Best drinking 2021+.

Vintage	17	
WR	7	
Drink	19-25	DRY $79 –V

China Girl by Crown Range Cellar Central Otago Pinot Noir ★★★★☆

The powerful 2016 vintage (★★★★★) was hand-picked on Chinaman's Terrace, at Bendigo, and matured for a year in French oak casks (30 per cent new). Deep ruby, it is fragrant, mouthfilling and vibrantly fruity, with ripe plum and spice flavours, showing excellent concentration, fresh acidity, good complexity and a lasting finish. Still youthful, it's a savoury, well-structured red with obvious potential; open 2020+.

DRY $65 –V

Churton Marlborough Pinot Noir ★★★★☆

Estate-grown at an elevated site in the Waihopai Valley, hand-picked, fermented with indigenous yeasts and matured for 18 months in seasoned French oak barriques, this is 'a delicate, refined' Pinot Noir, according to winemaker Sam Weaver. Retasted in early 2019, the ruby-hued 2016 vintage (★★★★☆) is still youthful, but already very expressive. It is mouthfilling and savoury, with moderately concentrated, ripe cherry, spice and nut flavours, showing excellent complexity and harmony, and a finely textured, lingering finish. Certified organic.

Vintage	16	15	14	13	12	11	10
WR	6	6	NM	7	5	6	7
Drink	19-25	19-27	NM	19-28	19-22	19-25	19-27

DRY $39 V+

Churton The Abyss Marlborough Pinot Noir ★★★★★

The 2013 vintage (★★★★★) was estate-grown on an elevated site in the Waihopai Valley, on a north-east-facing clay slope which catches the early morning sun. Hand-picked from vines planted in 1999, fermented with indigenous yeasts and matured for 18 months in French oak casks (30 per cent new), it is deeply coloured and highly fragrant, with rich plum/spice flavours, earthy notes adding complexity, firm tannins and obvious potential. Best drinking 2020+. Certified organic. (The next vintage will be 2017.)

Vintage	17	16	15	14	13	12	11	10
WR	6	NM	NM	NM	7	NM	NM	7
Drink	19-27	NM	NM	NM	20-30	NM	NM	19-28

DRY $75 AV

Clark Estate Upper Wairau Marlborough Pinot Noir (★★★★)

Worth cellaring, the good-value 2017 vintage (★★★★) is a single-vineyard red, bright ruby, with good body and depth. It has fresh, youthful, plummy, spicy flavours, with savoury notes adding complexity, and a fairly firm finish. Open 2020+.

DRY $24 V+

Clericus Marlborough Wild Pinot Noir (★★★★☆)

Still unfolding, the 2017 vintage (★★★★☆) of this Wairau Valley red is deep ruby, with a fragrant, savoury, slightly herbal bouquet. Full-bodied, it has concentrated plum, herb and spice flavours, complex and savoury, fine-grained tannins and a lengthy finish. Best drinking mid-2020+. (From Clark Estate.)

DRY $42 AV

Clos de Ste Anne Naboth's Vineyard Pinot Noir   ★★★★

This Gisborne red from Millton is one of this country's northernmost quality Pinot Noirs. Grown at the hillside Clos de Ste Anne site at Manutuke, it is hand-harvested from vines up to 25 years old, fermented with indigenous yeasts, barrique-aged, and bottled without fining or filtering. Certified biodynamic, the 2015 vintage (★★★★) is ruby-hued, fragrant, mouthfilling and savoury, with ripe, strawberryish, spicy, nutty flavours, gentle acidity, and good complexity and harmony. Drink now or cellar.

 DRY $60 –V

Clos Henri Bel Echo Marlborough Pinot Noir – see Bel Echo
by Clos Henri Marlborough Pinot Noir

Clos Henri Marlborough Pinot Noir   ★★★★☆

From Henri Bourgeois, a top Loire Valley producer with a site near Renwick, the 2015 vintage (★★★★☆) was hand-picked and matured for a year in French oak casks. It has deep, fairly youthful colour. Savoury and complex, it is full-bodied and generous, with concentrated, plummy, spicy, slightly herbal and nutty flavours. Drinking well now, it will also reward cellaring. Certified organic.

Vintage	15
WR	7
Drink	19-26

 DRY $44 AV

Clos Henri Petit Clos Marlborough Pinot Noir   ★★★☆

Certified organic, the 2017 vintage (★★★★) is based on Clos Henri's youngest vines. Estate-grown and hand-harvested in the Wairau Valley, it was matured in large (7500-litre) French oak vats. Ruby-hued, it is an elegant red, mouthfilling and supple, with ripe cherry, plum and spice flavours, showing some savoury complexity, and velvety tannins. Best drinking 2020+.

Vintage	17
WR	6
Drink	19-22

 DRY $26 AV

Clos Marguerite Marlborough Pinot Noir   ★★★★

The sturdy, generous 2015 vintage (★★★★☆) of this estate-grown, Awatere Valley red is the finest yet. Hand-harvested, it was matured for a year in French oak barrels (partly new). Full coloured, it is fragrant and mouthfilling, with concentrated, plummy, spicy flavours, fresh acidity and very good complexity. Drink now or cellar.

DRY $52 –V

Cloudy Bay New Zealand Pinot Noir   ★★★★☆

Consistently classy. Grown at sites on the cooler, more clay-influenced south side of the Wairau Valley, the 2017 vintage (★★★★☆) was matured in French oak barriques (25 per cent new). Full, bright ruby, it is fragrant, mouthfilling, fresh and supple, with plum, cherry and spice flavours, showing good complexity, delicacy and vigour. Still youthful, it's a finely structured wine, likely to be at its best 2021+.

Vintage	17	16	15	14
WR	6	7	7	6
Drink	19-25	19-26	19-25	19-21

 DRY $41 AV

Cloudy Bay Te Wahi Central Otago Pinot Noir   ★★★★★

Delicious drinking now onwards, the 2015 vintage (★★★★★), retasted in 2019, was estate-grown in the Calvert Vineyard at Bannockburn and Northburn Vineyard, on the east bank of Lake Dunstan. Fermented with indigenous yeasts, it was matured for a year in French oak barriques (35 per cent new). Deep, bright ruby, it is a powerful, sturdy, complex red with a savoury bouquet, concentrated, well-ripened cherry, plum, spice and nut flavours, good complexity and a long, rounded finish. The 2016 vintage (★★★★★) was matured for a year in French oak barriques (30 per cent new). Deep ruby, it is mouthfilling and sweet-fruited, with cherry, plum and spice flavours, savoury and harmonious, and a long, smooth finish. A very age-worthy red, it's well worth cellaring to 2021+. The 2017 vintage (★★★★★) is a powerful, softly seductive red. Deeply coloured, it is mouthfilling, concentrated and supple, with rich cherry, plum, spice and nut flavours, youthful and very harmonious. Best drinking 2022+.

Vintage	17	16	15	14
WR	7	7	7	7
Drink	19-27	19-26	19-25	19-24

 DRY $99 –V

Coal Pit Tiwha Central Otago Pinot Noir   ★★★★★

The very graceful 2017 vintage (★★★★★) was estate-grown and hand-picked at Gibbston, over 400 metres above sea level, and matured for a year in French oak casks (40 per cent new). Floral and deeply coloured, it is sweet-fruited, with fine-grained tannins, moderate acidity and bold, vibrant red-berry, plum, spice, dried-herb and nut flavours. Retasted in March 2019, it is already drinking well, but likely to be long-lived. A concentrated, very harmonious wine, it's well worth cellaring to at least 2021. Drinking well early, the 2018 vintage (★★★★☆) is a bright ruby, elegant, supple wine, full-bodied, with ripe sweet-fruit flavours, gentle acidity, good complexity and a well-rounded finish.

Vintage	17	16	15	14	13	12	11	10
WR	7	6	6	7	7	6	5	7
Drink	19-25	19-23	19-22	19-22	19-21	19-20	P	P

 DRY $57 AV

Coopers Creek Marlborough Pinot Noir   ★★★☆

Offering very good value, the 2016 vintage (★★★★) is a fragrant, full-bodied wine, drinking well now. Bright ruby, it is sweet-fruited and savoury, with strong, ripe cherry, plum and spice flavours, showing considerable complexity.

 DRY $23 V+

Coopers Creek Select Vineyards Razorback Central Otago Pinot Noir ★★★

The briefly oak-matured 2016 vintage (★★★☆) is a ruby-hued, full-bodied wine with very good depth of ripe, plummy, spicy, slightly nutty flavours, considerable complexity and a slightly chewy finish. Best drinking 2020.

 DRY $28 –V

Craft Farm Martinborough Pinot Noir (★★★★)

Already drinking well, but worth cellaring, the 2017 vintage (★★★★) is a single-vineyard red, matured for over a year in French oak casks (50 per cent new). Deep ruby, it is savoury and complex, with ripe plum, herb, spice and nut flavours, showing very good depth and harmony. Best drinking 2020+.

 DRY $48 –V

Crafters Union Depth & Finesse Central Otago Pinot Noir (★★★☆)

Enjoyable young, but also worth cellaring, the 2016 vintage (★★★☆) was oak-aged. Deep ruby, it is fragrant and vibrantly fruity, with generous, cherryish, plummy flavours, moderate complexity and a well-rounded finish. (From Constellation NZ.)

Vintage	16
WR	5
Drink	P

 DRY $25 AV

Craggy Range Te Muna Road Vineyard Martinborough Pinot Noir ★★★★★

The impressive 2016 vintage (★★★★★) was estate-grown, hand-picked and matured for nine months in French oak barriques (23 per cent new). Forward in its appeal, it is deep ruby, mouthfilling and sweet-fruited, with concentrated, plummy, spicy, nutty flavours, fine-grained tannins, and excellent complexity and harmony. Drink now or cellar.

 DRY $46 AV

Crater Rim, The, Omihi Rise Waipara Pinot Noir (★★★★☆)

Still unfolding, the 2014 vintage (★★★★☆), tasted in mid-2019, is a single-vineyard, North Canterbury red. Full and bright in colour, it is mouthfilling, with good concentration of ripe cherry, plum, spice and nut flavours, complex, firm and savoury. Open mid-2020+.

DRY $35 V+

Crater Rim, The, Rata Vineyard Banks Peninsula Pinot Noir (★★★★☆)

Grown in the Kaituna Valley, on Banks Peninsula, the 2015 vintage (★★★★☆) of this Canterbury wine is ruby-hued, with a fragrant, complex bouquet. Mouthfilling, it is savoury, slightly herbal and nutty, in a firm, concentrated, structured style, well worth cellaring to 2021+.

 DRY $39 V+

Crater Rim, The, Waipara Valley Pinot Noir ★★★★

Estate-grown in North Canterbury, the youthful 2016 vintage (★★★★) was matured for over a year in French oak barriques (partly new). Full, bright ruby, it has an attractive, fragrant, savoury bouquet. Mouthfilling, it has fresh, ripe cherry, plum and spice flavours, showing good complexity, and a very harmonious finish. Best drinking 2021+.

DRY $28 V+

Crown Range Cellar Signature Selection Grant Taylor
Central Otago Pinot Noir ★★★★★

The 2016 vintage (★★★★★) is very rare – only 100 cases were produced. Grown in the Gibbston sub-region, it was crafted by pioneer Central Otago winemaker Grant Taylor (owner of the Valli brand). Matured for a year in French oak casks (30 per cent new), it is a very refined and graceful red, ruby-hued, with an enticingly scented bouquet. Mouthfilling and supple, with ripe cherry, plum and spice flavours, fresh acidity and finely integrated oak, it's a very youthful, 'feminine' style of Pinot Noir, well worth cellaring to 2020+.

Vintage	16	15	14
WR	6	6	6
Drink	19-26	19-25	19-24

DRY $150 –V

Dashwood by Vavasour Marlborough Pinot Noir ★★★☆

Already enjoyable, the 2018 vintage (★★★☆) is bright ruby, fragrant, sweet-fruited and supple. Oak-aged for nine months, it is full-bodied, with very good depth of cherry, plum and spice flavours, a touch of complexity, and lots of drink-young charm.

DRY $22 V+

Delegat Awatere Valley Pinot Noir ★★★★

Offering great value – as in previous years – the 2017 vintage (★★★★) was estate-grown in Marlborough and matured for a year in French oak barriques (new and one year old). Invitingly scented, it is a ruby-hued, strongly varietal wine, sweet-fruited and finely textured, with youthful, cherryish, plummy flavours, gentle tannins and a smooth finish. Drink now to 2020.

DRY $25 V+

Delta Hatters Hill Marlborough Pinot Noir ★★★★☆

The 2017 vintage (★★★★☆) was estate-grown in the Waihopai Valley, hand-picked and matured in French oak casks (one-third new). Deeply coloured, it is mouthfilling, rich and vibrantly fruity, with plummy, spicy flavours, showing excellent ripeness and depth, and fine-grained tannins. A powerful, youthful red, it should be long-lived. Best drinking 2021+.

DRY $35 V+

Delta Marlborough Pinot Noir   ★★★★

The 2017 vintage (★★★★) is a single-vineyard red, grown at the mouth of the Waihopai Valley. Partly (50 per cent) French oak-aged, it is deep ruby, fresh and full-bodied, with vibrant, ripe cherry, plum and spice flavours, showing good concentration, some savoury complexity and the structure to age. A great buy in the sub-$20 range.

DRY $19 V+

Devil's Staircase Central Otago Pinot Noir   ★★★☆

From Rockburn, this skilfully crafted, drink-young charmer is matured in tanks, without oak, 'to retain bright fruit'. Deep ruby, with a fresh, fragrant bouquet, the 2018 vintage (★★★☆) is full-bodied, with ripe plum and spice flavours, gentle tannins, and very good depth. It's already enjoyable.

DRY $30 –V

Doctors Flat Central Otago Pinot Noir   ★★★★★

The highly age-worthy 2016 vintage (★★★★★) is a single-vineyard red, estate-grown at Bannockburn, matured for a year in French oak barrels (25 per cent new), and bottled without fining or filtering. Deep ruby, it is mouthfilling, savoury and supple, with concentrated, ripe cherry, plum and spice flavours and a finely structured, lasting finish. Best drinking 2021+.

Vintage	16	15	14	13
WR	7	7	7	6
Drink	19-24	19-23	19-22	19-21

DRY $47 AV

Doctors', The, Marlborough Pinot Noir   (★★)

Crafted as a very low alcohol style (9.5 per cent), the 2018 vintage (★★) is pale ruby, with fresh, light, red-berry and spice flavours. It lacks any real stuffing or richness, but offers smooth, easy drinking. (From Forrest Estate.)

DRY $25 –V

Dog Point Vineyard Marlborough Pinot Noir   ★★★★★

This classy, finely structured red is estate-grown on the south side of the Wairau Valley, hand-picked and matured for 18 months in French oak barriques (35 per cent new in 2017). The 2017 vintage (★★★★☆) is a very deeply coloured, age-worthy wine. Weighty and supple, it has concentrated, vibrant cherry, plum and spice flavours, complex and savoury, and a finely balanced, harmonious finish. Best drinking 2022+. Certified organic.

Vintage	17	16	15	14	13	12	11	10
WR	7	7	6	7	7	7	5	7
Drink	19-27	19-26	19-25	19-25	19-25	19-24	P	19-22

DRY $40 V+

Domain Road Bannockburn Central Otago Pinot Noir ★★★★☆

The 2017 vintage (★★★★☆) is a powerful young red, estate-grown, hand-harvested and matured for 10 months in French oak casks (26 per cent new). Deeply coloured, it is vibrantly fruity, with concentrated cherry, plum and spice flavours, good tannin support, and obvious cellaring potential; open 2021+.

DRY $40 AV

Domain Road Defiance Single Vineyard Central Otago Pinot Noir ★★★★☆

The 2017 vintage (★★★★★) is a powerful, single-vineyard Bannockburn red, hand-picked and matured for 10 months in French oak casks (29 per cent new). Deep and youthful in colour, it is highly fragrant, with dense, youthful cherry, plum and spice flavours, showing excellent vigour, concentration and structure. Best drinking 2022+.

Vintage	17	16
WR	7	6
Drink	19-28	19-26

DRY $65 –V

Domain Road Paradise Single Vineyard Bannockburn Pinot Noir (★★★★★)

The 2013 vintage (★★★★★) is Domain Road's 'premier wine'. Matured for 13 months in French oak casks (33 per cent new), it has full, bright, moderately youthful colour. Mouthfilling and concentrated, it has dense cherry, plum, spice and nut flavours, showing excellent complexity, and a long, savoury, firmly structured finish. Set for a long life, it's well worth cellaring to 2021+.

Vintage	13
WR	6
Drink	19-23

DRY $85 AV

Domaine-Thomson Explorer Central Otago Pinot Noir ★★★★

Offering top value, the classy 2018 vintage (★★★★☆) was estate-grown at Lowburn, in the Cromwell Basin, and matured for eight months in French oak casks (20 per cent new). Bright ruby, it is fragrant and full-bodied, with strong, ripe, plummy, spicy flavours, showing excellent depth, complexity and harmony. As good as many Central Otago Pinot Noirs priced far higher, it's a 'serious' but very approachable red; best drinking 2021+.

DRY $29 V+

Domaine-Thomson Rows 1–37 Single Clone Central Otago Pinot Noir (★★★★★)

Still on sale, the 2014 vintage (★★★★★) was estate-grown at Lowburn. Selected from a 0.8-hectare block of clone 777 vines, planted in 2000, it was matured for 10 months in French oak barrrels (25 per cent new). Deeply coloured, it is full-bodied, with generous, ripe cherry, plum and spice flavours, showing excellent complexity. A very savoury wine with good tannin backbone, it's likely to be long-lived. Certified organic.

Vintage	14
WR	7
Drink	19-28

DRY $75 AV

Dry Gully Central Otago Pinot Noir   (★★★★☆)

Offering good value, the 2017 vintage (★★★★☆) of this Alexandra red is deeply coloured, with a fresh, fragrant bouquet. Full-bodied and fruit-packed, it has generous, vibrant, plummy, spicy flavours, nutty, savoury notes adding complexity, and good tannin support. Best drinking mid-2020+.

 DRY $32 V+

Dry River Martinborough Pinot Noir   ★★★★★

Dark and densely flavoured, this Martinborough red ranks among New Zealand's greatest Pinot Noirs. It is grown in three company-owned vineyards – Dry River Estate, Craighall and Lovat – on the Martinborough Terrace, and most of the vines are over 20 years old. Matured for a year in French oak hogsheads (20 to 30 per cent new), it is a slower-developing wine than other New Zealand Pinot Noirs, but matures superbly. Tasted in June 2018, the 2016 vintage (★★★★★) has a real sense of youthful drive. Highly fragrant, it is sweet-fruited, with very intense, vibrant plum and spice flavours, savoury notes adding complexity, and a long, tightly structured finish. Still extremely youthful, it is crying out for cellaring; open 2021+. The 2017 vintage (★★★★☆) was matured for a year in French oak hogsheads (20 per cent new). Bright ruby, it is a finely scented, elegant wine with very youthful, vibrant cherry, plum and spice flavours, woven with fresh acidity, gentle tannins and a finely poised finish. Still a baby, it's well worth cellaring to 2022 onwards.

Vintage	17	16	15	14	13	12	11	10
WR	6	7	7	7	7	6	7	7
Drink	19-29	19-29	19-28	19-27	19-27	19-25	19-25	19-24

DRY $90 AV

Durvillea by Astrolabe Marlborough Pinot Noir   ★★★☆

Offering great value, the 2018 vintage (★★★☆) is a regional blend, mostly hand-picked and matured in French oak barriques of varying ages. Ruby-hued, it is mouthfilling and supple, with cherry, plum and spice flavours, some savoury notes adding complexity, and lots of drink-young appeal.

Vintage	18
WR	6
Drink	19-24

DRY $20 V+

Eaton Marlborough Pinot Noir   (★★★★)

Grown in the upper Waihopai Valley, the 2018 vintage (★★★★) is a single-vineyard red, hand-picked, matured for 11 months in two oak barrels (one new), and bottled unfined and unfiltered. It has light, slightly developed colour. Fragrant, with a hint of herbs, it is savoury, with moderately concentrated cherry and spice flavours, and nutty notes adding complexity. It's already quite open and expressive.

Vintage	18
WR	6
Drink	20-23

DRY $48 –V

Eight Ranges Central Otago Pinot Noir ★★★★

Showing good cellaring potential, the 2017 vintage (★★★★☆) is a single-vineyard red, grown at Alexandra and matured in French oak barrels. Deep ruby, it is fragrant, sweet-fruited and fresh, with mouthfilling body, strong, youthful, plummy, spicy flavours, showing excellent concentration and complexity, and a moderately firm finish. Best drinking 2021+. (From Tussock Ridge.)

DRY $38 AV

Eight Ranges Trail Rider Central Otago Pinot Noir (★★★★)

Delicious young, the 2018 vintage (★★★★) from this Alexandra-based producer was matured in French oak (24 per cent new). Bright ruby, it is fragrant and full-bodied, with ripe cherry, plum and spice flavours, nutty, savoury notes adding complexity, and gentle tannins. An elegant, youthful red, it should be at its best 2021+.

DRY $30 AV

Elder, The, Martinborough Pinot Noir ★★★★★

Estate-grown in the Hanson Vineyard, at Te Muna, the 2016 vintage (★★★★★) is a very graceful red, likely to be long-lived. Deep ruby, it is weighty, sweet-fruited and supple, with rich cherry, plum, berry and spice flavours, savoury notes adding complexity, balanced acidity, and a lingering finish. Best drinking 2021+.

DRY $62 AV

Eradus Awatere Valley Marlborough Pinot Noir ★★★☆

A good drink-young style, the 2019 vintage (★★★☆) is boldly fruity, with gentle tannins and strong, vibrant, plummy, spicy flavours.

DRY $22 V+

Escarpment Kupe by Escarpment Pinot Noir ★★★★★

This flagship, estate-grown red is based on vines closely planted at Te Muna, near Martinborough, in 1999, and matured in French oak barriques (typically 50 per cent new). At its best, it is dark and densely flavoured, with lovely texture and length. The most recent vintage I have tasted was the 2012 (★★★★), in 2014. From a very cool growing season, it's a generous, supple wine, medium-bodied, with a savoury, spicy, earthy complexity, and hints of herbs and tamarillos, but less powerful, concentrated, ripe-tasting and lush than top vintages.

DRY $115 –V

Escarpment Martinborough Pinot Noir ★★★★★

This 'district' blend is the third-tier label, after the single-vineyard and flagship Kupe reds, but top vintages can be highly impressive. The most recent vintage I have tasted was the 2012 (★★★★), in 2014. From a very cool summer, it was quite forward in its appeal – ruby-hued, savoury and supple, in a moderately concentrated style with cherry, plum and spice flavours and a slightly herbal twist.

DRY $46 AV

Esk Valley Marlborough Pinot Noir ★★★★

The attractive 2017 vintage (★★★★) is a single-vineyard red, grown in the Omaka Valley and matured for 11 months in French oak barriques (16 per cent new). Bright ruby, it is fragrant, mouthfilling and supple, with generous, vibrant, cherryish, plummy flavours, showing good complexity, and a well-rounded finish. Offering good value, it's a drink-now or cellaring proposition.

Vintage	18	17
WR	5	5
Drink	19-21	19-23

 DRY $26 V+

Falconhead Marlborough Pinot Noir ★★★

The slightly gutsy 2018 vintage (★★★) is ruby-hued, with spicy, slightly nutty flavours, showing considerable complexity, and a fairly firm finish. Drink 2020+.

 DRY $18 V+

Fancrest Estate North Canterbury Pinot Noir ★★★☆

Certified organic, matured in old oak casks, and bottled unfined and unfiltered, the 2015 vintage (★★★★) was handled with 'exceptionally low sulphite levels'. It has deep, slightly cloudy colour. A distinctive wine with a restrained bouquet, it is mouthfilling, concentrated, structured and complex, in a very savoury style, spicy and firm.

 DRY $45 –V

Fancrest Estate Reserve North Canterbury Pinot Noir (★★★★☆)

Certified organic, the distinctive 2015 vintage (★★★★☆) was matured for two years in old oak casks and bottled unfined and unfiltered, with 'exceptionally low sulphite levels'. It has full, fairly mature colour. A powerful, savoury, mouthfilling wine (14.5 per cent alcohol), it has concentrated flavours, ripe and spicy, a hint of liquorice, good complexity, and a firm, long finish. Full of personality, it's a drink-now or cellaring proposition.

Vintage	15
WR	6
Drink	23-28

 DRY $49 –V

Felton Road Bannockburn Central Otago Pinot Noir ★★★★★

The Bannockburn winery's 'standard' Pinot Noir is a distinguished wine, blended from its four sites in the district. Matured in French oak casks (27 per cent new in 2018), it is fermented with indigenous yeasts and bottled without fining or filtering. Barrel-aged for 13 months, the 2018 vintage (★★★★★) is bright ruby, with a highly scented bouquet. Savoury and supple, with deep cherry, plum, spice and nut flavours, it's a very harmonious red, with a finely textured, lasting finish. Already very approachable, it should be at its best 2021+.

Vintage	18	17	16	15	14	13	12	11	10
WR	7	7	7	7	7	7	7	7	7
Drink	19-29	19-28	19-27	19-26	19-25	19-24	19-26	19-23	19-22

 DRY $68 AV

Felton Road Block 3 Central Otago Pinot Noir   ★★★★★

Grown at Bannockburn, on a north-facing slope 270 metres above sea level, this is a majestic Central Otago wine, among the finest Pinot Noirs in the country. The mature vines are cultivated in front of the winery, in a section of the vineyard where the clay content is relatively high, giving 'dried-herbs and ripe fruit characters'. The wine is matured for about a year in Burgundy oak barrels (30 per cent new in 2018), and bottled without fining or filtration. The 2018 vintage (★★★★★) is a lovely, very harmonious young red. Deep ruby, it is mouthfilling, with highly concentrated, ripe plum, cherry, spice and nut flavours, complex and savoury, and a rich, seamless finish. Best drinking 2023+.

Vintage	18	17	16	15	14	13	12	11	10
WR	7	7	7	7	7	7	7	7	7
Drink	19-34	19-33	19-32	19-31	19-30	19-24	19-26	19-23	19-22

 DRY $109 AV

Felton Road Block 5 Pinot Noir   ★★★★★

This is winemaker Blair Walter's favourite Felton Road red. Grown in a 'special' block of The Elms Vineyard at Bannockburn, in Central Otago, it is matured for a year or longer in French oak barriques (17 months in 30 per cent new barrels in 2018), and bottled unfined and unfiltered. The 2018 vintage (★★★★★) is a deep ruby, highly scented wine, mouthfilling and supple, with a strong surge of cherry, plum and spice flavours. Complex and savoury, it's a very harmonious red, already delicious but likely to be at its best 2023+.

Vintage	18	17	16	15	14	13	12	11	10
WR	7	7	6	7	7	7	7	7	7
Drink	19-34	19-33	19-30	19-31	19-30	19-27	19-26	19-23	19-22

 DRY $109 AV

Felton Road Calvert Pinot Noir   ★★★★★

Grown in the Calvert Vineyard at Bannockburn – 1 kilometre east of the winery – matured in French oak barriques (30 per cent new in 2018), and bottled unfined and unfiltered, the 2018 vintage (★★★★★) is already delicious. Deep ruby, it is highly fragrant, rich and supple. A refined young red, it has concentrated cherry, plum and spice flavours, a subtle seasoning of oak, and excellent vibrancy and harmony.

Vintage	18	17	16	15	14	13	12	11	10
WR	7	7	6	7	7	7	7	7	7
Drink	19-34	19-33	19-30	19-31	19-28	19-24	19-26	19-23	19-22

 DRY $81 AV

Felton Road Cornish Point Pinot Noir   ★★★★★

From the company-owned Cornish Point Vineyard at the eastern end of Bannockburn, 6 kilometres from the winery, this is always one of my favourite Felton Road reds. The 2018 vintage (★★★★★) was matured for 13 months in French oak barriques (30 per cent new), and bottled without fining or filtering. A very refined wine, it is perfumed and smooth-flowing, with deep colour, concentrated, plummy, spicy flavours, finely integrated oak, gentle acidity, and a rich, very harmonious finish. Best drinking 2022+.

Vintage	18	17	16	15	14	13	12	11	10
WR	7	7	7	7	7	7	7	7	7
Drink	19-32	19-31	19-30	19-29	19-28	19-24	19-26	19-23	19-22

 DRY $81 AV

Flaxmore Moutere Pinot Noir   (★★★)

Estate-grown and hand-picked in the Moutere hills, the 2018 vintage (★★★) was oak-aged for nine months. Light ruby, with a hint of development showing, it has fresh tamarillo and spice aromas, leading into a light to medium-bodied red with fresh acidity, a hint of herbs, some savoury complexity and plenty of flavour. Best drinking 2020.

 DRY $29 –V

Folding Hill Bendigo Central Otago Pinot Noir   ★★★★★

Highly refined, the youthful 2016 vintage (★★★★★) was hand-harvested, matured for 10 months in French oak barriques (25 per cent new), and bottled unfined and unfiltered. Attractively perfumed, it is deep ruby, with rich, vibrant cherry, plum, spice and nut flavours, very harmonious and persistent. Best drinking 2021+.

Vintage	16	15
WR	6	7
Drink	19-26	19-27

 DRY $45 AV

Folding Hill Orchard Block Bendigo Central Otago Pinot Noir   ★★★★☆

The tightly structured, youthful 2015 vintage (★★★★☆) was estate-grown, hand-picked in 'the most sheltered part of the vineyard', matured for 20 months in French oak barrels (partly new), and bottled unfined and unfiltered. Bright ruby, with a highly fragrant, perfumed bouquet, it has strong, ripe cherry, plum, spice and nut flavours, with a firm tannin grip. It needs time; open 2022+.

Vintage	15	14
WR	6	7
Drink	19-26	19-27

 DRY $55 –V

Folium Marlborough Pinot Noir   ★★★★☆

Estate-grown in the Brancott Valley, the 2018 vintage (★★★★) was matured in French oak casks (10 per cent new). Bright ruby, it is youthful, with moderately concentrated, vibrant cherry, plum and spice flavours, fresh acidity, savoury notes adding complexity, and obvious cellaring potential. Best drinking 2021+.

Vintage	18	17	16
WR	4	5	5
Drink	19-25	19-25	19-25

 DRY $32 V+

Folium Reserve Marlborough Pinot Noir   ★★★★★

The classy 2017 vintage (★★★★★) of this Brancott Valley red was hand-harvested and matured in French oak casks (33 per cent new). Deep ruby, it is fragrant, generous and savoury, with concentrated cherry, plum and spice flavours, showing good complexity, fresh acidity and a well-structured, powerful finish. Very age-worthy, it should be at its best 2022+.

Vintage	17	16	15
WR	6	5	6
Drink	20-30	20-30	20-30

 DRY $40 V+

Forrest Marlborough Pinot Noir ★★★★

The 2018 vintage (★★★★) was grown in the Southern Valleys and aged in French oak barrels (20 per cent new). Bright ruby, it is fresh and full-bodied, with youthful cherry, plum and spice flavours, showing good complexity, and a moderately firm finish. Best drinking 2021+.

 DRY $30 AV

Framingham Marlborough Pinot Noir ★★★★

This wine is 'feminine', says winemaker Andrew Hedley, meaning it is elegant, rather than powerful. The 2015 vintage (★★★★) was grown at seven sites, mostly on the south side of the Wairau Valley, and matured for 10 months in French oak barriques (20 per cent new). A refined, supple wine, with ripe cherry, plum and spice flavours, it shows excellent depth and complexity, with lots of early drinking appeal.

Vintage	15	14
WR	7	6
Drink	19-21	19-20

 DRY $30 AV

Fromm Churton Vineyard Marlborough Pinot Noir ★★★★★

The 2017 vintage (★★★★★) is rare – only five barrels were made. Grown organically in the Churton Vineyard, in the Waihopai Valley, it was hand-picked from east-facing clay slopes, fermented with indigenous yeasts, oak-matured, and bottled unfined and unfiltered. Full, bright ruby, it is fresh and smooth-flowing, with strong, vibrant plum, cherry and spice flavours, and a finely poised, long finish. A generous, savoury, supple red, with a real sense of youthful drive, it should be at its best 2021+.

 DRY $55 AV

Fromm Clayvin Vineyard Pinot Noir ★★★★★

This acclaimed Marlborough red is grown and hand-picked on north-facing clay slopes at Clayvin Vineyard, in the Brancott Valley, fermented with indigenous yeasts, matured in French oak barriques, and bottled without fining or filtering. In its youth, it is more floral and charming than its Fromm Vineyard stablemate. Certified organic, the very youthful, vigorous 2017 vintage (★★★★★) is rare – only eight barrels were produced. Deeply coloured, it is full-bodied and sweet-fruited, with very deep, plummy, spicy flavours, earthy, savoury notes adding complexity, fresh acidity, supple tannins, and a lovely combination of power and grace. Full of potential, it should be at its best 2022+.

Vintage	16	15	14	13	12	11	10
WR	7	7	6	7	7	7	7
Drink	19-28	19-27	19-25	19-25	19-26	19-23	19-24

 DRY $85 AV

Fromm Cuvée 'H' Marlborough Pinot Noir ★★★★★

Certified organic, the lovely 2017 vintage (★★★★★) is labelled in honour of Hätsch Kalberer, Fromm's winemaker since the first vintage in 1992. Designed as 'a mindful blend of what our single-vineyard wines offer as a composite', it is a classy wine, full-coloured, with generous, vibrant, youthful cherry, plum and spice flavours, finely structured, supple and persistent. Still a baby, it has obvious cellaring potential; best drinking 2022+.

DRY $65 AV

Fromm Fromm Vineyard Pinot Noir ★★★★★

Winemaker Hätsch Kalberer describes this Marlborough red as 'not a typical New World style, but the truest expression of terroir you could find'. In the Fromm Vineyard near Renwick, in the heart of the Wairau Valley, many clones of Pinot Noir are close-planted on a flat site with alluvial topsoils overlying layers of clay and free-draining gravels. The wine is fermented with indigenous yeasts, matured for 18 months in Burgundy oak barrels (six in 2017), and bottled unfined and unfiltered. Certified organic, the impressive 2017 vintage (★★★★★) looks set for a very long life. Full-coloured, it is savoury, ripe and finely structured, with deep plum, spice and nut flavours. A more graceful, supple red than some earlier vintages, with power through the palate, it's a top vintage, well worth cellaring to 2021+.

Vintage	16	15	14	13	12	11	10
WR	7	7	6	7	7	6	7
Drink	19-28	19-27	19-26	19-26	19-25	19-22	19-23

DRY $85 –V

Fromm La Strada Marlborough Pinot Noir ★★★★☆

This wine is made to be ready for drinking upon release, by 'steering the fermentation towards more fruit expression and moderate tannins and structure'. Certified organic, the 2016 vintage (★★★★☆) is a multi-site blend, hand-picked from vines in the Wairau, Brancott and Waihopai valleys, and matured for 14 to 16 months in mostly seasoned oak barrels. It is savoury and complex, with concentrated, ripe, plummy, spicy flavours, gentle tannins, and loads of drink-young appeal. Certified organic.

Vintage	16	15	14	13	12
WR	6	7	6	7	7
Drink	19-23	19-22	19-21	19-20	P

DRY $40 AV

Fromm Marlborough Pinot Noir (★★★★☆)

Certified organic, the 2017 vintage (★★★★☆) is a blend of grapes hand-picked from four vineyards – Quarters, Churton, Yarrum and Fromm – in three districts. Matured for 14 to 16 months in French oak barriques (less than 10 per cent new), it is bright ruby, full-bodied and complex, with concentrated, ripe, youthful, savoury, slightly nutty flavours and a firmly structured finish. Best drinking 2021+.

DRY $43 AV

Fromm Quarters Vineyard Marlborough Pinot Noir ★★★★★

Certified organic, the rare 2017 vintage (★★★★★) was hand-harvested in the lower Brancott Valley, fermented with indigenous yeasts, and matured in three French oak barriques (yielding a total production of 900 bottles). Full-coloured, it is a classy young red, mouthfilling, rich and finely structured, with dense, berryish, spicy, nutty flavours, complex and persistent. A refined, highly approachable and very harmonious wine, it's already delicious, but likely to be at its best 2021+.

Vintage	17	16	15
WR	7	6	7
Drink	19-27	19-25	19-25

 DRY $55 AV

Gale Force Marlborough Pinot Noir (★★★)

Grown in the Wairau Valley, the 2017 vintage (★★★) is bargain-priced. Bright ruby, it is full-bodied and vibrantly fruity, with youthful vigour, good depth of fresh, plummy, slightly herbal flavours, and a touch of complexity. Drink now to 2020. (From Clark Estate.)

 DRY $15 V+

Georges Road Williams Hill Waipara Pinot Noir ★★★★

The deeply coloured 2016 vintage (★★★★☆) is a single-vineyard red, hand-picked on the eastern slopes of the Waipara Valley and matured for 16 months in French oak casks (25 per cent new). A powerful, youthful, fruit-packed red, it has bold, plummy, spicy flavours, good tannin backbone and obvious cellaring potential; open 2021+.

DRY $36 AV

Georgetown Vineyard Central Otago Pinot Noir ★★★★☆

Grown at the Cromwell end of the Kawarau Gorge, this single-vineyard red is typically full of personality. I tasted the 2016, 2015, 2013 and 2011 vintages in 2018. The elegant, age-worthy 2016 vintage (★★★★☆) is deep ruby, with a fragrant, complex bouquet, mouthfilling body and rich, plummy, spicy, slightly herbal and nutty flavours. Firm, savoury and youthful, it's well worth cellaring. The 2015 vintage (★★★★) shows good depth of plum, spice and herb flavours, in a savoury, complex style; drink now or cellar. My pick is the lovely, skilfully crafted 2013 vintage (★★★★★). Still bright and youthful in colour, it is very graceful and vigorous, sweet-fruited and generous, with mouthfilling body, concentrated, plummy, gently spiced flavours and a finely poised, persistent finish. It should be at its peak 2020+.

 DRY $38 V+

Gibbston Valley China Terrace Bendigo Central Otago Pinot Noir ★★★★★

Estate-grown at altitude (320 metres above sea level) in the China Terrace Vineyard, at Bendigo, the 2017 vintage (★★★★★) was hand-picked and matured for 10 months in French oak casks (22 per cent new). A graceful, highly refined red, it is sweet-fruited and supple, with vibrant cherry, plum and spice flavours, complex, strong and savoury, and a scented bouquet. Delicious young, but capable of lengthy cellaring, it's best opened mid-2020+.

Vintage	17	16	15	14	13	12	11	10
WR	7	6	7	7	7	7	7	7
Drink	19-28	19-27	19-27	19-26	19-25	19-23	19-22	19-20

DRY $65 AV

Gibbston Valley Glenlee Central Otago Pinot Noir   ★★★★☆

A single-vineyard red, grown at Gibbston, the classy 2016 vintage (★★★★★) was hand-picked, fermented with indigenous yeasts and matured in French oak barriques (26 per cent new). Deep ruby, it is fragrant and finely textured, with rich, ripe, vibrant cherry, plum and spice flavours, oak complexity and obvious potential. A very elegant, 'feminine' style of Pinot Noir, it's well worth cellaring to 2020+.

Vintage	16	15	14	13	12	11
WR	6	NM	7	7	7	7
Drink	19-25	NM	19-24	19-20	19-23	19-22

Gibbston Valley Gold River Central Otago Pinot Noir   ★★★★

This is the winery's 'lighter' red, for 'immediate enjoyment'. The 2017 vintage (★★★★) was grown at Gibbston (50 per cent) and Bendigo (50 per cent), hand-picked and barrel-aged for nine months. Bright ruby, with an inviting floral, fresh bouquet, it is sweet-fruited and supple, with ripe, plummy, spicy flavours, showing considerable complexity, and a smooth, very harmonious finish.

Gibbston Valley GV Collection Central Otago Pinot Noir   ★★★★★

This replaces the former 'Gibbston Valley Central Otago Pinot Noir' label. The rewarding 2017 vintage (★★★★★) is a blend of Bendigo (50 per cent), Pisa (46 per cent) and Gibbston (4 per cent) grapes, hand-picked and matured for 10 months in French oak casks (23 per cent new). Full, bright ruby, it is fragrant and supple, with strong, ripe cherry, plum and spice flavours, showing good complexity, supple tannins, and a finely balanced, persistent finish. Already very approachable, it's best opened mid-2020+.

Gibbston Valley Le Maitre Gibbston Central Otago Pinot Noir   ★★★★★

Grown in the Home Block at Gibbston, where the oldest vines were planted in 1983, the 2017 vintage (★★★★★), certified organic, was matured for 10 months in French oak casks (33 per cent new). Bright ruby, it is highly fragrant, with concentrated, very vibrant cherry, plum and spice flavours, a vague hint of herbs, balanced acidity, and a long, supple finish. Still youthful, it's a very refined red, well worth cellaring to at least 2021.

Vintage	17	16	15	14	13	12	11
WR	7	7	7	7	7	7	7
Drink	19-28	19-27	19-26	19-25	19-20	19-23	19-22

Gibbston Valley Reserve Central Otago Pinot Noir ★★★★★

At its best, this Central Otago red is mouthfilling and savoury, with superb concentration of sweet-tasting, plummy fruit and lovely harmony. The grapes have been drawn from various sub-regions and vineyards over the years and yields have been very low (under 5 tonnes/hectare). The 2016 vintage (★★★★★) was grown at Bendigo. Deeply coloured, it is powerful and sturdy (14.5 per cent alcohol), with lovely depth of fresh, plummy, spicy flavours, oak complexity, supple, ripe tannins and a resounding finish. Still youthful, it's best cellared to 2021+.

Vintage	16	15
WR	7	7
Drink	19-26	19-25

DRY $120 AV

Gibbston Valley School House Central Otago Pinot Noir ★★★★★

This consistently classy red is estate-grown in the late-ripening School House Vineyard, at Bendigo, an extremely elevated site (up to 420 metres above sea level). The 2017 vintage (★★★★★) was hand-picked and matured for 10 months in French oak casks (28 per cent new). Deep ruby, it is mouthfilling, vibrantly fruity and youthful, with well-ripened cherry, plum and spice flavours, showing excellent concentration, savoury, earthy notes adding complexity, and good tannin backbone. A very age-worthy wine, it's well worth cellaring to 2022+. Certified organic.

Vintage	17	16	15	14	13	12	11	10
WR	7	7	7	7	7	7	7	7
Drink	19-28	19-27	19-27	19-26	19-25	19-23	19-22	19-20

DRY $65 AV

Gladstone Vineyard Blair Patrick Single Vineyard Wairarapa Pinot Noir (★★★★★)

The debut 2018 vintage (★★★★★) was matured for a year in French oak casks (35 per cent new). Deep ruby, it is highly fragrant and very refined, in a savoury, youthful, tight-knit style with impressive complexity, fresh acidity and a long, structured finish. Best drinking 2022+.

Vintage	18
WR	6
Drink	21-30

DRY $100 –V

Gladstone Vineyard Dakins Road Single Vineyard Wairarapa Pinot Noir (★★★★★)

Finely scented, the debut 2018 vintage (★★★★★) was matured for a year in French oak casks (35 per cent new). Bright ruby, it is a savoury, youthful, well-structured red, with cherry, plum and spice flavours, showing excellent complexity, and a long life ahead. Best drinking 2021+.

DRY $80 –V

Gladstone Vineyard Pinot Noir ★★★★☆

Estate-grown and hand-harvested in the northern Wairarapa, and matured for a year in French oak casks (20 per cent new), the 2018 vintage (★★★★☆) is ruby-hued, scented and supple. A very harmonious red, it has ripe cherry, plum and spice flavours, well-integrated oak, very good complexity and lots of current-drinking appeal. Best drinking 2021+.

DRY $45 –V

Glasnevin Limited Release Waipara Valley Pinot Noir ★★★★☆

The 2016 vintage (★★★★), matured for 14 months in seasoned French oak barriques, is freshly scented, sturdy and vibrantly fruity, with strong, ripe, spicy flavours, hints of raisins and liquorice, and good tannin backbone.

Vintage	16	15
WR	6	6
Drink	19-27	19-24

 DRY $35 V+

Gold Digger Central Otago Pinot Noir ★★★★

The 2018 vintage (★★★★) is a single-vineyard red, hand-picked and matured in French and Hungarian oak casks (14 per cent new). Bright ruby, with a fragrant bouquet, it is mouthfilling and supple, with generous, ripe cherry, plum and spice flavours, showing good complexity. It's already drinking well. (From Maori Point Wines.)

 DRY $30 AV

Goldwater Marlborough Pinot Noir ★★★☆

Offering excellent value, the 2018 vintage (★★★★) was French oak-matured for nine months. An elegant, full-bodied wine, it is bright ruby, with strong, youthful cherry, plum and spice flavours, fresh acidity, gentle tannins and good immediacy. Drink now or cellar.

 DRY $25 AV

Grasshopper Rock Earnscleugh Vineyard Central Otago Pinot Noir ★★★★★

Estate-grown in Alexandra, this is typically a great buy. From vines planted in 2003, the 2017 vintage (★★★★★) was matured for 10 months in French oak barriques (28 per cent new). Still very youthful, it is deeply coloured. A powerful young red, it has intense, vibrant cherry, plum and spice flavours, savoury and earthy notes adding complexity, firm tannins, and excellent freshness, density and length. Open 2020 onwards.

Vintage	17	16	15	14	13	12	11	10
WR	7	7	7	6	6	7	7	7
Drink	19-28	19-28	19-28	19-24	19-25	19-22	19-24	19-24

 DRY $40 V+

Green Songs Waipara Valley North Canterbury Pinot Noir (★★★★)

The 2017 vintage (★★★★) from this Nelson-based producer was grown at Waipara and matured for a year in French oak casks (30 per cent new). Deep ruby, with a fresh bouquet of herbs and spices, it is full-bodied, with very good depth of cherry, plum and spice flavours, savoury, earthy notes adding complexity, and a moderately firm finish.

DRY $40 –V

Greenhough Hope Vineyard Nelson Pinot Noir ★★★★★

One of Nelson's greatest reds, at its best powerful, rich and long-lived. It is estate-grown and hand-picked on an elevated terrace of the south-eastern Waimea Plains, where the vines, planted in gravelly loam clays, have an average age of over 20 years. Yields are very low – 4 to 5 tonnes of grapes per hectare – and the wine is matured for about a year in French oak barriques (15 per cent new in 2017). Certified organic, the 2017 vintage (★★★★☆) was bottled unfined and unfiltered. Bright ruby, it is mouthfilling, with strong, plummy, spicy flavours, complex and savoury. A youthful, well-structured red with cellaring potential, it should be at its best 2021+.

DRY $46 AV

Greenhough Nelson Pinot Noir ★★★★

The 2016 vintage (★★★★) was hand-picked in the Home and Morison vineyards at Hope, and matured for a year in French oak barriques and puncheons (15 per cent new). Ruby-hued, it is fresh, with very good depth of plummy, spicy, nutty flavours, savoury and complex, and a moderately firm finish. Best drinking 2020+.

Vintage	16	15	14	13
WR	6	6	7	6
Drink	19-21	19-21	19-20	P

DRY $30 AV

Greenhough Stone's Throw Nelson Pinot Noir (★★★★)

From two sites – including the home vineyard – just a 'stone's throw' apart on the Waimea Plains, the debut 2017 vintage (★★★★) was matured for 11 months in French oak barriques (13 per cent new). Deep ruby, it is fragrant, fresh and full-bodied, with good concentration of cherry, plum and spice flavours, fresh and smooth. Best drinking mid-2020+.

DRY $30 AV

Greyrock New Zealand Pinot Noir (★★★)

The 2019 vintage (★★★) was grown in Hawke's Bay. Enjoyable young, it is ruby-hued and fragrant, with good body, fresh, generous, berry and spice flavours, gentle tannins and a smooth finish. (From Sileni.)

DRY $19 AV

Greyrock Te Koru New Zealand Pinot Noir (★★★)

Tasted at six months old, the 2019 vintage (★★★) was grown in Hawke's Bay. Ruby-hued, it is very smooth, with ripe, berryish, slightly nutty flavours, hints of herbs and spices, youthful vigour and decent depth. Best drinking mid-2020+. (From Sileni.)

DRY $20 AV

Greystone Thomas Brothers Waipara Valley Pinot Noir ★★★★★

The classy 2016 vintage (★★★★★), grown in the steep Brothers Block, was hand-picked at over 24 brix, fermented with indigenous yeasts and matured for 15 months in French oak barriques (50 per cent new). Already delicious, it is deep ruby and fragrant, with highly concentrated, vibrant cherry, plum and spice flavours, notably savoury and complex. Combining power and grace, it's still youthful; best drinking 2021+. (There is no 2017 vintage.)

Vintage	16	15
WR	7	6
Drink	19-29	19-30

 DRY $99 AV

Greystone Vineyard Ferment Pinot Noir ★★★★★

This classy red is estate-grown and hand-picked at Waipara, in North Canterbury, and made by fermenting the grapes in the vineyard, using indigenous yeasts. Matured in old oak barriques for 16 months, the 2017 vintage (★★★★★) is ruby-hued, mouthfilling and highly complex, with concentrated, notably savoury, cherryish, spicy, nutty flavours. Already very expressive, it's certified organic.

 DRY $70 AV

Greystone Waipara Valley Pinot Noir ★★★★★

Certified organic, the impressive 2017 vintage (★★★★★) was estate-grown, hand-harvested and matured for 10 months in French oak barriques. Deep ruby, with a fragrant, savoury bouquet, it is mouthfilling and highly complex, with strong, plummy, spicy, nutty flavours and a fairly firm finish. Already drinking well, it's also age-worthy and should be at its best 2021+.

 DRY $42 V+

Greywacke Marlborough Pinot Noir ★★★★★

Grown at elevated sites in the Southern Valleys, hand-harvested and matured for 18 months in French oak barriques (33 per cent new), the 2016 vintage (★★★★★) is deeply coloured, with a fragrant, fruit-packed, slightly earthy bouquet. A powerful, very youthful red, it has bold, vibrant, cherryish, plummy flavours, hints of herbs and spices, and a long, finely textured finish; best drinking 2021+. The 2017 vintage (★★★★★) is deeply coloured, with a fragrant, savoury bouquet. Full-bodied, it is powerful, with very deep cherry, plum and spice flavours, showing excellent complexity, and a finely structured, long finish. Best drinking 2022+.

Vintage	17	16	15	14	13	12	11	10
WR	6	6	6	6	6	6	6	6
Drink	19-25	19-24	19-23	19-22	19-21	19-21	P	P

DRY $47 AV

Grove Mill Wairau Valley Marlborough Pinot Noir   ★★★☆

The easy-drinking 2018 vintage (★★★☆) was matured for 10 months in French oak barriques (20 per cent new). Full, bright ruby, it is mouthfilling and sweet-fruited, with cherry, plum and spice flavours, oak complexity and a well-rounded finish. Deep ruby, the 2017 vintage (★★★☆) is a fresh, full-bodied red with generous, ripe plum/spice flavours, a hint of herbs and gentle tannins. Still youthful, it should break into full stride mid-2020+.

DRY $23 V+

Haha Marlborough Pinot Noir   ★★★

The 2018 vintage (★★☆) is an easy-drinking style, light ruby, fresh and supple. Grown in the Awatere and upper Wairau valleys, it was partly (35 per cent) barrel-aged. Enjoyable young, it is ripe and rounded, with a slightly earthy streak and solid depth of cherryish, slightly spicy and nutty flavours.

DRY $25 –V

Hans Family Estate Marlborough Pinot Noir   ★★★★☆

The 2013 vintage (★★★★) was estate-grown on the north side of the Wairau Valley, fermented with indigenous yeasts, matured for 20 months in French oak barriques, and bottled unfined and unfiltered. Full-coloured, with a hint of maturity, it is mouthfilling, savoury and concentrated, with cherry, plum and spice flavours, fresh acidity and good tannin support. Approaching its peak, it's certified organic.

DRY $53 –V

Hans Herzog Marlborough Pinot Noir Grand Duc   ★★★★★

The highly impressive 2015 vintage (★★★★★) was estate-grown in the Wairau Valley, hand-harvested, matured for 22 months in French oak barriques, and bottled unfined and unfiltered. Fragrant and deeply coloured, it is sweet-fruited and complex, with finely balanced tannins and deep cherry, plum, spice and nut flavours. A powerful, savoury red, it's currently delicious, but should be at its best 2021+. Certified organic.

DRY $69 AV

Hawkshead Bannockburn Central Otago Pinot Noir   ★★★★☆

The impressive 2015 vintage (★★★★★) was matured for 11 months in French oak casks (30 per cent new). Deep ruby, with an invitingly scented bouquet, it is mouthfilling, savoury and supple, with ripe plum, strawberry and spice flavours, hints of coffee and nuts, fine-grained tannins, and excellent depth and complexity. Deliciously rich and smooth, it's a drink-now or cellaring proposition.

DRY $65 –V

Hawkshead Central Otago Pinot Noir   ★★★☆

The 2018 vintage (★★★☆) was hand-harvested at various sites and matured for eight months in French oak barriques (25 per cent new). Ruby-hued, it is moderately rich, with fresh, plummy, spicy, slightly herbal aromas, gentle tannins, considerable complexity, and lots of drink-young charm.

DRY $44 –V

Hawkshead Gibbston First Vines Central Otago Pinot Noir   ★★★★☆

Estate-grown at Gibbston, the 2015 vintage (★★★★☆) was hand-harvested and matured for nearly a year in French oak casks (33 per cent new). Full and fairly youthful in colour, it has a fragrant, slightly herbal bouquet. Mouthfilling, vibrantly fruity and supple, with very good complexity, it's a finely poised wine with fresh acidity and a lingering finish. Best drinking 2020+.

DRY $65 –V

Huntaway Reserve Marlborough Pinot Noir   (★★★☆)

Retasted in 2019, the easy-drinking 2017 vintage (★★★☆) was barrel-matured. Bright ruby, it is full-bodied, vibrantly fruity and supple, with good depth of ripe, cherryish, spicy flavours, in a moderately complex style, drinking well now.

DRY $22 V+

Hunter's Marlborough Pinot Noir   ★★★☆

Typically a supple, charming red. The 2016 vintage (★★★☆) was grown in the Southern Valleys, hand-picked and matured for 10 months in French oak casks (25 per cent new). Light ruby, it is a gentle, savoury wine, with moderately rich cherry, plum and spice flavours, showing considerable complexity, and smooth tannins. Best drinking 2020+.

Vintage	16
WR	5
Drink	19-21

DRY $29 AV

Hunting Lodge, The, Central Otago Single Vineyard Pinot Noir   (★★★★★)

The 2017 vintage (★★★★★) from this Waimauku, West Auckland-based producer is instantly likeable. Grown and hand-picked at a single vineyard at Bendigo, it was fermented with indigenous yeasts and matured for 11 months in French oak barriques (25 per cent new). Promoted as a red 'with broad shoulders yet soft hands', it has rich, purple-flushed colour. Finely crafted, it is sweet-fruited, with concentrated, cherryish, plummy flavours, balanced acidity, gentle tannins, and a seductively rich and seamless finish. Well worth cellaring.

DRY $39 V+

Hunting Lodge, The, Expressions Marlborough Pinot Noir   (★★★☆)

Drinking well in its youth, the 2018 vintage (★★★☆) is a light to medium-bodied, elegant Pinot Noir, grown in the Southern Valleys and French oak-aged for 10 months (25 per cent new). Ruby-hued, it is supple, with ripe, cherryish, slightly spicy and nutty flavours, showing a distinct touch of complexity, and good harmony.

DRY $24 V+

Hunting Lodge, The, Marlborough Single Vineyard Pinot Noir   (★★★★☆)

The refined 2017 vintage (★★★★☆) was hand-picked in the Southern Valleys and matured for 10 months in French oak barriques (35 per cent new). Ruby-hued, it is fragrant, sweet-fruited and full-bodied, with cherry, plum, spice and nut flavours, showing good complexity, gentle tannins and a finely poised finish. Best drinking 2020+.

DRY $38 V+

Impromptu Central Otago Pinot Noir ★★★★

From Misha's Vineyard, this estate-grown Bendigo red is made in a 'more upfront, sweet-fruited' style than its similarly priced stablemate, Misha's Vineyard Cantata Pinot Noir. The age-worthy 2017 vintage (★★★★) was matured for a year in French oak hogsheads (8 per cent new). Ruby-hued, with a fragrant, savoury bouquet, it has ripe cherry, plum and spice flavours, showing good complexity, and a fairly firm finish. Best drinking mid-2020+.

Vintage	17	16	15	14	13	12	11	10
WR	6	7	7	6	6	7	5	7
Drink	19-27	19-26	19-25	19-24	19-23	19-22	19-21	19-21

 DRY $30 AV

Invivo Central Otago Pinot Noir ★★★★

The 2018 vintage (★★★☆) is already enjoyable. Fragrant and savoury, with fullish, slightly developed colour, it is moderately rich, with berryish, spicy, nutty flavours, oak complexity and a fairly firm finish. Drink now or cellar.

 DRY $25 V+

Invivo Michelle's Central Otago Pinot Noir ★★★★☆

Already drinking well, but also age-worthy, the 2017 vintage (★★★★☆) is rare – only five barrels were made. Grown at Bannockburn, it is mouthfilling, very sweet-fruited and supple, with deep, well-ripened cherry and plum flavours, a hint of liquorice, savoury notes adding complexity, gentle acidity and a rich, well-rounded finish.

Vintage	17	16	15	14
WR	7	7	7	7
Drink	19-25	19-25	19-24	19-23

 DRY $40 AV

Jackson Estate Gum Emperor Single Vineyard
Waihopai Valley Marlborough Pinot Noir ★★★★

Still on sale, the 2013 vintage (★★★★) is ruby-hued, with some development showing. Firmly structured, it is savoury, with plummy, berryish, nutty flavours, fresh acidity and good complexity. Best drinking mid-2020+.

Vintage	13
WR	6
Drink	20-30

 DRY $48 –V

Jackson Estate Homestead Marlborough Pinot Noir ★★★☆

Offering good value, the 2017 vintage was partly barrel-aged. Bright ruby, it has a fragrant, slightly herbal bouquet, leading into a full-bodied wine with good concentration of cherry, plum and spice flavours, slightly earthy notes adding complexity, and a fairly firm finish. Best drinking 2021+.

Vintage	17
WR	4
Drink	20-22

DRY $23 V+

Jackson Estate Somerset Single Vineyard
Waihopai Valley Marlborough Pinot Noir

Still on sale, the 2013 vintage (★★★) is mature, with strong flavours showing some savoury complexity, but is also slightly austere, with a lack of fruit sweetness and firm, grippy tannins.

DRY $50 –V

Jackson Estate Vintage Widow Marlborough Pinot Noir

Offering good value, the 2016 vintage (★★★★☆) was hand-harvested in the Southern Valleys and matured in French oak barriques. Bright ruby, it is highly fragrant, sweet-fruited and supple, with strong cherry, plum and spice flavours, showing very good complexity. An elegant, savoury red, it's delicious now, but age-worthy too. The 2015 vintage (★★★★☆) is also good value. Fragrant and full-coloured, it is mouthfilling, sweet-fruited, savoury and supple, with cherry, plum and spice flavours, showing excellent complexity and harmony. Drink now or cellar.

Vintage	16	15
WR	5	5
Drink	20-30	20-30

DRY $34 V+

Johanneshof Maybern Single Vineyard Marlborough Pinot Noir

Estate-grown on a steep (30 degrees), north-facing slope at Koromiko, between Picton and Blenheim, the 2016 vintage (★★★★) of this distinctive wine was hand-picked, fermented with indigenous yeasts and barrel-aged. Deep ruby, it is full-bodied, sweet-fruited and moderately firm, with strong plum, spice, herb and nut flavours, oak complexity and good length. Best drinking 2020+.

DRY $43 –V

John Forrest Collection Bannockburn Pinot Noir ★★★★★

The powerful 2014 vintage (★★★★★) is a dense, youthful red, matured for 15 months in French oak casks (30 per cent new). Deeply coloured, it has bold, very ripe cherry and plum flavours, a hint of liquorice, and good tannin backbone. Built for the long haul, it's well worth cellaring to 2021+.

DRY $65 AV

John Forrest Collection Waitaki Valley Pinot Noir

On sale now, the 2013 vintage (★★★★) is full-coloured, with some development showing, and a fragrant, spicy, slightly leafy bouquet. Showing good concentration, it has plummy, herbal flavours, excellent complexity, and current-drinking appeal.

DRY $65 –V

Johner Estate Gladstone Pinot Noir ★★★★

Estate-grown in the northern Wairarapa, matured for a year in French oak barrels (25 per cent new), and bottled unfined and unfiltered, the 2017 vintage (★★★★) is a ruby-hued, full-bodied red, showing good complexity. It is savoury, with generous, plummy, spicy flavours, seasoned with nutty oak, a hint of herbs, and a well-rounded finish. Best drinking mid-2020+.

Vintage	17
WR	5
Drink	19-25

DRY $39 AV

Johner Estate Gladstone Reserve Pinot Noir ★★★★☆

The 2016 vintage (★★★★☆) is a single-vineyard, estate-grown Wairarapa red, hand-harvested from the oldest vines, matured for a year in French oak barrels (80 per cent new), and bottled unfined and unfiltered. Ruby-hued, it is mouthfilling, savoury and supple, with concentrated cherry, plum, spice and nut flavours, showing excellent complexity and harmony.

Vintage	16	15	14
WR	6	7	7
Drink	19-27	19-26	19-25

DRY $60 –V

Johner Estate Wairarapa Pinot Noir ★★★☆

Labelled as a 'soft and very approachable' style, the 2017 vintage (★★★☆) was matured for a year in seasoned oak barrels. Ruby-hued, it is fragrant and mouthfilling, with cherryish, spicy, slightly nutty flavours, hints of herbs and tamarillos, considerable complexity and a smooth finish. Drink now onwards.

Vintage	17
WR	5
Drink	19-22

DRY $26 AV

Judge Rock Alexandra Central Otago Pinot Noir ★★★★☆

This single-vineyard red is estate-grown at Alexandra and French oak-matured. The 2015 vintage (★★★★☆) is ruby-hued, with mouthfilling body, fresh acidity, generous cherry, plum, dried-herb and spice flavours, and fine-grained tannins. An age-worthy wine, it's likely to be at its best 2020+.

DRY $45 AV

Jules Taylor Marlborough Pinot Noir ★★★★

Made in a 'fruit-forward' style, the 2018 vintage (★★★★) was mostly hand-picked and partly barrel-aged. Bright ruby, it is youthful, with very good body and depth of ripe cherry, plum and spice flavours, nutty, savoury notes adding complexity, and a well-rounded finish. It needs a bit more time; open mid-2020+.

Vintage	18	17	16	15	14
WR	5	6	6	6	6
Drink	19-23	19-22	19-21	19-20	19-20

DRY $35 AV

Jules Taylor OTQ Limited Release Single Vineyard Marlborough Pinot Noir   ★★★★☆

Made 'On The Quiet', the bold 2017 vintage (★★★★☆) was grown in the Wrekin Vineyard, in the Fairhall Valley, and matured in French oak barriques (33 per cent new). Full-coloured, it is mouthfilling, fresh and fruit-packed, with concentrated plum and spice flavours, a hint of liquorice, and a fairly firm finish. Still very youthful, it's well worth cellaring to 2021+.

Vintage	17	16	15
WR	6	6	6
Drink	19-24	19-22	19-20

DRY $45 –V

Kahurangi Estate Mt Arthur Reserve Nelson Pinot Noir   (★★★★)

The fresh, youthful 2017 vintage (★★★★) is full-coloured, with mouthfilling body, very good depth of ripe plum, spice and nut flavours, oak complexity and a moderately firm finish. Still unfolding, it should be at its best mid-2021+.

DRY $35 AV

Kaimira Estate Vintner's Selection Brightwater Pinot Noir   ★★★☆

Certified organic, the youthful 2017 vintage (★★★★) was estate-grown in Nelson and matured for 10 months in French oak barrels (20 per cent new). Deep ruby, with a spicy fragrance, it has strong, fresh, berryish, spicy flavours, showing good complexity, and obvious cellaring potential. Best drinking 2021+.

DRY $30 –V

Kalex Alex Kaufman Central Otago Pinot Noir   ★★★★☆

The impressive 2015 vintage (★★★★☆) was hand-harvested and matured in French oak casks (33 per cent new). Deeply coloured, it is mouthfilling, with concentrated, cherryish, spicy flavours, complex and savoury, and a lasting, finely structured finish. Retasted in 2019, it is still very fresh and likely to be at its best for drinking 2021+.

DRY $40 AV

Kereru Martinborough Pinot Noir   (★★★★)

Hand-picked and barrel-matured, the 2014 vintage (★★★★) is bright ruby, with a fragrant bouquet. Drinking well now, it has ripe cherry, plum and spice flavours, showing very good complexity and depth, and a smooth finish. (From Porters Estate.)

DRY $35 AV

Kim Crawford Marlborough Pinot Noir   ★★★☆

Ruby-hued, the 2016 vintage (★★★☆) is a mouthfilling, moderately complex style, with good depth of ripe cherry, plum and spice flavours, slightly toasty and nutty notes, and a fairly firm finish.

DRY $24 V+

Kina Beach Vineyard Nelson Pinot Noir   (★★☆)

Still on sale, the easy-drinking 2015 vintage (★★☆) is a single-vineyard red, barrel-aged for a year and bottled unfined and unfiltered. It has light, slightly developed colour, a slightly leafy bouquet, and a herbal thread running through its cherryish, plummy flavours. Fruity and smooth, it's ready to roll.

Vintage	15
WR	7
Drink	19-20

 DRY $29 –V

Koha Marlborough Pinot Noir   ★★★

The 2018 vintage (★★☆) has lightish, slightly developed colour. Matured in oak barrels (26 per cent new), it has decent depth of ripe cherry and spice flavours, fresh acidity, earthy notes and a fairly firm finish. (From te Pā.)

Vintage	18
WR	6
Drink	19-29

 DRY $24 –V

Konrad Marlborough Pinot Noir   ★★★☆

Certified organic, the 2016 vintage (★★★☆) is a single-vineyard red, estate-grown in the Waihopai Valley and matured in French oak barriques (partly new). Deep ruby, it is sweet-fruited, with strong, vibrant, plummy flavours to the fore, moderate complexity, and some cellaring potential. Best drinking 2020+.

 DRY $30 –V

Kōparepare Marlborough Pinot Noir   (★★★)

Enjoyable now, the 2017 vintage (★★★) is made by Whitehaven for LegaSea, to help fund its work to restore inshore fisheries to abundance. Tasted in mid-2019, it is a light ruby, medium-bodied style,with ripe cherry, plum and spice flavours, slightly savoury notes adding complexity and a well-rounded finish. Priced right.

 DRY $20 AV

Kumeu River Hunting Hill Pinot Noir   ★★★★

Grown on the slopes above Mate's Vineyard, directly over the road from the winery at Kumeu, the 2017 vintage (★★★★☆), barrel-matured for a year, is a rare example of classy Pinot Noir from the Auckland region. Deep, bright ruby, it is fragrant and vibrantly fruity, with generous, cherryish, plummy flavours, fresh acidity and a lingering, well-rounded finish. Still youthful, it's a refined red, well worth cellaring to 2020+.

Vintage	17
WR	7
Drink	19-21

DRY $50 –V

Kumeu River Rays Road Pinot Noir   (★★★★)

From the company's elevated, north-facing vineyard in Hawke's Bay, the 2018 vintage (★★★★) was hand-picked and matured for a year in French oak barrels. Bright ruby, it is savoury and supple, with ripe cherry, plum, spice and nut flavours, showing very good complexity, and fine-grained tannins. Less exuberantly fruity than South Island styles, it's well worth cellaring. Best drinking 2021+.

Vintage	18
WR	5
Drink	20-25

Kumeu Village Hawke's Bay Pinot Noir   (★★★☆)

The 2018 vintage (★★★☆) was estate-grown at a cool, elevated site in Hawke's Bay, and handled without oak barrels. A light to medium-bodied, supple red, it has good depth of lively cherry, plum and spice flavours, finely balanced for early drinking. Good value.

Kuru Kuru Central Otago Pinot Noir   ★★★★☆

Drinking well now, the 2016 vintage (★★★★) is a blend of Bendigo and Alexandra grapes, French oak-aged for nine months. Ruby-hued, with a hint of development, it is mouthfilling and savoury, with generous, spicy, nutty flavours, balanced tannins and very good complexity. (From Tarras Vineyards.)

Lake Chalice Marlborough Pinot Noir   ★★★☆

Enjoyable young, the 2016 vintage (★★★☆) was grown in the Eyrie Vineyard, in the Southern Valleys. Bright ruby, it is mouthfilling, sweet-fruited, vibrant and smooth, with gentle tannins and ripe cherry, plum and spice flavours, showing very good depth.

DRY $20 V+

Lake Chalice The Falcon Marlborough Pinot Noir   (★★★☆)

Bargain-priced, the 2017 vintage (★★★☆) was grown principally in the Eyrie Vineyard, in the Waihopai Valley, and matured for eight months in French oak barriques. Deep, bright ruby, it is fragrant and supple, with mouthfilling body, fresh acidity, very good depth of youthful cherry/plum flavours and well-integrated oak. Best drinking 2021+.

Lake Chalice The Raptor Marlborough Pinot Noir   ★★★★

Fleshy and flavoursome, the 2016 vintage (★★★★) is a single-vineyard red, grown in the lower Waihopai Valley. Bright ruby, it is mouthfilling and savoury, with good concentration of cherry, plum and spice flavours and a finely balanced, smooth finish. Enjoyable now, it should be at its best 2020+.

Lake Hayes Central Otago Pinot Noir   ★★★★

From Amisfield, the attractive 2016 vintage (★★★★) was estate-grown at Pisa and partly barrel-aged. Deep ruby, with a fragrant bouquet, hinting of herbs and spices, it is full-bodied, generous and supple, with ripe-fruit flavours, showing good delicacy and harmony, some savoury complexity, and a well-rounded finish.

DRY $30 AV

Last Shepherd, The, Central Otago Pinot Noir   ★★★☆

Fresh and supple, the youthful 2018 vintage (★★★☆) is already enjoyable, but worth cellaring. Bright, light ruby, it is a lively, skilfully balanced red, with moderately concentrated, ripe cherry, plum and spice flavours, gentle tannins and an easy-drinking charm. (From Pernod Ricard NZ.)

DRY $25 AV

Lawson's Dry Hills Marlborough Pinot Noir   ★★★☆

The 2018 vintage (★★★☆) was estate-grown and matured for 10 months in French oak barrels (10 per cent new). Bright ruby, it is mouthfilling, with good depth of cherry, plum, spice and nut flavours, showing considerable complexity, and a moderately firm finish. Best drinking 2021+.

Vintage	18	17
WR	6	6
Drink	19-21	19-21

DRY $25 AV

Lawson's Dry Hills Reserve Marlborough Pinot Noir   ★★★★☆

Still very youthful, the great-value 2017 vintage (★★★★★) was grown at two sites in the Waihopai Valley and matured in French oak barriques (25 per cent new). Deep ruby, it is mouthfilling, concentrated and fruit-packed, with deep, plummy, spicy flavours, a firm underlay of tannin and the structure to mature well. Best drinking 2021+. The 2015 vintage (★★★★☆), retasted in 2019, is also a very good buy. Deep ruby, with a fragrant, complex bouquet, it is full-bodied, with generous, ripe plum/spice flavours, finely balanced tannins and a long life ahead.

Vintage	17
WR	7
Drink	19-25

DRY $30 V+

Left Field Marlborough Pinot Noir   ★★★☆

Offering good value, the 2017 vintage (★★★☆) was matured in seasoned French oak barrels (75 per cent) and tanks (25 per cent). Ruby-hued, it is vibrantly fruity, with good depth of plummy, spicy flavours, finely balanced for early drinking. (From Te Awa.)

Vintage	17
WR	5
Drink	19-22

DRY $18 V+

Leo Nelson Pinot Noir

The 2017 vintage (★★★☆) comes 'with 13 per cent alcohol by volume and 750 ml of enjoyment'. Enjoyable young, it is a bright ruby, freshly scented wine, with very good body and depth of vibrant, plummy flavours, showing a distinct touch of complexity.

DRY $20 V+

Leveret Estate Hawke's Bay Pinot Noir

Ruby-hued, the 2015 vintage (★★★) was barrel-aged for a year. A mouthfilling, supple red, enjoyable now, it has fresh, gentle, strawberryish, spicy flavours and a touch of complexity.

DRY $23 AV

Leveret Estate Marlborough Pinot Noir ★★★

Already drinking well, the 2018 vintage (★★★) was barrel-aged for a year. It has lightish, slightly developed colour. Full-bodied, it has nutty, spicy flavours, showing considerable complexity.

Vintage	14	13
WR	5	6
Drink	19-20	P

DRY $23 AV

Leveret Estate Reserve Hawke's Bay Pinot Noir ★★★☆

Still on sale, the generous 2014 vintage (★★★★) has bright, deep ruby colour. Mouthfilling and vibrantly fruity, it is maturing well, with good concentration of fresh, slightly spicy and nutty flavours, showing considerable complexity, and a smooth finish.

Vintage	14	13
WR	7	7
Drink	19-24	P

DRY $27 AV

Leveret Estate Reserve Marlborough Pinot Noir ★★★

The 2015 vintage (★★★☆) was matured for two years in French oak casks (63 per cent new). Bright ruby, it is full-bodied and supple, with good flavour depth, savoury, nutty notes adding complexity, and lots of current-drinking appeal.

DRY $27 –V

Lime Rock Central Hawke's Bay Pinot Noir ★★★★

I tasted the 2013 to 2016 vintages in 2017. Matured in French oak barriques (20 to 40 per cent new), the wines were all drinking well, in an elegant, mid-weight style with vivid varietal characteristics and proven aging ability. The 2016 vintage (★★★★) is ruby-hued and sweet-fruited, with vibrant cherry, plum and spice flavours, some funky notes adding complexity, and a long finish. The 2015 vintage (★★★★) is ruby-hued, savoury, ripe and supple, with very good complexity.

Vintage	16	15	14	13
WR	7	6	7	7
Drink	19-30	19-20	19-24	19-24

DRY $42 –V

Lime Rock White Knuckle Hill Central Hawke's Bay Pinot Noir   ★★★★☆

Showing plenty of personality, the 2013 vintage (★★★★☆) was matured in French oak barriques (20 per cent new). Ruby-hued, with a hint of maturity, it is very savoury, with mouthfilling body, dense, ripe cherry, plum and spice flavours, good tannin support, and excellent complexity and length.

Vintage	13
WR	7
Drink	19-30

 DRY $59 –V

Lindis River Central Otago Pinot Noir   (★★★★☆)

Estate-grown in the Ardgour Valley, at Tarras, the 2014 vintage (★★★★☆) was hand-picked and French oak-aged for a year. Ruby-hued, it is still youthful, with a fragrant bouquet. An elegant, supple red, it has vibrant cherry, plum and spice flavours, showing good, savoury complexity, fresh acidity and the structure to mature well; best drinking 2020+.

 DRY $40 AV

Loop Road Central Otago Pinot Noir   ★★★★

Enjoyable young, but also well worth cellaring, the 2017 vintage (★★★★) was grown in the Bendigo and Pisa districts of the Cromwell Basin and barrel-aged for 10 months. Bright ruby, it is fragrant, full-bodied and smooth, with generous, ripe cherry, plum and spice flavours, savoury notes adding complexity, and excellent harmony. (From Quartz Reef.)

Vintage	17
WR	6
Drink	19-22

 DRY $35 AV

Lowburn Ferry Home Block Central Otago Pinot Noir   ★★★★★

This single-vineyard red is estate-grown and hand-picked at Lowburn, in the Cromwell Basin. The elegant 2016 vintage (★★★★☆) was matured for 10 months in French oak barriques (30 per cent new). Deep ruby, it is mouthfilling and concentrated, with ripe cherry, plum and spice flavours, vibrant and youthful, well-integrated oak, fresh acidity, and a supple, long finish. Best drinking 2020 onwards.

Vintage	16	15	14	13	12
WR	7	7	7	7	7
Drink	19-23	19-22	19-21	19-20	19-20

 DRY $50 AV

Luminary, The, Wairarapa Pinot Noir   ★★★☆

From Palliser Estate, the 2017 vintage (★★★) is designed for sale in supermarkets. A blend of fruit grown at Gladstone, in the northern Wairarapa (89 per cent) and Martinborough (11 per cent), it's a lightly oaked wine; only 11 per cent was barrel-aged. Ruby-hued, it's an easy-drinking style, light and supple, with gentle, ripe, plummy flavours, fresh acidity, and some spicy, earthy notes adding a touch of complexity.

 DRY $20 V+

Luna Blue Rock Vineyard Martinborough Pinot Noir   (★★★★★)

From a hillside vineyard originally planted in 1986, the graceful 2016 vintage (★★★★★) was matured for a year in French oak casks (30 per cent new), and bottled unfined and unfiltered. Bright ruby, it is a perfumed, 'feminine' style, with generous cherry, plum and spice flavours, a hint of herbs, and a real sense of youthful drive. A wine of substance, poise and potential, it should be at its best 2020+.

Vintage	16
WR	5
Drink	19-25

 DRY $50 AV

Luna Eclipse Martinborough Pinot Noir   (★★★★★)

The powerful 2016 vintage (★★★★★) was grown on the Martinborough Terrace, matured for a year in French oak casks (30 per cent new), and bottled unfined and unfiltered. The colour is deep and youthful; the palate is substantial and firmly structured, with mouthfilling body, generous, ripe, plummy, spicy, slightly earthy flavours, showing excellent complexity, good tannin backbone, and obvious cellaring potential. Best drinking 2021+.

Vintage	16
WR	5
Drink	19-25

 DRY $50 AV

Luna Martinborough Pinot Noir   ★★★★

Offering top value, the 2017 vintage (★★★★) was made for early enjoyment, but is age-worthy too. Matured for a year in French oak casks (10 per cent new), it is ruby-hued and full-bodied, with strong, ripe, berryish, plummy, spicy flavours and a savoury, moderately firm finish. Best drinking mid-2020+.

Vintage	17	16
WR	6	5
Drink	19-23	19-22

 DRY $24 V+

LV by Louis Vavasour Marlborough Pinot Noir   (★★★★)

Deep ruby, the attractive, easy-drinking 2016 vintage (★★★★) is ensconced in a very heavy, punted bottle, but the wine is lighter. Mouthfilling and supple, it has generous plum, herb and spice flavours, showing good ripeness, complexity and harmony, and a smooth finish.

 DRY $64 –V

Madam Sass Central Otago Pinot Noir   (★★★☆)

The 2017 vintage (★★★☆) was estate-grown in the Claim 431 Vineyard at Bendigo, and matured in an even split of tanks and seasoned oak barrels. Deep, bright ruby, it is full-bodied and fruit-packed, with vibrant cherry, plum and spice flavours. A generous red with lots of youthful impact, it should be at its best 2020+. (From Accolade Wines.)

DRY $25 AV

Mahi Marlborough Pinot Noir ★★★★

The refined, finely textured 2017 vintage (★★★★) was hand-picked at three sites, fermented with indigenous yeasts, and matured for 13 months in French oak barrels. Bright ruby, it is a fragrant, supple, youthful wine, with ripe plum, spice and nut flavours, showing good complexity, and a lingering finish. Best drinking 2020+.

Vintage	18	17
WR	6	6
Drink	19-24	19-24

DRY $34 AV

Main Divide North Canterbury Pinot Noir ★★★★

A consistently rewarding, great-value red from Pegasus Bay. The 2016 vintage (★★★★) was grown at Waipara. Matured for 18 months in French oak barriques, it is bright ruby, fragrant and supple, with generous, plummy, slightly nutty flavours, well-integrated oak adding complexity, and lots of current-drinking appeal. As good as many $35 Pinot Noirs, it should be at its best mid-2020+.

Vintage	16	15	14	13	12	11	10
WR	7	7	6	7	7	5	7
Drink	19-26	19-28	19-23	19-23	19-20	P	19-20

DRY $25 V+

Main Divide Tehau Reserve Waipara Valley Pinot Noir ★★★★

Still on sale, the attractive 2014 vintage (★★★★) was fermented with indigenous yeasts and matured for 18 months in French oak barriques (30 per cent new). Deep ruby, it is mouthfilling, with generous, plummy, spicy flavours and ripe, supple tannins. (From Pegasus Bay.)

Vintage	14
WR	6
Drink	19-24

DRY $33 AV

Manu Marlborough Pinot Noir (★★★☆)

The ruby-hued, fragrant 2017 vintage (★★★☆) was barrel-aged for eight months. Age-worthy, it is lively, with good depth of berryish, spicy flavours, showing some savoury complexity, and finely balanced tannins. Drink now or cellar. (From Steve Bird.)

DRY $28 AV

Maori Point Central Otago Pinot Noir ★★★★☆

The age-worthy 2016 vintage (★★★★) of this single-vineyard wine was grown at Tarras, in the Cromwell Basin, and matured in French oak barrels (24 per cent new). Ruby-hued, it is fragrant and savoury, with youthful, ripe, plummy, gently spicy and nutty flavours, oak complexity and a finely balanced finish. Best drinking 2020+. The 2017 vintage (★★★★★) is the finest yet. Deep ruby, it is fresh, full-bodied, savoury and supple, with concentrated, ripe cherry, plum and spice flavours, showing very good complexity, and a finely poised, long finish. Already delicious, it should be at its best 2021+.

Vintage	17	16
WR	7	5
Drink	21-25	20-23

DRY $42 AV

Maori Point Grand Reserve Professors' Block Central Otago Pinot Noir   (★★★★☆)

Delicious now, the 2015 vintage (★★★★☆) is a rare, estate-grown red, matured for two years in four French oak barrels (50 per cent new), and bottled unfined and unfiltered. Ruby-hued, it is an elegant, savoury, supple wine, with strong cherry, plum and spice flavours, nutty and complex. Showing some maturity, it's a drink-now or cellaring proposition.

DRY $70 –V

Maori Point Reserve Central Otago Pinot Noir   (★★★★★)

The fragrant, silky-textured 2014 vintage (★★★★★) was estate-grown at Tarras, in the Cromwell Basin. Barrel-selected, it is a delicious, very harmonious and 'complete' red, with deep, ripe plum, cherry and nut flavours, savoury and lingering. Drink now or cellar.

DRY $64 AV

Map Maker Marlborough Pinot Noir   ★★★☆

From Staete Landt, the 2016 vintage (★★★☆) was estate-grown and hand-picked at Rapaura, and matured in French oak barriques. Bright ruby, it is attractively scented, with ripe cherry, plum and spice flavours, and some savoury notes adding a touch of complexity. Drink now to 2020.

Vintage	16
WR	5
Drink	19-23

DRY $26 AV

Margrain Home Block Martinborough Pinot Noir   ★★★★☆

The elegant 2016 vintage (★★★★☆) was harvested from mature vines and matured in French oak barriques. Deeply coloured, it is still youthful, with concentrated, vibrant cherry, plum and spice flavours, a hint of liquorice, savoury notes adding complexity, and good tannin backbone. Well worth cellaring, it should be at its best 2021+.

DRY $45 –V

Margrain Reserve Martinborough Pinot Noir   ★★★★☆

The classy 2015 vintage (★★★★★) is a single-vineyard wine, matured for 18 months in French oak barriques (30 per cent new). A powerful young red, it is deep ruby, with mouthfilling body, strong, very ripe plum/spice flavours, a hint of liquorice, fairly firm tannins and a lasting finish. Best drinking 2020+.

Vintage	15
WR	7
Drink	19-28

DRY $65 –V

Margrain River's Edge Martinborough Pinot Noir   ★★★☆

Designed for early drinking, this wine is estate-grown and 'barrel selected for its smoothness and charm'. The attractive 2016 vintage (★★★★) is ruby-hued, full-bodied, generous and supple, with fresh, cherryish, plummy, spicy flavours and a finely textured finish. Best drinking 2020.

DRY $26 AV

Martinborough Vineyard Home Block Pinot Noir ★★★★★

The elegant, silky-textured 2017 vintage (★★★★★) was matured for a year in French oak casks (23 per cent new). Deep ruby, with a perfumed, savoury bouquet, it is mouthfilling and supple, with excellent weight and concentration of cherry, plum, spice and nut flavours. A refined, complex, very harmonious red, it's already delicious, but well worth cellaring.

Vintage	17	16	15
WR	7	7	7
Drink	19-30	19-31	19-30

DRY $63 AV

Martinborough Vineyard Marie Zelie Reserve Pinot Noir ★★★★★

The intriguing 2013 vintage (★★★★★) is the first since 2010. Hand-picked from the oldest vines and matured in French oak barriques, it is all about refinement, rather than sheer power. Light ruby in hue, it is very finely perfumed, with cherry, red-berry and nut flavours, highly complex, very savoury and harmonious. A gentle, persuasive, persistent wine, it's likely to be at its best 2020+.

DRY $225 –V

Martinborough Vineyard Te Tera Pinot Noir ★★★★

Te Tera ('The Other') is designed for early drinking, compared to its stablemates. The 2018 vintage (★★★★) was matured for 10 months in French oak barrels (14 per cent new). Bright ruby, it is softly mouthfilling, with ripe cherry, plum and spice flavours, oak complexity, and very gentle tannins. Already highly enjoyable, it's an excellent example of the 'drink-young' style.

Vintage	18	17
WR	7	7
Drink	19-25	19-22

DRY $30 AV

Matahiwi Estate Holly Wairarapa Pinot Noir ★★★★

The 2018 vintage (★★★★) was matured for a year in French oak casks (23 per cent new). Bright ruby, it is full-bodied and supple, with fresh, generous cherry and spice flavours, hints of tamarillos and nuts, oak complexity and a smooth finish. Still youthful, it should be at its best 2021+.

Vintage	18
WR	6
Drink	22-28

DRY $40 –V

Matt Connell Bendigo Single Vineyard Central Otago Pinot Noir ★★★★★

The lovely 2017 vintage (★★★★★) was matured for 10 months in French oak barriques (25 per cent new). It's a rare wine – only 820 bottles were produced. Deep ruby, it is full-bodied, concentrated and structured, with rich cherry, plum, spice and nut flavours, showing excellent complexity, and a finely poised, persistent finish. Best drinking 2021+.

DRY $67 AV

Matt Connell Wines Rendition Central Otago Pinot Noir   ★★★★★

Mouthfilling, richly flavoured and supple, the 2017 vintage (★★★★★) was grown at Bendigo and Lowburn, hand-harvested, matured for 10 months in French oak barriques (25 per cent new), and bottled unfined and unfiltered. Deep ruby, floral, vibrant and sweet-fruited, it is very finely textured, with concentrated, plummy, spicy flavours, hints of herbs and nuts, and well-integrated oak adding complexity. An age-worthy red, it's also delicious young.

DRY $44 V+

Maude Central Otago Pinot Noir   ★★★★☆

The 2017 vintage (★★★★☆) is a deep ruby, finely structured red, hand-harvested, matured for 10 months in French oak barriques (30 per cent new), and bottled unfined and unfiltered. Poised and youthful, it is fragrant and full-bodied, with fresh, ripe cherry, plum and spice flavours, good complexity and obvious potential; best drinking 2021+. The 2018 vintage (★★★★☆) was French oak-aged (25 per cent new). Bright ruby, it is fragrant, fresh and savoury, with generous cherry, plum and spice flavours, oak complexity and fine-grained tannins. Open mid-2021+.

Vintage	18	17	16	15	14
WR	5	7	7	5	7
Drink	19-25	20-30	20-28	19-22	19-28

DRY $38 V+

Maude Mt Maude Vineyard Wanaka Reserve Central Otago Pinot Noir   ★★★★★

Estate-grown at Wanaka, this wine is hand-picked from vines planted in 1994. The 2015 vintage (★★★★☆) was matured for 16 months in French oak casks (40 per cent new). Ruby-hued, it is floral, savoury and complex, with strawberry and spice flavours, hints of dried herbs and nuts, and a fairly firm finish. A distinctive, very age-worthy red, with some ethereal notes, it should be at its best 2020+.

Vintage	15	14	13	12	11	10
WR	5	7	6	5	4	7
Drink	20-24	20-26	20-24	19-24	19-22	19-22

DRY $65 AV

Maude Mt Maude Wanaka Reserve EMW Pinot Noir   (★★★★☆)

'EMW' means 'East meets West' – in this case, two blocks in the estate's Mt Maude Vineyard at Wanaka, in Central Otago. Matured in French oak casks (10 per cent new), the 2017 vintage (★★★★☆) is deeply coloured, with a fragrant, slightly herbal bouquet. A very age-worthy, structured red, it is mouthfilling, with berry, herb and spice flavours, showing excellent complexity, and a firm foundation of tannin. Best drinking 2021+.

DRY $45 –V

Maude Mt Maude Wanaka Reserve Kids Block Pinot Noir   (★★★★★)

Invitingly fragrant, the 2016 vintage (★★★★★) is based on estate-grown vines planted in 2000. Matured in French oak casks (30 per cent new), it is still unfolding. Ruby-hued, savoury and mouthfilling, with ripe cherry, plum, spice and nut flavours, finely balanced tannins and impressive complexity, it should be at its best 2021+.

DRY $45 AV

Maui Waipara Pinot Noir

The 2018 vintage (★★☆) has lightish colour, showing considerable development. It's a full-bodied, slightly rustic and austere wine, with plenty of firm, spicy flavour, but lacks a bit of charm. (From Tiki.)

DRY $20 –V

Mediator, The, by Urlar Gladstone Pinot Noir

Delicious young, the 2017 vintage (★★★★) was grown in the northern Wairarapa, hand-harvested and matured in French oak casks (15 per cent new). Full, bright ruby, it is scented and supple, with good intensity of vibrant cherry and plum flavours, and a real sense of youthful drive.

DRY $33 AV

Milcrest Estate Nelson Pinot Noir

The 2016 vintage (★★★☆) is enjoyable now. Full-coloured, it is fragrant, generous and smooth, with ripe, plummy, slightly savoury flavours.

DRY $29 –V

Milcrest Estate Reserve Nelson Pinot Noir (★★★★)

The 2014 vintage (★★★★) was grown on the Kina Peninsula and matured for 11 months in French oak barrels. Full-bodied and smooth, it has strong, ripe cherry, plum and spice flavours, nutty and savoury notes adding complexity, and good tannin support. It's enjoyable now.

DRY $36 AV

Mills Reef Reserve Marlborough Pinot Noir

The 2017 vintage (★★★☆) was matured for three months in French (mostly) and American oak hogsheads (27 per cent new). Bright ruby, it is a fresh, medium-bodied red, buoyantly fruity, with cherryish, plummy, slightly spicy flavours, showing very good depth. Best drinking 2020+.

Vintage	17
WR	5
Drink	19-21

DRY $25 AV

Millton Clos de Ste Anne Naboth's Vineyard Pinot Noir –
see Clos de Ste Anne Naboth's Vineyard Pinot Noir

Millton La Cote Gisborne Pinot Noir

Certified organic, the 2016 vintage (★★★★☆) was estate-grown in the Clos de Ste Anne vineyard, hand-picked, barrel-aged, and bottled unfined and unfiltered. A wine of real presence, it is bright ruby, very savoury and harmonious, with layers of ripe, plummy, spicy, nutty flavours. Offering fine value, it's already delicious. Certified organic.

Vintage	16	15	14
WR	6	6	6
Drink	19-21	19-20	P

DRY $32 V+

Misha's Vineyard Cantata Central Otago Pinot Noir   ★★★★☆

Designed principally for 'on-premise' sale in restaurants, this label offers consistently good value. Estate-grown at Bendigo, the 2017 vintage (★★★★) was fermented with indigenous yeasts and matured in French oak hogsheads (14 per cent new). Ruby-hued, it is floral and supple, with mouthfilling body and fresh, youthful cherry, plum and spice flavours, showing very good ripeness and complexity. A vibrantly fruity, finely textured, very harmonious red, it's already drinking well, but should be at its best 2020+.

Vintage	17	16	15
WR	6	7	7
Drink	19-29	19-28	19-28

DRY $30 V+

Misha's Vineyard The High Note Central Otago Pinot Noir   ★★★★★

Estate-grown at Bendigo, in the Cromwell Basin, the very graceful 2017 vintage (★★★★★) was hand-harvested from 14-year-old vines and matured for a year in French oak hogsheads (28 per cent new). Deep ruby, it is invitingly fragrant, with cherryish, plummy, spicy, slightly nutty flavours, showing impressive complexity, fresh acidity and a lingering, savoury, supple finish. Still youthful, it's well worth cellaring to 2022+.

Vintage	17	16	15	14	13	12	11	10
WR	6	7	7	6	6	7	5	7
Drink	19-28	19-29	19-28	19-27	19-26	19-25	19-22	19-23

DRY $45 AV

Misha's Vineyard Verismo Central Otago Pinot Noir   ★★★★☆

This 'reserve style', estate-grown Bendigo red is oak-aged longer, with greater exposure to new oak, than its High Note stablemate. On sale now, the 2013 vintage (★★★★★) was matured for 18 months in French oak hogsheads (40 per cent new). It has deep, moderately youthful colour and a highly fragrant, complex bouquet. Set for a long life, it has concentrated plum, spice and nut flavours, showing lovely balance and depth, supple tannins and a powerful finish.

Vintage	13	12	11	10
WR	6	7	5	7
Drink	19-27	19-26	19-24	19-24

DRY $75 –V

Mission Barrique Reserve Marlborough Pinot Noir   ★★★★

Enjoyable young, the 2018 vintage (★★★★) was estate-grown in the Awatere Valley and matured for a year in French oak casks. Bright ruby, it is fresh and supple, with generous, ripe cherry, plum and spice flavours, a hint of herbs, oak complexity, gentle tannins and good harmony. Best drinking 2021+.

Vintage	18
WR	5
Drink	20-28

DRY $30 AV

Mission Marlborough Pinot Noir (★★★)

Already drinking well, the 2018 vintage (★★★) is a 'fruit-driven' (lightly oaked) style. Bright, light ruby, it is medium-bodied, with good depth of fresh, berryish, slightly spicy flavours, showing a touch of savoury, nutty complexity, and a smooth finish.

DRY $18 V+

Mission Vineyard Selection Marlborough Pinot Noir ★★★☆

Offering good value, the 2016 vintage (★★★★) was estate-grown in the Awatere Valley. Full, bright ruby, it has a fragrant bouquet of herbs and spices. Mouthfilling, with generous, plummy, spicy flavours, showing good complexity, and a lingering finish, it's a drink-now or cellaring proposition.

DRY $22 V+

Misty Cove Signature Marlborough Pinot Noir ★★★☆

Estate-grown on the north side of the Wairau Valley, the 2016 vintage (★★★☆) is packaged in a heavy bottle. Light ruby, it has fragrant strawberry/spice aromas, leading into a medium to full-bodied, sweet-fruited and supple wine, with ripe, plummy, slightly nutty flavours, showing some savoury complexity. Enjoyable young.

DRY $25 –V

Mondillo Bella Reserve Central Otago Pinot Noir ★★★★★

The lush, sturdy, velvety 2017 vintage (★★★★★) was estate-grown and hand-selected at Bendigo, and matured for 19 months in French oak barriques (one year old). Deeply coloured, it is softly mouthfilling, with seductively rich, ripe cherry/plum flavours, gentle acidity, and a very harmonious, rounded finish.

DRY $95 AV

Mondillo Central Otago Pinot Noir ★★★★★

Already delicious, the 2017 vintage (★★★★★) is a rich, savoury, supple Bendigo red, estate-grown and matured for 10 months in French oak barrels (25 per cent new). Deeply coloured, with a fragrant, berryish, spicy bouquet, it is a powerful, sturdy wine, with generous, ripe cherry, plum, spice and nut flavours, finely integrated oak, good complexity and a well-rounded finish.

Vintage	17	16	15	14	13	12	11	10
WR	7	7	7	7	7	7	6	7
Drink	19-23	19-22	19-22	19-22	19-22	19-20	P	P

DRY $45 AV

Monowai Hawke's Bay Pinot Noir (★★★)

Grown at Crownthorpe and aged in French oak barrels, the 2016 vintage (★★★) is a ruby-hued red, with good depth of flavour, slightly nutty and spicy notes adding complexity, and moderately firm tannins. Ready.

DRY $23 AV

Monowai Upper Reaches Hawke's Bay Pinot Noir (★★★☆)

The 2015 vintage (★★★☆) is a Crownthorpe-grown red, matured for a year in new to two-year-old French oak casks. Ruby-hued, it is lively, with very good depth of plum, berry, spice and nut flavours, fresh acidity and a fairly firm finish. Ready.

DRY $35 –V

Montana Reserve Waipara Pinot Noir (★★★☆)

Looking for a good, affordable Pinot Noir? The 2017 vintage (★★★☆) of this North Canterbury red is ruby-hued and mouthfilling, with good depth of ripe, plummy, spicy flavours, showing some savoury complexity, and a smooth finish. It's drinking well now.

DRY $17 V+

Morton Estate [Black Label] Marlborough Pinot Noir (★★★☆)

Showing considerable complexity, the 2016 vintage (★★★☆) has full, fairly youthful colour. Mouthfilling, it has good depth of ripe, plummy, spicy, nutty flavours, fresh and savoury.

DRY $23 AV

Mount Brown Estates Grand Reserve North Canterbury Pinot Noir ★★★★

Well worth cellaring, the 2017 vintage (★★★★) is an estate-grown red, matured for 18 months in French oak barriques (25 per cent new). Full-coloured, with a complex bouquet, it is mouthfilling and savoury, with fresh acidity and strong, ripe, spicy, slightly nutty flavours.

Vintage	17
WR	5
Drink	19-24

DRY $30 AV

Mount Brown Estates North Canterbury Pinot Noir ★★★☆

Past releases of this good-value red were called 'Waipara Valley', but the 2018 vintage (★★★☆) is labelled 'North Canterbury'. Barrel-aged for a year, it is ruby-hued, fresh and lively, with good depth of plummy, spicy flavours, showing some savoury complexity. Enjoyable young.

Vintage	18
WR	4
Drink	19-24

DRY $20 V+

Mount Edward Central Otago Pinot Noir ★★★★★

The classy 2016 vintage (★★★★★) of this regional blend was fermented with indigenous yeasts, matured for 11 months in French oak casks (15 per cent new), and bottled unfined and unfiltered. Deep ruby, it is fragrant, savoury and supple, with ripe cherry, plum, spice and nut flavours, showing excellent complexity and harmony. A very refined and age-worthy wine, it should be at its best 2020+. Certified organic.

Vintage	16
WR	7
Drink	19-28

DRY $49 AV

Mount Edward Muirkirk Vineyard Pinot Noir   (★★★★★)

Grown at Bannockburn, the 2015 vintage (★★★★★) was barrel-aged, and bottled without fining or filtration. Full, bright ruby, it is highly fragrant and finely textured. A mouthfilling, youthful, sweet-fruited wine, it has a lovely spread of cherryish, spicy, complex flavours, gentle tannins, and a smooth, long, very harmonious finish. Best drinking 2021+.

Vintage	15
WR	7
Drink	19-30

 DRY $75 AV

Mount Riley Marlborough Pinot Noir   ★★★☆

The 2017 vintage (★★★☆) is skilfully crafted. Matured for nine months in French oak barriques, it is ruby-hued, mouthfilling, fresh and lively, with ripe cherry, plum and spice flavours, some savoury notes, and a finely balanced finish. Showing good weight and depth, it's bargain-priced.

 DRY $20 V+

Mount Riley Seventeen Valley Marlborough Pinot Noir   ★★★★

The 2015 vintage (★★★★☆) is a single-vineyard red, hand-picked in the Southern Valleys and matured for 10 months in French oak barrels (partly new). Ruby-hued, it is fragrant and softly mouthfilling, with strawberry and spice flavours, seasoned with nutty oak, and excellent complexity and harmony.

 DRY $39 AV

Moutere Hills Nelson Pinot Noir   ★★★★

The 2017 vintage (★★★★) is a single-vineyard red, hand-picked at Upper Moutere and matured for 11 months in French oak. Fragrant and generous, it is youthful, with strong, plummy, spicy, slightly nutty flavours, showing good complexity. Best drinking 2020+.

 DRY $34 AV

Moutere Hills Sarau Reserve Nelson Pinot Noir   ★★★★☆

Likely to be long-lived, the 2015 vintage (★★★★☆) is an estate-grown red, hand-harvested at Upper Moutere and matured for 11 months in French oak casks. It has fullish, slightly developed colour. Mouthfilling, it has generous, ripe, plummy, cherryish, spicy flavours, a slightly earthy streak, and the structure and depth to mature well. Best drinking 2020+.

 DRY $55 –V

Mt Beautiful North Canterbury Pinot Noir   ★★★★

The classy, youthful 2017 vintage (★★★★☆) was estate-grown at Cheviot, north of Waipara, and matured for a year in seasoned French oak barriques. Bright ruby, it is fragrant and mouthfilling, with concentrated, ripe, plummy, gently spicy flavours, a hint of herbs, good complexity and ripe, supple tannins. Best drinking 2020+.

Vintage	17	16	15
WR	6	7	6
Drink	19-25	19-27	19-25

DRY $32 AV

Mt Difficulty Bannockburn Central Otago Pinot Noir   ★★★★★

This is one of the region's highest-profile reds. Matured for a year in French oak casks (25 per cent new), the 2017 vintage (★★★★★) is full-coloured and youthful, with fresh, strong cherry, plum and spice flavours, earthy, savoury notes adding complexity, good tannin backbone and obvious cellaring potential. Best drinking 2021+.

Vintage	17	16	15	14	13
WR	6	6	6	6	6
Drink	19-32	19-28	19-27	19-26	19-25

Mt Difficulty Ghost Town Bendigo Pinot Noir   ★★★★★

The very youthful 2017 vintage (★★★★★) is a single-vineyard red, grown on Chinaman's Terrace, at Bendigo, and matured for a year in French oak barrels (25 per cent new). An elegant, concentrated wine, bright ruby, it is mouthfilling and vibrantly fruity, with rich, ripe cherry, plum and spice flavours, nutty oak adding complexity, supple tannins, and good cellaring potential. Best drinking 2022+.

Vintage	17
WR	6
Drink	19-32

Mt Difficulty Havoc Farm Gibbston Pinot Noir   (★★★★★)

Full of youthful drive, the elegant 2016 vintage (★★★★★) is a single-vineyard red, grown over 400 metres above sea level at Gibbston, and matured for 15 months in French oak casks (27 per cent new). The colour is deep and purple-flushed; the bouquet is highly fragrant, with hints of berries and herbs. A classic sub-regional style, it has concentrated, cherryish, plummy, spicy flavours, with a long, finely structured finish. It should blossom with cellaring.

Vintage	16
WR	6
Drink	19-30

Mt Difficulty Long Gully Bannockburn Central Otago Pinot Noir   ★★★★★

From vines planted in 1992, the 2017 vintage (★★★★★) is a single-vineyard red, matured for 15 months in French oak casks (25 per cent new). Deeply coloured, with a fragrant, spicy bouquet, it's a powerful, classy young red, with deep cherry, plum and spice flavours, finely integrated oak, impressive complexity and a well-structured, long finish. Best drinking 2022+.

Vintage	17
WR	6
Drink	19-32

Mt Difficulty Mansons Farm Bannockburn Pinot Noir   ★★★★★

Described on the label as 'dark and brooding', the powerful 2016 vintage (★★★★★) was matured for 14 months in French oak barrels (27 per cent new). Bright ruby, it is mouthfilling and savoury, with concentrated, ripe, plummy, spicy, nutty flavours, showing excellent complexity, and a lasting finish. Likely to be long-lived, it should be at its best 2021+.

 DRY $110 AV

Mt Difficulty Packspur Lowburn Valley Pinot Noir   (★★★★★)

From the oldest vineyard at Lowburn, in the Cromwell Basin, the graceful 2017 vintage (★★★★★) was grown at 360 to 380 metres above sea level and matured for 15 months in French oak barrels (25 per cent new). Full, bright ruby, it is an elegant, mouthfilling and supple red, with youthful cherry, plum and spice flavours, woven with fresh acidity, good complexity and a long, silky-smooth finish.

Vintage	17
WR	5
Drink	19-32

 DRY $75 AV

Mt Difficulty Pipeclay Terrace Bannockburn Pinot Noir   ★★★★★

From vines planted in 1996, the 2017 vintage (★★★★★) was matured for 15 months in French oak barrels (25 per cent new). Deep ruby, it is mouthfilling and very youthful, in a powerful, but approachable, style, with youthful cherry, plum, spice and nut flavours, savoury notes adding complexity, and a vigorous, lasting finish. Best drinking 2022+.

Vintage	17
WR	6
Drink	19-32

 DRY $110 AV

Mt Difficulty Target Gully Bannockburn Pinot Noir   ★★★★★

The 2016 vintage (★★★★☆), from vines planted in 1994, is a single-vineyard red, matured for 15 months in French oak casks (27 per cent new). Full ruby, it has strong cherry, plum and spice flavours, nutty and savoury, good complexity and a smooth finish. Fairly forward in its appeal, it's already drinking well.

Vintage	16
WR	5
Drink	19-30

DRY $110 –V

Mt Rosa Central Otago Pinot Noir ★★★★☆

Highly approachable already, the 2016 vintage (★★★★) is a moderately youthful Gibbston red, matured for 10 months in French oak casks (10 per cent new). Ruby-hued, it is sweet-fruited, with ripe cherry, plum and spice flavours, earthy, savoury notes adding complexity, and a smooth finish. The 2014 vintage (★★★★☆) has fairly mature colour. Developing well, it is savoury and complex, with generous cherry, plum, spice and herb flavours. It's probably at its peak.

Vintage	16	14
WR	3	5
Drink	21-24	19-22

DRY $40 AV

Mud House Central Otago Pinot Noir ★★★★

Estate-grown at Bendigo, in the Claim 431 Vineyard, and matured in tanks and French oak barriques, the 2018 vintage (★★★☆) is a lively, youthful red. On sale as early as December 2018, it has very good depth of ripe cherry, plum and spice flavours, showing some savoury complexity. Best drinking 2020+.

DRY $20 V+

Mud House Estate Claim 431 Vineyard Central Otago Pinot Noir ★★★★☆

The very graceful 2016 vintage (★★★★☆) was estate-grown at Bendigo, hand-picked and matured for a year in French oak barriques (20 per cent new). Deep ruby, it is a vibrant, youthful wine, with concentrated cherry, plum and spice flavours, fresh acidity, finely integrated oak, and a tight, lingering finish. Best drinking mid-2020+.

DRY $33 V+

Mud House Sub Region Series The Narrows Marlborough Pinot Noir ★★★☆

Worth cellaring, the 2017 vintage (★★★☆) was grown in the upper Wairau Valley and partly matured in new French oak barrels. Bright ruby, with a slightly earthy, rustic bouquet, it is full-bodied, with strong, plummy, spicy flavours, showing some complexity, and a fairly firm finish.

DRY $20 V+

Muddy Water Waipara Pinot Noir ★★★★☆

Certified organic, the perfumed, good-value 2017 vintage (★★★★★) was harvested principally from vines planted in 1993, hand-picked, matured for 14 months in French oak barriques (30 per cent new), and bottled unfined and unfiltered. Full, bright ruby, it is very savoury, fresh and youthful, with dense, ripe cherry, plum and spice flavours, seasoned with nutty oak, fine-grained tannins, and strong personality. Best drinking 2021+.

DRY $40 AV

Nanny Goat Vineyard Central Otago Pinot Noir ★★★★

Still youthful, the 2018 vintage (★★★★) is bright ruby, mouthfilling and vibrantly fruity, with strong cherry, plum and spice flavours, oak complexity and finely balanced tannins. Best drinking 2021+.

DRY $36 AV

Nanny Goat Vineyard Super Nanny Central Otago Pinot Noir   (★★★★★)

Deep ruby, the 2018 vintage (★★★★★) has an inviting, savoury fragrance. Mouthfilling, concentrated and supple, it's a powerful, high-impact style, with strong, ripe fruit flavours, savoury notes adding complexity, good supporting tannins, and obvious potential. Best drinking 2021+.

DRY $55 AV

Nautilus Clay Hills Vineyard Marlborough Pinot Noir   ★★★★☆

The delicious 2016 vintage (★★★★★) is a single-vineyard red, grown in the Southern Valleys and matured in French oak casks (33 per cent new). Deep ruby, it is full-bodied and fleshy, with rich, ripe cherry, plum, spice and nut flavours. Finely textured, it's a very harmonious red, well worth cellaring, but already a lovely mouthful.

Vintage	16
WR	7
Drink	19-26

DRY $70 –V

Nautilus Southern Valleys Marlborough Pinot Noir   ★★★★☆

The fresh, graceful 2016 vintage (★★★★☆) was matured in French oak barrels (30 per cent new). Fragrant and full-bodied, with strong, vibrant cherry, plum and spice flavours, showing excellent depth, ripeness, complexity and harmony, it should be at its best for drinking 2020+.

Vintage	16	15	14
WR	6	7	7
Drink	19-26	19-23	19-22

DRY $44 AV

Neck of the Woods Gibbston Central Otago Pinot Noir   (★★★★☆)

Offering good value, the 2016 vintage (★★★★☆) is a single-vineyard red, grown at Gibbston and matured for over a year in French oak casks (25 per cent new). Deep ruby, it is sturdy and firmly structured, with a fragrant bouquet, concentrated, ripe, berryish, spicy flavours, fresh acidity, and excellent depth and complexity. Still youthful, it should be at its best 2020+.

DRY $37 V+

Neudorf Moutere Pinot Noir   ★★★★★

Typically a very classy Nelson red. It is hand-picked from 'older vines' at Upper Moutere, fermented with indigenous yeasts, matured for 10 to 12 months in French oak barriques (22 per cent new in 2017), and usually bottled without fining or filtering. The full ruby 2017 vintage (★★★★★) has a savoury, complex bouquet. Mouthfilling and supple, it has strong, ripe cherry, plum and spice flavours, showing good complexity, gentle acidity and tannins, and a smooth, very harmonious finish. A 'forward' vintage, it's already drinking well. Certified organic.

Vintage	17	16	15	14	13	12	11	10
WR	6	6	7	6	6	7	6	7
Drink	19-24	19-23	19-22	19-21	19-20	19-23	P	P

DRY $65 AV

Neudorf Tom's Block Nelson Pinot Noir   ★★★★☆

Typically good value, this is an ideal introduction to the Neudorf Pinot Noir style. The 2016 vintage (★★★★☆), hand-harvested at three Moutere sites, was matured for 10 months in French oak barriques (22 per cent new), and bottled without fining or filtration. Enjoyable in its youth, it is ruby-hued, savoury and supple, with delicious cherry, spice and nut flavours, a hint of herbs, gentle tannins, good complexity and a fragrant bouquet.

Vintage	16	15	14	13	12	11	10
WR	7	7	6	6	7	6	7
Drink	19-23	19-22	19-21	19-20	P	P	P

 DRY $33 V+

Nevis Bluff Reserve Central Otago Pinot Noir   ★★★★

The 2014 vintage (★★★★) was matured for a year in French oak casks (35 per cent new). Ruby-hued, with some development showing, it is fragrant and full-bodied, with strong cherry, plum, spice and herb flavours, and nutty oak adding complexity. Best drinking 2020+.

Vintage	14
WR	6
Drink	19-22

 DRY $85 –V

Nga Waka Martinborough Lease Block Pinot Noir   ★★★★★

The delightful 2016 vintage (★★★★★) is a single-vineyard red, from vines planted in 1999. Matured for a year in French oak casks (40 per cent new), it is a deep ruby, velvety, perfumed wine. Full-bodied and seductively smooth, with strong, ripe plum/spice flavours, complex and savoury, it's already delicious, but well worth cellaring.

Vintage	16	15	14
WR	7	6	7
Drink	19-25	19-24	19-23

DRY $50 AV

Nga Waka Martinborough Pinot Noir   ★★★★

The highly attractive 2016 vintage (★★★★☆) was matured for a year in French oak casks (30 per cent new). Deep ruby, it is floral, mouthfilling, sweet-fruited and savoury, with cherry, plum and spice flavours, showing excellent depth and harmony. Drink now or cellar.

Vintage	16	15	14	13
WR	6	6	7	7
Drink	19-25	19-24	19-23	P

 DRY $40 –V

Nikau Point Reserve Marlborough Pinot Noir   ★★★

Priced sharply, the 2018 vintage (★★★☆) offers very easy drinking. Bright ruby, it is mouthfilling and supple, with youthful, ripe cherry, plum and spice flavours, showing good depth, a touch of complexity and a smooth finish. Best drinking mid-2020+.

 DRY $16 V+

Nockie's Palette Georgetown Central Otago Pinot Noir   (★★★★☆)

Well worth cellaring, the youthful 2016 vintage (★★★★☆) is a single-vineyard red, estate-grown at the eastern end of the Kawarau Gorge. Bright ruby, it is fragrant and savoury, with good intensity of ripe plum and spice flavours, oak complexity, fresh acidity, and a long, finely structured finish. Best drinking 2021+.

DRY $38 V+

Nor'Wester by Greystone North Canterbury Pinot Noir   ★★★★☆

From vineyards 'scattered across the region', the refined and harmonious 2017 vintage (★★★★☆) was grown at Waipara, fermented with indigenous yeasts and matured for 10 months in French oak barriques. Fragrant and savoury, it is full-bodied, with youthful, ripe, plummy, spicy flavours, showing greater richness and complexity than most sub-$30 Pinot Noirs, and the structure to mature well. Best drinking 2021+.

DRY $29 V+

Odyssey Marlborough Pinot Noir   ★★★☆

Certified organic, the 2016 vintage (★★★☆) was estate-grown in the upper Brancott Valley and matured in French oak barriques (10 per cent new). Ruby-hued, with a hint of development, it is mouthfilling, with good depth of plummy, spicy, nutty flavours, fairly firm tannins, and some savoury complexity. Drink now to 2020.

DRY $25 AV

Odyssey Reserve Iliad Marlborough Pinot Noir   ★★★★☆

Still unfolding, the 2017 vintage (★★★★☆) was estate-grown and hand-picked at the top of the Brancott Valley, and matured in French oak casks (30 per cent new). Fragrant, with bright, youthful colour, it is savoury and firmly structured, with concentrated plum, spice and nut flavours, good tannin backbone, and obvious potential; best drinking mid-2021+.

Vintage	16	DRY $32 V+
WR	6	
Drink	19-24	

Old House Vineyards Falcon Hill Nelson Pinot Noir   (★★★★☆)

The elegant, youthful 2017 vintage (★★★★☆) was estate-grown at Upper Moutere, fermented with indigenous yeasts and matured for 11 months in French oak casks. Deep ruby, with a fragrant, savoury bouquet, it is mouthfilling and sweet-fruited, with generous, ripe plum, spice and nut flavours, showing excellent concentration and complexity. Best drinking mid-2020+.

Vintage	17	DRY $39 V+
WR	7	
Drink	19-30	

Old House Vineyards Fantail New Zealand Pinot Noir   (★★★★)

Estate-grown in Nelson, the 2018 vintage (★★★★) was hand-picked and French oak-aged for 11 months. Bright ruby, it is sweet-fruited, savoury and supple, with ripe cherry, plum and spice flavours, gently seasoned with oak, and lots of drink-young appeal. Best drinking mid-2020+.

Vintage	18	DRY $24 V+
WR	6	
Drink	19-27	

Omeo Hidden Valley Single Vineyard Central Otago Pinot Noir   ★★★★☆

The age-worthy 2016 vintage (★★★★☆) is a top buy. A single-vineyard wine, grown at Alexandra, it was matured for 10 months in seasoned French oak casks. Bright ruby, it is mouthfilling, ripe and savoury, with generous, youthful cherry, plum and spice flavours, finely integrated oak, and excellent complexity and harmony.

 DRY $30 V+

Opawa Marlborough Pinot Noir   ★★★☆

From Nautilus, the very youthful 2018 vintage (★★★☆) was grown in the Wairau Valley and barrel-matured (12 per cent new). Bright ruby, it is full-bodied, with very good depth of cherry, plum and spice flavours, showing considerable complexity, some earthy, 'funky' notes and a fairly firm finish. Best drinking mid-2020+.

 DRY $30 –V

Ostler Caroline's Waitaki Valley Pinot Noir   ★★★★☆

Estate-grown in North Otago, the impressive 2016 vintage (★★★★☆) is a powerful young red, deeply coloured. Full-bodied, it has concentrated, ripe, plummy flavours to the fore, hints of herbs and liquorice, a subtle seasoning of oak, and gentle tannins. Best drinking 2020+.

 DRY $59 –V

Oyster Bay Marlborough Pinot Noir   ★★★☆

The 2018 vintage (★★★☆) was grown in the Wairau and Awatere valleys, and French oak-matured for nearly a year. Bright ruby, it is fragrant and softly mouthfilling, with generous cherry, plum and spice flavours, showing some savoury complexity, and lots of drink-young appeal.

 DRY $25 AV

Pā Road Marlborough Pinot Noir   ★★★

The 2018 vintage (★★☆) was partly barrel-aged. A fresh, light-bodied style, it has moderate depth of cherry, nut and spice flavours, with a fairly firm finish. Drink young.

DRY $18 V+

Paddy Borthwick Left Hand New Zealand Pinot Noir ★★★★☆

Estate-grown in the Wairarapa, this very rare red (70 cases per year) gives left-handed winemaker Braden Crosby the chance to express his 'logical, precise' approach. Matured in French oak casks (35 per cent new), the 2016 vintage (★★★★☆) is bright ruby, with a vibrantly fruity bouquet. Mouthfilling, it is still youthful, with concentrated cherry/plum flavours, fresh acidity and silky tannins. It should be long-lived. Best drinking 2020+.

DRY $75 –V

Paddy Borthwick New Zealand Pinot Noir ★★★★

Grown in the Wairarapa, the 2016 vintage (★★★★☆) is a single-vineyard red, deeply coloured and mouthfilling. A powerful wine, it has highly concentrated, ripe plum and dried-herb flavours, well-integrated oak, and the structure to mature well. Still youthful, it's best cellared to 2020+.

DRY $35 AV

Paddy Borthwick Right Hand New Zealand Pinot Noir ★★★★☆

Estate-grown, this is a rare wine (only 70 cases per year), made by Wairarapa winemaker Paddy Borthwick, an 'intuitive, impulsive', right-handed vigneron. The 2016 vintage (★★★★★) was matured in French oak casks (35 per cent new). Deep ruby, it is a youthful, fairly firm red, with highly impressive concentration and complexity. Mouthfilling, savoury and structured, with a firm finish, it's well worth cellaring to 2021+.

DRY $50 –V

Palliser Estate Martinborough Pinot Noir ★★★★★

This is typically an enticingly perfumed, notably elegant and harmonious red. The 2017 vintage (★★★★☆) was mostly grown at Wharekauhau, south of Martinborough, and matured for 10 months in French oak barrels (27 per cent new). An attractively scented, engaging young red, it is light ruby, with ripe cherry, plum, spice and nut flavours, showing good complexity, and a harmonious, persistent finish.

DRY $58 AV

Palliser Pencarrow Martinborough Pinot Noir –
see Pencarrow Martinborough Pinot Noir

Pegasus Bay North Canterbury Pinot Noir ★★★★★

This is one of North Canterbury's greatest Pinot Noirs, typically very rich in body and flavour. Many of the vines are over 25 years old and the wine is matured for 18 to 22 months in French oak barriques (about 40 per cent new). The 2016 vintage (★★★★★) is a fragrant, deep ruby wine, full-bodied and rich. It has deep cherry and plum flavours, with hints of herbs and spices, fresh acidity, and a very harmonious finish. Already delicious, it should be at its best 2020+. The 2017 vintage (★★★★★) is full-coloured and finely perfumed. Mouthfilling, sweet-fruited, savoury and supple, it is still very youthful, with concentrated, ripe cherry, plum and spice flavours, oak complexity and a rich, smooth finish. Best drinking 2022+.

DRY $51 AV

Pegasus Bay Prima Donna Aged Release Pinot Noir   (★★★★★)

A decade old when it was rereleased in 2019, the 2009 vintage (★★★★★) was estate-grown at Waipara, in North Canterbury, and matured for 18 months in French oak barriques (40 per cent new). It has full, moderately mature colour, with a highly fragrant, complex bouquet. Currently delicious, it is deep and soft, with concentrated, cherryish, nutty flavours, very complex and savoury, and a harmonious, velvet-smooth finish. Hard to resist.

DRY $120 AV

Pegasus Bay Prima Donna Pinot Noir   ★★★★★

For its top Waipara red, Pegasus Bay wants 'a heavenly voice, a shapely body and a velvety nose'. Based on the oldest vines, it is matured for 15 to 20 months in French oak barriques (50 per cent new). The deeply coloured 2016 vintage (★★★★★) is mouthfilling and sweet-fruited, with vibrant cherry, plum and spice flavours, concentrated, savoury and supple, that build to a powerful finish. Still very youthful, it needs time; open 2022+.

Vintage	16	15	14	13	12	11	10
WR	6	6	NM	6	7	6	7
Drink	19-30	19-34	NM	19-28	19-28	19-23	19-25

DRY $95 AV

Pencarrow Martinborough Pinot Noir   ★★★★

This is Palliser Estate's second-tier label, but in most years it is impressive and offers good value. The 2017 vintage (★★★★) is a graceful young red, mostly estate-grown and aged for 10 months in barrels (18 per cent new). Ruby-hued, it is an elegant, supple wine with cherryish, plummy flavours, some savoury notes, and good complexity and harmony.

DRY $30 AV

People's, The, Central Otago Pinot Noir   ★★★

From Constellation NZ, the 2017 vintage (★★★) is a medium-bodied red, with deep ruby colour. Fragrant, it is vibrant and youthful, with good depth of cherry, plum and spice flavours, showing a touch of complexity, and a fairly firm finish.

DRY $24 AV

Peregrine Central Otago Pinot Noir   ★★★★★

Outstanding in top seasons, this classic red is grown mostly in the Cromwell Basin but also at Gibbston. The refined 2016 vintage (★★★★★) is a youthful blend of Bendigo (45 per cent), Pisa (47 per cent) and Gibbston (8 per cent) grapes. Barrel-aged for 10 months, it is deep ruby and attractively scented, with strong, vibrant cherry/plum flavours, oak complexity, impressive delicacy and a lasting finish. Best drinking 2020+.

DRY $45 AV

Peter Yealands Reserve Awatere Valley Marlborough Pinot Noir   ★★★☆

The 2016 vintage (★★★☆) is enjoyable young. Partly barrel-aged, it is ruby-hued, fresh and softly mouthfilling, with vibrant red-berry, spice and dried-herb flavours, a touch of complexity, and a well-rounded finish.

DRY $22 V+

Pick & Shovel Reserve Central Otago Pinot Noir   (★★★☆)

A drink-young charmer, the 2018 vintage (★★★☆) is ruby-hued, fresh and very harmonious, with ripe, moderately concentrated flavours, showing some savoury complexity, and a smooth finish.

 DRY $28 AV

Pinot Naturel by Fromm   ★★★★

Certified organic, the 2018 vintage (★★★★) is an 'uncomplicated' red from Fromm that 'can be drunk young and slightly cooler'. Grown and hand-harvested in Marlborough, it was fermented with indigenous yeasts and bottled without fining or filtering, with 'minimal sulphur at bottling to ensure stability'. Bright ruby, it is a generous, supple red, fresh and lively, with strong, plummy flavours, showing some complexity, and a smooth finish. Already delicious.

 DRY $32 AV

Pisa Range Estate Black Poplar Block Pinot Noir   ★★★★★

Estate-grown at Pisa Flats, north of Cromwell, in Central Otago, this classy, enticingly scented wine is well worth discovering. The 2015 vintage (★★★★★) was picked from the oldest vines and matured for a year in French oak barriques (33 per cent new). A fragrant, powerful red, it is deeply coloured. Robust (15 per cent alcohol), it is youthful, fresh, sweet-fruited and concentrated, with very ripe plum, spice and slight liquorice flavours, and good tannin support. Best drinking 2021+.

Vintage	15	14	13	12	11	10
WR	7	6	7	6	NM	6
Drink	19-25	19-26	19-25	19-23	NM	19-23

 DRY $56 AV

Porters Estate Martinborough Pinot Noir   ★★★★

I tasted the 2014, 2015 and 2016 vintages together in August 2019. Hand-picked and matured in French oak barriques (partly new), the 2016 vintage (★★★★) is bright ruby, mouthfilling and spicy, with cherry, plum and nut flavours, a hint of tamarillo, good complexity and a moderately firm finish. My favourite is the 2015 vintage (★★★★☆), a powerful, savoury, deeply coloured wine with concentrated cherry, plum and spice flavours, slightly earthy notes adding complexity, and good cellaring potential. Still unfolding, the 2014 vintage (★★★★) is mouthfilling and generous, earthy and savoury, with good flavour complexity and the structure to age well.

Vintage	16	15	14
WR	6	6	6
Drink	20-30	20-27	19-22

 DRY $45 –V

Porters Reserve Martinborough Pinot Noir   (★★★★★)

Still developing, the impressive 2015 vintage (★★★★★) was hand-picked and matured in French oak barriques (partly new). Deep, bright ruby, it is mouthfilling and concentrated, with rich cherry, plum, spice and nut flavours, complex and savoury, and a well-structured, moderately firm finish. Best drinking 2022+.

Vintage	15
WR	7
Drink	20-30

DRY $75 AV

Prophet's Rock Home Vineyard Central Otago Pinot Noir ★★★★★

This consistently rewarding red is estate-grown at a high-altitude site at Bendigo, in the Cromwell Basin. Barrel-aged for 17 months (35 per cent new oak) and bottled unfiltered, the classy 2014 vintage (★★★★★) has full, fairly youthful colour. Mouthfilling, it is notably savoury and complex, with ripe plum, spice and nut flavours, concentrated, silky-textured and sustained. The 2015 vintage (★★★★★) is a very graceful, full-coloured and sweet-fruited wine, with youthful, concentrated, complex flavours, showing lovely richness and harmony. Best drinking 2021+.

Vintage	15	14	13
WR	7	7	7
Drink	19-27	19-28	19-26

Prophet's Rock Infusion Central Otago Pinot Noir (★★★★)

Delicious now, the 2017 vintage (★★★★☆) was estate-grown at Bendigo. All freshness and suppleness, it was 'made without the normal extraction from the grape skins during fermentation. Instead, the wine was fermented using indigenous wild yeast in old barrels, after being pressed and removed from its skins.' Veering in style towards rosé or Beaujolais, it's a pale red, floral, bone-dry wine with gentle berry and spice flavours, supple and lingering. Well worth discovering.

Prophet's Rock Retrospect Pinot Noir ★★★★★

The 2014 vintage (★★★★★) of this Central Otago red was designed to be released at five years old. Estate-grown at Bendigo and barrel-aged (33 per cent new French oak), it is full-coloured, with a hint of development. Savoury, sweet-fruited and supple, with cherryish, plummy, spicy flavours, showing excellent complexity, it's currently delicious, but also worth cellaring.

Providore Central Otago Pinot Noir (★★★★☆)

The fruit-packed 2017 vintage (★★★★☆) is boldly coloured, vibrant, very rich and supple. Still youthful, with impressively concentrated, plummy, spicy flavours and a well-rounded finish, it's an age-worthy red, likely to be at its best mid-2020+.

Providore First Edition Central Otago Pinot Noir (★★★★)

Grown mostly at Gibbston and partly oak-aged, the 2018 vintage (★★★★) is bright ruby, floral and boldly fruity, with generous, plummy, slightly spicy flavours, gentle tannins, and lots of drink-young charm.

Pruner's Reward, The, Waipara Valley Pinot Noir ★★★☆

From Bellbird Spring, the savoury 2016 vintage (★★★★) was matured for a year in French oak casks (15 per cent new). Ruby-hued, with a hint of development, it is drinking well now, with ripe cherry, spice and nut flavours, showing very good vigour, depth and harmony.

DRY $27 AV

Pyramid Valley Angel Flower Pinot Noir   ★★★★☆

Showing some early maturity, the 2016 vintage (★★★★☆) was estate-grown on an elevated, north-facing slope at Waikari, in North Canterbury. Matured for a year in French oak casks (10 per cent new), and bottled unfined and unfiltered, it has a savoury, slightly herbal bouquet. Mouthfilling, it is a very savoury rather than vibrantly fruity wine, spicy, herbal and complex, with fine-grained tannins, and excellent flavour depth and harmony. Best drinking now to 2021.

DRY $130 –V

Pyramid Valley Central Otago Pinot Noir   (★★★★☆)

The debut 2017 vintage (★★★★☆) was hand-harvested in the Manata Vineyard, at Lowburn, and matured for 10 months in French oak barriques (10 per cent new). Deep, bright ruby, with a fragrant, fresh, berryish, spicy bouquet, it is mouthfilling and fruit-packed, with good concentration of youthful, plummy, spicy flavours. Savoury and complex, with a structured, lengthy finish, it should be at its best 2021+.

DRY $45 –V

Pyramid Valley Earth Smoke Pinot Noir   ★★★★★

Estate-grown on an east-facing block at Waikari, in North Canterbury, the 2016 vintage (★★★★★) was matured for a year in French oak barrels (10 per cent new). Full of personality, it has deep, moderately developed colour. Drinking well now, but also worth cellaring, it is mouthfilling, savoury and complex, with spicy, slightly herbal flavours, showing excellent depth and harmony.

DRY $130 –V

Pyramid Valley Vineyards Growers Collection Calrossie
Vineyard Marlborough Pinot Noir   (★★★★☆)

From 'slopes in the hills between the Awatere and Wairau Valleys', the youthful 2016 vintage (★★★★☆) was matured in old oak barriques and bottled without fining or filtering. Deep ruby, it has a fragrant, slightly spicy and smoky bouquet. Mouthfilling, with deep, ripe, plummy, spicy flavours, an earthy streak and gentle tannins, it is savoury, with excellent vigour, complexity and potential; best drinking 2020+.

DRY $45 –V

Quartz Reef Bendigo Estate Franz Ferdinand Pinot Noir   (★★★★★)

The weighty, savoury 2015 vintage (★★★★★) was selected from the most eastern block of the estate vineyard – the first to catch the morning sun – and barrel-matured for 15 months. Ruby-hued, with a fragrant, spicy, nutty bouquet, it is sturdy and vigorous, with rich, ripe, plummy, spicy flavours, revealing impressive complexity, fine-grained tannins, and a very harmonious, persistent finish. Best drinking 2020+. (Certified organic and biodynamic.)

DRY $120 AV

Quartz Reef Bendigo Estate Otto Pinot Noir   (★★★★★)

The lovely 2017 vintage (★★★★★) was estate-grown at Bendigo, in Central Otago, and matured in one-year-old French oak casks. Deeply coloured, with an enticingly perfumed, savoury bouquet, it is full-bodied and youthful, with concentrated, well-ripened cherry, plum and spice flavours, revealing superb complexity, depth and harmony, and a finely textured, lasting finish. Already drinking well, it should be very long-lived; open 2021+.

 DRY $120 AV

Quartz Reef Bendigo Estate Single Ferment Pinot Noir   ★★★★★

Certified organic and biodynamic, the memorable 2017 vintage (★★★★★) is 'a single ferment . . . personally selected by Rudi Bauer as it best expresses the Bendigo Estate vineyard'. Estate-grown and hand-picked at Bendigo, in Central Otago, it was matured in French oak casks (50 per cent new), and bottled unfined and unfiltered. Deep and youthful in colour, it is highly fragrant, weighty and very savoury, with ripe cherry, plum and spice flavours, showing notable density, complexity and harmony. A very 'complete' wine, set to flourish for a decade, it's already a lovely mouthful.

Vintage	17	16
WR	7	7
Drink	19-24	19-24

 DRY $85 AV

🍇🍇🍇

Quartz Reef Bendigo Estate Single Vineyard Central Otago Pinot Noir   ★★★★★

Certified biodynamic, the refined, youthful 2017 vintage (★★★★★) was estate-grown at Bendigo, hand-picked and matured in French oak barriques (28 per cent new). Deeply coloured, it is invitingly perfumed, with strong, ripe fruit flavours, vibrant and supple, excellent complexity, and a long, finely poised finish. Already drinking well, it should be at its best from 2021 onwards.

Vintage	18	16	15	14	13
WR	6	6	6	7	7
Drink	19-24	19-21	19-22	19-20	P

 DRY $49 AV

 🍇🍇

Quest Farm Home Vineyard Central Otago Pinot Noir   (★★★★)

Still on sale, the 2014 vintage (★★★★) was estate-grown at the base of the Pisa Range, in the Cromwell Basin, and barrel-aged. Ruby-hued, with some development showing, it is highly fragrant, mouthfilling and savoury, with cherryish, gently spicy and nutty flavours, showing good complexity. A graceful red, it's drinking well now.

DRY $38 AV

Rabbit Ranch Central Otago Pinot Noir   ★★★☆

Enjoyable young, the 2017 vintage (★★★☆) is bright ruby, fresh and supple, in a middleweight style with ripe cherry, plum and spice flavours, a touch of complexity and good depth. Drink now to 2020. (From Chard Farm.)

 DRY $27 AV

Rapaura Springs Limestone Terrace Marlborough Pinot Noir   ★★★★☆

The 2018 vintage (★★★★) is a single-vineyard, Awatere Valley wine. Matured in French oak casks (32 per cent new), it is a ruby-hued, very graceful red, with cherry, plum and spice flavours, showing good complexity, and gentle tannins. Best drinking mid-2020+.

Vintage	18	DRY $50 –V
WR	6	
Drink	19-25	

Rapaura Springs Reserve Central Otago Pinot Noir   ★★★☆

The ruby-hued, vibrant, supple 2018 vintage (★★★☆) was matured in French and Hungarian oak. Still youthful, it has very satisfying depth of fresh, ripe cherry, plum and spice flavours, showing some savoury complexity, and a smooth finish. Best drinking mid-2020+.

Vintage	18	17	16	15	14	13	12	11	DRY $33 –V
WR	6	7	6	7	5	7	6	6	
Drink	19-24	19-25	19-23	19-22	19-20	19-20	19-20	P	

Rapaura Springs Reserve Marlborough Pinot Noir   ★★★☆

Already enjoyable, the 2018 vintage (★★★☆) of this regional blend was handled with French and Hungarian oak. Ruby-hued, it is a fresh, supple, medium-bodied red with well-ripened cherry, plum and spice flavours, nutty, savoury notes adding complexity, gentle tannins and a very smooth, harmonious finish.

Vintage	18	17	16	15	DRY $29 AV
WR	6	5	7	7	
Drink	19-24	19-23	19-25	19-22	

Rapaura Springs Rohe Awatere Pinot Noir   (★★★☆)

Bright ruby, the 2018 vintage (★★★☆) was grown in the Awatere Valley and matured in French oak casks (38 per cent new). Still very youthful, it has gentle cherry, spice and nut flavours, showing good complexity, and a fairly firm finish. Best drinking 2021+.

Vintage	18	DRY $37 –V
WR	6	
Drink	19-25	

Rapaura Springs Rohe Southern Valleys Marlborough Pinot Noir   (★★★★)

Well worth cellaring, the 2018 vintage (★★★★) was matured in French oak barrels (56 per cent new). Full, bright ruby, it is fragrant and supple, with youthful, ripe cherry, plum and spice flavours, showing very good depth, and gentle tannins. A graceful red, it should be at its best 2021+.

Vintage	18	DRY $37 AV
WR	6	
Drink	19-25	

Renato Nelson Pinot Noir   ★★★☆

The age-worthy 2017 vintage (★★★★) was hand-picked at Kina and aged for 10 months in French oak barriques (25 per cent new). Bright ruby, it is mouthfilling and sweet-fruited, with very good depth of ripe cherry, plum and spice flavours, nutty and savoury notes adding complexity, and a finely textured, very harmonious finish. Good value.

Vintage	17	16	15	14	13
WR	6	5	NM	7	5
Drink	19-23	19-22	NM	19-21	P

DRY $25 AV

Rendition Central Otago Pinot Noir   (★★★★☆)

Delicious young, the debut 2016 vintage (★★★★☆) from Matt Connell offers an enticing blend of richness and early approachability. Hand-picked at Bendigo and Lowburn, it was matured for 10 months in French oak barriques (25 per cent new). Deeply coloured, it is mouthfilling, sweet-fruited and vibrantly fruity, with very generous, plummy, slightly spicy flavours, savoury notes adding complexity, and a silky-smooth finish.

DRY $44 AV

Rimu Grove Nelson Pinot Noir   ★★★★☆

Estate-grown near Mapua, on the Nelson coast, this is typically a rich wine with plenty of personality. The 2017 vintage (★★★★), French oak-matured for 11 months, is already drinking well. A 'forward' year, it is mouthfilling and supple, with generous, savoury, nutty flavours, showing good complexity, and gentle tannins. Best drinking 2020.

Vintage	17	16	15	14	13	12	11	10
WR	7	6	7	7	7	7	7	7
Drink	20-32	19-30	19-30	19-30	19-30	19-30	19-27	19-25

DRY $52 –V

Rimu Grove Synergy Nelson Pinot Noir   (★★★★★)

The powerful 2015 vintage (★★★★★) was estate-grown at Moutere and French oak-matured. Deep and bright in colour, it is rich and complex, with concentrated, very ripe plum/spice flavours, hints of herbs and nuts, silky-smooth tannins, and great depth through the palate. Drink now or cellar.

Vintage	15
WR	7
Drink	19-35

DRY $98 –V

Rippon Emma's Block Pinot Noir   ★★★★★

From an east-facing slope, this Lake Wanaka wine has 'animated femininity', according to winemaker Nick Mills. It is typically barrel-aged for two winters in Central Otago and bottled unfined and unfiltered. The 2015 vintage (★★★★★) is still very youthful. Full-coloured, with strong cherry, plum and spice flavours, it has a real sense of power and potential. Savoury and complex, with supple tannins, it's well worth cellaring to 2021+.

DRY $105 AV

Rippon 'Rippon' Mature Vine Central Otago Pinot Noir ★★★★★

This Lake Wanaka red has a long, proud history. Estate-grown but not a single-block wine – winemaker Nick Mills views it as 'the farm voice' – it is typically a very elegant, 'feminine' style, rather than a blockbuster. Hand-picked from ungrafted vines planted between 1985 and 1991, the 2015 vintage (★★★★★) was fermented with indigenous yeasts, matured in French oak barrels, and bottled unfined and unfiltered. A wine with a powerful presence, it is deeply coloured, fragrant and weighty, with concentrated plum/spice flavours, savoury and structured. A very harmonious wine, it should be long-lived; open 2020+.

DRY $65 AV

Rippon Tinker's Field Mature Vine Pinot Noir ★★★★★

Named after Rippon's co-founder, Rolfe Mills ('Tink' to his friends), this exceptional wine is based on 'the oldest vines on the property'. Grown on a north-facing slope at Lake Wanaka, in Central Otago, it is matured for 17 months in French oak barriques (30 per cent new), and bottled without fining or filtering. The 2015 vintage (★★★★★) is a deeply coloured, notably weighty and savoury red, with rich plum/spice flavours and impressive complexity. Firmly structured, it should be long-lived; open 2022+.

DRY $115 AV

Riverby Estate Marlborough Pinot Noir ★★★★

This good-value, single-vineyard red is grown in the heart of the Wairau Valley and French oak-aged. The 2017 vintage (★★★★) is a bright ruby, medium to full-bodied red, with ripe cherry, plum, spice and nut flavours, showing very good complexity and harmony. Drink now onwards.

Vintage	17
WR	6
Drink	19-27

DRY $27 V+

Riverby Estate Reserve Marlborough Pinot Noir ★★★★

The youthful 2015 vintage (★★★★☆) of this single-vineyard, Rapaura red was hand-picked and matured for 15 months in French oak casks (45 per cent new). Ruby-hued, it is mouthfilling, with good concentration of ripe, savoury, nutty, cherryish, plummy flavours, showing good complexity, and a fairly firm finish. Best drinking mid-2020+.

Vintage	15
WR	6
Drink	20-30

DRY $35 AV

Riwaka River Estate Resurgence Nelson Pinot Noir ★★★★

The 2015 vintage (★★★★) of this single-vineyard red has a fragrant, savoury, slightly herbal bouquet. Deep ruby, it is full-bodied and smooth, with very satisfying depth of cherry, plum, spice and nut flavours, showing good complexity.

DRY $35 AV

Roaring Meg Central Otago Pinot Noir   ★★★

From Mt Difficulty, the 2018 vintage (★★★★) of this highly popular red was hand-picked and matured for nine months in French oak casks (18 per cent new). Full, bright ruby, it is fresh, sweet-fruited, savoury and supple, with good concentration of berry, plum and spice flavours, showing considerable complexity. Enjoyable young, it should be at its best mid-2020+.

 DRY $32 AV

Rock Ferry 3rd Rock Central Otago Pinot Noir   ★★★★★

Estate-grown at a high-altitude site at Bendigo, in the Cromwell Basin, the impressive 2016 vintage (★★★★★) was matured for a year in French oak barriques (25 per cent new). Deep ruby, with a fragrant, spicy, savoury bouquet, it is mouthfilling and sweet-fruited, with concentrated, vibrant cherry, plum and spice flavours, revealing excellent complexity, and good tannin support. A lovely young red, approachable now, it should be at its best 2021+.

 DRY $45 AV

Rock Ferry Trig Hill Vineyard Pinot Noir   ★★★★★

The classy young 2016 vintage (★★★★★) was estate-grown, 400 metres above sea level, at Bendigo, in Central Otago, hand-picked and barrel-aged. Deep ruby, it is finely scented and weighty, with deep cherry, plum and spice flavours, oak complexity, and a long, finely structured finish. Best drinking 2022+. Certified organic.

 DRY $65 AV

Rock N Pillar Central Otago Pinot Noir   (★★★★)

Enjoyable young but worth cellaring, the 2017 vintage (★★★★) is a single-vineyard Alexandra red. Deeply coloured, with fresh cherry, plum and herb aromas and flavours, gently seasoned with French oak, it is a lively wine, generous and supple.

 DRY $32 AV

Rockburn Central Otago Pinot Noir   ★★★★★

This consistently stylish blend of Cromwell Basin (mostly) and Gibbston grapes typically has concentrated cherry, plum and dried-herb flavours, silky-textured and perfumed. Estate-grown in the Parkburn Vineyard (88 per cent) and Gibbston Valley Back Road Vineyard (12 per cent), the impressive 2017 vintage (★★★★★) was matured for 10 months in French oak casks (35 per cent new). Deep ruby, it has an inviting, fragrant bouquet of plums, spices and nuts. Mouthfilling and sweet-fruited, with deep, well-ripened plum, cherry and spice flavours, it is savoury and complex, with lovely harmony. A classy, youthful wine with obvious cellaring potential, it should be long-lived; best drinking 2020+.

Vintage	17	16	15
WR	6	7	6
Drink	19-26	19-27	19-26

DRY $50 AV

Rockburn Nine Barrels Central Otago Pinot Noir   (★★★★★)

The very classy 2015 vintage (★★★★★) is a single-vineyard red, grown at Parkburn, in the Cromwell Basin. Based entirely on the 10/5 clone, it was fermented with indigenous yeasts and matured for 16 months in French oak casks (33 per cent new). Full, bright ruby, it is mouthfilling, savoury and supple, with generous, ripe cherry, plum and spice flavours, showing lovely depth, complexity and harmony. Finely textured, it's a very 'complete' wine, already drinking well.

Vintage	15	DRY $95 AV
WR	7	
Drink	18-30	

Rockburn Six Barrels Central Otago Pinot Noir   (★★★★★)

Still very youthful, the 2017 vintage (★★★★★) is a deeply coloured, single-vineyard red, grown at Gibbston and barrel-aged in French oak (30 per cent new). Lush and silky-textured, it has a fresh, fragrant bouquet of spices and herbs. Mouthfilling, with concentrated plum, herb and spice flavours, balanced acidity, gentle tannins and a finely poised, savoury, lasting finish, it should be at its best from 2022 onwards.

Vintage	17	DRY $95 AV
WR	7	
Drink	19-30	

Rockburn The Art Central Otago Pinot Noir   (★★★★★)

Distinctive and thought-provoking, the 2016 vintage (★★★★★) is a single-vineyard red, grown at Bannockburn and matured for 10 months in French oak casks (43 per cent new), followed by 'extended aging in old barrels'. Full-coloured, with some development showing, it is highly fragrant and very savoury, in an elegant style with fresh acidity, a hint of herbs, excellent complexity and a very long, finely textured finish. It's already delicious.

Vintage	16	DRY $99 AV
WR	7	
Drink	19-30	

Rockburn The Chosen Central Otago Single Vineyard Pinot Noir   (★★★★★)

'Crafted for immediate enjoyment', the 2018 vintage (★★★★★) is a graceful Gibbston red, from a notably early-ripening season. It was matured for 10 months in French oak barrels (15 per cent new). Bright ruby, it is fragrant and softly mouthfilling, with deep, very ripe plum, spice and herb flavours, savoury, nutty notes adding complexity, gentle acidity and a long, well-rounded finish. Weighty, rich and harmonious, it's already delicious.

Vintage	18	DRY $65 AV
WR	7	
Drink	19-23	

Rocky Point Central Otago Pinot Noir ★★★★☆

From Prophet's Rock, the 2017 vintage (★★★★☆) was hand-harvested at Bendigo, fermented with indigenous yeasts and matured in French oak casks. Fragrant and full-coloured, it is buoyantly fruity and supple, with fresh, cherryish, plummy, spicy flavours, showing excellent depth and harmony. A lovely young red, it's already drinking well.

DRY $30 V+

Rongopai Estate Premium Selection Marlborough Pinot Noir ★★☆

Light, fresh and fruity, the 2017 vintage (★★☆) is a simple style of Pinot Noir, priced accordingly. Enjoyable young, it has cherry, plum and herb flavours, woven with fresh acidity, and a smooth finish. (From Babich.)

DRY $16 AV

Ruru Central Otago Pinot Noir ★★★☆

The attractive, sharply priced 2018 vintage (★★★★) is a single-vineyard red, estate-grown at Alexandra and matured for 10 months in French oak casks (20 per cent new). Bright ruby, with ripe, cherryish, plummy, spicy flavours, it is fresh and lively, with nutty, savoury notes adding complexity. Drink now or cellar.

DRY $26 AV

Ruru Reserve Central Otago Pinot Noir (★★★★☆)

Well worth cellaring, the 2017 vintage (★★★★☆) of this Alexandra red was matured for 10 months in French oak barrels (20 per cent new). Deep ruby, with a fragrant, savoury bouquet, it is full-bodied and sweet-fruited, with youthful cherry, plum and spice flavours, showing excellent concentration and complexity, supple tannins and a long finish.

DRY $45 –V

Russian Jack Martinborough Pinot Noir ★★★

Enjoyable young, the 2018 vintage (★★★) was mostly barrel-aged. Ruby-hued, it is softly mouthfilling, with ripe cherry, plum and spice flavours in a gentle, easy-drinking style. (From Martinborough Vineyard.)

Vintage	18
WR	6
Drink	19-24

DRY $25 –V

Sacred Hill Single Vineyard Marlborough Pinot Noir (★★☆)

The 2018 vintage (★★☆) was picked with 'a degree of raisining' and matured for 10 months in French oak barrels (25 per cent new). It has light, advanced colour. Softly mouthfilling, with hints of cherries, herbs and spices, showing a touch of complexity, it's a very 'forward' wine, disappointing for the price.

DRY $28 –V

Saddleback Central Otago Pinot Noir ★★★★

Offering good value, the 2017 vintage (★★★★) is a blend of Pisa (50 per cent), Bendigo (39 per cent) and Gibbston (11 per cent) grapes, matured in seasoned French oak barrels. Full-coloured, it is mouthfilling and fruit-packed, with strong, plummy, spicy flavours, gentle tannins and lots of drink-young charm. Best drinking 2020+.

DRY $29 V+

Saint Clair Marlborough Pinot Noir ★★★☆

The 2016 vintage (★★★☆), grown in the Southern Valleys, is a bright ruby, mouthfilling, supple red, with ripe cherry, plum and spice flavours, showing some nutty, savoury complexity. A very harmonious wine, it's drinking well now.

DRY $26 AV

Saint Clair Omaka Reserve Marlborough Pinot Noir ★★★★☆

This is Saint Clair's top Pinot Noir, but understanding where the grapes were grown can be a challenge. Despite the prominence of 'Omaka' (a prestigious district for Pinot Noir, on the south side of the Wairau Valley) on its front label, past vintages have been grown in the Ure Valley, the Waihopai Valley and 'carefully selected vineyards'. The bold 2017 vintage (★★★★☆) is a single-vineyard red, grown in the Southern Valleys and matured for 10 months in French oak barrels (40 per cent new). Deeply coloured, it is a generous, upfront style, mouthfilling and sweet-fruited, with rich, ripe, plummy flavours, a hint of liquorice, and a smooth finish.

DRY $38 V+

Saint Clair Origin Marlborough Pinot Noir (★★★★)

Saint Clair's Origin red is partly barrel-aged. The 2017 vintage (★★★★) is fresh, mouthfilling, vibrantly fruity and supple, with strong, ripe, plummy, spicy flavours and a fragrant bouquet.

DRY $25 V+

Saint Clair Pioneer Block 10 Twin Hills Omaka Valley Marlborough Pinot Noir ★★★★

The 2016 vintage (★★★★) is an Omaka Valley red, matured in French oak barriques. Enjoyable young, it is bright ruby, full-bodied and smooth, with fresh, ripe cherry, plum and dried-herb flavours, nutty and savoury notes adding complexity, gentle tannins and a silky-smooth, persistent finish.

DRY $38 AV

Saint Clair Pioneer Block 14 Doctor's Creek Marlborough Pinot Noir ★★★★☆

Built to last, the 2017 vintage (★★★★☆) is a youthful red, estate-grown at Fairhall, south-west of Blenheim. Deep ruby, it is mouthfilling, with concentrated, vibrant ripe-berry and spice flavours, nutty and earthy notes adding complexity, and obvious potential. Best drinking 2021+.

DRY $38 V+

Saint Clair Pioneer Block 15 Strip Block Marlborough Pinot Noir   ★★★★☆

Grown in the lower reaches of the Waihopai Valley, the 2017 vintage (★★★★☆) is a mouthfilling, concentrated, youthful red. Deep ruby, it has strong, ripe, plummy, spicy flavours, showing good complexity, savoury notes and a fairly firm finish. Best drinking 2021+.

 DRY $38 V+

Saint Clair Pioneer Block 22 Barn Block Marlborough Pinot Noir   ★★★★☆

Grown on the southern edge of the Wairau Valley, and matured in French oak barriques, the 2015 vintage (★★★★☆) is a deep ruby, generous, finely textured red, with concentrated cherry, plum and spice flavours, ripe and supple, and a seasoning of smoky, savoury oak adding complexity. Well worth cellaring.

 DRY $38 V+

Saint Clair Pioneer Block 23 Master Block Marlborough Pinot Noir   ★★★★☆

The classy, elegant 2017 vintage (★★★★★) was grown in Benmorven Vineyard, in the Southern Valleys. Bright ruby, it is very fresh, lively and supple, with strong, ripe, cherryish flavours, seasoned with nutty oak, good complexity, and a finely textured, poised, persistent finish. Best drinking 2020+.

 DRY $38 V+

Sanctuary Marlborough Pinot Noir   ★★★☆

Ruby-hued, the 2017 vintage (★★★) was matured in an even split of tanks and old French oak barriques. Light and supple, it is sweet-fruited, with fresh cherry and spice flavours, showing a touch of complexity. It's drinking well now.

Vintage	18
WR	5
Drink	19-25

 DRY $25 AV

Satyr Foothills Hawke's Bay Pinot Noir   ★★★★

The 2015 vintage (★★★★) was grown at coastal and elevated, inland sites, and matured in French oak barrels (20 per cent new). Full ruby, it is very vibrant and supple, with a strong surge of fresh cherry, plum and spice flavours, and gentle tannins. A graceful red with youthful vigour, it should be at its best 2020+. (From Sileni.)

DRY $34 AV

Saving Grace Pinot Noir   (★★★☆)

Attractive young, the 2018 vintage (★★★☆) is a single-vineyard red, grown in North Canterbury, barrel-aged for nine months, and bottled unfined and unfiltered. Ruby-hued, it is medium-bodied, with moderately concentrated, cherryish flavours, showing some savoury complexity, gentle tannins and a very smooth finish. (From Waipara Hills, this label is mostly for restaurants.)

 DRY $25 AV

Scott Base Central Otago Pinot Noir ★★★★

Estate-grown in the Cromwell Basin, the 2017 vintage (★★★★) was matured in French oak barriques (35 per cent new). Ruby-hued, it is mouthfilling and fruit-packed, with strong plum, spice and nut flavours, showing good complexity. A fresh, vigorous, youthful wine, it needs time; open 2020+. (From Allan Scott.)

DRY $38 AV

Selaks Reserve South Island Pinot Noir ★★☆

Priced right, the light ruby 2017 vintage (★★☆) offers smooth, easy drinking, with plummy, spicy, slightly earthy flavours.

DRY $16 AV

Selaks The Taste Collection Marlborough Velvety Pinot Noir (★★★☆)

The attractive 2016 vintage (★★★☆) was partly barrel-aged. Ruby-hued, it is mouthfilling, vibrantly fruity and smooth, with ripe, plummy, spicy, slightly toasty flavours, showing some savoury complexity, and fine-grained tannins.

Vintage	16
WR	6
Drink	19-21

DRY $22 V+

Shaky Bridge Pioneer Series Central Otago Pinot Noir (★★★★)

The fragrant, generous 2017 vintage (★★★★) was grown at several sites in the Alexandra Basin and barrel-aged. The colour is deep and purple-flushed; the palate is fresh and youthful, with strong, plummy, cherryish flavours and a seductively smooth finish. A very good example of the 'fruit-driven' style, it's priced sharply. Best drinking 2020+.

DRY $25 V+

Sileni Cellar Selection Hawke's Bay Pinot Noir ★★★

The easy-drinking 2019 vintage (★★★) has a Beaujolais-like charm. Bright ruby, it is medium-bodied and vibrantly fruity, with lively cherry, plum and spice flavours, fresh and finely balanced.

DRY $19 AV

Sileni Exceptional Selection Hawke's Bay Pinot Noir ★★★★

The 2017 vintage (★★★☆) has moderately youthful, ruby colour. Mouthfilling and fleshy, it has strong, ripe cherry, plum and spice flavours, hints of liquorice and nutty oak, and a fairly firm finish. Drinking well now, but worth cellaring, the 2016 vintage (★★★★) is full-bodied and sweet-fruited, with generous cherry, plum and spice flavours. Best drinking 2021+.

DRY $70 –V

Sileni Grand Reserve Plateau Hawke's Bay Pinot Noir ★★★★

Grown in the elevated, inland Plateau Vineyard, the 2018 vintage (★★★★) was barrel-aged. Bright ruby, it is fragrant and supple, with vibrant cherry, plum and spice flavours, showing very good complexity, vigour and depth. Best drinking 2021+.

DRY $32 AV

Sileni Grand Reserve Springstone Hawke's Bay Pinot Noir   ★★★★

Grown in the inland, elevated Mangatahi district, the 2017 vintage (★★★☆) is ruby-hued, with a hint of development. It has strong, ripe cherry, plum, spice and nut flavours, showing good complexity, and a firm, slightly 'grippy' finish.

Sisters Ridge North Canterbury Pinot Noir   (★★★☆)

From Mt Beautiful, the 2017 vintage (★★★☆) was French oak-aged for 10 months. Offering great value, it is a bright ruby, medium-bodied red with youthful, ripe cherry, plum and spice flavours, a hint of herbs, fresh acidity, and some complexity and cellaring potential. Best drinking 2020+.

Soho Havana Yarrum Vineyard Marlborough Pinot Noir   ★★★★

Still youthful, the 2017 vintage (★★★★) is a mouthfilling, supple red, hand-picked and French oak-matured (25 per cent new). Full, bright ruby, it has ripe, cherryish, plummy, slightly spicy flavours, showing good concentration, nutty, savoury notes adding complexity, and obvious potential. Open mid-2020+.

Soho McQueen Central Otago Pinot Noir   ★★★★☆

Already drinking well, the 2017 vintage (★★★★☆) is an attractively perfumed red, hand-picked at Gibbston, Bannockburn and Bendigo, and matured in French oak casks (25 per cent new). Full, bright ruby, it is mouthfilling and supple, with vibrant plum, dried-herb and spice flavours, showing good complexity and harmony.

Spinyback Nelson Pinot Noir   ★★★

Still on sale, the 2015 vintage (★★★☆) is deep ruby, mouthfilling and firmly structured, with good depth of ripe plummy, spicy flavours, showing some complexity. Ready.

Spy Valley Envoy Johnson Vineyard Waihopai Valley Marlborough Pinot Noir   ★★★★★

The 2016 vintage (★★★★★) was estate-grown in the Waihopai Valley, hand-harvested and matured in French oak barrels for 18 months. Ruby-hued, it is mouthfilling and supple, with deep, ripe, plummy, spicy flavours, showing excellent complexity, and a long, finely textured finish. A subtle, very age-worthy wine, it should break into full stride 2021+.

Vintage	16	15	14	13	12	11	10
WR	6	6	6	NM	7	7	6
Drink	19-25	19-23	19-20	NM	P	P	P

DRY $55 AV

Spy Valley Envoy Outpost Vineyard Omaka Valley
Marlborough Pinot Noir

From hill-grown vines in the Omaka Valley, the classy 2015 vintage (★★★★★) was hand-picked, fermented with indigenous yeasts and matured for 16 months in French oak casks. Deeply coloured, it is mouthfilling, sweet-fruited and concentrated, with ripe cherry, plum, spice and nut flavours, complex and savoury, which build to a smooth, lasting finish. A delicious, classy, finely structured red, it should mature gracefully; open 2020+.

Vintage	15	14	13	12	11	10
WR	6	6	6	7	6	6
Drink	19-25	19-20	P	P	P	P

DRY $55 AV

Spy Valley Southern Valleys Marlborough Pinot Noir

Offering good value, the 2016 vintage (★★★★☆) was estate-grown in the Waihopai Valley and Omaka Valley, and matured for 11 months in French oak barrels. Ruby-hued, it is a savoury, sweet-fruited wine, with mouthfilling body and strong, plummy, spicy flavours, showing excellent complexity, harmony and length. Drink now or cellar.

Vintage	16	15	14	13
WR	7	6	6	6
Drink	19-23	19-23	19-20	P

DRY $33 V+

Stables Reserve Ngatarawa Hawke's Bay Pinot Noir ★★★

Priced sharply, the 2018 vintage (★★★☆) is a bright ruby, softly mouthfilling red, savoury and sweet-fruited, with cherry, plum and spice flavours, showing considerable complexity, and a smooth finish. Drink now to 2021.

DRY $20 AV

Staete Landt State of Grace Marlborough Pinot Noir ★★★★

The age-worthy 2016 vintage (★★★★) was hand-picked at Rapaura, on the north side of the Wairau Valley, and matured in French oak barriques. Bright ruby, it is mouthfilling and savoury, with ripe plum/spice flavours and a lingering, fairly firm finish. Best drinking 2020+.

Vintage	16
WR	5
Drink	19-25

DRY $35 AV

Starborough Family Estate Marlborough Pinot Noir ★★★★

The youthful 2018 vintage (★★★☆) was grown in the Awatere and Wairau valleys, and matured in French oak casks (25 per cent new). Bright ruby, it is moderately concentrated, with youthful, ripe cherry, plum and spice flavours, showing a distinct touch of complexity, and a fairly firm finish. Best drinking mid-2020+.

DRY $28 V+

Stoneleigh Latitude Marlborough Pinot Noir   ★★★

Celebrating the 'Golden Mile' along Rapaura Road, on the stony north side of the Wairau Valley, the 2017 vintage (★★★☆) is a deep ruby, medium to full-bodied wine. It is moderately concentrated, with plummy, spicy flavours, showing a touch of complexity, and good harmony. Drink now onwards.

DRY $20 AV

Stoneleigh Marlborough Pinot Noir   ★★☆

From Pernod Ricard NZ, this red is grown on the relatively warm north side of the Wairau Valley. The 2017 vintage (★★☆) is ruby-hued, with slightly earthy aromas. Medium to full-bodied, it has decent depth of ripe plum and spice flavours, and a smooth finish. Enjoyable young.

DRY $16 AV

Sugar Loaf Marlborough Pinot Noir   (★★★☆)

The 2017 vintage (★★★☆) from this Rapaura-based producer was grown in the Southern Valleys and matured in French oak casks (30 per cent new). Ruby-hued, it is fragrant, fresh and youthful, with satisfying depth of plum, berry and spice flavours, savoury notes adding complexity, and a moderately firm finish. Best drinking 2020+.

DRY $28 AV

Summerhouse Central Otago Pinot Noir   ★★★☆

The 2017 vintage (★★★☆) is a full-bodied and smooth, drink-young charmer. Deep ruby, it is vibrantly fruity, with a slightly earthy streak and generous, cherryish, plummy flavours.

DRY $25 AV

Summerhouse Marlborough Pinot Noir   ★★★☆

The 2018 vintage (★★★☆) was matured in French oak barriques (20 per cent new). Bright ruby, it is mouthfilling and sweet-fruited, with very good depth of fresh cherry, plum and spice flavours, showing considerable complexity. Drink now onwards.

Vintage	18
WR	6
Drink	19-25

DRY $33 –V

Surveyor Thomson Single Vineyard Central Otago Pinot Noir   ★★★★☆

From Domaine-Thomson, at Lowburn, the highly attractive 2015 vintage (★★★★★) was matured for 10 months in French oak barrels (35 per cent new). It has full, moderately youthful colour, with a welcoming fragrance. Full-bodied and savoury, with deep, ripe cherry, plum and spice flavours, showing excellent complexity and harmony, it's delicious now, but should also reward cellaring.

DRY $55 –V

Takapoto Estate Central Otago Pinot Noir

The 2014 vintage (★★★★) was grown at Gibbston, hand-harvested, matured in French oak casks (66 per cent new), and bottled unfined and unfiltered. Full-coloured, with a fresh, herbal bouquet, it is rich, vibrantly fruity and smooth, in a moderately complex style, showing very good depth and harmony. Drink now onwards.

DRY $70 –V

Tarras Vineyards Central Otago Pinot Noir

Estate-grown in The Canyon Vineyard at Bendigo, the 2017 vintage (★★★★☆) is an attractively scented, age-worthy red. Full, bright ruby, it is mouthfilling, savoury and supple, with strong cherry, plum and spice flavours, finely balanced tannins and impressive complexity. Best drinking 2021+.

DRY $40 AV

Tarras Vineyards The Canyon Single Vineyard Central Otago Pinot Noir

The enticingly fragrant, full-bodied 2016 vintage (★★★★★) was estate-grown at Bendigo and matured for nine months in French oak casks (32 per cent new). Full, bright ruby, it is vibrant, concentrated and savoury, with fresh, rich cherry, plum and spice flavours, showing excellent complexity, and a finely structured, lasting finish. Best drinking 2020+.

DRY $65 AV

Tatty Bogler Waitaki Valley North Otago Pinot Noir ★★★★

The 2016 vintage (★★★★) was matured for 10 months in French oak casks (20 per cent new). It has full, moderately youthful colour and a fresh, fragrant, slightly leafy bouquet. Full-bodied, it is vibrantly fruity, with strong plum, spice and herb flavours, fresh acidity, oak complexity and a moderately firm finish. (From Forrest Estate.)

DRY $45 –V

Te Awanga Estate Hawke's Bay Pinot Noir

The 2015 vintage (★★★☆) was oak-matured for six months. Ruby-hued, with some development showing, it is probably at its peak. Full-bodied and savoury, with hints of spices and mushrooms adding complexity, it has very good depth and a fairly firm finish.

DRY $25 AV

Te Awanga Estate One Off Red Planet Martinborough Pinot Noir

Drinking well now, but still developing, the 2016 vintage (★★★★) was barrel-aged for 18 months. Ruby-hued, it is moderately youthful, with mouthfilling body and cherry, plum, spice and nut flavours, showing good complexity. Best drinking 2021+.

DRY $35 AV

Te Kairanga John Martin Martinborough Pinot Noir ★★★★★

This typically impressive red is based on the 'best vineyard parcels'. The 2017 vintage (★★★★☆) was matured in French oak barrels (25 per cent new). Deep ruby, it is fresh and vibrant, with very youthful, cherryish, spicy, nutty flavours, showing good complexity. Savoury and supple, it's well worth cellaring to 2021+.

Vintage	17	16	15	14	13
WR	7	6	7	7	7
Drink	20-27	19-27	19-25	19-25	19-24

 DRY $46 –V

Te Kairanga Martinborough Pinot Noir ★★★★

The 2018 vintage (★★★★) was matured in French oak casks (19 per cent new). Ruby-hued, it is sweet-fruited and supple, in a moderately rich style with excellent elegance and harmony, and plenty of drink-young charm.

 DRY $30 AV

Te Kairanga Runholder Martinborough Pinot Noir ★★★★☆

Estate-grown and matured in French oak casks (20 per cent new), the 2018 vintage (★★★★☆) is a youthful red, but already drinking well. Bright ruby, it is savoury, sweet-fruited and supple, with cherry, spice and nut flavours, good complexity and excellent depth. Best drinking 2021+.

Vintage	18	17
WR	6	5
Drink	20-25	19-25

 DRY $35 V+

Te Kano Central Otago Pinot Noir (★★★★★)

The powerful yet elegant 2017 vintage (★★★★★) was grown at two sites at Bannockburn, French oak-aged for 11 months, and bottled unfined and unfiltered. Deep ruby, it is highly perfumed and full-bodied, with real density of ripe-fruit flavours, oak-derived complexity and the structure to mature well over the long haul. Best drinking 2021+.

 DRY $65 AV

Te Mata Estate Alma Hawke's Bay Pinot Noir (★★★★★)

The highly auspicious 2018 vintage (★★★★★) marks Te Mata's first plunge into the production of top-end Pinot Noir, a variety not commonly linked to Hawke's Bay, but cultivated in the region since the nineteenth century. Estate-grown inland, at the Woodthorpe Terraces Vineyard in the Dartmoor Valley, it was matured in French oak casks (over 50 per cent new). Deeply coloured, it is mouthfilling and savoury, with rich cherry, plum and spice flavours, and fine, supple tannins. A powerful, youthful, dense, well-structured red, it's well worth cellaring to 2022+.

Vintage	18
WR	6
Drink	19-29

 DRY $60 AV

Te Mata Estate Vineyards Hawke's Bay Pinot Noir (★★★★)

Still very youthful, the 2018 vintage (★★★★) was matured for 11 months in French oak casks (partly new). Deep ruby, it is mouthfilling and sweet-fruited, with concentrated, ripe plum, spice and nut flavours, showing good complexity, and the structure to mature well. Best drinking 2021+.

Vintage	18
WR	6
Drink	19-22

 DRY $30 AV

te Pā Marlborough Pinot Noir ★★★★

Still unfolding, the youthful 2017 vintage (★★★★) was hand-harvested on the south side of the Wairau Valley and matured in French oak barrels. Bright ruby, it is mouthfilling, with very good depth of vibrant cherry, plum and spice flavours, a hint of herbs, savoury notes adding complexity, and a moderately firm finish. Best drinking mid-2020+.

 DRY $30 AV

te Pā Reserve Collection Taylor River Marlborough Pinot Noir (★★★★☆)

The powerful 2017 vintage (★★★★☆) was fully barrel-aged. Bright ruby, it is mouthfilling, with rich, plummy, spicy flavours, woven with fresh acidity, a hint of liquorice, and a well-structured finish. An age-worthy red, it should be at its best 2021+.

 DRY $45 –V

Ted by Mount Edward Central Otago Pinot Noir ★★★★

Certified organic, the 2016 vintage (★★★★) is bright ruby, with a fragrant, savoury, slightly herbal bouquet. Showing good complexity, it is mouthfilling and fairly supple, with generous cherry, plum and spice flavours, a hint of herbs, and plenty of current-drinking appeal. Best drinking 2020.

 DRY $35 AV

Terra Sancta Estate Bannockburn Central Otago Pinot Noir ★★★★☆

The lively, very youthful 2017 vintage (★★★★☆) was estate-grown at Bannockburn and matured in French oak barriques (10 per cent new). Deep ruby, with a slightly earthy bouquet, it is fresh and concentrated, with strong, vibrant cherry, plum and spice flavours, good power through the palate and a well-structured finish. Best drinking 2021+.

Vintage	17	16	15	14	13
WR	7	7	7	7	6
Drink	19-28	19-23	19-26	19-22	19-20

DRY $35 V+

Terra Sancta Jackson's Block Bannockburn Central Otago Pinot Noir ★★★★★

The impressive 2017 vintage (★★★★★) is a single-block, single-clone red, matured in French oak barriques (20 per cent new). Full, bright ruby, it is very refined, rich and supple, with intense cherry, plum and spice flavours and a long finish. It should be long-lived; open 2022+.

Vintage	17	16	15	14	13	12	11
WR	7	7	6	6	5	7	7
Drink	19-30	19-28	19-25	19-24	19-20	19-24	19-20

DRY $50 AV

Terra Sancta Mysterious Diggings Bannockburn Central Otago Pinot Noir ★★★★

The savoury 2018 vintage (★★★★☆) is already drinking well. Estate-grown and matured in seasoned French oak barrels, it is ruby-hued, with ripe cherry, plum, spice and nut flavours, showing good complexity, and finely balanced tannins. Best drinking mid-2020+.

Vintage	18	17	16	15
WR	6	6	7	6
Drink	19-23	19-21	19-23	P

DRY $27 V+

Terra Sancta Shingle Beach Bannockburn Central Otago Pinot Noir ★★★★☆

From a block of mature, close-planted vines, the 2016 vintage (★★★★☆) was matured in French oak puncheons (20 per cent new). Light ruby, it is a fragrant, savoury, middleweight red, with cherryish, spicy, slightly herbal flavours, showing excellent complexity. It's already very expressive; drink now to 2028.

Vintage	16	15	14	13	12
WR	7	7	6	7	7
Drink	19-28	19-26	19-24	19-23	19-22

DRY $45 –V

Terra Sancta Slapjack Block Bannockburn Pinot Noir ★★★★★

From the oldest vines in Bannockburn, planted in 1991, and matured in French oak barriques (20 per cent new), the outstanding 2017 vintage (★★★★★) was bottled unfined and unfiltered. A deeply coloured, powerful young red, it is rich, sweet-fruited, complex and smooth-flowing, with impressive flavour density and an invitingly perfumed bouquet. Already delicious, it has obvious cellaring potential, and should be at its best 2022+.

Vintage	17	16	15	14	13	12	11
WR	7	7	7	7	6	7	7
Drink	19-30	19-28	19-30	19-25	19-24	19-24	19-25

DRY $80 AV

Terrace Edge Waipara Valley Pinot Noir ★★★★☆

A consistently attractive red, priced sharply. Certified organic, the youthful 2016 vintage (★★★★☆) was hand-picked, fermented with indigenous yeasts and matured for 11 months in French oak casks (25 per cent new). Bright ruby, it is fragrant, full-bodied, sweet-fruited and savoury, with generous cherry, plum and spice flavours, showing good complexity and harmony. Best drinking 2021+.

DRY $30 V+

Thornbury Central Otago Pinot Noir ★★★★

The graceful 2017 vintage (★★★☆) was grown at Bannockburn (60 per cent) and Bendigo (40 per cent), hand-picked, matured in French oak barriques (27 per cent new) until spring, then aged longer in barrels. Full, bright ruby, it is vibrant and smooth, with cherry, plum and spice flavours, showing a touch of complexity, and very good depth.

Vintage	18	17	16
WR	5	6	6
Drink	19-23	19-23	19-21

DRY $26 V+

Three Miners Warden's Court Central Otago Pinot Noir (★★★★)

Estate-grown between Alexandra and Clyde, the 2016 vintage (★★★★) was hand-picked and matured in French oak barriques (29 per cent new). Ruby-hued, it is medium to full-bodied, with moderately rich, cherryish, spicy, slightly nutty flavours, showing good complexity and harmony, and a smooth finish. Drink now onwards.

DRY $38 AV

Three Paddles Martinborough Pinot Noir ★★★★

From Nga Waka, this second-tier red is a rewarding, drink-young style. The 2017 vintage (★★★★) was French oak-aged for a year (20 per cent new). Fragrant, with a spicy bouquet, it is ruby-hued, with generous, ripe, plummy, spicy flavours, savoury notes adding complexity, and finely balanced tannins. Best drinking 2021+.

Vintage	17	16	15	14	13
WR	6	6	6	7	7
Drink	19-23	19-22	19-22	19-21	19-20

DRY $28 V+

Tiki Estate Single Vineyard Waipara Pinot Noir (★★★★)

Enjoyable now, but still youthful, the 2017 vintage (★★★★) was matured in French oak barriques. Bright ruby, it is fragrant, savoury and supple, with cherry, plum and spice flavours, seasoned with nutty oak, finely balanced tannins and good complexity. Best drinking mid-2020+.

Vintage	17
WR	6
Drink	19-21

DRY $27 V+

Tiki Estate Waipara Pinot Noir (★★★☆)

Enjoyable young, the 2018 vintage (★★★☆) was barrel-aged. Ruby-hued, it is sweet-fruited and smooth, with gentle cherry, plum, spice and nut flavours, showing some savoury complexity. Best drinking mid-2021+.

Vintage	18
WR	6
Drink	19-21

DRY $24 V+

Tiki Koro Central Otago Pinot Noir   ★★★★

The youthful 2018 vintage (★★★★) was matured for 10 months in French oak barriques. Bright ruby, it is fresh, vibrantly fruity and supple, with ripe cherry, plum, spice and nut flavours, showing considerable complexity, and obvious cellaring potential. Best drinking 2021+.

Vintage	18
WR	6
Drink	19-21

DRY $35 AV

Tiki Koro Waipara Pinot Noir   (★★★★)

French oak-aged for 18 months, the 2016 vintage (★★★★) is a mouthfilling, ruby-hued red with generous, ripe plum, cherry and spice flavours, showing good complexity, fresh acidity and a finely balanced finish. It's drinking well now.

Vintage	16
WR	6
Drink	19-21

DRY $35 AV

Tohu Awatere Valley Marlborough Pinot Noir   ★★★☆

The 2018 vintage (★★★☆) was grown in the Awatere Valley and matured in French oak barriques (20 per cent new). Light ruby, it is mouthfilling and supple, in a moderately concentrated style with ripe, plummy, spicy, slightly nutty flavours, showing some complexity, and good harmony.

Vintage	18
WR	5
Drink	20-25

DRY $25 AV

Tohu Rore Reserve Marlborough Pinot Noir   ★★★★

The 2017 vintage (★★★★) is a single-vineyard red, estate-grown in the upper Awatere Valley and matured in French oak barriques. Deeply coloured, it is mouthfilling and very vibrant, with good concentration of ripe cherry, plum and spice flavours. A fruit-packed, supple, age-worthy wine, it should be at its best mid-2020+.

DRY $35 AV

Tohu Single Vineyard Whenua Awa Awatere Valley Marlborough Pinot Noir   (★★★★☆)

The very age-worthy 2017 vintage (★★★★☆) was estate-grown in the upper Awatere Valley. Deep, bright ruby, it is fragrant and savoury, with concentrated plum, cherry, spice and herb flavours, seasoned with nutty oak, fresh acidity and very good complexity. Best drinking 2021+.

DRY $42 AV

Tohu Single Vineyard Whenua Matua Upper Moutere Nelson Pinot Noir   (★★★★)

The elegant 2017 vintage (★★★★) is ruby-hued, with a fragrant, savoury bouquet. Medium-bodied, it has lots of current-drinking appeal, with ripe cherry, spice and nut flavours, gentle tannins and a well-rounded, very harmonious finish.

 DRY $30 AV

Toi Toi Clutha Central Otago Pinot Noir   ★★★☆

Exuberantly fruity, the 2018 vintage (★★★☆) is a good, drink-young style. Deep ruby, it is mouthfilling and supple, with generous, vibrant, plummy, slightly spicy flavours, gentle acidity and an ultra-smooth finish.

 DRY $27 AV

Toi Toi Reserve Central Otago Pinot Noir   ★★★☆

The 2018 vintage (★★★★) is a single-vineyard red, hand-picked at Lowburn and matured for 14 months in French oak barrels. Full, bright ruby, it is mouthfilling, sweet-fruited and vibrant, with very youthful cherry, plum and spice flavours, seasoned with oak, considerable complexity, fresh acidity and lots of youthful vigour. Open 2021+.

 DRY $40 –V

Toi Toi Winemakers Selection Central Otago Pinot Noir   (★★★★)

The fragrant, youthful 2018 vintage (★★★★) is deep ruby, with mouthfilling body, strong, ripe, cherryish, gently spicy flavours, savoury notes adding complexity, and a fairly firm finish. Well worth cellaring, it should be at its best 2021+.

 DRY $33 AV

Two Paddocks Central Otago Pinot Noir   ★★★★★

The latest vintages are the best yet. Grown at the company's sites at Bannockburn (68 per cent), Alexandra (26 per cent) and Gibbston (6 per cent), and matured in French oak casks (20 per cent), the 2016 vintage (★★★★★) is deep ruby, fresh, youthful and savoury, with vibrant, plummy, spicy, nutty, slightly earthy flavours, showing excellent complexity, and a well-structured, long finish. It's well worth cellaring. Delicious now, the 2015 vintage (★★★★★) was grown at Bannockburn (62 per cent), Alexandra (30 per cent) and Gibbston (8 per cent), and matured in French oak casks (25 per cent new). Ruby-hued, it is a fragrant, very graceful red with cherry, plum and spice flavours, hints of herbs and nuts, excellent complexity, and a savoury, lingering finish. A very 'complete' wine.

DRY $55 AV

Two Paddocks Proprietor's Reserve The First Paddock
Central Otago Pinot Noir   ★★★★★

The highly impressive 2016 vintage (★★★★★) was estate-grown at Gibbston, hand-harvested from vines planted in 1993, and matured in French oak barrels (30 per cent new). Deeply coloured, it is an enticingly fragrant, full-bodied wine, with an array of cherry, plum, spice and herb flavours, finely balanced tannins and a savoury, supple finish. An elegant, concentrated and lively red, it should be long-lived; best drinking 2020+.

 DRY $85 AV

Two Paddocks Proprietor's Reserve The Fusilier
Bannockburn Vineyard Pinot Noir ★★★★★

The 2016 vintage (★★★★★) was estate-grown at Bannockburn, hand-picked, fermented with indigenous yeasts and matured in French oak barriques (28 per cent new). Bright ruby, it is an attractively scented, elegant rather than powerful style, very savoury and complex, with fresh acidity and ripe cherry, plum, spice and nut flavours, showing excellent vigour and harmony.

 DRY $85 AV

Two Paddocks Proprietor's Reserve The Last Chance
Earnscleugh Vineyard Pinot Noir ★★★★★

Estate-grown at Alexandra, in 'possibly the world's most southerly vineyard', the 2016 vintage (★★★★★) was hand-picked, fermented with indigenous yeasts and matured in French oak barriques (25 per cent new). Full of personality, it is bright ruby, with a spicy, slightly earthy bouquet. Mouthfilling, generous and savoury, it has strong plum, herb and nut flavours, good tannin backbone, an earthy streak, and excellent complexity and harmony. Best drinking 2020+.

 DRY $85 AV

Two Rivers of Marlborough Tributary Pinot Noir ★★★★

The 2017 vintage (★★★★☆) is a single-vineyard red, hand-picked in the Southern Valleys, matured for 11 months in French oak barrels (25 per cent new), and bottled unfined and unfiltered. Deep, bright ruby, it is fragrant, savoury and complex, in a very elegant style with ripe, berryish, slightly spicy and nutty flavours, fine-grained tannins and good aging potential. Best drinking mid-2020+.

Vintage	17	16	15
WR	7	6	6
Drink	19-24	19-23	19-20

 DRY $36 AV

Two Sisters Central Otago Pinot Noir ★★★★

The 2016 vintage (★★★★☆) is a refined, single-vineyard wine from Lowburn, in the Cromwell Basin. Hand-harvested, fermented with indigenous yeasts and matured in French oak casks (33 per cent new), it is bright ruby, fresh and youthful, in a medium-bodied style with cherry, plum, spice and nut flavours, showing good complexity, finely balanced tannins, and obvious potential. Best drinking 2021+.

 DRY $50 –V

Universe Central Otago Pinot Noir ★★★☆

The very easy-drinking 2018 vintage (★★★☆), from an Auckland-based producer, was grown in the Alexandra sub-region and French oak-aged. Ruby-hued, it is softly mouthfilling and sweet-fruited, with satisfying depth of fresh, youthful cherry, plum and spice flavours, savoury notes adding complexity, gentle tannins and some cellaring potential; best drinking mid-2020+.

 DRY $28 AV

Urlar Gladstone Pinot Noir ★★★★☆

Certified organic, this distinctive, savoury red is estate-grown in the northern Wairarapa. The 2017 vintage (★★★★★) was hand-picked, matured for 10 months in French oak barriques (45 per cent new), and bottled unfined and unfiltered. Retasted in mid-2019, it is full, bright ruby, with a finely scented bouquet. An immediately engaging style, with deep cherry, plum, spice and nut flavours, slightly earthy notes adding complexity and a softly textured finish, it's full of personality. Best drinking 2020+.

Vintage	17
WR	6
Drink	19-26

 DRY $45 –V

Urlar Select Parcels Gladstone Pinot Noir ★★★★★

Certified organic, the lovely 2017 vintage (★★★★★) was estate-grown in the northern Wairarapa, hand-picked and matured in French oak barriques (45 per cent new). Retasted in mid-2019, it is a refined wine, still very youthful. Deeply coloured, it is invitingly scented, very savoury and supple, with concentrated cherry, plum and spice flavours, finely structured and harmonious. Full of aging potential, it should be at its best 2022+.

Vintage	17
WR	6
Drink	19-29

 DRY $60 AV

Valli Bannockburn Vineyard Central Otago Pinot Noir ★★★★★

The powerful 2018 vintage (★★★★☆) is a very savoury, firmly structured red, hand-harvested, matured for 11 months in French oak casks (30 per cent new), and bottled unfined and unfiltered. Deep ruby, it is full-bodied, with strong, well-ripened cherry, plum, spice and nut flavours, fresh acidity and a tight finish. Best drinking 2022+.

Vintage	18	17	16	15	14	13	12	11	10
WR	7	6	7	6	7	7	7	6	6
Drink	20-30	19-30	19-28	19-27	19-26	19-26	19-25	19-24	19-23

 DRY $69 AV

Valli Bendigo Vineyard Central Otago Pinot Noir ★★★★★

The powerful, sweet-fruited 2018 vintage (★★★★★) was hand-picked, matured for nearly a year in French oak casks (30 per cent new), and bottled unfined and unfiltered. Deep, bright ruby, it is sturdy and concentrated, with strong, ripe plum, cherry and nut flavours, well-structured, youthful and long. Best drinking 2023+.

Vintage	18	17	16	15	14	13	12	11	10
WR	7	7	7	6	7	7	7	5	6
Drink	20-30	19-30	19-26	19-25	19-25	19-25	19-24	19-23	19-23

DRY $69 AV

Valli Burn Cottage Vineyard Central Otago Pinot Noir ★★★★★

The very classy 2017 vintage (★★★★★) is part of a collaboration between Valli and Burn Cottage, involving access to each other's grapes to explore key aspects of terroir. From vines planted in 2008 near Lowburn, it was matured in French oak barriques (25 per cent new), and bottled unfined and unfiltered. A 'complete' wine, it is very fragrant and concentrated, with dense, vibrant cherry, plum and spice flavours, fine tannins and lovely harmony. Best drinking 2020+.

Vintage	17
WR	5
Drink	19-28

DRY $69 AV

Valli Gibbston Vineyard Otago Pinot Noir ★★★★★

The refined, graceful, very youthful 2018 vintage (★★★★★) was hand-harvested, matured for 11 months in French oak casks (30 per cent new), and bottled unfined and unfiltered. Ruby-hued, it is floral, savoury and supple, with vibrant, berryish, spicy, nutty, slightly herbal flavours, woven with fresh acidity, impressive complexity and a lasting finish. Best drinking 2022+.

Vintage	18	17	16	15	14	13	12	11	10
WR	7	7	7	7	7	7	6	7	7
Drink	20-33	19-32	19-25	19-24	19-25	19-25	19-23	19-24	19-23

DRY $69 AV

Valli Waitaki Vineyard Otago Pinot Noir ★★★★☆

Still very youthful, the 2018 vintage (★★★★☆) is a ruby-hued red, hand-harvested, matured for 11 months in French oak casks (30 per cent new), and bottled unfined and unfiltered. Elegant and supple, it has vibrant cherry, plum, spice and nut flavours, fresh acidity, savoury notes adding complexity and a lingering finish. Best drinking 2021+.

Vintage	18	17	16	15	14	13	12	11	10
WR	7	5	7	6	7	7	7	5	6
Drink	19-27	19-26	19-26	19-25	19-25	19-25	19-25	19-23	19-23

DRY $69 –V

Vavasour Awatere Valley Marlborough Pinot Noir ★★★★

The very youthful 2018 vintage (★★★★) is bright ruby, mouthfilling and supple. Matured for nine months in French oak casks (22 per cent new), it is sweet-fruited and vibrant, with cherryish, plummy, spicy flavours, fresh acidity and a very harmonious finish. Best drinking mid-2020+.

Vintage	18	17
WR	6	6
Drink	19-26	19-25

 DRY $30 AV

Vavasour Felix's Vineyard Awatere Valley Marlborough Pinot Noir ★★★★☆

From vines planted in 2003 within The Favourite Vineyard, the 2017 vintage (★★★★☆) was matured for 14 months in French oak barriques. Deep and youthful in colour, it is a weighty, bold Pinot Noir, packed with cherryish, plummy, slightly herbal flavours. Still very youthful, it's a finely balanced wine with obvious potential; open 2021+.

Vintage	17
WR	7
Drink	19-30

DRY $41 AV

Vidal Reserve Marlborough Pinot Noir ★★★★

Delicious young, the top-value 2017 vintage (★★★★) was grown in the Wairau Valley (86 per cent) and Awatere Valley (14 per cent), and matured for a year in French oak barriques (12 per cent new). Bright ruby, it is fragrant, rich and harmonious, with strong cherry, plum and spice flavours, complex and savoury, and a well-rounded finish.

Vintage	17	16	15	14	13
WR	6	6	7	6	7
Drink	19-23	19-21	19-20	P	P

DRY $25 V+

Villa Maria Cellar Selection Marlborough Pinot Noir ★★★★

This is typically one of the country's best-value Pinot Noirs. The 2017 vintage (★★★★) was grown in the Wairau and Awatere valleys, and matured for 10 months in French oak barriques (15 per cent new). Bright ruby, it is a graceful red, mouthfilling, with ripe cherry, plum and spice flavours, savoury notes adding complexity, fine-grained tannins and great drinkability.

Vintage	17	16
WR	6	6
Drink	19-22	19-20

 DRY $26 V+

Villa Maria Private Bin Marlborough Pinot Noir ★★★☆

Offering fine value, the 2017 vintage (★★★☆) was grown in the Wairau and Awatere valleys, and partly barrel-aged. Enjoyable young, it is bright ruby, with slightly spicy aromas. A fresh, medium-bodied style, it has good depth of plummy, spicy flavours and a well-rounded finish.

Vintage	17	16	15	14	13
WR	5	5	5	6	6
Drink	19-20	19-20	19-20	19-20	P

 DRY $20 V+

Villa Maria Reserve Marlborough Pinot Noir   ★★★★★

Launched from 2000, this label swiftly won recognition as one of the region's boldest, lushest reds. Grown in the Awatere Valley and the Southern Valleys, it is hand-picked and matured in French oak barriques (22 per cent new in 2017). The 2017 vintage (★★★★★) is a very graceful, 'complete' red. Deep ruby, with a fragrant, complex bouquet, it is weighty, sweet-fruited and supple, with deep cherry, plum, spice and nut flavours, earthy, savoury notes adding complexity, and a long, finely textured finish. Already delicious, it should break into full stride 2020+.

Vintage	17	16
WR	7	7
Drink	19-22	19-22

 DRY $50 AV

Villa Maria Single Vineyard Seddon Marlborough Pinot Noir   ★★★★★

From an Awatere Valley site further inland and higher than its stablemate (below), the very classy 2015 vintage (★★★★★) was hand-picked, fermented with indigenous yeasts, and matured for 14 months in French oak barriques (23 per cent new). A lovely wine, it is rich and silky-textured, with deep cherry, plum and dried-herb flavours, complex, harmonious and lasting.

Vintage	15	14	13	12	11	10
WR	7	7	7	7	7	7
Drink	19-22	19-22	19-20	19-22	P	P

 DRY $60 AV

Villa Maria Single Vineyard Southern Clays Marlborough Pinot Noir   ★★★★★

From gentle, north-facing slopes on the south side of the Wairau Valley, the deep ruby 2017 vintage (★★★★☆) was matured in French oak barriques (23 per cent new). A very graceful, fragrant and supple red, it is full-bodied, with vibrant, cherryish, plummy, spicy flavours, showing good complexity, fresh acidity and a smooth finish. Best drinking mid-2020+.

Vintage	17
WR	7
Drink	19-25

DRY $60 AV

Villa Maria Single Vineyard Taylors Pass Marlborough Pinot Noir   ★★★★★

Estate-grown in the upper Awatere Valley, the elegant 2015 vintage (★★★★☆) was hand-picked and matured for 14 months in French oak barriques (25 per cent new). Fresh and vibrantly fruity, it has generous cherry, plum and spice flavours, woven with lively acidity, finely integrated oak adding complexity, and obvious cellaring potential. Open 2020+.

Vintage	16	15	14	13	12	11	10
WR	7	7	7	7	7	7	7
Drink	19-25	19-22	19-22	19-20	19-22	P	P

 DRY $55 AV

Volcanic Hills Central Otago Pinot Noir   (★★★★)

Still unfolding, the 2017 vintage (★★★★) is a fresh, vibrant, supple red, French oak-aged for a year. Deep ruby, it has very good vigour and concentration, with cherry, plum and spice flavours, a hint of herbs, savoury notes adding complexity and a finely balanced finish.

DRY $40 –V

Waimea Nelson Pinot Noir   ★★★☆

The 2017 vintage (★★★☆) was estate-grown on the Waimea Plains and barrel-aged. Bright ruby, it is fresh and lively, with good depth of youthful, plummy, spicy flavours, showing a touch of complexity. It's drinking well now.

DRY $25 AV

Waipara Hills Waipara Valley Pinot Noir   ★★★☆

The 2017 vintage (★★★☆) is a lightly oaked style, bright ruby and invitingly scented, with vibrant cherry and plum flavours, fresh and smooth. Delicious young.

DRY $17 V+

Wairau River Marlborough Pinot Noir   ★★★☆

Estate-grown on the north side of the Wairau Valley, the 2017 vintage (★★★☆) was barrel-aged. Full, bright ruby, it is mouthfilling and fleshy, with very good depth of plummy, slightly spicy flavours, ripe and rounded.

Vintage	17	16	15	14
WR	6	6	6	6
Drink	19-23	19-21	19-20	19-20

 DRY $25 AV

Wairau River Reserve Marlborough Pinot Noir   ★★★★

Estate-grown at two sites on the banks of the Wairau River, the 2016 vintage (★★★★) was matured in French oak casks and bottled unfined and unfiltered. Deep ruby, it is very fragrant, with rich, ripe plum/spice flavours, showing good complexity. Finely balanced, it's still unfolding and should reward cellaring to at least 2020.

Vintage	16	15	14
WR	6	6	7
Drink	19-24	19-22	19-23

DRY $40 –V

Walnut Block Nutcracker Marlborough Pinot Noir   ★★★★

Certified organic, the youthful 2017 vintage (★★★★) was hand-harvested, matured for a year in French oak casks (20 per cent new), and bottled unfined and unfiltered. Deep ruby, it is fragrant, with moderately concentrated, savoury, nutty flavours, showing good complexity, and a fairly firm finish. Best drinking 2021+.

Vintage	17	16	15
WR	7	7	6
Drink	19-24	19-23	19-22

 DRY $42 –V

Whitehaven Greg Southern Valleys Single Vineyard Marlborough Pinot Noir ★★★★★

The classy 2017 vintage (★★★★★) was hand-harvested, matured for 10 months in French oak barrels, and bottled unfined and unfiltered. Deeply coloured, it is fragrant, full-bodied and supple, in a very savoury style with youthful, ripe flavours, showing excellent depth, complexity and harmony, and a long finish. Best drinking 2021+.

 DRY $55 AV

Whitehaven Marlborough Pinot Noir ★★★★

The attractive 2016 vintage (★★★★) is bright ruby, with a fragrant, spicy bouquet. Mouthfilling, sweet-fruited and supple, it is fresh and vibrant, with very good depth, complexity and harmony, and a finely balanced, smooth finish.

 DRY $35 AV

Wild Earth Central Otago Pinot Noir ★★★★★

Delicious now, but also very age-worthy, the 2017 vintage (★★★★★) is a single-vineyard, Bannockburn red, hand-picked and matured for a year in French oak casks (27 per cent new). Full, bright ruby, it is a powerful, young, sweet-fruited and savoury wine, with a fragrant, slightly earthy bouquet and fresh, deep cherry, plum, spice and nut flavours, combining charm and complexity.

 DRY $40 V+

Wither Hills Marlborough Pinot Noir ★★★☆

Priced right, the 2017 vintage (★★★☆) is a bright ruby, fresh and supple red, with moderately rich, cherryish, spicy, slightly nutty flavours, showing some savoury complexity. Drink now or cellar. (In a vertical tasting of the 2016, 2011, 2007 and 1997 vintages, held in 2019, the standout was the sturdy, highly concentrated 2007 vintage (★★★★★), which has a bold, Syrah-like richness.)

 DRY $22 V+

Wither Hills Single Vineyard Taylor River Marlborough Pinot Noir ★★★★

Offering good value, the 2016 vintage (★★★★) is described on the back label as 'masculine, dense, chewy', but is far more approachable than that. Retasted in mid-2019, it is bright ruby, mouthfilling and sweet-fruited, with generous cherry, plum and spice flavours, showing very good complexity, and a finely balanced, lingering finish. Best drinking 2020+.

 DRY $26 V+

Wither Hills The Honourable Marlborough Pinot Noir (★★★★☆)

Released in 2018, the debut 2014 vintage (★★★★☆) is sold as 'our finest Pinot Noir'. Deep ruby, with some development showing, it is mouthfilling, with concentrated, still fairly fresh plum, spice, herb and nut flavours, showing good complexity. Drink now to 2020.

 DRY $75 –V

Wooing Tree Beetle Juice Central Otago Pinot Noir   ★★★★

Designed for early enjoyment, this single-vineyard Cromwell red is hand-picked and matured for eight or nine months in French oak casks (24 per cent new in 2016). The 2017 vintage (★★★★☆) is deeply coloured, with fresh, plummy, slightly spicy aromas. Full-bodied and fruit-packed, it is sweet-fruited and supple, in a 'full-on' style, with concentrated cherry, plum and spice flavours. Offering good value, it's already delicious.

Wooing Tree Central Otago Pinot Noir   ★★★★★

This single-vineyard Cromwell red is typically classy. The deeply coloured 2017 vintage (★★★★☆) was French oak-aged for 11 months. Full-bodied, it is youthful, with concentrated, vibrant, plummy, spicy, slightly nutty flavours, showing very good complexity, fresh acidity and fine-grained tannins. Well worth cellaring, it should be at its best 2021+.

Wooing Tree Sandstorm Reserve Single Vineyard Central Otago Pinot Noir   ★★★★★

Estate-grown at Cromwell, this wine is hand-picked from especially low-yielding vines. Matured for a year in French oak casks (33 per cent new), the 2015 vintage (★★★★☆) is deep ruby, floral, weighty, sweet-fruited and supple. It has strong, cherryish, plummy flavours, complex and savoury, and gentle tannins. Retasted in April 2018, the 2013 vintage (★★★★★) is maturing very gracefully. Moderately youthful in colour, it is a finely scented, mouthfilling red, concentrated, very savoury and complex, with notable vigour and depth. Best drinking 2020+.

Yealands Estate Single Vineyard Awatere Valley Marlborough Pinot Noir   ★★★★

Estate-grown, the 2018 vintage (★★★☆) is a ruby-hued, harmonious red. Vibrantly fruity and moderately concentrated, it has a distinct touch of complexity, gentle tannins and lots of drink-young charm.

Zephyr Marlborough Pinot Noir   ★★★★

The finely poised, youthful 2018 vintage (★★★★☆) was hand-picked at two sites in the Southern Valleys. Ruby-hued, it is sweet-fruited and supple, with generous, cherryish, spicy flavours, nutty, savoury notes adding complexity, and a very harmonious, lingering finish. Best drinking 2021+.

DRY $33 AV

Pinotage

Popular in New Zealand in the 1960s and 1970s, Pinotage is today overshadowed by more glamorous varieties, with just 19 hectares of bearing vines in 2020. Pinotage now ranks as the country's ninth most extensively planted red-wine variety, behind even Pinot Meunier and Tempranillo.

Pinotage is a cross of the great Burgundian grape, Pinot Noir, and Cinsaut, a heavy-cropping variety popular in the south of France. Cinsaut's typically 'meaty, chunky sort of flavour' (in Jancis Robinson's words) is also characteristic of Pinotage. Valued for its reasonably early-ripening and disease-resistant qualities, and good yields, its plantings are mostly in Gisborne (32 per cent), Auckland (21 per cent), Hawke's Bay (18 per cent) and Northland (16 per cent).

A well-made Pinotage displays a slightly gamey bouquet and a smooth, berryish, peppery palate that can be reminiscent of a southern Rhône. It matures swiftly and usually peaks within two or three years of the vintage.

Karikari Estate Pinotage ★★★★

Estate-grown and hand-picked on the Karikari Peninsula, in the Far North, the 2016 vintage (★★★☆) was matured for 29 months in French, Hungarian and American oak barrels (30 per cent new). Fullish and moderately youthful in colour, with a slightly rustic bouquet, it is mouthfilling and firm, with ripe, moderately concentrated, spicy, slightly earthy flavours. A powerful, gutsy red, it's a drink-now or cellaring proposition.

 DRY $42 –V

Linden Estate Hawke's Bay Pinotage (★★★★)

The age-worthy 2016 vintage (★★★★) was estate-grown and hand-picked in the Esk Valley. Full-coloured, it is mouthfilling and savoury, with fresh, ripe, plummy, spicy flavours, showing good complexity.

 DRY $25 AV

Marsden Bay of Islands Pinotage ★★★☆

The deeply coloured, generous 2015 vintage (★★★☆) was hand-harvested from 25-year-old vines in Northland and oak-aged for over a year. It has ripe, plummy, spicy, slightly gamey flavours, seasoned with sweet oak, in a soft, very drinkable style.

Vintage	15
WR	6
Drink	19-22

 DRY $28 –V

Muddy Water Waipara Pinotage ★★★★★

The impressive 2016 vintage (★★★★★) tastes like a cross between Pinot Noir and Syrah. Harvested at a soaring 25.2 brix, it was hand-picked, fermented with indigenous yeasts, matured for 10 months in French oak barrels (25 per cent new), and bottled unfined and unfiltered. Full-coloured, it's a strapping red (15 per cent alcohol), but not heavy, with a fragrant, plummy, spicy bouquet. Rich, savoury and soft, it is sweet-fruited and vibrant, with dense, youthful berry, spice and slight liquorice flavours, gentle tannins, and obvious potential.

 DRY $65 –V

Waitapu Estate Reef View Northland Pinotage   (★★★★☆)

Hand-picked and French oak-aged for a year, the 2015 vintage (★★★★☆), tasted in early 2019, is fragrant and full-bodied. A top example of the variety, it has full, bright, youthful colour, generous, berryish, spicy, slightly earthy flavours, showing good complexity, gentle tannins and great drinkability.

DRY $28 AV

Sangiovese

Sangiovese, Italy's most extensively planted red-wine variety, is a rarity in New Zealand. Cultivated as a workhorse grape throughout central Italy, in Tuscany it is the foundation of such famous reds as Chianti and Brunello di Montalcino. Here, Sangiovese has sometimes been confused with Montepulciano and its plantings are not expanding. Only 6 hectares of Sangiovese vines will be bearing in 2020, mostly in Auckland and Hawke's Bay.

Black Barn Concetta Sangiovese/Montepulciano (★★★★★)

Named after co-founder Concetta Lombardi, the 2015 vintage (★★★★★), now on sale, is an age-worthy, Hawke's Bay blend of Sangiovese (60 per cent) and Montelpulciano (40 per cent), oak-aged for three years. Full-coloured, with a fragrant, fresh, spicy bouquet, it is sturdy, youthful and vibrant, with deep, well-ripened blackcurrant, plum, spice and nut flavours, finely integrated oak, and impressive complexity and harmony.

DRY $85 –V

St Laurent

This Austrian variety is known for its deeply coloured, silky-smooth reds. It buds early, so is prone to frost damage, but ripens well ahead of Pinot Noir. Judge Rock imported the vine in 2001, but St Laurent is still extremely rare in New Zealand, with just 1 hectare of bearing vines in 2020, clustered in Waipara, Otago and Marlborough.

Hans Herzog Marlborough St Laurent ★★★★☆

Certified organic, the 2016 vintage (★★★★☆) was estate-grown in the Wairau Valley, matured for two years in French oak barriques, and bottled unfined and unfiltered. Deeply coloured, it is fragrant, full-bodied and supple, with vibrant blackcurrant and red-berry flavours, gently seasoned with oak, gentle tannins and loads of current-drinking appeal.

DRY $64 –V

Syrah

Hawke's Bay and the upper North Island (especially Waiheke Island) have a hot, new-ish red-wine variety, attracting growing international acclaim. The classic 'Syrah' of the Rhône Valley, in France, and Australian 'Shiraz' are in fact the same variety. On the rocky, baking slopes of the upper Rhône Valley, and in several Australian states, this noble grape yields red wines renowned for their outstanding depth of cassis, plum and black-pepper flavours.

Syrah was well known in New Zealand a century ago. Government viticulturist S.F. Anderson wrote in 1917 that Shiraz was being 'grown in nearly all our vineyards [but] the trouble with this variety has been an unevenness in ripening its fruit'. For today's winemakers, the problem has not changed: Syrah has never favoured a too-cool growing environment (wines that are not fully ripe show distinct tomato or tamarillo characters). It needs sites that are relatively hot during the day and retain the heat at night, achieving ripeness in Hawke's Bay late in the season, at about the same time as Cabernet Sauvignon. To curb its natural vigour, stony, dry, low-fertility sites or warm hillside sites are crucial.

In 2020 some 443 hectares of Syrah will be bearing – a steep rise from 62 hectares in 2000. Syrah is now New Zealand's third most widely planted red-wine variety, behind Pinot Noir and Merlot, but well ahead of Cabernet Sauvignon, Malbec and Cabernet Franc. Over 75 per cent of the vines are in Hawke's Bay, with most of the rest in Auckland and Northland (although there are pockets as far south as Central Otago).

Syrah's potential in this country's warmer vineyard sites is finally being tapped. The top wines possess rich, vibrant blackcurrant, plum and black-pepper flavours, with an enticingly floral bouquet, and are winning growing international applause.

Could Syrah replace Bordeaux-style Merlot and Cabernet Sauvignon-based blends over the next decade or two as the principal red-wine style from Hawke's Bay and the upper North Island? Don't rule it out.

144 Islands Northland Syrah (★★★★☆)

Full of personality, the 2017 vintage (★★★★☆) is a single-vineyard red, grown near Kerikeri, matured in French oak barrels (one year old), and bottled unfined and unfiltered. Deep and youthful in colour, it is full-bodied, with concentrated, vibrant, plummy, spicy flavours, a hint of liquorice, finely balanced tannins and a long finish. Best drinking 2021+.

DRY $35 AV

Alpha Domus The Barnstormer Hawke's Bay Syrah ★★★★

Matured for a year in predominantly French oak barriques, the 2016 vintage (★★★★) was designed as a 'fruit-driven' style. Full-coloured, it is fragrant, mouthfilling and vibrantly fruity, with generous plum, spice and black-pepper flavours to the fore, well-integrated oak and considerable complexity.

Vintage	16	15
WR	5	6
Drink	19-21	19-21

DRY $35 –V

Ash Ridge Doppio Chave Syrah ★★★★★

Refined, deeply coloured and very age-worthy, the 2015 vintage (★★★★★) is based on the Chave clone of Syrah, estate-grown in the Bridge Pa Triangle of Hawke's Bay, barrel-aged, and bottled unfined and unfiltered. Perfumed and supple, it is a classy red with strong, ripe plum and black-pepper flavours, showing excellent complexity and harmony. A lovely young wine, it should be at its best 2020+.

DRY $75 AV

Ash Ridge Doppio MS Syrah ★★★★☆

The 2015 vintage (★★★★☆) is based on the MS (Mass Selection) clone of Syrah. Like its Doppio stablemate (see above), but slightly less refined, it was estate-grown in the Bridge Pa Triangle of Hawke's Bay, barrel-aged, and bottled unfined and unfiltered. Dark and youthful in colour, it is still youthful, with concentrated, peppery, plummy flavours, hints of herbs and nuts, good complexity, and a finely textured finish. Best drinking 2020+.

 DRY $75 –V

Ash Ridge Estate Hawke's Bay Syrah ★★★☆

Estate-grown in the Bridge Pa Triangle, this label is Ash Ridge's top-selling wine. Barrel-aged in French and American oak, the 2017 vintage (★★★) is the only Syrah produced that season. Bright ruby, it is medium-bodied, with fresh, plummy, spicy flavours, a hint of tamarillo, some savoury complexity, and a smooth finish.

DRY $20 AV

Ash Ridge Premium Estate Hawke's Bay Syrah ★★★★☆

The attractive 2016 vintage (★★★★) was matured for 18 months in predominantly French oak casks (15 per cent new). Deep ruby, with a fragrant, peppery bouquet, it is medium to full-bodied, with good density of plummy, spicy flavours, considerable complexity and supple tannins. Drink now or cellar.

 DRY $30 AV

Ash Ridge Reserve Hawke's Bay Syrah ★★★★☆

The very elegant 2016 vintage (★★★★☆) was estate-grown in the Bridge Pa Triangle, barrel-aged, and bottled unfined and unfiltered. Deeply coloured, with a fragrant, peppery bouquet, it is medium to full-bodied, with good intensity of youthful, plummy, spicy, peppery flavours, fresh acidity, savoury notes adding complexity and fine, supple tannins. Best drinking 2021+.

 DRY $50 –V

Askerne Hawke's Bay Syrah ★★★☆

Delivering excellent value, the 2016 vintage (★★★★) is a refined young red, matured for 18 months in barrels (30 per cent new). Full-coloured, it is mouthfilling, with good density of plummy, peppery flavour and a long, spicy finish. Best drinking 2020+. The 2015 vintage (★★★☆) is still youthful. Floral, vibrantly fruity and supple, it is a medium-bodied, moderately concentrated wine, with fresh acidity and savoury, slightly toasty, well-spiced flavours.

 DRY $23 AV

Awaroa Melba Peach Waiheke Island Syrah ★★★★★

The 2015 vintage (★★★★★) is a concentrated, finely textured Waiheke Island red. Well worth cellaring, it has rich blackberry, spice, liquorice and toasty oak flavours, fine-grained tannins, and excellent balance and length.

Vintage	15	14	13	12	11	10
WR	6	7	7	5	NM	7
Drink	19-22	19-22	19-21	P	NM	19-24

 DRY $65 AV

Awaroa Waiheke Island Syrah

Delicious now but also well worth cellaring, the dark, sturdy 2016 vintage (★★★★★) was hand-picked and matured for a year in French oak barriques. It has concentrated plum and black-pepper flavours, with a hint of liquorice. Fragrant and spicy, it has slightly earthy notes adding complexity and a long, structured finish.

DRY $45 –V

Babich Black Label Hawke's Bay Syrah

Designed principally for 'on-premise' consumption (in restaurants), the deep ruby 2017 vintage (★★★☆) was French oak-aged for seven months. Retasted in April 2019, it is medium-bodied, fresh and supple, with vibrant berry, plum and black-pepper flavours, a hint of tamarillo, and a slightly nutty, smooth finish. Enjoyable young.

Vintage	17
WR	5
Drink	19-23

DRY $23 AV

Babich Hawke's Bay Syrah ★★★

An attractive, drink-young style, the 2018 vintage (★★★) is a medium-bodied red, vibrant and supple, with youthful, plummy, spicy flavours, fresh acidity and gentle tannins.

Vintage	18
WR	7
Drink	19-23

DRY $20 –V

Babich Winemakers' Reserve Hawke's Bay Syrah ★★★★☆

The 2017 vintage (★★★★) is a fresh, full-bodied red, grown in the Bridge Pa Triangle and matured for eight months in French oak barrels (25 per cent new). Retasted in April 2019, it is deep ruby, with a fragrant, peppery bouquet. It has strong, youthful, plummy, spicy flavours, showing good complexity, and a backbone of fine-grained tannins. A 'forward' vintage, but also worth cellaring, it should be at its best 2021+.

Vintage	17
WR	5
Drink	19-23

DRY $35 AV

Blank Canvas Hawke's Bay Syrah

Well worth cellaring, the 2015 vintage (★★★★☆) was made by co-fermenting Syrah from the Gimblett Gravels with Grüner Veltliner skins from Marlborough ('this results in deeper colour, smoother texture'), and then matured for 10 months in French oak casks (partly new). Dark and purple-flushed, with a fresh, peppery fragrance, it is mouthfilling and vibrantly fruity, with strong, youthful plum and spice flavours, lively acidity, and excellent concentration and structure. Best drinking 2020+.

DRY $45 –V

Boulder Bay Syrah (★★★★☆)

Estate-grown on Moturoa Island, in the Bay of Islands, the 2015 vintage (★★★★☆) is a rare Northland red, worth discovering. Still unfolding, it has deep, bright, moderately youthful colour, with a fragrant, ripe, spicy bouquet. Fresh and full-bodied, it is sweet-fruited, with strong, plummy, berryish, spicy flavours, a hint of liquorice, good tannin backbone and a lasting finish. Best drinking 2021+.

 DRY $35 AV

Brookfields Back Block Hawke's Bay Syrah ★★★★

Offering great value, the 2018 vintage (★★★★☆) was grown on a 'north-facing, very hot site' and barrel-aged for eight months. Full-coloured, mouthfilling and smooth, it's a highly approachable red, but also shows excellent concentration and structure. Finely textured, with strong, plummy, spicy flavours, oak complexity and impressive harmony, it's a drink-now or cellaring proposition.

Vintage	18
WR	7
Drink	19-26

 DRY $20 V+

Brookfields Hillside Syrah ★★★★★

This distinguished red is grown on a sheltered, north-facing slope between Maraekakaho and Bridge Pa, in Hawke's Bay (described by winemaker Peter Robertson as 'surreal – a chosen site'). The 2016 vintage (★★★★★), matured in new French (mostly) and American oak casks, has deep, youthful colour and a fragrant bouquet, with hints of spices and liquorice. Powerful and well-structured, with concentrated, vibrant, plummy, spicy flavours, braced by firm tannins, it is built for cellaring and should flourish for at least a decade; open 2021+.

Vintage	16	15	14	13
WR	7	7	7	7
Drink	21-27	20-26	19-25	19-23

DRY $47 AV

Byrne Puketotara Northland Syrah (★★★☆)

The 2015 vintage (★★★☆) was grown in the Fat Pig Vineyard and matured in old French oak casks. Full and bright in colour, it has a spicy bouquet, leading into a medium-bodied red with fresh, strong, plummy, nutty, distinctly peppery flavours, showing considerable complexity.

DRY $24 AV

Byrne Te Puna Northland Syrah (★★★★★)

From a coastal site, overlooking Te Puna Inlet, the impressive 2015 vintage (★★★★★) was matured in French oak casks (50 per cent new) and bottled unfiltered. Deeply coloured, it has a fragrant, plummy, spicy, nutty bouquet. Sturdy (14.5 per cent alcohol), it is powerful, sweet-fruited and concentrated, with a strong surge of fresh, ripe plum, pepper and liquorice flavours. An arresting wine, it should be long-lived.

 DRY $42 AV

Byrne Waingaro Northland Syrah   (★★★★★)

Offering fine value, the 2015 vintage (★★★★★) is a single-vineyard red, blended with Viognier (4 per cent) and matured in French oak barriques (one-third new). Full-coloured, it is perfumed, weighty and savoury, with excellent depth of blackcurrant, plum, liquorice and spice flavours, seasoned with toasty oak, and ripe, supple tannins. Full of personality, it's well worth cellaring.

Church Road 1 Single Vineyard Gimblett Gravels Syrah   (★★★★★)

The 2016 vintage (★★★★★) is hard to resist. Matured for 18 months in French oak barriques (30 per cent new), it is dark and softly mouthfilling, with beautifully rich, ripe blackcurrant, plum and spice flavours, and a velvet-smooth, lasting finish. Likely to be at its best from 2022 onwards, it's already a memorable mouthful. (Note: only available in 'travel retail and cellar door/online'.)

Church Road Grand Reserve Hawke's Bay Syrah   ★★★★★

Lovely already, but full of potential, the 2016 vintage (★★★★★) of this Gimblett Gravels red was matured for 17 months in French oak barriques. It has bold, youthful colour, with a spicy, highly fragrant bouquet. Very rich and supple, it is packed with blackcurrant, plum and black-pepper flavours, in a dense, yet smooth, style with a long, spicy finish. Best drinking 2021+. The 2017 vintage (★★★★★) is deeply coloured, fragrant and full-bodied, with dense, youthful plum and black-pepper flavours, seasoned with toasty oak, hints of liquorice and dark chocolate, and fine-grained tannins. Open 2022+.

Church Road Hawke's Bay Syrah   ★★★★

The 2017 vintage (★★★★) is a great buy. Deeply coloured, it has an attractive, fresh, spicy bouquet. Medium to full-bodied, with strong plum and black-pepper flavours, savoury notes adding complexity and fine-grained tannins, it's a drink-now or cellaring proposition.

Church Road McDonald Series Hawke's Bay Syrah   ★★★★★

The 2017 vintage (★★★★☆) is an age-worthy, intensely varietal red, grown in the Gimblett Gravels and Bridge Pa Triangle. Deeply coloured, with a highly fragrant, fresh, spicy bouquet, it is mouthfilling, with strong, youthful plum and black-pepper flavours, showing good complexity, and a long finish. Best drinking 2021+.

Church Road Tom Syrah   ★★★★★

Syrah is the latest addition to Church Road's elite Tom range. Released in September 2019, the third, 2015 vintage (★★★★★) was mostly (82.5 per cent) estate-grown in the Redstone Vineyard, in the Bridge Pa Triangle of Hawke's Bay; 17.5 per cent was grown in the Gimblett

Gravels. Matured for 22 months in French oak barrels (42 per cent new), it has deep, bright, purple-flushed colour and a highly fragrant, floral bouquet. A very elegant, supple, youthful and harmonious red, it is densely packed, with concentrated plum, spice and black-pepper flavours, a hint of liquorice, and a long, refined finish. Already dangerously drinkable, it's well worth cellaring to at least 2022.

DRY $220 –V

Clearview Cape Kidnappers Hawke's Bay Syrah   ★★★★

The youthful 2017 vintage (★★★☆) is a bright ruby red, grown at Te Awanga and matured in French oak casks (10 per cent new). A medium-bodied style, approachable young, it is fresh, vibrantly fruity and smooth, with good depth of ripe berry, plum and black-pepper flavours, savoury notes adding complexity and gentle tannins. Best drinking 2020+.

DRY $27 AV

Clos de Ste Anne The Crucible Syrah   ★★★★★

The 2015 vintage (★★★★★) is impressive. Grown biodynamically in Millton's elevated Clos de Ste Anne Vineyard in Gisborne, it was hand-harvested, co-fermented with Viognier (5 per cent), and matured in large, seasoned French oak casks. Deeply coloured, it is floral and full-bodied, with plum, spice and black-pepper flavours, hints of earth and dark chocolate, and notable depth, complexity and harmony. A very distinctive red, it's already delicious.

DRY $75 AV

Coopers Creek Hawke's Bay Syrah   ★★★☆

With its full, bright, youthful colour and plummy, peppery aromas, the 2016 vintage (★★★☆) is a clearly varietal red. Medium-bodied, it is vibrantly fruity, with good depth of spicy flavours and gentle tannins. Best drinking 2020.

DRY $22 AV

Coopers Creek Reserve Hawke's Bay Syrah   ★★★★★

Set for a long life, the 2018 vintage (★★★★★) is a powerful, highly refined red, grown in the Chalk Ridge vineyard, on the edge of the Havelock North hills. Hand-harvested and matured for a year in French oak casks (45 per cent new), it is dark and invitingly fragrant, with dense, youthful, well-ripened plum, spice and black-pepper flavours, a hint of liquorice, and a very rich, harmonious finish. Open 2023+.

Vintage	13
WR	7
Drink	19-24

DRY $60 AV

Coopers Creek Select Vineyards Chalk Ridge Hawke's Bay Syrah   ★★★★☆

The good-value 2018 vintage (★★★★☆) is a sturdy, finely structured, highly fragrant red, hand-picked, blended with a splash of Viognier (1.3 per cent) and matured for a year in French oak casks (27 per cent new). It has excellent concentration of plum, spice and black-pepper flavours, showing good complexity, and a lasting finish. Best drinking 2022+. Drinking well now, but still youthful, the 2017 vintage (★★★★) has fresh, peppery aromas, leading into a mouthfilling, supple wine with vibrant plum and black-pepper flavours, a hint of liquorice, and very good depth.

Craft Farm Hawke's Bay Syrah   ★★★★☆

From a hillside site overlooking Bridge Pa, the 2016 vintage (★★★★☆) is full-coloured, with a fresh, spicy, very varietal bouquet. Mouthfilling and supple, it has excellent depth of plummy, peppery flavours, oak complexity, and a very harmonious, lingering finish. Best drinking 2020+.

Craggy Range Gimblett Gravels Single Vineyard Hawke's Bay Syrah   ★★★★★

This label is overshadowed by the reputation of its stablemate, Le Sol, but proves the power, structure and finesse that can be achieved with Syrah grown in the Gimblett Gravels of Hawke's Bay. The 2016 vintage (★★★★☆) was matured for 16 months in French oak barriques (20 per cent new). Dense and youthful in colour, it has a floral, peppery fragrance. Mouthfilling and vibrant, with good density of plum, spice and black-pepper flavours, fresh and firm, it's a classy young red, best cellared to 2020+.

Craggy Range Le Sol Syrah – see Craggy Range Le Sol in the Branded and Other Red Wines section

De La Terre Hawke's Bay Syrah   ★★★★

The 2016 vintage (★★★★) was estate-grown at Havelock North and barrel-aged. Full-coloured, it is fragrant and supple, with vibrant, spicy flavours, showing excellent vigour and depth, and a finely balanced, lingering finish.

De La Terre Reserve Hawke's Bay Syrah   ★★★★☆

The youthful 2016 vintage (★★★★) was estate-grown at Havelock North and matured for 18 months in French oak barriques (40 per cent new). Full-coloured, it has generous, vibrant, well-spiced aromas and flavours. Plummy and peppery, with fresh acidity, good complexity and supple tannins, it should be at its best 2021+.

Vintage	16
WR	6
Drink	19-25

Dry River Lovat Vineyard Martinborough Syrah ★★★★★

The memorable 2016 vintage (★★★★★) is the best yet. An arresting wine, it is densely coloured and highly fragrant, with spice and liquorice aromas. Bursting with potential, it has exceptional depth of vibrant plum, spice and black-pepper flavours, buried tannins and a long, lovely finish. It should flourish for a decade or longer. Best drinking 2023+.

Vintage	13	12	11	10
WR	7	NM	6	6
Drink	19-29	NM	19-26	19-20

DRY $70 AV

Elephant Hill Airavata Hawke's Bay Syrah ★★★★★

An emerging star. The very classy, stylish 2015 vintage (★★★★★) was estate-grown and hand-harvested in the Gimblett Gravels (71 per cent) and at Te Awanga (29 per cent), co-fermented with a splash of Viognier (1.7 per cent of the blend), and matured for 26 months in French oak casks (40 per cent new). It has deep, bright, youthful colour, with a beautifully fragrant, fresh, spicy bouquet. A full-bodied, graceful, supple red, it has concentrated, plummy, slightly peppery and nutty flavours, savoury notes adding complexity, and a very harmonious, finely textured, persistent finish. Already delicious, but still unfolding, it should break into full stride from 2022 onwards.

DRY $120 AV

Elephant Hill Hawke's Bay Syrah ★★★★☆

The 2015 vintage (★★★★☆) was grown in the Gimblett Gravels, at Te Awanga and in the Bridge Pa Triangle, blended with Viognier (1 per cent), and matured for 13 months in French oak casks (30 per cent new). Deeply coloured, it is fragrant and full-bodied, with deep, ripe plum and black-pepper flavours, fresh and supple, and a long, spicy finish. Finely structured, with good density, it should be at its best 2020+.

Vintage	15
WR	6
Drink	19-25

DRY $34 AV

Elephant Hill Reserve Hawke's Bay Syrah ★★★★★

The classy, youthful 2015 vintage (★★★★★) was hand-picked in the Bridge Pa Triangle (56 per cent), at Te Awanga (30 per cent) and in the Gimblett Gravels (14 per cent), and matured in French oak casks (25 per cent new). Still a baby, it is deeply coloured, fragrant, rich and supple, with a lovely surge of ripe plum, blackcurrant and spice flavours, hints of liquorice and nuts, and a velvety texture. Showing obvious cellaring potential, it should break into full stride 2020+.

DRY $54 AV

Elephant Hill Stone Hawke's Bay Syrah   (★★★★★)

The 2017 vintage (★★★★★) is a rare red – only 840 bottles were produced. Estate-grown in the Gimblett Gravels and blended with a splash of Viognier (1 per cent), it was matured for two years in French oak casks (40 per cent new). Deeply coloured and fragrant, it is densely packed, with concentrated, plummy, spicy flavours, finely textured and long. Best drinking 2022+. (To be released in May 2020.)

DRY $75 AV

Esk Valley Winemakers Reserve Gimblett Gravels Hawke's Bay Syrah   ★★★★★

The classy young 2016 vintage (★★★★★) was grown in the Cornerstone Vineyard, hand-picked, fermented with indigenous yeasts and matured for 15 months in French oak barriques (30 per cent new). Dark and purple-flushed, with fragrant plum and spice aromas, it is sturdy and well structured, with concentrated, youthful plum and black-pepper flavours, good tannin backbone, and lovely harmony and length.

Vintage	16	15	14	13	12	11	10
WR	7	NM	7	7	NM	NM	7
Drink	19-30	NM	19-30	19-25	NM	NM	19-25

DRY $60 AV

Falconhead Hawke's Bay Syrah   ★★★

Barrel-aged for 20 months, the 2016 vintage (★★★) is a medium to full-bodied style, with distinctly spicy, slightly earthy flavours, showing good depth, and a fairly firm finish. It's enjoyable now.

Vintage	14	13
WR	7	7
Drink	19-20	19-20

DRY $17 AV

Fromm La Strada Marlborough Syrah   ★★★★☆

A cool-climate, 'fruit-driven' style – with style. The 2016 vintage (★★★★☆), which includes a splash of Viognier, is certified organic. From various sites in the Wairau Valley, it was hand-picked and matured for 16 to 18 months in barriques and puncheons (almost all seasoned, rather than new). Still youthful, it's a very fragrant red, full-bodied, with ripe plum, spice and black-pepper flavours, slightly earthy notes, gentle tannins, and excellent depth and harmony. Best drinking 2020+.

Vintage	16	15	14	13	12	11
WR	7	7	7	7	7	7
Drink	19-23	19-22	19-21	19-21	19-20	19-20

DRY $40 –V

Fromm Marlborough Syrah   (★★★★)

Certified organic, the 2017 vintage (★★★★) was hand-harvested, blended with a splash of Viognier (2 per cent), fermented with indigenous yeasts, and matured for 19 months in French oak barrels (less than 10 per cent new). Fullish in colour, it is a fresh, medium-bodied wine, vividly varietal, with strong, plummy, peppery flavours, gentle acidity and supple tannins. Already enjoyable, it should be at its best 2021+.

DRY $38 –V

Fromm Syrah Fromm Vineyard ★★★★★

Estate-grown in the Wairau Valley, Marlborough, hand-harvested from mature vines, and co-fermented with a splash of Viognier (2 per cent), the 2016 vintage (★★★★★) is a rare red (only six barrels were produced). Certified organic, it is deeply coloured, mouthfilling and concentrated, with ripe blackcurrant, plum and spice flavours, fine-grained tannins, and a long, finely structured finish. A classy young red, it should be very long-lived; best drinking 2021+.

DRY $63 AV

Georges Road Cuvée 43 Waipara Syrah (★★★★)

Estate-grown and hand-harvested, the 2016 vintage (★★★★) was matured for 19 months in French oak casks (33 per cent new). Dark and youthful in colour, it is fragrant and full-bodied, with mouthfilling body and fresh, concentrated flavours, brambly and spicy, with a hint of herbs. Best drinking 2020+.

DRY $50 –V

Greyrock Te Koru Hawke's Bay Syrah (★★★☆)

The 2018 vintage (★★★☆) has bright, fullish colour. A fresh, medium-bodied style, it is youthful, with ripe, moderately concentrated, plummy, spicy flavours, some savoury notes adding complexity and finely balanced tannins. Best drinking 2021+.

DRY $20 AV

Haha Hawke's Bay Syrah (★★★☆)

Delicious young, the 2018 vintage (★★★☆) is a floral, ruby-hued red. Vibrantly fruity and supple, it is medium to full-bodied, with gentle tannins, good depth of fresh, youthful, plummy, spicy flavours and a rather Pinot Noir-ish charm.

DRY $25 –V

Hopesgrove Single Vineyard Hawke's Bay Silver Lining Syrah ★★★★★

Still unfolding, the 2014 vintage (★★★★★), tasted in mid-2019, was estate-grown, hand-picked and matured for 28 months in French oak casks (66 per cent new). Deeply coloured, it has a real sense of youthful potential. Mouthfilling and supple, with concentrated, plummy, spicy flavours, complex and savoury, it should be at its best 2021+.

Vintage	14
WR	6
Drink	19-29

DRY $65 AV

Hopesgrove Single Vineyard Hawke's Bay Syrah (★★★★☆)

The youthful 2015 vintage (★★★★☆), tasted in mid-2019, was estate-grown, hand-harvested and matured for 20 months in French oak casks (33 per cent new). Full-coloured, with a fragrant, fresh, spicy bouquet, it is an elegant red, with plummy, spicy flavours, showing good concentration and vigour, savoury notes adding complexity, and good aging potential. Best drinking 2021+.

DRY $40 –V

Huntaway Reserve Hawke's Bay Syrah   (★★★☆)

The 2017 vintage (★★★☆) is a barrel-matured, medium to full-bodied red. Fullish in colour, it is distinctly spicy, with good depth of berry/plum flavours, a hint of tamarillo, savoury notes adding complexity and gentle tannins. Enjoyable young.

DRY $22 AV

John Forrest Collection Gimblett Gravels Hawke's Bay Syrah   ★★★★★

The very classy 2014 vintage (★★★★★) was grown in the Cornerstone Vineyard and matured for 20 months in oak casks (40 per cent new). It has bold, still purplish colour. A notably powerful, lush wine, it has dense, very ripe plum, blackcurrant and liquorice flavours, good tannin backbone, and a finely textured, very harmonious finish. Already delicious, it should be at its best for drinking 2021+.

DRY $80 AV

Johner Estate Reserve Gladstone Syrah   (★★★★☆)

The powerful 2016 vintage (★★★★☆) was barrel-aged for a year (20 per cent new oak), and bottled unfined and unfiltered. Deeply coloured, it has a fragrant bouquet of plums, herbs and liquorice. Bold and youthful, it is concentrated and clearly varietal, with a hint of tamarillo, nutty oak adding complexty, and good tannin backbone. Best 2021+.

Vintage	16
WR	7
Drink	19-23

DRY $50 –V

Karikari Estate Syrah   ★★★☆

The 2016 vintage (★★★) was estate-grown on the Karikari Peninsula in Northland, hand-picked and matured for 18 months in French (mostly) and American oak casks (partly new). It has fullish, fairly mature colour. A very northern style, it is gutsy, ripe and slightly raisiny, with advanced flavours of liquorice, spice and nuts, firm and ready.

DRY $45 –V

Kidnapper Cliffs Gimblett Gravels Hawke's Bay Syrah   (★★★★★)

From Te Awa, the 2013 vintage (★★★★★), released in 2017, is a classy red, estate-grown, hand-picked, fermented with indigenous yeasts and matured for 20 months in French oak hogsheads (35 per cent new). Deeply coloured, with a highly fragrant bouquet, it is mouthfilling, with deep, ripe plum, spice and black-pepper flavours, fine-grained tannins and excellent complexity. A savoury, very harmonious and age-worthy red, it should be at its best 2020+.

DRY $70 AV

La Collina Syrah ★★★★★

La Collina ('The Hill') is grown at Bilancia's steep, early-ripening site on the northern slopes of Roys Hill, overlooking the Gimblett Gravels, Hawke's Bay, co-fermented with Viognier skins (but not their juice, giving a tiny Viognier component in the final blend), and matured for 20 to 24 months in 85 per cent new (but 'low-impact') French oak barriques. A majestic red, it ranks among the country's very finest Syrahs. The 2015 vintage (★★★★★) is full-coloured, with a floral, complex bouquet. Still youthful, it is savoury, with strong, ripe, plummy, spicy flavours, fine-grained tannins, and a lasting finish. Open 2020+.

Vintage	15	14	13	12	11	10
WR	7	7	7	NM	NM	7
Drink	19-28	19-27	19-30	NM	NM	19-28

 DRY $120 AV

Landing [The] Bay of Islands Syrah ★★★★☆

The 2015 vintage (★★★★☆) is a classy, coastal Northland red, estate-grown and matured for 18 months in French oak barriques (30 per cent new). Deep and still youthful in colour, it is fragrant, weighty and concentrated, with ripe, plummy, spicy flavours, showing impressive vigour, balance and depth. Best drinking 2020+.

 DRY $40 –V

Last Shepherd Hawke's Bay Syrah (★★★)

Attractive young, the 2017 vintage (★★★) is a lively, medium-bodied red. Deeply coloured, it has satisfying depth of berry, plum and spice flavours, woven with fresh acidity, and a smooth finish. (From Pernod-Ricard NZ.)

 DRY $23 –V

Left Field Hawke's Bay Syrah ★★★☆

The elegant 2016 vintage (★★★★) was grown in the Te Awa Vineyard and matured for 20 months in French and American oak hogsheads (10 per cent new). Deep ruby, it is full-bodied and smooth, with plum, spice and nut flavours, showing excellent depth and harmony. (From Te Awa, owned by Villa Maria.)

Vintage	16	15	14
WR	5	5	5
Drink	19-23	19-21	19-20

 DRY $26 –V

Leveret Estate Hawke's Bay Syrah ★★★☆

The full-bodied 2016 vintage (★★★☆) is an easy-drinking red, barrel-aged for a year. It has very good depth of plummy, spicy flavours, with nutty, savoury notes adding complexity, and a smooth finish.

Vintage	14	13
WR	6	7
Drink	19-22	19-20

DRY $24 AV

Leveret Estate Reserve Hawke's Bay Syrah   ★★★★

The youthful 2015 vintage (★★★★) was matured for two years in French oak casks (80 per cent new). Full-coloured, it is mouthfilling, with strong, fresh, plummy, spicy flavours, slightly earthy notes adding complexity, and finely balanced tannins. Best drinking 2020+.

Vintage	14	13
WR	6	7
Drink	19-22	19-22

 DRY $26 AV

Luna Blue Rock Martinborough Syrah   ★★★★☆

The 2017 vintage (★★★★) was harvested from 20-year-old vines on a 'precipitous, north-facing slope', south of Martinborough. Matured for 18 months in French oak casks (25 per cent new), it was bottled unfined and unfiltered. Deep ruby, it is floral, with a very spicy fragrance. Fresh and vibrantly fruity, with plummy, spicy, distinctly peppery flavours, balanced tannins, and lots of youthful vigour, it's well worth cellaring; best drinking 2021+.

 DRY $45 –V

Mahurangi River Winery Matakana Syrah   ★★★★

The 2016 vintage (★★★☆) is floral and supple, with very good depth of plummy, spicy flavours, and earthy notes adding a touch of complexity.

 DRY $30 –V

Maison Noire Hawke's Bay Syrah   ★★★★

The 2016 vintage (★★★☆), grown at Te Awanga and on hills overlooking the Gimblett Gravels, was matured for a year in French oak barrels (25 per cent new). Ruby-hued, with a fragrant bouquet, it is a medium-bodied style, with lively plum and spice flavours, a hint of liquorice, fresh acidity, some savoury notes adding complexity, and good length. Best drinking 2020+.

Vintage	16	15
WR	5	5
Drink	19-21	19-21

 DRY $25 AV

Man O' War Waiheke Island Dreadnought Syrah   ★★★★★

Estate-grown at the eastern end of the island, the powerful 2015 vintage (★★★★★) was matured in French oak puncheons (35 per cent new). Dark, mouthfilling and fragrant, it is concentrated, sweet-fruited and tightly structured, with ripe plum, pepper and blackcurrant flavours, showing good complexity, slightly earthy notes, a seasoning of nutty oak, and good tannin backbone.

Vintage	15	14
WR	5	6
Drink	19-22	19-21

DRY $55 AV

Marsden Bay of Islands Vigot Syrah ★★★★

The 2015 vintage (★★★★) is a dark Northland red, matured for 16 months in oak casks. Strongly varietal, it has a fragrant, spicy bouquet, leading into a sturdy, fresh, sweet-fruited wine with good concentration of plum, spice and slight liquorice flavours, and a finely balanced finish.

Vintage	15	14	13
WR	6	6	6
Drink	19-23	19-20	P

DRY $40 –V

Martinborough Vineyard Martinborough Syrah/Viognier ★★★★

The elegant 2017 vintage (★★★★☆) includes a splash of Viognier (4 per cent). Matured for a year in French oak casks (33 per cent new), it has fullish colour and a fragrant, peppery bouquet. A fresh, medium to full-bodied wine, it has youthful plum, spice and slight tamarillo flavours, showing good complexity, and a long, spicy finish.

Vintage	17	16
WR	7	7
Drink	19-30	19-30

DRY $45 –V

Matahiwi Estate Hawke's Bay Syrah (★★★★)

The floral, supple, finely textured 2018 vintage (★★★★) was grown in the Bridge Pa Triangle and matured for a year in old French oak barrels. Deep ruby, it's already drinking well, with plummy, spicy flavours, showing excellent complexity and harmony. Best drinking 2021+.

Vintage	18
WR	6
Drink	19-22

DRY $30 –V

Milcrest Estate Nelson Syrah ★★★☆

Still on sale, the 2014 vintage (★★★☆) is a single-vineyard red, matured for 11 months in French and American oak casks. Full-coloured, it is fresh and medium-bodied, with good depth of plummy, spicy flavours, lively acidity and considerable complexity. Retasted in mid to late 2018, it's maturing well. Best drinking 2020+.

DRY $35 –V

Mills Reef Arthur Edmund Gimblett Gravels Syrah (★★★★★)

Released in late 2018, the debut 2013 vintage (★★★★★) is rare – only about 1000 bottles were produced. Deeply coloured and highly fragrant, it was estate-grown at two sites in Mere Road, and matured for 20 months in French and American oak hogsheads (100 per cent new). Highly refined, it is mouthfilling and sweet-fruited, with deep, notably youthful plum and spice flavours, and a long, very smooth-flowing finish. Already approachable, it should be very long-lived; open 2023+.

DRY $350 –V

Mills Reef Elspeth Gimblett Gravels Hawke's Bay Syrah   ★★★★☆

In top vintages, this is one of Hawke's Bay's greatest Syrahs. Retasted in early 2019, the 2016 vintage (★★★★☆) was matured for 17 months in French oak casks (5 per cent new). Already approachable, it is a graceful, supple red, full-coloured, with a plummy, spicy fragrance. It has strong plum and black-pepper flavours, in a clearly varietal, elegant style.

Vintage	16
WR	7
Drink	19-24

 DRY $49 –V

Mills Reef Estate Hawke's Bay Syrah   ★★★

A drink-young charmer, the 2018 vintage (★★★) is a single-vineyard red, matured for seven months in French and American oak casks. Bright ruby, it is floral and supple, in a medium-bodied style with ripe, plummy, distinctly spicy flavours, a touch of complexity and gentle tannins.

 DRY $19 AV

Mills Reef Reserve Gimblett Gravels Hawke's Bay Syrah   ★★★★

Fresh and full-bodied, the 2018 vintage (★★★★) is an age-worthy red, matured in a mix of American (56 per cent) and French (44 per cent) oak casks (26 per cent new). Full-coloured, it has strong black-pepper and plum aromas and flavours, showing very good complexity, hints of liquorice and dark chocolate, and a moderately firm finish. Best drinking 2021+.

 DRY $25 AV

Mission Barrique Reserve Gimblett Gravels Syrah   ★★★★

The 2016 vintage (★★★★) was estate-grown in Hawke's Bay and matured in French oak casks. Full-coloured, it is mouthfilling and savoury, with concentrated, ripe plum, spice and black-pepper flavours, good tannin support, and excellent complexity and depth.

Vintage	16	15
WR	5	5
Drink	19-23	19-22

 DRY $29 AV

Mission Hawke's Bay Syrah   ★★★

Enjoyable young, but still unfolding, the 2018 vintage (★★★☆) is a fresh, medium-bodied red, deep ruby, with a spicy, slightly earthy bouquet. Strongly varietal, it has good depth of plummy, spicy flavours, slightly savoury notes and a long, peppery finish. Good value.

 DRY $16 V+

Mission Huchet Gimblett Gravels Syrah   ★★★★★

Named in honour of nineteenth-century winemaker Cyprian Huchet, the 2013 vintage (★★★★★) is a powerful red with a fragrant, spicy bouquet. Estate-grown in Mere Road, in the Gimblett Gravels, and French oak-matured for 18 months (33 per cent new), it is deeply coloured, with a fragrant, spicy bouquet. Mouthfilling, it has richly varietal, concentrated blackcurrant, plum and spice flavours, fine-grained tannins, and a very harmonious finish. An elegant red with a long future, it should be at its best 2020+.

Vintage	13	12	11	10		DRY $130 –V
WR	7	NM	NM	6		
Drink	19-25	NM	NM	19-23		

Mission Jewelstone Hawke's Bay Syrah ★★★★★

Already delicious, but still very age-worthy, the 2016 vintage (★★★★★) is a single-vineyard red, estate-grown at Mere Road, in the Gimblett Gravels, and matured for a year in French oak casks (30 per cent new). Deep and youthful in colour, it is floral, concentrated and supple, with rich blackcurrant and spice flavours, savoury, earthy, nutty notes adding complexity, and a smooth, persistent finish. Best drinking 2021+. Certified organic.

Vintage	16	15	14	13	DRY $50 AV
WR	7	7	7	7	
Drink	19-31	19-31	19-30	19-30	

Mission Vineyard Selection Hawke's Bay Syrah ★★★☆

The elegant, deeply coloured 2016 vintage (★★★★) was predominantly estate-grown in the Gimblett Gravels and mostly (90 per cent) barrel-matured. Full-coloured, it is a fragrant, medium to full-bodied wine, fresh and vibrantly fruity, with strong plum, spice and black-pepper flavours, oak complexity, supple tannins, and lots of drink-young appeal.

DRY $20 AV

Mt Difficulty Ghost Town Bendigo Central Otago Syrah (★★★★)

Syrah is a rare beast in Central Otago, but the 2017 vintage (★★★★) of this single-vineyard red is an auspicious debut. Matured for a year in French oak casks (25 per cent new), it is full-coloured and mouthfilling, with generous, youthful plum and spice flavours, a hint of tamarillo, savoury notes adding complexity and good tannin backbone. Best drinking 2021+.

Vintage	17	DRY $26 AV
WR	5	
Drink	19-32	

Nikau Point Reserve Hawke's Bay Syrah ★★☆

Probably best drunk young, the estate-grown 2017 vintage (★★☆) was barrel-aged for nine months. Medium-bodied, with lightish, moderately youthful colour, it has solid depth of berry and spice flavours, with a fairly firm finish.

DRY $16 AV

Obsidian Reserve Waiheke Island Syrah ★★★★★

Currently delicious, the impressive, boldly coloured 2014 vintage (★★★★★) was matured for a year in French oak casks. A fragrant, powerful, sweet-fruited red, it has commanding mouthfeel (14.5 per cent alcohol), with dense, ripe plum, liquorice and spice flavours, and a well-rounded finish. Full of personality, it's a drink-now or cellaring proposition. The 2015 vintage (★★★★☆) was matured for a year in French oak barriques (40 per cent new). Deeply coloured, it is fragrant, with generous, youthful plum, spice and slight tamarillo flavours, fine-grained tannins, savoury notes adding complexity, and very good potential.

Vintage	15	14	13	12
WR	5	6	7	5
Drink	19-23	19-23	19-23	19-20

DRY $63 AV

Okahu Estate Syrah   ★★★★

Still on sale, the 2014 vintage (★★★★) of this Northland red is generous and savoury, with fine-grained tannins, good weight and strong, ripe plum/spice flavours.

DRY $39 –V

Omata Estate Reserve Russell Syrah   (★★★★☆)

The powerful 2015 vintage (★★★★☆) was estate-grown at Russell, in Northland, and French oak-aged. Harvested at an advanced stage of ripeness (26 brix), it is dark, with a very fragrant, spicy bouquet. Robust (15 per cent alcohol), it has concentrated, plummy, spicy flavours, fresh and supple, and obvious cellaring potential; best drinking 2020+.

DRY $46 –V

Omata Estate Russell Syrah   ★★★☆

The 2016 vintage (★★★) was estate-grown at Russell, in Northland, and French oak-aged. Bright ruby, it is a medium-bodied, vibrantly fruity red, with fresh acidity and plummy, smooth flavours.

DRY $36 –V

Pask Declaration Hawke's Bay Syrah   ★★★★☆

Estate-grown in Gimblett Road and matured in French oak casks (80 per cent new), the 2014 vintage (★★★★★) is maturing very gracefully. Deeply coloured, it is fragrant and mouthfilling, with concentrated plum, spice and nut flavours, complex and finely textured, that build across the palate to a lasting finish. Best drinking 2020+.

Vintage	14
WR	7
Drink	20-30

DRY $50 –V

Pask Gimblett Gravels Hawke's Bay Syrah   ★★★☆

The 2018 vintage (★★★) is a medium-bodied red, matured for 10 months in French oak casks (20 per cent new). Bright ruby, with a fresh, peppery fragrance, it is vibrantly fruity and supple, with lively, plummy, spicy flavours and lots of drink-young charm.

Vintage	18
WR	4
Drink	20-23

DRY $22 AV

Passage Rock Reserve Waiheke Island Syrah ★★★★★

One of Waiheke's most awarded reds. Estate-grown, the 2015 vintage (★★★★★) was matured for a year in French oak barriques (30 per cent new). Deeply coloured, it has a fragrant, spicy, complex bouquet. Sturdy and strongly varietal, it has deep, plummy, peppery flavours, showing excellent complexity, ripe tannins and a long, savoury finish. Combining power and elegance, it should be at its best 2022+.

Vintage	15	
WR	6	
Drink	20-25	

DRY $65 AV

Passage Rock Waiheke Island Syrah ★★★★★

This Waiheke Island red is consistently rewarding. The 2017 vintage (★★★★☆) was matured for a year in small French oak barrels (30 per cent new). Full-coloured, fresh and mouthfilling, it is strongly varietal, with a fresh, peppery fragrance. It has good density of plum, spice and black-pepper flavours, seasoned with nutty oak, good complexity and refined tannins. Best drinking 2021+.

Vintage	17	
WR	5	
Drink	19-25	

DRY $35 V+

Pont, Le, Grand Vin Rouge Syrah (★★★★☆)

The 2014 vintage (★★★★☆) is a top Gisborne-grown red. Hand-picked at Patutahi, blended with a small portion of Merlot and French oak-matured for 30 months, it is full-coloured, fresh and mouthfilling, with generous, plummy, spicy flavours, good vigour, savoury notes adding complexity, and a firm backbone of tannin. It should be long-lived.

DRY $36 AV

Pukeora Estate Ruahine Range Central Hawke's Bay Syrah (★★★★)

Only two barrels were made of the elegant 2015 vintage (★★★★). Estate-grown at altitude, hand-picked and matured for 20 months in French oak barriques (50 per cent new), it has deep, youthful, purple-flushed colour and a fragrant, spicy bouquet. Mouthfilling and vibrantly fruity, with fresh, strong berry and spice flavours, good tannin backbone and a long, tightly structured finish, it's well worth cellaring to 2020+.

DRY $30 –V

Quarter Acre Hawke's Bay Syrah ★★★★★

Drinking well now, but still unfolding, the classy 2017 vintage (★★★★★) was hand-picked and matured for nine months in French oak barriques. Full-coloured, it is highly fragrant and mouthfilling, with concentrated, plummy, spicy flavours, fresh acidity and a supple, very harmonious finish. More refined and subtle – less pungently varietal – than many Hawke's Bay Syrahs, it should be at its best 2021+.

DRY $40 AV

Ra Nui Maid's Quarters Marlborough Syrah (★★★★)

The elegant 2016 vintage (★★★★) is a single-vineyard red, hand-harvested and matured for a year in French oak barriques (20 per cent new). Bright ruby, with a peppery fragrance, it is vibrantly fruity, with good depth of fresh, plummy, spicy flavours, nutty notes adding complexity, and gentle tannins. A distinctly cool-climate style of Syrah, it should be at its best 2020+.

DRY $45 –V

Rangatira Reserve Gimblett Gravels Syrah (★★★★☆)

The 2015 vintage (★★★★☆) is a single-vineyard Hawke's Bay red, matured for 18 months in French oak barriques (30 per cent new). It's a youthful, mouthfilling, full-coloured wine, with generous, ripe plum, spice and slight liquorice flavours, a hint of herbs, oak complexity, fine-grained tannins and a long finish. Best drinking 2020+. (From Ka Tahi.)

DRY $30 AV

Redmetal Vineyards Basket Press Hawke's Bay Syrah ★★★★☆

Estate-grown in the Bridge Pa Triangle, the 2018 vintage (★★★★) was barrique-aged for 10 months (35 per cent new). Full-coloured, fragrant and supple, it has strong, plummy, spicy flavours, fresh and youthful, and gentle tannins. Already enjoyable, it should be at its best 2021+.

Vintage	18
WR	4
Drink	20-26

DRY $42 –V

Redmetal Vineyards Bridge Pa Triangle Hawke's Bay Syrah ★★★☆

An excellent example of the drink-young style, the 2018 vintage (★★★★) was lightly oak-influenced. Bright ruby, with fresh, peppery aromas, it is medium-bodied, with very good depth of plummy, spicy flavours, lively and smooth. A graceful young red, it's a drink-now or cellaring proposition.

DRY $24 AV

Sacred Hill Deerstalkers Hawke's Bay Syrah ★★★★★

Estate-grown and hand-picked in the Gimblett Gravels, fermented with indigenous yeasts and matured for 16 months in French oak barriques and puncheons (35 per cent new), the 2015 vintage (★★★★★) is deeply coloured, with a scented, distinctly peppery bouquet. Mouthfilling, it has fresh, concentrated flavours of plums, spices and nuts, with supple tannins and a long, finely textured finish. Highly approachable in its youth, it's also well worth cellaring; best drinking 2020+.

Vintage	15	14	13	12	11	10
WR	7	7	7	6	NM	7
Drink	19-30	19-24	19-22	19-20	NM	P

DRY $60 AV

Sacred Hill Reserve Hawke's Bay Syrah   ★★★☆

A 'fruit-driven' style, the 2015 vintage (★★★) was matured for eight months in seasoned French barrels. Ruby-hued, it is peppery and slightly herbal, in a smooth, vibrantly fruity style, offering easy, early drinking. The 2016 vintage (★★★☆) was French oak-aged for eight months. Full-coloured, it is mouthfilling, with generous plum, spice and slight tamarillo flavours, showing considerable complexity, and gentle tannins.

Vintage	16	15
WR	5	6
Drink	P	P

 DRY $30 –V

Sacred Hill Single Vineyard Hawke's Bay Syrah   (★★★☆)

Enjoyable young, the 2018 vintage (★★★☆) was estate-grown in the Gimblett Gravels and matured for eight months in French oak barrels (20 per cent new). Full-coloured, with a fragrant, peppery bouquet, it is mouthfilling and vibrantly fruity, with fresh, plummy, spicy flavours, showing a touch of complexity, very good depth and a smooth finish.

 DRY $28 –V

Saint Clair James Sinclair Gimblett Gravels Hawke's Bay Syrah   ★★★☆

The 2018 vintage (★★★☆) is full-coloured, with a fresh, spicy bouquet. Medium-bodied, it is vibrantly fruity, with plummy, spicy flavours, showing clear-cut varietal characteristics, a gentle seasoning of oak and a smooth finish.

DRY $28 –V

Sileni Cellar Selection Hawke's Bay Syrah   ★★★

The 2018 vintage (★★★) is a ruby-hued, medium-bodied red, with fresh, ripe, plummy, spicy aromas and flavours, gentle tannins, and good balance and depth. Enjoyable young.

DRY $20 –V

Sileni Exceptional Vintage Hawke's Bay Syrah   (★★★★★)

The delicious 2013 vintage (★★★★★) was matured for 10 months in French oak casks (60 per cent new). Dark and mouthfilling, with sweet-fruit characters and concentrated blackcurrant, plum, spice and liquorice flavours, it's an impressively weighty and complex red, finely textured and long.

Vintage	13
WR	7
Drink	19-23

 DRY $70 AV

Sileni Grand Reserve Peak Hawke's Bay Syrah   ★★★★

Already drinking well, the supple 2018 vintage (★★★★☆) is full-coloured, fragrant and finely balanced. It has concentrated plum and black-pepper flavours, showing good complexity, gentle tannins, and a long, spicy finish.

 DRY $35 –V

Smith & Sheth Cru Heretaunga Syrah   (★★★★☆)

The graceful, supple 2017 vintage (★★★★☆) was grown in the Gimblett Gravels and matured for 18 months in oak barriques (40 per cent new). Dark and purple-flushed, with a fresh, spicy fragrance, it is medium to full-bodied, with strong, vibrant, plummy, spicy flavours, finely integrated oak and obvious cellaring potential. Best drinking 2022+.

 DRY $40 AV

Smith & Sheth Cru Omahu Syrah   ★★★★★

Built for cellaring, the 2015 vintage (★★★★★) is an 'old vine' Gimblett Gravels red, barrique-matured. Deep and bright in colour, with a fragrant, plummy, peppery bouquet, it is a full-bodied, clearly varietal wine, concentrated, savoury, complex and structured. Best drinking 2021+.

 DRY $55 AV

Squawking Magpie Gimblett Gravels Syrah   (★★★★☆)

The very age-worthy 2017 vintage (★★★★☆) is a single-vineyard red, matured for 15 months in French oak casks (22 per cent new). Full-coloured, it is a strongly varietal, medium to full-bodied red, with concentrated plum, spice and black-pepper flavours, a hint of tamarillo, good tannin backbone and excellent complexity. Best drinking 2022+.

 DRY $34 AV

Stables Ngatarawa Reserve Hawke's Bay Syrah   (★★★★)

Bargain-priced, the 2018 vintage (★★★★) is a fragrant, full-bodied red that includes minor portions of Merlot (8 per cent), Malbec (4 per cent) and Cabernet Franc (2 per cent). Full-coloured, with a plummy, spicy bouquet, it is youthful, with concentrated plum and black-pepper flavours and a fairly firm, long finish. Best drinking 2021+.

 DRY $20 V+

Staete Landt Arie Marlborough Syrah   ★★★★

The 2015 vintage (★★★★☆) was estate-grown at Rapaura, hand-harvested and matured for 17 months in French oak barriques. Full-coloured, it is mouthfilling and flowing, with strong plum and spice flavours, peppery and lingering. Showing good personality, it's currently delicious, but also worth cellaring.

Vintage	15
WR	7
Drink	19-28

 DRY $49 –V

Stonecroft Crofters Gimblett Gravels Hawke's Bay Syrah   ★★★★

Certified organic, the 2018 vintage (★★★★) was grown in three vineyards and partly (50 per cent) matured for five months in French oak barrels. Designed for early consumption, it is deep ruby, with a fresh, spicy bouquet. Medium-bodied, with very good depth of plummy, spicy flavours, showing some savoury complexity, it's a harmonious, supple, age-worthy red, that many Pinot Noir lovers would enjoy. Best drinking 2020+.

DRY $24 V+

Stonecroft Gimblett Gravels Hawke's Bay Reserve Syrah ★★★★★

Certified organic, the 2016 vintage (★★★★★) was estate-grown at two sites, hand-picked and matured for 20 months in French oak barriques (40 per cent new). Built to last, it is a lovely young wine, full-coloured, fragrant, concentrated and supple, with plum, blackcurrant and spice flavours, showing excellent complexity, and fine-grained tannins. Best drinking 2021+.

Vintage	16	15	14	13	12	11	10
WR	7	7	7	7	6	NM	7
Drink	21-28	19-27	19-26	19-25	19-24	NM	19-23

DRY $60 AV

Stonecroft Gimblett Gravels Hawke's Bay Serine Syrah ★★★★

Certified organic, the youthful 2016 vintage (★★★★) was estate-grown at Mere Road and Roys Hill, hand-picked, fermented with indigenous yeasts and matured for 20 months in French oak barrels (20 per cent new). Full-coloured, it is floral and supple, with rich, plummy, gently spicy flavours, woven with fresh acidity, and savoury notes adding complexity. Already highly approachable, it should be at its best 2020+.

Vintage	16	15	14	13	12	11	10
WR	7	7	6	7	5	NM	7
Drink	19-23	19-23	19-21	19-21	19-20	NM	P

DRY $31 –V

Stonecroft Gimblett Gravels Hawke's Bay Undressed Syrah ★★★★

Certified organic, the 'preservative-free' (no added sulphur) 2018 vintage (★★★☆) is a youthful, single-vineyard red, hand-picked in Mere Road and matured for five months in French oak barrels (20 per cent new). Bright ruby, with peppery aromas, it is medium-bodied, with vibrant, plummy, spicy flavours, showing considerable complexity, fresh acidity and supple tannins. Best drinking 2020+.

DRY $31 –V

Stonyridge Pilgrim Waiheke Island Syrah/Mourvedre/Viognier/Grenache ★★★★★

This distinguished Rhône-style blend is estate-grown at Onetangi and matured for a year in French oak barriques (30 per cent new in 2015). The 2015 vintage (★★★★★) is delicious now, but also well worth cellaring. Deeply coloured, it is sturdy (14.5 per cent alcohol), vibrantly fruity and supple, with dense plum and spice flavours, complex and savoury, and ripe, supple tannins. Very finely textured and harmonious, it's already highly approachable, but should be at its best 2020+.

Vintage	15
WR	7
Drink	19-25

DRY $95 AV

Summerhouse Marlborough Syrah   ★★★☆

The easy-drinking 2016 vintage (★★★☆) was matured for 10 months in French oak barriques, seasoned and new. Full-coloured, it is mouthfilling, with generous plum, berry, herb and tamarillo flavours, showing considerable complexity. Drink now or cellar.

Vintage	16	15
WR	6	7
Drink	19-25	19-26

 DRY $29 –V

Te Awa Single Estate Hawke's Bay Syrah   ★★★★☆

The 2017 vintage (★★★★) of this Gimblett Gravels red was matured for 14 months in French oak hogsheads (35 per cent new). Deep ruby, savoury and spicy, it is full-bodied and lively, with good density of youthful plum and black-pepper flavours, slightly earthy notes, and a firmly structured finish. Best drinking 2021+.

Vintage	17	16	15	14	13
WR	6	7	NM	7	7
Drink	19-28	19-28	NM	19-24	19-23

 DRY $30 AV

Te Awanga Estate Hawke's Bay Syrah   (★★★)

Ruby-hued, the 2017 vintage (★★★) is a fresh, medium-bodied red, oak-aged for six months. Still youthful, it has vibrant, berryish, plummy, spicy flavours, threaded with lively acidity, and nutty notes adding a touch of complexity. Best drinking 2020+.

 DRY $28 –V

Te Awanga Estate The Loom Reserve Hawke's Bay Syrah   (★★★★)

From young vines on a north-facing slope near the coast, the youthful 2017 vintage (★★★★) was oak-aged for 15 months. Full-coloured, it is fresh and supple, in a medium to full-bodied style with strong, vibrant, plummy, spicy flavours, fresh acidity and a long finish. Well worth cellaring, it should be at its best from 2021 onwards.

 DRY $35 –V

Te Mata Estate Bullnose Syrah   ★★★★★

Grown in the Bullnose and Isosceles vineyards, in the Bridge Pa Triangle inland from Hastings, in Hawke's Bay, this classy red is hand-picked and matured for 15 to 16 months in French oak barriques (about 35 per cent new). Unlike its Estate Vineyards stablemate (below), it is not blended with Viognier, and the vines for the Bullnose label are cropped lower. The elegant 2016 vintage (★★★★☆) is deeply coloured and invitingly fragrant. Rich and supple, with strong, vibrant plum and spice flavours, it's a clearly varietal, very harmonious red, already drinking well, but well worth cellaring to 2021+.

Vintage	16	15	14	13	12	11	10
WR	6	7	7	7	7	6	7
Drink	19-24	19-25	19-24	19-23	19-21	P	P

 DRY $75 AV

Te Mata Estate Vineyards Hawke's Bay Syrah ★★★★

The 2018 vintage (★★★★) is highly enjoyable in its youth. Estate-grown in the Woodthorpe Terraces Vineyard and in the Bridge Pa Triangle, it was matured in French oak barrels for five months. Bright ruby, with a floral, slightly peppery fragrance, it is medium to full-bodied, with vibrant plum and black-pepper flavours, showing a distinct touch of complexity, savoury notes and gentle tannins. A very harmonious red, it's already delicious.

Vintage	18
WR	6
Drink	19-21

 DRY $20 V+

Terrace Edge Waipara Valley Syrah ★★★★

Grown on a '45-degree north-facing "roasted slope"' and matured for over a year in French oak (25 per cent new), the 2016 vintage (★★★★) has a fragrant, peppery, slightly herbal bouquet. Sturdy (14.5 per cent alcohol) and generous, it has strong, spicy flavours, hints of herbs, liquorice and nuts, and lots of drink-young appeal. Retasted in March 2019, the 2015 vintage (★★★★☆) is maturing well. Certified organic, it is a powerful, weighty red (14.5 per cent alcohol) with deep, bright colour. Fragrant, with rich, plummy, spicy, peppery, slightly earthy and herbal flavours, it's a well-structured, supple red, likely to be at its best 2021+.

Vintage	16	15
WR	7	7
Drink	19-25	19-26

 DRY $31 –V

Theory & Practice Hawke's Bay Syrah ★★★★

If you like Pinot Noir, try this. The 2016 vintage (★★★★) was hand-picked 'south of Hastings', fermented with indigenous yeasts and matured for 20 months in French oak barrels (20 per cent new). A floral, softly mouthfilling red, it is deep ruby, with vibrant berry and spice flavours, a slightly peppery streak, gentle tannins, and loads of drink-young charm. (There is no 2017.)

 DRY $25 AV

Thomas Waiheke Island Syrah (★★★★)

Still unfolding, the 2015 vintage (★★★★) of this estate-grown red was matured for 15 months in French oak barriques (50 per cent new). Full-coloured, with a floral, spicy bouquet, it is medium-bodied, with vibrant, berryish, spicy flavours, savoury notes adding complexity, and supple tannins. An elegant style, it should be at its best 2021+.

 DRY $56 –V

Tohu Hawke's Bay Syrah ★★★☆

Still developing, the attractive 2015 vintage (★★★★) was hand-picked and matured for 15 months in old French oak barriques. Deeply coloured, with a fragrant, spicy bouquet, it is mouthfilling and vibrant, with good concentration of plum and spice flavours, oak complexity, and obvious cellaring potential; best drinking 2020+.

DRY $28 –V

Toño Mas O Menos Hawke's Bay Syrah/Tempranillo   (★★★★)

Designed as 'a modern take on Spanish winemaking heritage', the 2016 vintage (★★★★) is a blend of Syrah and Tempranillo, with a splash of Cabernet Sauvignon. Matured for two years in old barrels and bottled unfined and unfiltered, it is deeply coloured, fragrant and full-bodied, with strong, vibrant, plummy, spicy flavours and ripe, supple tannins. A distinctive wine, it offers good drinking now to 2021.

DRY $19 V+

Trinity Hill Gimblett Gravels Syrah   ★★★★★

The 2018 vintage (★★★★☆) is a very age-worthy, supple, medium-bodied red with a floral, peppery bouquet. Estate-grown, hand-harvested and blended with a splash of Viognier (2 per cent), it was matured for eight months in a mix of French oak barriques and 5000-litre oak ovals. Still purple-flushed, it is strongly varietal, with concentrated, plummy, peppery flavours, gently seasoned with oak, a hint of liquorice and gentle tannins. Best drinking 2021+.

DRY $40 AV

Trinity Hill Homage Hawke's Bay Syrah   ★★★★★

One of the country's most distinguished – and expensive – reds. Still a baby, the 2017 vintage (★★★★★) was estate-grown in the Gimblett Gravels and matured for 15 months in French oak ovals and barriques. It has deep, purple-flushed colour and a highly scented, peppery bouquet. Mouthfilling, vibrantly fruity and supple, with deep plum and black-pepper flavours, seasoned with nutty oak, it builds across the palate to a very long, harmonious, spicy finish.

Vintage	17	16	15	14	13	12	11	10
WR	7	7	7	7	7	NM	NM	7
Drink	19-29	19-28	19-27	19-25	19-25	NM	NM	19-25

DRY $145 AV

Vidal Legacy Hawke's Bay Syrah   ★★★★★

The estate-grown 2016 vintage (★★★★★) was hand-harvested from 18-year-old vines in the Omahu Gravels and Twyford Gravels vineyards, in the Gimblett Gravels, and matured for 20 months in French oak barriques (43 per cent new). Dark and purple-flushed, it is enticingly floral, with lifted plum and black-pepper aromas. Concentrated and vibrantly fruity, it is richly varietal and smoothly textured, with fresh, concentrated plum, berry and pepper flavours, and a long, spicy finish. Best drinking 2021+.

Vintage	16
WR	7
Drink	19-28

DRY $75 AV

Vidal Reserve Gimblett Gravels Hawke's Bay Syrah   ★★★★

The 2017 vintage (★★★★) was estate-grown and matured for 17 months in French oak barriques (30 per cent new). Full-coloured, it is mouthfilling and vibrant, with very good intensity of youthful, plummy, spicy flavour, oak complexity, fresh acidity and the structure to age well. Best drinking 2021+.

Vintage	17	16	15	14	13	12	11	10
WR	6	7	7	7	7	6	6	7
Drink	19-22	19-23	19-23	19-23	19-22	P	P	P

DRY $27 AV

Vidal Soler Gimblett Gravels Hawke's Bay Syrah   (★★★★★)

The debut 2017 vintage (★★★★★) is a classic cellaring style. Estate-grown at two sites in the Gimblett Gravels, it was matured for 18 months in French oak barriques (36 per cent new). Deeply coloured, with a fragrant, peppery bouquet, it is savoury, complex and well-structured, with concentrated, plummy, spicy, slightly earthy flavours, woven with fresh acidity, and good tannin backbone. Finely poised and youthful, with obvious potential, it should be at its best 2022+.

Vintage	17
WR	6
Drink	19-22

DRY $35 V+

View East Waiheke Island Syrah   (★★★★)

The 2016 vintage (★★★★) was matured for 10 months in French oak casks (33 per cent new). Full-coloured, it's an elegant wine, mouthfilling, with strong plum and spice flavours and a fresh, lingering finish. Best drinking 2020+.

DRY $50 –V

Villa Maria Cellar Selection Hawke's Bay Syrah   ★★★★

The very youthful 2018 vintage (★★★★) was matured for a year in French oak barriques (25 per cent new). Full-coloured, it is mouthfilling and supple, with fresh acidity and strong, vibrant plum and black-pepper flavours. Well worth cellaring, it should be at its best 2021+.

Vintage	18	17	16	15	14	13	12
WR	7	6	6	7	7	7	6
Drink	19-25	19-24	19-23	19-23	19-24	19-22	19-20

DRY $25 AV

Villa Maria Private Bin Hawke's Bay Syrah   ★★★☆

The 2018 vintage (★★★☆) is a highly approachable red, bright ruby, fresh and smooth. Medium to full-bodied, it has plenty of ripe, plummy, peppery flavour, some savoury notes adding a touch of complexity, and a well-rounded finish.

DRY $20 AV

Villa Maria Reserve Gimblett Gravels Hawke's Bay Syrah   ★★★★★

The 2016 vintage (★★★★★) was estate-grown at two sites and matured for 17 months in French oak barriques (30 per cent new). A powerful, fleshy yet elegant wine, it has concentrated plum/spice flavours, ripe and smooth, and excellent depth, vigour and harmony. Still available, the 2014 vintage (★★★★★), retasted in 2019, is a highly perfumed, powerful red, currently a pleasure to drink, but still unfolding. Dark and full-bodied, it has dense, beautifully ripe flavours of plums, spices, black pepper and nuts, a hint of liquorice, firm tannins and a lasting finish.

Vintage	16	15	14
WR	7	NM	7
Drink	19-26	NM	19-26

DRY $60 AV

Waitapu Estate Reef View Northland Syrah   (★★★☆)

The 2015 vintage (★★★☆), tasted in early 2019, is a medium-bodied, vibrantly fruity red, deep ruby, with a distinctly spicy bouquet. Estate-grown and French oak-aged for a year, it is still developing, with ripe, plummy, spicy flavours, fresh acidity, and savoury notes adding complexity. Open 2020+.

DRY $28 –V

Tannat

Although extremely rare in New Zealand, Tannat is well known in south-west France, especially as a key ingredient in the dark, firm, tannic reds of Madiran. Tannat is also a star variety in Uruguay, yielding firm, fragrant reds with rich blackberry flavours. According to New Zealand Winegrowers' *Vineyard Register Report 2017–2020*, only 2 hectares of Tannat vines will be bearing in 2020, in Northland, Hawke's Bay and Auckland.

De La Terre Reserve Hawke's Bay Tannat ★★★★☆

The distinctive 2016 vintage (★★★★★) has a compelling presence. Grown and hand-harvested at Havelock North, it was matured for 16 months in French and Hungarian oak barriques (30 per cent new). Dark and purple-flushed, it is fragrant, bold and fruit-packed, with fresh, vibrant plum, spice and slight liquorice flavours, good tannin backbone, and obvious potential; open 2021+.

DRY $45 –V

Tempranillo

The star grape of Rioja, Tempranillo is grown extensively across northern and central Spain, where it yields strawberry, spice and tobacco-flavoured reds, full of personality. Barrel-aged versions mature well, developing great complexity. The great Spanish variety is starting to spread into the New World, but is still rare in New Zealand, with 20 hectares of bearing vines in 2020, mostly in Hawke's Bay (12 hectares) and Marlborough (3 hectares).

Brennan Gibbston Central Otago Tempranillo (★★★★☆)

Already drinking well, the impressive 2018 vintage (★★★★☆) is New Zealand's southernmost Tempranillo. Deeply coloured, with a fragrant bouquet, it is mouthfilling, sweet-fruited, savoury and supple, with generous, plummy, berryish flavours, a hint of herbs, and excellent depth, complexity and harmony.

DRY $45 –V

Church Road McDonald Series Hawke's Bay Tempranillo ★★★★★

The powerful 2015 vintage (★★★★☆) is a deeply coloured red, estate-grown in the Redstone Vineyard, in the Bridge Pa Triangle, barrel-aged, and bottled unfined and unfiltered. It is a strapping wine (15.5 per cent alcohol), rich and smooth, with deep blackcurrant, plum and spice flavours, gentle tannins, and a well-rounded finish. Drink now or cellar.

DRY $28 V+

Dry River Craighall Vineyard Martinborough Tempranillo ★★★★☆

'In style the wine sits between our Pinot Noir and Syrah,' says Dry River. The highly impressive 2016 vintage (★★★★★) has promisingly deep, purple-flushed colour. Likely to be long-lived, it is mouthfilling, with dense, vibrant, plummy, spicy flavours, a hint of liquorice, a fairly firm finish and a fragrant bouquet. Best drinking 2022+.

DRY $69 –V

Hans Herzog Marlborough Tempranillo ★★★★★

The lovely 2015 vintage (★★★★★) was estate-grown in the Wairau Valley, matured for 30 months in French oak barriques, and bottled unfined and unfiltered. Full-coloured, it is mouthfilling and savoury, with deep blackcurrant, plum and spice flavours, showing excellent ripeness and complexity. Drink now or cellar.

Vintage	14	13	12	11	10
WR	7	7	7	7	7
Drink	19-24	19-23	19-22	19-21	19-22

DRY $53 AV

Marsden Bay of Islands Tempranillo ★★★☆

The 2015 vintage (★★★☆) is a Northland red, matured for a year in French oak barriques. Full and moderately youthful in colour, it is mouthfilling and sweet-fruited, in a slightly gutsy style with ripe plum and spice flavours, a hint of liquorice and a firm finish.

Vintage	15	14
WR	6	6
Drink	19-21	19-22

DRY $37 –V

Mount Brown Tempranillo

Estate-grown at Waipara, the 2016 vintage (★★★☆) is a vibrantly fruity red, full-coloured, with a ripe, slightly earthy bouquet. Enjoyable young, it has very satisfying depth of plummy, spicy, slightly nutty flavours, woven with fresh acidity, and gentle tannins.

DRY $20 AV

Obsidian Estate Waiheke Island Tempranillo ★★★★

The firm, youthful 2018 vintage (★★★★) was grown at Onetangi and matured for 10 months in French and American oak barriques. Full-coloured, it is mouthfilling and savoury, with strong, ripe, berryish, spicy flavours, fresh acidity and good complexity. Best drinking 2021+.

DRY $42 –V

Rock Ferry Trig Hill Vineyard Tempranillo ★★★★

Certified organic, the 2015 vintage (★★★★) was estate-grown at Bendigo, in Central Otago, fermented with indigenous yeasts, and matured for 20 months in French oak puncheons (20 per cent new). Fragrant and full-coloured, it has strong, plummy, spicy flavours to the fore, hints of herbs and nuts, very good complexity and a smooth finish. Drinking well now, it's also worth cellaring.

DRY $45 –V

Te Awa Single Estate Hawke's Bay Tempranillo ★★★★☆

The 2016 vintage (★★★★) is a Gimblett Gravels red, matured in French and American oak barriques (20 per cent new). Offering lots of current-drinking appeal, it is deeply coloured and vibrantly fruity, with good intensity of fresh, berryish, plummy flavours, and a seductively smooth finish.

Vintage	16
WR	7
Drink	19-28

DRY $35 AV

Trinity Hill Gimblett Gravels Hawke's Bay Tempranillo ★★★★☆

The classy young 2017 vintage (★★★★★) was matured for 16 months in American oak barriques (partly new). Full-coloured, with a fragrant, berryish, spicy bouquet, it is mouthfilling, with excellent density of vibrant blackcurrant, plum and spice flavours, earthy, savoury notes adding complexity, good tannin backbone, and a long, spicy finish. Best 2021+.

DRY $40 –V

Yealands Estate Single Vineyard Awatere Valley Marlborough Tempranillo ★★★★

Already drinking well, the 2018 vintage (★★★☆) is an estate-grown red, ruby-hued and vibrantly fruity, with satisfying depth of ripe plum, berry and spice flavours, some savoury notes adding complexity, and a smooth finish.

DRY $26 AV

Touriga Nacional

Touriga Nacional is the most prized blending variety in the traditional ports of the Douro Valley of Portugal, and is also used widely in the Dao region for table reds. The low-cropping vines produce small berries that yield sturdy, concentrated, structured wines with high tannin levels. However, Touriga Nacional is extremely rare here and is not listed separately in New Zealand Winegrowers' *Vineyard Register Report 2017–2020*.

Trinity Hill Gimblett Gravels Touriga (★★★★★)

This non-vintage, Hawke's Bay wine is a 'port style', blended from Touriga Nacional – the key variety in classic port – Touriga Francesca and Tinta Roriz. From base wines back to 2004, matured in oak barrels for two to nine years, it has dense, inky colour. Highly fragrant, it is robust (19 per cent alcohol), with notably concentrated, spicy, plummy flavours. Overflowing with fruit, it is not a mellow style, but still a lovely mouthful – sweet and delicious.

SW $70 (500ML) AV

Zinfandel

In California, where it is extensively planted, Zinfandel produces muscular, heady reds that can approach a dry port style. It is believed to be identical to the Primitivo variety, which yields highly characterful, warm, spicy reds in southern Italy. There will be only 2 hectares of bearing Zinfandel vines in New Zealand in 2020, clustered in Hawke's Bay, with no expansion projected. Alan Limmer, formerly of Stonecroft winery in Hawke's Bay, believes 'Zin' has potential here, 'if you can stand the stress of growing a grape that falls apart at the first sign of a dubious weather map!'

Stonecroft Gimblett Gravels Hawke's Bay Zinfandel ★★★☆

Certified organic, the 2017 vintage (★★★☆) was estate-grown at Roys Hill, hand-harvested from mature vines and aged for 18 months in seasoned American oak casks. It is fresh and lively, with youthful, lightish colour. A medium-bodied red, with a fresh, spicy fragrance, it has berryish, spicy flavours, showing considerable complexity, and a firm finish. Already enjoyable, it's a drink-now or cellaring proposition.

		DRY $31 –V
Vintage	17	
WR	6	
Drink	19-23	

Zweigelt

Austria's most popular red-wine variety is a crossing of Blaufränkisch and St Laurent. It's a naturally high-yielding variety, but cropped lower can produce appealing, velvety reds, usually at their best when young. Zweigelt is extremely rare in New Zealand, with 3 hectares believed to be planted, mostly in Nelson and Marlborough (but the variety is not listed separately in New Zealand Winegrowers' *Vineyard Register Report 2017–2020*).

Hans Herzog Marlborough Zweigelt ★★★★☆

Maturing superbly, the youthful 2014 vintage (★★★★★) was estate-grown on the north side of the Wairau Valley and matured for 18 months in French oak barriques. Dark and purple-flushed, with a fragrant bouquet of blackcurrants and spices, it is a powerful wine. Fleshy, sweet-fruited and smooth, it is packed with cassis, plum and spice flavours, with savoury notes adding complexity, and obvious potential. Certified organic.

Vintage	14	13	12	11	10
WR	7	7	7	7	7
Drink	19-26	19-25	19-24	19-23	19-21

 DRY $53 –V

Seifried Nelson Zweigelt ★★★

The easy-drinking 2018 vintage (★★☆) was matured for a year in new and seasoned French oak barriques. Light and moderately youthful in colour, it is a pleasant, smooth red, with moderate depth of berryish, slightly spicy and nutty flavours. (Early 2020 release.)

Vintage	14
WR	5
Drink	P

DRY $18 AV

Index of Wine Brands

This index should be especially useful when you are visiting wineries as a quick way to find the reviews of each company's range of wines. It also provides links between different wine brands made by the same producer (for example, Amisfield and Lake Hayes).